THE STRANGEST FAMILY

THE PRIVATE LIVES OF GEORGE III, QUEEN CHARLOTTE AND THE HANOVERIANS

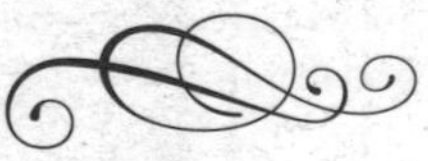

JANICE HADLOW

William Collins
An imprint of HarperCollins*Publishers*
77–85 Fulham Palace Road
London W6 8JB
WilliamCollinsBooks.com

First published in Great Britain by William Collins in 2014

1 3 5 7 9 8 6 4 2

A catalogue record for this book is
available from the British Library.

ISBN 978-0-00-716519-3

Endpapers: A Series of Fifteen Portraits of the Royal Family, 1782
(oil on canvas, by Thomas Gainsborough), Royal Collection Trust
© Her Majesty Queen Elizabeth II, 2014/Bridgeman Images

Printed and bound in Great Britain by
Clays Ltd, St Ives plc

MIX
Paper from
responsible sources
FSC® C007454

FSC™ is a non-profit international organisation established to promote the responsible management of the world's forests. Products carrying the FSC label are independently certified to assure consumers that they come from forests that are managed to meet the social, economic and ecological needs of present and future generations, and other controlled sources.

Find out more about HarperCollins and the environment at
www.harpercollins.co.uk/green

Contents

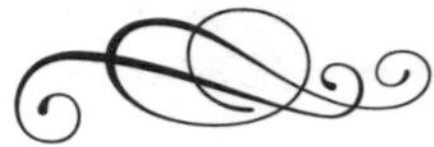

FOR MARTIN, ALEXANDER AND LOUIS,
AND FOR MY PARENTS, WHO DID NOT LIVE TO READ IT

Author's Note

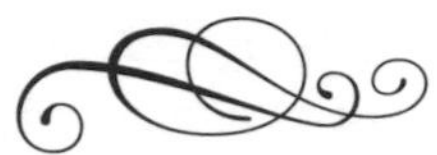

WHEN QUEEN CHARLOTTE WAS ASKED by the artist, botanist and diarist Mrs Delany why she had appointed the writer Fanny Burney to the post of assistant dresser in her household, she answered with characteristic clarity: 'I was led to think of Miss Burney first by her books, then by seeing her, then by hearing how much she was loved by her friends, but chiefly by her friendship for you.' If questioned about why I wrote this book, I am not sure I could answer with such confident precision. In one sense, it simply crept up on me, emerging from a long love affair with the period and the people who lived in it.

I have always been fascinated by history. I studied it at university, where I was taught by some exceptional and inspiring teachers. As a television producer, I have made many history programmes, covering all aspects of the past – from the ancient world to times within living memory. I have worked with some of the most eminent British historians, witnessing at first-hand their knowledge and passion for a huge variety of subject areas. But it was always the eighteenth century that had first place in my heart. I had immersed myself in the politics of the period at college, but its appeal went far beyond what my reading delivered for me. Like so many others, I was drawn to it partly by the wonderful things made in it: the incomparable architecture that created austerely elegant palaces for the great, and airy, comfortable homes for the 'middling sort'. I coveted the objects that went into those houses, from the sturdily beautiful furniture to the delicate blue-and-white coffee cups intended to sit proudly on all those much-polished tea tables. I admired the art of the period too, especially the portraiture, whether it was the clear-eyed intensity of Allan Ramsay, the bravura gestures of Joshua Reynolds, or the tender luminosity of Thomas Gainsborough. Those eighteenth-century men and women rich enough to afford it never tired of having themselves painted. If I had been one of them, I would have chosen Thomas Lawrence for my portrait. Who wouldn't want to see themselves through Lawrence's humane yet flattering eye, which infused even the most unpromising sitter with a sense of spirit and passion? I would have worn a red velvet dress, as both princesses Caroline and Sophia did when they sat for Lawrence, and hoped for a similarly impressive result: both women gaze directly out from their pictures, proud, commanding and smoulderingly bold. The portraits do not quite capture their true characters, at least as revealed in their letters; but what an image to look upon when your spirits needed a boost.

But much as I responded to the things the period produced, my real desire was to understand the people who lived in it. It was the men and women of what is often called the long eighteenth century – which runs from the accession of George I in 1714 to the death of George IV in 1830 – who really captivated me. Caught between the religious intensity of the seventeenth century and the earnest high-mindedness of the Victorians, this was a society in which I felt very much at home. I enjoyed its bustle and energy, and liked being in the company of its garrulous, argumentative and emotional inhabitants. The contradictions of their world intrigued me. On the one hand, they loved order, politeness, restraint. On the other, they were loud, forthright and often violent. The sedate drawing rooms of the rich looked out onto streets where passions could and did run very high. The poor, in both town and country, had a tough time of it, although they too seem to have shared something of the assertive confidence of the wealthy. For most of the middling sort, however, and especially for the rich, there was good reason to be bullish. This was a period in which there was money to be made, and a new kind of life to be lived. It is the experiences of these people – those who built the houses, big and small, laid out the gardens, commissioned the pictures, bought the furniture – that I have come to know best.

I knew them first by their books, and above all, through the work of Jane Austen. My earliest encounters with the authentic voice of the time came through her novels; the first eighteenth-century people I felt I really knew were the Bennetts of Longbourn, the Elliots of Kellynch Hall, Admiral and Mrs Croft, Mr Elton and his dreadful wife.

From fiction, it was a short jump to the world of real people. I think I began with James Boswell's *London Journal*. That was my introduction to the vast and compelling world of eighteenth-century diaries and correspondence in which I have been happily immersed ever since. There are two reasons why I love nothing better than a collection of letters or a lengthy journal. Firstly, I'm gripped by the unfolding human story they capture, the narrative of real life as it is actually lived, the biggest events pressed hard up against the small details of the everyday round, matters of love and marriage, birth and death interspersed with accounts of dinner parties and shopping trips, the ups and downs of relationships, the likes and dislikes, triumphs and failures that are the stuff of all human experience. I always want to know what happened next, how things turned out. Did the marriage for which everyone had planned and schemed take place? Was it a success? Did the baby that seemed so sickly survive? Did the business venture prosper? Was a husband ever found for the awkward youngest sister, or a profession for the lacklustre youngest son?

Secondly, I so enjoy the way the letter- and diary-writers tell their stories. The eighteenth-century voice, in its most formal mode, can be stately and remote; but in more relaxed correspondence, the prevailing tone is quite different. Letters between family and friends have an immediacy and a directness that rarely fail to engage the reader. Educated eighteenth-century writers were extremely candid: there were few subjects that they considered off limits. They were intensely interested in themselves and their own concerns, thinking nothing of filling page after page with detailed analyses of their health, their thoughts, and the nature of their relationships, marital, professional or political. They were tremendous gossips. Some of them were also very funny, caustic, satiric, masters (and mistresses) of an ironic tone that feels very modern in its knowingness and is still able to raise a smile after so many years.

It is very easy, reading their letters, to feel that the people who wrote them are just like us. For me, that is part of the appeal of the period, and it is, to some extent, true. But in other ways, the reality of their lives is almost impossible for contemporary readers to appreciate. In the midst of a world that seems so sophisticated and so recognisable, eighteenth-century people encountered on a daily basis experiences which would horrify a modern sensibility. Outside the well-managed homes of the better-off, extremes of poverty and the brutal and degrading treatment of the powerless and vulnerable were everywhere to be found. Even the richest families lived with the constant spectre of sickness, pain and death and could not protect themselves against the disease that decimated a nursery, the accident that felled a promising young man or the complications that killed a mother in childbirth. There is a drumbeat of darkness in all the correspondence of this period that makes a modern reader pause to give thanks for penicillin and anaesthesia.

Many of the letter-writers who so assiduously chronicled the ebb and flow of family life were women. Then, as is perhaps still the case now, it was women who worked hardest to cement the social relationships that held scattered families and friends together. One of the ways they did this was by writing to everyone in their social circle, passing on news, advice and scandal, describing their feelings and speculating on the motives and emotions of those around them. This sprawling world of the family, especially the lives of women and children, is the territory I have always found most compelling. I am fascinated by the inner life of this intimate place and am endlessly curious about how it worked. I always want to find out who was happy and who was not, how duty was balanced with self-interest, and how power worked across the generations.

It was via these paths that I eventually came to fix upon the grandest family of them all as a suitable subject for a book. I had always been interested in George III, that much-misunderstood man, in whom apparently contradictory characteristics were so often combined: good-natured but obstinate, kind but severe, humane but unforgiving, stolid but with the occasional ability to deliver an unexpectedly sharp and penetrating insight. At first, however, it was the story of his wife and daughters that most attracted me. Queen Charlotte's reputation was, both in her own time and afterwards, equivocal at best. In her lifetime, she endured a very bad press, excoriated by her critics as a plain, bad-tempered harridan, miserly and avaricious, interested principally in the preservation of rigid court etiquette and the taking of copious amounts of snuff. The real story, as her letters and the diaries and correspondence of those around her reveal, was rather different. Charlotte was never easy to love or, in later life, to live with, but she had a great deal to bear. She was a very clever woman in an age that found clever woman unsettling. Her intellectual appetite was unequalled by any of her successors, but could never be expressed in a way that threatened established expectations about how queens were supposed to behave. She spent nearly twenty years of her life in a state of almost constant pregnancy. In public she embraced this as the destiny of a royal wife; but, as her private correspondence makes clear, she resented the decades spent in child-bearing. Before it was crushed by the horror of the king's illness, from which she never really recovered, and the pressures of her public role, which she sometimes found almost impossible to endure, her personality was much more attractive, sprightly, humorous and playful.

The lives of her six daughters seemed to contemporaries to contain little of interest except for the occasional whiff of scandal. They lingered unmarried for so long that they were described even by their own niece as 'a parcel of old maids'. Their narrative is perhaps more familiar now – they were the subject of a group biography by Flora Fraser in 2004 – and it is clear that beneath the apparently bland uneventfulness of their existence, the princesses too were subject to strong emotions which were often expressed in circumstances of great personal drama. Their lives were dominated by their struggles to balance what they saw as their duty to their parents with some degree of self-determination and freedom to make their own choices. Where did the obligations they owed to their mother and father end? When – if ever – might they be allowed to follow their own desire for love and happiness? These contests were largely fought out in the secluded privacy of home – 'the nunnery' as one of the princesses bitterly described it – which perhaps made the sisters' trials less visible than those of their more flamboyant brothers, but they were no less the product of powerful and often disruptive feelings.

These were extraordinary stories in themselves, and ones I longed to tell. But the more I read, the more I was convinced that the experiences of the female royals could really be appreciated only as part of a much wider canvas. The experiences of Charlotte and indeed all her children – the sons as much as the daughters – could not be understood without exploring the personality, expectations and ambitions of the king. It was George III, both as father and monarch, who established the framework and set the emotional temperature for all the relationships within the royal family. And, as I soon discovered, his ideas about how he wanted his family to work, and what he thought could be achieved if his vision were to succeed, went far beyond the happiness he hoped it would bring to his private world.

George was unlike nearly all his Hanoverian predecessors in his desire for a quiet domestic life. As a young man, he yearned for his own version of the family life he thought so many of his subjects enjoyed: an emotionally fulfilling, mutually satisfying partnership between husband and wife, and respectful but affectionate relations with their children. This was an ideal that suited his dutiful, faithful character, and which he genuinely hoped would make him and his relatives happy. But he also hoped that by changing the way the royal family lived, by turning his back on the tradition of adultery, bad faith and rancour that he believed had marked the private lives of his predecessors, he could reform the very idea of kingship itself. The values he and his wife and children embraced in private would become those which defined the monarchy's public role. Their good behaviour would give the institution meaning and purpose, connecting it with the hopes, aspirations and expectations of the people they ruled. The benefits he hoped he and his family would enjoy as individuals by living a happy, calm and rational family life would be mirrored by a similarly positive impact on the national imagination. In his thinking about his family, for the king, the personal was always inextricably linked to the political.

As I hope this book shows, there were many good things that emerged from George's genuinely benign intentions. But, as will also be seen, his vision imposed on his family a host of new obligations and pressures. George, Charlotte and their children were the first generation of royals to be faced with the task of attempting to live a truly private life on the public stage, of reconciling the values of domesticity with the requirements of a crown. The book's title, *The Strangest Family*, partly reflects the opinions of close observers and indeed of family members themselves that among the royals were to be found some very distinctive, strong-willed and colourful characters; but it also recognises the paradox at the heart of modern monarchy. For most people, the family represents the most intimate and personal of spheres. For royalty, it is also the defining aspect of their public identity. The modern idea of monarchy owes far more to George III and his conception of the royal role than is often realised.

His insight did much to ensure the survival of the Crown, linking it to the hearts and minds of the British in ways of which he would surely have approved. But, in other respects, his descendants still find themselves trying to square the circle he created, attempting to enjoy a family life defined by private virtues, yet obliged to do so in the unflinching glare of public scrutiny.

Although the experiences of George, Charlotte and their children are at the heart of this book, I have ranged beyond their stories to include those of their immediate forebears. It is impossible to appreciate what George III was attempting to achieve without understanding the moral world he sought so decisively to reject. In doing so, I was fascinated by the complicated marriage of George II and his wife Caroline (another clever Hanoverian queen), a stormy relationship coloured by passion, jealousy and deceit in fairly equal measure. Their hatred for their eldest son Frederick, operatic in its intensity, still makes shocking reading after so many years. I have also looked forward in time to include in some detail the story of George III's only legitimate grandchild, Princess Charlotte. Hers is a sensibility very different from that of her predecessors: she was a young woman of romantic inclination, devoted to the works of Lord Byron and given to flirtations with unsuitable officers. The clash of wills between the young Charlotte and her grandmother, the queen, is one in which two very different interpretations of royal, and indeed female, duty collide, with an outcome as unexpected as it is touching.

I did not set out to write a book that ranged so far across the generations and included so many large and powerful personalities. I believe, however, that without that level of scale and ambition, it would be impossible to do justice to the story I wanted to tell. Besides, I have always loved a family saga. That is the narrative that dominates the diaries and correspondence that have been my window onto the reality of eighteenth-century lives. I have tried to use those sources to let the characters in this book speak, as far as possible, for themselves. I like it best when their voices are heard as clearly and as directly as possible. It will be up to the reader to decide if I have succeeded.

Bath, July 2014

'But it is a very strange family, at least the children – sons and daughters'

SYLVESTER DOUGLAS, Lord Glenbervie, diarist

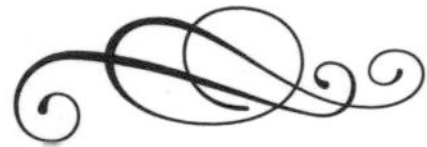

'No family was ever composed of such odd people, I believe, as they all draw different ways, and there have happened such extraordinary things, that in any other family, public or private, are never heard of before'

PRINCESS CHARLOTTE, daughter of George IV

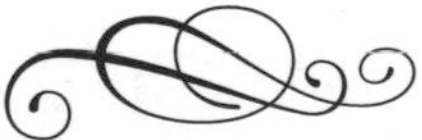

'Laughing, [she] added that she knew but one family that was more odd, and she would not name that family for the world'

PRINCESS AUGUSTA, mother of George III

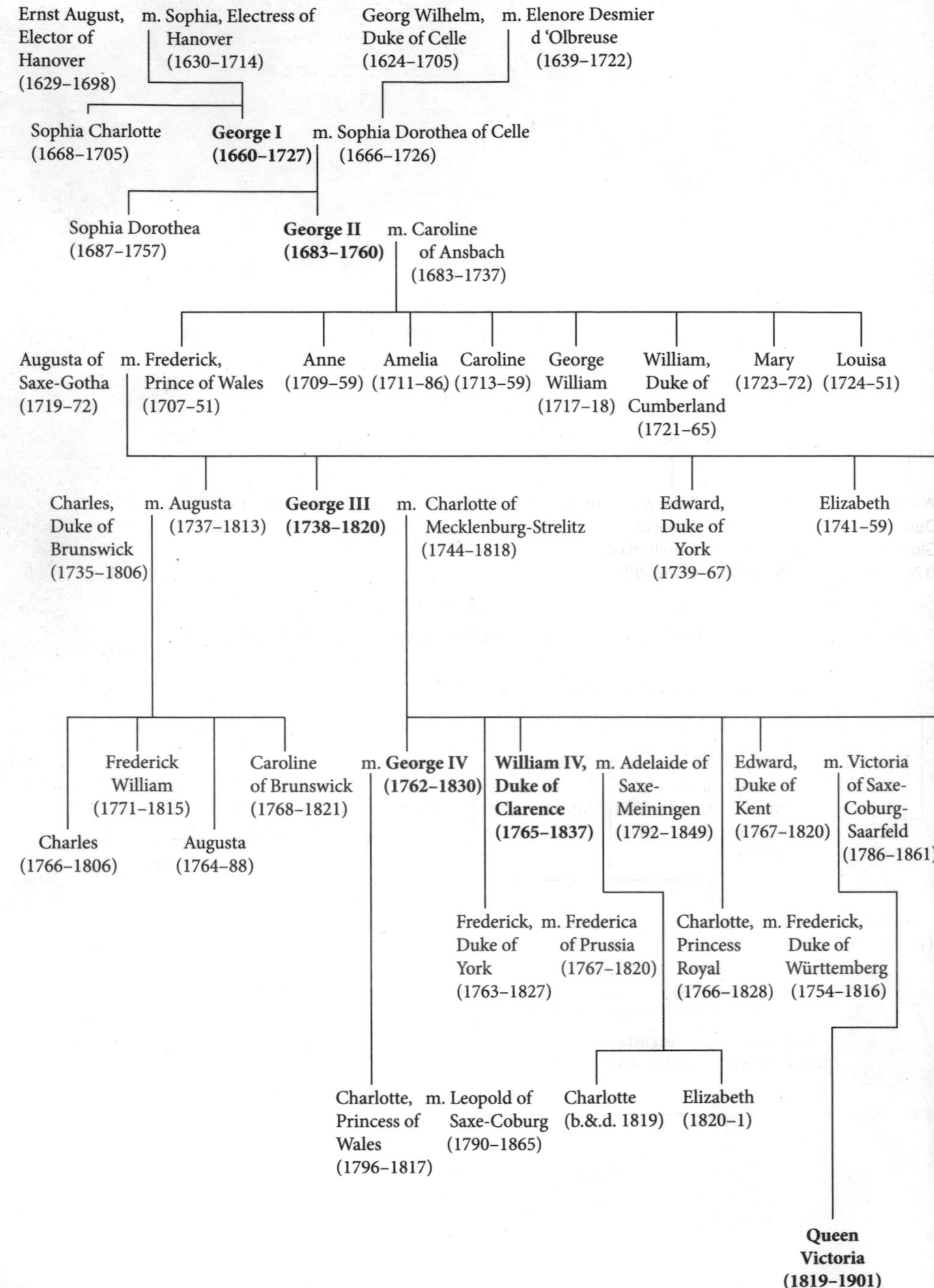
Ernst August, Elector of Hanover (1629–1698)
m. Sophia, Electress of Hanover (1630–1714)
Georg Wilhelm, Duke of Celle (1624–1705)
m. Elenore Desmier d 'Olbreuse (1639–1722)
Sophia Charlotte (1668–1705)
George I (1660–1727)
m. Sophia Dorothea of Celle (1666–1726)
Sophia Dorothea (1687–1757)
George II (1683–1760)
m. Caroline of Ansbach (1683–1737)
Augusta of Saxe-Gotha (1719–72)
m. Frederick, Prince of Wales (1707–51)
Anne (1709–59)
Amelia (1711–86)
Caroline (1713–59)
George William (1717–18)
William, Duke of Cumberland (1721–65)
Mary (1723–72)
Louisa (1724–51)
Charles, Duke of Brunswick (1735–1806)
m. Augusta (1737–1813)
George III (1738–1820)
m. Charlotte of Mecklenburg-Strelitz (1744–1818)
Edward, Duke of York (1739–67)
Elizabeth (1741–59)
Frederick William (1771–1815)
Caroline of Brunswick (1768–1821)
m. George IV (1762–1830)
William IV, Duke of Clarence (1765–1837)
m. Adelaide of Saxe-Meiningen (1792–1849)
Edward, Duke of Kent (1767–1820)
m. Victoria of Saxe-Coburg-Saarfeld (1786–1861)
Charles (1766–1806)
Augusta (1764–88)
Frederick, Duke of York (1763–1827)
m. Frederica of Prussia (1767–1820)
Charlotte, Princess Royal (1766–1828)
m. Frederick, Duke of Württemberg (1754–1816)
Charlotte, Princess of Wales (1796–1817)
m. Leopold of Saxe-Coburg (1790–1865)
Charlotte (b.&d. 1819)
Elizabeth (1820–1)
Queen Victoria (1819–1901)

The House of Hanover

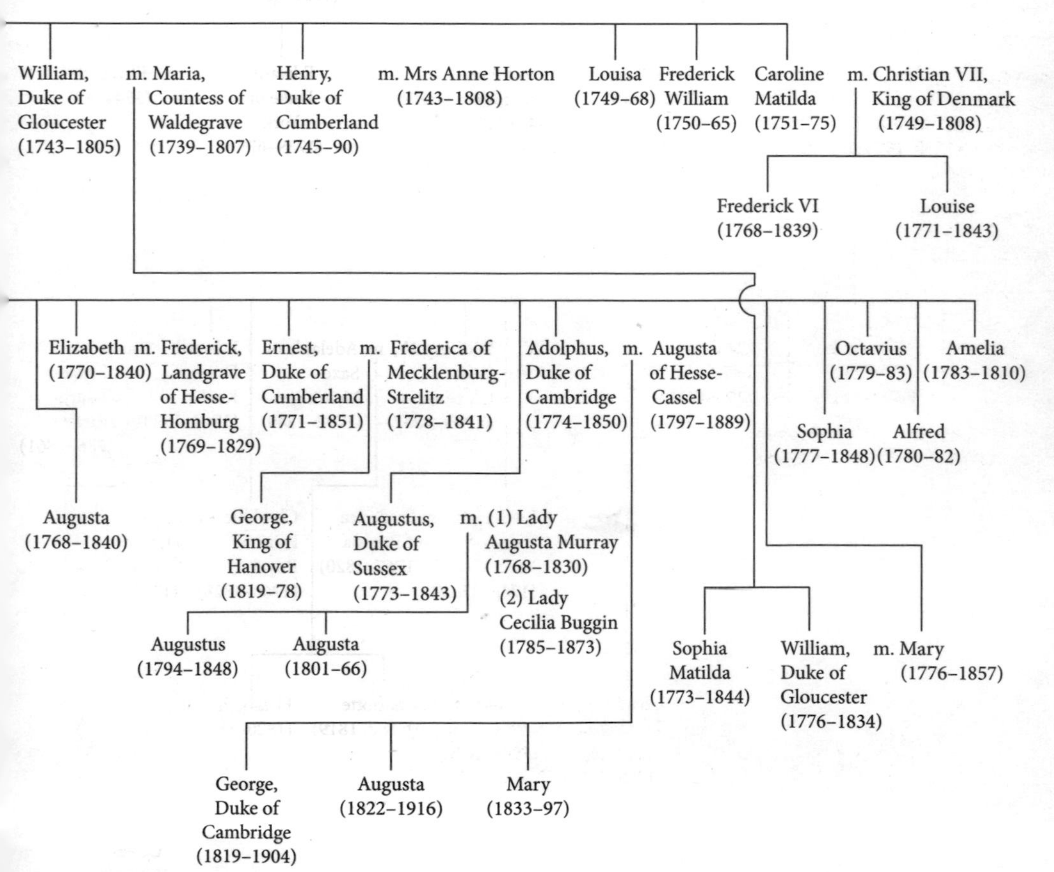

Prologue

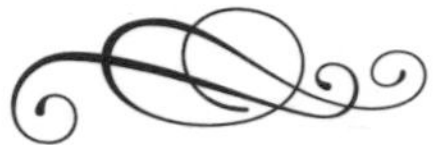

FORTY-FOUR YEARS AFTER THE EVENT took place that altered his life for ever, George III could still recall with forensic clarity exactly how it happened. On Saturday 25 October 1760, he had set off from his house in Kew to travel to London. He had not gone far when he was stopped by a man he did not recognise, who pulled a note out of his pocket and handed it to him. It was, George remembered, 'a piece of coarse, white-brown paper, with the name Schroeder written on it, and nothing more'. He knew instantly what this terse and grubby communication signified. It was sent by a German servant of his elderly grandfather, George II; using 'a private mark agreed between them', it informed the young man that the old king was dying, and that he should prepare to inherit the crown.[1]

To avoid raising alarm, George warned his entourage to say nothing about what had passed, and began to gallop back to Kew. Before he reached home, a second messenger approached him, bearing a letter from his aunt Amelia, the old king's spinster daughter. With blunt punctiliousness, she had addressed it 'To His Majesty'; George did not need to open it to understand that his grandfather was dead and that he had come into his inheritance. Amelia was probably the first person to call him by the title he would now bear for the rest of his life. With a similarly precise observation of the formalities, he signed his reply to her 'GR' – Georgius Rex. When he had set out for London that morning, he was the Prince of Wales, a young man of twenty-two embarking on a day of ordinary business, with no reason to suppose the life of perpetual anticipation and apprehension which he had endured since childhood was about to come to an end. The message contained in that 'coarse, white-brown paper' changed all that, turning him into the ruler of one of the most powerful nations in the world. 'A most extraordinary thing is just happened to me,' he scribbled breathlessly in a letter he wrote immediately after receiving the news.[2] He was right. His long apprenticeship was over. He was king at last, and the mission for which he had been preparing himself for so many years could now begin in earnest.

*

The prospects for the new reign looked exceptionally bright. 'No British monarch,' the diarist Horace Walpole later declared, 'has ascended the throne with so many advantages as George III.'[3] The new king was very fortunate in his timing. Had his predecessor died just a few years earlier, Walpole's bullish optimism would have been inconceivable. Since the mid-1750s, Britain had been embroiled in a territorial struggle between the monarchies of Europe which, by 1756, had metamorphosed into a conflict of international proportions. During the Seven Years War, in North America, the Caribbean and India, the British fought the French in a clash of would-be global superpowers to establish strategic mastery over whole continents. Things started badly for the British, but with the appointment of the buccaneering William Pitt as first (later known as 'prime') minister in 1757, the tide was decisively turned. In the course of a year, the French surrendered valuable sugar-producing islands in the West Indies, lost the Battle of Quebec, which challenged their cherished pre-eminence in Canada, and saw their fleet decisively beaten by the Royal Navy at Quiberon Bay. It was hardly surprising that 1759 became known as 'the year of victories'. As news of fresh triumphs continued to roll in, even the British themselves seemed somewhat taken aback by the scale and speed of their achievement. When the French capitulated at Pondicherry in 1761, which effectively forced them out of India, Walpole was not sure he could absorb any more success. 'I don't know how the Romans did, but I cannot support two victories every week.'[4]

Britain's confidence on the international stage was mirrored by a similarly robust sense of self-worth at home. César de Saussure, a Swiss traveller who visited Britain in 1727, was struck even then by the unshakeable sense of pride the British displayed in themselves and all their works: 'I do not think that there is a people more prejudiced in its own favour than the British people. They look upon foreigners in general with contempt and think nothing is done as well elsewhere as it is in their own country.'[5] The British had no difficulty in identifying the source of their good fortune: their political liberty, guaranteed to them by birthright and history, and enshrined in a constitutional settlement which protected them equally from the despotism of absolutist kings and the anarchy of the mob. De Saussure observed that the English 'value this gift more than all the joys of life, and would sacrifice everything to retain it'. Nor was this passionate attachment confined to the political classes. Even the poor, who could not vote, 'will give you to understand that there is no country in the world where such perfect freedom may be enjoyed as in England'.[6]

Liberty was not an unmixed blessing, however. Whilst foreign visitors found much to admire in the constitutional freedoms the British enjoyed, they were far more ambivalent when confronted with the impact of these ideas on the mass of the population. The assertive, aggressive, unapologetic behaviour of the urban poor, particularly in London, shocked observers used to more decorous (or more cowed) communities. De Saussure thought ordinary Londoners disrespectful, rowdy and threatening, 'of a very brutal and insolent nature, and very quarrelsome'. He was horrified by their habitual drunkenness and casual violence, but was most disturbed by their lack of respect for their social superiors. He noted – perhaps as a result of painful personal experience – that a finely dressed man, especially one 'with a plume in his hat or his hair tied in a bow', risked verbal abuse and worse if he walked alone through the poorer streets. On holidays such as Lord Mayor's Day, 'He is sure, not only of being jeered at and being be-spattered with mud, but, as likely as not, dead dogs and cats will be thrown at him, for the mob makes a provision beforehand of these playthings, so that they may amuse themselves with them on the great day.'[7]

The energetically expressed opinions of the crowd frequently went far beyond contempt for the sartorial pretensions of the rich. Mobilised in large numbers, the freeborn Englishman was given to demonstrations of popular feeling that were often violent. Issues of political and religious controversy (particularly those which were thought to undermine the dual foundations of British freedom – the

Protestant settlement and a limited monarchy) brought men and women on to the streets to make their views loudly known. Throughout the eighteenth century, the threat of disorder and disturbance was as much a part of the life of British politics as the parliamentary vote. As they went about the process of government, the great and the good were abused, threatened and sometimes physically manhandled; parades were staged, effigies burnt, stones thrown, windows broken, carriages overturned, property destroyed; there were injuries and sometimes deaths. The practice of liberty could be a rough business on the streets of George III's Britain.

If Britain in 1760, was a volatile and sometimes intimidating place, it was also an increasingly wealthy one. Almost every visitor commented on the general air of comfortable prosperity that manifested itself in the clean and well-appointed private houses, the luxurious inns and, above all, in the quality of the roads. Unlike most European highways, these were well engineered and very extensive, linking not just the great cities, but smaller market towns and villages. They were paid for by tolls, and regularly maintained. Foreigners were amazed to discover that travel, such an ordeal everywhere else, had in large areas of England become a leisurely communal pleasure. One bemused observer noted that even on a Sunday evening, the roads outside London were packed with people on the move, visiting, travelling, or simply taking the air. 'Carriages of every kind … succeeded each other without interruption and with such rapidity that the whole picture looked like magic; it certainly showed a degree of wealth and extent of population, of which one had no notion in France.'[8]

From the moment of their arrival, travellers to Britain were struck by the sheer busyness of the place. They were astonished by the air of perpetual activity, not just on the roads, but in the teeming streets; in the ports dominated by the masts of tightly packed ships; on the new canal systems, thronged with burdened barges; in the parks and pleasure gardens, where rich and poor mingled in huge numbers in pursuit of a good time. In fact, mid-eighteenth-century Britain had yet to experience the rapid growth in population that would see its towns and cities grow to unprecedented size in the next hundred years. There were around 7.5 million people living in England, Scotland and Wales in 1750. France, a much larger country, supported far greater numbers; in the same year, its population reached 25 million. The universal impression of Britain as a crowded, bustling community arose less from the absolute numbers of its inhabitants than from a far more significant development – the extraordinary size and influence of its capital city.

Although Britain was not yet a heavily populated country, it was already a strongly metropolitan one. London doubled in size between 1600 and 1800; by the end of the seventeenth century, it was the largest city in western Europe. By 1750, only 2.5 per cent of Frenchmen lived in Paris; in comparison, London housed 11 per cent of the population.[9] An unprecedented proportion of Britons were Londoners, whether by birth or immigration. Still more had some experience of metropolitan life, even if they subsequently left it behind them. It has been calculated that one in six of the population of mid-eighteenth-century Britain had lived in London at some stage in their lives.[10] The magnetic attraction of the capital was overwhelming, especially to foreign visitors. Most travellers went straight there, and few ventured beyond the southern counties which were already becoming the capital's dependent hinterlands. Their experiences were dominated by the time they spent in the capital, which shaped profoundly their perceptions of the country as a whole.

The lure of London was not confined to foreigners. Like so many other ambitious young men of the time, James Boswell was convinced that the only proper existence for an eager striver like himself was one lived to the full in London. He could not wait to leave his native Edinburgh behind and embrace all the possibilities London offered. Arriving at its outskirts in 1762, he was beside himself with anticipation, declaring that 'I was all life and joy!' As his carriage descended Highgate Hill, 'I gave three huzzas and we went briskly in.'[11] It was Boswell's great patron Samuel Johnson – himself a grateful emigrant from the staid Midlands – who famously linked the appetite for London's pleasures to the enjoyment of life itself. From his first arrival in town, Boswell did all he could to demonstrate the truth of Johnson's observation. Subject headings from the index to the *London Journal* that Boswell wrote during his stay between November 1762 and August 1763 give a taste of the capital's gamey appeal: 'Artists exhibitions, billiards, bleeding, Bow St magistrates court, card-playing, catch singing, circulating library, cock-fighting, concert, damning a play, Guards on parade, horseback rides, intrigues, Newgate prison, prostitution, royal menagerie, Mrs Salmon's waxworks, surgeons and their fees, Tyburn, execution at, watermen rowing for prizes.'[12]

London's reputation as the place where anything was on offer and where everything seemed achievable was then, as it is now, the key to much of its pungent attraction. But it promised far more than entertaining diversions. The growth of the capital was driven by the extraordinary number of roles it performed. It was the focus of the nation's politics. The king lived there, it was where Parliament assembled, and it was there that the political classes expected to fight their battles and win their arguments. At court at St James's, in the government offices at Whitehall, the debating chambers at Westminster, they planned their strategies and marshalled their supporters; in the conversations of the coffee houses and taverns, in the great mansions of aristocratic grandees and sometimes on the volatile, riotous streets, the successes and failures of their policies were forcibly and mercilessly assessed. London was also a magnet for anyone interested in the making and management of that other great lever of power: money. The capital was home to Europe's most sophisticated banking system, and to the busiest, most innovative and ambitious financial markets in the world. The wealthy moneymen of the City of London – known derisively as 'Cits', whose nouveau-riche antics were ruthlessly caricatured by contemporary satirists – had long overtaken the Dutch as the brokers, bankers and insurers of international choice. But London's commerce went far beyond the buying and selling of money. It was a thriving market place for the selling of goods as well as services. It was a great port, a major destination for shipping, whose crowded forests of masts packed into the Thames docks astonished foreign visitors and were a striking visual reminder of the other great preoccupation of eighteenth-century Britons: trade.

The whole of Europe benefited from an upturn in international trade in the middle years of the eighteenth century, but no nation did so with such spectacular results as Britain. British merchants dealt in a vast and ever-expanding range of goods. New essentials – such as tea, coffee and sugar – came into the country, whilst a host of exports – from textiles to metalwares to Josiah Wedgwood's competitively priced china – flowed out.

Other British entrepreneurs undertook a darker business. Slavery was 'one of the staple trades of Englishmen', and the great ports of Bristol and Liverpool were largely built on its tainted dividends.[13] The huge returns generated by such ventures, whether trading in people or in things, ramped up confidence, creating a perfect storm of enthusiasm for the very idea of commerce itself. 'There never was,' observed Samuel Johnson, 'from earliest ages, a time in which trade so much engaged the attention of mankind, or commercial gain was sought after with such general emulation.'[14] In Britain this was experienced with particular intensity; the nation's sense of itself as a great trading nation was, in the mid-eighteenth century, firmly and irrevocably embedded in its identity as a free and enterprising people. Part of the appeal was a simple one: trade made a great number of investors a great deal of money, but it played a role in the construction of an idea of Britishness that went far beyond the advantage of individual profit. The fruits of commercial enterprise were widely believed to underwrite all the constitutional advantages which made Britain so specially favoured among nations. The private wealth it generated, which could not be taken away by taxation unless approved by Parliament, acted as a bulwark against the ambitions of despotic power at home. A poor and hungry people was not a free people, and was easily corrupted by the bribes or threats of overmighty rulers. The profits of trade paid for a strong navy, which kept the seas safe for British exports abroad, but, unlike a standing army, could never be used to threaten the integrity of domestic politics. It delivered a prosperity which, as early economists already understood, kept the wheels and ploughs of industry turning. There was no aspect of the distinctive British way of life which it did not touch. It was little wonder that at every convivial supper or political gathering of the period, once a toast had been drunk to the king, it was the invocation 'To trade's increase!' that was greeted with the most heartfelt and passionate sense of shared feeling.

The wealth produced from the profits of trade was to be seen in all the great commercial centres of Britain – Liverpool, Bristol and Glasgow – which expanded rapidly in the 1760s and beyond. The influence of new money was also evident in the development of pleasure resorts such as Bath and Cheltenham, towns which existed largely as a way to spend profits made elsewhere. Then as now, it was through property – the building, designing and furnishing of houses – that individual prosperity found its most visible expression. These were the years in which the urban centres of Britain were rebuilt and re-imagined as the rich, the genteel and the polite moved surely and steadily out of the old city quarters, leaving behind their uncomfortable proximity with dirty trades and the insolent poor, constructing for themselves new houses built in terraces and squares, on clean, classical lines, punctuated by parks and gardens. Across the monied hotspots of Britain, the process was endlessly and elegantly replicated, from Edinburgh to Dublin to Newcastle, creating a vision of town life whose ordered, light and spacious appeal endures to this day.

The changes to the landscape of mid-eighteenth-century life were not confined to the cities. There was as yet little obvious sign of the revolution in industrial production that would transform Britain out of all recognition during George III's long reign. In the valleys of Coalbrookdale and the iron foundries of Wales, in the workshops of the Midlands and the mills of Lancashire, new technologies were being developed – engines, looms and furnaces – which would recast the relationship between humanity and the natural world, ushering in production on a hitherto unimaginable scale; but it would be at least another twenty years before these became the dominant and visible signature of British economic expansion.

But for most contemporaries, it was the farm, not the factory, which, after trade, was seen as the most forceful engine of change. For over a generation, it had been improvements in agriculture which had underpinned prosperity. The green, rural countryside that forms such an elegiac backdrop to so much Georgian art was in fact one of the most intensively managed landscapes in Europe. The application of scientific methods to farming – especially new fertilisation techniques which overcame the need to let fields lie fallow for years at a time – transformed crop yields and increased profits, providing a tempting incentive to consolidate smaller holdings into larger and more efficient businesses. For some, the result of these changes was impoverishment: families who had once owned small plots of land were forced off them and into the day labour market, subject to the fluctuating needs of the season and the whims of the farmer's overseer. For others, the result was cheaper food and much more of it. This left them with more disposable income to spend; for perhaps the first time in history, significant numbers of ordinary people had money to buy goods beyond the basic necessities of life. Their purchases in turn put more money into the hands of those who made the things they bought, and the outcome was a steady but significant increase in both the wealth and buying power of 'the poor and middling sorts'.

This steady diffusion of prosperity was obvious to anyone visiting Britain. Every observer noted that there was clearly a good deal of new money around. Among the very rich, it was apparent in the construction of great new country houses, and in the seemingly limitless demand for luxurious objects to put in them: clocks and carpets, portraits and brocades, china and silverware, chairs, tables and sideboards. What struck foreign visitors most powerfully, however, was the degree to which the middle classes, and even some of the poor, shared in the general sense of improved wellbeing. In the opinion of one German writer in the 1770s, the 'luxury' enjoyed by the middle and lower classes 'had risen to such a pitch as never before seen in the world'.[15] A few years later, a Russian traveller compared the general wellbeing he saw in London with the gulf between rich and poor he had witnessed in France. 'How different this is from Paris! There vastness and filth, here simplicity and astonishing cleanliness; there wealth and poverty in continual contrast, here a general air of sufficiency; there palaces out of which crawls poverty, here tiny brick cottages with an air of dignity and tranquillity, lord and artisan almost indistinguishable in their immaculate dress.'[16]

As he went on to remind his readers, squalor and poverty were of course still to be found in eighteenth-century England, but most foreign observers agreed that a larger proportion of the British now seemed to have escaped the worst deprivations that were the general experience of the European poor. Back in the 1720s, de Saussure had observed with surprise that 'the lower classes are usually well dressed, wearing good cloth and linen. You never see wooden shoes in England, and the poorest individuals never go with naked feet.'[17] Indeed, in England, the wearing of 'wooden shoes' was indelibly associated with the desperate poverty held to be the inevitable product of life under Catholic absolute monarchies. The passionate cry of: 'No popery and no wooden shoes!', which so often resounded through the streets of eighteenth-century London, was an expression of the conviction held by even the poorest Britons that they enjoyed a standard of living of which their foreign counterparts could only dream.

The small prosperity of small people created the demand for ever larger numbers of affordable goods. British manufacturers soon showed themselves eager and adaptable enough to supply them. Unlike many of its grander European competitors, the British market did not just cater to the super-rich – to 'the magnificence of princes'. It was just as interested in selling to new customers, less wealthy but more numerous. Matthew Boulton, the great Birmingham-based producer of the buckles and buttons that were an essential part of every eighteenth-century wardrobe, had no doubt which of the two kinds of buyer he valued most. 'We think it of far more consequence to supply the People than the Nobility only … We think that they will do more towards supporting a great Manufactory than all the Lords of The Nation.'[18] Boulton understood that an entire new market had emerged, a new generation of purchasers, looking to achieve their own moderately priced vision of the good life, and he and others were ready and willing to supply it. 'Thus it is,' wrote the clergyman and economist Josiah Tucker, 'that the English … have better conveniences in their houses and affect to have far more in quantity of clean, neat furniture and a greater variety, such as carpets, screens, window curtains, chamber bells, polished brass locks, fenders etc., (things hardly known abroad amongst persons of such rank) than are to be found in any country in Europe.'[19] These simple and often extraordinarily resilient objects, designed to appeal to the taste of modest eighteenth-century buyers, were made in such numbers that any frequenter of modern auction rooms or antique shops will be familiar with them. Those that have survived the uses and abuses of 250 years are often beautiful to look at and still desirable things to own. They are also mute witness to the power of a quiet revolution which began to transform British experience just as George III began his reign. He was the first king to rule over a nation of consumers.

The Britain in which the young king acceded in 1760 was an assertive and forceful society, sometimes brash and overbearing in the robustness of its self-belief. It was not an easy place in which to be poor, vulnerable, sensitive or a failure; but for those who could stand the pace, and who were not among the losers crushed by the relentlessness of its forward movement, the experience of being British in the mid-eighteenth century was dominated by a sense of energetic exhilaration, an acute consciousness of an upward trajectory towards levels of international power and domestic wealth that were unthinkable only a generation before. The experience of the nation thus mirrored that of its inhabitants; both now found themselves in possession of assets that had arrived with swift and surprising speed. Horace Walpole caught the mood perfectly. 'You would not know your country again,' he wrote to a friend who had long lived abroad. 'You left it as a private island living upon its means. You would find it now capital of the world.'[20]

*

In such circumstances, the accession of a youthful king, whose vitality seemed to reflect the ambition of the country he ruled, was greeted with unconstrained enthusiasm. George II had been on the throne since 1727. He was an old man, aged seventy-six at the time of his death, who belonged to the old world. Of the new monarch, Philip, 4th Earl of Chesterfield, usually the most detached and cynical of observers, wrote that he was the king of 'his united and unanimous people, and enjoys their confidence and love to such a degree that were I not as fully convinced as I am of His Majesty's heart and the moderation of his will, I should tremble for the liberties of my country'.[21]

Impressions of the young man at the centre of this whirlwind of attention were universally positive, contrasting his affability with the curmudgeonly attitudes of his elderly predecessor. Walpole, who rushed to court to get an early look at his new ruler, was pleased with what he found: 'This sovereign don't stand in one spot, with his eyes fixed royally on the ground and dropping bits of German news; he walks about and speaks to everybody.'[22]

The polite and considerate monarch had not yet grown into the bulky figure he would become in early middle age, the familiar image of florid imperturbability whose prominent blue eyes gaze so resolutely from later portraits. Although he was not conventionally handsome, the Duchess of Northumberland, who knew him well, described him tactfully as 'tall and robust, more graceful than genteel'. The family tendency towards fat, against which George struggled diligently throughout his life, meant that he would never look the part of either romantic hero or fashion plate. He had strong, white teeth, evidently enough of a rarity, even in aristocratic circles, to merit approving comment by a number of observers. His hair, when neither powdered nor hidden beneath a wig, was considered one of his best points. It was, the duchess recorded, 'a light auburn, which grew very handsomely to his face'. She also admired his clear and healthy complexion, but noted that in common with others of his age, 'he had now and then a few pimples out'. For the duchess, however, it was George's demeanour that mattered more. 'There was a noble openness in his countenance, blended with a cheerful good-natured affability,' which trumped his prosaic appearance and even gave him a certain fugitive charm.[23] The portrait that best captures the elusive quality of George's appeal was made a few years before his accession by the

Swiss painter Jean-Etienne Liotard. Delicately rendered in pastels, it does not flatter – the man George would later become is visible in the round lineaments of his face, the fullness of his mouth and the protuberance of his eyes – but it captures brilliantly the clear-eyed, healthy, pink-and-white freshness of his youthful self.

George's looks were only part of the story. In the opening weeks of his reign, admiration for the new king's 'open and honest countenance' was exceeded only by approval of the unstudied excellence of his behaviour. Everyone who saw him in the immediate aftermath of his grandfather's death commented on the considerate correctness of all his actions. 'He has behaved with the greatest propriety, dignity and decency,' observed Walpole.[24] He knew how to carry himself respectfully at solemn moments, but onlookers were also struck by his ability to strike a lighter note. His unforced, natural warmth of character was particularly admired. Lady Susan Fox-Strangways, who saw him often at court, approvingly observed in him 'a look of happiness and good humour that pleases everyone – and me in particular.'[25]

The grace and cheerfulness that George displayed in these days of excitement and promise were more than the temporary product of a moment; he was an essentially good-hearted man, who tried to observe the decencies of gentlemanly behaviour even in the darkest and most trying times of his reign. However, the polite, easy candour celebrated by so many observers in those early days was only part of who he really was. There was a sombre, more thoughtful cast to his character, which Liotard's portrait caught as acutely as it did the new-minted freshness of his features. The young George stares watchfully out from the canvas, with an air of wary self-containment. This is a serious man, with a serious purpose in mind – there is no hint of frivolity or light-heartedness in his measured expression. For all its tenderness, it is also an image of quiet, sustained – even steely – determination; and it was a better indicator of what lay in George's mind as he contemplated the future than all the benign gestures with which he navigated the immediate aftermath of his grandfather's death. For George III came to the throne determined to do more than merely replace George II. He aspired to be not just the next king, but a new kind of king.

As heir to the crown, George had spent much of his youth transfixed by the inevitability of his destiny, trying to comprehend what was expected of him. What was the true purpose of kingship in the modern world? Why had he been called upon to undertake this extraordinary and unasked-for burden? How could he discharge it as providence intended, fulfilling his duty to God, to himself and to his subjects? The answers to these questions, he eventually concluded, encompassed far more than the narrowly political concerns that had absorbed the energies of his predecessors. Their obsession with the day-to-day management of political business, the ups and downs and ins and outs of ministerial fortunes, had obscured the unique and singular meaning of sovereignty. The job of a king, George had decided, was no less than to graft moral purpose on to the nation's polity. It was his role to act as the conscience of the country, and the guardian of its true interests. He was, George believed, the active agent of principle in public life, a figure intimately connected with the daily workings of politics and yet with a significance far beyond them. It was his duty to remind politicians what the point of politics was and, through his interventions and understanding, to direct them beyond their personal and party interests towards a larger and more lasting common good.

This interpretation of his task did more than influence George's public life; it also profoundly shaped his sense of his duties as a private man. How could a king act as a moral compass to others if he did not live a moral life himself? George's idea of kingship thus reached far beyond a purely public dimension; it contained within itself a powerful personal imperative too. There was a direct connection between his actions in the political world and his conduct at home. He could not act as a force for good in the national interest if he was unable to live by right principles in his private life.

George's desire to see these ideas reflected in his actions as king was to put a great deal of pressure on the established order of politics in the years immediately after his accession; but it was their impact on the intimate world of the royal family that would prove far more revolutionary and of much greater lasting significance. He knew that to deliver the moral authority he needed to justify his vision, he would need to create a new kind of family life for himself. This meant redefining the personal relationships at its heart, reshaping what it meant to be a royal husband, wife, son or daughter. This would involve a greater emphasis on meeting high moral standards, a greater stress on duty, obligation and conscience. But he would also attempt to introduce into these roles something of the human warmth and emotional authenticity he believed non-royals found in them, hoping to provide for his wife and his children the solace and affection that seemed so singularly lacking in the lives of his immediate predecessors.

Because in becoming a new kind of king, George recognised that he would also have to become a new kind of Hanoverian. He understood that his idea of kingship required him to turn his back on his family's past, rejecting a malign inheritance of emotional dysfunction that had been handed down from generation to generation. Both his great-grandfather, George I, and grandfather, George II, had hated their sons with a passion bordering on madness. None of his male relations had been faithful to his wife. Every Hanoverian prince kept a succession of mistresses with scant concern for the feelings of his spouse, who responded with either mute resignation or loud and furious cries of dismay. The children of these unhappy unions were, unsurprisingly, rarely happy themselves. Drawn into feuds between their parents, they were angry, jealous and disaffected. They schemed and quarrelled between themselves and seemed destined to repeat the behaviour that had destroyed any chance of contentment for their parents. As George saw it, this legacy of amoral, cynical behaviour had warped and corrupted the Hanoverians, crippling their effectiveness as rulers and making their private lives miserable. It had made them bad kings and bad people. It had set husband against wife, father against son, sister against brother. It had thwarted their ambitions and corrupted their affections, leaving in its wake nothing but bitterness.

George planned to put an end to the whole painful cycle. On the very day he became king, he sent for his uncle, William, Duke of Cumberland, the victor of Culloden, with whom he had had many differences in the past, and announced his intention to outlaw the old habits of spite and bad faith. Walpole heard that George had been most explicit in signalling the magnitude of the change, telling the duke that 'it had not been common in their family to live well together, but that he was determined to live well with all his family'.[26] It was such a public declaration that everyone appreciated its significance.

George's intention to reform the way his family related to one another underpinned all the decisions he made about his private life in the years that followed. It dictated his choice of a wife, and shaped the ambitions he had for their relationship within marriage. It influenced his attitude to fatherhood, and was the foundation upon which he based the upbringing of his small children. It governed the way the young princes and princesses were educated and laid down a pattern of behaviour they were expected to follow as adults. Alongside his profound Christian faith – another distinction that marked him out from his forebears – it informed almost every action he took in relation to his intimate, personal world.

At one level, his devotion to the project grew out of something deeper than conscious strategy; it was a manifestation of the most enduring aspects of his personality, a reflection of the qualities of exacting, dutiful conscientiousness that were indivisible from his character. George acted as he did because he was who he was. But his desire for change owed as much to his sense of history as to the promptings of his nature. He was profoundly aware of his family's failings and believed passionately that it was his duty to reject the pattern of behaviour they had bequeathed to him. For that reason, the lives of George's predecessors are worth exploring, in all their dissolute, chaotic extraordinariness. They were the mirror image of everything George thought valuable and true in human relationships – a dark vision of just how wrong things could go when all sense of discipline, restraint and honest affection was lost. To appreciate what motivated the most upright of the Hanoverians, it is necessary to understand something of the people against whom he so firmly defined himself.

CHAPTER 1

The Strangest Family

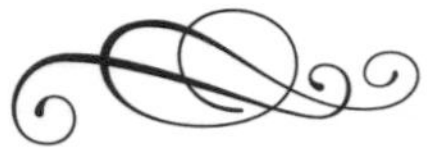

GEORGE III'S FIRST SPEECH FROM the throne was a resounding declaration of his particular fitness to take up the task before him. 'Born and educated in this country,' he pronounced, 'I glory in the name of Britain.'[1] It was not a statement any of his immediate predecessors could have made, which was of course precisely why he said it. From the very earliest days of his reign, he sought to mark himself out from his Hanoverian forebears. Neither George I nor George II had been born in Britain, and neither ever thought of the country as home. Their true *Heimat* was Hanover, a princely state in northern Germany in whose flat farmlands the dynasty had its ancestral roots. They both thought of themselves first and foremost as electors of Hanover; their kingship of England, Scotland and Ireland came very much second in their hearts.

When George III became monarch, the family had been somewhat reluctantly seated on the throne for only forty-six years. The crown of Great Britain had not been a prize they had expected to inherit, but they had done so with the death of Queen Anne in 1714. Anne was the daughter of James II, the last Stuart king, who was forced off his throne in 1688 when his Catholicism became unacceptable to the Protestant English. In the Glorious Revolution that followed, the Dutch prince William of Orange, nephew and son-in-law of the deposed James, was invited to become king, with the stipulation that henceforth, only a Protestant could become sovereign, a qualification still in force today. Anne, who succeeded the childless William, was known with cruel irony as 'the teeming Princess of Denmark'. Her pregnancies were many, but, despite an appalling catalogue of gynaecological endurance, she had no living children to show for it; she lost five babies in infancy and suffered thirteen miscarriages. When her only surviving child, the eleven-year-old Duke of Gloucester, died in 1700, it was clear that an heir must be looked for elsewhere.

The defenders of the Glorious Revolution did not find it easy to identify a suitably qualified candidate. Catholicism ruled out James II's exiled son, who had otherwise by far the strongest claim, as well as fifty-six other religiously unacceptable potential heirs. Eventually, it was decided to offer the crown to Electress Sophia of Hanover. A daughter of Charles I's sister Elizabeth, in purely dynastic terms her claim was weaker than those of many more directly related contenders, but her impeccable Protestant credentials won the day, and it was her name and that of her descendants which was enshrined in the Act of Settlement of 1701 as heirs to the crown if Queen Anne should die without a child. When Anne's health, exhausted by a lifetime of fruitless childbearing, fatally gave out in 1714, the electress was already dead, so the succession passed to her eldest son, George Louis. He was crowned in London later that year as George I.

It was not an entirely popular choice. The Jacobites – supporters of the old Stuart monarchy – rioted in at least twenty English towns. It was worse in Scotland, still smarting with outraged national grievance at the Act of Union, which linked the nations together in 1707, and whose simmering discontents erupted into the uprisings of 1715 and 1745. Although on those occasions it looked as if Hanoverians might be forced back to the electorate that was always their first love, they hung on, somewhat despite themselves, and it was their dynasty that ruled Britain until the death of George III's son, William IV, in 1837.

As a child, the diarist Horace Walpole, who wrote so voluminously about George I's successors, had a brief encounter with the first of the Hanoverians. His father, Sir Robert Walpole, was George's first minister, and as such was able to gratify for his son 'the first vehement inclination that I ever expressed … to see the king'. He was taken in the evening to St James's Palace and, after supper, informally introduced to the monarch. The ten-year-old Horace 'knelt down and kissed his hand, he said a few words to me, and my conductress led me back to my mother'. Writing nearly seventy years later, Walpole recalled that 'the person of the king is as perfect in my memory, as if I saw him but yesterday. It was that of an elderly man, rather pale and exactly like his pictures and coins; tall; of an aspect rather good than august; and with a dark tie wig, a plain coat, waistcoat and breeches of a snuff-coloured cloth, with stockings of the same colour, and a blue riband all over.' He had, he thought in retrospect, been remarkably indulged, for the king 'took me up in his arms, kissed me and chatted some time'.[2]

Walpole, who in later life liked to think of himself as almost a republican, and who observed that he had 'never since felt any enthusiasm for royal persons', was clearly captivated. But there was another side to the king who seemed so kind and genial to the starstruck small boy. For it was George I who must bear much of the responsibility for nurturing the tradition of Hanoverian family hatred that was to bequeath such a miserable inheritance to future generations.

*

George I's own experience of family life was hardly a happy one. His father, Ernst August, was a man of calculating ambition, dominated by the all-pervasive desire to see his dukedom of Hanover elevated to the far greater status of an electorate. His many children were raised in an atmosphere of military discipline, expected to display absolute obedience to his will and utter devotion to the grand project of dynastic consolidation. He seldom saw any of them alone or in informal circumstances; unsurprisingly, they were said to be 'solemn and restrained' in his presence.[3] Ernst's wife Sophia, whose antecedents were ultimately to bring the crown of Great Britain into the family's possession, was a far more relaxed and sympathetic character than her unbending husband – Walpole described her as 'a woman of parts and great vivacity' – but she too submitted without question to her husband's severe dictatorship.[4] Any resistance on her part had been undone by love. She had expected very little from her arranged marriage, and when, against all her expectations, Ernst proved a passionate and enthusiastic lover, Sophia could not believe her luck. From her wedding night onwards, for the rest of her life, she was completely in thrall to her husband's judgement, never venturing to set her own considerable intellect against any of his schemes. Ernst's numerous affairs with other women caused her much pain – in middle age, she wrote sadly that she could not believe she had ever been so foolish as to imagine he would remain faithful to her for ever – yet she fought hard to preserve her primacy in his eyes. She was much tried by his long relationship with the malicious Countess von Platen, who subjected her over many years to a litany of carefully calculated public insults; but Sophia's commitment to the errant Ernst August never wavered. She once declared that she would 'gladly have followed him to the Antipodes'.[5]

Sophia's dogged devotion won her no part at all in her husband's political strategising. He acknowledged the sharpness of her mind but denied her any active role in his schemes. She was 'without influence' in family affairs and allowed no say in the making of even the most significant decisions. When Ernst decided to disinherit his many younger sons in order to consolidate all the family possessions in the hands of George, the eldest, Sophia could do nothing to protect their interests. Angry and betrayed, three of the brothers left Ernst's court and signed on as soldiers in the Imperial service. Within a few years, all had died in battle, to the despairing grief of their mother. She was equally powerless when Ernst began to make marriage plans for the favoured George. Ernst had long before decided that his eldest son would marry his cousin, Sophia Dorothea of Celle, thus uniting two branches of the family dukedoms into a single greater state.

For all its desirability as a political alliance, it was obvious to anyone who knew them that George and Sophia Dorothea were hardly well matched. Sophia Dorothea, who was only eleven when the marriage was first proposed, had been brought up from her earliest days in a relaxed atmosphere of indulgence and luxury. Her father, a very different man from his single-minded brother Ernst, had married for love a woman considered beneath him in the complicated gradations of princely hierarchy, and had sacrificed the opportunity for further aggrandisement as a result. Sophia Dorothea, the only child of this love match, grew up into a beautiful woman – sophisticated, conscious of her attractiveness, and considered very French in her tastes. She loved to be amused and entertained, and was said to be obsessed by fashion. Lively and good-looking, she had no shortage of suitors. Her prospective mother-in-law regarded her balefully; she was sure she would not find a soulmate in her reserved and cautious eldest son.

Sophia, who described herself as 'a nearly stupidly fond mother', was devoted to the silent and watchful George.[6] She admired her son's deep sense of responsibility and his formidable devotion to duty. Others found him harder to appreciate. His cousin, the Duchess of Orléans, thought him 'ordinarily neither cheerful nor friendly, dry and crabbed'. She complained that 'his words have to be squeezed out of him', that he was suspicious, proud, parsimonious and had 'no natural good-heartedness'.[7] Sophia maintained that those who thought her son sullen simply did not understand him; they did not see that, beneath his undemonstrative surface, he took things much to heart, and was far more sensitive than he was prepared to show. But she knew him well enough to suspect that he was not the best partner for the outgoing Sophia Dorothea, who loved playful conversation, sought out cheerful company and had a taste for extravagant entertainments. The prospective bride's mother had similar misgivings; but neither could persuade their respective husbands to take their concerns seriously.

George himself had little to say on the subject. It was widely supposed that he would have been happy to be left alone with his mistress, a sister of the Countess von Platen, who had – as it were – continued the family business, becoming the son's lover, as her sister was the father's. However, obedience, not self-fulfilment, came first in the young George's mind. He had seen Sophia Dorothea, and had apparently been impressed by her good looks; but there is little doubt that he would have taken her anyway, regardless of any personal qualities, once his father had wished it. His mother once remarked that 'George would marry a cripple if he could serve the House of Brunswick'.[8] In 1682, the ill-matched couple did the bidding of their fathers, and were married. Sophia Dorothea was sixteen, her groom five years older.

At first they seem to have made the best of things, and in 1683 Sophia Dorothea gave birth to a son, George August. Such speedy provision of a healthy male heir raised her immeasurably in Ernst's eyes, and for a few years Sophia Dorothea's life was probably not unpleasant. Under the eye of her satisfied father-in-law, she enjoyed court life at the elaborate palace of Herrenhausen, relishing the parties, masques and concerts Ernst August laid on there to magnify his grandeur. She saw very little of her husband. George's great passion was the army, which took him away on active service for long periods. When Ernst August took his entire court to Italy for a year, Sophia Dorothea went on the extended holiday without her husband. Reunited with George on her return, she conceived a daughter who was named after her. But thrown back into each other's company, the strategy of polite coexistence the couple had maintained with some success began to fall apart. Bored and frustrated, Sophia Dorothea began to behave badly; she picked quarrels, caused scenes and was outspokenly impatient of the etiquette that ruled court life, apparently driven both to dominate and to despise the circumstances in which she lived. One observer called her '*une beauté tyrannique*'.[9]

Her unhappiness was given an edge of anger when she discovered that her taciturn husband had taken another mistress, and one whom he seemed genuinely to love. Melusine von Schulenberg had none of Sophia Dorothea's physical attractions – she was tall and thin, nicknamed 'the scarecrow' by George's mother – but she was calm, malleable and good-natured, in contrast to Sophia Dorothea's more febrile character. She sought to manage George's moods, and make his life easier, whilst his wife seemed only to cause him difficulties. Sophia Dorothea was bitterly humiliated by her husband's public preference for a woman far less beautiful and of lower social status than herself, and she refused to adopt the wronged wife's traditional stance of dignified resignation. She scolded her resentful husband, made scenes at court, and complained to her father-in-law. In doing so, not only did she earn the lasting resentment of George's mother (who could not see why she should not submit quietly to marital infidelity, as she had done), but also made enemies of the powerful Platen women, who disliked Sophia Dorothea's wilder accusations against mistresses and their wiles. Unhappy, rejected and isolated amongst people who were embarrassed and annoyed by her indiscreet outbursts, Sophia Dorothea was in a very vulnerable state. It is perhaps not surprising that she was so quickly persuaded to do the very worst and dangerous thing she could have done in such circumstances: fall in love with another man.

It was at this inauspicious moment that 'the famous and beautiful' Count Philip von Königsmark arrived at the Hanoverian court. He was a Swedish aristocrat, rich, handsome, clever, witty and assured, an archetypal sophisticated bad boy who had gambled, fought and drunk his way across Europe before enlisting as an officer in the Hanoverian service. He was everything Sophia Dorothea's dour husband was not, and was obviously attracted to her. They enjoyed each other's company, and when he left to join the army, he began to write to her. Soon the letters they exchanged were those of lovers. At first, they were careful

– 'If I were not writing to a person for whom my respect is as great as my love,' wrote Königsmark, 'I should find better terms to express my passion' – but as their relationship grew more intense, they became less discreet.[10]

When Königsmark returned, they snatched meetings in corridors, and exchanged glances in ballrooms. People noticed. They became the object of gossip, spread avidly by the Platens. Eventually, even Sophia Dorothea's mother heard the talk, and begged her daughter to break off the affair. She refused, and for over two years sustained her love for the count through occasional meetings and lengthy correspondence, in which she did not hesitate to declare the strength of her feelings, even confessing she would like to abandon her empty, unsatisfactory life. 'I thought a thousand times of following you,' she wrote, 'what would I not give to be able to do it, and always be with you. But I should be too happy and there is no such bliss in this world.'[11]

Yet for all her declaration of its impossibility, the idea of starting a new life with Königsmark became an obsession for her. By 1694, both her parents were aware that she wanted to end her twelve-year marriage. Rumours of an impending elopement transfixed the court. Königsmark's recent appointment as commander of a Saxon regiment seemed to offer the couple both the resources and the opportunity to run away together.

Then in July events came to a sudden and horrible conclusion. Whilst drunk, Königsmark was heard publicly discussing the affair; as a result, he was ordered, allegedly by Ernst August himself, to leave Hanover that very night. He was then seen entering the palace, apparently to say goodbye to his lover. Horace Walpole later heard that with the assistance of Sophia Dorothea's ladies, 'he was suffered to kiss her hand before his abrupt departure, and was actually introduced by them into her bedchamber the next morning before she rose.'[12] Others maintained he never reached his rendezvous. What is certain is that after his late-night arrival at the Leine palace, Königsmark was never seen again.

Exactly what happened to him remains a mystery. It was widely suspected he had been murdered; his remains were supposed to have been thrown into a river in a sack weighted with stones.[13] Nothing was ever definitively proved, and rumours concerning Königsmark's fate circulated around the princely courts of Europe for years. Walpole, however, believed he knew the truth. A generation later, when Sophia

Dorothea's son George II ordered alterations to be made to his mother's old apartments at Leine, Walpole was told that the builders made a gruesome discovery: 'The body of Königsmark was discovered under the floor of the Electoral Princess's dressing room, the count probably having been strangled the instant he left her, and his body secreted there.'[14] This discreditable story was, asserted Walpole, 'hushed up', but he claimed that his father, Sir Robert, had heard it directly from George II's wife, Queen Caroline.

Whatever Königsmark's fate, it is hard to believe that Ernst August played no part in it. The payment of large sums of money by Ernst to a small group of loyal courtiers shortly after the event seems more than coincidental. Ernst certainly had sufficient motive at least to connive at the killing. After a lifetime of planning and scheming, he had finally achieved the coveted status of elector only two years before, in 1692. The humiliation of his son at the hands of an adulterous wife did not form part of his plan for the continued upward rise of his family's power and influence. It is unlikely, however, that his role in the affair will ever finally be established. The role played by Sophia Dorothea's husband in her lover's disappearance is even harder to assess. Perhaps intentionally, George was away from court at the time of Königsmark's disappearance. But if he was ignorant of any plans to dispose of the count, he was fully complicit in what now happened to his wife.

Sophia Dorothea was hustled away to a remote castle at Ahlden, Lower Saxony, where she was kept isolated in the strictest confinement. Letters from her were found at Königsmark's house, and shown to her father who, as a result of what they disclosed, effectively abandoned her. Her mother was refused access to her. Immured alone at Ahlden, she was questioned over and over again about the precise nature of her relationship with Königsmark. She always denied that she had committed what she called '*le crime*', but the couple's correspondence contradicted her assertions. In them, Königsmark made it clear how much he hated the thought of Sophia Dorothea having sex – or, as he put it, '*monter à cheval*' – with her husband. In her replies, Sophia Dorothea reassured him that George was a very poor lover in comparison with himself, and added vehemently that she longed for George to die in battle. It is probable that George was shown these letters, which may explain some of the harshness with which Sophia Dorothea was treated in the months that followed.[15]

At first, it was hard to know what to do with George's errant wife. In the end, she was persuaded to become the unwitting author of her own misery. She was encouraged to ask for a separation from her husband, which she did almost willingly, on the grounds that 'she despaired of ever overcoming the aversion the prince has for several years evinced towards her'.[16] It is unlikely she knew at this stage that Königsmark was dead; naively, she may still have hoped to be reunited with him after a separation had taken place. Armed with his wife's declaration, in December 1694, George was quickly able to obtain a divorce. Sophia Dorothea hoped that afterwards she would be allowed quietly 'to retire from the world', expecting to live with her mother at Celle; instead she was returned to Ahlden, where she was locked up and, in all but name, imprisoned.

Any reminders of Sophia Dorothea's presence were ruthlessly and systematically erased from the Hanoverian court. Her name was struck out of prayers, and all portraits of her taken down. She had become a non-person, and disappeared into a confinement from which she would never emerge. She had not been allowed to say goodbye to her children – twelve-year-old George and seven-year-old Sophia Dorothea – before she was taken away. She would not see them again. Her name was never mentioned to them, and they were forbidden to speak of her. She was permitted to take portraits of them with her, which she regarded as her most precious possessions. When Ernst August died, and her ex-husband inherited his title, she wrote to him, begging to be allowed to see her children. He did not reply. 'He is so cold, he turns everything to ice,' commented the Duchess of Orléans sadly.

For the first two years, Sophia Dorothea was held entirely inside the Ahlden castle. Later, she was able to walk outside for half an hour a day. George did not deprive her of money and she lived in some luxury, dressed in the fashionable clothes she had always loved. There were few people to admire them, however. No visitors were permitted. Sophia's only contact with her family was through the eighty-one pictures of her relations that she had hung on her walls, including one of her ex-husband. She did not read a letter that had not been scrutinised by her gaoler first. Surrounded by a small entourage of elderly ladies, Sophia went nowhere unattended. The boredom of her life seems to have overwhelmed her, and she sought sensation wherever she could find it. On rare outings in her state carriage, she always asked to have the horses driven at the highest possible speed. Her mother, who had been tireless in her appeals to see her daughter, was eventually allowed to visit her; but after her death, Sophia Dorothea saw no one. In 1714, when George crossed the North Sea to take up his new responsibilities in Britain, it was suggested to him that he might now relax the conditions under which his ex-wife dragged out her existence; but he was implacable. Sophia Dorothea endured this shadow of a life for thirty-one years. In 1726, she became seriously ill. Her attendants tried to raise her spirits by showing her the portraits of her children, but when this much relied-upon source of comfort failed, they realised she was dying. A few days later, she was dead.

If George was troubled by guilt at any point throughout her long exile, he gave no sign of it. He never commented on his ill-starred marriage, nor its tragic end. He did not marry again, but lived in apparently placid contentment with Melusine von Schulenberg, whom he later ennobled as the Duchess of Kendal.

Yet there remained in George's carefully preserved, quiet life an unignorable reminder of a partnership he had never wanted, and which had caused him such public humiliation. The two children he had fathered with Sophia Dorothea could not be expunged or denied. His daughter he seems to have regarded benignly, although she played almost no part in his daily life; but his relationship with his son could not be similarly consigned to the margins of his public world. As his heir, the young Prince George represented a dynastic and political fact which George was compelled to acknowledge. But he could not – and would not – be brought to love the boy.

*

As a child, the prince had been very attractive. An English visitor to Hanover said he had 'a very winning countenance'. He was small and slender, with fair hair and pale skin, a lively and inquisitive boy. 'He speaks very gracefully, and with the greatest easiness imaginable, nor does his great vivacity let him be ignorant of anything.'[17] He was highly strung, racked by intense emotions, much subject to 'blushes and tears'. It was impossible not to see in the son the image of his mother, and this sealed his father's inveterate dislike for him. In later life, Prince George acknowledged in the most matter-of-fact way that his father 'had always hated him and used him ill'. Disdain, ridicule and indifference were familiar fare. He could think of only one occasion when the old man had found anything complimentary to say about him, and despite its characteristically barbed quality, he quoted it with poignantly transparent pride. As the courtier and diarist, John, Lord Hervey, recounted: 'When Lord Sunderland had tried to fix some lie on him, the late king (his father) had answered, "No, no. I know my son; he is not a liar, he is mad, but he is an honest man."'[18]

It was hardly surprising that by the time he was an adult, George disliked his father as much as his father seemed to despise him. It was plain to everyone who considered it that the great, undiscussed, unresolved nightmare of Sophia Dorothea's ruined life lay at the heart of their mutual resentment. 'Whether the prince's attachment to his mother embittered his mind against his father,' mused Walpole, 'or whether hatred of his father occasioned his devotion to her, I do not pretend to know.'[19] Prince George was as silent on the painful subject of Sophia Dorothea as was his father. Hervey, who knew him very well when he was king, noticed that although 'he discoursed so constantly and so openly of himself', there was one subject that was never brought up. He touched on everything 'except what related to his mother, whom on no occasion I ever heard him mention, not even inadvertently, or indirectly, as if such a person never existed'.[20]

Prince George grew into a volatile and unpredictable young man. His temper, which worsened as he grew older, was always explosive. Unlike his taciturn father, who suppressed his brooding antagonisms, his son's rages were more flamboyant affairs. Always a great talker, the prince's volubility ran away with him when he was cross; anger provoked in him diatribes of eloquent fury. When words failed him, he was known to throw his wig off and kick it around the room in frustration. It was hardly surprising that, as the Duchess of Marlborough recorded, he was sometimes considered 'a little bit cracked'.[21] In comparison with his father, who never said more than he needed to, George was effusive, in bad moods and good. His happiness was expressed with as much noise and passion as his anger, as anyone who antagonised him soon discovered. His feelings were always strong, and his inability to control them often made him appear ridiculous.

Beneath the frequent empty bluster, though, were more solid qualities. He was genuinely brave, not afraid to do what he thought was right, even at the cost of his reputation. He did not bear political grudges, and had little of his father's unforgiving rancour. Horace Walpole believed 'he had fewer sensations of revenge ... than any man who ever sat upon a throne'.[22] His physical courage was considerable. Trained as a soldier, he served as a cavalry officer with John, 1st Duke of Marlborough, at the Battle of Oudenarde in 1708, when he was twenty-four. He was engaged in the thick of the fighting, charging at the head of his troops, and, when his horse was shot from under him, he mounted another and plunged back into the mêlée. Marlborough thought he had behaved with distinction, and wrote to tell his father so.[23] But the elder George refused to allow his son a permanent military role, which bitterly disappointed the prince and did nothing to improve relations between them.

For the rest of his life, George remained devoted to the soldierly ideal. Nothing interested him more than the business of warfare – from grand strategy to the design of a medal or the cut of a uniform. He jealously guarded his right to make senior army appointments, and his love of pomp and pageantry was perhaps a way of staying close to a world from which politics excluded him. In his forties, the desire to be back in the field still burnt just as brightly as it had in his youth. Hervey recalled that he declared 'almost daily and hourly' to Sir Robert Walpole that 'it was with his sword alone that he desired to keep the balance of Europe; that war and action were his sole pleasures; that age was coming on fast to him ... He could not bear, he said, the thought of growing old in peace.' In response, Walpole patiently pointed out that 'it would not be a very agreeable incident for the King of Great Britain' to find himself 'running again through Westphalia with 70,000 Prussians at his heels'.[24] (George had his way in the end: in 1743, when he was sixty, and Walpole was no longer around to thwart him, he led troops victoriously into battle once more, against the French at Dettingen near Frankfurt. He was the last British king to do so, a fact that would have delighted him perhaps more than any other accolade.)

George was never a scholar, and loved to boast of his disdain for intellectual ideas. 'He often used to brag of the contempt he had for books and letters,' recalled Hervey, 'saying how much he hated all that stuff from his infancy.' He said he despised reading even as a child, because he 'felt as if he was doing something mean and below him'.[25] But for all his distrust of the outward manifestations of the life of the mind, George's antipathy concealed a sharp intellect. He spoke four languages – German, English, French and Italian – and had a quick tongue in all of them. He was a ready deliverer of woundingly pungent phrases or mocking observations, some of which suggested that he read rather more than he was prepared to admit. Like all his family, he loved music (he would become a devoted patron of Handel), but he had no patience with abstract analytical thinking. He was untouched by the new ideas of the Enlightenment that excited so many of his contemporaries, and seems to have been as little interested in traditional religious beliefs as in the philosophical attitudes that had just begun to undermine them. Like his father, he had no real religious feeling, and throughout his life he demonstrated a steady indifference to all things spiritual – with a single exception: he was, as Horace Walpole incredulously reported, prey to a host of superstitious and supernatural fears. 'He had yet implicit faith in the German notion of vampires,' the diarist noted, 'and has more than once been angry with my father for speaking irreverently of these imaginary bloodsuckers.'[26]

George was not an easy man to understand. Bravery and bombast, principle and passion struggled for mastery in his nature, yet beneath the often grating bravado that defined so much of his behaviour, there occasionally emerged a glimpse of a rather different man: calmer, less swayed by the intensity of feelings he found so hard to control, a more reflective character capable of far greater emotional acuity than he usually revealed. For most of his life, George kept those parts of his personality hidden beneath the image he had created of himself as a blunt, instinctual, plain-speaking man of action. The contrast between this persona and the remote, sinuous unreachableness that defined his father's character could not have been more extreme. By his every word and action, George sought to present himself as a very different kind of man, demonstrating both to himself and to those about him that he was not destined to repeat the destructive mistakes of his predecessor. He would do things differently; and nowhere more so than in the selection of a wife.

Prince George told his father that he would not make a purely political marriage, but expected to have some say in the choice of a suitable spouse. Somewhat surprisingly, his declaration met with no opposition; perhaps the elder George, lacking in empathy though he was, had no wish to repeat the disastrous outcome of his own forced match. It did not take his son long to fix on the woman he thought would suit him. Caroline, daughter of the Margrave of Ansbach, was highly sought after in the German marriage market. Tall and stately, with an abundance of fair hair and a substantial bosom (said to be the finest in Europe), she had recently refused a very impressive offer from the Archduke Charles, heir to the Holy Roman Emperor. She had baulked at the prospect of converting to Catholicism, and had thus waved goodbye to one of the oldest and grandest of royal titles. Her reputation for beauty – and also for intelligence, for she was said to have debated the issue of her possible religious conversion with incisive skill – was probably well known to George, as Caroline had for many years lived in the Berlin household of his father's sister, Sophia Charlotte, queen in Prussia. Orphaned aged thirteen, Caroline had grown up under the protection of George's aunt and his grandmother, Electress Sophia of Hanover. The electress had long hoped to see her grandson married to Caroline, although she 'doubted that God will let me be so happy'. She did everything she could to force God's hand, though, and was clearly successful in piquing the young George's interest in marrying her protégée. 'I think the prince likes the idea also,' she observed hopefully, 'for in talking to him about her, he said "I am very glad that you desire her for me."'[27]

When George raised the possibility of marrying Caroline, his father insisted his son should meet her first, and suggested that he do so in disguise, so that he could make an honest assessment of her person and character. In June 1705, George obediently travelled to Ansbach, where he was presented to the unsuspecting Caroline as a Hanoverian nobleman. He was smitten at their very first meeting. As intemperate in passion as in so much else, George insisted for the rest of his life that he had fallen in love with Caroline the moment he saw her. Without declaring himself, he hurried back to Hanover, and urged his father to open negotiations for her hand. Uncharacteristically compliant, the elder George agreed without argument. Significantly, he was concerned to ensure that Caroline shared his son's enthusiasm for the match, stressing to the diplomatic negotiators that 'her inclinations should be assured first of all'.[28] It did not take long for everyone to be satisfied on that point. Once the identity of the young man whom she had met under such unusual circumstances was explained, it was clear that Caroline had seen something she liked in the intense, emphatic stranger. Perhaps she was impressed by the directness of his desire for her. Perhaps the prospect of marrying the heir presumptive to the British crown appealed more than becoming Holy Roman Empress; she was always considered an ambitious woman, and marriage to George undoubtedly promised access to considerable power and influence, with the additional benefit that it did not require her to become a Catholic. Perhaps she simply felt she could not refuse another well-connected marital prospect. For whatever reason, her consent was quickly given; and George and Caroline were married in Hanover in the early autumn.

Their marriage could not have been more different from that of George's parents. From the very beginning, his young wife was the central focus of his life. In 1707, when she contracted smallpox, he nursed her throughout the illness, imperilling his own health as a consequence. Two years later, when Caroline gave birth to their eldest daughter, Anne, he wrote her a loving letter from which the warmth of his affection still radiates. 'The peace of my life depends on knowing you in good health, and upon the conviction of your continued affection for me. I shall endeavour to attract it,' he assured her, 'by all imaginable passion and love, and I shall never omit any way of showing you that no one could be more wholly yours.'[29] Theirs was a partnership founded on passion – on George's side at least. 'It is certain,' wrote Horace Walpole, 'that the king always preferred the queen's person to any other woman; nor ever described his idea of beauty, but that he drew a picture of his wife.'[30] For the rest of his life, Caroline exerted a physical attraction over him that was never truly extinguished, even when her youthful prettiness had been compromised by childbearing and her stately dignity edged into fat. Caroline was proud of her sexual hold over her husband; when she was over fifty, she showed Robert Walpole a letter George had written to her from Hanover which 'spoke of his extreme impatience for their meeting; and in a style that would have made one believe him the rival of Hercules' vigour and her of Venus' beauty, her person being mentioned in the most exalted strains of rapture.'[31]

Caroline responded to the blitzkrieg of George's passion by surrendering herself entirely to it. She never looked at another man, and did everything she could to keep her mercurial husband satisfied. Her submission to him went far beyond the purely physical. From the day of her marriage until the day she died, over thirty years later, she rarely had a thought or performed an action that was not designed in some way to please him: 'To him she sacrificed her time, for him she breathed every inclination; she looked, spake and breathed but for him, was a weathercock to every blast of his uncertain temper.'[32] Whether she did this out of love, or whether as a means of exercising through her husband the power and influence otherwise denied her as a woman, was the subject of constant speculation. Most thought that power played a large part in her calculations.

The complicated intensity of their relationship fascinated all those who witnessed it, and many contemporaries sought to explain and unpick its curious dynamic, the strange combination of attraction, manipulation and destructiveness that characterised their life together. For all the self-absorption of the couple at its centre, this was far from a conventionally happy marriage. Between George's sexual thraldom and Caroline's self-abnegating submission, some very dark currents seemed to flow; and many of those who found themselves caught in the eddies and undertows thus created were permanently damaged by the experience, not least the couple's children, none of whom could be said to have emerged happily from the private world their parents created for themselves.

Perhaps theirs would have always been a marriage characterised by internal tension. It was, in many ways, an example of the attraction of opposites. They did not even look very well matched. Caroline was far taller than her husband, whose lack of height, slender build and love of overdressed magnificence inevitably attracted the epithet 'dapper'. She was dignified and magisterial, though large in later life. One observer likened Caroline and her Maids of Honour, all dressed in pink, making their way through a crowded court, to a lobster pursued by shrimps. Caroline had little interest in the physical pursuits that George enjoyed, although she gamely accompanied him on his favourite stag hunts. Left to herself, Caroline preferred less punishing activities. She was a dedicated and accomplished gardener, later laying out and improving the parks at Richmond and Kew. George, who did not share her interest, refused to look at her ambitious plans, declaring that he 'did not care how she flung away her own revenue'. He did not know that, having long ago exhausted her own resources in pursuing her gardening passions, she had persuaded Robert Walpole to subsidise her projects from Treasury funds.

While Caroline had no idea how to manage her own income, and was always in debt, George's attitude to expenditure was very different: he was a compulsive hoarder of cash, regarded by most people who knew him as mean in a way unbefitting the grandeur of his position. Although his sympathies could be engaged by worthy causes – he contributed £2,000 to help establish London's Foundling Hospital – George was always a more reluctant donor than his wife. It was all but impossible to prise money out of his hands; he even sought to wriggle out of annuities he had promised to pay his own daughters. Hervey thought it was hard to say whether passion for armies or for money predominated in his mind: 'he could never have enough of either, and could seldom be persuaded to part with either, though he had more of both than he had any occasion to employ.'[33]

Walpole once observed that George would rather have found a guinea in his pocket than have a work of literature dedicated to him. In contrast to the resolute philistinism of her husband, Caroline was completely at home in the world of books and ideas. She had 'read a great deal', noted Hervey with approval. 'She understood good writing too, in English, the harmony of numbers in verse, the beauty of style in prose, and the force and propriety of terms much better than anyone who has only heard her speak English would ever have thought possible. She had a most incredible memory, and was learned both in ancient and modern history as the most learned men.'[34] Caroline was an intellectual woman who had been raised among other intellectual women. In the household in which she had grown up, the Electress Sophia and her daughter Sophia Charlotte had created a remarkable salon in which the greatest minds of their generation were invited to discuss the philosophical questions of the day. As a girl, Caroline had been an eager participant in the debates and arguments that dominated the days of these thoughtful princesses. The mathematician and philosopher Gottfried Leibniz acted as the resident in-house thinker of the Hanoverian women at Sophia Charlotte's palace. He liked the young Caroline, although he sometimes found himself at the sharp end of her wit and thought her a little too fond of scoring points of argument at the expense of others. 'I have a most bitter tongue,' confessed Caroline in later years. There was little evidence here of the traditional pursuits of royal women – the fascination with scandal, needlework, dress and display that Caroline described dismissively as 'paltry'. Instead, Sophia Charlotte turned her mind to bigger questions – 'the why of why', as Leibniz called it. No subject was off limits, and a scepticism towards traditional theology was much in evidence. (On her deathbed, Sophia Charlotte, who died at the age of only thirty-seven, refused the ministrations of a priest. 'Do not pity me,' she told those gathered around her, including a heartbroken Caroline; 'I am going at last to satisfy my curiosity about the origin of things which even Leibniz could never explain to me, to understand space, infinity, being and nothingness.'[35])

This was not a world in which Caroline's husband would have felt at ease. Although Walpole believed George's 'understanding was not near so deficient as it was imagined', intellectual discussion bored and unsettled him.[36] When she became queen, Caroline sought to recreate in London the salon she had found so stimulating as a girl in Berlin; but the scorn of her husband cast a shadow over her efforts. Hervey noted with regret that she did not dare allow herself to indulge in the philosophical discussions she so enjoyed, 'for fear of the king, who often rebuked her for dabbling in all that learned nonsense (as he called it)'.[37] Nor did he share her artistic interests. Once, when George was away in Hanover, Caroline and Hervey took 'several very bad pictures out of the great Drawing Room at Kensington, and put very good ones in their place'. When George returned he was furious, and insisted that Hervey have 'every new picture taken away and all the old ones replaced'. When asked if any of the newly transplanted paintings might be allowed to remain, the king was adamant all must go, especially 'the picture with the dirty frame over the door, and the three nasty little children'. Thus dismissing Van Dyck's masterly portrait of the children of Charles I, he told the disdainful Hervey that he especially wanted the painting of his 'gigantic fat Venus' returned. 'I am not as nice as your lordship. I like my fat Venus much better than anything you have given me instead of her.'[38]

Caroline was not the first royal wife to find herself married to a man whose mind did not match her own. Her Berlin mentor, Sophia Charlotte, found little common intellectual ground with her own princely husband, who, like Caroline's George, preferred the study of pageantry and military decorations to the contemplation of big ideas. 'Leibniz talked to me today of the infinitely little,' Sophia once remarked. 'My God, as though I did not know enough about that already.'[39] Such a comment would never have escaped Caroline's lips. She decided early in their marriage that her intellect, of which she was justifiably proud, would never be used to undermine her husband, but would be dedicated instead to the strengthening and consolidation of their partnership. From the day she married George, she saw the preservation of their union and the advancement of their interests as the paramount duty of her role as his wife. She began as she meant to go on. As soon as she arrived in Hanover as a married woman, she took lessons in English, and persuaded her learning-averse husband to do the same. Leibniz heard that Caroline 'had a decided turn for that language' and that George was also making excellent progress. While he never lost his 'his bluff Westphalian accent', George was, Walpole thought, later to speak the language with far more 'correctness' than his wife. Caroline's determination to master the language of the people she would one day rule was only part of a wider campaign to win their hearts and minds. She had already begun to plan for the moment when her father-in-law would inherit the British crown, and she and George would become Prince and Princess of Wales. The British envoy to Hanover noted that she behaved with special courtesy to British visitors; she employed British ladies in her household; ordered English novels to read; and had even begun to drink tea.

Her father-in-law viewed all these acts with the deepest suspicion, believing, with some justification, that his son and daughter-in-law were seeking to secure their own position at the cost of his own. When Queen Anne's government somewhat unwisely offered the title of Duke of Cambridge to Prince George, his father was incensed, seeing it as a sign that his future British subjects sought the favour of his son more than they did his own. It hardened his resolve to treat the prince 'as a person of no consequence'; nor did it make him feel more warmly disposed towards Caroline. Recognising her intelligence, he was convinced she encouraged the prince in what he regarded as acts of defiance, and referred to her as '*cette diablesse Mme la Princesse*'.

Caroline's success in providing the dynasty with a male heir in 1707 did nothing to alter her father-in-law's hostile attitude. On the contrary, the rejoicings in both England and Hanover that greeted the baby Frederick's arrival only increased his suspicion of their popularity, and he refused to pay for any celebrations to mark the child's birth. The appearance of a succession of other children – all daughters – between 1709 and 1713 was similarly ignored; and by the time the long-awaited call to Britain arrived in 1714, with the death of Queen Anne, the breach between the king and the prince was wider than ever.

*

The future George I arrived in London first, accompanied by his son. The three young princesses came next, with Caroline herself following on last. Her tardy departure perhaps reflected a reluctance to leave her only son, who, George I had decreed, would not travel with the rest of the family to London. Frederick was to stay in Hanover as a living reminder to the Hanoverians that their ruling family had not deserted them. Although he was only seven years old, Frederick was expected to preside over state functions, sitting alongside a large portrait of his elector grandfather propped up on a chair. He was not to see his family again for nearly fourteen years.

Once in London, it was quickly evident that the new king would much rather have stayed in Hanover with his grandson and his portrait. His new subjects were far from united in welcoming the incoming ruling family, some of them making their preference for the exiled Stuarts very apparent by word, gesture or riot. George I, for his part, was equally unenthused. He disliked England and its inhabitants from the start. It was soon noticed that 'the king has no predilection for the English nation and never receives in private any English of either sex', preferring to spend his time with his mistress, smoking a pipe and drinking German beer.[40] His inability to speak the language isolated him – he was said to conduct political business with Robert Walpole in Latin – and he did not understand the complicated and somewhat ambivalent status of an English king, which left him with the strong conviction that the first objective of his new countrymen was to rob and insult him. The French ambassador reported that such was George's dislike of his new kingdom that he did not consider it anything more 'than a temporary possession to be made the most of whilst it lasts, rather than a perpetual inheritance to himself and his family'.[41]

His son and his wife took a very different view. From the moment of their arrival, they strove to do all they could to impress and conciliate their new countrymen. The prince, though not yet completely fluent in English, showed a winning desire to improve, and would help himself out when words failed him 'with a world of action'. He and Caroline were effusive in their praise for their new homeland, the prince calling the English 'the best, the handsomest, the best shaped, the best natured and lovingest people in the world; if anyone would make their court to him, it must be by telling him he was like an Englishman'.[42] Caroline, who was already regarded as 'so charming that she could make anyone love her if she would', employed a more vivid turn of phrase, declaring that she 'would as soon live on a dunghill as return to Hanover'.[43]

It was hardly surprising that, as the courtier Peter Wentworth observed: 'I find all backward in speaking to the king but ready enough to speak to the prince.'[44] King George could not fail to be aware of the contrast between his embattled and unpopular position, and that of his son and daughter-in-law. The result was inevitable. The Duchess of Orléans, an avid transmitter of all the royal gossip of Europe, heard that things had gone from bad to worse between George I and his son. 'His quarrel with the Prince of Wales gets worse every day. I always thought him harsh when he was in Germany, but English air has hardened him still more.'[45]

George and Caroline must bear some of the blame for what happened next. In making the contrast between their own reception and that of George I quite so plain, they had not, perhaps, behaved in the most tactful manner; they had burnished their own reputations and secured their own interests with scant consideration for the impact it would have on the new king. They must have realised their actions would elicit some response from a man whose brooding character they both knew very well. But they cannot have expected him to strike against them in the way that he did, in an action that was to echo miserably through the family for the rest of their lives.

It began with what should have been a celebration. On 13 November 1717, Caroline gave birth to a second son, a long-awaited boy after so many daughters, and the first Hanoverian to be born in Britain. The prince was delighted, and made arrangements for a grand christening. He asked his father and his uncle, the Prince-Bishop of Osnabrück, to stand as the baby's godfathers. To this the king initially agreed; but just before the ceremony, the king insisted that the prince-bishop be replaced by the Duke of Newcastle, a politician he knew his son particularly disliked. Furious at what he perceived as a gross humiliation, the young George smouldered his way through the proceedings, held in Caroline's bedroom. Walpole heard from his friend Lady Suffolk, who had been one of the shocked spectators, exactly what followed: 'No sooner had the bishop closed the ceremony, than the prince crossing the feet of the bed in a rage, stepped up to the Duke of Newcastle, and holding up his hand and forefinger in a menacing attitude, said, "You are a rascal, but I shall find you out," meaning in broken English, "I shall find a time to be revenged."'[46] Newcastle, deeply disconcerted, asserted that the prince had challenged him to fight a duel, a very serious offence within the precincts of a royal palace. He complained to the king, who had been present but had not understood a word of what was said. George I immediately decided to regard his son's words in the worst possible light. He told the prince to consider himself under arrest and confined both George and Caroline to their apartments.

Prince George, alarmed by the escalating gravity of the situation, wrote an unequivocally submissive letter to his father, admitting that he had used those words to Newcastle, but denying that they were intended to provoke a duel and begging forgiveness. The king was unmoved; he ordered the prince to leave the palace immediately. The princess, he said, could remain only if she promised to have no further communication with her husband. He then informed the distraught couple that under no circumstances would their children leave with them. Even the newborn baby was to be left behind. 'You are charged to say to the princess,' declared the king to his son, 'that it is my will that my grandson and my granddaughters are to stay at St James's.'[47] When Caroline declined to abandon her husband, the baby prince, only a few weeks old, was taken from his mother's arms. The couple's daughters, aged nine, seven and five, were sent to bid their parents a formal farewell. The princess was so overwrought that she fainted; her ladies thought she was about to die.

Separated from their children and exiled from their home, the couple composed a desperate appeal to the king. It made no difference. Saying that their professions of respect and subservience were enough 'to make him vomit', the elder George demanded that the prince sign a formal renunciation of his children, giving them up to his guardianship. When he refused, the king deprived the prince and princess of their guard of honour, wrote to all foreign courts and embassies informing them that no one would be welcomed by him who had anything to do with his son, and ordered anyone who held posts in both his and his son's households – from chamberlain to rat-catcher – to surrender one of them, for he would employ nobody who worked for the prince.

At St James's, Caroline's baby son, taken away from his mother in such distressing circumstances, suddenly fell ill. As the child grew steadily worse, the doctors called in to treat him begged the king to send for his mother. He refused to do so, until finally persuaded that if the boy died, it would reflect extremely badly on him. He relented enough to permit the princess to see her child, but with the proviso that the baby must be removed to Kensington, as he did not want her to come to St James's. The journey proved too much for the weakened child, and before his frantic mother could get to him, he died, 'of choking and coughing', on 17 February 1718. In her grief, Caroline was said to have cried out that she did not believe her son had died of natural causes; but a post-mortem – admittedly undertaken by court physicians who owed their livings to the king – seemed to show that the child had a congenital weakness and could not have lived long.

The distraught parents were unable to draw any consolation from their surviving children. Their son Frederick was far away in Hanover; their daughters were closeted in St James's, where the king, clearly thinking the situation a permanent one, had appointed the widowed Countess of Portland to look after them. They were not badly treated; but, having effectively lost both her sons, Caroline found the enforced separation from her daughters all but unbearable. The prince wrote constantly to his father, attempting to raise sympathy for his wife's plight: 'Pity the poor princess and suffer her not to think that the children which she shall with labour and sorrow bring into the world, if the hand of heaven spare them, are immediately to be torn from her, and instead of comforts and blessings, be made an occasion of grief and affliction to her.' Eventually the king relented, and allowed Caroline to visit her daughters once a week; but he would not extend the same privilege to his son. 'If the detaining of my children from me is meant as a punishment,' the prince wrote sadly, 'I confess it is of itself a very severe method of expressing Your Majesty's resentment.'[48] Six months later, the prince had still been denied any opportunity to see his daughters. Missing their father as much as he missed them, the little girls picked a basket of cherries from the gardens at Kensington, and managed to send them to him with a message 'that their hearts and thoughts were always with their dear Papa.'[49] The prince was said to have wept when he received their present.

Not content with persecuting his son by dividing his family, the king also pursued him with all the legal and political tools at his disposal. When he attempted to force the prince to pay for the upkeep of the daughters he had forcibly removed from him, George sought to raise the legality of the seizure in the courts, but was assured that the law would favour the king. His father's enmity seemed to know no rational bounds. In Berlin, the king's sister heard gossip that he was attempting to disinherit the prince on the grounds that he was not his true child. He was certainly known to have consulted the Lord Chancellor to discover if it was possible to debar him from succeeding to the electorate of Hanover; the Chancellor thought not. This unwelcome opinion may have driven him to consider less orthodox methods of marginalising his son. Years later, when the old king was dead and Caroline was queen, she told Sir Robert Walpole that by chance she had discovered in George I's private papers a document written by Charles Stanhope, an Undersecretary of State, which discussed a far more direct method of proceeding. The prince was 'to be seized and Lord Berkeley will take him on board ship and convey him to any part of the world that Your Majesty shall direct'.[50] Berkeley was First Lord of the Admiralty in 1717, and his family held extensive lands in Carolina. Like the Hanover disinheritance plan, it came to nothing, and relied for its veracity entirely on Caroline's testimony; but it is a measure of the king's angry discontent with his son that such a ludicrous scheme could seem credible, even to his hostile and embittered daughter-in-law.

When Sir Robert Walpole came to power a few years later, in 1721, relations between the king and his son's family were still deadlocked in bitter hostility. The new first minister was convinced the situation, at once tragic and ridiculous, would have to change. Not only was it damaging to the emotional wellbeing of all those caught up in it; more worryingly, to Walpole's detached politician's eye, it also posed a threat to the precarious reputation of the newly installed royal house. This was not how the eighteenth century's supreme ministerial pragmatist thought public life should be conducted; if the king and his son could not be brought to love each other, they could surely be made to see the benefits of a formal reconciliation that would ensure some degree of political calm. Walpole worked on the king with all his unparalleled powers of persuasion; he did the same with the prince, and made some progress with both. But it was Caroline who proved most resistant to his appeals. She demanded that the restoration of her children be made a condition of any public declaration of peace with her father-in-law. In the face of Walpole's protestations that George I would never agree, and that it was better to take things step by step, she was implacable. 'Mr Walpole,' she assured him, 'this is no jesting matter with me; you will hear of my complaints every day and hour and in every place if I have not my children again.'[51]

Horace Walpole thought Caroline's 'resolution' was as strong as her understanding – and left to herself, it seems unlikely that she would ever have given up her demands for her children's return – but she was undermined by the person from whom she might have expected the most support. The prince, tempted by the offer of the substantial income Walpole had squeezed out of the king, and an apparently honourable way out of the political wilderness, was prepared to compromise, and, despite his wife's opposition, accepted terms that did not include the restitution of his daughters. He and Caroline would be allowed to visit the girls whenever they wished, but they were to remain living with their grandfather at St James's Palace. Caroline was devastated. The courtier Lady Cowper witnessed her grief: 'She cried and said, "I see how these things go; I must be the sufferer at last, and have no power to help myself; I can say, since the hour that I was born, that I have never lived a day without suffering."'[52]

Caroline's outburst said as much about her future prospects as her present unhappiness. Her husband had demonstrated in the most painful way possible that he lacked her capacity both for deep feeling and for consistent, considered action. It was not that George did not love his daughters – he was genuinely distressed by their absence, and felt the loss of their company – but he was not prepared to sacrifice all his interests on their behalf. Nor, much as he loved his wife, would he allow her openly to dictate how he should behave in the public sphere. It was a hard lesson that Caroline took much to heart. Even on matters that touched them in the very core of their being, the prince could not necessarily be depended upon to do either the right or the politic thing. That did not make her abandon the partnership to which she had committed when she married him, but she was compelled to accept that what could not be achieved by the open alliance of equals might be much better delivered by management and manipulation.

The king expressed a similar view when the reconciliation was finally achieved, and the prince was formally received by his father in a ceremony that reminded Lady Cowper of 'two armies in battle array'. George I saw his son privately for only a painful ten minutes, but devoted over an hour to haranguing his daughter-in-law on her failures. 'She could have made the prince better if she would,' he declared; and he hoped she would do so from now on. Caroline had reached much the same conclusion. For the next twenty years, she did all she could to ensure that her husband was encouraged and persuaded to follow paths that she believed served the best interests of their crown. By the time Lord Hervey watched her do it, she had turned it into a fine art. 'She knew … how to instil her own sentiments, whilst she affected to receive His Majesty's; she could appear convinced whilst she was controverting, and obedient when she was ruling; by this means, her dexterity and address made it impossible for anybody to persuade him what was truly the case, and that while she was seemingly in every occasion giving up her opinion to his, she was always in reality turning his opinion and bending his will to hers.'[53]

In one sense, it was not an unsuccessful policy. Her patience and self-effacement ensured that Caroline was able to achieve much of what she wanted in her management of her husband. Above all, she preserved the unity of their partnership. Throughout all their tribulations, in private and in public, she strained every sinew to prevent any permanent rupture dividing them. Whether the threat came from a discontented father, a predatory mistress, an unsatisfactory child, or a potentially disruptive politician, Caroline devoted all her skills to neutralising any possibility of a serious breach between them. It was clear to her that they were infinitely stronger as a like-minded couple than as competing individuals who would inevitably become the focus for antagonistic and destructive opposition. But although in later years she took some pride in the tireless efforts she had directed to maintaining their solidarity, she was aware that it had not been achieved without cost. To be locked into a pattern of perpetual cozening and cajolery was wounding and exhausting for her and demeaning for her husband. It kept them together; but it was not the best foundation upon which to base a marriage. In the end, despite the strength of the feelings that united them, both she and George were, in their different ways, warped and belittled by it.

As Caroline had feared, her elder daughters were never restored to her while the old king lived. She went on to have other children: William in 1721, Mary in 1723 and finally Louisa in 1724. But it was not until George I died, in 1727, from a stroke suffered while travelling through the German countryside he loved, that Anne, Amelia and Caroline came back to live with their parents again. By then it was too late to establish the stable home life that Caroline had hoped to provide for them. Before they had been taken from her, she had been a careful mother to her girls. 'No want of care, or failure or neglect in any part of their education can be imputed to the princess,' her husband had written in one of his many fruitless appeals to his father.[54] Caroline's daughters would never waver in their devotion to her; but their long estrangement from their father – and the constant criticism of his behaviour which they heard from their grandfather for nearly a decade – meant that on their return his eldest daughters regarded him with distinctly sceptical eyes. When they saw for themselves how he treated their mother – the strange mixture of obsession and disdain, passion and resentment, respect and rudeness, the destructive combination of warring emotions that had come to characterise George's attitude to his wife – any tenderness they once had for him soon evaporated. It was hardly an attractive vision of domestic happiness with which to begin a new reign.

CHAPTER 2

A Passionate Partnership

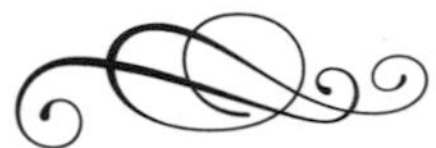

GEORGE AND CAROLINE WERE AT their summer retreat at Richmond Lodge on 25 June 1727, when Robert Walpole arrived with the news of George I's death. It was the middle of a hot day, and the royal couple were asleep; their attendants were extremely reluctant to wake them, but George was eventually persuaded to emerge from his bedroom and discover that he was now king.

It was only seven months since George's estranged mother had died in the castle at Ahlden. Although George could never bring himself to speak about Sophia Dorothea, he did make a single gesture towards her memory that suggests much of what he felt but could not say. The day after the news arrived of his father's death, the courtier Lady Suffolk told Walpole she was startled 'at seeing hung up in the new queen's dressing room a whole-length portrait of a lady in royal robes; and in the bed-chamber a half-length of the same person, neither of which Lady Suffolk had seen before'.[1] The pictures were of Sophia Dorothea. Her son must have salvaged them from the general destruction of all her images ordered by his father a generation before. 'The prince had kept them concealed, not daring to produce them in his father's lifetime.' Now George was king, and his mother was restored – albeit without comment – to a place of honour within the private heart of the family. Walpole heard that if she had lived long enough to witness his accession, George 'had purposed to have brought her over and declared her queen dowager'. Her death had denied him the opportunity to release his mother from her long captivity, to act as the agent of her freedom. Perhaps it was some small satisfaction to see her image where he had been unable to see her person; it was certainly a gesture of defiance towards the man who kept her from him, and a declaration of loyalty and affection towards his mother that he had never been able to make while his father lived.

The new king and queen were crowned in October, in a typically eighteenth-century ceremony that combined grandeur with chaos. Tickets were sold in advance for the event, and small booths erected around Westminster for the selling of coffee to the anticipated crowds.[2] The Swiss traveller de Saussure went to watch and noted that it took two hours for the royal procession to wend its way to the abbey. Handel's *Zadok the Priest* – which would be performed at every subsequent coronation – was given its first airing in the course of the ceremony, at which George and Caroline appeared sumptuously clothed and loaded down with jewellery, some of it, as it later appeared, borrowed for the day. The choristers were not considered to have acquitted themselves well – at one point, they were heard to be singing different anthems. After the ceremony was over and the grander participants had left, de Saussure watched as a hungrier crowd moved methodically over the remains of the event, carrying away anything that could be either eaten or sold.[3]

*

By the time John, Lord Hervey, joined George and Caroline's court in 1730, the couple had been on the throne for three years, and married for twenty-five. The patterns of their lives, both as king and queen and husband and wife, were thus very well established when Hervey began to chronicle them. Hervey's official court title was vice chamberlain. He later described his job dismissively as one that required him to do no more than 'to carry candles and set chairs', but in practice, it was a far from nominal office, giving him direct responsibility for the management and upkeep of all the royal palaces. It certainly did not imply any shortcomings in social status. Hervey was extremely well connected, heir to the Earl of Bristol, and an aristocrat of unimpeachable Whig principles. He was also a man who made a career from defying expectations and outraging traditional moralists. There was nothing conventional about any aspect of Hervey's life.

Even in a family considered remarkable for the production of extraordinary people – Lady Mary Wortley Montagu once declared that 'this world consists of men, women and Herveys' – he stood out above the rest. He married one of the most beautiful women of his generation, and had eight children by her; he conducted casual affairs with a host of other fashionable ladies of the court; but the great love of his life was another man. His sexuality was a barely concealed secret. Slight and slender, he had been considered outstandingly attractive as a young man. In later life, he used cosmetics to enhance his fading looks, with results that were not always successful. Inevitably, Hervey attracted attention, not all of it admiring. The Duchess of Marlborough once referred scornfully to his 'painted face with not a tooth in his head'.[4] In spiteful verse, Alexander Pope described him as an 'amphibious thing', 'a painted child of dirt that stinks and stings'. He was caricatured everywhere in prose as 'Lord Fanny'. One of his many enemies described him as a 'delicate little hermaphrodite, a pretty little Master Miss'.[5]

Perhaps it was the complexities of his own life that gave Hervey such a profound curiosity for the oddities of others. Certainly, it seems to have been what kept him so firmly in George and Caroline's orbit for so many years. His warmest relationship was with Caroline, with whom he spent nearly all his time. He was a clever man, well read and accomplished, equally at home in the worlds of politics, ideas and culture. Caroline, starved of intellectual companionship, found him stimulating and amusing, enjoying his dry, mordant humour which closely reflected her own. Both loved to gossip, and could be unsparing in the cruelty of the comments they directed at those they disliked. The queen indulged her favourite to an extraordinary degree, encouraging his frankness and sharing some of her most intimate thoughts with him. Alone among her courtiers, he was encouraged to contradict her. According to his own account, she soon came to consider Hervey as indispensable to her happiness, calling him 'her child, her pupil and her charge'.[6]

Although Hervey's principal loyalty was always to Caroline, he was just as interested in her husband, who seems to have regarded the constant presence in his household of this unusual figure entirely benignly. For all his loudly declared prejudices, George II was not, it seems, much troubled by the private lives of those around him. Perhaps he simply did not notice, as his self-absorption gave him little interest in contemplating the behaviour of others. In this, he was very different from Hervey, who found the family he lived with endlessly fascinating. Throughout his time at court he kept a detailed journal of everything that he witnessed there. He later assembled the entries into a memoir that contained everything he thought important or illuminating about the years he had spent in such intimate proximity with the royal family. The result was a three-volume work dominated by two overpowering central figures. Hervey records in compelling detail, over nearly a thousand pages, the words and actions of George and Caroline, who emerge as the flawed anti-heroes of his writings, appallingly larger than life; and, as Hervey effortlessly demonstrated, caught in a web of deceit, obsession and self-destruction that bound them together just as powerfully as it destroyed them. Hervey was George and Caroline's Boswell; the work he left behind him is a portrait of the dark and often bitter thing their marriage had become.

Hervey did not pretend to be objective in his judgements. He was always, at heart, Caroline's man, magnifying her good qualities – especially her wit and intelligence – whilst contrasting them with the boorish outbursts of her irritable husband. George is not well served by Hervey's account of him, which makes much of his bumptiousness and self-regard, and has less to say about his more admirable characteristics: his diligence, his bravery, his occasional flashes of genuine charity. And yet for all the bright colouration of Hervey's rendering, neither George nor Caroline emerges from his pages as a caricature. George is depicted as a complicated figure, defensive of his own virtues, naively unaware of the impression his behaviour makes on others, exacting, punctilious, somewhat of a bore; but also honest, pragmatic, and capable of considerable tenderness when his emotions were engaged. Above all, Hervey captured the deep ambivalence of his feelings for his wife – at once passionately in love and yet uneasy and ashamed at the degree of his dependency on her.

In Caroline, Hervey depicted a woman of strong and subtle intellect, the possessor of a forceful mind too often bent to trivial purposes. She could be wickedly funny, and perceptive – entertaining company for those who could keep up and were not provoked by her sharp tongue. This was the Caroline whom Hervey adored, the queenly wit who could cap a classical quotation whilst laughing unashamedly at his gossip. But he was not afraid to record a steelier side of her personality, a brusque hardness that sometimes shocked even the worldly Hervey with its cruel edge. The power of her hatred impressed itself upon him as much as the strength of her mind. And yet it was her situation that most evoked his pity: a woman who had concealed the cleverness that defined her beneath a lifelong subjection to the smallest and most mundane of her husband's wishes, the better to manipulate him into doing what she wished; and who, as a result, became as much her husband's victim as his puppet master.

Hervey had no doubt that, whatever it had cost her to establish it, Caroline's influence extended way beyond the intimate family circle. As soon as George II was crowned, 'the whole world began to feel that it was her will which was the sole spring on which every movement in the court turned; and though His Majesty lost no opportunity to declare that the queen never meddled with his business, yet nobody believed it ... since everybody knew that she not only meddled with business, but directed everything that fell under that name, either at home or abroad'.[7] Horace Walpole's account seems to confirm Hervey's assertion that Caroline was indeed a discreet but efficient manipulator of influence, a hidden power behind the throne. Walpole asserted that his father, Sir Robert, would often discuss matters of policy privately with the queen before raising them with the king. Both understood the importance of concealing their machinations from George, who was extremely sensitive to any suggestion of interference from his wife. If Walpole arrived for an audience with the king when Caroline was present, she would curtsey politely and offer to leave. Walpole argued that George was entirely deceived by this carefully choreographed piece of theatre, declaring naively to his first minister: 'there, you see how much I am governed by my wife, as they say I am'. Caroline played her own part to perfection. 'Oh sir,' she replied, 'I must indeed be vain to pretend to govern Your Majesty.'[8] But as George's comments reveal, the idea that it was Caroline and not he who drove forward the business of government was not confined to the inner sanctum of the court. With evident satisfaction, Hervey transcribed into his journals a popular poetic jibe that summed up the perceived balance of power between George II and his wife:

You may strut, dapper George, but 'twill all be in vain,
We know 'tis Queen Caroline and not you that reign –
You govern no more than Don Philip of Spain,
Then if you would have us fall down and adore you,
Lock up your fat spouse, as your dad did before you.[9]

Recent scholarship has tended to turn a sceptical eye on some of the more extravagant claims made for Caroline's role as the *éminence grise* of British politics. Historians have suggested that both Hervey and Walpole had their own reasons for accentuating her role and diminishing that of her husband; as Caroline's most devoted admirer, Hervey was keen to elevate her virtues in comparison to what he regarded as the emptier pretensions of her husband. Sir Robert Walpole, too, was strongly identified with Caroline, having allied himself with her very early in her husband's reign. He had quickly recognised that it was she who exerted the most influence over the king and had worked very hard to recruit her into his orbit. With characteristic bluntness, he later congratulated himself in having taken 'the right sow by the ear'. Once established as her ally, it suited him to talk up her influence, thus magnifying his own access to the apparent wellsprings of power. It was also perhaps the case that George was unlucky in those areas of policy in which he did excel. The image of George II as an ineffectual ruler, overshadowed by his wife, was made more credible by the relative indifference of so many of his new subjects to those areas in which he exerted genuine influence: military strategy and the complicated politics of princely Germany. Both were of some significance to the exercise of kingship in eighteenth-century Europe; but neither Hervey nor Walpole was particularly interested in them, and until recently, most historians have tended to share their perceptions.

George's reputation has been considerably enhanced by a new interest in these aspects of his reign; but in re-evaluating his role, it would be wrong to excise Caroline altogether from the landscape of political life. When the king was away on his frequent and often lengthy trips to his Hanoverian electorate, on every occasion until her death, it was Caroline who was given responsibility for heading the Regency Council which governed in George's absence.[10] This involved her directly in the daily business of politics, and required her to spend a great deal of time in the company of politicians. Her relationship with the wily and effective Sir Robert Walpole spanned a decade, and was built on a foundation of wary but mutual respect that ended only with her final illness. As Hervey observed, Caroline positively enjoyed political life. Her philosophical readings had given her an interest in the theory of political organisation, and she liked to reflect on the constitutional peculiarities of her adopted home. 'My God,' she once declared to Hervey, 'what a figure this poor island would make in Europe if it were not for its government! ... Who the devil do you think would take you all, or think you worth having, that had anything else, if you had not your liberties?'[11]

Caroline was astute enough to recognise that this was the kind of eulogy a British monarch was required to deliver in order to retain the affections of the people; but it does not seem to have been a particularly honest reflection of her private opinions. Hervey thought that in her heart, the queen's politics were closer to those of her husband. George was suspicious of the constitutional settlement over which he was obliged to preside, and 'looked upon all the English as king-killers and republicans, grudged them their riches as well as their liberty [and] thought them all overpaid'. He much preferred the way things were done in Hanover, for 'there he rewarded people for doing their duty and serving him well, but here he was obliged to enrich people for being rascals and buy them not to cut his throat'.[12] To Hervey, Caroline expressed similar frustrations with the limits of royal power, as the Glorious Revolution had defined it, complaining that in England, a king was 'no more than the humble servant of Parliament, the pensioner of his people, and a puppet of sovereignty that was forced to go to them for every shilling he wanted, that was obliged to court those who were always abusing him, and could do nothing himself'.[13] In public, she was far more measured. 'The business of princes,' she declared, 'is to make the whole go on, and not to encourage or suffer silly, impertinent, personal piques between their servants to hinder the business of government being done.'[14] For Caroline, the world of politics as she understood it bore a striking resemblance to the life she had made for herself at home. In the end, both came down to questions of management.

Whatever the reality of Caroline's political role, it is hard to imagine that George was indifferent to the powerful contemporary perception that in matters of government, it was she and not he who was in charge. For a man whose self-esteem was so dependent on the respect and admiration of others, this must have been a painful experience. To be found wanting in the arena where men – and royal men in particular – were expected to excel, unchallenged by even the brightest of women, was particularly humiliating. In the public world, as he came to recognise, there seemed little he could do about it. The more he denied it, the more it seemed as if it might be true. But George knew that there were other areas of his and Caroline's life together where he remained effortlessly dominant, where his primacy was secure and uncompromised: in the most intimate dimension of their private world there was no question whose will it was that governed, and who was required to submit to it.

From the earliest years of their marriage, George had taken mistresses. He did so not because he did not love Caroline, but because he was afraid that otherwise it might look as if he loved her too much. Horace Walpole thought he 'was more attracted by a silly idea he entertained of gallantry being becoming, than by a love of variety'. His infidelities made him seem more a man of the world and less of a besotted husband. When he was Prince of Wales, George followed long-established tradition in selecting his lovers from the household of his wife. He did not go about the process with great subtlety. Having decided to approach Mary Bellenden, one of Caroline's Maids of Honour – 'incontestably the most agreeable, the most insinuating, and the most likeable woman of her time' – George favoured the direct method. Knowing that she could not pay her bills, he sat beside her one night and 'took out his purse and counted his money. He repeated the numeration; the giddy Bellenden lost her patience, and cried out, "Sir, I cannot bear it! If you count your money any more, I will go out of the room."'[15] In the end Mary Bellenden's poverty conquered her irritation; but the time she spent as George's mistress turned out to be unrewarding in every way. He was too mean to make her relationship financially rewarding, too disengaged to give her any real pleasure, and unwilling to award her the status of Principal Mistress. As soon as she could, Mary Bellenden found a husband to marry, and exchanged the role of unhappy royal mistress for that of respectable wife.

She was succeeded in the post by Lady Suffolk, whom George and Caroline had known since the early days of their marriage in Hanover. She had been Mrs Howard then, and had arrived at their court accompanied by a violent and drunken husband, and so poor that she had been forced to sell her own hair to raise money. She was beautiful, elegant, cultivated and entertaining (as an elderly woman, grand and formidable, she was one of Horace Walpole's most valued friends). For over a decade she was George's principal mistress. She was also one of the queen's bedchamber women, which meant that wife and mistress spent a great deal of time in each other's company, an experience neither of them enjoyed.

The difficulties of the situation would have been exacerbated by George's indifference to the established rules of polite behaviour. He conducted his affair without the slightest attempt at discretion. With the methodical exactitude that characterised everything he did, he made his way to Lady Suffolk's apartment at seven every evening, in full view of the court. If he found he was too early, he would pace about, looking at his watch, until it was exactly the right time for their assignation to begin. Perhaps it was some consolation to Caroline that this hardly suggested a relationship driven by great passion. Hervey thought the king kept it up 'as a necessary appurtenance to his grandeur as a prince rather than an addition to his pleasure as a man.' He added that there were many at court who doubted whether the couple had a sexual relationship at all.[16] Whatever the nature of the affair, it certainly did not seem to cool George's ardour for his wife; and the much-tried Lady Suffolk often found herself caught in the crossfire of his angry attraction for Caroline. 'It happened more than once,' reported Walpole, 'that the king, coming in to the room while the queen was dressing, has snatched off the handkerchief, and turning rudely to Mrs Howard, has cried, "Because you have an ugly neck yourself, you seek to hide the queen's!"'[17]

Hervey thought that for all the offence Lady Suffolk's presence gave to the queen's dignity, Caroline had, with some effort, resigned herself to her rival's existence. 'Knowing the vanity of her husband's temper, and that he must have some woman for the world to believe he lay with, she wisely suffered one to remain in that situation whom she despised, and had got the better of, for fear of making room for a successor whom he might really love, and who might get the better of her.'[18] Certainly, when, in 1734, the king finally tired of his now middle-aged mistress, and Lady Suffolk sought to avoid the inevitable by quitting the court before she was asked to leave, it was Caroline who tried to persuade her to stay. In a lengthy private interview she urged her 'to take a week to consider of the business. And give me your word that you will not read any romances in that time.'[19] Lady Suffolk was not to be won over. She had had enough of her half-affair with a man she suspected had only ever wanted her as a mistress in order to demonstrate his independence from his wife. The king, who complained to Caroline that he could not understand 'why you will not let me part with an old deaf woman, of whom I am weary', was pleased to see her go.

Although Caroline's daughters were similarly glad to see Lady Suffolk – whom they all hated – disappear from their own and their mother's lives, it was their father towards whom they felt the most animus, despising him for his humiliating treatment of the queen. Anne, the cleverest and most outspoken of the sisters, made it the basis of a lasting and deeply felt dislike of the king, on which she would often expatiate to Hervey, venting her disdain in a resounding, freeform litany of the many things that she hated about him. 'His passion, his pride, his vanity, his giving himself airs about women, the impossibility of being easy with him, his affectation of heroism, his unreasonable, simple, uncertain, disagreeable and often shocking behaviour to the queen, the difficulty of entertaining him, his insisting upon other people's conversation who were to entertain him being always new and his own always the same thing over and over again ...'[20] The depth of her contempt for George made her hope he would not stay too long without a mistress. 'I wish with all my heart he would take somebody else,' she told Hervey, 'that Mama might be a little relieved from the ennui of seeing him forever in her room.'[21] This was to happen sooner than Anne can have imagined, and with consequences for her mother that she would never have wished for.

Among George II's most jealously guarded pleasures were the regular visits he made back to his electorate – trips he called his *Hanover-reisen*. Caroline did not go with him, staying instead in Britain as his regent; she never saw Germany again after leaving in 1714. While at Herrenhausen in 1735, George met Amalie von Wallmoden, a young, fashionable married woman. He fell in love with her at first sight, with an immediacy and intensity that resembled his first meeting with Caroline some thirty years earlier. It was soon clear to everyone that his passion for 'the Wallmoden' was of an entirely different order to anything he had felt for previous lovers. He was soon in the grip of a powerful obsession for her that dominated all his thoughts.

Caroline knew this better than anyone else, because George wrote to tell her all about it. Whenever he was away, George wrote constantly to his wife, with letters 'of sometimes sixty pages, and never less than forty, filled with an hourly account of everything he saw, heard thought or did'. Hervey thought this correspondence 'crammed with minute trifling circumstances unworthy of a man to write, but even more of a woman to read'.[22] George would sometimes instruct Caroline to show relevant passages 'to the fat man', which meant that the portly politician Robert Walpole saw for himself a great deal of what passed between the couple. He knew, as a result, that there was virtually nothing the king did not tell the queen, including all the most intimate details of his love affairs. Their correspondence also revealed that George required far more from Caroline than a dignified complaisance in the face of his infidelities; he also expected her to assist him in the pursuit of promising new affairs. 'There was one letter,' Walpole told Hervey, 'in which he desired the queen to contrive, if she could, that the prince of Modena, who was to come at the latter end of the year to England, might bring his wife with him; and the reason he gave, was that he had heard her highness was pretty free with her person.' It therefore came as no surprise to the queen to now receive 'so minute a description' of her husband's new mistress, 'that had the queen been a painter she might have drawn her rival's picture at 600 miles distance'.[23]

At first, Caroline attempted to dismiss George's new affair as she had done those that preceded it, but when he lingered on in Hanover, she began to grow increasingly concerned. And when at last he arrived reluctantly back in London, summoned home by his anxious ministers, she realised just how serious the situation had become, and to what degree her carefully managed primacy in his eyes was now threatened by his mistress in Germany.

Caroline might have imagined that she had already experienced most of what a royal marriage could require from a royal wife, but the humiliations, both public and private, she was now to endure at her husband's hands were beyond anything she had yet encountered. George had always treated her brusquely in public. Hervey thought he was 'perpetually so harsh and rough, that she could never speak one word uncontradicted, nor do any act unreproved'.[24] Caroline's response was to retreat into a posture of even greater submission, but her abnegation served only to spur George into even greater irritation.

However innocuous the subject of conversation, the king would direct it into an attack on his wife. When Hervey and Caroline tried to draw him into a discussion on whether it was right to tip servants when one visited the houses of friends, that too turned into a rant, with the king declaring that the queen should not be venturing beyond her home in pursuit of pleasure. His whole family came under the lash of his ill humour. A few days later, he 'snubbed the queen, who was drinking chocolate, for being always stuffing; the princess Emily [as Amelia was informally known] for not hearing him, the princess Caroline for being grown fat, the Duke of Cumberland for standing awkwardly, Lord Hervey for not knowing what relation the Prince of Sultzbach was to the elector Palatine, then carried the queen to walk, and be re-snubbed, in the garden'. On the rare occasions when the king's mood lightened, 'it was only to relate the scenes of his happy loves when he was at Hanover'.[25] George had brought over from Germany a series of paintings that depicted 'all his amorous amusements' with Mme de Wallmoden, which he had framed and placed in the queen's dressing room. In the evenings, before an embarrassed Hervey and a 'peevish' Caroline, 'he would take a candle in his own royal hand, and tell ... the story of these pictures'. To distract the queen, Hervey would 'make grimaces' over the king's shoulder; but his jokes did little to rouse her spirits. George did not understand why his wife could not enter his amours with the same enthusiasm he did. 'You must love the Wallmoden,' he once instructed her, 'for she loves me.'

When the king returned to Hanover the following year, it looked to an apprehensive Hervey as though Caroline had finally had enough and, provoked beyond endurance, intended to adopt a less conciliatory policy towards her husband. She began to write to him less regularly, and her letters, which had previously run to thirty pages or more, now barely exceeded seven or eight. When news reached England that Mme de Wallmoden had given birth to a son, Hervey feared that Caroline might lose control of her husband altogether. He 'begged Sir Robert Walpole to do something or other to prevent her going on in a way that would destroy her'. Walpole thought 'that nothing could ever quite destroy her power with the king'; but he was merciless in the advice he subsequently dispensed to a tearful Caroline: she must abandon any attempt to express her displeasure, or declare her own injured feelings. 'It was too late in her life to try new methods, and she was never to hope now to keep her power with the king by reversing those methods by which she had gained it.' She must conquer her bitterness and replace indignation with submission. 'Nothing but soothing, complying, softening, bending, and submitting could do any good.' And he added a final directive to his comprehensive recipe of humiliation: 'She must press the king to bring this woman to England. He taught her this hard lesson till she wept.'[26]

The strategist in Caroline could see the benefits of having George back in Britain again, where he would be susceptible to her influence; but the aggrieved, betrayed wife in her resisted. The struggle between the two warring dimensions of Caroline's character was short and sharp, and it was the queen and the politician who emerged victorious. Caroline wrote 'a most submissive and tender letter' to George 'assuring him she had nothing but his interest and his pleasure at heart' and making 'an earnest request that he would bring Mme de Wallmoden to England, giving assurances that his wife's conduct to his mistress should be everything he desired'.[27] As Robert Walpole had predicted, once Caroline had declared her utter surrender to his will, George's hostility began to melt away. He replied immediately with a host of conciliatory expressions. 'You know my passions, my dear Caroline. You understand my frailties. There is nothing hidden in my heart from you.' Robert Walpole, who was shown the letter, told Hervey that 'it was so well written, that if the king was only to write to women and never to strut or talk to them, he believed His Majesty would get the better of all the men in the world with them'.[28]

When the king at last returned to London, 'the warmest of all his rays were directed at the queen. He said no man ever had so affectionate and meritorious a wife or so faithful an able a friend'. Mme de Wallmoden 'seemed to those who knew the king best to be quite forgot'.[29] Aged over fifty, Caroline had managed to seduce her straying husband home again. That was undoubtedly a triumph of sorts, but she could not have been unaware of the high price she had paid – and indeed, had always paid – for the maintenance of their precarious marital status quo. There were many things she knew her husband admired about her: her energy; her beauty, even; could he but admit it, the intellect that she had so tirelessly directed towards the success of their partnership – but none of this mattered as much to George as her willingness to deny all her best qualities in an absolute emotional submission to his will. He knew that with a glance or a frown, and above all with the threat of departure, he could bring her to heel; in the private heartland of their marriage, true power resided firmly where it had always been – in his hands.

It is true that Caroline had very few options in responding to George's behaviour, as she had no desire to follow her mother-in-law into the post-marital wilderness; but her desire to keep the affections of her errant husband was more than simply the product of pragmatic considerations. She was genuinely distressed by his temporary abandonment of her, and was delighted when he came back. She was proud that the king had returned not only to court, but also to her bed, joyfully informing Robert Walpole of the fact so that he could appreciate the completeness of her victory. George was a difficult man to love, and he tried the fortitude of his wife severely in the thirty years they spent together. Yet during all that time, he remained the dominating figure in her life, crowding out all competing emotional claims. When forced by her father-in-law to make the appalling choice between her husband and her daughters, Caroline had unhesitatingly chosen George, declaring 'her children were not a grain of sand compared to him'.[30] It was not that she did not care for her girls; she loved her daughters deeply, but it was her relationship with her husband that occupied all her time and absorbed all her emotional energy. There was not much room left for anyone else.

*

If the relationship between George and Caroline was complex, and not conducive to happiness, it was as nothing compared to the misery that resulted from their dealings with Frederick, their eldest son. Some of the problems they encountered were not entirely of their own making; the operation of eighteenth-century politics inevitably placed the heir to the throne in opposition to his father. On reaching maturity he soon became the focus around which disgruntled politicians gathered, eager to stake their claim to the future. He could make a great deal of trouble for the king and his ministers if he was disposed to do so, and very few heirs found themselves able to resist that temptation. All this George and Caroline knew very well from their own difficult days as Prince and Princess of Wales; once they inherited the crown, however, they expunged all recollection of that period from their joint memory, and expected their son to behave with a political rectitude that had not characterised their own behaviour when they occupied his position. But their attitude to the prince went far beyond the discontents and difficulties that came with their constitutional roles. They treated Frederick with a venom that exceeded any legitimate political frustration, and conceived a hatred for him that became almost pathological in its intensity.

As with so much Hanoverian unhappiness, its origins lay in the actions of George I. He had kept his small grandson in Hanover, forbidding his parents to visit him there, and allowing them no say in his education and upbringing. When Frederick was sixteen, George I had begun to negotiate a marriage between his grandson and the Princess of Prussia. In a gesture of deliberate and insulting exclusion, the boy's father was not consulted, nor even informed of the project. Back in England, the younger George watched the king load on to Frederick a host of honours and titles which had never been extended to him, and began to wonder whether it would be Frederick and not himself who would eventually inherit the electorate. None of these slights made him look fondly on his absent son. As the Duchess of Orléans astutely commented, it seemed to guarantee that the filial hatred that had defined one generation would be passed on to the next: 'The young prince in Hanover may not meet with much love, for if the Prince of Wales has to bear his mother's sins, perhaps he may have to answer for the grandfather's.'[31]

In the years the young prince had been separated from his family, distance had not made his father's heart grow fonder. Frederick grew up a remote cipher, a blank page on which George could project all the anger he felt against his own father, with whom the boy was forever damagingly identified. He did not know him, and felt nothing for him but the suspicion he instinctively reached for when faced with a rival of unknown and possibly damaging intent. He showed no desire at all to bring the young man back into his life. When he succeeded to the throne, it had been widely expected that Frederick would immediately be summoned to attend the coronation; but it took a parliamentary address to persuade the new king to do so.

After a long and hazardous journey through the winter landscapes of north Germany, the young prince finally arrived in England in December 1727. He was greeted with scant ceremony and a very cool welcome. When he reached London, there were no officials to greet him and no royal coach to transport him to St James's Palace; he was obliged to hire a hackney coach and make his own way to his mother's apartments.[32] At first, he and his estranged family seem to have managed their new and somewhat uncomfortable proximity with some success. Frederick spent time with his mother, in private and in public, and played his part well at formal events such as the celebrations for the queen's birthday. The king was satisfied too, but for rather different reasons. In his early encounters, he had found the inoffensive reality of his son far less intimidating than the threatening image he had conjured up in the boy's absence. 'He was quite pleased with him, as a new thing, felt him quite in his power.' He was said to have told Robert Walpole, with a tellingly contemptuous air: 'I think this is a son I need not be much afraid of.'[33]

Whilst he took pains to behave well under the scrutinising eyes of his parents, the twenty-one-year-old Frederick was keen to take advantage of the opportunities London offered, in characteristically Hanoverian style. He had left behind him in Germany an established mistress, Mme d'Elitz, who was said to have served both his father and his grandfather as lovers before him; now he turned his attentions further afield. He began affairs with an opera singer, with the daughter of an apothecary, and with a woman who played the hautboy. One night, venturing into St James's Park in search of female company, he met a girl who robbed him of his wallet, twenty-two guineas and his royal seal; he was forced to advertise for the seal's return, promising that no questions would be asked of whoever brought it back to him. In all these encounters he retained a combination of adolescent innocence and boastfulness, qualities he was not to lose until well beyond his first youth. 'He was not over nice in his choice,' commented Lord Egmont, who became a close friend, 'and talks more of his feats in this way than he acts.'[34] He was rowdy and boisterous at times; with a group of other rich young men, he would race through the night-time streets, breaking the windows of respectable householders. The eccentric Duchess of Buckingham was said to have fired grapeshot at him when her glass was broken. She placed an advertisement in the *Daily Gazette*, 'to assure those who offered insults of this kind to her or her house that they should be received suitably to their conduct, and not to their rank.'[35] For the rest of his life Frederick never lost his taste for somewhat crude practical jokes and pranks; a strategically placed bucket of water emptied on the head of an unsuspecting friend would always raise a laugh from him.

In later years, when their hostility to their son was firmly established, George and Caroline were keen to suggest that his behaviour had been wicked and untrustworthy from his very earliest days. Caroline once confided to Robert Walpole, with tears in her eyes, the opinion of Frederick's old tutor in Hanover, whom she said had told her that her son had 'the most vicious nature and false heart that ever man had, nor are his vices those of a gentleman but the mean, base tricks of a knavish footman.'[36] But while Frederick was hardly a paragon of goodness, there is little to suggest that he committed sins any worse than those common to young men of his age and situation. Others who met him did not share his tutor's apocalyptically bleak judgement. The intrepid traveller Lady Mary Worley Montagu had been introduced to him when he was a child in Hanover and found 'something so very engaging and easy in his behaviour that he needs no advantage of rank to appear impressed.'[37] A decade later, Lady Bristol, Lord Hervey's mother, met the prince during his first weeks in London, and had been equally impressed. He was, she thought, 'the most agreeable young man that it is possible to imagine, without being the least handsome, his person very little, but very well made and genteel, a liveliness in his eyes that is indescribable, and the most obliging address that can be conceived.'[38]

From the moment Hervey himself arrived back in England from a Grand Tour of Italy in 1729, he laid siege to the prince, doing all he could to win his affection. Frederick fell as quickly under Hervey's spell as his mother was later to do. A few years older than the prince, Hervey was all the things the rather gauche young man was not – well travelled, assured, articulate, sophisticated, naturally at home in the elegant world. By the time Hervey's third son was born in 1730, the two men were such close friends that, with the prince's blessing, Hervey named the boy after him. They were seen everywhere together and supported each other through a variety of tribulations. When Hervey, whose health was always troublesome, collapsed 'as if I had been shot' in a fit at the prince's feet, Frederick abandoned all other commitments to stay with his friend until he recovered. 'The prince sat with me all day yesterday,' Hervey wrote with satisfaction, 'and has promised to do so again today.'[39] Hervey returned the favour when Frederick in his turn fell ill. After he recovered, he presented Hervey with a gold snuffbox bearing his portrait and invited him down to his country retreat at Kew, where they played at ninepins all day. They were now so close that they had dropped any formal titles; the prince wrote to Hervey in playful tones as 'my dear chicken' or 'my lord chicken'.[40]

By the summer of 1731, the relationship between Hervey and Frederick had become so intimate and so affectionate that Hervey's established lover began to grow uneasy about it. Stephen Fox – known to his friends as Ste – was the brother of the politician Henry Fox and the uncle of the famous Charles. He and Hervey had been involved in a passionate affair for nearly five years, even though Ste shared few of Hervey's interests. Where Hervey was happiest in the intrigue and incident of the city, Ste was a dedicated countryman, who could rarely be persuaded to leave his Somerset estate. Hervey's wife Molly, who knew all about their relationship, said that 'unless one could be metamorphosed into a bird or a hare, [Ste] will have nothing to say to one'.[41] When they were apart, Hervey wrote constantly to Ste, doing all he could to convey his love for him in words. 'I hear you in the deadliest silence and see you in the deepest darkness,' he assured him. 'For my own part, my mind never goes naked but in your territories.'[42] Now Ste began to wonder whether the prince was edging him out of Hervey's affections. When Hervey unguardedly told Ste how much he cared for the prince, Ste exploded in an outburst of jealousy and recrimination. Shocked by Ste's response, Hervey did all he could to mollify his wounded feelings. 'When I said I loved 7 [his codeword for the prince] as much as I loved you, I lied egregiously; I am as incapable of wishing to love anybody else so well as I am of wishing to love you less.'[43] He insisted that Ste would always be his only real love, assuring him 'that since first I knew you I have been yours without repenting, and still am, and ever shall be undividedly, and indissolubly yours'. Eventually, the storm passed.

While it is hard to know how conscious Frederick was of the effect he had on Hervey, it is difficult to imagine that he had no understanding of the emotions he had stirred up. When Hervey wrote to Frederick describing himself as Hephaistion, every educated man of the time would have known that Hephaistion was the male lover of a great prince, Alexander the Great. It is also perhaps significant that the pages which cover the period of greatest intimacy between Hervey and Frederick were removed and destroyed by Hervey's grandson when he inherited Hervey's memoirs. Considering the graphic and unflinching nature of what he left untouched, the excised section must have contained details he regarded as even more scandalous than what remains.

In the end, it was a row over a woman, not a man, that put an end to Frederick and Hervey's friendship. None of the three men involved in the complicated triangle that played itself out in 1731–32 saw their relationship with each other as debarring them from affairs with women. All three married, and between them they produced a tribe of children. Down in Somerset, Ste preferred hunting and shooting to the active pursuit of women; neither Frederick nor Hervey saw any reason to interrupt their more conventional predatory habits. 'What game you poach, sir,' Hervey wrote archly to the prince, 'what you hunt, what you catch, or what runs into your mouth, I don't pretend to guess.'[44] But when he discovered that Frederick had successfully seduced a woman he regarded as a conquest of his own, Hervey was incensed.

Anne Vane, one of Queen Caroline's Maids of Honour, had been Hervey's mistress since 1730. She was not considered much of a prize. 'She is a fat and ill-shaped dwarf,' said one uncharitable witness, 'who has nothing good to recommend her that I know.'[45] It was hardly a passionate affair; Hervey described her to Ste as 'a little ragout that, though it is not one's favourite dish, will prevent one either dying of hunger or choosing to fast.'[46] Yet when he discovered that the prince had set her up in a house in Soho he was furious. It was not a thwarted sense of possessiveness on Hervey's part. Anne Vane had so many lovers that when she became pregnant, three men claimed paternity of the baby, though it was the prince who was widely considered best entitled to that credit. Hervey was more hurt by what he considered the prince's betrayal than Anne Vane's faithlessness. When Frederick began to spend more and more time with Anne and less and less with his old friend, Hervey's anger turned to desperation. In a last-ditch attempt to win back the favour that was so visibly ebbing away, he wrote a blistering letter to his ex-mistress, threatening to tell the prince everything he knew about her unless she promised to help reinstate him in Frederick's good books. Anne collapsed with shock, and on her recovery, showed the letter to Frederick, who was extremely angry and never forgave Hervey. The breach between the two men was immediate and irrevocable; their years of friendship were swept away and replaced by volleys of insult and invective, claim and counterclaim, professions of outraged honour and betrayed loyalty. In the summer of 1732, Anne gave birth to a son, who was ostentatiously named Fitzfrederick. Frederick installed her in a palatial house in Grosvenor Square and gave her an annual allowance of £3,000.[47] It was a very public demonstration of the transfer of his affections.

Reluctantly accepting that he had no real future with the son, Hervey now concentrated his attention on Frederick's mother, who responded eagerly to his overtures. When the prince protested that 'it was extremely hard a man the whole world knew had been so impertinent to him, and whom he never spoke to, should be picked out by the queen for her constant companion', his complaints were ignored. Hervey later maintained that despite their quarrel, he would sometimes take Frederick's side, arguing his case before the prince's increasingly ill-disposed parents. He was candid enough to admit that he did this not as 'an affectation of false generosity but merely from prudence and regard to himself'. He knew, he said, how common it was in families 'for suspended affection to revive itself' and did not want to find himself excoriated by both sides of a reunited dynasty.[48] But as relations between the prince and his parents grew more bitter, Hervey took full advantage of the opportunities offered by his position around the queen to take revenge upon his erstwhile friend. He became one of the prince's greatest enemies in a household in which there was considerable competition for that title, egging Caroline on to ever greater and more shocking declarations of anger and disgust with Frederick.

In the end he supplanted the prince in every aspect of his mother's affection. As Caroline knew, Hervey disliked his own mother, whom he thought a loud and silly woman. 'Your mother,' she once told him, 'is a brute that deserves just such a beast as my son. I hope I do not; and I wish with all my soul we could change, that they who are alike might go together, and that you and I might belong to one another.'[49] Hervey, who did all he could to present himself to Caroline as the child she truly deserved, once ventured to suggest the possibility directly. 'Supposing I had had the honour to be born Your Majesty's son –' 'I wish to God you had,' interrupted the queen. Few conversations could have given him such a sense of deep and vengeful satisfaction.

In later years, there was a great deal of speculation about what had provoked the hatred that came to define the relations between the king and queen and their eldest son. Lord Hardwicke, the Lord Chancellor from 1737 to 1756, hinted at the existence of 'certain passages between him and the king' that he said were 'of too high and secret a nature' ever to be placed in writing. But for all the desire to find a single compelling explanation for their behaviour, there was in fact no one decisive event which produced the rapid decline in even nominal goodwill between George, Caroline and Frederick.

Instead, it was a number of considerations that exacerbated an already unhappy situation. The family history of suspicion, betrayal and distrust weighed heavily upon Frederick's parents. There were few examples in their own past of disinterested, affectionate conduct or calm self-effacement to guide or inspire them. George's temper was irritable and easily provoked, especially by those he thought should be unquestioningly subordinate to his will. These private discontents were magnified by a political culture which anticipated and indeed positively rewarded a separation of interests between the king and his heir. Once embarked upon, it was all but impossible to prevent these public breaches from taking on a very personal dimension. 'It ran a little in the blood of the family to hate the eldest son,' summarised Horace Walpole, with succinct understatement.[50] But as Walpole also understood, there was a more immediate trigger for the king's first eruption of fury at his son, and that issue was money.

When Frederick came of age, George II allowed him around £40,000 per annum from the Civil List. Frederick considered this inadequate, especially when compared to the £100,000 his father had received when he was Prince of Wales. Even Hervey had some sympathy with Frederick's position. He pointed out to Caroline that 'the best friends to her, the king and the administration were of the opinion that the prince had not enough money allowed him, and whilst he was so straitened in his circumstances, it was impossible he should ever be quiet.'[51] Hervey hoped that the queen would work her magic upon her husband and persuade him to adopt a more generous stance. Caroline was, at this point, better disposed towards Frederick than her husband, preferring to think of him as badly advised rather than malicious in intent. 'Poor creature,' she told Hervey, 'with not a bad heart, he is induced by knaves and fools to blow him up to do things that are as unlike an honest man as a wise one.'[52] Caroline insisted that she had often interceded on his behalf with his father, assuring Frederick that 'she wanted nothing so much as their being well together.' She had, she declared, 'sunk several circumstances the king had not seen and softened things that he had' in order to present her son in the best possible light. She did this even though she saw no signs that Frederick appreciated her efforts. When Hervey told her that 'it always had been his opinion, and still was so, that the prince loved Her Majesty in his heart', she was sceptical. She agreed that 'he has no inveterate hatred to me, but for love, I cannot say I see any great signs of it'.[53]

The king's response was both more straightforward and more hostile. He had no sympathy with his son's demands. Frederick had already run up huge debts in Hanover which he had no prospect of repaying without his father's help. George also argued that the larger allowance he had received as Prince of Wales had been required to support a growing family, whilst his son was responsible for no one but himself. Frederick's persistence in pursuing a comparable sum confirmed all his father's early apprehensions about the ambition and opportunism of his heir; he suspected the cash was intended to further Frederick's political ends, financing an opposition that would inevitably be directed against him. Soon the king refused to speak to his son at all. 'He hated to talk of him almost as much as to talk to him,' observed Hervey; but he made his feelings known by 'laying it on him pretty thick' in more oblique references. 'One very often sees a father a very brave man, and the son a scoundrel,' the king once declared to a group of embarrassed listeners, 'a father very honest and his son a great knave; the father a man of truth and the son a great liar; in short, a father that has all sorts of good qualities and a son that is good for nothing.' Hervey noticed that the king stopped short, 'feeling that he had pushed it too far', and noted that in some cases 'it was just the reverse, and that very disagreeable fathers sometimes had very agreeable men for their sons. I suppose,' remarked Hervey, 'that in this case he thought of his own father.'[54]

George's behaviour helped to usher in precisely the situation he had feared: soon, the prince stood at the centre of an organised coalition of ambitious politicians keen to use his grievances as a means of attacking his father's administration. Far from being a token figurehead, the prince was an active participant in the development of an opposition strategy, doing all he could to attract supporters to his cause. He was successful in luring some of the brightest talents of the rising generation into his orbit; recognising that time was on his side, he did all he could to win over the young. His friend and adviser Lord Egmont said he had even tried to attract into his camp the headmaster of Westminster School, as it was considered such a breeding ground for the politicians of the future.

Slowly, the prince began to feel his potential strength. When Robert Walpole's government found itself unable to carry the controversial Excise Bill through Parliament in 1737, Frederick declined to come to his father's assistance by ordering his supporters to vote with the ministers. It was his first public clash with the king. Walpole, alarmed at the precedent it set for the future, tried to coax him towards more dutiful behaviour by offering to raise the vexed issue of his allowance with Parliament. But Frederick was not interested; he was not to be bought off with promises, and was prepared to wait for a better opportunity to emerge.

The king did not react well to his son's defiance. For some time he had not spoken to Frederick. Now, when forced into his company, he could not be brought to make the smallest acknowledgement of his presence. 'Whenever the prince was in a room with the king,' observed Hervey, 'it put one in mind of stories one has heard of ghosts that appear to part of the company and are invisible to the rest; and in this manner, wherever the prince stood, though the king passed ever so near, it always seemed as if the king thought the place the prince filled a void space.'[55] George later told Hervey that he had once asked Caroline whether she thought 'the beast was his son'. He did not mean to impugn her fidelity; drawing perhaps on the same vision of the world that fuelled his belief in vampires, he explained that he thought Frederick might be what the Germans called 'a *Wechselbalg*' – a changeling.[56]

George's exasperation was increased by the apparent indifference with which his son appeared to receive the snubs and insults meted out to him. While his father fumed at St James's, Frederick turned with annoyingly blithe unconcern to his own pleasures. He was a skilled cricketer, captaining the Surrey team and – to Hervey's fastidious disgust – regularly playing alongside gardeners and grooms. He shared with most of his family a passionate love of music, although, unlike his father, he liked to perform as well as listen. He was an accomplished cellist and in 1734 gave impromptu concerts once or twice a week at Kensington Palace for anyone who turned up to enjoy them – including, noted a horrified Hervey (who compared Frederick to Nero playing his fiddle), 'all the underling servants and rabble of the palace'.[57] Like his mother, he loved books and read widely in subjects ranging from politics to philosophy to theology. Like her too, he relished an argument and was a sharp and nimble debater. Frederick even dabbled in writing himself. When he and Hervey were still friends, they had produced an undistinguished drama, *The Modish Couple*, which lasted only a few nights when performed on stage, and had closed amidst protests from a furious audience demanding their money back.

In 1734, the prince approached the king and asked permission to marry. George refused at first, citing Frederick's 'childish and silly' behaviour as his justification; he vetoed a plan for the prince to reopen negotiations for the Princess of Prussia, famously remarking that he did not think grafting a coxcomb on to a halfwit would improve the breed. But on returning from one of his regular trips to Hanover in 1736, George announced that during his visit, he had seen the Princess Augusta of Saxe-Gotha, and thought she would make a suitable wife for his son. The prince answered 'with great duty, decency and propriety, that whatever his majesty thought a proper match for his son would be acceptable to him'. In the midst of his affair with Mme de Wallmoden, the king was keen to return to Hanover as soon as possible, and demanded that the match take place immediately.

A few months later, Augusta arrived in London. She was seventeen years old, gawky, naive and alone: she 'suffered to bring nobody but a single man with her'. Hervey observed she was 'rather tall and had health and youth enough in her face, joined to a very modest and good-natured look, to make her countenance not disagreeable'; but his practised seducer's eye found 'her arms long, and her motions awkward, and in spite of all her finery of jewels and brocade' she had 'an ordinary air which trappings could not cover or exalt'.[58] She spoke not a word of English; her mother explained that it had not been thought necessary to teach her, believing that 'the Hanover family having been above twenty years on the throne, to be sure most people in England must now speak German'.[59]

Nervous and inexperienced as she was, Augusta made a good beginning by prostrating herself on the floor in front of the king, who found this extreme form of respect entirely to his liking. She summoned enough courage to support herself through the rigours of the marriage ceremony, and she endured the jocular formality of a public wedding night with a man she had never met before with phlegmatic resignation. The young couple were led to their chamber and undressed with great ceremony. Once they were established in bed, the court processed past them, offering congratulations and ribald remarks about what was to come next. The prince was observed to eat glass after glass of jelly, which was thought to be an aphrodisiac; 'every time he took one', Hervey noted disdainfully, 'turning about and laughing and winking at some of his servants'. He also wore a nightcap 'some inches higher than any grenadiers cap in the whole army'. The next morning, the queen gossiped away to Hervey 'with her usual enjoyment, on the glasses of jelly and the nightcap', saying that one had made her sick and the other had made her laugh. They both thought Augusta looked so refreshed that 'they concluded she had slept very sound'.[60]

The prince's marriage marked a new phase in the deterioration of relationships within the royal family, and brought out into the open the covert warfare that had been waged between parents and son for so many years. Now Frederick felt himself strong enough to go on the offensive, and did so through the medium of his naive young wife. Whenever the couple attended chapel, the prince ensured that they always arrived after the king and queen. To reach her seat, Augusta had to push past Caroline and oblige her to get up. It took a direct order from the king to put a stop to this petty campaign of attrition. Caroline did not blame her new daughter-in-law, saying that she knew she 'did nothing without the prince's order'. There was no harm in Augusta, Caroline assured Hervey: 'she never meant to offend, was very modest and very respectful', but it was 'her want of understanding' that made her such exhausting company. She was perhaps not surprised to hear from one of her daughters that Augusta spent a large part of each day 'playing with a great jointed baby', dressing and undressing it in full view of an incredulous crowd of servants, who, like the queen, thought a married woman should be beyond playing with dolls.

When the prince announced that his wife was pregnant, Caroline simply refused to believe it. She had for some time harboured doubts about her son's capacity to sire a child; now her curiosity developed into a strange, fixed obsession. She insisted to Hervey that she did not believe the marriage had ever been consummated, and questioned him remorselessly to discover what he knew about Frederick's sexual prowess. It was a subject she had already discussed directly with her son, who, she told Hervey, 'sometimes spoke of himself in these matters as if he were Hercules, and at other times as if he were four-score'. Frederick had recently confided in her details 'of an operation that he had had performed upon him by his surgeon', and added that he had 'got nasty distempers by women'; but she suspected both were lies intended to distract attention from the reality of his impotence. She was sure little Fitzfrederick, the prince's alleged child by Anne Vane, was really Hervey's. Hervey replied that Fitzfrederick was not his child and that from what Anne Vane had told him, he assured Caroline there was no reason why he should not be Frederick's. 'She used to describe the prince in these matters as ignorant to a degree inconceivable, but not impotent.'[61]

Unconvinced, Caroline asked for a second opinion: could Hervey 'get some intelligence' from Lady Dudley, who 'has slept with half the town' and might know if Frederick 'was like other men or not'? When Hervey refused to do so, the queen tried another approach. Had Frederick ever asked him to father a child on his behalf? Hervey told her he had not. If he had been asked, Caroline persisted, would such a thing be possible? Hervey thought it might be, but only if the marriage had actually been consummated, 'for though I believe I may put one man upon her for another', he doubted whether he could fool a woman who had never had a lover. Would it be possible to deceive her if both men were agreed to carry out the plan? It would take about a month, mused Hervey, during which 'I would advise the prince to go to bed several hours after his wife, and to pretend to get up with a flux several times in the night, to perfume himself always with the same predominant smell, and by the help of these tricks, it would be very easy.' It would be easier if the man was the same size as the husband and did not speak during the process. Caroline was so shocked by the ease with which Hervey thought the deception might be managed that she delivered a rare rebuke to him: 'I love you mightily, my dear Lord Hervey, but if I thought you would get a little Hervey on the Princess of Saxe-Gotha … I could not bear it, nor do I know what I should be capable of doing.'[62]

Caroline seems to have convinced herself that her son was preparing some deception in relation to his wife's pregnancy, whether at the point of conception or delivery. As the months went by, she questioned Augusta about her condition, but could get no sensible answers from her. To everything she asked – how long she had been pregnant, when she expected to give birth – the princess replied simply that she did not know. The prince had clearly instructed her to tell his mother nothing. But Caroline was determined the couple would not evade her scrutiny. She knew Frederick wanted the birth to take place at St James's, rather than at Hampton Court where the family were currently in residence. Wherever it happened, Caroline was certain she would be there: 'At her labour I positively will be … I will be sure it is her child.'[63]

She had reckoned without her son's lunatic determination to outwit her. On 31 July 1736, the prince and princess dined formally with the king and queen at Hampton Court. Later that night, the princess's labour began. Frederick immediately ordered a carriage to take his wife, himself, three of the princess's ladies and Vreid, the man-midwife, to London, away from the prying eyes of his mother. Augusta's waters broke as the prince carried her down the corridor. Ignoring the princess's desperate pleas to be left where she was, Frederick bundled his labouring wife into the coach, all the time murmuring, 'Courage, courage' in her ear. It was quite the worst thing Frederick ever did in his life, and he was lucky that Augusta did not die as a result of his actions. 'At about ten this cargo arrived in town,' wrote Hervey. 'Notwithstanding all the handkerchiefs that had been thrust up Her Royal Highness's petticoats in the coach, her clothes were in such a state with the filthy inundations which attend these circumstances … that the prince ordered all the lights put out that people might not see … the nasty oracular evidence of his folly.' There were no sheets in the unprepared house, so Augusta was finally delivered between two tablecloths. At nearly eleven o'clock, she gave birth to 'a little rat of a girl, about the bigness of a large toothpick case.'[64]

After the birth the prince informed his parents, back at Hampton Court, what had happened. The queen could not believe it; the king was furious, shouting, 'You see now, with all your wisdom how they have outwitted you! This is all your fault! A false child will be put upon you and how will you answer to your children!'[65] Pausing only to dress and to pick up Lord Hervey, Caroline went immediately to London, where she spoke politely to the exhausted princess and kissed the tiny baby. She said nothing to Frederick, other than to observe that 'it was a miracle the princess and the child had not been killed'.[66] Then she turned around and returned to Hampton Court. She had no doubts, she told Hervey, that the 'poor ugly little she-mouse' she had seen at St James's was indeed the princess's child. Had it been 'a brave, jolly boy I should not have been cured of my suspicions'. But her relief that there had been 'no chairman's brat' wished on them did nothing to make the birth an event that brought the family together.

Frederick named his new daughter Augusta, pointedly failing to pay his mother the compliment of naming the first-born girl in her honour. But even without the ill feeling surrounding her arrival, there would have been no reconciliation between the generations. Some time before her birth, Frederick had decided to raise again the long-disputed issue of his allowance in Parliament, and against all expectations, he had been successful in making the subject a Commons motion. His father's response to the prospect of having his financial affairs publicly (and no doubt critically) discussed was predictably apoplectic. Caroline's reaction was more surprising. It had been plain for some time that her attitude to Frederick had hardened considerably. When Hervey asked her if her views on her son had indeed changed over the last year, Caroline agreed most vehemently that they had, telling him that she now believed 'my dear firstborn is the greatest ass and the greatest liar and the greatest *canaille* and the greatest beast in the world, and I most heartily wish he was out of it'.[67]

Now Caroline exploded, releasing a pent-up torrent of reproach and resentment. 'Her invectives against her son were of the incessant and of the strongest kind,' wrote Hervey, who witnessed them at first hand. As the parliamentary vote drew nearer, and the prospect of the prince's victory looked more likely, the queen's rage grew increasingly intemperate. She and her unmarried daughter, Caroline, worked themselves up into ever more passionate denunciations of Frederick. 'They neither of them made much ceremony of wishing a hundred times a day that the prince might drop down dead of an apoplexy, the queen cursing the hour of his birth, and the princess declaring she grudged him every hour he continued to breathe.' The young Caroline, who was said to nurture a deep and unrequited passion for Lord Hervey, had quickly absorbed her parents' hostility towards her eldest brother; she claimed always to have detested him, provoked by his duplicity, his selfishness and his demeaning and destructive pursuit of money. She told Hervey 'that he was a nauseous beast (those were her words) who cared for nobody but his nauseous self', adding that Hervey was a fool for ever having loved him. When the prince refused the political mediations of Robert Walpole, saying he was determined to pursue his claim, the queen declared her son was 'the lowest, stinking coward in the world ... I know if I was asleep, or if he could come behind me, he is capable of shooting me through the head, or stabbing me in the back.'[68]

On the day of the vote, even the usually unshockable Hervey was taken aback by the venom of the queen's attack. As Frederick walked across a courtyard, Caroline watched him. 'Reddening with rage, she said, "Look, there he goes – that wretch! – that villain! – I wish the ground would open this moment and sink that monster to the lowest reaches of hell." Seeing Hervey's startled face she added: 'You stare at me; but I assure you that if my wishes and prayers had any effects; and the maledictions of a mother signified anything, his days would not be very happy or very long.'[69] In the end, the prince lost the motion by the narrow margin of thirty votes; but it was too late now for anything to mend the gulf that divided him from the rest of his family.

There was a tragic echo of the past in what happened next. The king decided Frederick's behaviour had been so provocative that he was to be expelled from the precincts of all the royal palaces. He instructed Hervey, in his role as Vice Chamberlain, to make the necessary arrangements. Hervey based his actions on the instructions that had been drawn up to manage the ejection of George and Caroline from the same palaces almost twenty years before. There was, however, one area in which the king did not intend to follow the harsh example of his father. 'Sir Robert Walpole told Lord Hervey that the resolution was to leave the child with the princess, and not to take it (as the late king had taken the king's children upon the quarrel in the last reign) lest any accident might happen to this little royal animal.'[70] Hervey went about his task with gusto, and admitted that he 'was not a little pleased with a commission that put it in his power to make use of the king's power and authority to gratify and express his resentment against the prince.'[71] But even he was surprised when the king expressly refused to allow Frederick and Augusta any 'chests or other such things' from the royal apartments. When Hervey said that surely he did not mean them to carry away their clothes in linen baskets, George retorted: 'Why not? A basket is good enough for them.'[72]

On the day of the prince's departure, Hervey joined the royal family as they sat round the breakfast table contemplating what was about to happen. 'I am weary of the puppy's name,' declared the king. 'I wish I was never to hear it again, but at least I shall not be plagued any more with seeing his nasty face.' He told Caroline that he could forgive everything he had done to him, but could never forget the injury done to her. 'I never loved the puppy well enough to have him ungrateful to me but to you he is a monster and the greatest villain ever born.' Princess Caroline, elaborating on what was a familiarly obsessive theme, hoped her brother would burst so that they could mourn 'with smiling faces and crepe and hoods for him'. The queen was adamant that she was unmoved by her son's impending exile: 'God knows in my heart, I feel no more for him than if he was no relation, and if I was to see him in hell, I should feel no more for him than I should for any rogue that was there.' And yet, she added, 'once I would have given up all my other children for him. I was fond of that monster, I looked on him as if he had been the happiness of my life, and now I wish that he had never been born … I hope in God I shall never see the monster's face again.' [73] She never did.

*

'There was a strange affectation of incapacity of being sick that ran through the royal family,' Hervey observed, 'which they carried so far that no one of them was more willing to own any other of the family being ill than to acknowledge themselves to be.' Hervey had seen the king 'get out of his bed choking and with a sore throat and in a high fever, only to dress and have a levee'. He expected Caroline to do the same. 'With all his fondness for the queen, he used to make her in the like circumstances commit the like extravagances.'[74]

Throughout the summer of 1737, Hervey noticed that Caroline was often unwell. On 9 November, whilst inspecting her newly completed library at St James's Palace, she was taken seriously ill. 'She called her complaint the colic, her stomach and bowels giving her great pain. She came home, took Daffy's elixir, but … was in such pain and so uneasy with frequent retchings to vomit, that she went to bed.' Like the dutiful warhorse she was, she forced herself to attend that day's formal Drawing Room, but she admitted to Lord Hervey that she was not 'able to entertain people' and prepared to take her leave. Before she could do so, the king reminded her that she had not spoken to the Duchess of Norfolk. The queen 'made her excuses' to the duchess, 'who was the last person she ever spoke to in public', then retired to her room.[75]

Hervey, of course, went with her. He was, as he proudly recalled, 'never out of the queen's apartment for above four or five hours at most during her whole illness'. He loved Caroline as much as he loved anyone, except Ste; but he did not allow his affection to get in the way of his merciless reporter's eye. The candid details of her suffering that fill his account of the queen's long and painful death demonstrate how hard it was to die with dignity in the eighteenth century, and how little medicine could do, either to cure or to alleviate distress. It also illustrates very poignantly the strength of the complicated ties that had bound Caroline to her husband for so long, and the true depth of his feelings for her. He never showed her so clearly that he loved her as when she was dying; but even then, his passion was tempered by anger – an impotent frustration in the face of her weakness and suffering that was, in its own warped way, what it had always been – a furious demonstration of his need for her.

From the beginning of her sickness, George refused to leave his wife. He had his bedding brought into her room and laid it on the floor, so that he could be near her. Sometimes, 'inconveniently to both himself and the queen', he would 'lay on the queen's bed all night in his nightgown, where he could not sleep, nor she turn around'.[76] He scolded her when pain made her shift about in bed. 'How the devil should you sleep when you can never lie still a moment? … Nobody can sleep in that manner and that is always your way; you never take the proper method to get what you want and then you wonder that you have it not.'[77] He begged her to eat, and although she could not hold anything in her stomach, she tried to take something to please him. When she brought it up, 'he used peevishly to say, "How is it possible that you should not know whether you like a thing or not? If you do not like it, why do you call for it?"' Once, in front of an appalled Hervey, he told her she looked like a calf whose throat had just been cut.

Hervey thought these 'sudden sallies of temper' were 'unaccountable'. He did not understand that they were a product of George's increasing desperation, for his anger mounted as his wife grew steadily worse. At first, no one knew exactly what was wrong. She would not allow any doctors to attend her and permitted no one to examine her. When they were alone, Hervey often heard her cry: 'I have an ill which nobody knows of!' He took that to mean 'nothing more than she felt what she could not describe'.

Her husband knew better. As days went by, and Caroline 'complained more than ever of the racking pains she felt in her belly', George decided enough was enough. He whispered to her that 'he was afraid her illness proceeded from a thing he had promised never to speak of to her again; but that her life being in danger', he was obliged to tell everything he knew. Caroline 'begged and entreated him with great earnestness that he would not', but the king sent for Ranby the surgeon 'and told him that the queen had a rupture at her navel, and bid him examine her'. It took Ranby only a few minutes to confirm the diagnosis. Caroline 'made no answer but lay down and turned her head to the other side, and as the king told me, he thinks it was the only tear she shed while she was ill'.[78]

George told Hervey that he had first noticed the injury fourteen years before, after Caroline had given birth to their last child, Louisa. She told him 'it was nothing more than what was common for almost every woman to have had after a hard labour'. When it did not improve, he had urged her to consult a doctor, but she refused and begged him to say no more about it. When he came back from his extended trip to Hanover in 1736, he thought it had become much worse. He told her he was certain it was a rupture. Caroline responded with uncharacteristic fury, 'telling me it was no such thing, and that I fancied she had a nasty distemper, which she was sure she had not, and spoke more peevishly to me than she had ever done in her life'. The more he begged her to 'let somebody see it', the more determined she became to reveal it to no one. 'I at last told her I wished she might not repent her obstinacy, but promised her I would never mention this subject to her again as long as I lived.' These conversations took place at the height of the king's passionate affair with Mme de Wallmoden, and even the determinedly unimaginative George suspected that his infidelity had coloured the way his words had been received by his hurt and resentful wife. 'In as plain insinuations as he could,' he told Hervey that Caroline believed it was because of her injury that he had 'grown weary of her person'. Hervey was astonished that 'an ill-timed coquetry at fifty-four that would hardly have been acceptable at twenty-five' had been allowed to exacerbate the queen's complaint; but he was forced to accept the truth of it. 'Several things she afterwards said to the king in her illness … plainly demonstrated how strongly these apprehensions of making her person distasteful to the king had worked upon her.'[79]

Caroline suffered from an umbilical hernia, a condition in which internal pressure or congenital weakness forces part of the intestine through the stomach wall. As she told George, it can be caused by difficult labour, or through other side effects of pregnancy. Now it can be resolved by an operation usually simple enough to be performed as day surgery. In the eighteenth century, there was little that could be done. The doctors debated how best to proceed. One proposed 'cutting a hole in her navel big enough to thrust the gut back into its place, which Ranby opposed, saying all the guts, on such an operation, would come out of the body, in a moment, on to the bed'. The wound had begun to mortify, and Caroline was subjected to a great deal of pointless agony as the doctors tried to cut away the infected areas around it. But they all knew there was nothing useful that could be done; and Ranby soon told George that the queen could not survive.

Caroline knew it too. She had declared from the beginning of her illness that she was dying. She summoned her family around her to take leave of them, and said goodbye to them one by one. 'She took a ruby ring from her finger that the king had given her at her coronation and putting it on his said, "This is the last thing I have to give you – naked I came to you and naked I go from you."' As the king wept, she urged him to marry again, 'upon which his sobs began to rise, and his tears to fall with double vehemence. Whilst in the midst of this passion, wiping his eyes and sobbing between every word, he got out the answer. "*Non – j'aurai – des – maîtresses*." To which the queen made no other reply than "*Mon Dieu! Cela n'empêche pas*."'[80] In death, Caroline was as resigned as she had been in life to the curious mixture of passion and selfishness with which her husband had declared his devotion to her.

There was one conspicuous absentee from her deathbed farewells. As soon as he heard his mother was ill, Frederick asked permission to come and see her. George was incensed, telling Hervey that if the prince appeared at St James's, 'I order you to go to the scoundrel, and tell him I wonder at his impudence for daring to come here … Bid him go about his business, for his poor mother is not in a condition to see him now act his false, whining cringing tricks.'[81] However, when the queen asked if there had been any messages from Frederick, the king relented. He would do anything to please his dying wife, even to the extent of admitting his hated son back into the house from which he had been so recently ejected. He told Caroline 'that if she had the least mind to see her son, he had no objection to it, and begging her to do just what she liked'. Caroline was implacable. She told George she would not see him again, and that if she grew worse 'and was weak enough to talk of seeing him, I beg, sir, that you will conclude that I dote and rave'. She did neither; Hervey reported that until the moment of her death she never spoke of the prince 'but always with detestation'. She told the king and her daughter that 'at least I shall have one comfort in having my eyes eternally closed – I shall never see that monster again'.

She finally died, after ten days of suffering, on 20 November. George 'kissed the face and hands of the lifeless body several times' and went silently to his apartments, which he did not leave for several weeks. He took Hervey with him, and 'during this retirement … showed a tenderness of which the world thought him utterly incapable'. Everything he did and said, thought Hervey, proved how much he had loved and admired the woman he had lost. Hervey was amazed to hear the usually blunt and unsentimental king describe so feelingly what she had meant to him, 'the tender manner in which he related a thousand old stories relating to his first seeing the queen, his marriage with her, the way in which they had lived at Hanover, his behaviour to her when she had had smallpox and his risking his life by getting it off her (which he did) rather than leave her'.[82]

He also recalled more recent times, 'and repeated every day, her merits in every capacity with regard to him'. Unsurprisingly, he praised her complete submission to his will. 'He firmly believed, she never, since he first knew her, ever thought of anything she was to do or say, but with the view of doing or saying it in what manner it would be most agreeable to his pleasure or serviceable to his interest.' But he also acknowledged 'that she had been of more use to him as a minister than any other body had ever been to him or any other prince'. It was an astute assessment of Caroline's virtues in the public world; yet it was in her role as the lodestone of his private world that he knew he would miss her most. 'She was the best wife, the best mother, the best companion, the best friend and the best woman that ever was born.'

He firmly believed that 'he had never seen her out of humour in his life, though he had passed more hours with her than he believed any two other people in the world had ever passed together, and that he had never been tired in her company one minute'. He concluded with a compliment which Caroline would surely have understood was the highest accolade he could bestow on her: 'He was sure that he could have been happy with no other woman upon earth for a wife, and that if she had not been his wife, he had rather had her for his mistress than any other woman he had ever been acquainted with.'[83]

George and Caroline's had been an unconventional kind of marriage; but George could say, with some justification, that it had delivered for him an experience of happiness that had been so conspicuously denied to his mother and father. Even at their worst times, he and Caroline had never been less than a partnership, one which, for all the turbulence within it, was held together by the powerful dynamic of their mutual attraction. But they had extended none of that sense of inclusiveness to their son, and as George sat grieving for his wife, he might have reflected that he found himself in much the same position as his father had been before him: a man alone, alienated from a son he distrusted and despised. It would now be left to the generation that came after them to try to repair what George and Caroline had left undone. Frederick's wife Augusta was pregnant again by the time the queen died. Caroline did not live to see the birth of her first grandson in June 1738. Frederick named the baby George, after his grandfather. It remained to be seen whether he had learnt more from the treatment he had received at the hands of his parents than George and Caroline had done; and whether he could prevent the legacy of bitterness that had so darkened his own life from surfacing to cast a similar shadow over that of his son.

CHAPTER 3

Son and Heir

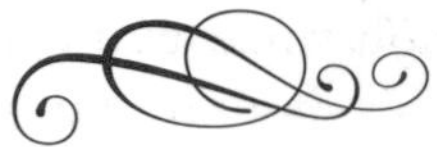

FREDERICK AND AUGUSTA'S FIRST SON, George, was born on 24 May 1738 at Norfolk House in St James's Square. He was a seven months' child, and 'so weakly at the time of his birth, that serious apprehensions were entertained that it would be impossible to rear him'.[1] He was baptised that night, noted the diarist Lord Egmont, 'there being a doubt that he could live', but like his sister before him, the baby George clung tenaciously to life.[2] In later years, he had no doubt whom he had to thank for his survival: Mary Smith, his wet nurse, 'the fine, healthy, fresh-coloured wife of a gardener'. When she died in 1773, George was still conscious of the debt of gratitude he bore her. 'She suckled me,' he recalled, 'and to her great attention my having been reared is greatly owing.'[3] When told that etiquette made it impossible for the infant George to sleep with her, she had 'instantly revolted, and in terms both warm and blunt, she thus expressed herself: "Not sleep with me! Then you may nurse the boy yourselves!"'[4] The forthright Mary Smith won the battle, and with it the unwavering affection of the prince.

In 1743, Frederick moved his growing family – another son Edward had been born in 1739, and six other children were to follow, in almost annual succession over the next decade – to a bigger establishment. Leicester House, a large but ugly building, stood on the north side of what is now Leicester Square. It was not the most fashionable of neighbourhoods, being rather too near louche Soho for the politest society, and Frederick was by far its grandest inhabitant. His neighbours were businessmen, musicians and artists, most notably William Hogarth who had his studios across the square at number 32. Frederick was not short of places to live – he spent a great deal of money on nearby Carlton House, and rented properties for the summer on the Thames at Kew and at Cliveden – but it was Leicester House that became his principal residence. It was where he held informal court, assembling around him a group of ambitious young men who were as impatient as he was with his father's government. With their support, Leicester House became the basis for Frederick's political operations, the campaign headquarters from which he directed his attacks on the king's ministers with such sustained effort that the term 'Leicester House' soon became synonymous with the very idea of princely political opposition. But the Soho property was also a family home; all Frederick and Augusta's children grew up there, and their eldest son George seems to have retained an affection for it; he used it as his London house until very shortly before he became king.

George II never visited. He remained estranged from his son, although with the death of Queen Caroline some of the furious antipathy that had characterised their relationship ebbed away. The king occupied himself with his cards, his mistress and his military campaigns. His only engagement with Frederick was through the distancing formalities of party politics, where the two fought out their differences by ministerial and opposition proxies. They took care never to meet. Horace Walpole was once at a fashionable party where the usual precautions had somehow failed, and Frederick and his father were both embarrassingly present ('There was so little company that I was afraid they would be forced to walk about together'), but this was a rare occurrence.[5] Beyond the public stage of politics, the prince and the king lived carefully segregated existences.

Although he was now both paterfamilias and politician, Frederick continued to conduct his life with the same breezy goodwill and indifference to criticism that had so infuriated his parents when he was younger. If his ability to tell people what they wanted to hear coined him a reputation for duplicity, and his relaxed attitude to matters of political principle led to accusations of inconstancy, he was also singularly lacking in the anger and suppressed rage that had characterised so much of his parents' lives. If he was resentful at their treatment of him, he concealed it very well; in public he appeared to be entirely unmarked by their baroque hostility. He was the least bitter of the early Hanoverians and, as such, seemed to have the best opportunity to the break the inheritance of dynastic unhappiness which his parents had passed on to him with such relish. In many ways, and with profound consequences for the development of his eldest son's character, Frederick rose to the challenge. In his attitude to his wife and family, he represents a crucial and often underestimated bridge between the very different worlds of George II and George III.

Frederick's conception of family life did not, however, extend to the practice of conjugal fidelity. He was his father's son in that, at least. One of his favourites was Grace, Lady Middlesex, whom Horace Walpole described as 'very short, very plain, and very yellow'. But, as Walpole saw, none of these affairs really mattered; they certainly did not disrupt the settled ecology of Frederick's marriage, as those of his father had done: 'Though these mistresses were pretty much declared, he was a good husband.' Augusta, sensibly in Walpole's opinion, ignored the transient lovers and reaped the benefits as a result. 'The quiet inoffensive good sense of the princess (who had never said a foolish thing, nor done a disobliging one since the day of her arrival) ... was always likely to have preserved her ascendancy over him.'[6] Frederick's relationship with his wife had none of the obsessive, jealous intensity that marked his father's feelings for his mother; nor did it have about it the toxic undercurrents that damaged so many of those who came into too close contact with his parents' passion.

His marriage was entirely lacking in the drama that characterised George and Caroline's union, yet there is little doubt that Frederick loved and desired his wife. The prince, who was proud of his literary talents, wrote a series of verses to Augusta celebrating her physical charms, including 'those breasts that swell to meet my love,/That easy sloping waist, that form divine'. But as the poem made clear, it was not her body for which her husband most admired her: 'No – 'tis the gentleness of mind, that love,/so kindly answering my desire/ ... That thus has set my soul on fire.'[7] It was Augusta's mild, unchallenging personality that Frederick found particularly appealing. From the earliest days of their marriage he had been delighted to discover that his wife was everything his mother was not: calm and pliable, with no discernible tastes or ambitions other than those her husband encouraged her to share. Her docility was one of her chief attractions, as Augusta herself seems clearly to have understood. Throughout their marriage, she never did or said anything to discommode or contradict him. One of the prince's friends, in a parody of Frederick's uxorious verses, added to the list of Augusta's virtues 'that all-consenting tongue,/that never puts me in the wrong'.[8]

Augusta's willingness to please extended not just to what she said but also to what she did. She patiently indulged her husband in all his interests and foibles; in return, he found a place for her at the centre of his life. She accompanied him on all his excursions. Sometimes twice a week, they went to formal masquerades at Ranelagh pleasure gardens, where the princess, usually very modestly dressed, appeared 'covered with diamonds'. Augusta gamely joined her husband in his pursuit of less grand entertainments. They went together to investigate the infamous Cock Lane Ghost, whose alleged spectral manifestation drew large crowds nightly (though the spirit failed to appear for them). She was also a dutiful participant in the pranks that Frederick enjoyed so much, reacting with the expected surprise when taken by him to visit a fortune teller, who turned out to be their children's dancing master in heavy disguise. The politician George Dodington, who occupied a prominent place in the prince's entourage, joined them on a typical day out in June 1750: 'To Spitalfields, to see the manufactures of silk, and to Mr Carr's shop in the morning. In the afternoon, the same company … to Norwood Forest to see a settlement of gypsies. We returned and went to Bettesworth the conjuror's in hackney coaches – not finding him, we went in search of the little Dutchman, but were disappointed; and concluded by supping with Mrs Cannon, the princess's midwife.'[9]

If the princess found Frederick's pursuit of the eccentric and the exotic exhausting, she would never have said so. Perhaps she took more pleasure in their shared botanical interests. She and Frederick laid out the foundations of what is now Kew Gardens, jointly commissioning a summerhouse in the fashionable Chinese style, decorated with illustrations of the life of Confucius. Like her mother-in-law, Augusta's only real extravagance was her spending on the gardens, where she built on the work Caroline had begun, erecting an orangery and completing the famous pagoda.

She played a less significant part in her husband's other interests. For all his enduring fascination with low-life, Frederick was also a sophisticated consumer of high culture and keen to be seen as an urbane and discerning man of taste. He was a patron of the architect William Kent, and employed him to remodel the interior of his houses in his severe, classical style. In contrast to his father's boasted indifference to the quality of the paintings that hung on his walls, Frederick was a thoughtful collector of pictures, buying two Van Dycks and two landscapes by Rubens. Horace Walpole, who was not well disposed to the prince, regarded his artistic ambitions as mere pretension until Frederick asked to see the catalogue Walpole had drawn up of his father's extensive art collection at Houghton Hall in Norfolk. To his surprise, Walpole was impressed by the prince's knowledge and appreciation: 'He turned to me and said such a crowd of civil things that I did not know what to answer; he commended the style of quotations; said I had sent him back to his Livy.'[10]

Frederick was his mother's son in his respect for intellectuals, if in little else. Like her, he enjoyed the company of writers. A keen amateur author himself (besides the poem written for Augusta and the disastrous play co-written with Hervey, he had a host of other works to his name), he sought out the company of John Gay, whose *Beggar's Opera*, with its attack on Robert Walpole and the king, was attractive to him both culturally and politically, and James Thomson, whose poem *The Seasons* was hugely popular in the 1730s, and often visited Alexander Pope at his home in Twickenham. When Pope fell asleep in the middle of one of Frederick's disquisitions on literature, the prince was not offended but stole discreetly away.

Built on the foundation of their stable marriage, and enlivened by the energy and diversity of the prince's interests, Frederick and Augusta's household was a comparatively happy place in which to raise children. It was certainly an improvement on Frederick's, or indeed on his father's, experiences of childhood. There seems little doubt that this was a conscious effort on Frederick's part; he was determined to create for his own family the life he had never enjoyed himself as a boy. He was an attentive and affectionate parent, who enjoyed the company of his wife and children and was not afraid to show it. 'He played the part of the father and husband well,' wrote one appreciative visitor, 'always happy in the bosom of his family, left them with regret and met them again with smiles, kisses and tears.'[11] When the Bishop of Salisbury went to dinner with Frederick and Augusta, he was impressed to see that afterwards the children were called in, 'and were made to repeat several beautiful passages out of plays and poems' whilst their proud parents looked on. Beguiled by this unaccustomed image of royal family harmony, the bishop declared 'he had never passed a more agreeable day in his whole life'.[12] Frederick was particularly attached to his two eldest boys. When he was away, he was a diligent correspondent, his letters suffused with a warm informality. Writing to 'dear George' in 1748, he signed himself 'your friend and father'. To 'dear Edward' he 'rejoiced to find that you have been so good both. Pray God it may continue. Nothing gives a father who loves his children so well as I do so much satisfaction as to hear they improve, or are likely to make a figure in this world.'[13] 'Pray God,' he once wrote, more wistfully, 'that you may grow in every respect above me – good night, my dear children'.[14]

Frederick involved himself in every aspect of his children's lives. In the country, whether at Kew or Cliveden, he arranged sports for them. There were skittles and rounders – played inside the house if wet, amidst the formal elegance of William Kent's interiors. Everyone, including the girls, played cricket. All visitors were expected to join in, with neither age, dignity nor excess weight conferring exemption. When the rotund politician Dodington visited Kew in October 1750, he found himself reluctantly conscripted into a game. Further exercise for the royal children was provided by gardening. Each of them had a small plot to tend, but tilling the soil was not confined to the young. Here too, as the unhappy Dodington discovered, guests were compelled to do their bit, hoeing and digging with the rest of the family. 'All of us, men, women and children worked at the same place,' Dodington noted on 28 February 1750, adding the mournful postscript, 'Cold dinner.'[15] Having endured the perils of the cricket pitch and the rigours of the garden plot, visitors were also expected to join willingly in the practical jokes and horseplay for which Frederick never lost his taste. Dodington, who was almost as fat as he was tall, once allowed Frederick to wrap him in a blanket and roll him downstairs. The prince's inner circle was not a place where ambitious politicians could expect to stand on their dignity.

In the evenings, the prince staged elaborate nightly theatricals in which all the family took part. Dodington recorded each night's offering in his diary; the range of works was extensive, encompassing the classics – *Macbeth*, *Tartuffe*, *Henry IV* – to forgotten lighter pieces such as *The Lottery* or *The Morning Bride*. James Quin, a London actor, was recruited to coach the royal children in their performances. Many years later, when George III made his first speech from the throne as king, Quin commented with pride that ''Twas I that taught the boy to speak.'[16] One of Frederick's favourite pieces was Addison's *Cato*, whose Prologue, with its enthusiastic endorsement of the principles of political liberty, was usually given to the young George to recite, as he did for the first time in 1749 at the age of eleven.

> Should this superior to my years be thought,
> Know – 'tis the first great lesson I was taught,
> What, tho' a boy! It may in truth be said,
> A boy in England bred,
> Where freedom becomes the earliest state,
> For there the love of liberty's innate.

If Frederick's tastes shaped the leisure hours of his children, he was just as active in managing their education. He himself drew up a scholastic timetable, 'The Hours of the Two Eldest Princes', which laid out when and what George and Edward were to be taught, and appointed the Reverend Francis Ayscough as their tutor. Ayscough, a doctor of divinity, was not very inspiring, but the boys made steady progress under his instruction, and by the time he was eight, George could speak and write English and German. Frederick had the two boys painted with their tutor, who looms above them, formal in black clerical dress. Grey classical pillars rise behind them. The overwhelming impression is of chilly dourness; this was not, it seems, an atmosphere in which learning was likely to deliver either pleasure or excitement.

Then, in 1749 – the same year that the carefully coached eleven-year-old George delivered his eulogy on English liberty – Frederick replaced Ayscough with a far abler man. George Lewis Scott was a barrister and an extremely accomplished mathematician, and his arrival signified the prince's intention to accelerate his sons' academic progress. Their working day was long – they were required to translate a passage from Caesar's *Commentaries* before breakfast – and the curriculum broad, including geometry, arithmetic, dancing and French. Greek was introduced for the first time, and after dinner, the boys were to read 'useful and entertaining books, such as Addison's works, and particularly his political papers'.[17]

The more demanding timetable reflected a new sense of urgency that had entered Frederick's thinking, particularly in relation to his eldest son. At the beginning of 1749, he had composed a paper intended for the guidance of his heir. Its intentions were clearly set out in the title the prince gave it: 'Instructions for my son George, drawn by myself, for his good, and that of my family, for that of his people, according to the ideas of my grandfather and best friend, George I.' It was addressed directly and personally to his son. If Frederick were to die before he could himself elaborate on its contents to the boy, it was to be held by Augusta, 'who will read it to you from time to time, and will give it to you when you come of age to get the crown'. 'My design,' Frederick promised, 'is not to leave you a sermon as is undoubtedly done by persons of my rank. 'Tis not out of vanity I write this; it is out of love to you, and to the public. It is for your good and for that of the people you are to govern, that I leave this to you.'[18] What followed was a detailed blueprint for good government, as seen through Frederick's eyes. It sought to impress on George the nature of his future duties as king, head of his family, and father of the people. It stressed the importance of identifying himself with the country he would one day rule ('Convince the Nation that you are not only an Englishman born and bred, but that you are also this by inclination').[19] It urged him to decrease the national debt, and to separate the electorate of Hanover from Great Britain to minimise involvement in European wars.[20] Such policies would reduce expenditure, making the king more solvent, less dependent on forging alliances with political parties, and free to pursue policies of his own devising. These, Frederick asserted, would be more likely to reflect the true national interest than the existing system, reliant as it was on the management of a host of often conflicting and selfish sectional interests. When presented to his son later as part of a wider constitutional framework, these were ideas that would prove very compelling to the young George; but what prompted his father to articulate them at that time, in a form that suggested so powerfully a kind of political last will and testament?

Although Frederick was only forty-two when he wrote the document, the 1740s had been a punishing decade for him and his followers. They had enjoyed some successes, most notably, and most pleasing from the perspective of Leicester House, the fall of George II's favoured minister Robert Walpole in 1742. The prince did not entirely engineer Walpole's defeat, but when begged by the king to save him, he refused to help the stricken politician. It had proved hard to capitalise on such triumphs. George II had denied Frederick a role in the army, both in the Continental wars of the mid-1740s and during the Jacobite rising of 1745. On both occasions he was forced to watch, humiliated, from the sidelines as his father and his younger brother William, Duke of Cumberland, rode to victory respectively at Dettingen and Culloden. Then, in 1747, Frederick's followers were roundly defeated at the general election.

By the end of the decade, he was forced to come to terms with the ambivalence of his position. As Prince of Wales he was master of an alternative court, with over two hundred household posts at his disposal and the promise of preferment once he, eventually, came to power; but although he might be able to undermine or even destroy administrations, he could never be part of them himself. He could break, but he could not build; or at least, not until the king died. Dodington, now acting as one of the prince's advisers, counselled waiting; but as he approached middle age, Fredrick's appetite for the struggle seems, surely and steadily, to have ebbed away. Perhaps he suspected that the chances of achieving his ambitions were always going to be limited by the circumstances of his birth. He knew that, unlike his son, he could never be 'an Englishman born and bred', and gradually, he began to transfer his hopes for the fulfilment of his long-term goals beyond the possibilities offered by his own reign, concentrating instead on that of his heir. Writing his letter of 'Instructions' marked the beginning of that process. It was a sign of both what he hoped his son might one day achieve, and what he had gradually abandoned for himself. And if it marked the level of his ambitions for George, it was also perhaps a measure of his concern. He spelt out his blueprint for the future with such clarity perhaps because he had begun to doubt whether, without such precise guidance, the boy would ever be capable of achieving it. For, as he grew older, George did not seem to anyone – and possibly not even to his father – quite the stuff of which successful kings were made.

*

Though never a voluble child, with age George became steadily shyer, more awkward and withdrawn. He was 'silent, modest and easily abashed', said Louisa Stuart, whose father, the Earl of Bute, was one of Frederick's intimate circle. She maintained that George's parents, frustrated by his reticence, much preferred his brother Edward. 'He was decidedly their favourite, and their preference of him to his elder brother openly avowed.'[21] Edward was everything his older brother was not: confident, cheerful, talkative and spirited. Horace Walpole, who knew Edward well in later life, described him tellingly as 'a sayer of things'. His natural confidence, thought Louisa Stuart, 'was hourly strengthened by encouragement, which enabled him to join in or interrupt conversation and always say something which the obsequious hearers were ready to applaud'. It was very different for his diffident elder brother. 'If he ever faltered out an opinion, it was passed by unnoticed; sometimes it was knocked down at once with – "Do hold your tongue, George, don't talk like a fool."'[22]

Frederick, it seemed, for all his genuine affection for his children, was still Hanoverian enough to prefer the spare to the heir. He was never deliberately harsh to his mute and anxious eldest son; but he was often exasperated by his unresponsiveness, and failed to understand its causes. He insisted to the boy that his 'great fault' was 'that nonchalance you have of not caring enough to please'.[23] He did not see that there was not a scrap of insouciance in George's make-up, and that his son's diffidence arose not from nonchalance but from a paralysing lack of confidence in his ability to fulfil his destiny. For Louisa Stuart, Frederick was less to blame than his wife. Beneath the compliant surface she presented to the world, Augusta nurtured a severe and unflinching personality, with a strong tendency to judge others harshly. It was Augusta, she said, who was 'too impressed by vivacity and confidence' and who failed to see that 'diffidence was often the product of a truly thoughtful understanding'. She did not recognise the true strengths of her stolid elder son, 'whose real good sense, innate rectitude, unspeakably kind heart, and genuine manliness of spirit were overlooked in his youth, and indeed, not appreciated till a much later time'.[24]

Had Frederick lived, the warmth of the genuine affection he felt for all his children might eventually have buoyed up the spirits of his tremulous heir; George might have matured under the protection of a father who, for all his criticism of his son's shortcomings and lack of insight into their causes, nevertheless saw the protection of the boy's long-term interests as his most important responsibility. But at the beginning of March 1751, the prince caught a cold. A week later, on the 13th, Dodington noted in his diary that 'the prince did not appear, having a return of pain in his side'.[25] He was probably suffering from pneumonia. For a few days, he seemed to improve. Augusta, who was five months pregnant, informed Egmont that Frederick 'was getting much better, and only wanted time to recover his strength'. She added that 'he was always frightened for himself when he was the least out of order, but that she had laughed him out of it, and would never humour him in these fancies'. She hoped her attempts to raise his spirits had worked as Frederick now declared that 'he should not die in this bout, but for the future, would take more care of himself'.[26]

Dodington called at Leicester House on the 20th, and he too was reassured on hearing that Frederick 'was much better and had slept eight hours the night before'. Everyone's optimism was unfounded. Later that night, at a quarter to ten, Frederick died. The end came with shocking swiftness. Dodington reported that 'until half an hour before he was very cheerful, asked to see some of his friends, ate some bread and butter and drank coffee'.[27] Walpole heard a similar story. The prince seemed to be over the worst and beginning to improve when he was suddenly overcome with a fit of coughing. At first, Dr Wilmot, who attended him, thought this was a good sign, telling him hopefully: 'Sir, you have brought up all the phlegm; I hope this will be over in a quarter of an hour, and that your highness will have a good night.' But Hawkins, the second doctor, was less optimistic, declaring ominously: 'Here is something I don't like.' The cough became increasingly violent. Frederick, panicking, declared that he was dying. His German valet, who held him in his arms, 'felt him shiver and cried, "Good God! The prince is going." The princess, who was at the foot of the bed, snatched up a candle, but before she got to him, he was dead.'[28] He was forty-four years old.

The king received the news of Frederick's death as he sat playing cards. George had not remarried; he had kept his promise to his dying queen, taking a mistress rather than a wife. He had sent for Mme de Wallmoden, who divorced her husband and in 1740 was given the title of the Countess of Yarmouth. It was to her that the king turned first. 'He went down to Lady Yarmouth looking extremely pale and shocked, and only said, "*Il est mort!*"'[29] Once the horror of the moment had passed, the king, who was too self-absorbed to be a hypocrite, did not pretend to be grieved. He had hated his son for years, and his sudden and unexpected death provoked no remorse for his behaviour. As 1751 drew to a close, he commented with characteristic candour: 'This has been a fatal year to my family. I have lost my eldest son, but I was glad of it.'[30] It was his final comment on a relationship which had begun in suspicion, matured into vicious acrimony and ended with estrangement. He felt neither guilt nor regret for what had happened, and never referred to Frederick again.

The prince's funeral was the final reflection of his father's disdain. It was, thought Dodington, a shameful affair, 'which sunk me so low that for the first hour, I was incapable of making any observation'. No food was provided for those of his household who stood loyally by Frederick's body as he lay in state; they 'were forced to bespeak a great cold dinner from a common tavern in the neighbourhood'. No arrangements had been made to shelter mourners from the rain as they walked from the House of Lords to Westminster Abbey. The funeral service itself 'was performed without anthem or organ' and neither the king nor Frederick's brother the Duke of Cumberland attended.[31] Even in the performance of his last duty to his son, George II could find no generosity of spirit.

He appeared in a better light on his first visit to Frederick's bereaved wife and children, when he was clearly moved by their stricken condition. 'A chair of state was provided for him,' reported Walpole, 'but he refused it; and sat by the princess on the couch, embraced and wept with her. He would not suffer Lady Augusta to kiss his hand, but embraced her, and gave it to her brothers, and told them, "They must be brave boys, obedient to their mother, and deserve the fortune to which they were born."'[32] It was a rare display of emotional sympathy from the king; but as the family sat huddled in their misery, they all knew that significant decisions must now be made about their future.

The most obvious solution would have been for the king to take over the upbringing and education of the young prince, bringing the boy to live with him at St James's. At the same time, it might have been expected that the Duke of Cumberland would be made regent. As the king's eldest surviving son, he would have been well placed to act for his father during his frequent absences in Hanover, and to be appointed guardian to the young George if the king had died while he was still a minor. In the event, none of these arrangements ever happened. They had been rendered politically impossible by the momentous events of 1745/46, the consequences of which were to have a profound effect on the lives of George, Augusta and indeed all of Frederick's remaining family.

*

William, Duke of Cumberland, was loved by his parents with an intensity matched only by their disdain for his brother Frederick. Mirroring the actions of George I, it was rumoured that George II had once consulted the Lord Chancellor to discover if it would be constitutionally possible to disinherit his eldest son in favour of William. The disappointing answer he was said to have received did nothing to weaken the affection he felt for Cumberland, who shared many of his interests, particularly his passion for the army. Cumberland had been given all the military experience that Frederick persuaded himself he craved and had been denied. He was a capable soldier and at the age of only twenty-three was appointed captain general. 'Poor boy!' commented Walpole, 'he is most Brunswickly happy with all his drums and trumpets.'[33] When Charles Edward Stuart raised his standard in Scotland in 1745, Cumberland was the obvious candidate to put down a rebellion aimed directly at the survival of the Hanoverian dynasty. His reputation would never recover from the victory he won.

The possibility of regime change seemed a very real one as Bonnie Prince Charlie's troops swept first through Scotland and then through northern England in the winter of 1745. As Carlisle, Lancaster and Preston fell, panic engulfed London. Even Horace Walpole was shaken out of his usual pose of ironic detachment, putting all his trust in the duke's 'lion's courage, vast vigilance … and great military genius'.[34] After Charles Stuart made the unexpected decision to turn back at Derby, Cumberland chased his army back to Scotland, where the two forces met on 16 April 1746 at Culloden. The duke's victory over the exhausted Jacobites was total, and the aftermath of the battle exceptionally brutal, as Cumberland's soldiers bayoneted wounded survivors. This was only a prelude to an extensive campaign of terror, intended by Cumberland to eradicate all possibility of another uprising. 'Do not imagine,' the duke wrote, 'that threatening military execution and other things are pleasing to do, but nothing will go down without it. Mild measures will not do.'[35] He was not alone in thinking extreme actions were called for. 'I make no difficulty of declaring my opinion,' declared Lord Chesterfield, 'that the commander-in-chief should be ordered to give no quarter but to pursue the rebels wherever he finds 'em.'[36] Cumberland's troops pursued the defeated Scots into the glens and remote settlements of the Highlands, burning and murdering as they went, killing not just men of fighting age, but women, children, and even the cattle that supported them.

At first, Cumberland was fêted for the completeness of his victory. Handel composed *See, the Conquering Hero Comes* to mark his triumph; the duke was mobbed in the street, celebrated as the defender of constitutional monarchy. But as accounts began to arrive in London describing the methods by which he had achieved his success – and as the initial relief at the removal of the Jacobite threat began to fade – a sense of popular unease mounted. The atrocities appalled a public who, with the threat of a restored Stuart monarchy now behind them, did not feel liberty had been best protected by uncontrolled rape and murder. Simultaneously, suspicion of what Cumberland's true intentions might be began to mount. At the head of a vicious and unstoppable army, what might he not attempt? Could he use it to break opposition as thoroughly in England as he had done in Scotland, and seize power for himself?

Frederick, who saw Cumberland's success as a direct threat to him, did all he could to fuel hostility to his brother. He financed a pamphlet laying out in detail all the excesses committed by Cumberland's troops, and his adviser Egmont wrote another, arguing that the emboldened duke's next step would indeed be to mount a coup d'état. This was a complete fiction, but a very powerful one, that struck alarm into the hearts of otherwise rational politicians for nearly twenty years. In eighteen months, Cumberland was transformed in the public perception from conquering hero to 'the Butcher', a cruel German militarist with tyrannical ambitions and, unless his access to power was closely controlled, both the desire and the means to make them real.

So overwhelming was this scenario, even at the time of Frederick's death five years after Culloden, that it made Cumberland unemployable in England. The king railed impotently against what he regarded as the traducing of his favourite, declaring that 'it was the lies they told, and in particular this Egmont, about my son, for the service he did this country, which raised the clamour against him'; but he knew nothing could be done about it.[37] He understood the political realities well enough to understand that Cumberland could never now be made regent. The disgraced duke bore his exclusion stoically in public – 'I shall submit because the king commands it' – but in private confessed himself deeply humiliated, wishing 'that the name William could be blotted out of the English annals'.[38]

If he could not name Cumberland regent, the king had little choice but to appoint an otherwise most unlikely candidate, Augusta, who now held the title of princess dowager. And if she was thought competent to act in that capacity, he could hardly justify removing his heir from her control. Thus, against all expectation, the young Prince George was allowed to stay in the company of his mother. This decision was to have an extraordinary effect on the shaping of his character; as much as the premature death of his father, it was to determine the kind of man he became. Had he been exposed, while still a boy, to the worldly challenges of life at George II's court, very different aspects of his personality might have emerged. Instead, he was allowed to retreat with Augusta into an increasingly remote and cloistered existence.

His mother's intention was to protect him, and George – anxious and easily intimidated – was keen to be protected. He had responded to news of his father's death with a sense of shock so profound that it was physical in its intensity. 'I feel it here,' he declared, laying his hand on his chest, 'just as I did when I saw the two workmen fall from the scaffold at Kew.'[39] He did not like his grandfather, whom he rightly suspected was irritated by his shyness and lack of confidence. (On one occasion, the king's frustration may have taken more violent form; a generation later, walking round Hampton Court, George III's son, the Duke of Sussex, mused: 'I wonder in which one of these rooms it was that George II struck my father? The blow so disgusted him that he could never afterwards think of it as a residence.'[40]) But when George II arrived at Leicester House in the days after Frederick's death, 'with an abundance of speeches and a kind behaviour to the princess and the children', his sympathy seemed so genuine that even the cautious prince was partially won over. He declared that 'he should not be frightened any more with his grandpa.'[41]

Despite this, it is hard to believe that George II could ever have changed the habits of a lifetime and transformed himself into the steady, supportive father figure of which his heir stood in such deep need over the next few years. Certainly the prince did not think so. For all the king's new-found concern, his timid grandson had no wish to test the depth of his solicitude by joining him at St James's. He made it clear he preferred to live with his mother. Yet, although the prospect of staying with Augusta no doubt offered security to a young boy badly in need of solace, it was far from an ideal solution. The life

Augusta made for her son, isolated from the world he would one day be expected to dominate, did nothing to prepare him for the role that his father's death had made so terrifyingly imminent. The complicated politics that had ensured George remained in his mother's care may not, in the long run, have done him much of a favour.

*

Until Frederick's sudden death, the defining quality of Augusta, Princess of Wales, was her apparent passivity. She seemed to have no real personality of her own, but was entirely under the control of her husband. Hervey, who once memorably described her as 'this gilded piece of royal conjugality', claimed that she played no active role in his political life. Frederick, he reported, had once observed that 'a prince should never talk to a woman of politics' and that 'he would never make himself the ridiculous figure his father had done in letting his wife govern him or meddle with business, which no woman was fit for'.[42] George II, on the other hand, who always suspected there was more to his daughter-in-law than met the eye, used to declare: 'You none of you know this woman, and none of you will know her until after I am dead!'[43]

The king was not wrong in alleging that Augusta was not quite the demure innocent she seemed. For all Frederick's protestations, she was no stranger to his political ambitions during the late 1740s. She hosted the dinners at which he and his supporters thrashed out their strategies and engineered their alliances; she was discreet, trustworthy and, above all, unquestioningly loyal, identifying herself completely with her husband's strategising. Significantly, it was to Augusta, and not to one of his trusted advisers, that Frederick entrusted his 'Instructions', encapsulating the programme he expected his eldest son to implement in due course, and it was she who was charged with explaining them to his heir and keeping them fresh in his mind. And after Frederick's shocking demise, it was she who took brisk and immediate measures to destroy any incriminating material that might compromise his followers and his family.

As the historian John Bullion has shown, in the hours immediately following his death, she showed herself to be more of a politician than any of his dazed friends. While Frederick lay dead in the next room, she summoned Lord Egmont and outlined a decisive plan of action to be followed in the next few vital hours. 'She did not know, but the king might seize the prince's papers – they were at Carlton House – and that we might be ruined by these papers.' She probably had in mind a document Frederick had drawn up in 1750 that was a blueprint for action in the event of the king's death and described in some detail appointments that were to be made and policies followed. She gave Egmont the key to three trunks, told him to retrieve the papers and bring them back to her; she even gave him a pillowcase in which to carry them. When Egmont returned, she burnt the papers in front of him. Only then did she begin to consider what to do about her husband's body, or inform the king of his death.[44]

Having dealt with the most pressing threat to her family's security, she proceeded to manage her father-in-law too. When he arrived at Leicester House, 'she received him alone, sitting with her eyes fixed: thanked the king much, and said she would write as soon as she was able; and in the meantime, recommended her miserable self and children to him.'[45] Always pleased to be treated with the respect he thought he deserved, the king warmed to her submission, as she must have known he would. 'The king and she both took their parts at once; she, of flinging herself entirely in his hands, and studying nothing but his pleasure; but minding what interest she got with him to the advantage of her own and the prince's friends.'[46] When she heard that the king had decided to allow George to stay with her, she did not forget to write and tell him how thankful she was.

Although Augusta was astute enough to have kept hold of her son, she had no idea what to do with him once she had him. She had no vision for his development, no sense of how best to equip him to face his destiny with confidence. She was not a strategic thinker; without imaginative leadership, Augusta's instincts were always defensive. She had neither the desire nor the capacity to forge alliances or build networks of friendship and support for her son. Hers was an inward-looking nature, suspicious of those she did not know and habitually secretive. Dodington, who came to know her very well, thought the defining quality of her character was prudence, 'not opening herself much to anybody, and of great caution to whom she opens herself at all.'[47] As a result, her motives were often opaque, and her true feelings more so. Lord Cobham thought her 'the only woman he could never find out; all he discovered about her was that she hated those she paid court to.'[48]

If she was an enigma, she was an increasingly sombre one. No longer obliged to accompany Frederick into the wider world, she quickly lost the habit of pleasure; she went nowhere and saw no one. But she did not appear to miss the life that had been taken from her with such cruel suddenness. Instead, she seemed to relish the opportunity to dispense with the trappings of her old existence, and emerge as a sober woman of early middle age, unencumbered now by the obligation to please or conciliate anyone but herself. Nothing illustrates more starkly the gulf between these two versions of Augusta than two contrasting portraits. In 1736, she was painted in a conventionally fashionable pose. Overwhelmed by the stiff ornateness of her dress, she is a tiny doll-like figure, rigid and stranded in the gloom of an oppressive grey interior. Of her personality, there is no sense at all. In 1754, when Augusta chose her own artist, the result could not have been more different. Jean-Etienne Liotard's portrait is not an image designed to flatter. Augusta is simply dressed; she wears no jewellery, and her hair is pulled back sharply from her forehead. Its defining quality is its cool candour. Augusta's gaze is wary; her whole posture suggests a guarded, watchful reticence. She does not seem a woman eager for enjoyment or delight; and it is perhaps possible to read in her expression a hint of the debilitating combination of anxiety and suspicion with which she came to view the world in the long years of her widowhood.

These were not the happiest qualities on which to build a family life, and it must have been quickly apparent to Augusta's children that, as the halo of their father's warmth and sociability dimmed, their world grew inexorably chillier. The amateur theatricals, the compulsory team sports, the trips and treats and jokery, the noise and lively bustle of their father's daily round all gradually ebbed away. They were replaced by a carefully cultivated seclusion, in which all the pleasures were small ones.

One of the few people allowed to intrude into this increasingly remote and withdrawn existence was George Dodington, whom Augusta adopted as chief confidant after her husband's death. A much-tried member of Frederick's entourage, Dodington's greatest asset was his understanding of the practical business of politics, drawn from a lifetime of holding office and the management of parliamentary interests, although he had many other sterling qualities: he was loyal, witty and humane, an ugly man with a complicated love life and a naive enthusiasm for extravagant grandeur. Walpole described his house in Hammersmith as a monument to rich, bad taste, crammed full of marble busts and statues, and dominated by a fireplace decorated with marble icicles. It is not hard to see why Frederick, with his predilection for the eccentric, should have enjoyed his company. That Augusta too soon came to value and rely upon him is further testament to her carefully concealed political acumen. Beneath his unprepossessing exterior, Dodington nurtured a sharp mind and a wealth of experience. He was an excellent ally for a woman who believed herself more or less friendless, a seasoned adviser who could help her navigate her way through the difficulties that lay ahead. Perhaps Augusta also recognised in him some of the warmth and conviviality that was in such short supply elsewhere in her household.

Dodington clearly missed his late patron's relaxed expansiveness. He often struggled to penetrate Augusta's ingrained reticence, but did all he could to support and encourage her. He recorded his somewhat stuttering progress in his diary, a rueful chronicle of his efforts to persuade Augusta to adopt what he saw as politic courses of action. It was not an easy task. He soon saw there was no chance at all that Frederick's death might have opened the way for a serious reconciliation with the rest of the royal family. Beneath the blandly compliant surface she presented to her in-laws throughout her married life, Augusta hid a settled dislike and disrespect for all her Hanoverian relations which was evident from the earliest days of her widowhood. In 1752, she and Dodington were enjoying a gossip about the Dorset family. Dodington opined that 'there were oddnesses about them that were peculiar to that family, and that I had often told them so. She said that there was something odd about them, and laughing, [she] added that she knew but one family that was more odd, and she would not name that family for the world.'[49] It was a rare moment of playfulness – and the only instance of Augusta's laughter in the whole of Dodington's diary. Her antipathy was usually expressed with far greater resentment, seen most starkly in her attitude to the king. As Frederick's wife, she had shared in all the humiliations that had been heaped upon him by his father; then, for over a decade, she had witnessed all her husband's attempts to harass and embarrass George through the medium of politics. Her husband's hostility and suspicion had defined her attitude to her father-in-law for twenty years, and continued to do so long after he was dead.

Augusta knew these were views that could have no outward expression. She told Dodington she fully understood 'that, to be sure, it was hers and her family's business to keep well with the king'.[50] In public, she assiduously cultivated the role of dutiful daughter-in-law, obedient and tractable; but in private, she had nothing but contempt for her father-in-law. She was bitterly angry that George had refused to settle Frederick's debts, which she considered a slight to his posthumous reputation, and furious when he refused to release to her the revenues from the Duchy of Cornwall that he had claimed for himself after the prince's death. As she described how she had berated and harangued the king on the vexed subject, Dodington's politician's spirits sank; he was not surprised to hear that George rarely visited now. His absence did nothing to make Augusta's heart grow fonder. Over a period of six months, Dodington heard her speak favourably of the king only once, and considered it so remarkable that he made a special note of it.

She was equally dismissive of the Duke of Cumberland, whom she referred to with heavy irony as 'her great, great fat friend', and who had also refused to assist in paying Frederick's debts.[51] She rebuffed all his attempts to build a friendship with his nephew. Augusta rarely missed an opportunity to mock or belittle the duke. 'The young Prince George had a great appetite; he was asked if he wanted to be as gross as his uncle? Every vice, every condescension was imputed to the duke, that the prince might be stimulated to avoid them.'[52] More seriously, Augusta accepted absolutely the popular belief – encouraged so assiduously by her husband – that Cumberland harboured unconstitutional designs on the throne. She drilled these into Prince George, who, as the sole obstacle standing in the way of such ambitions, regarded his uncle with nervous trepidation. Once, during a rare meeting alone with his nephew, Cumberland pulled down some weapons he had displayed on his wall to show the young prince; George 'turned pale, and trembled and thought his uncle was going to murder him'. Cumberland was horrified and 'complained to the princess of the impressions that had been instilled into the child against him'.[53] It was not until after he succeeded to the throne that George shook off the distrust of his uncle nurtured in him by his mother.

Augusta soon found herself without friends. She could not seek the support of opposition politicians except at the risk of provoking the king to remove the prince from her care, and she was too deeply imbued with her husband's opinions to seek allies from within the royal family. It was a tricky situation for which Dodington could see no immediate resolution. He begged Augusta not to act precipitately, and she assured him that she would do nothing rash and had made no dangerous alliances, insisting that she had 'no connexions at all'. Dodington found this only too easy to believe. Isolated as she was, without friends, family or supporters, there was little he could offer her except patience, meaning she had no choice but to wait for the king to die. In the privacy of his diary, Dodington was more pessimistic about her prospects, recording his stark belief that she must 'become nothing'.

*

As Frederick's family drifted gradually but inexorably away from both their surviving royal relations and the active political heartland, they had only themselves to rely upon for company. In the mid-1750s, all Augusta and Frederick's children were still alive; fourteen years separated the eldest, Augusta, from the youngest, baby Caroline, born five months after her father's death and named to please her grandfather. In the 1930s, the historian Romney Sedgwick commented that 'as a eugenic experiment, the marriage could not be considered a success'. His remark, though callous, contained an element of truth. Five of Frederick and Augusta's offspring died either in childhood or in their twenties, and two were sickly from birth. Elizabeth, the second daughter, was thought by Walpole to have been the most intelligent of all the family – 'her parts and applications were extraordinary' – but her figure 'was so very unfortunate that it would have been impossible for her to be happy'.[54] She died in 1759, probably from appendicitis. Louisa, the third daughter, died at nineteen, having suffered from such bad health that even her aunt, Princess Amelia, 'thought it happier for her that she was dead'.[55] The youngest son, Frederick, 'a most promising youth', according to Walpole, died at sixteen of consumption.

Prince George was considered to be one of the best looking of Frederick's family; he was also, as a child and a young man, among the healthiest. His elder sister Augusta, whose grasp on life had seemed so tenuous after the thoughtless theatrics surrounding her birth, grew into an equally resilient child, although her looks were never much admired. Walpole thought 'she was not handsome, but tall enough, and not ill-made; with the German whiteness of hair and complexion so glaring in the royal family, and with their thick yet precipitate Westphalian accent'.[56] She was eager, lively and boisterous, resembling her brother Edward in her love of a joke. William, Duke of Gloucester, the third brother, was as fair as Augusta and Edward, but of a very different disposition. Walpole, who knew him well, summed him up as 'reserved, serious, pious, of the most decent and sober deportment'. He closely resembled his eldest brother, whose favourite sibling he later became. Henry, who became Duke of Cumberland after his uncle's death, was small like his father 'but did not want beauty'. He had, however, 'the babbling disposition of his brother York, though without the parts or condescension of the latter'. His youth, concluded Walpole severely, 'had all its faults, and gave no better promises'.[57] The toddler Caroline was remarkable at this stage only for her beauty; the 'German whiteness' that contemporaries found so 'glaring' in her brothers and sisters had in her become a golden blonde. Taken together with her blue eyes and round, pink face, she was by far the prettiest of the family.

Dodington's diary is peppered with glimpses of 'the children', flitting silently round the edges of the world in which he and Augusta occupied centre stage. Always mute, they move as an undifferentiated royal pack. 'The children' are sent to prayers; 'the children' come in to dine; 'the children' retire. Occasionally, the older siblings emerged from the group and joined their mother in simple, family pleasures and games. Dodington was excessively proud of his occasional invitations to join the family in such informal moments, and recorded them with palpable satisfaction. In November 1753, he went to Leicester House 'expecting a small company and a little music; but found no one but Her Royal Highness. She made me draw up a stool, and sit by the fire with her. Soon after came the Prince of Wales and Prince Edward and then the Lady Augusta, all quite undressed, and took their stools and sat round the fire with us. We sat talking of familiar occurrences of all kinds till between 10 and 11, with ease and unreservedness and unconstraint, as if one had dropped into a sister's house that had a family to pass the evening.'

Gentle, unforced intimacy of this kind represented Augusta's household at its best. But while Dodington strongly approved of such warm domestic scenes, he knew in his heart that they were only part of what was required to prepare the older boys for their future lives. He added a wistful postscript to his lyrical description of his quiet night at home with royalty. 'It was much to be wished,' he wrote, 'that the princes conversed familiarly with more people of a certain knowledge of the world.'[58] At a time when George should have been learning how to conduct himself in society, he was utterly removed from it. By 1754, when George was sixteen, even Augusta had begun to worry that the narrow existence she had created for her son was failing him. She confessed to Dodington that she too 'wished he saw more company – but whom of the young people were fit?'[59] She recognised that her eldest son needed more experience of life, but could not reconcile this with her increasingly dark vision of what lay beyond the secure walls of home. For Augusta, whose character took on an ever bleaker cast in the years after her husband's death, the world was a wicked and threatening place and it was her first duty to protect her children from its wiles. Wherever she looked, she saw only moral bankruptcy. She complained at great length to Dodington of the 'universal profligacy' of the youthful aristocrats who might, in other circumstances, have become her children's friends. The men were bad enough, but the women were even worse, 'so indecent, so low, so cheap.'[60] Beyond the inner circle of the family, everyone's behaviour, motives and desires were suspect; no one was really to be trusted. Exposed to temptation, even her own sons might not have the inner strength to resist it. The preservation of an untested virtue, secured by isolation and retirement, was thus the key foundation of their upbringing. 'No boys,' commented William, Duke of Gloucester, in middle age, 'were ever brought up in a greater ignorance of evil than the king and myself ... We retained all our native innocence.'[61] In the end, Augusta's instinctual desire to protect her children from the lures of the world proved stronger than her rational understanding that they must one day learn to master it.

If Prince George's social and family life did little to equip him for the future, he was equally unprepared in almost every other practical dimension of kingship. As a young man, he was bitter about the failings he believed had left him so exposed. 'I will frankly own,' he wrote in 1758, 'that through the negligence, if not wickedness of those around me in earlier days ... I have not that degree of knowledge and experience of business one of my age might reasonably have acquired.'[62] His formal education had certainly been a haphazard affair. After Frederick's death, it was underpinned by no coherent plan and driven by political considerations as much as by the desire to equip the boy with a foundation of useful knowledge. The king had replaced George's tutors with his own appointees; only George Scott, who did most of the actual teaching, survived as part of the new team. As the prince's governor, George II appointed his friend Simon, Earl Harcourt, a loyal courtier whose principal task was to ensure that the prince was encouraged neither to venerate nor to follow the policies of his dead father. He was otherwise undistinguished, memorably described by Walpole as 'civil and sheepish'.[63] Thomas Hayter, Bishop of Norwich, filled the role of preceptor. His pupil had nothing but contempt for him, describing him in later life as 'unworthy … more fitted to be a Jesuit than an English bishop'.[64] A third new appointment was Andrew Stone, who became sub-governor. Stone, like Harcourt, was a political choice; he was the fixer and general factotum of the Duke of Newcastle, who served regularly as George II's first minister, and could be expected to pass back to St James's detailed reports of events at Leicester House.

Under this top-heavy array, George and his brother Edward were set to work. Their lessons began at seven in the morning, and ranged, as they had always done, well beyond the traditional curriculum. However, the more modern subjects – including science, which George particularly enjoyed – did not displace the traditional concentration on the classics. Caesar's *Commentaries* remained a familiar if unwelcome feature of the princes' daily routine, much to George's frustration. '*Monsieur Caesar*,' he wrote in the margins of one of his laborious translations, '*je vous souhaite au diable*.' ('I wish you to hell.'[65]) As his later life was to demonstrate, George had a lively mind, and as an adult would find pleasure in a wide range of intellectual pursuits; but he found little to engage his imagination in what he was taught as a boy. He lacked the aptitude to master ancient languages, and was, in general, poor at rote learning. His fascination for practical and mechanical tasks was regarded as further evidence of his intellectual dullness. Only in music did he shine, playing the German flute with self-absorbed pleasure. All the siblings were accomplished amateur musicians, the girls singing and playing the harpsichord. The love of music was one of the few passions he shared with his father, and one which would outlast his sanity. In all other areas of educational endeavour, especially those that required feats of memory, George was generally regarded as a failure, his apathy and inattention exasperating his instructors.

Augusta knew, as did almost everyone else in the political world, that her eldest son was not making the progress expected of him: 'His education had given her much pain. His book-learning she was no judge of, but she supposed it small or useless.'[66] She thought her sons had not been well served by their instructors. Bishop Hayter may have been 'a mighty learned man', but he did not seem to Augusta 'to be very proper to convey knowledge to children; he had not the clearness she thought necessary … his thoughts seemed to be too many for his words'.[67] She told Dodington that she had repeatedly attempted to challenge Lord Harcourt directly about what was happening, but he simply avoided her. She finally cornered him one night at St James's, 'and got between the door and him, and took him by the coat'; even then the slippery earl escaped her grasp with a platitude. She disliked Harcourt, not only for his elusiveness, but because he 'always spoke to the children of their father and his actions in so disrespectful a manner as to send them to her almost ready to cry'.[68]

Stone, in contrast, 'always behaved very well to her and the children and though it would be treason if it were to be known, always spoke of the late prince with the greatest respect'.[69] But even he seemed to have a curious idea of what was required of him. 'She once desired him to inform the prince about the constitution,' wrote Dodington, 'but he declined it, to avoid giving offence to the Bishop of Norwich. That she had mentioned it again, and he had declined it, as not being his province.' When Dodington asked Augusta what Stone's province was, 'she said she did not know, she supposed to go before him upstairs, to walk with him, sometimes seldomer to ride with him and then to dine with him'.[70]

George's tutors had reason to be nervous when called upon to offer interpretations of the constitution to the heir to the throne. At the end of 1752, Harcourt and Hayter turned on their colleagues Stone and Scott and accused them of Jacobite sympathies, claiming they were covertly indoctrinating George with absolutist principles. They offered no real evidence for their charges, and could persuade neither the king nor his first minister, Newcastle, to believe them. Both promptly resigned, but the recriminations surrounding the affair dragged on for over a year, and were not resolved until Stone had appeared before the Privy Council and the matter had been raised in the House of Lords. It was easy for Dodington to declare with passion that 'what I wanted most was that his Royal Highness should begin to learn the usages and knowledge of the world; be informed of the general frame and nature of government and the constitution, and the general course and manner of business.'[71] But, as the cautious Stone had understood when he refused Augusta's direct invitation to do just that, attempting the political education of princes was a far riskier undertaking than teaching them Latin.

With the departure of Harcourt and Hayter, the king was determined to make one last effort to turn his fourteen-year-old grandson into the kind of heir he thought he deserved. Prince George's hesitant and self-conscious appearances at the formal Drawing Rooms did not impress his grandfather, who had forgotten many of the tender professions he had made at the time of Frederick's death. Unless taken in hand, he feared the prince would be fit for nothing but to read the Bible to his mother. He approached James, Earl Waldegrave, who had been a Lord of the Bedchamber in his household, and asked him to become the prince's new governor. Confident, experienced and expansive, Waldegrave was a very different character from the ineffectual Harcourt, and his sophisticated presence introduced an unfamiliar flavour into Augusta's circle. At first, everyone seemed to welcome both it and him, and Waldegrave used this early advantage to effect something of a revolution in the prince's education. He recognised immediately that the most important task was to engage George's fitful attention, and sought to do this by offering him a vision of knowledge that went beyond the traditional forms of learning his pupil found so unengaging. 'As a right system of education seemed impossible,' Waldegrave recalled in his *Memoirs*, 'the best which could be hoped for was to give him true notions of common things; to instruct him by conversation, rather than books; and sometimes, under the disguise of amusement, to entice him to the pursuit of more serious studies.'[72]

Waldegrave thought that George might work harder if he enjoyed himself more. Unlike any of his previous instructors, he was convinced that beneath the habitual indolence, the prince had potential. The present glaring shortcomings in his character were, Waldegrave believed, less a reflection of his true nature and more the inevitable product of the circumscribed life he led: 'I found HRH uncommonly full of princely prejudices, contracted in the nursery and improved by the society of bedchamber women and pages of the back-stairs.'[73]

Wider experience of the world might cure many of the faults that others had found so intractable.

As time went on, however, it became clear to Waldegrave that the kind of change he advocated – a relaxation of the regime of seclusion, a more active participation in society – would never be countenanced by Augusta. For all her anxieties about her eldest son's education, she would not sacrifice any of her own prejudices to see it improved. She did not expect her authority to be challenged by her son's governor. She explained to Dodington that she considered the post – and Waldegrave, while he occupied it – 'as a sort of pageant, a man of quality for show, etc.'[74] Faced with her blank resistance, Waldegrave's new measures ran slowly but steadily into the ground. Although he was supported in his endeavours by 'men of sense, men of learning and worthy good men', Waldegrave eventually concluded he could do nothing to make a real difference: 'The mother and the nursery always prevailed.'[75]

By the mid-1750s, George's formal education had done little more than confirm in the self-conscious boy an even greater sense of his own shortcomings. Morbidly aware of his faults, especially those of 'lethargy' and 'indolence' with which he was so often charged, he seemed incapable of rousing himself to do anything about them. He had, thought Waldegrave, 'a kind of unhappiness in his temper, which if it be not conquered before it has taken too deep a root, will be a source of frequent anxiety'. The prince's apparent preference for solitude concerned Waldegrave, especially as he suspected the boy chose to be alone the better to contemplate his misery: 'he becomes sullen and silent and retires to his closet, not to compose his mind by study, or contemplation, but merely to indulge the melancholy enjoyment of his own ill humour'.[76] He had no friends except his brother Edward, to whom he was very close. To everyone else, he revealed nothing of himself. The retired life he and his mother shared had certainly not forged a strong emotional bond between them. When Dodington asked her 'what she took the real disposition of the prince to be', Augusta replied that Dodington 'knew him almost as well as she did'.[77]

As he drifted irrevocably towards a destiny that terrified him, George retreated further and further into a private world of remote introspection. Transfixed with apprehension by the prospect before him, lethargy overwhelmed him. Neither his tutors nor his family knew what to do about it, or understood that his much-criticised indolence was less a sign of laziness than a strategy to avoid engaging with a future he knew he could not avoid. By the time he was sixteen, in 1754, he had erected around himself a tough carapace of emotional detachment which no one could penetrate. But George's life was about to be transformed by someone who would instil in him a new vision of who he was; and, for the first time, offer the anxious boy an inspirational idea of what he might become. He encountered the man who would change his life for ever.

*

John Stuart, 3rd Earl of Bute, was a well-connected aristocrat related to some the grandest names in Scottish politics, including the powerful Dukes of Argyll. For a man whose career was so dominated by the fact of his Scottishness, he spent a surprising amount of his early life in England. He was educated at Eton alongside Horace Walpole, who was later to paint such a malign picture of him in his *Memoirs of the Reign of King George III*. Bute married early, and for love: in 1736, at the age of twenty-three, he eloped with the only daughter of Lady Mary Wortley Montagu. The girl's furious father refused to make any financial provision for his disobedient daughter and her new husband. When his irascible father-in-law died some twenty years later, Bute inherited all his money and became extremely rich; but as a young man, he was always short of funds. Contemporaries were certain that only poverty – or 'a gloomy sort of madness' – could have induced him to take up residence on the remote island that bore his name. In the years before the Romantics induced the literate public to admire the wilderness, it was assumed no sensible modern man would choose to live so far from civilisation. Bute's critics, of whom even in his earliest days there were many, asserted that his personality was ideally suited to his faraway, chilly home. 'His disposition,' one remarked, 'was naturally retired and severe.'[78] Others mocked his pomposity and high opinion of himself, his 'theatrical air of the greatest importance', his 'look and manner of speaking' which, regardless of the subject, 'was equally pompous, slow and sententious.'[79] On his island, Bute pursued the literary and scientific studies that were the mark of the aristocratic eighteenth-century intellectual, including 'natural philosophy, mines, fossils, a smattering of mechanics, a little metaphysics'. His enemies claimed that this was all typical self-aggrandisement and that he had in fact 'a very false taste in everything'.[80] It was true that Bute was something of an intellectual dilettante, but in the field of botany, which was his great passion, he possessed real authority. His nine-volume *Botanical Tables Containing the Families of British Plants*, completed in 1785, created a system of classification that was a genuine contribution to scholarship.

In 1746, Bute left his island and headed south, hoping perhaps to improve his financial prospects. Once in London, he was soon noticed, but it was not the power of his mind that attracted attention. 'Lord Bute, when young possessed a very handsome person,' recalled the politician and diplomat Nathaniel Wraxall, 'of which advantage he was not insensible; and he used to pass many hours a day, as his enemies asserted, occupied in contemplating the symmetry of his own legs, during his solitary walks by the Thames.'[81] Bute's portraits – in which his legs are indeed always displayed to advantage – confirm that he was a very attractive man. Tall, slim and with a dark-eyed intensity of expression, it is not hard to see why he was so sought after. It may have been his looks that caught the eye of the Prince of Wales. It was said that Bute first met Frederick at Egham races, when the prince invited him in from a rainstorm to join the royal party at cards. Soon he was a regular attendee at all the prince's parties, and had unbent sufficiently to play the part of Lothario in one of Frederick's private theatrical performances. The prince seemed to enjoy his company, and Bute was admitted to the inner circle of his court. Walpole asserted that Frederick eventually grew tired of Bute's pretensions, 'and a little before his death, he said to him, "Bute, you would make an excellent ambassador in some proud little court where there is nothing to do."'[82] But whatever his occasional frustrations, Frederick thought enough of the earl to make him a Lord of the Bedchamber in his household, and it was only the prince's sudden demise that seemed to put an end to Bute's ambitions, as it did to those of so many others.

After Frederick's death, Bute stayed in contact with his widow. Augusta shared his botanical interests, and he advised her on the planting of her gardens at Kew. He is never mentioned in Dodington's diary, perhaps because Dodington correctly identified him as a rival for Augusta's confidence. As the years passed, Bute's influence grew and grew, until, by 1755, he had supplanted Dodington and all other contenders for the princess's favour. He had also won over her son, and without telling anyone, least of all the king, Augusta quietly instructed Bute to begin acting as George's tutor. For all his experience in the ways of courts, Waldegrave, the official incumbent, seems to have had no idea what was happening until it was too late. Once he realised just how thoroughly he had been supplanted, Waldegrave was determined to leave with as much dignity as he could muster. The king pressed Waldegrave to stay. He was resolutely opposed to the inclusion of Bute – an intimate of Frederick's – in the household of his grandson, particularly in a position of such influence; but Waldegrave knew there was nothing to be done. In 1756, the prince reached the age of eighteen and could no longer be treated as a child. Reluctantly, the king bowed to the inevitable, and Bute was appointed Groom of the Stole, head of the new independent establishment set up for George. To show his displeasure, the king refused to present Bute with the gold key that was the badge of his new office, but gave it to the Duke of Grafton – who slipped it into Bute's pocket and told him not to mind.

When Horace Walpole wrote his highly partisan account of the early reign of George III, he maintained that there was far more to Bute's appointment than anyone had realised at the time; it was, he claimed, the opening act in a plot aimed to do nothing less than suborn the whole constitution. In Walpole's version of events, Augusta and Bute – 'a passionate, domineering woman and a favourite without talents' – conspired together to bring down the established political settlement. They intended first to indoctrinate the supine heir with absolutist principles, and then to marginalise him by ensuring his isolation from the world. All this was to be achieved in the most gradual and surreptitious manner. Ignorant and manipulated, George would remain as titular head of state; but behind him, real power would reside in the hands of Bute and Augusta. To add an extra frisson to a story already rich in classical parallels, Walpole insisted that Augusta and Bute were lovers, 'his connection with the princess an object of scandal'. Elsewhere he was more blunt, declaring: 'I am as much convinced of an amorous connexion between Bute and the princess dowager as if I had seen them together.'[83]

Related with all the passion he could muster, in Walpole's hands this proved to be a remarkably potent narrative. For nearly two hundred years, until interrogated and revised by the work of twentieth-century historians, it was to influence thinking about George's years as Prince of Wales and as a young king; and the reputations of

Bute and Augusta are still coloured by Walpole's bilious account of their alleged actions and motives. But in writing the *Memoirs*, Walpole's purpose was scarcely that of a disinterested historian. First and foremost, he wrote to make a political point. Walpole was a Whig, passionately opposed to what he saw as the autocratic principles embraced by his Tory opponents, who, he had no doubt, desired nothing so much as to restore the pretensions and privileges of the deposed Stuarts. He was, he said, not quite a republican, but certainly favoured 'a most limited monarchy', and was perpetually on the look-out for evidence of plots hatched by the powerful and unscrupulous to undermine the hard-won liberties of free-born Britons. To that extent, the *Memoirs*, couched throughout in a tone of shrill outrage quite unlike Walpole's accustomed smooth, ironic style, are best considered as a warning of what might happen rather than an account of what did – a chilling fable of political nightmare designed to appal loyal constitutionalists. Less portentously, Walpole also wrote to pay off a grudge. He considered he had been wronged by Bute, who had refused to grant him a sinecure Walpole believed he was owed: 'I was I confess, much provoked by this … and took occasion of fomenting ill humour against the favourite.'[84]

Much of what resulted from this incendiary combination of intentions was simply nonsense, and often directly contradicted what Walpole had himself written in earlier days. In truth, there was no plot; Augusta was not 'ardently fond of power'; neither she nor Bute was scheming to overturn the constitution; and it is extremely unlikely that they were lovers. But if the central proposition of Walpole's argument was a fiction, that did not mean that everything he wrote was pure invention. The *Memoirs* exerted such a powerful appeal because Walpole drew on existing rumours that were very widely believed at the time; and because, sometimes, beneath Walpole's wilder assertions there lay buried a tiny kernel of truth.

Thus, Walpole seemed on sure ground when describing the isolation in which George had been brought up, and the extraordinary precautions taken to keep him away from wider intercourse with the world. He was correct in his assertion that much of this policy had been driven by Augusta. He was wrong about her motives – the extreme retirement she imposed on her son was a protective cordon sanitaire, not a covert means of dominating him – but the prince's isolation was observable to everyone in the political world, and of as much concern to Augusta's few allies as it was to her enemies. Walpole was also right to assert that within the secluded walls of Kew and Leicester House, the future shape of George's kingship was indeed the subject of intense discussion; but these reflections were directed towards an outcome very different from Walpole's apocalyptic image of treasonous constitutional conspiracy. Finally, he was accurate in his suspicion that there was a passionate relationship at the heart of the prince's household. But it was not, in fact, the one he went on to describe with such relish.

The stories about Bute and Augusta had been in circulation long before Walpole's *Memoirs* appeared. Waldegrave, who never forgot or forgave the way he was humiliatingly ejected from his post around the prince, seems to have been the origin of many of them. 'No one of the most inflammable vengeance, or the coolest resentment could harbour more bitter hatred than he did for the king's mother and favourite,' wrote Walpole with a hint of appalled admiration.[85] For the rest of her life, as a result of these rumours, Augusta was mercilessly pilloried as a brazen adulteress; in newspapers, pamphlets, and above all in satirical caricatures, she was depicted as Bute's mistress. One print showed her as a half-naked tightrope walker, skirt hitched up to her thighs, suggestively penetrated by a pole with a boot (a play on Bute's name) attached to it. It was hardly surprising that Prince George was horrified 'by the cruel manner' in which his mother was treated, 'which I will not forget or forgive till the day of my death.'[86]

However, for all the salacious speculation surrounding their relationship, it seems hard to believe that Bute and Augusta ever had an affair. Although Augusta clearly admired the attractive earl, writing to him with an enthusiasm and warmth that few of her other letters betray, to embark on anything more than friendship would have been quite alien to her character. She was too cautious, too conscious of her standing in the world, too controlled and reserved to have taken the extraordinary risk such a relationship would have entailed. But, in the complex interplay of the political and the personal that transformed the tone of Augusta's family in the latter years of the 1750s, there was one person who surrendered himself entirely to an unexpected and completely overpowering affection. The diffident young Prince George had finally found someone to love.

Bute had been acting as George's informal tutor for less than a year before it was plain that he had achieved what no one had been able to do before: win the trust and affection of the withdrawn prince. Augusta was delighted. 'I cannot express the joy I feel to see he has gained the confidence and friendship of my son,' she wrote in the summer of 1756, with uncharacteristically transparent pleasure.[87] The prince himself was equally fervent, writing almost ecstatically to Bute that 'I know few things I ought to be more thankful to the Great Power above, than for having pleased Him to send you and help me in these difficult times.'[88]

This was the first of many letters the prince wrote to Bute over nearly a decade; its tone of incredulous gratitude, its sense of sheer good fortune at the very fact of Bute's presence, was one that would be replicated constantly over the years. Their correspondence illuminates the painful intensity of George's feelings for the earl, from his speedy capitulation to the onslaught of Bute's persuasive charm, to the submissive devotion that characterised the prince's later relationship with this charismatic, demanding and sometimes mercurial figure. George's letters also offer a remarkably candid picture of his state of mind as a young man. He opened his heart to Bute in a way he had done to no one before, and would never do again after he and the earl had parted. Many of his letters make uncomfortable reading; they reveal an isolated and deeply unhappy character, consumed by a sense of his own inadequacies, and desperate to find someone who would lead him out of the fog of despair into which he was sinking. George knew he was drifting, fearful and rudderless, towards a future which approached with a horrible inevitability. He was very quickly convinced that Bute was the only person who could deliver him from the state of paralysed inertia in which he had existed since his father's death. 'I hope, my dear Lord,' he wrote pleadingly, 'you will conduct me through this difficult road and bring me to the goal. I will exactly follow your advice, without which I will inevitably sink.'[89]

He knew he needed someone to supply the determination and resilience in which he suspected he was so shamefully deficient. He was delighted – and profoundly relieved – to find a mentor to whom he could surrender himself absolutely, to whose better judgement he could happily submit. Without such a guide, he believed his prospects looked bleak indeed. 'If I should mount the throne without the assistance of a friend, I should be in the most dreadful of situations,' he assured the earl in 1758.[90]

Bute also offered George genuine warmth and affection. His enthusiastic declarations of regard, his energetic and apparently disinterested commitment to his wellbeing, exploded into the prince's arid, sentimental life. George's devotion to Bute soon became the most important relationship in his life. 'I shall never change in that, nor will I bear to be the least deprived of your company,' he insisted vehemently.[91] The growing intensity of the prince's feelings was reflected not just in the content of his letters to Bute, but also in the way he addressed him. At first, he was 'my dear Lord', a term of conventional courtly politeness; soon this warmed into 'my dear Friend'; but very quickly, the strength of the prince's feelings were made even plainer. All obstacles, he wrote to the earl with unembarrassed devotion, could and would be overcome, 'whilst my Dearest is near me'.[92] Bute was not just mentor and role model to the prince; he was also the first person to unearth George's hitherto deeply buried but strong emotions.

Bute broke through the prince's habitual reserve partly by what he did, and partly by who he was. He was a compellingly attractive figure to a fatherless, faltering boy: handsome, assured and experienced, he was everything George knew he was not. Augusta, who was suspicious of almost everyone, admired and respected Bute, and the earl was unequivocal in his praise of George's dead father, declaring that he had gloried in being known as Frederick's friend. Unlike many of his predecessors, Bute actually seemed to like the prince, and he approached the prospect of training him for kingship with a galvanising enthusiasm. 'You have condescended to take me into your friendship,' he told the prince, 'don't think it arrogance if I say I will deserve it.'[93] Bute's breezy optimism about the task before him was in stark contrast to the dour resignation of previous instructors. 'Use will make everything easy,' he confidently assured his faltering charge.[94]

Leaving Latin behind at last, George and Bute embarked on a course of more contemporary study. Bute encouraged the prince to investigate finance and economics, and together they read a series of lectures by the jurist William Blackstone that was to form the basis of his magisterial work on the origins of English common law. Bute even ventured confidently where Andrew Stone had feared to tread. George's essay, 'Thoughts on the English Constitution', included opinions that might have reassured Walpole, had he read it, so impeccably Whiggish were its sentiments. The Glorious Revolution had, the prince wrote, rescued Britain 'from the iron rod of arbitrary power', while Oliver Cromwell was described, somewhat improbably by the heir to the throne, as 'a friend of justice and virtue'.[95]

Whilst Bute's more liberal definition of 'what is fit for you to know' undeniably piqued George's interest, it was his bigger ideas that consolidated his hold over the prince and secured his pre-eminent place in George's mind and heart. The most significant of these was one which would transform the prince's prospects and offer him a way out of the despondency that had threatened to overwhelm him since his father's death. In the late 1750s, Bute proposed nothing less than a new way of understanding the role of monarchy, offering George an enticingly credible picture of the kind of ruler he might aspire to become. For the first time he was presented with a concept of kingship that seemed within his capacity to achieve, that spoke to his strengths rather than his failings. It changed the nature of George's engagement, not just with Bute but, more significantly, with himself. It gave him something to aim for and believe in; the delivery of this vision was 'the goal' that George believed was the purpose of his partnership with Bute. Indeed, it far outlasted his relationship with the earl; until his final descent into insanity half a century later, it established the principles by which he lived his life as a public and private man.

In Bute's ideal, the role of the king was not simply to act as an influential player in the complex interplay of party rivalry that dominated politics in mid-eighteenth-century Britain. It was the monarch's job to rise above all that, to transcend faction and self-interest, and devote himself instead to the impartial advancement of the national good. This was not an original argument; it derived from Henry, Viscount Bolingbroke's extremely influential *Idea of a Patriot King*, written in 1738 (though not published until 1749). Frederick had been much taken with Bolingbroke's ideas, and the 'Instructions' he wrote as a political testimony for his son drew strongly on many of Bolingbroke's conclusions, but Frederick was primarily concerned with the practical political implications of Bolingbroke's ideas. The 'Instructions' is mostly a list of recommendations intended to secure for a king the necessary independence to escape the control of politicians, most of which revolve around money: don't fight too many wars, and separate Hanover, a drain on resources, from Great Britain as soon as possible.

Bute too was interested in the exercise of power; but, always drawn towards philosophy, he was even more fascinated by its origins, and sought to formulate a coherent, modern explanation for the very existence of kingship itself. Choosing those measures which best reflected the ambitions of a 'patriot' king was secondary, in his mind, to establishing the justification by which such a king held the reins of government in the first place. For Bute, the answer was simple: it was the virtue of the king – the goodness of his actions, as both a public and a private man – that formed the source of all his power. Virtue was clearly the best protection for an established ruler; a good king was uniquely positioned to win the love and loyalty of his people, making it possible for him to appeal credibly to the sense of national purpose that went beyond the narrower interests of party politicians. But the connection between morals and monarchy went deeper than that. Virtue was not just an attribute of good kingship; it was also the quality from which kings derived their authority. And the virtues Bute had in mind were not cold civic ones peculiar to the political world, of necessity and expediency. They were the moral standards which all human beings were held to, those which regulated the actions of all decent men and women. Kingship offered no exemption from moral conduct; on the contrary, more was expected of kings because so much more had been given to them. Moral behaviour in the public realm was therefore indivisible from its practice in the private world. To be a good king, it was essential to try to be a good man.

The place where private virtue was most clearly expressed, for Bute as for most of his contemporaries, was within the family. Here, in the unit that was the basic building block of society, the moral life was most easily and most rewardingly to be experienced. The good king would naturally enjoy a family life based on shared moral principles. Indeed, for Bute, authority had itself actually originated within the confines of the family. 'In the first ages of the world,' as he explained to George, private and public virtue had been one and the same thing; in this pre-political Eden, there was no distinction between the two, as government and family were not yet divided: 'Parental fondness, filial piety and brotherly affection engrossed the mind; government subsisted only in the father's management of the family, to whom the eldest son succeeding, became at once the prince and parent of his brethren.'

Everything began to go wrong when families lost their natural moral compass: 'Vice crept in. Love, ambition, cruelty with envy, malice and the like produced unnatural parents, disobedient children, diffidence and hatred between near relations.' It all sounded remarkably like the home lives of George's Hanoverian predecessors, as Bute perhaps intended that it should. The failure of self-regulating family virtue forced men to create artificial forms of authority – 'hence villages, towns and laws' – but as communities grew bigger, their rulers moved further and further away from the moral principles that were the proper foundation of power. The consequences were dire, both for the ruled and their rulers: 'Unhappy people, but more unhappy kings.'[96] The amoral exercise of power ruined those who practised it. 'They could never feel the joy arising from a good and compassionate action … they could never hear the warm, honest voice of friendship, the tender affections and calls of nature, nor the more endearing sounds of love, but here, the scene's too black, let me draw the curtain.'[97]

For Bute, the lesson of history was clear: good government originated in the actions of good men. What was needed now, he concluded, was a return to such fundamental first principles. He summed up his programme succinctly: 'Virtue, religion, joined to nobility of sentiment, will support a prince better and make a people happier than all the abilities of an Augustus with the heart of Tiberius; the inference I draw from this is, that a prince ought to endeavour in all his thoughts and actions to excel his people in virtue, generosity, and nobility of sentiment.' This is the source of his authority and the justification for his rule. Only then will his subjects feel that 'he merits by his own virtue and not by the fickle dice of fortune the vast superiority he enjoys above them.'[98]

George embraced Bute's thinking enthusiastically – and also perhaps with a sense of relief. He might have doubts about his intellectual capacity, and about his ability to dominate powerful and aggressive politicians, but he was more confident of legitimising his position by the morality of his actions. He suspected he was not particularly clever, but he was enough of his mother's son to believe that he could be good – and perhaps more so than other men. He grasped at this possibility, and never let it go. It rallied his depressed spirits, jolted him out of a near-catatonic state of despair. It gave him a belief in himself and an explanation for his strange and unsettling destiny. It invested his future role with a meaning and significance it had so profoundly lacked before.

Bute's vision of kingship transformed George's perception of his future and shaped his behaviour as a public man for the rest of his life. Inevitably, it also dictated the terms on which his private life was conducted. He was unsparing in his interpretation of what the virtuous life meant for a king. He rarely flinched from the necessity to do the right rather than the pleasurable or easy thing, and he insisted on the absolute primacy of duty over personal desire and obligation over happiness. In time, these convictions came to form the essence of his personality, the DNA of who he was; and when he came to have a family, the lives of his wife and children were governed by the same rigorous requirements of virtue. As a father, a husband, a brother or a son, he was answerable to the same immutable moral code that governed his actions as a king. Bute taught him that in his case, the personal was always political; and it was a lesson he never forgot.

All this was to come later, however. When he took up his post, Bute was acutely aware of just how far short his charge fell from the princely ideal that was the central requirement of his monarchical vision. From the moment of his arrival, he set out to rebuild the prince's tentative, disengaged personality, using a potent combination of threat and affection to do so. His first target was the prince's lethargy, the subject of so much ineffectual criticism from Waldegrave and previous tutors. Bute was tenacious in his attempts to persuade George to show some energy and commitment to his studies; but it was a slow process, and one which required all the earl's considerable powers of persuasion. By 1757, he had begun to make some progress, and the prince assured him: 'I do here in the most solemn manner declare that I will entirely throw aside this my greatest enemy, and that you shall instantly find a change.'[99] It was not just George's academic dilatoriness that Bute sought to tackle; he also attempted to root out other potentially damaging aspects of his personality that might compromise his authority when he came to be king. His pathological and disabling shyness must and would be conquered. Again, George declared himself ready to take up the challenge. He promised Bute that he was now determined to 'act the man in everything, to repeat whatever I am to say with spirit and not blushing and afraid as I have hitherto.'[100]

Although George confessed he was sometimes 'extremely hurt, at the many truths' Bute told him, he did not doubt that Bute's 'constant endeavours to point out these things in me that are likely to destroy any attempts at raising my character' were for his own good, 'a painful, though necessary office'.[101] They were also, in George's eyes, a sign of the depth of Bute's regard for him, since only someone who really loved him would be prepared to criticise him so readily. 'Flatterers, courtiers or ministers are easily got,' his father had explained to him in his 'Instructions', 'but a true friend is hard to be found. The only rule I can give you to try them by, is that they will tell you the truth.' If George discovered such an honest man, he should do all he could to keep him, even if that required him to bear 'some moments of disagreeable contradictions to your passions'.[102]

George had no difficulty in submitting to Bute's comprehensive programme of self-improvement, sadly convinced that all the criticisms were deserved. His opinion of himself could not have been lower. He was, he confessed, 'not partial to myself', regularly describing both his actions and himself as despicable. 'I act wrong perhaps in most things,' he observed, adding that he might be best advised to 'retire, to some distant region where in solitude I might for the rest of my life think on the faults I have committed, that I might repent of them'.[103] He was afraid that he was 'of such an unhappy nature, that if I cannot in good measure alter that, let me be ever so learned in what is necessary for a king to know, I shall make but a very poor and despicable figure'.[104] When he contemplated his many shortcomings and failures, he was amazed that Bute was prepared to remain with him at all.

The idea that Bute might leave – that his patience with his underachieving charge might exhaust itself – threw the prince into paroxysms of anxiety. Bute seems often to have deployed the idea of potential abandonment as a means of reminding George of the totality of his dependency. The merest suggestion of it was enough, George admitted, to 'put me on the rack', declaring that the prospect was 'too much for mortal man to bear'.[105] His self-esteem was so low that George was sure that if Bute were to depart, he would have only himself to blame. 'If you should resolve to set me adrift, I could not upbraid you,' he wrote resignedly, 'as it is the natural consequence of my faults, and not want of friendship in you.'[106] George was endlessly solicitous about Bute's health: the possibility of losing him through illness or even death was a horrifying prospect that loomed large in George's nervous imagination; his letters are full of enquiries and imprecations about the earl's wellbeing. When Bute and his entire family fell seriously ill with 'a malignant sore throat', the prince was beside himself with worry. He took refuge in his conviction that 'you, from your upright conduct, have some right to hope for particular assistance from the great Author of us all'.[107] It was inconceivable that God would not value Bute's virtues as highly as George did; when the earl recovered, George presented his doctors with specially struck gold medals of himself to mark his appreciation of their care.

From the mid-1750s to the time of his accession, the entire object of George's existence was to reshape and remodel himself into the type of man who could fulfil the role of king, as Bute had so alluringly redefined it; but this internal reformation was not accompanied by a change in his way of life. He remained closeted at home with his mother and the earl, and for all Bute's desire to reform the prince's personality, he left many of George's deepest beliefs untouched – partly because he shared some of them himself. One of the reasons George found Bute so congenial was because he endorsed so much of the vision of the world that the prince had inherited from his mother. For all his confidence in the righteousness of his prescriptions, and for all the energy and enthusiasm with which he argued them, there was in Bute himself a core of austerity and reserve. He was not a naturally sociable man, preferring to judge society – often rather severely – than to engage with it. He had a natural sympathy with the suspicion and apprehension with which Augusta encountered anything beyond the narrow bounds of her immediate family. He offered George no alternative perspective, but instead confirmed the prince's pessimism about the moral worth and motives of others, a bleak scepticism that was to endure throughout his life. 'This,' wrote George, 'is I believe, the wickedest age that ever was seen; an honest man must wish himself out of it; I begin to be sick of things I daily see; for ingratitude, avarice and ambition are the principles men act by.'[108]

Bute's counsels did nothing to dilute the mix of fear and contempt with which the prince contemplated the world he must one day join. 'I look upon the majority of politicians as intent on their own private interests rather than of the public,' George wrote with grim certainty.[109] William Pitt, his grandfather's minister, was 'the blackest of hearts'. His uncle, Cumberland, was still, George believed, capable of mounting a coup d'état to prevent his accession: 'in the hands of these myrmidons of the blackest kind, I imagine any invader with a handful of men might put himself on the throne and establish despotism here.'[110] He had fully absorbed Augusta's deep-seated hostility to his grandfather and, like her, could not find a good word to say about 'this Old Man'. George II's behaviour was 'shuffling' and 'unworthy of a British monarch; the conduct of this old king makes me ashamed of being his grandson.'[111] There was only one man deserving of George's confidence, and that was Bute. 'As for honesty,' he told Bute, 'I have already lived long enough to know you are the only man I shall ever meet who possesses that quality and who at all times prefers my interest to their own; if I were to utter all the sentiments of my heart on that subject, you would be troubled with quires of paper.'[112]

By 1759, Bute's ascendancy over the prince seemed complete. The prospect of translating their political ideas into practice once George II was dead offered a beacon of hope which sustained them through adversity – it had been agreed at the very outset of their relationship that Bute was to become First Lord of the Treasury when George was king. But in that year, the earl's authority was challenged from a direction that neither he and nor perhaps George himself had anticipated.

*

In the winter, conducting one of his regular inventories of George's state of mind, Bute became convinced the prince was hiding something from him. Pressed to declare himself, George was cautious at first, but eventually began a hesitant explanation of his mood. At first, he confined himself to generalities. 'You have often accused me of growing grave and thoughtful,' he confessed. 'It is entirely owing to a daily increasing admiration of the fair sex, which I am attempting with all the philosophy and resolution I am capable of, to keep under. I should be ashamed,' he wrote ruefully, 'after having so long resisted the charms of those divine creatures, now to become their prey.'[113] There was no doubt that the twenty-one-year-old George was still a virgin. His younger brother Edward, far more like his father and grandfather in his tastes, had eagerly embarked on affairs as soon as he had escaped the schoolroom, but George had thus far remained true to his mother's principles of self-denial and restraint. Walpole believed that if she could, Augusta would have preferred to keep her son perpetually away from the lures of designing women: 'Could she have chained up his body as she did his mind, it is probable that she would have preferred him to remain single.' But the worldly diarist thought he knew the Hanoverian temperament well enough to be convinced this was an impossible objective. 'Though his chastity had hitherto remained to all appearances inviolate, notwithstanding his age and sanguine complexion, it was not to be expected such a fast could be longer observed.'[114] Certainly this was how the prince himself felt, confessing to Bute that he found repressing his desires harder and harder. 'You will plainly feel how strong a struggle there is between the boiling youth of 21 years and prudence.' He hoped 'the last will ever keep the upper hand, indeed if I can but weather it, marriage will put a stop to this conflict in my breast'.[115]

As Bute suspected, George's disquiet reflected something more than a general sense of frustration. Incapable of concealing anything of importance from Bute, he wrote another letter which confessed all. 'What I now lay before you, I never intend to communicate to anyone; the truth is, the Duke of Richmond's sister arrived from Ireland towards the middle of November. I was struck with her first appearance at St James's, and my passion has increased every time I have since beheld her; her voice is sweet, she seems sensible ... in short, she is everything I can form to myself lovely.' Since then, his life had hardly been his own: 'I am grown daily unhappy, sleep has left me, which was never before interrupted by any reverse of fortune.' He could not bear to see other men speak to her. 'The other day, I heard it suggested that the Duke of Marlborough made up to her. I shifted my grief till I retired to my chamber where I remained for several hours in the depth of despair.' His love and his intentions were, he insisted, entirely honourable: 'I protest before God, I never have had any improper thoughts with regard to her; I don't deny having flattered myself with hopes that one day or another you would consent to my raising her to a throne. Thus I mince nothing to you.'[116]

Lady Sarah Lennox, daughter of the Duke of Richmond (which title her brother inherited), was almost as well connected as George himself. Her grandfather was a son of Charles II and his mistress Louise de Kérouaille. She had four sisters, three of whom had done very well in the marriage market. The eldest, Caroline, was wife to the politician Henry Fox, and mother to Charles. Emily had married the Earl of Kildare, and Louisa had made an alliance with an Irish landowner, Thomas Connolly. From her youth, Sarah was one of the liveliest members of a famously lively family. As a very small child, she had caught the eye of George II. He had invited her to the palace where she would watch the king at his favourite pastime, 'counting his money which he used to receive regularly every morning'. Once, with heavy-handed playfulness, he had 'snatched her up in his arms, and after depositing her in a large china jar, shut down the lid to prove her courage'.[117] When her response was to sing loudly rather than to cry, he was delighted.

When her mother died, Sarah went to live with her sister, Lady Kildare, in Ireland. She did not return to court until she was fourteen. George II, who had not forgotten her, was pleased to see her back, but 'began to joke and play with her as if she were still a child of five. She naturally coloured up and shrank from this unaccustomed familiarity, became abashed and silent.' The king was disappointed and declared: 'Pooh! She's grown quite stupid!'[118]

Those who found themselves on the receiving end of his grandfather's insensitivity aroused the sympathy of the Prince of Wales. 'It was at that moment the young prince … was struck with admiration and pity; feelings that ripened into an attachment which never left him until the day of his death.'[119] That was the account Sarah gave to her son in 1837, and which he transcribed with reverential filial piety. In letters she wrote to her sisters at the time, Sarah was not so sentimental. After her first meeting with George, she described her clothes – blue and black feathers, black silk gown and cream lace ruffles – with far more detail than her encounter with the prince. She hardly spoke to him at all. Too shy to approach her directly, the prince had instead approached her older sister Caroline, stumbling out unaccustomed praises of her beauty and charm.

George was not the only man to find Sarah Lennox mesmerisingly attractive. It was hard to pin down the exact nature of her appeal, which was not always apparent at first sight. Her sisters failed to understand it at all. 'To my taste,' wrote Emily, 'Sarah is merely a pretty, lively looking girl and that is all. She has not one good feature … her face is so little and squeezed, which never turns out pretty.'[120] Her brother-in-law Henry Fox thought otherwise. 'Her beauty is not easily described,' he wrote, 'otherwise than by saying that she had the finest complexion, the most beautiful hair, and prettiest person that was ever seen, with a sprightly and fine air, a pretty mouth, remarkably fine teeth, and an excess of bloom in her cheeks, little eyes – but that is not describing her, for her great beauty was a peculiarity of countenance that made her at the same time different from and prettier than any other girl I ever saw.'[121] Horace Walpole saw her once as she acted in amateur theatricals at Holland House; his detached connoisseur's eye caught something of her intense erotic promise: 'When Lady Sarah was all in white, with her hair about her ears and on the ground, no Magdalen by Caravaggio was half so lovely and expressive.'[122] Sarah, unfazed by the comparison to a fallen woman, declared its author 'charming'. She liked Walpole, she said with disarming honesty, because he liked her.

This cheerful willingness to find good in all those who found good in her no doubt smoothed her encounters with the awkward Prince of Wales. They met at formal Drawing Rooms and private balls, and George's attention was so marked that it was soon noticed by the sharp-eyed Henry Fox. At this point, he did not take it seriously; it was no more than an opportunity for a good tease. 'Mr Fox says [George] is in love with me, and diverts himself extremely,' Sarah told Emily wryly.[123]

Bute, however, knew that George's feelings were anything but a joke. Having declared them to his mentor, George was now desperate to know whether Sarah Lennox could be considered a suitable candidate for marriage. It seems never to have occurred to him that this was a decision he might make for himself. He submitted himself absolutely to Bute's judgement, assuring him that no matter what the earl concluded, he would abide by his decision. He hoped for a favourable answer, but insisted that their relationship would not be affected if it were not so: 'If I must either lose my friend or my love, I shall give up the latter, for I esteem your friendship above all earthly joy.'[124] The rational part of him must have known what Bute's answer would be. It was inconceivable that he should marry anyone but a Protestant foreign princess; an alliance between the royal house and an English aristocratic family would overthrow the complex balance of political power on which the mechanics of the constitutional settlement depended.

To marry into a family that included Henry Fox was, if possible, even more outrageously improbable. Henry was the brother of Stephen Fox, the lover of Lord Hervey, the laconic Ste, who had been driven into a jealous fury by the ambiguous relationship between Hervey and Prince Frederick. Henry Fox was one of the most controversial politicians of his day: able, amoral and considered spectacularly corrupt, even by the relaxed standards of eighteenth-century governmental probity. A man described by the Corporation of the City of London as a 'public defaulter of unaccounted millions' was unlikely to prove a suitable brother-in-law to the heir to the throne. Bute's judgement was therefore as unsurprising as it was uncompromising: 'God knows, my dear sir, I with the utmost grief tell it you, the case admits of not the smallest doubt.' He urged George to consider 'who you are, what is your birthright, what you wish to be'. If he examined his heart, he would understand why the thing he hoped for could never happen. The prince declared himself reluctantly persuaded that Bute was right. 'I have now more obligations to him than ever; he has thoroughly convinced me of the impossibility of ever marrying a countrywoman.' He had been recalled to a proper sense of duty. 'The interest of my country shall ever be my first care, my own inclinations shall ever submit to it; I am born for the happiness or misery of a great nation, and consequently must often act contrary to my passions.'[125]

George's renunciation was made easier by the fact that he did not see the object of his passion for some months. The next time he did so, he was no longer Prince of Wales but king. George II died in October 1760; Sarah Lennox went to court in 1761, when all the talk was of the impending coronation. As soon as he saw her again, all George's hard-won resolution ebbed away, as 'the boiling youth' in him made him forget all the promises he had made to Bute. Despite his undertaking to give her up, he took the unprecedented step of declaring to her best friend the unchanged nature of his feelings for Sarah. One night at court, he cornered Lady Susan Fox-Strangways, another member of the extensive Fox clan. The conversation that followed was so extraordinary that Lady Susan repeated it to Henry Fox, who transcribed it. The king asked Lady Susan if she would not like to see a coronation. She replied that she would.

K: Won't it be a finer sight when there is a queen?

LS: To be sure, sir.

K: I have had a great many applications from abroad, but I don't like them. I have had none at home. I should like that better.

LS: (Nothing, frightened)

K: What do you think of your friend? You know who I mean; don't you think her fittest?

LS: Think, sir?

K: I think none so fit.

Fox then said that George 'went across the room to Lady Sarah, and bid her ask her friend what he had been saying and make her tell her all.'[126]

The fifteen-year-old Sarah, never very impressed by George's attentions, had been conducting a freelance flirtation of her own, which had just come to an end, and she was in no mood to be polite to other suitors, even royal ones. When George approached her at court soon after, she rebuffed all his attempts to discuss the conversation he had had with Lady Susan. When he asked whether she had spoken to her friend, she replied monosyllabically that she had. Did she approve of what she had heard? Fox reported that 'She made no answer, but looked as cross as she could. HM affronted, left her, seemed confused, and left the Drawing Room.'[127]

Fox worked away, trying to discover the true state of George's feelings for Lady Sarah. Despite the unfortunate snub, they seemed to Fox as strong as ever. He was less certain, however, of where they might lead. Fox told his wife that he was not sure whether George really intended to marry her, adding that 'whether Lady Sarah shall be told of what I am sure of, I leave to the reader's discretion.'[128] If a crown was out of the question, it might be worth Sarah settling for the role of royal mistress. At the Birthday Ball a few months later, Fox's hopes of the ultimate prize revived once more. 'He had no eyes but for her, and hardly talked to anyone else … all eyes were fixed on them, and the next morning all tongues observing on the particularity of his behaviour.'[129] But after over a year of encouraging signals, there was still no sign of any meaningful declaration from the king. Determined to bring matters to a head, Lady Sarah was sent back to court with very precise instructions to do all she could to extract from her vague suitor some concrete sense of his intentions. As she explained to Lady Susan, Fox had coached her to perfection: 'I must pluck up my spirits, and if I am asked if I have thought of … or if I approve of … I am to look him in the face and with an earnest but good-humoured countenance, say "that I don't know what I ought to think". If the meaning is explained, I must say "that I can hardly believe it" and so forth.' It was all very demanding. 'In short, I must show I wish it to be explained, without seeming to suggest any *other* meaning; what a task it is. God send that I may be enabled to go through with it. I am allowed to mutter a little, provided that the words *astonished*, *surprised*, *understand* and *meaning* are heard.'[130]

Yet for all Lady Sarah's careful preparation, she could not get near the king, and nothing came of it. Then, at the end of June 1761, the king made yet another of his cryptically encouraging remarks, this time to Sarah's sister Emily, telling her: 'For God's sake, remember what I said to Lady Susan … and believe that I have the strongest attachment.' A few days later, Fox was dumbstruck to be told that the meeting of the Privy Council summoned for 8 July was 'to declare His Majesty's intention to marry a Princess of Mecklenburg!'[131]

No one could believe it, least of all Sarah. On the day after the meeting – and its purpose – had been announced, 'the hypocrite had the face to come up and speak to me with all the good humour in the world, and seemed to want to speak to me but was afraid. There is something so astonishing in all this that I can hardly believe …'[132] For months, Lady Sarah and Fox puzzled and obsessed over what the strange and confusing episode had meant. Lady Sarah could not help but feel humiliated, but was determined not to let others see it. 'Luckily for me, I did not love him, and only liked him, nor did the title weigh anything with me; or so little at least, that my disappointment did not affect my spirits above one hour or two, I believe.'[133] If that was an exaggeration born of bravado, it was nonetheless true that she had recovered her spirits sufficiently to accept without a qualm the invitation to act as one of the bridesmaids at George's wedding a few months later. 'Well, Sal,' sighed Fox, making his own final comment on the whole affair, 'you are the first virgin' – or as he jokingly pronounced it, 'the first *vargin*' – 'in England, and you shall take your place in spite of them all, and the king shall behold your pretty face and weep.'[134]

Had either Fox or Lady Sarah asked George to explain his behaviour, it is hard to know what he might have said. No one could deny that his conduct had not been strictly honourable. Although he had not made a direct proposal of marriage, he had come pretty close to it, and he had certainly encouraged Sarah to think of him as some kind of suitor when he was not, as he knew only too well, in a position to offer any respectable outcome to their developing relationship. By January 1761, preliminary enquiries had begun in Germany to find him a woman he could marry, but, despite all his assurances to Bute and to himself, he was still irresistibly drawn to Sarah Lennox, dropping suggestions and making promises that he knew he could not keep. When, in the spring, he made his fateful declaration to Lady

Susan Fox-Strangways, he was privately reading reports evaluating the looks and characters of every German Protestant princess of marriageable age. His formal proposal to the Princess of Mecklenburg was accepted on 17 June, only days before he made yet another of his insistent speeches to Sarah's sister Emily, beseeching her to 'believe that I have the strongest attachment'.

George's motives, in the end, remain opaque; but perhaps he explained his actions to himself by considering them as the contradictory product of the two conflicting aspects of his identity. The king in him submitted, as he knew he must, to an arranged marriage with a woman he had never seen; but the 'boiling youth of 21 years' found it harder to accept that he 'must often act contrary to my passions', and that to 'the interest of my country … my own inclinations shall ever submit'. In 1760–61, for the first and only time in his life, George allowed his heart to rule his head and followed the call of instinct, not obligation. He knew from the beginning which way it would end, recognising that he was formed for duty not rebellion. However, before the world of *you shall* closed inevitably and finally over the prospect of *you could*, he enjoyed a brief flirtation with the alternative. While he kept his sanity, he would never stray again.

CHAPTER 4

The Right Wife

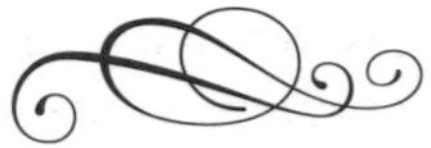

DEATH HAD COME SUDDENLY UPON George II, with very little regard for his dignity. Horace Walpole heard that the last day of the king's life had been conducted with the same punctiliousness which had marked all his actions. At six in the morning he had been served his breakfast chocolate. 'At seven, for everything with him was exact and periodic, he went to his closet to dismiss it.' When he did not emerge from his private lavatory, his valet, Schroeder, grew alarmed. Drawing closer to the door, he 'heard something like a groan. He ran in, and found the king on the floor.' He had cut the right side of his face as he collapsed. Schroeder may have been the author of the laconic coded note hurriedly sent to the young Prince of Wales informing him what had happened to his grandfather. The stricken king did not respond to his valet, nor to the anxious ministrations of his servants, who carried him back to the more decorous surroundings of his bedroom. By the time they had summoned his spinster daughter Amelia, he was beyond help. Amelia's sight was very poor, and when she saw her father laid on his bed she did not realise he was already dead. Walpole was told that 'they had not closed his eyes.' Amelia bent down, 'close to his face and concluded he spoke to her, though she could not hear him – guess what a shock when she found out the truth.'[1]

George II was the first reigning monarch to have died in England for nearly fifty years. His funeral was intended to be an event both sombre and imposing, reflecting the dignity of the office of kingship and the mourning of a bereaved nation. It was held at night, and began with suitable solemnity, accompanied by muffled drum rolls and bells tolling in the darkness. Walpole, who could never resist the lure of a ceremony, was present throughout the proceedings. He thought the early stages were very impressive, and was moved, despite himself, by the severe choreography that marked the coffin's journey to Westminster Abbey. But once inside the chapel, he was sorry to see that discipline and decorum fell apart: 'No order was observed; people sat or stood where they could or would; the yeoman of the guard were crying out for help, oppressed by the immense weight of the coffin; the bishop read sadly, and blundered in the prayers.' The dead king, with his obsessive devotion to the niceties of correct behaviour, would have been appalled. Walpole noticed that only the Duke of Cumberland – the chief mourner and the son George II had loved above all his other children – behaved as his father would have wished. 'His leg extremely bad, yet forced to stand upon it nearly two hours; his face bloated and distorted by his late paralytic stroke … Yet he bore it all with firm and unaffected countenance.'

The same could not be said for the Duke of Newcastle, who had served as the late king's first minister, and whose grief was flamboyantly unconstrained. 'He fell back into a fit of crying the moment he came into the chapel, and flung himself back in his stall, the Archbishop hovering over him with a smelling-bottle.' The sardonic Walpole noticed that Newcastle's distress did not prevent him from surreptitiously making himself as comfortable as he could in cold and clammy circumstances. When Cumberland tried to shift his position, 'feeling himself weighed down, and turning round, he found it was the Duke of Newcastle standing on his train to avoid the chill of the marble.'[2]

For all the incipient disorder that so often overwhelmed even the most sober eighteenth-century spectacles, the final act of the funeral was a moment of genuine pathos. The king had always intended that he would be buried alongside his long-dead wife. Now, as his remains were placed in the grave next to hers, it was apparent that their two coffins had been constructed without sides, so that their bones would eventually mingle. Twenty-three years after her death, George and Caroline were united once more.

Mourning for George II was subdued. His death had been expected for so long – he was seventy-six when he died, the oldest king to sit on the throne since Edward the Confessor – that the public response to it was inevitably muted. The Duke of Newcastle, whose tears were perhaps more heartfelt than Walpole allowed, was one of the few who seemed genuinely moved, declaring that he 'had lost the best king, the best master, the best friend that ever a subject had'.[3] Most other verdicts were distinctly cooler; in many of his obituaries, it was George's least attractive characteristics – his parsimony, his boorishness and his proudly declared lack of intellectual refinement – which featured most prominently. Walpole thought his disdain for the literary world had a very direct and adverse impact on his posthumous reputation, musing that if he had pensioned more writers, he might have enjoyed a better press at the time of his death. As it was, George had never laid himself out to court approval, and his character was not one that attracted easy plaudits or unmixed admiration. In death, as in life, he remained a difficult man to love.

However, there were some among his contemporaries who looked beyond his very visible failings and eccentricities and recognised qualities of greater worth. Lord Waldegrave, once the reluctant governor to the unhappy Prince of Wales, was convinced that with time, 'those specks and blemishes that sully the brightest characters' would be forgotten and George would be remembered as a king 'under whose government the people have enjoyed the greatest happiness'.[4] Elizabeth Montagu, an intellectual with no inherent admiration for kings, was another who praised the late king's somewhat undervalued virtues: 'With him, our laws and liberties were safe; he possessed to a great degree the confidence of his people and the respect of foreign governments; and a certain steadiness of character made him of great consequence in these unsettled times.' He had not, she admitted, been a particularly heroic figure – 'his character would not afford subject for epic poetry' – but she thought him none the worse for that. Indeed, she wondered if his lack of interest in the lofty and the ideal was not his best quality, praising his conviction that 'common sense [was] the best panegyric'.[5]

The old king was certainly not much regretted by the man who succeeded him. Relations between George II and his heir had not been good in the years leading up to his death. The unstoppable ascendancy of Bute had alarmed the king, who distrusted him, and the fervency of the prince's devotion left no room in his emotional life for any other male authority figure. In private, the young George was intimidated and repelled by the king's loud, blustering invective; in his public role, he longed, as had his father before him, to be released from the frustrations which curtailed his political actions as Prince of Wales. Only his grandfather's death could deliver him from this limbo, and he and Bute awaited the inevitable with ill-disguised eagerness. In 1758, when George II fell seriously ill, one observer commented on the excitement with which the prince's household greeted the news, 'how sure' they were 'that it was all over, and in what spirits they were in'.[6]

As his opinion of the king sank ever lower, the prince was determined that there was one area of his life over which his grandfather should have no influence. 'I can never agree to marry whilst this Old Man lives,' he told Bute. 'I will rather undergo anything ever so disagreeable than put my trust in him for a matter of such delicacy.' It was probably for this reason that, even after Bute had decisively scuppered his hopes of marrying Sarah Lennox, he made no public move to find a more acceptable spouse. In private, however, he was more pragmatic, preparing for the inescapable eventuality of an arranged marriage even as he carried on his doomed flirtation with the unattainable Sarah. Safely secluded from any potential interference from his grandfather, the prince had begun to explore more realistic matrimonial prospects. Closeted with his mother, he was spending his evenings 'looking in the *New Berlin Almanack* for princesses, where three new ones have been found, as yet unthought of'.[7]

When the much-anticipated moment of his grandfather's death finally arrived, one of George's first acts was to promote the issue of his marriage to the top of his personal agenda. He had maintained an extraordinary discipline over his desires, but did not intend to wait any longer than was absolutely necessary to become a virtuous and properly satisfied husband. Even before the old king's funeral had taken place, George summoned Baron Munchausen, the Hanoverian minister in London, and instructed him to begin investigating potential candidates for the vacant position of Queen of England.

George had a very clear idea of the kind of woman he was looking for: he hoped to find a helpmeet and a companion who would share his vision of a morally regenerated monarchy, and who would be happy to play her allotted role in his great domestic project. Physical attraction did not rank particularly high on his list of requirements; and he was not interested in women of fashion, influenced perhaps by his great-grandfather's unhappy experience with a high-maintenance beauty. He told Munchausen he hoped his future wife would have a good general understanding, but stipulated she should have no taste for politics. He had no desire to be managed in public life by an intellectual superior, which he suspected had been his grandfather's fate. Not over-confident in the strength of his own character, the attributes he sought in a woman were mild, calm, unassuming ones; but equally he hoped for something more than mere colourless docility. He was keen to find a spouse who would actively appreciate his seriousness of mind, and welcome the continence and discipline which he intended should be the defining qualities of his adult life. A strong religious sense, a deep-rooted understanding of the importance of duty, and a willingness unhesitatingly to identify her interests with his own were also of prime importance. Years before, his mother had rejected a princess proposed by the old king as a possible wife for his grandson: Augusta was concerned the girl would take after her mother, intriguing, meddling and 'the most sarcastical person in the world'. She knew 'such a character would not do for George'. A loud, uncooperative, pleasure-seeking woman 'would not only hurt him in his public life but make him uneasy in his private situation'.[8] George knew his mother was right. If he was to have any chance of reforming kingship from within, a great deal depended on his finding the right wife.

The pool of possibilities was not large: a British king had to marry a Protestant, ruling out an alliance with the great nation states of France and Spain. George II's daughters had taken husbands from Holland and Denmark, and a princess of Denmark was briefly considered, until she was discovered to be already promised, and dropped out of the running. Otherwise, George concentrated his search entirely within German principalities and dukedoms. Germany was the spiritual home of his dynasty; it had provided wives for his father, grandfather and great-grandfather; he was personally related to many of the ducal and princely rulers, and through them could expect to access useful knowledge about the characters and dispositions of potential brides. Germany was not only known territory for George; it was also one in which he was unequivocally the dominant suitor. He was an incomparably attractive catch, ruling a country that was richer and more powerful than most of the small princely states put together. There was little doubt that anyone he approached would consent to his invitation; the only difficulty lay in deciding whom to ask.

When the king first approached him, Munchausen had been able to think of only two princesses who might match his requirements. One, Elizabeth of Brunswick-Wolfenbüttel, was the younger sister of the girl who had been proposed to George as a potential wife by his grandfather several years before, and briskly rejected. Elizabeth was only fourteen, but her youth was only part of the reason George was reluctant to consider her. Her prospects were irrevocably tainted in his eyes by the old king's attempts to bring about the earlier alliance, and he was obstinately prejudiced against the whole family as a result. Munchausen's only other immediate candidate was Frederica Louise of Saxe-Gotha. She was nineteen – a suitable age – and Munchausen had heard many good things about her; however, he felt constrained to add that, like her mother, she was reputed to be very interested in philosophy. George replied with some vehemence that this description made the princess repugnant to him from every point of view.[9] He added that he was not at all discouraged by the shortcomings of these first contenders, assuring Munchausen that, perhaps as a result of his study of the *New Berlin Almanack*, he knew there were many other princesses to consider.

Bute later presented Munchausen with a list, drawn up in George's handwriting, of the marriageable princesses who had caught his eye. Armed with these names, Munchausen was directed to begin the search in earnest. He was told to ask his brother, chief minister in Hanover, to make discreet enquiries about the character and disposition of all the women on the list. Bute emphasised that speed was of the essence. The king wanted the matter resolved as soon as possible, and so, for his own reasons, did Bute. He had seen how severely Sarah Lennox had tried George's determination not to involve himself with women, and understood that marriage could be delayed no longer. Both he and Augusta had done all they could to instil in the young man a deep-seated conviction that it was one of his most important duties to avoid entanglements with designing females, and, responsive as he always was to the pull of obligation, George had so far complied; but both anticipated with apprehension the possible advent of a mistress, with her own agenda to pursue and her own relatives to advance. A lover was thus far more to be feared than a wife, and it was not surprising that Bute confided to Munchausen that he could not be happy until he saw the young king happily married. He dreaded the danger of his being led astray, he told the minister, out of the good way in which he had been at such pains to keep him.[10]

Munchausen's brother, himself an experienced politician, responded immediately to the sense of urgency communicated by both George and Bute and sent back a report containing his initial findings on the front-runners. Frederica of Saxe-Gotha, whose philosophical interests had so dismayed the king, was firmly dismissed: Munchausen had heard she was scarred by smallpox; he confided privately to his brother that she was rumoured to be deformed. More promising was Philippa of Schwedt, sixteen years old and a niece of Frederick the Great. Caroline of Darmstadt was considered to be worth further investigation. Munchausen was keen to keep Elizabeth of Brunswick-Wolfenbüttel as a possibility, despite discouraging signals from the king. She was reputed to be very beautiful. It was true she was young, but Munchausen insisted she was very well developed for her age, although he admitted it might require a proper medical opinion to determine her potential childbearing capacity.[11]

Almost as an afterthought, Munchausen added an idea of his own: Sophia Charlotte, of the tiny duchy of Mecklenburg-Strelitz, looked promising. He had heard she was quiet, unassuming, of unimpeachable respectability, and was said to have been very properly educated by her mother, '*une princesse d'un esprit solide*'. He undertook to find out more about all the princesses, preferably from those who had actually met them, and, if possible, from an Englishman, who might be expected to have a better understanding of the king's taste. His own preference was for the Princesses of Brunswick and Schwedt; he doubted whether any of the others had been brought up in circumstances of sufficient grandeur to prepare them for the role of Queen of England.[12] George and Bute did not entirely agree. Having read Munchausen's report, they instructed him to concentrate on the Princesses of Schwedt, Darmstadt and Mecklenburg-Strelitz, and to consider the Brunswick princess only if all other options failed. Bute told Munchausen her youth counted against her, but Munchausen believed it was the continued association of her family with George II's wishes that had set the king's mind against her. George, it seemed, and as he declared, was determined not to be 'be-Wolfenbüttled'.

It took Munchausen some weeks to complete the next stage of his enquiries, and it was not until January 1761 that a detailed report arrived in London. It put an end to the chances of Philippa of Schwedt.

Although she was said to be handsome, it also described her as '*d'une humeur opiniatre et peu prévenante*': 'stubborn' and 'inconsiderate' were not words George wanted to hear used about a prospective wife, and her name disappeared from his thinking. 'I am under the greatest obligation to your brother,' he told Munchausen. 'What would I have risked if I had not hit upon so honest a man. I now abandon the idea.' That left only the Princesses of Mecklenburg-Strelitz and Darmstadt. Charlotte of Mecklenburg-Strelitz was said to have a very good character, but Munchausen was still anxious that, having been raised in a very small, undistinguished court, she was too provincial to be seriously considered. The king's own preference, at this point, was for Caroline of Darmstadt; if further reports on her were favourable, he confided to Bute that she would be his choice. Meanwhile, he continued to urge haste on everyone concerned. 'The king's longing and impatience increase daily,' Munchausen told his brother, 'and he has today calculated how long it will take for this letter to reach *mon cher frère* and for him to send an answer.'[13]

When the much-awaited dispatch arrived, it was a great disappointment. It had little positive to say about Caroline's character, asserting that her own mother had described her 'as stubborn and ill-tempered to the greatest degree'. The same report was, however, far more encouraging about the other candidate, 'giving a very amiable character of the Princess of Strelitz'. George was encouraged, insisting that he did not share Munchausen's anxieties about the limitations of her upbringing. It was her character that mattered to him, not her background. He told Bute that if she was as sensible as was reported, 'a little of England's air will soon give her the deportment necessary for a British queen'.[14]

The relaxed jocularity of George's tone defined the attitude with which he set about the prosecution of what he called 'my business'. Indeed, as the search for a spouse progressed, there is a definite sense in his correspondence that he was rather enjoying it. For such a timid and inexperienced man, the prospect of making an unhindered choice from a parade of marriageable young women, none of whom was likely to reject him, was clearly an attractive one. In the role of prospective husband, he found a new confidence, secure in his worth and in the power of his position. He had no difficulty in outlining the qualities necessary to satisfy him, nor in rejecting candidates who failed to live up to his very exacting requirements. As a spouse, he intended to be an altogether more assertive character than he had been as a son. In finding the partner he thought he deserved, he showed himself capable of making decisions with none of the anxiety or lethargy that had paralysed his actions in earlier life. This was an enterprise in which George did not intend to fail.

In the spring, the king's search began to move towards a conclusion. In May, Caroline of Darmstadt was finally and decisively eliminated from his thinking, as disturbing new facts emerged about her family. The apparent piety of her father and his court had at first seemed attractive to George, who hoped his wife would share his own strong Christian convictions. But fresh information put a far darker complexion on the family's spiritual pursuits. The king was horrified to learn that the Prince of Darmstadt had been drawn into the orbit of a group of religious visionaries who had driven him to the edge of reason. George had been told that these '*visionnaires*' had 'got about the princess's father, have persuaded him to quit his family in great measure, lest the hereditary princess should prevent their strange schemes; they have brought the prince very near the borders of madness, and draw his money to that degree from him, that his children are often in want of necessaries such as stockings, etc.'. He had also discovered that 'this princess was talked of last year' for another prince, who had 'refused her on account of her strange father and grandfather'.[15] Was George prepared to take a risk another man had already declined?

He brooded for a fortnight, then on 20 May he wrote to Bute with his final decision: 'The family of the Princess of Darmstadt has given me such melancholy thoughts of what may perhaps be in the blood.' The possibility of madness was not an inheritance any ruler wanted to import into his bloodline, and put an end to the candidacy of Caroline of Darmstadt. As a result, the seventeen-year-old Charlotte of Mecklenburg-Strelitz, who had begun as a complete outsider – little more than a chance addition to Munchausen's list – ended up bearing away the crown. 'I trouble my Dearest Friend with the enclosed account of the Princess of Strelitz,' wrote George. 'I own it is not in every particular as I could wish, but yet I am resolved to fix here.'[16]

*

In the eighteenth century, Mecklenburg-Strelitz was considered very much a rural backwater. The duchy was then about the size of Sussex, and in the hierarchy of German princely states was in the second or perhaps even third division. Such was its reputation for mud and provinciality that it was sometimes referred to by heavy-handed contemporary jokers as 'Mecklenburg-Strawlitter'. In 1736, when he was still Crown Prince of Prussia, Frederick the Great paid a surprise call on the Mecklenburg dukes, arriving unannounced at the family castle of Mirow. There was little evidence of the Prussian military discipline that reigned in Berlin. He wrote to his father that, 'Coming on to the drawbridge, I perceived an old stocking-knitter disguised as a grenadier, with his cap, cartridge and musket laid aside so that they might not hinder his knitting.' Gaining access to the castle proved a task in itself. 'After knocking almost half an hour to no purpose, there peered out at last an exceedingly old woman. She was so terrified that she slammed the door in our faces.' When Frederick finally met someone with enough self-possession to take him to the ducal family, he was promptly invited to dinner.

At the duke's table, Frederick was surprised to see some of the ladies darning stockings during the meal.[17] He was even more shocked to discover that sewing was not an activity confined to the female members of the family. The duke himself was a passionate devotee of needlework, said to embroider his own dressing gowns in his spare time, having achieved considerable skill in the art through years of practice. This was an eccentric pursuit for an aristocratic man (Frederick clearly thought it evidence of mild derangement) but neither the duke nor his relatives seemed embarrassed by it. On the contrary, over supper, madness formed the principal subject of discussion. 'At table, there was talk of nothing but of all the German princes who are not right in their wits – as Mirow himself is reputed to be. There was Weimar, Gotha, Waldeck, Hoym and the whole lot brought on the carpet; and after our good host had got considerably drunk, he lovingly promised me that he and his whole family will come to visit me.'[18] It was fortunate for George III's future wife that none of these rumours reached the ears of the king, finely attuned as they were to any hint of inherited mental instability.

This was the world into which Princess Sophia Charlotte was born in 1744. The embroidering duke was her grandfather. Life was quiet for the Mecklenburg family in their compact palace, so small that

Frederick had mistaken it for the parsonage. Charlotte had four brothers and an elder sister, Christiane (who at twenty-five was considered too old to be a wife for the twenty-two-year-old George III). Her father's death, in 1752, when she was only eight, must have disturbed the placid passing of the days, but little else seems to have impacted on an early life distinguished by its lack of event. 'The princess lived in the greatest retirement,' one contemporary observer noted. 'She dressed only in a *robe de chambre*, except on Sundays, on which day she put on her best gown and after service, which was very long, took an airing in a coach and six, attended by guards. She was not yet allowed to dine in public.'[19] Charlotte's mornings were devoted to the reigning family passion, sewing, in one of its many ornamental forms; she was inducted into the discipline of the needle very early, and never lost her taste for it when she was both older and grander. 'Queen Charlotte, as we know, always had her piece of work in hand,' recalled one of her more unctuous biographers. What had been in her grandfather adduced as possible evidence of insanity was regarded in Charlotte as an admirable demonstration of female industry. Her sewing skills, however, did not displace more academically minded pursuits. Charlotte's mother took the education of her daughters seriously, and by the time Charlotte was seven she was already in the schoolroom. The sisters were instructed by Mme de Grabow, a poet whose local fame had earned her the title of 'the German Sappho.'[20] Besides teaching poetic composition and the rudiments of French – then considered an essential part of a polite education – Mme de Grabow also gave lessons in Latin. This was an unusual subject for girls: classical learning was generally considered the exclusive preserve of masculine study. Charlotte and Christiane were also taught theology by a Dr Gentzner, but the study of religion seems to have been secondary to his real passion, which was natural history. He was an accomplished botanist who awakened a similar enthusiasm in Charlotte. From her youth, she was a keen collector of plant specimens, preserving those she found most interesting in voluminous sketch books.

By the time she was in her early teens, Charlotte had already developed the bookish tastes that would stay with her for the rest of her life. She was a voracious reader, devouring serious works of literature, theology and philosophy; whatever she could beg, buy or borrow she would consume with an intensity that belied her otherwise docile demeanour. But her intellectual journeys were undertaken alone. The remoteness of Mecklenburg ensured she had no access to sophisticated thinking of the kind that had so stimulated Queen Caroline. Her parents were committed Lutherans who viewed with deep suspicion any form of study which sought to question the foundations of sacred truths. There was no Leibniz at the small, rural court to stretch her mind, and no protective cadre of like-minded, clever women to encourage her curiosity. Perhaps as a result of her intellectual isolation, Charlotte drew very different conclusions from her reading. Without the debate and provocation that had encouraged Caroline to explore unorthodox opinion, Charlotte's values were unchallenged by what she read. Unlike Caroline, who was always suspected of harbouring suspiciously radical ideas about the truth of revealed religion, Charlotte's intellectual explorations never undermined the traditional beliefs in which she had been so scrupulously raised. Her studies made her a bluestocking,[21] but she was never a *philosophe*. While she immersed herself in the products of the Enlightenment, she did not endorse its implied social and political progressivism. She once returned a copy of one of Voltaire's book to a correspondent, announcing primly: 'I do not want anything more of his.'[22]

Her moral world remained that of her parents and grandparents, in which obligation was more important than personal happiness, and religion was the only meaningful expression of faith. She was a conservative, politically, morally and spiritually, most at ease in the confines of the established order, and unsettled by any attempts to undermine its power. These were qualities which would have appealed very strongly to George, who prized them in himself. Nor would he have been necessarily dismayed by her literary interests. It was not so much intellectual capacity itself which he distrusted in women, as the desire to give it a public, and above all a political, meaning. Charlotte never sought to build a reputation for herself as a clever woman; hers were private passions, pursued with decorous and entirely characteristic self-effacement. Indeed, when Colonel David Graeme, sent by the king to Mecklenburg to begin the formal negotiations for her hand, first met her he was underwhelmed by her accomplishments. He thought she spoke French 'but middling well', and was surprised that she had no knowledge at all of English. He saw too, as Munchausen had warned, she possessed little of the social polish that more urbane girls of her age and status could usually command. That Charlotte had talents, Graeme was sure; he just did not believe they had been fostered as they deserved. Only one of her skills truly impressed him: he was intrigued to discover that she had taught herself to play the glockenspiel, an instrument of which Graeme had never heard. It produced, he explained, 'a bright and agreeable sound'.[23]

Two weeks after George had made his decision to 'fix here', he had instructed Graeme, a friend of Bute's, to set out for the duchy, taking with him the formal offer of marriage. It was a slow journey, the roads 'either overflowing with water or deep sand', and it took Graeme more than a fortnight to get there. When he arrived, he was horrified to find that the widowed Duchess of Mecklenburg, to whom he had been told to explain his mission, was seriously ill. A series of 'violent cramps' had, he wrote to Bute, confined her to bed and 'deprived her of speech'.[24] Graeme carried with him a letter from the Dowager Princess Augusta, proposing her son as a husband for Charlotte. Unable to carry the document directly to the duchess, he entrusted it to Charlotte's sister Christiane, who read it to her sick mother. When Graeme met the rest of the family at dinner later that night, it was plain that everyone now knew about the offer of marriage except the person most concerned by it. They had decided to tell Charlotte nothing, so that 'by having no disturbance in her mind, she would converse more freely', and Graeme could observe her natural behaviour. Unconscious of his scrutiny, Charlotte clearly acquitted herself well and some time after dinner was informed of the possible future that awaited her.

How she responded to this extraordinary announcement is not known. The story that she sat stoically silent, unmoved, without looking up from her sewing, is probably apocryphal. Her family were certainly far less restrained. They recognised what an unlooked-for opportunity had fallen into their laps, and were desperate to grasp it with both hands. Only Christiane must have found it hard to join in the general rejoicing. The terms of the marriage treaty forbade any other member of Charlotte's family from marrying an English subject; having been thwarted in his own desire to marry 'a countrywoman', the king wanted no ambitious British in-laws intriguing from the sidelines. This put an abrupt end to Christiane's romance with the Duke of Roxburghe, who had met her whilst travelling in Germany, and 'had formed an attachment to her which was returned'.[25] Unable to marry each other, neither Christiane nor the duke ever married anyone else. He dedicated his life to the collection of rare books; she became a cloistered royal spinster, an unacknowledged casualty of her younger sister's marital good fortune.

Christiane's fate registered not at all on the rest of the Mecklenburg family, who hastened to reply to a list of questions posed in Augusta's letter. Alongside the formal declarations of the princess's age, religion and availability – her brother eagerly confirmed that she was engaged to no one else – Graeme sent back to London a more intimate report of his own. Intended for the king's eyes, this was in effect a candid, first-hand portrait of Charlotte. Inevitably, it began with an assessment of her looks. No one ever thought Charlotte a beauty, and throughout her life her supposed plainness was remorselessly and woundingly satirised. In middle age, she was depicted in cruel caricatures as a crow-like hag, or a bony, miserly witch, an emaciated spider, all arms, legs and chin. Even as a young woman, she was often described as plain and charmless. Recalling her first arrival in England, the diarist Sylvester Douglas, Lord Glenbervie, thought Charlotte presented a very unappealing figure: 'She was very ill-dressed, and wore neither rouge nor powder … her hair used to be combed tight over a roller, which showed the skin through the roots, than which nothing can be more frightful.'[26]

Graeme's pen portrait of her was more kind. She was very slender, he wrote, and of medium height; her complexion was 'delicate and fine, with an abundance of red, not to be called a high bloom but as much as, in my opinion, there should be at her age, and sufficient to relieve the lustre of a very fine white'. Her hair, one of her best features, was a pale brown. Her nose was acceptable in shape and size, but her mouth, later to attract the delighted attention of the caricaturists, was, he admitted, 'rather large'. She had a little growing still to do. She was just seventeen, and 'the appearance of her person is not quite that of a woman fully formed, nor may it be expected at her age, though the bosom is full enough for her age and person'. She was, he had been told, healthy, and carried herself well, 'the whole figure straight, genteel and easy, all her actions and carriage natural and unaffected'. In conclusion, he declared, as so many others were to later do, that 'she is not a beauty', but 'what is little inferior, she is amiable, and her face rather agreeable than otherwise'.[27]

If Graeme was cautious in his careful evaluation of Charlotte's looks, he was far more effusive in his description of her character. The more time he spent with her, the more he grew to like her. He warmed to her artlessness, and was delighted when she sent him a bowl of cherries as a present. When her sick mother died only days after the marriage offer had been received, Graeme was moved by Charlotte's 'flowing tears'; she confided in him that the duchess's last words had been a wish for her happiness, and declared herself ready 'to render herself worthy of that station ... before tears again stopped her utterance'. Throughout her grief, he noted with approval, she showed 'not the least spark of hauteur'. Her unworldly rectitude amused him. He was amazed to discover with what detail she had researched the services of the Anglican Church before solemnly assuring him that she would have no difficulty in conforming to them. He could not imagine that she could be so seriously attached to 'some inessential points' that they would prevent her 'paving the way to a throne'.[28]

If she was sometimes guilty of taking herself too seriously, this was not the dominant note in her character; as a young woman, Charlotte was lively and even playful in company. Lord Harcourt admitted that 'our queen that is to be' had seen very little of the world, but thought she demonstrated qualities more important than those of sophistication and experience. 'Her good sense, vivacity and cheerfulness, I daresay will recommend her to the king and to the whole British nation.'[29] Charlotte certainly demonstrated a fervent desire to win the approval of both her future husband and her prospective subjects. When the British navy won a victory in the West Indies in July 1761, she wrote enthusiastically to Graeme, describing how she and her sister had danced till midnight to celebrate. Her feelings, she wrote, were exactly those that the wife of the King of Great Britain should be, sharing in the happiness of not just the king himself, 'but of all his worthy nation ... there are times when the heart speaks, and this is how my heart feels this morning'. Graeme forwarded her letter to Bute as proof of her 'frank open heart', adding his hope that 'her good humour and good spirits' should never 'suffer any interruption or change'.[30]

For others, it was her calm good temper that attracted most plaudits. Munchausen, to whom more than anyone she owed her good fortune, was struck by the sweetness of her disposition, if not the polish and sparkle of her conversation. 'It cannot be pretended she should entertain people in a brilliant manner,' he observed, 'but she is gracious and kind to everyone.' He noticed that her servants and entourage adored her and that 'never since her tenderest childhood did she arouse in anyone the slightest ill humour'.[31] Charlotte's marriage prospects had plucked her from obscurity and made her an object of political interest to other European states. Baron Wrangel, a Swedish diplomat reporting on her to his government, painted a similar picture of placid good temper and innocence. 'She has a good and generous heart ... but no idea of the value of money.' She spent a lot of her time with servants, and was unguarded in her conversations with them, a fact that might, he thought, be used to gather intelligence about her; but she was not herself either a strategist or schemer. 'She has no knowledge of politics, and no idea of intrigues, or of the interests of princes.' That, he believed, was one of the reasons she had been chosen, since 'she will never involve Britain in the affairs of the Continent'.[32] To some extent, Wrangel was correct in his analysis. The relative insignificance of Mecklenburg meant that in marrying one of its princesses, George was unlikely to become embroiled in the complicated pattern of alliance and dispute that dominated relationships between the larger and more powerful German princely states.

But it was Charlotte's character as much as her dynastic neutrality that consolidated her appeal for the king. It was her simplicity, upon which all who met her commented with such approval, her lack of sophistication, of contention or wilfulness, that commended her most strongly to Graeme and, through his reports, to her future husband. Young, inexperienced, untutored in the ways of courts or politics, her naivety emerged not as the disadvantage Munchausen had feared, but as her most powerfully attractive quality, an enticingly blank page for a man to write upon. She was 'mild', 'soft and pliable', Graeme enthused, 'capable of taking any impression, of being moulded into any form'.[33] Little similar flexibility was to be expected from her husband, who saw himself as the secure stake around which his wife would twine. George would supply the worldly judgement and direction their relationship would require; he did not hope or wish to find such qualities in his wife. Charlotte's lack of looks, money, sophistication and influence counted for nothing; on the contrary, they amplified the key promise of her pliability – and it was that which ultimately secured her the crown.

'The more I resolve in my mind the affair, the more I wish to have it immediately concluded,' wrote George to Bute at the end of June. Now he had made his choice, he was impatient to be married; but he was also keen to spare his bride the prospect of having to face both coronation and wedding services in intimidating succession. The coronation was planned for September. He hoped Charlotte could arrive in London a month beforehand, allowing time for the wedding and a short honeymoon. With no time to lose, the machinery of government and protocol was put in motion, and the Privy Council was summoned to meet on 8 July. When they assembled, they were informed of the king's intention 'to demand in marriage the Princess of Mecklenburg-Strelitz, a princess distinguished by every eminent virtue and amiable endowment'. This was the meeting that so shocked Henry Fox and put an abrupt end to Sarah Lennox's royal romance. It caught even the unflappable Walpole by surprise, and as a result he had only the baldest news about the impending nuptials to pass on to his extensive network of correspondents. 'All I can tell you of truth is that Lord Harcourt goes to fetch the princess and comes back as her Master of the Horse. She is to be here in August, and the coronation on the 22nd September.'[34]

The choice of Lord Harcourt as the official charged with negotiating the marriage treaty, and bringing Charlotte to her new home in England, was surprising – Harcourt himself confessed that 'this office I expected about as much as I did the Bishopric of London, then vacant'. His last contact with the king had been as his louche and ineffectual governor, when George was Prince of Wales. It was Harcourt who had so successfully and infuriatingly given the dowager princess the repeated brush-off, despite all her persistent attempts to pin him down and find out exactly what he was doing with her son. It was a mystery to everyone why George had chosen him, but somehow fitting that the appointment seems to have arisen from what Harcourt had not done rather than as the result of some more positive action. The king was said to have told Harcourt that as he was the only man not to have solicited him for a place when he inherited the throne, he had always had it in mind to do something for him. It was definitely a plum of a job; Harcourt was given the title Master of the Horse to the new queen's household, and was granted the huge sum of £4,000 to pay for his trip.

He arrived in Strelitz on 14 July. The next day, final details were agreed and the marriage treaty was 'despatched away to England'. Harcourt was pleased to see how hard the ducal family had exerted themselves to mark the occasion and was particularly impressed by a grand banquet, held the night the treaty was signed. The palace and gardens were lit with 40,000 lamps; even the small town of Neustrelitz illuminated its lanes and backstreets to celebrate. To conclude the event, Charlotte made a speech of thanks which ended with a formal leave-taking of her family. It 'so forcibly impressed many of the bystanders that their wet cheeks could only tell what they felt'. Colonel Graeme – who was among the damp-eyed spectators – was moved to uncharacteristic emotion, writing to Bute that he was convinced 'no marriage can afford a greater prospect of happiness'.[35] When the day came to leave, Charlotte departed in great style. Lord Harcourt's carriage led the way, followed by Charlotte's; in the third carriage came 'the ladies', including two '*femmes des chambres*', Juliana Schwellenberg and Johanna Hagerdorn. George had been reluctant to allow Charlotte to bring any of her old servants with her to England. 'I own I hope they will be quiet people,' he told Bute gloomily, 'for by my own experience I have seen these women meddle much more than they ought to do.'[36]

Back in London, the king's enthusiasm mounted daily. He had acquired a portrait of Charlotte and was said to be 'mighty fond of it, but won't let any mortal look at it'.[37] Although George had little interest in fashion, he concerned himself in the provision of a suitable wardrobe for his bride. 'Graeme ought to get a very exact measure of her,' he told Bute, 'accompanied with a very explicit account of every particular, that her clothes may be made here.'[38] He knew that the styles of a remote German court would not survive the critical scrutiny of the London beau monde. The usual method of ordering clothes by proxy was to send one's stays to the dressmaker, who would use them as a form of measurement, but such was the austerity of Charlotte's upbringing that she had only a single pair, which clearly could not be spared. Graeme sent her measurements instead, passing them on to Lady Bute, who was to ensure that new gowns – and presumably a few extra pairs of stays – would be waiting for Charlotte when she arrived in England.

The atmosphere of apprehension and excitement in London had reached fever pitch well before Charlotte had even set out from Mecklenburg. The announcement of the royal wedding had been followed by news of a great victory in India, where the British and French were contesting for supremacy in the subcontinent. The capture of Pondicherry, the principal French base in the south, marked a decisive upturn in British fortunes, and had inflamed the national mood of manic self-congratulation even further. Even the usually detached Walpole was caught up in the celebratory atmosphere. 'I don't know where I am,' he confessed. 'It is all royal marriages, coronations and victories; they come tumbling so over one another from distant parts of the globe that it looks just like the handiwork of a lady romance writer to whom it costs nothing but a little false geography to make the Great Mogul fall in love with a Princess of Mecklenburg and defeat two marshals of France as he rides post on an elephant to his nuptials.'[39]

The man at the centre of the mounting excitement sought to sublimate his eager impatience into practical organisation. George began to assemble the Hanoverian family jewels so they could be worn by his new wife, paying his uncle the Duke of Cumberland £50,000 to buy out Cumberland's share of his inheritance. The result was a collection of extraordinary richness. At the end of July, the Duchess of Northumberland was granted a discreet opportunity to examine it by Lady Bute, who had temporary custody of it, presumably in her role as the overseer of Charlotte's trousseau. The duchess, a wealthy woman well supplied with jewels of her own, was astonished by what she saw. 'There are an amazing number of pearls of a most beautiful colour and prodigious size. There are diamonds for the facings and robings of her gown, set in sprigs of flowers; her earrings are three drops, the diamonds of an immense size and fine water. The necklace consists of large brilliants set around … The middle drop of the earring costs £12,000.'[40]

George also appointed a household for his wife-to-be, a substantial establishment that included six Ladies of the Bedchamber, six Maids of Honour and six lower-ranking waiting women. The future queen was also provided with chamberlains, pages, gentleman ushers, surgeons, apothecaries, 'an operator for teeth' and two 'necessary women'. As well as a Master of the Horse, other staff included a treasurer, law officers and her own band of German musicians. At the top of this structure, he placed two intimidating women: the Duchess of Ancaster was to be Mistress of the Robes, the Duchess of Hamilton, Lady of the Bedchamber. Both were experienced beauties, veterans of court life, worldly sophisticates who might not have been the obvious choices to reassure and support a callow seventeen-year-old on her first arrival in a strange country; they were, in effect, Charlotte's introduction to the female world in which she would now be expected to make a life for herself, for the king had charged them with the task of crossing the Channel and accompanying the future queen home. Neither duchess was very happy about the idea, and neither proved the easiest of passengers. The Duchess of Hamilton insisted that her tame ass should accompany her on the journey, so that she should not be deprived of the medicinal benefits of its milk. 'The Duchess of Ancaster,' Walpole noted, 'only takes a surgeon and a midwife, as she is breeding and subject to hysteric fits.'[41]

The fleet assembled to carry the reluctant duchesses across to Germany sailed from Harwich and arrived at the mouth of the Elbe on 14 August 1761. On the 22nd, Charlotte was ready to embark. She had no experience of the sea – indeed, she had probably never seen it before – and therefore little idea what to expect on her journey. Her first voyage turned out to be anything but a smooth one. The weather was bad from the beginning, with gales, rain and thunder making the small fleet's progress slow and haphazard. As the days went on with no sign of the English coast, the discomfort of the journey took its toll, and the duchesses were soon observed 'to be very much out of order'; however, a very different story was told of Charlotte's response to the ordeal.[42] 'The queen was not at all affected with the storm, but bore the sea like a truly British queen,' gushed one contemporary press account; Walpole heard that she had been 'sick but half an hour; sung and played on the harpsichord all the voyage, and been cheerful the whole time.'[43]

In reality, Charlotte seems to have found the voyage just as prostrating as all the other passengers. When Lord Anson, who captained the *Royal Charlotte*, finally arrived in Harwich on 7 September, he wrote immediately to the Admiralty explaining that 'the princess being much fatigued made it absolutely necessary to land her royal highness here', and plans for a triumphal procession up the Thames to London were quietly abandoned. From Harwich she travelled to Colchester, where she was presented with a gift of candied eringo root – a kind of sea holly – which must have given her a rather strange idea of what was considered a delicacy in her new homeland. She spent the night at the home of Lord Abercorn in Witham, where she ate her first formal English dinner, with Lord Harcourt standing on one side of her chair and Lord Anson on the other, and the door 'wide open, that everybody might have the pleasure and satisfaction of seeing her.'[44]

After that, it was onwards to London, to St James's Palace and her destiny. The marriage ceremony was to take place that very evening. No wonder that, as her destination approached, she had little to say. 'When she caught the first glimpse of the palace, she grew frightened and turned pale; the Duchess of Hamilton smiled – the princess said, "My dear Duchess, you may laugh, you have been married twice but it is no joke to me."'[45]

There was little time for reflection. As soon as her arrival in town had been confirmed, all the city's pent-up desire for celebration exploded into a cacophony of sound. 'Madame Charlotte is this instant arrived!' scribbled Walpole as a delighted postscript to one of his omnipresent letters. 'The noise of coaches, chaises, horsemen, mob that have been to see her pass through the parks is so prodigious that I cannot distinguish the guns. I am going to be dressed, and before seven shall launch into the crowd. Pray for me!'[46] Walpole was not the only well-connected spectator determined to satisfy his curiosity. Everyone wanted to see the first meeting of the king and the princess. The Countess of Harrington watched it from over her garden wall, and passed on what she had seen to the Countess of Kildare, who in turn described it to her husband. Introduced to the king, Charlotte 'threw herself at his feet, he raised her up, embraced her and led her through the garden up the steps into the palace'.[47]

Some later reminiscences asserted that at the moment of their meeting, the king had been shocked by Charlotte's appearance. 'At the first sight of the German princess,' wrote one particularly hostile commentator, 'the king actually shrank from her gaze, for her countenance was of that cast that too plainly told of the nature of the spirit working within.'[48] Yet there is no suggestion in any contemporary account that George was disappointed in what he saw. Walpole, never disposed to be charitable, described Charlotte on first seeing her as 'sensible, cheerful and … remarkably genteel'.[49]

After the formal greetings, George led Charlotte into St James's to present her to his family. In pride of place was his mother Augusta; also present were his three sisters and three brothers, and his uncle, the Duke of Cumberland, welcomed back into the family now that his nephew sat securely on his throne. Charlotte was conducted to a lavish dinner which included partridges stuffed with truffles, venison in pastry, and sweetbreads. While the royals ate, the court began to assemble in preparation for the wedding ceremony. Most, including

Walpole and the Duchess of Northumberland, arrived at around seven o'clock. They had a long wait, on an exceptionally hot evening.

'The night was sultry,' wrote Walpole, dashing off his impressions of the event. 'About ten, the procession began to move towards the chapel and at eleven they all came into the Drawing Room.'[50] Then Charlotte appeared for the first time in a public role in England, dressed in an elaborate wedding gown which was subjected to a scrutiny almost as intense as that directed upon her looks. The dress was made of silver tissue, trimmed with silver and covered with diamonds, set off with a little cap of purple velvet. But for all its magnificence, Charlotte's outfit was a very poor fit; clearly, the measurements sent across from Mecklenburg had proved no substitute for the more accurate sizing that stays would have provided. The dress, burdened with heavy jewels, was far too large for Charlotte's slender frame. It was of course Walpole who recorded that her 'violet velvet mantle ... which was attempted to be fastened on her shoulders by a bunch of pearls dragged itself and almost the rest of her clothes halfway down her waist.'[51] The unhappy result was that 'the spectators knew as much of her upper half as the king himself'.[52]

Struggling with her clothes, the princess was led by the Duke of York through the assembled crowd of courtiers towards the chapel where the wedding was to take place. As she made her way, her nerve began to fail her and her hands shook. 'Courage, Princess, courage,' urged the duke.[53] An even more intimidating experience followed, as she was plunged into a heaving rout of intensely curious strangers. She had enough self-possession to kiss the peeresses, as etiquette demanded, but Lady Augusta, the king's sister, was 'forced to take her hand and give it to those who were to kiss it'.[54]

In a reversal of tradition, protocol demanded that the princess arrive first at the altar and wait for the king. When he entered, the service began. It was conducted in English, as George had required. The Archbishop of Canterbury later remembered: 'I called on him and the queen only by their Christian names. When I asked them the proper question, the king answered solemnly, laying his hand on his breast, and suggested to her to answer, "*Ich will*," which she did: but spoke audibly in no other part of the service.'[55] The marriage began as it was to continue, with George instructing his wife while she remained silent.

'The instant the king put on the ring,' reported the Duchess of Northumberland, 'a rocket was let fly from the top of the chapel as a signal for the discharge of the Park and Tower guns, which were immediately fired.' The princess had rallied somewhat. 'She talks a great deal,' observed Walpole, 'is easy, civil, and not disconcerted.' Her French, he thought, was only 'tolerable' but 'she exchanged much of that, and also of German, with the king and the Duke of York.'[56] She was also able to display her other accomplishments. 'The royal supper not being ready, the queen (at the king's request) played very prettily on the harpsichord,' and sang to the assembled family, who did not, the duchess had been told, 'get to bed till three in the morning.'[57]

To Charlotte, brought up in the staid uneventfulness of Mecklenburg, the day must have seemed as if it would never end. At its close, however, she was spared the ordeal endured by Augusta, her new mother-in-law, and other princesses before her. When she and the king entered their bedroom, they did so alone, and closed the door behind them. Their marriage was undeniably a public event, but what happened afterwards was private, with none of the public ribaldry that had accompanied George's parents on their wedding night. Walpole heard that the abandonment of the old rituals had been at Charlotte's insistence. 'The queen was very averse to going to bed, and at last articled that no one should retire with her but the Princess of Wales, and her two German women, and that no one should be admitted afterwards but the king.' When the dowager princess returned from the couple's bedchamber, she asked the Duke of Cumberland to sit with her for a while. The duke was tired and tetchy, and refused with bad grace. 'What should I stay for?' he demanded. 'If she cries out, I cannot help her.'[58]

Later, George and Charlotte were to find it much harder to navigate their way through the imprecise distinctions between the two dimensions of royal life – that which they inhabited as man and wife, and that which they occupied as king and queen – but the privacy of their first night together was a declaration of the optimism with which the pair entered the marriage state. Their union would not be like those of their predecessors: it would start in the way it was meant to go on – as a genuine partnership, forged in private intimacy.

*

The day after the wedding, Charlotte was presented at an official Drawing Room, designed to introduce her to the great and the good of the court. Walpole thought that George seemed in great spirits and delighted with his wife, talking to her 'continually, with the greatest good humour. It does not promise,' he noted with rare generosity, 'as if they two would be the most unhappy persons in England, from this event.'[59] A celebration ball was held that night where, according to the Duchess of Northumberland, 'everything was vastly well conducted; nor was it too hot, notwithstanding there were a vast many people, all very magnificently dressed'. In the midst of the minuets and country dances, the duchess was touched to see the king doing all he could to please his new wife. 'His Majesty this evening showed the most engaging attention towards the queen, even the taking of snuff (of which Her Majesty is very fond) which he detests and it made him sneeze prodigiously.'[60] At a second Drawing Room the following day, the duchess heard from George himself how very pleased he was. 'The king this day did me the honour to tell me that he thought himself too happy.'[61]

Gradually, Charlotte began to relax a little. Even the news that the aged, half-blind, Jacobite Earl of Westmorland had mistaken Sarah Lennox for the queen and tried to kiss her hand in error did not cast a pall over the proceedings. Sarah had pulled back her hand in horror, declaring, 'I am not the queen, sir!' 'No,' declared one wit, 'she is only the Pretender.'

None of this seems to have disturbed Charlotte's increasing assurance. She was even confident enough to turn a small social embarrassment into a mild joke. As the Duchess of Northumberland and other ladies 'attended Her Majesty back to her dressing room, her train caught the fender and drew it into the middle of the room. I disengaged her. She laughed very heartily and told me a droll story of the Princess of Prussia having drawn a lighted billet out of the chimney and carrying it through the apartment, firing the mat all the way.'[62]

'You don't presume to suppose, I hope,' wrote Walpole to a distant correspondent a few days after the wedding, 'that we are thinking of you, and wars and misfortunes and distresses in these festival times. Mr Pitt himself would be mobbed if he talked of anything but clothes and diamonds and bridesmaids.'[63] With the first round of ceremonies over, the royal couple spent a few days taking trips to Richmond and Kew. They clearly enjoyed themselves, since they were to return in later life, spending many summers at Kew, and establishing their growing family there, in what was regarded as a healthy rural outpost of London.

While they admired the views of the Thames, and the gardens William Kent had designed for George's grandmother Queen Caroline, elsewhere the preparations for the coronation continued apace. Walpole, whose appetite for royal ceremony was all but sated, complained of 'the gabble one heard about it for six weeks before', and referred to the whole event as 'a puppet show', but could not entirely divorce himself from the rising tide of excitement. 'If I was to entitle ages, I would call this the century of crowds,' he mused as people from across the country began to flood into London.[64]

*

Coronation Day began early. The Duchess of Northumberland 'rose at half past four, went to the queen's apartment at Westminster'. There she found Charlotte, once more weighed down with jewels, dressed with stiff formality complete with mother-of-pearl fan, but with her hair worn girlishly loose, discreetly supplemented with 'coronation locks', a false hair piece that had cost six guineas.[65]

The event opened with a procession from Westminster Hall to the abbey. When George and Charlotte arrived at the abbey door it was immediately clear that the ceremony promised to be just as chaotic as the late king's funeral. From the outset, nothing ran to plan, or to time. Many key props were missing: 'In the morning, they had forgot the sword of state, the chairs for the king and queen and their canopies.' When the king complained about the poor management, the Earl Marshal, who was responsible for organising the day, promised him solemnly that 'the next coronation would be regulated in the most exact manner imaginable'.[66] Gradually, however, things began to fall into place. At the abbey, the king's entry was greeted by the choir of Westminster School, who sang '*Vivat Regina Charlotte!*' and '*Vivat Georgius Rex!*' 'There was all sorts of music,' enthused one spectator, who had travelled down from Yorkshire for the day. 'It was a grand sound.'[67]

Alongside the nobility and courtiers, the abbey was packed with more ordinary visitors who had squeezed themselves into its precincts with the settled intention of enjoying every moment of what promised to be a long and satisfying day. One of those was the young William Hickey, whose father, a prosperous City lawyer, 'had engaged one of the nunneries, as they are called, in Westminster Abbey, for which he paid fifty guineas'.[68] The Hickey family was stationed in a panelled bolt-hole right up in the roof, from which they commanded 'an admirable view of the whole interior of the building'. They had anticipated the affair would be a long one, and had therefore arrived properly prepared. 'Provisions, consisting of cold fowls, ham, tongues, different meat pies, wines and liquors of various sorts were sent into the apartment the day before, and two servants were allowed to attend.' The twelve-strong party had found it an ordeal just getting to the abbey at all. 'Opposite the Horse Guards, we were stopped exactly an hour without moving a single inch. As we approached the abbey, the difficulties increased.' Crushed together by the crowds, coaches were constantly 'running against each other, whereby glasses and panels were demolished without number, the noise of which, accompanied by the screeches of the terrified ladies, was at times truly terrific'. The Hickey family took six hours to get to their niche, where they were glad to find 'a hot and comfortable breakfast waiting for us all'.

Some five hours later, at one o'clock, the king and queen at last arrived. Hickey had 'a capital view' of the actual crowning, but like almost everyone else in the abbey, he could not hear a word of what the archbishop was saying, and so decided that this was the perfect opportunity to enjoy lunch. 'As many thousands were out of the possibility of hearing a single syllable, they took that opportunity to eat their meal, when the general clattering of knives, forks, plates and glasses that ensued, produced a most ridiculous effect, and a universal bout of laughter followed.'[69]

Whatever else had been overlooked, some provision had been made for the more basic needs of the ceremony's principal players. For Walpole, 'of all the incidents of the day, perhaps the most diverting was what happened to the queen. She had a retiring chamber, with all the conveniences, prepared behind the altar. She went thither – in the most convenient, what found she but – the Duke of Newcastle!'[70] After about five hours, the coronation was finally over. The procession assembled again and, at about six o'clock, marched back to Westminster Hall for the banquet. The Duchess of Northumberland found the walk back through the dark and cold extremely trying. She was impatient for a meal, which she felt was now long overdue. 'No dinner to eat ... instead of profusion of geese etc., not wherewithal to fill one's belly.'[71] The coronation's organisers had planned the long delays as a prelude to a gesture intended to amaze the guests as they re-entered

Westminster Hall. More than 3,000 candles had been suspended from the ceiling of the hall; they were designed to be illuminated instantly by a complicated system of flax tapers, but the whole enterprise almost ended in disaster. The poet Thomas Gray, who was sitting in the hall, described how 'the instant the queen's canopy entered, fire was given to all the lustres at once by trains of prepared flax, that reached from one to another'; then, 'it rained fire upon the heads of nearly all the spectators (the flax falling in large flakes) and the ladies (queen and all) were in no small terrors'.[72]

As the guests brushed the charred remnants of flax out of their clothes and hair, there was plenty to distract them. The banquet finally arrived – three services of over a hundred dishes – and the royal party devoted themselves to their food. Gray noticed that the king and queen 'both eat like farmers', as they tucked into the venison served to them on gold plates. As nothing had been provided for the many spectators to eat, baskets and knotted handkerchiefs were lowered from the crowded balconies, and heaved back up weighted down with cold chickens or bottles of wine. For the second time during the Coronation Day, the event had turned into an informal shared feast.

When the banquet was over, the king and queen returned to St James's Palace to share a prosaic supper of bread and milk with a little gruel. There seems little doubt they did so with quiet, unaffected relief. In the previous few weeks, Charlotte had acquitted herself as well as anyone could expect. She had travelled across Europe to marry a stranger, and found him to be neither cold prig nor louche debauchee, but instead a serious, steady young man who had so far treated her with nothing but respectful affection. He, for his part, had found for himself a woman who, if she was neither a great beauty nor overburdened with fashionable accomplishments, had so far displayed a gratifying willingness to admire, esteem and obey him. No wonder the king was pleased.

In early September, when Charlotte, as yet unseen by him, was still crossing the turbulent North Sea, George had written hopefully to Bute, 'I now think my domestic happiness [is] in my own power.'[73] Now that the idea of a wife had turned into the reality of Charlotte, he was even more confident that married life, so long anticipated, would deliver everything he expected from it.

CHAPTER 5

A Modern Marriage

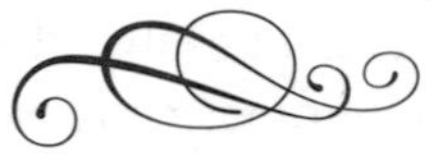

THE CARE WITH WHICH GEORGE had chosen his wife was a measure of the optimism with which he viewed the prospects for his marriage. He had always intended that it should be more than a purely dynastic union. Unlike so many of his royal predecessors, he was determined to find within it a personal happiness which would enrich and transform his private life. But he also hoped that his relationship with his new queen would have a public meaning too. It was central to his mission as king to set an example of virtuous behaviour that could inspire his subjects to replicate it in their own lives. The conduct of his marriage would be the strongest possible declaration of the principles in which he believed, a beacon of right-thinking and good practice which would illustrate in the most personal way what could be achieved when consideration, kindness and respect were established at the heart of the conjugal experience. In pursuing this ideal, George was not alone. Many other young couples of his generation sought to find in their marriages the qualities of affection and loyalty the king set out to achieve in his own partnership. In his attitude to this most important relationship, George was perhaps less royally unique and more reflective of the aspirations of many of his subjects than in almost any other dimension of his life.

This was not, however, always apparent in the marital practices of those closest to the king in social status. Among the upper reaches of the aristocracy, instances abounded of married couples displaying spectacular and well-publicised indifference to any of the established standards of moral probity. Plutocratic levels of wealth and a blithe sense of entitlement fostered a serene disregard for the marital conventions that regulated the actions of poorer, smaller people. The great aristocrats made their own rules. Lady Harley, the Countess of Oxford, had so many children by so many different lovers that her brood was dubbed the Harleian Miscellany, after the famous collection of antiquarian books. Her husband was unperturbed by her affairs, declaring that he found her 'frank candour' to be 'so amiable' that he entirely forgave her.[1] In the Pembroke marriage, it was the earl who was the unfaithful partner, eloping with his mistress but sending the baby boy produced by the liaison back to the family home, where he was affectionately cared for by Pembroke's much-tried countess.

A higher-profile example of marital conventions turned upside down was the talk of the country for most of its thirty-year duration. The relationship between the 5th Duke of Devonshire and his duchess, Georgiana, was a crowded one by any standards, including not only the ducal husband and wife but also Elizabeth Foster, who joined the Devonshire household as the duchess's best friend – some said lover – and eventually came to preside over it as the duke's acknowledged mistress, the mother of two of his children and, after Georgiana's death, his second wife. Unlike the long-suffering Lady Pembroke, who Horace Walpole thought had all the purity of a Madonna, Georgiana pursued her own relationships, most notably with the politician Charles Grey, by whom she had a daughter. The baby was raised by Grey's parents, but Georgiana's legitimate children were brought up at Chatsworth alongside those of her husband and his mistress.

For all its very public indifference to accepted standards, the Devonshire marriage came to an end in the traditional way, with the death of one of the partners. This was not the case with a relationship whose noisy dissolution scandalised a mesmerised public, and seemed to some outraged observers to have rewarded bad behaviour on all sides. The union of the Duke and Duchess of Grafton was a typical elite match. Augustus Fitzroy was heir to the Grafton dukedom; Anne Liddell was a rich man's daughter who brought a huge dowry of £40,000 to her new husband. It looked as though money had been the prime consideration in arranging the marriage, but the duchess claimed that she and the duke had been very much in love when first married in 1756. Whatever had brought them together, the Graftons were not happy for long. The duchess was soon complaining of the duke's gambling, drinking and adultery, and, perhaps hoping to shock him into better behaviour, she left him and retreated to her father's house. It proved a huge miscalculation on her part. Grafton immediately took up with Nancy Parsons, described by Horace Walpole as 'a girl distinguished by a most uncommon degree of prostitution', who was said to have earned a hundred guineas in a single week 'from different lovers, at a guinea a head'.[2] The duchess asked for, and received, a formal separation, whereupon the duke installed Nancy Parsons in her rooms and allowed her to wear the duchess's jewels and preside over her dinner table.

As a separated woman, only the most unimpeachable conduct would have shored up the duchess's tottering reputation; but she was only twenty-eight in 1765, and perhaps felt it was a little early to retire from the world, especially given the humiliating way in which she had been replaced by Nancy Parsons. Soon her 'flirtations' were the subject of disapproving gossip. She dallied with the Duke of Portland, who married someone else without telling her first. Then, in 1767, she met the Earl of Ossory at Brighton. They began an affair, and she found herself pregnant with his child. Despite his own well-publicised adultery, Grafton was outraged; perhaps his recent appointment as first minister had hardened his usually fluid moral resolve. He prosecuted the duchess for adultery and won. She was persuaded not to countersue in return for a generous allowance, and her agreement to hand over into Grafton's care the children from their marriage, who were taken from her as she lay in bed about to give birth to Ossory's baby. The Graftons were divorced by an Act of Parliament in 1769; three days later, the duchess married Ossory.

It was this last chapter in the duchess's chequered story that provoked most disapproval from guardians of conventional values. Princess Amelia, George II's plain-speaking spinster daughter, observed grimly that 'the frequency of these things amongst people of the highest rank had become a reproach to the nation'. She particularly objected to the duchess's remarriage, as it suggested that an adulterous affair could be transformed, via the agency of divorce, into a state of respectable matrimony. Princess Amelia was not the only member of the royal family who disapproved, especially when the reputation to be washed clean was that of the woman involved. The courtier and diarist Lady Mary Coke overheard the king ask the Lord Chancellor, the country's most senior legal officer, whether 'something might be thought of that would prevent the very bad conduct of the ladies, of which there had been very many instances lately'. Later she heard a rumour that 'His Majesty proposed a bill should be brought in, to prevent ladies divorced from their husbands from marrying again'.[3]

In the event, nothing more was heard of the king's desire to enforce female fidelity through parliamentary legislation, but George did all he could, by every other means at his disposal, to signal his distaste for the brittle, serial immorality practised so flamboyantly by so many of his loose-living aristocratic peers. The image of the worldly, sophisticated womaniser who took his pleasure with insouciant disregard for his marriage vows had been extremely attractive to George's father and grandfather, both of whom believed that their masculinity was enhanced by the tang of a little adultery; but George was immune to its appeal. He conformed to a very different eighteenth-century type, and, as a result, looked towards a very different vision of the married state. As the historian Amanda Vickery has shown, not all eighteenth-century men were amoral pleasure-seekers, drawing their gratification from the bottle, the hunt or the gaming table, believing, as Horace Walpole wrote of the Duke of Grafton, that 'the world should be postponed for a whore and a horse-race'.[4]

For many sober, conscientious, diligent young men, it was not through such expensive and ephemeral amusements that they hoped to establish their identity and position in the world; it was marriage with some respectable young woman which would allow them truly to come into their own and make their way in life. Marriage was not a burden to be endured, a restraint to be kicked against, but a prize towards which they endlessly planned and schemed. 'My imagination was excited with pleasurable ideas of what was coming,' wrote one eager groom for whom the longed-for day was at last in sight; 'There was not one thing on earth which gave me the slightest anxiety or doubt! Nothing but a delightful anticipation of happiness and independence!'[5] The yearning to find the right wife, with whom they could establish a home and raise a family, was, for men like these, an all-consuming desire, its achievement a source of lasting satisfaction.

Their outlook was one with which George III instinctively identified. He was socially conservative, sexually restrained, dutiful, exacting and often painfully self-aware. He was also loyal, decent and hungry for emotional warmth, if supplied on his own terms, and by a woman who would not intimidate or overwhelm him. The template towards which he was drawn, both by his character and his sense of his public mission, placed wedlock at the very pinnacle of human emotional experience. 'This state,' wrote the clergyman Wetenhall Wilkes in a bestselling pamphlet first published in 1741, and still in print when George and Charlotte were married twenty years later, 'is the completest image of heaven we can ever receive in this life, productive of the greatest pleasures we can enjoy on this earth.'[6]

This was a vision of matrimony in which, whilst considerations of property and money were not ignored, it was the harmony of the couple at its centre that mattered most. It was a union into which both partners entered willingly, with an equal commitment to making it work, a marital joint-enterprise in which husband and wife were both prepared to sacrifice individual needs and desires in order to secure the success of the wider family project. Both were prepared to involve themselves in the interests of the other, since shared tastes and mutually satisfying pursuits were considered to be the strongest bedrock upon which a happy marriage rested. Inside the partnership, the most propitious emotional climate was considered to be one of steady affection rather than volcanic eruptions of feeling. A firm endeavour to please was thought more significant than physical attraction, and generosity of spirit and mildness of temper most important of all.

The degree to which this model of matrimony – once dubbed by academics 'the companionate marriage' – was a new phenomenon which emerged in the mid-eighteenth century has been one of the most hotly contested debates in social history in recent years. Little credence is now given to the once widely accepted assertion that, before this date, most marriages were cold, commercial contracts, dominated by financial considerations, arranged by parents, and with little room within their bounds for affection. Nor is it now generally accepted that after about 1750 there was a universal warming up of the married state, with love becoming the principal basis for entering into wedlock. But whilst, in practice, marriage continued to contain within itself examples of success and failure, the concern to get things right, to try to identify the best possible preconditions for a stable and lasting relationship, was an obsessive preoccupation of many eighteenth-century writers, thinkers and moralists.

In the latter years of the eighteenth century, the poets and novelists of the Romantic movement celebrated the wilder transports of feeling as the means by which lovers underwent the most transcendent of human experiences, but an earlier generation took a more sceptical view. Most were concerned to balance the appeal of romantic love with a more pragmatic assessment of what made marriage work. Every mid-century writer offering advice to young people insisted that, despite what novels told them, unbridled passion was not a suitable foundation on which to build a stable relationship. Love, of the more turbulent kind at least, was a transient affair, not to be confused with the more solid virtues of lasting affection. They distrusted what they regarded as disorderly and disruptive emotions. The kind of desire later so powerfully celebrated by the Brontë sisters, which hurtled through ordinary life like a disruptive hurricane, was not at all to the taste of earlier moralists, who disapproved of its intemperate volatility and thought it a most unsuitable basis for the long-haul demands of married life. 'When you are of an age to think of settling,' wrote one mother to her daughter in an entirely typical example of maternal advice, 'let your attentions be placed in a sober, steady, religious man who will be tender and careful of you at all times.'[7]

A sensible parent would always have preferred the unexciting virtues of a George III – kindly, decent, disciplined – to the febrile glamour of a Grafton. In a society where only the richest and most powerful were able to contemplate divorce, choosing a suitable spouse was a matter of enormous significance. The perils involved in finding the right man is the subject of every one of Jane Austen's books, whose plots usually turn on the difficulties of distinguishing the genuinely worthy candidate from competitors of greater superficial attraction but less true value. To amplify the pitfalls, her novels usually feature a bitter portrait of an ill-matched couple, with *Pride and Prejudice*'s Mr and Mrs Bennett perhaps the most poignant example of the destructive effects of the fateful attraction of opposites. As Austen understood, there were no second chances in Georgian marital experience, except those supplied by the capricious agency of death.

If it was a good idea to choose a partner by the application of sense rather than sensibility, it was just as important to have a realistic expectation of what even the best marriage could deliver. A life of uninterrupted bliss was not to be looked for. Those most likely to enjoy the fruits of a successful marriage were those who set a limit on their aspirations for it. Writing to a close friend who had just announced her plans to marry, the bluestocking Elizabeth Carter was certain she was too intelligent to fall into such a trap, observing primly that 'you have too much sense to form any extravagant and romantic expectations of such a life of rapture as is inconsistent with human nature'. Carter was confident that her friend would enjoy far greater – if perhaps rather chillier – benefits as a result: 'The sober and steady mutual esteem and affection, from a plan of life regulated upon principles of duty will be yours.'[8] Wetenhall Wilkes warned his readers that 'The utmost happiness we can expect in this world is contentment, and if we aim at anything higher, we shall meet with nothing but grief and disappointment.'[9]

Most of those to whom Wilkes and his many counterparts directed their arguments were, on the whole, people like themselves: thoughtful, literate, leisured, with some property and income to dispose, with the time and means to make considered decisions about matrimony. They were not poor – for those without assets, marital choices were fewer and starker – but neither were they the great monied magnates who so often considered themselves beyond the reach of regulation and advice. In most cases, it was 'the middling sort' who were most engaged, both as practitioners and commentators, in debates about what constituted a good marriage; but even amongst the aristocracy, some partnerships were built upon foundations of which Wilkes and his many supporters would have entirely approved.

William Petty married Sophia Carteret in 1765. He was the Earl of Shelburne, she was an earl's daughter. They were not quite as rich as the Devonshires, but by any other standards, their income was huge. They owned property in London, Bath and Ireland, and their principal residence was Bowood in Wiltshire, a magnificent country house remodelled by Robert Adam. Within these majestic settings, they carved out for themselves a genuinely loving union, marked by shared interests, kindness and consideration, and, above all, a mutual commitment to the grand marital project.

Shelburne was one of those sober men who had looked forward to wedlock, and had been determined to make his marriage work. Like George III, he had had a difficult childhood, and was determined to create a happier world for his wife and children. In his public life, he was an ambitious politician, who was to serve the king briefly as first minister between 1782 and 1783, but in private, he was a thoughtful intellectual with a taste for the classics. In these scholarly pursuits, he found a willing partner in his wife. Sophia had been raised amongst educated women, and liked nothing more than to spend the evenings reading with her husband. Closeted in their apartments, away from the severe grandeur of the principal rooms, the couple jointly made their way through Thucydides or the works of David Hume. In this quiet intimacy, they enjoyed their happiest moments. 'Spent the whole evening tête-à-tête in my dressing room,' wrote Sophia in her diary. 'Nothing can be more comfortable than we have hitherto been.'[10] The Shelburnes had two children, but in giving birth to a third, Sophia died, at the age of only twenty-five. The earl never really recovered from her loss. He had carved on her tomb 'her price was above rubies'. It is impossible not to believe the words came from the heart.

The Shelburne marriage showed that affectionate, mutually supportive marriages were achievable not only by the middle classes. Aristocrats too could aspire to a model of matrimony that placed a loving alliance of husband and wife firmly at its heart. Perhaps the most surprising example of this is to be found in the later life of the Duke of Grafton. After his divorce, he cast off Nancy Parsons and married again. This time, Grafton proved a model husband, fathering twelve children. In 1789, the scandals of two decades before forgotten, he published a pamphlet urging a total reformation in the moral behaviour of the upper classes.

George's reserved and punctilious character would never have allowed him to follow the examples of the Devonshires or the Graftons, but he knew he would have no difficulty in conforming to the requirements of an alternative vision of conjugal life. The wedded happiness enjoyed by the Shelburnes – bookish, reserved, intimately self-absorbed – was exactly to his taste. This was the pattern he intended to follow in his own marriage, and he had done all he could to ensure that he would achieve it. Although he had no opportunity to get to know his wife before he married her, he sought out a woman whose character seemed likely to suit his own. Like other discerning suitors, he had rejected partners possessed of greater beauty or better connections in favour of a mild, obliging temper. He did this because he hoped his would be no aridly formal arrangement, but, as far as he could ensure it, a genuine union of like minds. He entered the married state eagerly, never doubting for a moment that it was within its bounds that he would achieve lasting happiness. From the outset, he was dedicated to the longest of long terms. Before he had even seen

Charlotte, George declared to Bute that he hoped he would be united with her for the rest of their lives.

*

Once safely and irrevocably joined to his new wife, the king set about creating the foundations for their future. They were to start their married life in St James's Palace, then the principal royal residence in central London. Originally built in the sixteenth century by Henry VIII, it had been subjected to numerous alterations over the years, and by the 1760s was a rambling warren of jumbled styles and tastes. Foreign visitors used to grander royal residences found it unprepossessing on the outside; within, it was neglected and shabby. George himself once referred to it as 'that dust trap'.[11] When Walpole was shown around it in 1758, he was astonished to find Queen Caroline's bedroom had been left as it had been at the time of her death twenty years before, 'down to the wood that had been laid for the fire on the day she died'.[12]

George fitted out a suite of rooms which included a bedchamber for which the royal furniture-makers built 'a very large mahogany four-post bedstead' with Corinthian columns. It took seven hundred yards of blue damask to cover the posts and make new valances and curtains. Five new mattresses were also ordered, stuffed with fine wool and the 'best curled hair'.[13] There was no dedicated bathroom, but there was a specially built tub, and in their dressing room the king had placed a selection of soaps, tooth sponges and lavender water. A flannel mat protected the carpets of Charlotte's closet when the hairdresser puffed powder on to her hair. Carved and gilded stands were bought for 'large glass basins of gold-fish' to stand upon; a card table was installed for the queen's German attendant, Mrs Schwellenberg, who was a keen player, and a small cushion was made for Charlotte's little dog, Presto, who followed her wherever she went.

From their smartened-up base at St James's, the young couple sallied out to show themselves to the world. In the early days of their marriage, they went everywhere together. It was a matter of surprise to Continental observers how frequently aristocratic English spouses were to be found in each other's company. 'Husband and wife are always together and share the same society,' noted the French traveller François de La Rochefoucauld somewhat incredulously. 'The very richest people do not keep more than four or six carriage horses, since they pay their visits together. It would be as ridiculous to do otherwise in England as it would be to go everywhere with your wife in Paris.'[14] George and Charlotte went together to a variety of public events. They were regular attendees at the theatre, particularly when the comedies the king preferred were performed. He was said to be 'in roars of laughter' when they watched David Garrick star in *The Rehearsal.* Charlotte loved the opera, and in the week after her marriage, declared her intention of attending productions once a week. When she proved true to her word, the opera's managers were forced to shift their timetables to accommodate her. Years later, Charlotte was to confide to her brother that she thought the standard of opera in London extremely poor, and that most of the singers sounded like parrots. She wisely kept these thoughts to herself, however, and in public showed nothing but enthusiasm for the musical productions of her newly adopted home.

Walpole thought it was Charlotte's taste for entertainment that drove much of the couple's sociability in the first days of their marriage. 'The queen is so gay that we shall not want sights,' he wrote, noting that 'two nights ago she carried the king to Ranelagh', the more decorous of London's two pleasure gardens.[15] The king's father had been a frequent visitor, but without the persuasion of his new wife it was unlikely his staider son would have chosen to go. George's presence there, against his natural inclination to avoid public revelry, was a real declaration of his willingness to please.

Their regular domestic entertainments were more low key, and focussed strongly on family. Once a week, George took his new wife with him on his visits to his mother. On Wednesdays, the queen held a regular concert, in a room that had been specially equipped for musical performance. 'The queen and Lady Augusta play on the harpsichord and sing, the Duke of York plays on the violincello and Prince William on the flute.' George did not perform in company, but only in private with Charlotte. 'The king never plays in concert,' noted the Duchess of Northumberland, 'but when they are alone, he sometimes accompanies her on the German flute.'[16]

George and Charlotte's shared interests made their moments of privacy all the more valuable to them. Their love of music was one of the strongest bonds between them in these early years. The queen played 'very prettily' on the harpsichord and took singing lessons twice a week from Johann Christian Bach, son of the great composer.

When the eight-year-old Mozart visited London in 1764, he and Charlotte played a duet together; he later dedicated some of his early sonatas to her. The king and queen were great readers and, like the Shelburnes at Bowood, spent many agreeable hours in George's growing library. Both were drawn to works of history and theology, and read easily in French and German. As Charlotte's English improved, she began to add the literature of her new homeland to the European titles she had hitherto enjoyed. The couple even had similar tastes in food. Terrified of succumbing to the family obesity, George was always extremely cautious about the amount he ate; but, like his wife, his natural preference was for simple, hearty meals prepared with the minimum of fuss. In 1762, the Duchess of Northumberland set down in her diary a typical royal menu: 'Their Majesties' constant table at this time was as follows, a soup removed with a large joint of meat and two other dishes such as pie or a broiled fowl and the like.' Accompaniments included 'pastry, spinach and sweetbreads, macaroons, scalloped oysters and the like'.[17]

These private pleasures perhaps seemed all the more precious because they were so rare. From the beginning of their marriage, quiet intimacy was something George and Charlotte had to fight to achieve. Most of their time was spent in full exposure to an intense and unblinking popular curiosity. In the performance of the formal duties that absorbed so much of their time, they were permanently on display; most of their private life was conducted in a semi-public world, where their behaviour was endlessly recorded, dissected and interpreted. The court was full of observers; many of the people closest to the royal couple hurried away from every encounter to place their impressions on paper, to be passed around friends and acquaintances, and discussed yet again at a distance.

St James's was a perfect embodiment of the contradictions and difficulties that surrounded George and Charlotte's attempts to carve out a domestic life for themselves. For all George's attempts to turn it into a home, it remained, first and foremost, a place of public business. All major royal events were held there; but most significantly, it was the venue for the twice-weekly Drawing Rooms that played such a crucial role in the rhythm of elite social and political life. Men and women both attended, in their best clothes, to compete for the notice and approbation of the king and queen. Politicians, military men and even the occasional author went there to further their interests, to demonstrate possession of favour or to attempt to recover it; women to confirm their position in polite society, or to be introduced into it via formal presentation to the queen. In theory, it was an exclusive gathering; in practice, it was very loosely policed, and anyone with the proper court dress and an appropriate air of command could talk their way in. 'I have got admittance a hundred times in my life,' boasted the MP George Selwyn, 'by ordering a door-keeper in a peremptory way to admit two gentlemen who have happened to stand near me in a crowd, and have been astonished at their access and my impudence.'[18]

The king was very frustrated by his inability to limit admission to the palace to those he thought had a right to be there. Then, in the summer of 1762, an incident occurred that demonstrated the impossibility of securing even the most private places in his life from unauthorised public access. 'I can't help troubling my dear friend with a very disagreeable subject,' he wrote to Lord Bute in July. 'On Saturday morning, a mean fellow came to [the bedchamber woman-in-waiting] Mrs Brudenell's room, and took nothing out of her drawers but the key to the queen's rooms, and made off into the passage.' Fortunately, he was seized by servants, but they 'very foolishly released him on restoring it'.[19] That night he was found again, lingering outside the queen's bedchamber. This time he was taken to the guards' room, where he was questioned. The Duchess of Northumberland reported that 'he said he came to see the king and queen and not to steal. Dropped some hints about how easy it would be to do the king a mischief. No arms, but an uncommonly long penknife upon him. Asked if he should not have been sorry to have alarmed the queen, he said why should she be alarmed? He meant her no ill … Asked if he should not be sorry to offend the king, said no, he was but a man like himself, and had but one life to lose, no more than he had.'[20] George, who would always be phlegmatic when faced with attempts on his own life, was horrified by the implied threat to the queen. 'If my dear friend sees what may be done,' he implored Bute, 'I wish he would order some steps to be taken.'[21]

In fact, George had concluded some time before that he must move out of St James's, and had been searching for a home more suitable to the married life he wanted for himself and Charlotte. Walpole had been anxious he might settle at Hampton Court, bringing all the bustle of court life far too close to his own quiet Thames-side house; but the king hated the old Tudor palace, perhaps because it was there that George II was said to have struck him. When it caught fire in 1770, he declared 'he should not be sorry had it been burnt down'.[22] Walpole breathed a sigh of relief: 'Strawberry Hill will remain in possession of its own tranquillity, and not become a cheesecake house to the palace; all I ask of princes is not to live within five miles of me.'[23]

Rather than relocating to an existing royal palace, George planned to buy something new and soon fixed upon a house built in 1702, standing in a fine position at the end of The Mall. Built of warm red brick, adorned with lead statues of classical worthies on its roof, and emblazoned on all four walls with mottoes in gold text, Buckingham House was a striking building. Surrounded by fields, it was, as one of its golden texts declared, *rus in urbe*. It was owned by Sir Charles Sheffield, a descendant of the Duke of Buckingham, who drove a hard bargain. The king paid £28,000 for the lease, a sum considered exorbitant by Lord Talbot, the Lord Steward, who, George observed to Bute, 'attacked the price given for the new house and everything that regards it'. That George, usually so careful with money, was prepared to lay out so much to secure the property was a measure of its importance to him. 'Bucks House,' he explained to Bute, 'is not meant for a palace, but as a retreat.'[24]

In many ways, this was George and Charlotte's first true home, and George began its refurbishment in 1762 with enormous energy and enthusiasm. 'I am so glad Sir Charles can remove so soon,' he wrote eagerly to Bute. 'The gardeners cannot begin too soon; all I want for the present is to have the outward walls planted, and a gravel walk round. I should imagine trees could be brought from Kensington that would nearly do.'[25] The gold mottoes, too exuberant for the king's plain taste, were to be painted over. He was horrified to discover that Sir Charles's servants had been bribed by the curious to let them see inside before the king and queen moved in and that it was now 'quite dirty'. Nothing escaped the king's attention, or diminished his desire to get the job done quickly. Inevitably, he turned to Bute – who in his day job was now George's first minister – to expedite matters. 'I send my Dear Friend a list of what is immediately wanted, I beg these things may be immediately put in hand, there is one article I had forgot, that is grates in all rooms that are furnished ... I have not touched upon what is necessary for enabling meat to be warmed up in the kitchen as that is an article I am totally unacquainted with.' It was unlikely the lofty and ascetic Bute would have been able to enlighten him. 'I cannot lay down my pen,' the king concluded breathlessly, 'without afresh recommending dispatch in preparing these things.'[26]

The result of all these efforts was a house furnished in a style of richly restrained elegance. It sought to blend grandeur with modern comforts, but it could never be described as simple or homely. Like the Shelburnes, George and Charlotte did not consider the pursuit of domestic happiness incompatible with interiors that reflected their elevated status. Walpole heard that the king and queen were 'stripping the other palaces to furnish' their new home, and Buckingham House was soon crammed with art treasures. Charlotte's apartments were laid out on the first floor, the most desirable space in any eighteenth-century house. Her drawing room was decorated in green and gold, the walls lined in a darker green damask specially chosen as a suitable background on which to display the Raphael cartoons, brought from Hampton Court. Elsewhere, the ceiling was decorated with a work by Gentileschi, representing the Muses paying court to Apollo. On the ground floor, the king had built for himself a grand new library and a 'mathematical room' which displayed his growing collection of clocks, coins and maps.

More personal touches were provided by the furniture made specially for the new house. The king ordered for Charlotte a music desk 'with a loose mahogany board to lie on the top, for the queen to draw off'; there were stands for bird cages, two 'mahogany houses for a turkey monkey' and a 'square deal tub' in which to wash the queen's dog. There was also 'a very handsome mahogany bookcase' that cleverly concealed its true purpose. On one side was a door that, when opened, led discreetly into a hidden water closet.[27] Outside, with a view of the fields where the king kept cows and sheep, was a scented carnation garden where the queen sat in warm weather. From the very beginning, the new palace was always strongly associated with Charlotte and her taste, and it was soon known as the Queen's House, a name it was to keep for the next fifty years.

In 1767, Caroline Girle, who had been among the crowds at the coronation and had since become a royal sightseer of remarkable persistence, 'went to see what is rather difficult to see at all, the queen's palace'. In the five years since George and Charlotte had moved in, the new house had become a sophisticated, opulent and comfortable home. Caroline noted the 'the capital pictures, the finest Dresden and other china, cabinets of more minute curiosities'. Managing to inspect even the queen's bedroom, she counted twenty-five watches, 'all highly adorned with jewels' in a case next to her bed. But what really impressed her was the fact that even though it was March, 'every room was full of roses, carnations, hyacinths, etc., dispersed in the prettiest manner imaginable in jars and different flower pots and stands'. She was also 'amazed to find so large a house so warm, but fires, it seems, are kept the whole day, even in closets'.[28] Buckingham House might not have presented the most flamboyant face to the world – the exacting La Rochefoucauld thought it was 'without ornamentation or architectural distinction' – but inside it was a model of discreet luxury that only the very largest amounts of money could achieve.

Within this setting of restrained richness, George and Charlotte soon established a private routine of extreme simplicity. Whenever they could, they abandoned their elaborate formal court dress for plainer, more comfortable clothes. Charlotte left her hair unpowdered and even persuaded George to abandon his wig. 'The king and queen's manner of life was very methodical and regular,' observed the Duchess of Northumberland. They spent as much time as they could alone together, a state they could best achieve by retreating to their bedroom. 'Whenever it was in their power, they went to bed by 11 o'clock,' wrote the duchess, who kept far later hours herself. 'The necessary woman first warming the bed, they had every night coals, chips etc., set by the chimney and they burnt a lamp in their room and had set by it a small wax taper.' The couple clearly slept in the same bed together, and seem to have done so for many years. George got up at dawn, as he was to do for the rest of his life. 'The king's alarum waked him before five o'clock, when he rose and lighted the fire, and went to bed again until the clock struck five, and by that time, the fire being a little burnt up, he rose and dressed himself, and went into the queen's dressing room, where he wrote till eight. What he wrote, no one knew.' When the queen got up and joined her husband, 'they breakfasted together, and that over, the king went downstairs. Their table was neither sumptuous nor elegant, and they always dined tête-à-tête.' The king, the duchess noted with amazement, 'at breakfast drank only one cup of tea and never ate anything'.[29]

Once the working day began, the king's time was not his own, and George's diligent attention to business meant that the hours left unoccupied to spend with Charlotte were limited. But when free to choose, he demonstrated unequivocally that what he really wanted was to be left alone with his wife. His fine home, renovated at huge expense, was designed to offer as much opportunity as possible for the pursuit of contented domestic retirement. There seems little doubt that the king's feelings for the woman at the centre of this meticulously created world were deep and genuine. When George fell ill in 1762, it was suggested that he leave London to improve his health. He told Bute bluntly this was impossible unless Charlotte accompanied him: 'Nothing in this world could make me go without her.' His love for his wife was as strong a feeling as any he had ever experienced. 'I know,' he confided in Bute, 'that the loss of her I have now would break my heart.'[30]

George's growing emotional involvement with his wife did not, in the first years of his marriage, do anything to lessen his dependency on Bute. The earl continued to play a central part in the king's life, not just as his political mentor, but also as a source of advice and support on his new-found responsibilities as a family man. George took few steps, even on the most trivial matters, without seeking the approval of his old friend. Did Bute think 'there was is any impropriety in my seeing *Henry V* at Covent Garden, in which the coronation is introduced?' He urged the earl to give the matter his speediest attention: 'I wish he would send me a line by ten o'clock tonight.'[31] If the queen's brother were to visit London, where was he to be lodged? 'I ask my Dear Friend, whether, being a younger brother, he may not with propriety live in a private house, what leads me to think this is that even my younger brothers do so.'[32] Issues of 'propriety' loomed large in George's mind; the difficulty of making the right decision made him anxious and he yearned for Bute's endorsement. Even small gestures of intimacy were, for the cautious and punctilious king, pregnant with unseen consequences, and routinely submitted to Bute's consideration. In May 1762, George wrote: 'The queen wishes very much that I would give her my picture in enamel to wear at her side in place of a watch. I see no impropriety in it, but wish he would, if he sees any, send me a word.'[33] What Charlotte thought of her husband's relationship with Bute is not known. The Duchess of Northumberland noted without further comment that after his marriage, the king still kept the earl's picture, 'in full-length, in his private closet.'[34]

*

The collapse of this relationship would be, without doubt, the single most significant event of George's early manhood, and a trauma which marked the king's character for the rest of his life. The abrupt, self-willed departure of Bute, and George's inability to prevent it, inflicted a deep wound on the king's sense of self and his relationship with others. The end of their partnership was as painful as a divorce, and neither man would ever be quite the same again.

This sad dissolution was all the more painful because, by 1761, everything promised so well. As soon after his accession as George could manage it, Bute had been appointed first minister: the earl now held the reins of government in his hands, and was at last in a position to turn the ideas he and George had discussed for so many years into practical politics. Both knew their first step would be to put an end to the Seven Years War, a conflict that had raged around the globe, encompassing conflict in Europe, naval battles in the West Indies and General Wolfe's victory in Quebec. As a proxy struggle for mastery between Britain and France, it had delivered a succession of strategic victories which made it popular amongst noisy patriots, but it was regarded by Bute and George as both bloody and expensive, draining national resources and undermining the crown by increasing debt. A king in thrall to City financiers, and the politicians who represented their views, could hardly pursue the public good with the disinterested energy Bute and George intended; but securing a peace treaty proved harder than either of them imagined, and the bruising apprenticeship it offered in the grubby realities of eighteenth-century politics, international and domestic, was to destroy the relationship between them that had been cemented with such deep affection over so many years.

The peace project was unpopular, and Bute's attempts to argue its virtues in Parliament failed. He was a poor speaker, and had no network of supporters on whom he could depend. Gradually, he concluded that if the Commons could not be persuaded to vote for peace, they must be convinced by other, cruder means. To the king's horror, Bute recommended bringing into government Henry Fox, whose shady reputation had been a significant factor in rejecting his close relation Sarah Lennox. Fox was the undisputed master of corrupt parliamentary practice, and Bute was sure he could deliver the peace that no one else could. The king reluctantly agreed. 'We must call in bad men to govern bad men,' he commented gloomily.

Fox's methods were as successful as Bute had suspected and the king had feared they would be. He offered pensions and salaried posts in government to win over supporters; to the less delicate, he offered straightforward cash payments, operating from the House of Commons pay office, and spending over £250,000 in bribes. At the same time, Fox engineered the dismissal of the Whig supporters of the war from almost every public office they held. The Duke of Devonshire, known as 'the prince of Whigs', was sacked from his job as Lord Chamberlain in the king's household. Whig dukes lost the lord lieutenancies of counties; Whig admirals fell from the Admiralty Board; even doormen and messengers who had gained their places through Whig patronage lost them overnight. In the space of a few days, Fox had 'turned out everyone whom Whig influence had brought into power except the king'.[35]

With the removal of all opposition so efficiently arranged, the peace was approved by the House of Commons by a majority of 319 votes to 65. It was a victory, but one in which neither the king nor Bute took much pleasure. This was not how they had imagined achieving 'the goal' in quieter days at Leicester House. The easy success of Fox's unashamed venality depressed Bute; but he was even more horrified by the venom with which he was now attacked as the chief architect of such an unpopular policy. 'The press is, with more vehemence than I ever knew, set to work against Lord Bute,' observed Sarah Lennox. 'The fire is fed with great industry and blown by a national prejudice which is inveterate and universal. He is most scurrilously abused as being a Scotsman and a favourite.'[36] In caricature after caricature, Bute was insultingly portrayed with all the attributes thought by the English to distinguish the Scots. He was shown as an impoverished wearer of a threadbare kilt, which managed to be both ludicrous and suggestive; he was depicted as an unprincipled, unashamed seeker of power and money, who would stop at nothing to achieve his ends. In one print, he is seen creeping into the dowager princess's bedroom at night; in another he pours poison into the sleeping king's ear. He would connive at adultery and even regicide, the caricaturists maintained, if either served his purposes.

Yet the violence of the press was as nothing compared to the physical intimidation to which Bute was exposed on the streets of London. Eighteenth-century politics was a feral business, and unpopular politicians were roughly handled by crowds as well as by newspapers and in prints. In 1761, on his way to the lord mayor's annual banquet, Bute's coach was recognised by his enemies who surrounded it with 'groans, hisses, yells, shouts of "No Scotch rogues!", "No Butes!"' The coach was pelted with mud and stones, and Bute feared he was about to be hauled out himself when the constables finally arrived. From then on, he surrounded himself with a posse of hired hard men, 'a gang of ruffians and bruisers', to protect him. Despite his precautions, he was attacked again in 1762 as he passed through the streets towards Westminster for the state opening of Parliament. This time, Walpole thought Bute had been lucky to have escaped with his life. The earl had had enough: in April 1763, he resigned.

His decision came as a shock to everyone except the king. George had known for some time that Bute had come to hate the political world he had once hoped to dominate. He begged him to reconsider, but Bute was determined to go. In a long letter he wrote to a friend a few months before his final departure, the earl laid out his reasons for leaving. The peace treaty was signed, 'the king has his sceptre in his hand ... and the helm, that demanded a bold, venturous hand may, at this peace, be managed by a child'. His health, he declared, was failing under 'the eternal, unpleasant labour of the mind and the impossibility of finding hours for exercise, the little time I get to sleep'. It was a shattering sense of disillusionment with the practical reality of politics that had made it impossible for him to carry on. He could no longer bear to be tainted by his involvement with men and measures that repelled him. 'In my opinion,' he wrote bitterly, 'the Angel Gabriel could not at present govern this country, but by means too long practised and such as my soul abhors.' As he could tolerate it no longer, 'therefore, in the bosom of victory', he went.[37]

George was devastated. Bute's resignation was 'the most cruel political blow that could have happened to me'.[38] He knew it marked the end of the great joint project of moral renewal which they had discussed, planned and longed for over the past decade. 'I own I had flattered myself that when the peace was once established, my D Friend would have assisted me in purging out corruption ... and that when we were both dead, our memories would have been esteemed to the end of time.' Now none of this would happen, for George could not do it alone. 'Instead of reformation, the ministers being vicious, the country will grow, if possible, worse, let me attack the irreligious, the covetous, etc. etc. as much as I please, that will have no effect.'[39]

Contemplating the departure of the man who had dominated his life for so long, the king was said to have sat for hours 'with his head reclining in his arm, without speaking a word'.[40] He never used the term 'betrayal', but it hovered in the air nonetheless. When called upon to give up the pursuit of private happiness for the greater good, George had done so uncomplainingly, in obedience to Bute's dictum that the sacrifice of Sarah Lennox was a necessary one. Now it appeared that Bute was unable – or unwilling – to do the same for him.

For a while after his departure, Bute and the king continued to correspond, with George still seeking the earl's advice as if nothing had changed. Their relationship staggered on, more polite form than substance, until, in 1766, George dealt it the final blow. He declined to meet Bute, who was still politically toxic, in order to avoid offending his current ministers. The earl could not believe it. He wrote to the king, begging him not to throw away the true affection that bound them together, even if he had no further role to play in public life. 'I say, sir, suffer me in this humiliated position to possess your friendship, independent of your power. I have never merited being deprived of that, which consists in the operation of the heart and soul ... Alas, my dear Sovereign, what other view or selfish purpose can I have? I have forever done with this bad public, my heart is half broke, and my health ruined ... The warmest wish I have remaining is to see you happy, respected and adored.'[41] George did not reply, and Bute did not write again.

The Dowager Princess Augusta once had a haunting dream: 'The window was open, and the moon, which was level to it, shook with a tremulous motion before her eyes, to her great disquiet. She bade Lord Bute to try and fix it. Extending his arms to stop its motion, it burst in his hands into a thousand fiery splinters, upon which, turning to the princess, he said reproachfully, "See, Madam, what you have brought me to."'[42] In the years he spent with Augusta and her son, Bute had done all he could 'to try and fix it'. He had offered George a credible vision of the kind of king he could be, and in doing so had transformed George's idea of himself and his destiny. But by leaving as he did, he confirmed many of George's deepest fears about the mutability of personal relationships. If leaving was an option, it was one that would be exercised eventually, with whatever professions of regret. 'I shall never meet with a friend in business again,' the king wrote mournfully upon his mentor's resignation.[43] In fact, Bute was probably the only friend George would ever have, in business or outside it. After the earl's departure, he did not look for one again. In future, all his significant emotional investments would be made amongst those who shared the lifelong obligation to the royal project. It was not by finding new friends that George hoped to fill the void left by Bute, but by turning to his family and, above all, to his wife.

For many years after Bute's ignominious departure, George's administrations were unstable and the source of much unhappiness to the young king, who considered himself bullied and oppressed by ministers forced upon him by political necessity. As George floundered, seemingly unable to find a way to work with anyone other than Bute, the popular mood grew increasingly hostile towards him. The corrupt means by which the peace had been achieved still rankled with both politicians and the press; accusations now circulated, asserting that the king's behaviour was unconstitutional and threatened the sovereignty of Parliament. The ill-advised decision to prosecute one of his most imaginatively abrasive critics, the formidable antagonist John Wilkes, made a difficult situation worse. It gave previously inchoate resentment a focus for its anger, and provoked rioting and disorder so violent and so widespread that it seemed to threaten the survival of the established system of government itself.

George was neither immune nor protected from the hurricane-like impact of popular political disapproval. The highly personalised invective that accompanied it was directed towards him with as much venom as it had once been towards Bute. Any appearance in public was an opportunity to insult or provoke him. On his way to visit his mother, 'the mob asked him if he was going to take suck'.[44] George and Charlotte were once at the theatre when the alarm for fire was raised. In the stalls, the result was mayhem, and some of the audience were injured; but far above in the royal box, Charlotte was unperturbed, assuming the chaos was no more than business as usual; 'she had not heard the expression of fire, and imagined they were saying impertinences to the king'.[45] Silence was just as potent a method of indicating disapproval. On his way to a City dinner, the king rode through wordless crowds who, once he had passed, cheered loudly and pointedly for their favourite, the successful wartime first minister, William Pitt. 'When he goes to the theatre, or goes out, or goes to the House, there is not a single applause,' noted Walpole.[46] The alternating experience of sinister silence or vociferous complaint was a seemingly inevitable aspect of royal experience, one that was simply to be ignored or endured.

In such circumstances, it is not surprising that George regarded the calm pleasures of his married life with such relief. It was also perhaps inevitable that he should come to associate his conjugal happiness with ideas of retreat and retirement. The private world he built with Charlotte was to be utterly distinct from the difficulties of his public existence. Her role was not to act as partner in resolving his problems, but to provide escape from them. George had no desire to see his wife drawn into the political factions and allegiances that permeated every crack and crevice of elite life. Nor had he any wish to see her follow in the footsteps of his grandmother, the busy, clever and managing Queen Caroline. Even his own mother, whose supposed political objectives were the subject of endless speculation, and whose alleged relationship with Lord Bute exposed her to public abuse of the crudest kind, was not considered a suitable role model for his wife. Indeed, if the Duke of Gloucester, the king's younger brother, is to be believed, George specifically warned Charlotte against having any dealings with the dowager princess. 'The very day the queen arrived,' the duke told Walpole, 'three hours afterwards when she was gone to be dressed for the wedding, I was left alone with the king, and he told me he had already given her a caution not to be alone with my mother, for she was an artful woman, and would try to govern her.'[47]

Whether as a result of the king's instructions or of the princess dowager's own self-contained and inward-looking nature, Charlotte was never on familiar terms with her mother-in-law. Nor did she build a relationship with George's eldest sister. Princess Augusta saw herself as a stout defender of the hegemony of the royal family, and had waged a doughty campaign against what she saw as Sarah Lennox's pretensions, laughing in her face in an attempt to warn her away from her infatuated brother. Walpole thought she was loud, indiscreet and 'much inclined to meddle in the private politics of the court'.[48] These qualities may have persuaded the king to extend to his sister the same chilly detachment he insisted Charlotte observe in regard to his mother. It was certainly the case that Charlotte and Augusta were never friends; thirty years later, Augusta was still complaining about her sister-in-law, describing her as 'an envious and intriguing spirit', who had disliked her mother and herself, 'was extremely jealous of them' and had alienated the king's affections from her.[49]

George's proscriptions extended far beyond his immediate family. In his anxiety to place his wife beyond politics, he erected around her a powerful social exclusion zone which left her in splendid isolation at the centre of the court over which she was expected to preside. In the early years of her marriage, Charlotte had no real friends at all, and was equally alone among the ladies of the court. The Ladies of the Bedchamber, whom she saw most regularly, were far older than the young queen, and having intrigued and campaigned for their positions around her, were often thoroughly bored with the role once they had secured it. One of them, Lady Egremont, described the dullness of the mornings they spent sitting in a formal circle around the queen with nothing to do but examine what each of them was wearing. 'She represented it as a very triste affair,' sniffed Lady Mary Coke primly.[50] With little else to think about, the ladies occupied themselves with the elegant prosecution of turf wars over excruciating issues of precedence. 'I went to court,' recorded the Duchess of Northumberland, a seasoned combatant in such battles, 'and the queen called before Lady Bolingbroke, who was lady-in-waiting, came in. The Duchess of Ancaster going in, I stepped before her and said I was the lady-in-waiting, which nettled her so much she would not speak to me after. The queen,' she noted with satisfaction, 'was very gracious.'[51]

The duchess's diaries are peppered with references to Charlotte's 'graciousness'. She admired her ladies' dresses; she politely showed them her jewels; she played and sang, smilingly acknowledging their praise. As Charlotte later explained to Lady Harcourt, her studied politeness was as much a result of the king's direction as her carefully imposed aloofness, for 'he allowed and encouraged me to be civil to all'.[52] Her goodwill was of necessity spread very evenly amongst those around her; anything expressive of an emotion warmer than bland disinterest on the queen's part led to nothing but strife. The mildest indication of genuine preference was sufficient to provoke gossip and recrimination for weeks. When Lady Bolingbroke appeared to have attracted Charlotte's favour, news of it became the subject of endless speculation and it was immediately reported that 'the other ladies, particularly Lady Egremont', were extremely jealous.[53]

Many years later, Charlotte considered George had been absolutely correct to insist that she held herself apart from those around her and made no close connections: 'I am not only sensible that he was right, but I feel thankful for it from the bottom of my heart.'[54] But as a young bride in a strange country, surrounded by the scrutiny of the ambitious, and forbidden to build friendships with those she found more sympathetic, it must have been a demanding proscription to obey. Isolated behind her enforced graciousness, Charlotte was a lonely figure in those early days. It was perhaps not surprising that, in the absence of other connections, her relationship with one of her servants became one of the most important in her life.

Juliana Schwellenberg was one of the two 'German women' Charlotte had brought over to England with her. Mrs Schwellenberg was in theory one of the queen's assistant dressers, but she rarely did any actual dressing herself; instead, she was in charge of Charlotte's Wardrobe – a significant department of the household – overseeing 'the persons therein employed and the regulation of the expenditure'. She insisted on being addressed as 'Madame', and liked to think of herself as 'Female Mentor to the queen'.[55] From the moment of her arrival, she was a controversial figure. In an early memoir of Charlotte, published shortly after her death in 1818, Mrs Schwellenberg was described as 'a well-educated woman, extremely courteous in her manner ... devotedly attached to the illustrious family with whom she lived'. Others found her less amenable. The novelist Fanny Burney, who suffered at her hands when she was at court in the 1780s, and disliked her as a result, created a picture of Mrs Schwellenberg in her journals as a true comic monster, an appallingly compelling mix of petty cruelties and absurd self-aggrandisement. She was unpopular with Charlotte's other servants, and involved in a wearying succession of rows and feuds. The king had always resented her presence and, after yet another explosion in the queen's household, he was reported to have 'desired she should be dismissed, and return to Germany with an allowance suitable to her position in that country'.[56] With surprising defiance, Charlotte begged him to reconsider. George relented, but made it a condition of her reprieve that Mrs Schwellenberg 'should not resist his commands, nor influence the queen's mind upon any subject'.[57]

'The Schwellenberg', as she was universally known, successfully weathered not just the king's disapproval, but that of almost everyone else at court. Impervious to decades of criticism and complaint, secure in the unwavering protection of the queen, she remained in her service until the day she died in 1797. Though she could never be described as Charlotte's friend, she was a loyal and devoted companion, and in her early days in England, the queen had few enough of those. She was a link with Charlotte's old home, almost the only person at court who had known Mecklenburg, and who missed its low-key charms. Above all, she was, with a single-minded intensity, dedicated entirely to the queen. She had no interest in cultivating wider alliances, impressing or conciliating other people, as her widespread unpopularity demonstrated. All that mattered was the preservation of her primacy with Charlotte. For all her eccentricities and shortcomings, Mrs Schwellenberg offered the queen a relationship in which Charlotte always came first, in which there could be no question of other, hidden allegiances. It was hardly surprising that Charlotte could not bear the prospect of losing her.

Charlotte's isolation grew more pronounced as the years went by. By the mid-1760s, it was apparent that her husband's passionate desire for a life of domestic retirement was not a passing phase but the guiding principle by which he intended to govern their time together. The rhythm of their year was soon well established. They spent the winter, whilst Parliament sat, in the luxurious privacy of Buckingham House. In the summer, they retreated to the even greater seclusion of Richmond Lodge in the countryside south-west of London, where they were reputed to spend their days very modestly. 'The court,' wrote Walpole in 1764, 'makes a strange figure. The recluse life led at Richmond, which is carried on to such an excess of privacy and economy, that the queen's *friseur* waits on them at supper, and four pounds only of beef are allowed for their soup, disgusts all sorts of people.'[58]

Walpole voiced a common contemporary response to the king and queen's increasing lack of visibility – a sense of disappointment that they had failed to deliver on their early promise to act as a lively focus for aristocratic life, using their place at the pinnacle of the pyramid of polite society to nurture a resurgence of cultural energy and excitement. Put simply, they had not turned out to be as much fun as everyone had hoped. Manipulating the facts to serve his own purpose, Walpole argued that the royal couple's seclusion had been forced upon them by Bute and his ally the princess dowager, the better to prosecute their intentions to subvert the constitution. Augusta, he asserted, had imposed 'strict laws of retirement' on her son. 'He was accessible to none of his court, but at the stated hours of business and ceremony; nor was any man but the favourite … allowed to converse with the king.'[59] This argument was nonsense, as Walpole himself well knew; but like so many of his pronouncements, the hollowness of his conclusions were disguised by the strength of the evidence he submitted to support them. As the Duchess of Northumberland's diary suggests, Walpole was not the only observer to find something both puzzling and troubling in the extremity of the king and queen's insular existence. 'His Majesty,' she wrote, 'was certainly naturally of a most cheerful, even sociable disposition, and a clear understanding, yet he lived in the utmost retirement.'[60] She, like Walpole, blamed Bute. Others attributed the king's taste for seclusion to the way he had been brought up, and linked it directly to the habits he had acquired under his mother's tutelage. But as one well-placed observer maintained, these explanations were only part of a more complicated story.

Years later, the Duke of Gloucester, the king's brother, declared that, contrary to what was popularly supposed, 'the retired life the king and queen led for the many first years of their marriage' was 'entirely the king's doing.'[61] The duke conceded that his mother, Augusta, had instilled in her eldest son an early distaste for loud, unregulated sociability – 'he had been locked up till he married, and taught to have a bad opinion of the world' – but maintained that George's preference for solitude arose from something more than habit. He sought out retirement, Gloucester thought, not just because it was what he was used to, but because it provided the best possible circumstances in which he could shape and mould the affections of his malleable young wife: 'That he was delighted in having under his own training a young innocent girl of 17, for such was the queen when she arrived, and that he determined she should be wholly devoted to him and that she have no other friend or society.' The king's prohibition of all other relationships was designed, in Gloucester's opinion, to make himself the uncontested focus of all her affections, to ensure she would 'depend on him and him alone.' It was to ensure the exclusivity of her love that Charlotte's early married years were spent largely alone, 'except for the Ladies of the Bedchamber, in a funeral circle.' For most of the time, 'she never had a soul to speak to except the king.'[62]

It is impossible not to feel that George's love for his wife in these early years was a strong and genuine emotion. For a man not given to extravagant declarations, he was uncharacteristically voluble in expressing the pleasure he took in her company. 'Every hour convinces me more and more of the treasure I have got,' he once wrote delightedly to Bute, describing his marriage 'as the source of my happiness as a private man'. However, as George's brother recognised, contained in the unfeigned reality of his sentiments was a whiff of emotional despotism.[63] His love for Charlotte was real, but it required from her an almost total resignation of self, a willingness to subsume all her interests in his, to submit utterly to his powerful instinct to own and control. As she quickly came to understand, George's affection was ruthlessly proprietorial. It is perhaps significant that the only recorded declaration of her own feelings in these early years was couched in language she must have known would please him most. Writing to Bute in May 1762, George had noted with satisfaction that Charlotte, 'with her usual affection, expressed herself as this effect ... that my conduct to her made her esteem herself as belonging to me and me only'.[64]

If there was a darker side to the ideal of affectionate marriage, it lay perhaps in the potential for extreme self-absorption and isolation on the part of the couple at its heart. A quiet domestic life, shared by two like-minded and reasonable people, could, if their privacy was too strictly and narrowly enforced, start to feel more like confinement than contentment. Gloucester was not the only observer to wonder whether that had not been Charlotte's experience. Mrs Mary Harcourt, who came from a family of courtiers and saw much of Charlotte in later life, agreed with his reading of events: 'Coming over, with natural good spirits, eagerly expecting to be queen of a gay court, finding herself confined in a convent, and hardly allowed to think without the leave of her husband, checked her spirits, made her fearful and cautious to an extreme, and when the time came that amusements were allowed, her mind was formed to a different manner of life.'[65] If there was a price to be paid for the success of George and Charlotte's marriage, it was clear from the outset that it would be Charlotte's duty to pay it.

In her younger days at least, Charlotte may have felt that too much attention from a husband was to be preferred to none at all, or to the routine humiliations of ill-concealed infidelities. Neither she nor

George could have been happy in the loosely amoral partnerships that were the experience of so many of their aristocratic contemporaries. They were, as they thankfully recognised, fortunate in sharing a much more positive view of marriage as the foundation of all social and personal happiness, and luckier still in that both were prepared to try to live up to the ideals they so eagerly embraced in theory. In the earliest years of their partnership, they were rewarded for their efforts and experienced some of the fullest pleasures that the eighteenth-century married state could offer. It was true that when scrutinised closely, their relationship already contained within it seeds of the difficulties that would later reshape it in altogether less glowing colours; but, by any standards – and especially those of other royal partnerships – they had embarked on their union with all the willingness to make it work that defined the most successful modern marriages. Confident in having found the right wife, secure in the happy state of his home, George was ready to begin the next stage of his great family project. 'I have now but one wish as a public man,' he confessed, 'and that is that God will make her fruitful.'[66]

CHAPTER 6

Fruitful

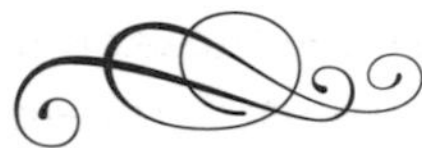

FROM THE VERY MOMENT GEORGE and Charlotte were married, speculation began about how long it would take them to produce an heir. Just after their wedding, Bute told the king that predictions had acquired a competitive edge. Wagers were being taken on their having a child before Bute's eldest daughter and her new husband, who had married the day before the royal couple. Though not a betting man, George was clearly confident enough of his own prowess cheerfully to take on all comers: 'The king told Lord Orford he should be glad to go his halves.'[1]

George won his bet. In February 1762, he confided to Bute that Charlotte 'had been forced to retire from Chapel and did not appear at the Drawing Room'. As the father of a large family himself, Bute would surely understand what had prompted her absence. 'My dearest friend is too conversant not to guess what this is,' he wrote excitedly. 'I say nothing, but deny nothing. She now calls with impatience for her dinner. I desire the whole of this may remain *entre nous*.'[2] There was little chance of that. A few weeks later, Horace Walpole had heard that the queen was 'breeding'; soon, everyone else in the fashionable and political worlds knew it too.

The confirmation of a first pregnancy was a mixed blessing for an eighteenth-century wife. On the one hand, it was a joyous event, a declaration of her status as a potential mother, still regarded as the most appropriate and fulfilling destiny for any woman; but it also pitched her into a world of dangerous – indeed life-threatening –

uncertainty. Even for someone as young and apparently healthy as Charlotte, the risks inherent in childbirth were considerable. Although recent scholarship has tended to revise downwards the numbers of women dying in labour – one study suggests the mortality risk was about 6 to 7 per cent across a woman's reproductive career – complications arising from childbirth were probably still the most common cause of death for women of child-rearing age.[3] Grimly matter-of-fact accounts of maternal suffering, frequently resulting in the loss of both mother and child, echo tragically throughout every collection of journals, diaries or letters of the eighteenth century. Every pregnant woman must have known someone – a sister, a friend or even her own mother – who had not survived the experience.

Nothing could offer absolute peace of mind for an anxious husband and wife about to embark on this unpredictable journey, but those who could afford it tried to insure themselves against disaster by seeking from the outset the best possible care. Usually, it was the woman herself, in conjunction with her female friends, who found and appointed the practitioners she wanted around her; but Charlotte had no network of family or acquaintances to guide her. In the spring, it was the king who made the first tentative enquiries, writing to Bute on 'a subject of much consequence to me now'. He wanted to know the name 'of the midwife Lady Bute made use of, after Mrs Cannon's death, that I may recommend her, if she is still able to attend ladies'.[4] The veteran Mrs Cannon had assisted Princess Augusta, delivering all her children, including George himself, and the king hoped to find someone similarly dependable to minister to Charlotte. In the event, Mrs Mary Draper was eventually engaged, but whether through the recommendation of Lady Bute is not known.

Mrs Draper was a well-regarded expert with an extensive clientele, and prosperous enough to own a substantial house in Soho. She was, as tradition prescribed, a grandmother with many years' direct experience of the process of childbirth. Like all midwives, her skills were acquired through practical experience rather than academic tuition; women were excluded from formal medical education in Britain.

For centuries, the delivery of children had remained the responsibility of female midwives like Mrs Draper; by the mid-eighteenth century, however, their primacy in the birthing chamber was increasingly challenged by the arrival of medically trained doctors. These 'man-midwives', as they were known, were the product of fifty years of philosophical enquiry, during which pregnancy had become a subject of consuming interest to scientists, surgeons and physicians. One of the first midwifery schools opened in 1739, in St James's, under eminent man-midwife Sir Richard Manningham. Anatomical study, especially knowledge gained from the dissection of dead bodies, had transformed the clinical understanding of female physiology. Ideas based on detailed observation rather than the received wisdom of the classical world had resulted in far greater understanding of the natural processes of pregnancy, from conception to birth; and this in turn had produced advances in the practical management of labour. A better appreciation of the function of the uterus and the position of the baby within it made possible the development of forceps, which, though not without risk in their application, nevertheless transformed outcomes in many cases of obstructed deliveries. Before their invention, the only way to prevent the death of the mother was to cut the child into pieces and remove it limb by limb from the womb; the skilled use of forceps now offered a potentially life-saving alternative for the woman and her baby.

The exclusion of women from the institutions which developed such techniques meant that much of the new expertise was not easily accessible to female midwives. Perhaps as a result, from the 1760s onwards, there was a decline in the status and authority of midwives, matched by a corresponding rise in that of their male counterparts or *accoucheurs*. This has been interpreted by some historians as a defeat inflicted on traditional female skills by the male authority of doctors, the destruction of a world of hard-won experience by an imposed professionalism which took the management of pregnancy out of the hands of women and placed it into an artificially medicalised world from which it has struggled ever since to escape. There may be some truth in this; not all *accoucheurs* were as expert as some of the midwives they displaced, and the more invasive techniques they practised did not always rebound to the benefit of mother or baby, especially when insufficient attention to cleanliness resulted in internal infection.

However, recent research suggests that from the mid-eighteenth century onwards, amongst those who could afford it, the medically trained man-midwife was overwhelmingly the choice of the pregnant woman herself.[5] The flight from total reliance upon the traditional midwife was not achieved as a result of a sustained male conspiracy to drive out them out; on the contrary, some husbands were suspicious of the motives and opportunities available to the man-midwife, 'these touching gentry', as one uneasy commentator described them. The decline of the midwife was a result of decisions made by women themselves, who were quickly convinced that the benefits of the professional specialist outweighed his shortcomings. Indeed, younger women may have welcomed the presence of a doctor as a means of freeing themselves from what could feel like the stifling weight of traditional practice imposed by their mothers and an older generation. By 1762, for nearly all aristocratic women, the appointment of a specialist doctor to oversee both pregnancy and labour was considered a necessity.

George and Charlotte were thus entirely in step with contemporary practice when, alongside Mrs Draper, they invited Dr William Hunter to manage the queen's pregnancy. Hunter, one of the many formidably clever Scots who did so much to shape eighteenth-century learning, had trained as a doctor in Edinburgh, then, as now, a centre of excellence in medicine. Always interested in gynaecology, he began his career investigating the female reproductive system by observing its function in animals. He made huge advances, both in understanding and practice, when studying in Paris, where he was allowed to work extensively on human corpses. Returning to London, he soon established a reputation as an inquisitive and energetic scientist. He was a brilliant dissector, and communicated his discoveries in electrifying talks; one of his pupils described him as 'the most perfect demonstrator as well as lecturer the world has ever known'. In 1774, he published the fruits of a lifetime of research in his book *The Anatomy of the Human Gravid Uterus*. Everything Hunter had learnt through decades of careful observation was encompassed in a series of precise and extraordinarily beautiful drawings which illustrated the progress of a child's development from foetus to full-term baby, and established for the first time that mother and child had separate blood supplies.[6]

Hunter was a man of phenomenal activity, with a finger in every philosophical or institutional pie; he was physician to the British Lying-In Hospital, owner of a private academy of anatomy, holder of numerous fellowships and a fervent acquirer of a vast collection of natural and mineral curiosities. He also ran a very successful – and extremely lucrative – private practice as a man-midwife. When George and Charlotte engaged him in 1762, he was a familiar presence in the grandest aristocratic homes, having attended, among others, the Pitts, Foxes, Norths and Graftons. His unparalleled physiological knowledge assisted him in his professional success, and his suave, discreet and calmly authoritative manner was also a huge asset in dealing with apprehensive patients; in Hunter, the qualities of the society doctor were combined with the rigour of a first-class scientist. It is hard to think that the king and queen could have made a better choice of attendant.

Hunter's wealth and consequence, his uncontested place as the tallest and grandest pillar of the burgeoning obstetric medical establishment, had not turned him into a medical conservative. In the journal he kept as a record of his experiences with his royal clients, he confidently declared that 'labour is not a disease'. From this strikingly modern conviction followed much of his management of Charlotte throughout her pregnancy. He was sceptical of the value of bloodletting, the eighteenth-century panacea for any physical problem, prescribing instead 'greater quiet' when Charlotte felt 'a kind of palpitation' at six months. He insisted the queen be excused further royal duties, stipulating that 'she should go no more to the Chapel or Drawing Room' and avoid 'everything that *could in the least* tire or hurry her'.[7]

Charlotte's pregnancy advanced without further incident until 12 August, when, some nine days after her due date, Hunter was called to St James's, 'at ½ after five in the morning'. At about the same time, the king scribbled 'a scrawl' to Bute telling him that 'the dear queen is very near her time' and adding that his mother was already there, to oversee proceedings. When Hunter arrived, some time after the eager dowager princess, he waited in one of the outer rooms with many others who claimed a right of attendance at royal births, including the Ladies of the Bedchamber, members of the Cabinet, and the Archbishop of Canterbury. Throughout Charlotte's delivery, the queen's *accoucheur* never actually entered the room where she gave birth. He was there to be called upon if matters took an unfavourable turn; until then, practical management of labour remained the territory of the midwife.

From time to time, as Charlotte's labour progressed, Mary Draper obligingly emerged to inform the doctor what was happening. 'A little after six, Mrs Draper came to us and told us that all was in a very natural way,' recorded Hunter, 'but that appearances indicated it would be slow.' To everyone's surprise, suddenly things began to move very quickly. 'At half an hour after seven, when I little expected it, from what Mrs Draper had told us, the prince was born.'[8] It was an entirely successful outcome, apparently achieved without great suffering on the mother's part. The Duchess of Northumberland, who was among the ladies congregated in the outer room, noted that 'the queen's labour was short (two hours) but severe', adding approvingly that 'she scarce cried out at all'.[9] As soon as the baby was born, 'the ladies went into the room, and soon after came the archbishop'. Only after the latter had seen enough to make a formal declaration that the child was truly the queen's was Hunter allowed into the delivery room to see the young prince. He 'examined him all over, and found him perfect, with every mark of health, and of a large size'.[10] The boy was given 'two large teaspoons-full of purging mixture' as a precaution, but Hunter thought he looked extremely well.

Whilst Hunter assessed the new baby, Charlotte's attendants argued about who should go and tell the king that he was now a father. Lord Huntingdon claimed the right, although, perhaps confused by the altercation, he promptly informed George that the baby was a girl, 'to which the king replied that he was but little anxious as to the sex of the child, so the queen was but safe'. Reassured about Charlotte, and corrected about the gender of the newborn, George 'went to the bedchamber, and soon after the child was brought out and shown to all, a strong, large pretty boy he is, as ever was seen'.[11] Everyone was overjoyed – the king, the ladies, the Cabinet, the archbishop and, of course, Dr Hunter, whose supervision had proved such an unalloyed triumph. But it was the woman at the centre of events who had most reason to feel both relieved and elated. Just eleven months after her marriage, Charlotte had fulfilled her primary dynastic purpose. She was the mother of a healthy heir – George, Prince of Wales – and, as an added bonus, was still alive herself.

In the days after the birth, Hunter again demonstrated his forward-looking approach in his treatment of the queen. Custom dictated that newly delivered women kept to their rooms for at least a month, battened down against mishap, with windows closed and every crevice stuffed tight against draughts. Their friends might visit them, but physical activity of any kind on their part was strictly discouraged. Hunter, however, sought to get Charlotte out of bed as soon as possible; but his patient proved to be more of a traditionalist than her doctor. Although there was clearly nothing wrong with her – Hunter thought her 'remarkably well', noting her 'cheerful spirits' and recording that she 'laughed heartily' – she refused to be dislodged from her bed. Disingenuously, she told Hunter that she was 'desirous of doing nothing but what he thought best', and then completely ignored his advice. She would not get up, nor would she eat the healthy meals he prescribed, telling him that 'she desired to live some days upon broth, caudle and tea rather than to eat chicken'.[12] Caudle, a gruel fortified with wine that was customarily given to new mothers, was clearly not regarded as highly by Hunter as it was by Charlotte. He told the queen that 'she should have no more draughts and she ought to get up'. Although Charlotte obediently spent 'an hour on the couch', she was soon back in bed again, and, noted an exasperated Hunter, 'still would not eat chicken'. It wasn't until 20 August that the queen finally left her bed. On the same day Hunter noted with satisfaction that she 'ate with appetite almost a whole chicken ... and felt quite well'.[13] Seeing this, he knew his job was over. Charlotte was soon back in her accustomed place besides her husband, who was delighted and perhaps a little surprised to see how little the experience of childbearing had changed her. 'The queen is just up,' George wrote to Bute, 'and is, thank heaven, very well and just as nimble as she was a year ago.' His son, too, was thriving. 'He never stirred for six hours last night, and seems three months older than yesterday.'[14]

Before the end of 1762, Charlotte was pregnant again. Hunter was pleased to be called upon to attend, but found there was very little for him to do. Her labour, when it came in August 1763, was once more short, but not as sharp as her first. 'After complaining lightly for about two hours, she was delivered, with three pains, of a fine boy.' Hunter was pleased with a second successful result, but embarrassed that the speedy turn of events had meant 'there was not time to call the proper people together'. He blamed this lapse in professionalism on Mrs Draper, with whom he was again working, in what was clearly an increasingly uneasy partnership. The midwife insisted it was not her fault, telling Hunter that 'the pains continued so trifling that she did not imagine the queen was near delivery till three strong pains came suddenly and close together and finished it'. Hunter was not convinced. '*This she said*,' he confided to his journal, his scepticism apparent in each heavily underlined word.[15]

The new baby was another healthy son, Frederick, later given the title Duke of York. 'He looked well,' reported Hunter, 'but was not as large as the Prince of Wales when born.' This time Hunter's advice seems to have been taken more seriously by Charlotte, who seemed far readier to adopt his post-partum practice. Only five days after the birth, Hunter was pleased to hear from the king 'that the queen had been down on the couch near two hours, without feeling in the least weak'. He was confident she was now totally converted to his regime.[16]

It was widely rumoured that Charlotte suffered a miscarriage at Richmond some time in 1764, but this proved a rare occurrence for her. A third pregnancy ran as smoothly as her first two, producing another boy, William, born in August 1765. To have delivered three flourishing sons in almost as many years was an achievement many eighteenth-century mothers would have envied; but to have secured the succession to the throne with such generous insurance against disaster surely gave Charlotte a sense both of satisfaction and profound gratitude. Across Europe, other princesses struggled year after year in exhausting and often futile attempts to supply the longed-for male heir, sacrificing their health in the process. The queen knew very well how desperate and destructive this desire could become. Her much-loved brother Charles shared none of Charlotte and George's prolific good luck in the production of sons. Charles's wife gave birth to daughter after daughter, none of whom could inherit the Mecklenburg duchy. In 1776, Charlotte wrote ruefully to him to congratulate him on the birth of yet another dynastically redundant girl: 'I had hoped that it might be a son, but God directs in all things, and that pleasure is reserved for another time.'[17] When, after three more labouring years, the princess finally gave birth to a boy, Charlotte was both delighted and relieved: 'Nothing in the world could give such pleasure and cause me such joy.' She hoped her brother would find in him 'all the joy and satisfaction I find in mine'. Her eldest sons were thriving, especially the Prince of Wales, who was 'as strong and well built as General Freytag, only a little bigger and very kind'.[18] But Charles's family would prove far less robust than Charlotte's sturdy brood: his first wife did not survive yet another pregnancy; a second son died in infancy; and in 1785, Charles's second wife, sister to his first, also lost her life in childbirth. Charlotte did not have to look far to realise how fortunate her own experience had been.

Confident in the healthy profusion of their sons, and with an irony that would not have been lost on their miserable Mecklenburg relations, George and Charlotte now wanted nothing so much as a daughter. When the queen was again pregnant in 1766, Lady Mary Coke, that well-connected habitué of the court, was assured by the four-year-old Prince of Wales that the coming baby would definitely be 'a little princess'. In the extensive journal in which she recorded with painstaking scrupulousness every detail of her encounters with the royal family, Lady Mary confessed her surprise at the family's hunger to provide themselves with a girl. 'I find that the king and queen are very desirous it should be one,' she noted, adding with incredulity that 'they hope they shall have no more sons.'[19] On 29 September, their wishes were gratified with the birth of Charlotte Augusta. The king and queen were instantly delighted with their baby girl and gave her the title of Princess Royal, which could be borne only by the eldest daughter of the monarch. This grand dignity soon eclipsed her own name; all her life she was known simply as 'Royal', which came to define the most important elements of her dignified and self-conscious character.

Royal had been ushered into the world as briskly as her brothers had been, but this time without the assistance of Mrs Draper. A few weeks before the event, Lady Mary Coke had heard that 'the queen was to be brought to bed by Dr Hunter, instead of the old woman, but that it was kept as great a secret as if the fate of the country depended on this change'.[20] For the first time, Hunter was in sole charge of the birth. A Mrs Johnson was employed as an assistant, but very much in a subordinate capacity. Hunter, who was to preside over every one of Charlotte's confinements until old age and incapacity made it impossible, was finally established as the source of all authority, both inside and outside the bedchamber.

The doctor was in attendance the following year when the queen's fourth son Edward – 'the largest child the queen has ever had' – was born. He was on duty again in 1768, when the smooth, conciliating manner for which he was so famous almost foundered in the face of the king's intense desire for another daughter. As Charlotte's confinement drew near, Hunter gamely attempted to prepare George for the possibility that such an outcome could not be guaranteed. Lady Mary Coke reported that he had suggested tentatively to the king that 'whoever sees those lovely princes above stairs must be glad to have another', to which George replied: 'Dr Hunter, I did not think I could be angry with you but I am; and I say, whoever sees that lovely child the Princess Royal above stairs must wish to have the fellow to her.'

Fortunately for Hunter, the baby was indeed another girl, 'the prettiest child the queen had had, but very small'. Her father did not mind the child's size; all that mattered was its sex. 'The king told Dr Hunter that he forgave him, and appeared extremely happy.'[21] Ten days after the birth, Lady Mary heard that the new baby was to be called 'Augusta, or Elizabeth, though the Prince of Wales has a mind it should be Louisa, and says he has desired it of the king; though whether he has as yet power with His Majesty to obtain his request, I really don't know'.[22] In this, as in so many things to come, the king did not see eye to eye with his eldest son; the new princess was named Augusta.

In 1770, the queen gave birth to a third daughter, Elizabeth. The celebrations that marked her arrival were muted in comparison to those that had greeted the Prince of Wales, or even the eldest sister Royal. The addition of a new child to the ever-expanding nursery had become almost an annual event, one to be marked by thankfulness for the healthy survival of mother and child, but not deserving of any special commemoration. Elizabeth was Charlotte's seventh child; as Charlotte dutifully followed what was now the accustomed rhythm of Hunter's post-natal regimen, she could not have known that she was not even halfway through a reproductive marathon that was to last for another thirteen years. A clutch of princes followed Elizabeth: Ernest in 1771, Augustus in 1773 and Adolphus in 1774. They were succeeded by two princesses, Mary in 1776 and Sophia in 1777, and two final princes, Octavius in 1779 and Alfred in 1780. Until the birth of her last child, Amelia, in 1783, Charlotte was pregnant on a more or less continuous basis for over two decades, with rarely more than an eighteen-month break between her deliveries. She had fifteen children, of whom thirteen would survive infancy. She had started early, of course: she was only eighteen when the Prince of Wales was born. The gap between her age and his was smaller than the twenty-one years that separated him from his youngest sister.

*

The size of their family was of immense significance in the creation of George and Charlotte's public persona. It was a vivid demonstration of their commitment to domestic values, a declaration of their devotion to each other, and a tribute to the remarkable fidelity of the king. Other European royals may have fathered as many children as he did, but unlike those of so many of his contemporaries, George's numerous progeny were all the legitimate offspring of his wife. Indeed, the teeming robustness of the king and queen's ever-increasing brood was seen by some commentators as a reward for their unswerving pursuit of the strictest moral conduct. At the same time, the exuberant vitality of the children themselves softened the image of what a well-conducted family life looked like, making good behaviour seem a little less static and severe, a little more lively, and perhaps even sometimes fun.

In practice, the sheer number of siblings the king and queen produced meant that the family very rarely operated as a single unit. From their earliest days, the children tended to divide into small groups. The two eldest sons, George and Frederick, only a year between them, were by far the closest, rarely spending a night apart from each other throughout their childhood. When they were little more than babies, the queen's cabinetmaker constructed for them a pair of twin beds 'under one tester' and surrounded by enveloping red velvet curtains in which the small princes slept together. As 'heir and spare' they clearly occupied a more elevated place in the family hierarchy than the other brothers; William, the next son, seems to have hovered rather yearningly outside the gilded partnership of the elder boys, constantly hoping – usually without success – to be admitted to their world. Edward and Ernest were often placed together, in classrooms and apartments, as were their younger brothers Adolphus and Augustus. The very youngest boys, Octavius and Alfred, were still in the nursery when the older princes were almost adults. The daughters' lives followed a similar pattern. Royal, Augusta and Elizabeth were treated very much as the senior princesses; they were educated together and lived separately from their younger sisters. Mary and Sophia, the middle daughters, formed a tightly knit pair, whilst Amelia, the baby of the family, occupied an especially privileged position, somewhere between pet and mascot, fussed over and admired by all.

These arrangements would have been familiar to other eighteenth-century children, many of whom grew up in similarly large families. The queen was one of ten children; the king one of nine. Lady Kildare, a sister of George's first love Sarah Lennox, produced twenty-two children during her two marriages. Mrs Tunstall, one of the royal housekeepers, had sixteen. Long after her own childbearing days were over,

Charlotte wrote to a friend that she had just met Sir John and Lady Wigram, 'father and mother of twenty children, all alive, their ages from thirty years to five months, and hopes to have four more to complete the two dozen'.[23] The king was a great advocate of big families. When the Countess of Aylesford, already the mother of nineteen children, was about to give birth yet again, George commented that he hoped 'two will be produced ... the more the better'.[24]

Where George and Charlotte were exceptional was in the number of their children who survived the perils of infancy and childhood. Death stalked the eighteenth-century nursery, with appalling consequences. The loss of 'beloved objects' was a miserable inevitability for many parents. To have lost only two of their fifteen made the king and queen extremely fortunate, as they knew from their own youthful experience. Four of the ten children born to Charlotte's parents were dead before they were two. Three of George's siblings died as teenagers. Twelve of Lady Kildare's twenty-two succumbed to childhood sickness, including her adored eldest son, Lord Ophaly, the heir to the earldom. Of Mrs Tunstall's sixteen babies, only a single daughter emerged alive from the schoolroom.

Evidence of the horrifying and seemingly unstoppable cull of the young and vulnerable is to be found in every aspect of eighteenth-century life; every family has its own story to tell of a 'fine child' taken with gut-wrenching suddenness, or of the hand-wringing powerlessness of parents witnessing a long and terminal decline. Particularly poignant in their testimony to the callous universality of loss are the pictures eighteenth-century parents had made of their children. Cheerful, thriving boys and girls gaze happily out of their portraits, but a distressingly large number of the subjects of these tender portraits did not long survive their completion. In Hogarth's famous depiction of the Graham children, baby Thomas, who reaches so eagerly for the cherries his sister holds, was dead before the painting was finished. A touchingly idealised vision on the canvas too often concealed the sad reality of childhood vulnerability.

Whilst it may not have been apparent to the mourning parents of the dead, a quiet demographic revolution had begun to make itself felt in the middle of the eighteenth century, shifting the chances of survival slowly but surely in favour of the child. This was particularly evident amongst the children of upper- and middle-class families, where it is estimated that infant death rates fell by around 30 per cent between 1750 and 1775.[25] In the comfortable homes of the better-off, improved nutrition and higher standards of cleanliness played an important part in accelerating this decline. And whilst many illnesses – particularly tuberculosis – remained resistant to the limited treatments offered by contemporary medicine, other diseases lost some of their ancient destructive force. The gradual withdrawal of plague from Europe and the introduction of early forms of inoculation against smallpox tempered the impact of two powerful epidemic killers of children. This did not mean that childhood became a risk-free experience; as late as the twentieth century, and perhaps until the widespread availability of penicillin, infancy remained a minefield of life-threatening dangers. Yet, for all the tragic instances of individual deaths, more and more wealthy eighteenth-century parents could expect to see larger numbers of their children survive into adulthood.

This extraordinary demographic shift triggered a great debate amongst social historians in the mid-twentieth century, who sought to understand its causes and explain its significance. Some, most notably Philip Aries and Lawrence Stone, argued that improved infant survival rates had an impact on contemporary behaviour that was nothing short of revolutionary, ushering in completely new ideas about the nature of childhood itself. They maintained that in medieval and pre-modern Europe, high levels of child mortality discouraged parents from forming close emotional bonds with their children. When chances of death were so high, it made little sense to invest either time or affection in the very young. Parents kept their distance; their dealings with their children were formal and hierarchical. The wealthy in particular had little personal contact with their young, contracting out the practical business of child-rearing to servants. It was only when death rates decreased in the mid-eighteenth century that this bleak picture began to change. Then, it is argued, parents were able to relax the barriers they had erected over the ages to protect themselves against the likelihood of loss. This in turn encouraged even greater survival rates, since fewer young children died when their wellbeing became the direct responsibility of their parents. In scarcely more than a generation, this process was said to have transformed thinking about children and their place in the world. From the 1750s onwards, the welfare of children, their interests, and even their pleasures, became the paramount aim of all concerned parents.

Since this theory was first articulated, other historians have criticised it as oversimplifying changes in family life. They have argued in favour of a more complex picture, stressing the variety and range of experiences across the ages. Recent scholarship has decisively, and often poignantly, demonstrated that parental affection was very far from being the unique product of any one era. The personal testimony of many pre-eighteenth-century mothers and fathers bears heartbreaking witness to the strength of their love for their vulnerable children, as well as to the depth of their despair when they lost them. No one reading Ben Jonson's raw poem, written in 1603 and mourning the loss of his seven-year-old son to plague, could doubt the sincerity of his love for his lost child:

> Farewell, thou child of my right hand, and joy;
> My sin was too much hope of thee, lov'd boy ...
> Rest in soft peace, and asked, say, here doth lie
> Ben Jonson his best piece of poetry ...

Few scholars now accept the principle of a general 'warming-up' of the emotional temperature of family relationships in this period. But it seems hard to deny that something important was happening to ideas about the relationship between parents and children during the eighteenth century. If parental affection and its impact on family relationships were not the exclusive creation of that period, they were certainly given new force and meaning during its latter decades. During these years, thinking about the duties and pleasures of parenthood had become one of the most keenly debated topics of the day, exercising philosophers, clerics, politicians, moralists and, above all, parents themselves. And what many of them concluded was that that there was little of more importance to society and individuals alike than the achievement of a happy family life.

Emerging from the accumulated observations and arguments of half a century's philosophical and polemical literature, a powerful image gradually took shape of the new model family most likely to deliver this optimistic outcome. At its heart was a complete reappraisal of the nature and meaning of childhood. Traditional religious teaching held that the young were born sinful; it was the duty of parents to civilise them and bring them to a knowledge of God, by chastisement if necessary. Enlightened thinkers took a very different view. For them, children were the embodiment of mankind's original innocence, pure and uncorrupted. They were much influenced by the philosopher John Locke, whose work *Some Thoughts Concerning Education*, published in 1693, did much to popularise the idea of the infant mind as a *tabula rasa*, a clean slate, which it was the task of its mentors carefully to shape and form. Enlightened parents hoped to prepare their children for entry into society without destroying any of the natural virtues with which they had been born. This, they were sure, was far better achieved by affection than any harshness. In the ideal, enlightened family, mothers and fathers exercised their authority gently; they were firm but fair, governing by tenderness not fear, prizing warmth over distance and friendly intimacy over cold authority. They understood that childhood was a unique and special state, with its own particular needs and requirements. The energy and uninhibitedness of children were to be celebrated, not denied. Lively play was to be encouraged, with specially designed toys and games provided to increase their pleasure.

William Hamley, whose descendants went on to run the great toyshop in London's Regent Street that still bears his name, opened his 'Noah's Ark' in High Holborn in 1760, stocking a vast variety of playthings for children of all ages, from tin soldiers to wax dolls and illustrated books for young readers. His first customers were better-off families from the newly built squares and terraces of the West End, prepared to pay handsomely to entertain their offspring. For the truly committed amongst these new consumers, their purchases were about something more than just the delight of the moment. Adding to their children's pleasure was also an investment in the future, since happy boys and girls were far more likely to develop into well-balanced adults, properly fitted to take their place in society. Adding to the enjoyments of your children thus delivered benefits that went far beyond the cheerful indulgence of a doting parent; it was also a forward-looking social duty. Making children happy was a good thing in itself since it was likely to nurture a new generation of fulfilled, content and well-balanced adults, happier in themselves and of far greater use to society.

This was a very seductive blueprint for eighteenth-century parents of a thoughtful cast of mind. It was made all the more appealing by the conviction of many of its advocates that it was easily and practicably achievable. In books and pamphlets, articles and treatises, advice abounded on how to turn the ideal into reality. All agreed that the conscientious parent must be prepared to interrogate and if necessary reject all institutions and thinking that interfered with natural behaviour and affection: established practices in childcare, in education, in discipline, in nutrition, even in the style of children's clothes – nothing was to be regarded as sacred. In pursuit of an uncorrupted upbringing for their sons and daughters, mothers and fathers were told they must be prepared to make great changes in their own lives, as well as those of their offspring.

Nowhere were these ideas more attractively synthesised than in the philosopher Jean-Jacques Rousseau's *Emile, ou de l'éducation* published in 1762. In dense and didactic detail, the book tells the story of Emile, a child of aristocratic parents, who is sent to the country to be raised as far away as possible from the malign, distorting effects of polite, urban life. He lives there in a state of almost complete isolation – significantly, the only book he is allowed is *Robinson Crusoe* – quarantined from customary practices of every kind. His food is plain, his clothing simple, and he spends most of his time outdoors. The cultivation of a strong and hardy body is given as much attention as the nurturing of his mind. As a small child his education is conducted entirely through practical experience, learning from what he sees around him. His spiritual instruction is designed to preserve his instinctual morality rather than expose him to revealed religion.

Emile was an immediate bestseller across Europe, unquestionably one of the most influential books of the century. It was bought even by those who disagreed with the radical political philosophy of Rousseau's earlier works. In Britain it became a publishing phenomenon, reviewed everywhere, serialised in magazines, and provoking intense and lively debate in correspondence columns about its virtues and deficiencies. The small part played by religion in Emile's upbringing displeased some commentators – it was publicly burnt in France as a result of what he had to say about the role of the Catholic Church – but this had no discernible effect on its popularity amongst British readers.

Rousseau always insisted he had not written the book as a practical guide, although that did not prevent some of his more committed admirers attempting to replicate Emile's experiences. Lady Kildare, a deep devotee, actually offered him a job as tutor to her children. When he declined, she embarked on the experiment without him, leaving her home at the heart of ascendancy Dublin, abandoning her role as a political hostess and decamping to the rural coast of Black Rock, where she attempted to raise her huge family in circumstances as close to Emile's as possible. Some readers were more sceptical: Lady Kildare's sister, Caroline Fox, declared there were 'more paradoxes, more absurdities' in it than almost any other book she had read – but perhaps the great majority of Rousseau's many readers sat somewhere between these two responses.[26] What they took away from *Emile* was a potent, if romanticised summation of Enlightenment ideas about family life, from which they cherry-picked those for which they felt the most sympathy, and adapted them as best they could into the requirements of real life. For, despite Rousseau's protests that he had not written a handbook, there is no doubt some of his audience did regard it as a prescriptive text and acted on what they believed to be his recommendations. Contemporary commentators attributed the rapid decline of the swaddling of babies in England, which had virtually disappeared by the end of the century, almost entirely to his criticism of the practice.

Equally influential was his forcefully expressed conviction that the welfare of children was the direct, personal responsibility of all conscientious parents. Rousseau had very harsh things to say about those who handed children over to the governance of servants and tutors. The nurturing and care of children was not a chore to be outsourced; it was the central obligation, and indeed one of the principal pleasures, of parenthood. In theory, bringing up the young was a duty incumbent on both parents; but Rousseau had little doubt that, in practice, it was the mother who had the most important role to play. 'In the union of the sexes,' he wrote, 'each contributes equally to the common aim, but not in the same way.' Both in physiology and temperament, nature had marked women out for a special role as nurturers and carers.

Rousseau maintained that among the rich and well-to-do, this first duty had been too often subordinated to the requirements of polite society, but was convinced any thoughtful woman would much prefer to undertake the care of her children herself, if allowed to do so. In the 1760s, and beyond, his message was ardently embraced by an ever-increasing number of aristocratic women. The Countess of Shelburne, secure in the happy intimacy of her model marriage, was as fulfilled as a mother as she was as a wife. She devoted her days to her toddler son in a way that would have surely won Rousseau's approval. She spent her mornings with the little boy, walking in the gardens with him 'without his nurse'. She watched him dine, and after he had slept returned to the nursery to 'teach him to spell words till it is time to dress for my own dinner'.[27]

George and Charlotte embarked on their own experiment with parenthood on the crest of the first wave of enthusiasm for the new thinking. *Emile* was published in the year of the Prince of Wales's birth. Like so many other young mothers of her age, Charlotte had a copy, which she added to a growing collection of other books on the subject that formed a substantial part of her private library. These were not ornamental acquisitions, but works Charlotte clearly knew well. In 1776, she sent her brother Charles 'a book which contains everything about how to care for children from the moment of their birth ... Have it translated, and return the original when you please. Follow a little of our method, and you will find that your children will soon grow stronger.'[28]

Charlotte was exactly the kind of intellectually minded, conscientious young woman for whom modern ideas about child-rearing exerted the strongest possible appeal. But, from the earliest days of her own motherhood, it was clear that her ability to implement Rousseau's principles would be limited by the customary practices the author deplored. Judged by his standards, Charlotte fell at the very first hurdle when she did not breastfeed her children. For Rousseau, breastfeeding was the touchstone of a woman's commitment to the whole ideal of better parenting, the source from which all resulting social benefits flowed. 'But let mothers deign to nurse their children,' he wrote in *Emile*, 'morals will reform themselves, nature's sentiments will be awakened in every breast, the state will be re-peopled.' Until the mid-eighteenth century, most women who could afford to do so hired wet nurses to feed their babies; in the years that followed, the climate steadily shifted in favour of mothers suckling their own children. By the end of the century, maternal breastfeeding had become the prevailing ideological orthodoxy.

'The first of the parental duties which nature points out to the mother is to be herself the nurse of her own offspring,' sternly opined the cleric Thomas Gisborne in 1797, in a widely read series of reflections on the duties of women. To hire a wet nurse except in cases of absolute physical incapacity 'is to evince a most shameful degree of selfishness and unnatural insensibility'.[29] The assumption that breast was best extended even to children themselves. Lady Kildare, that enthusiastic devotee of Rousseau's principles, had been forbidden to suckle her children as doctors feared it would affect her already poor sight; later, she found herself having to justify her lapse to her young son, as keen as Rousseau himself to draw conclusions about human behaviour from observation of the natural world. '"Mama, don't the mothers of calves give them suck?" "Yes," says I. "And why then did you not give me suck, for you are my mother, like the mothers of the little calves?"' Lady Kildare was hurt and ashamed. 'Now, was this not quite cutting? I was ready to cry, but I told him the naughty doctors would not let me.'[30]

Charlotte had no medical dispensation to excuse her from 'the first duty'. It is clear from Hunter's journal that she had plenty of milk with her first three babies, but there seems never to have been any question she would feed them herself. It may well have been regarded as incompatible with her public role, as it would have obliged her to neglect many of her official duties. It would also have absented her from the marital bed. Contemporary medical opinion considered sex during lactation extremely undesirable; it was thought adversely to affect the quality of the milk, as well as exhausting a woman already physically reduced by the demands of nursing. If a woman employed a wet nurse, she was generally regarded as ready to get back into sexual harness a month or so after giving birth. The feminist writer Mary Wollstonecraft, writing at the end of the century, noted scornfully that some husbands, 'devoid of sense and parental affection', refused to allow their wives to breastfeed because they were not prepared to endure the period of celibacy it required. Looking at the pattern of her pregnancies, there seems little doubt that this was Charlotte's experience; had she breastfed her own babies, she might well have produced fewer of them. Although the contraceptive effects of lactation itself remain a subject of debate, only the most demanding of eighteenth-century husbands would have expected his wife to resume sexual relations whilst she was still feeding a child. One way or another, Charlotte's practice of handing over her babies to wet nurses contributed to her extraordinary fertility.

It is of course possible that the decision not to breastfeed was not Charlotte's. Her mother-in-law, the Princess Dowager Augusta, was a powerful presence during Charlotte's first confinements, and, in common with most women of her generation, had made unquestioning use of a wet nurse, and may have been instrumental in ensuring her daughter-in-law followed her example. Certainly it was she who selected and vetted the woman who was to take on that role for Charlotte: Mrs Margaret Scott, the wife of a Kentish squire who had fallen on hard times. It was an important and well-rewarded post: the Duchess of Northumberland heard that Mrs Scott was 'to have £500 for the first year, and one or two for life. Her husband is to have £1,000 a year.' In return, Mrs Scott was to devote herself entirely to the prince to the exclusion of all other activity. 'She is neither to see, write to, nor receive any letters from any of her friends.'[31] Although the duchess thought she looked sickly (she had just given birth to her tenth child), under her care, the prince flourished. Perhaps because she seems to have played so little part in her appointment, Charlotte did not like her. Recalling Mrs Scott's regime in later years, the queen declared that she had been difficult from the start, meddling, argumentative and prone to stand on her dignity. Future wet nurses were chosen with regard more to calmness of disposition than claims of gentility.

Thomas Gisborne argued that failure to breastfeed often arose from want of affection on the mother's part. Such an accusation could not be levelled at Charlotte, who, within the restrictive bounds of royal behaviour, was an attentive parent to her first son. She asked to have him given to her as soon as he was born, and in later weeks was often to be seen carrying him in her arms. In 1763, every inch the proud mother, she presented the king with a wax head of his eldest son mounted on a column which gently rotated, so that the model could be seen from every side.

As childhood was increasingly seen as a uniquely precious and beautiful state, capturing its essence became the ambition of both patrons and artists alike – and, as domestically minded parents, the king and queen were at the very heart of this unfolding project. Charlotte and George celebrated their affection for their growing family in the pictures they commissioned. They had their family painted constantly, in a huge variety of media, and in every possible grouping, from intimate single portraits to large, ambitious conversation pieces. They embraced modern ideas about how best to portray the young, favouring painterly styles which encapsulated all the newest thinking about what it was to be a child. The decades during which their sons and daughters were born saw the depiction of children in art aspire towards an ever-greater informality, with a sense of joy and exuberance replacing the more stately images of previous years. By the 1780s, the subjects of youthful portraiture had, for the most part, moved out of the drawing room and into the open air, just as Rousseau recommended for their real-life counterparts. Children were shown romping with pets, digging the garden, playing cricket, picking fruit and generally having a high time of it. At the beginning of the period, painters such as Allan Ramsey (one of George's favourites) sought to convey a calmer, more restrained vision of domestic happiness. In 1764, he produced a delicate and tender picture of Charlotte and her two young sons. The queen and her boys are posed against a neutral grey background, anonymous yet undeniably grand; tall pillars loom out of the shadows. The centre of the picture glows with light, and framed within it sits the small family group, united and gently entwined with one another. The Prince of Wales, a sturdy toddler, leans against his mother's leg, a toy bow in his hand, whilst his younger brother Frederick perches on her lap. The queen's arm rests on her spinet; among the many papers piled upon it can be glimpsed a copy of John Locke's *Some Thoughts Concerning Education*. The tone is wistful, almost dream-like, and the very isolation of the trio emphasises the strength of the bond between them. At the same time, it quietly suggests the things that unite the family as a whole: a shared passion for music, an interest in learning and, above all, a depth of affection between parent and children that was the bedrock of their life together.

Twelve years later, in 1776, Benjamin West painted the six middle children in a very different style. West, best known for his epic historical canvases, sought to convey liveliness and energy rather than the hushed stillness of Ramsey's picture. The royal children are shown outside in a garden, transfixed by the antics of a small dog that attempts to catch a ball thrown by one of the boys. Prince Ernest holds the dog's lead; a drum and other toys lie discarded on the ground; no adult is present to demand they be picked up. The boys wear their hair long and unpowdered, and sport white open-collared shirts, a style that had become the virtual uniform of the modern, informally reared child. One of the princes is shown with his stockings falling down. The boys are clearly having a rather better time than their sisters, who look on with a slightly anxious, preoccupied air.

By 1785, in a picture by John Singleton Copley, even girls are allowed to have fun. The three youngest princesses are shown enjoying themselves in a wooded grove, where cheerful chaos rules. Three dogs bark and gambol, Princess Mary brandishes a tambourine, Sophia holds up her skirts, whilst the infant Amelia, in an elaborate baby carriage and even more elaborate hat, raises her hands in excited pleasure. The contrast with Ramsey's painting of twenty years earlier could not be greater. It is a noisy and energetic picture – the final effect is one of hectic gaiety rather than genuine unforced liveliness – which seeks to capture childish excitement in all its unruly excess. In its heightened emotionalism, Copley's work looks forward to the Romantics, whilst Ramsey's serene image has its heart in a more ordered, classical world.

Perhaps the most beautiful of the pictures which the king and queen had made of themselves and their children was one of the very simplest. Soon after the birth of the Princess Royal, Charlotte was drawn in pastels by Francis Cotes. She is shown holding her baby daughter, who lies sleeping in her arms. She wears simple clothes, her brown hair undressed, and she looks directly at the viewer, one finger delicately raised in a silent request not to wake the child. It is a beguiling and delicate vision of maternal affection, and was much praised when it was publicly exhibited in 1767. Lady Mary Coke thought it caught the queen's character and likeness better than any other picture: 'It was so like it could not be mistaken for any other person.'[32] Even Walpole, usually immune to the appeal of royal imagery, thought it 'incomparable'.[33] But the most appreciative of the picture's many admirers was the king himself. He had it placed in his bedchamber at the Queen's House, so he could enjoy it every day. When the family moved to Windsor, it went with him, and was still in his room in 1813, when he was too blind to see it clearly and not always lucid enough to remember what it depicted.

'I did not love my children when they were young,' George II once admitted; 'I hated to have them running into my room.'[34] In this, as in so many other ways, George III was very different from his grandfather. 'The king loves little babies,' one observer noted approvingly.[35] When his children were toddlers, he was an unaffectedly fond and surprisingly informal father. Mrs Scott remembered how the king would 'at times shed the dignity of a monarch in the natural impulse of a parent' and get down on to the floor in order to play with his young sons. Mrs Mary Delany, a close friend of the family, watched 'as the king carried around in his arms, by turns, Princess Sophia and the last Prince, Octavius'. Although Mrs Delany was very much of an older generation, she had nothing but praise for this open, uninhibited display of parental affection. 'I never saw more lovely children; nor a more pleasing sight than the king's fondness for them, and the queen's; they seem to have but one mind, and that is to have everyone happy around them. The king brought in his arms the little Octavius to me, who held out his hand to play with me, which, on my taking the liberty to kiss, he made me kiss his cheek.'[36] Nearly twenty years later, George's enthusiasm for playing with his smallest children seemed undiminished: in 1785, Mrs Delany spent an evening at Windsor with George and Charlotte and their youngest child, 'the beautiful babe Amelia', who took huge pleasure 'in playing with the king upon the carpet'.[37]

George was far from unique in both the strength of his feelings for his children and his willingness to show them. The domestic ideal was as attractive and as powerful for eighteenth-century men as it was for women. A man was never more of a man than when he was to be seen at the head of a fine family of numerous healthy children, and the pride and affection felt by fathers for their broods shine out from contemporary letters and diaries and infused all social classes. The aristocrat William Finch described to his wife his own well-meaning attempts to live up to the modern fatherly ideal. He and 'the pretty boy' played together when alone. 'He was cook in the kitchen this morning and dressed a dinner for me and when I had dined, I said, thank you Master Cook, He thought I had said Nasty Cook and I assure you, it was a good while before I could make it up.'[38] William Ramsden, a London schoolteacher, took open, glowing pleasure in the company of his son. Sitting 'on the arm of my wife's easy chair' in the nursery, contemplating his little boy, Ramsden felt his was 'a situation I would not change with the King of Prussia, no, not with a man a million times more to be envied, George the third, King of Great Britain'.[39]

George himself worked very hard to ensure that the pressures of his public role did not entirely crowd out pleasures of the kind so treasured by Ramsden. He was a regular visitor to his children's nursery, arriving before the official duties of the day claimed him, 'at the early hour of five in the morning, gently tapping at the door of their apartments to enquire how they spent the night'.[40] Even during the Gordon Riots of 1780, which saw London erupt in violence, prisons burning, the House of Commons barricaded and civil authority all but collapse,

George I: 'ordinarily neither cheerful nor friendly, dry and crabbed' (oil on copper, after Godfrey Kneller, c. 1714).

Sophia Dorothea of Celle: a high-maintenance beauty married to an undemonstrative man (mezzotint, by William Faithorne Jr, after Johann Kerseboom, early 18th century).

George II: passionate, forthright, irritable, but with 'fewer sensations of revenge ... than any man who ever sat upon a throne' (oil on canvas, by or after Thomas Worlidge, c. 1753).

Queen Caroline: clever, energetic, managing, and said to possess the best bosom in Europe (oil on canvas, by Jacopo Amigoni, 1735).

Frederick, Prince of Wales: 'I think this is a son I need not be much afraid of' (oil on canvas, by Philip Mercier, 1736).

Augusta, Princess of Wales: admired by her husband for her apparently obedient, docile nature – 'that all-consenting tongue,/that never puts me in the wrong' (oil on canvas, attributed to William Hogarth, c. 1736).

Prince George and Prince Edward with their tutor Francis Ayscough: an image of learning at its most chilly and severe (oil on canvas, by Richard Wilson, c. 1749).

John, 3rd Earl of Bute: tall, dark and brooding, the earl displays to advantage the legs of which he was so proud (oil on canvas, by Joshua Reynolds, 1773).

Queen Charlotte: 'not a beauty', but 'amiable, and her face rather agreeable than otherwise' (watercolour on ivory, unknown artist, c. 1761).

George, Prince of Wales: 'tall and robust, more graceful than genteel ... he had now and then a few pimples out' (pastel on vellum, by Jean-Etienne Liotard, 1754).

Augusta, Dowager Princess of Wales: Augusta as she chose to be depicted in middle age – unflinching and unadorned (pastel on paper, by Jean-Etienne Liotard, 1754).

George III: the defining depiction of the young king – the demand for copies of this picture was immense (oil on canvas, by Allan Ramsay, 1761).

Queen Charlotte: the official portrait in coronation robes – a less flattering image of the teenage queen (oil on canvas, by Allan Ramsay, 1761).

Queen Charlotte with Charlotte, Princess Royal: 'The Queen, fine; the Child, incomparable' – this picture was still hanging in the king's private apartments in 1813, during his final illness (pastel, by Francis Cotes, 1767).

Queen Charlotte with George, Prince of Wales, and Frederick, Duke of York: maternal affection expressed in the midst of looming grandeur – John Locke's *Some Thoughts Concerning Education* can be seen among the queen's papers (oil on canvas, by Allan Ramsay, c. 1764).

Prince Ernest, Prince Augustus, Princess Augusta, the infant Princess Mary, Prince Adolphus and Princess Elizabeth: the growing brood of royal children, with the princes wearing the open-collared, relaxed clothes of the modern, natural child (oil on canvas, by Benjamin West, 1776).

Princess Mary, Princess Amelia and Princess Sophia: the pleasures of boisterous play, which even princesses could now enjoy (oil on canvas, by John Singleton Copley, 1785).

the king found time 'to see his children, on whom he fondly doted'.[41] When he went to Portsmouth in 1778 to review the fleet, the queen wrote to tell him how badly he was missed by his young daughter, Mary. 'She desired me to call dear Papa; but after telling her that could not be, she desired to be lifted up and she called for at least half an hour, Papa coming, Papa comes! But seeing she was disappointed by receiving no answer, I desired her to tell me what I should say to the king in case I should write and she answered, Miny [Mary's nickname] say goody Papa, poor Papa.'[42]

The queen's relationship with her children was just as conscientious as that of the king. She was painstaking in her practical concern for their health and welfare: one of Charlotte's earliest biographers noted with approval her determination to be a real presence in her children's world, 'not leaving them, as some would have done, to the management of attendants, but indulging herself in their innocent prattle, sharing in their little amusements, and leading them carefully into the first paths of knowledge'.[43] The close personal attention Charlotte took in the direction of her children's upbringing soon made her a model of modern maternal solicitude, neatly summed up by a poem written in 1779:

> The queen, they say,
> Attends her nursery every day,
> And like a common mother, shares
> In all her infants' little cares.[44]

The punctiliousness of Charlotte's care of her children's minds and their bodies reflected her conviction that this was one of the most important duties of motherhood. But she found it much harder than her husband to lose herself in play and the informal pleasures of parenthood. She was more restrained in her dealings with her children, in public at least, rarely indulging in boisterous demonstrations of affection. The easy, relaxed displays of intimacy which characterised George's relationship with his young children were not Charlotte's style. Indeed, her very presence was sometimes enough to stop them. Mrs Scott, the Prince of Wales's wet nurse, maintained that 'on the approach of the queen (at all times dignified and strict, especially with the Duke of York), His Majesty would assume a royal demeanour' and put an end to the games on the floor.[45]

Charlotte's somewhat chilly restraint, her refusal to lose the dignity of the queen to the spontaneity of motherhood, does not necessarily indicate want of deep feelings on her part, so much as an inability to express them in public. Over the years, her husband had become far less self-conscious, acquiring a degree of imperturbability that gave him the confidence to abandon the constraints of formal behaviour when it suited him. Charlotte never mastered this very important royal skill. Her exacting, dutiful temperament shrank away from the gaze of observers, and she quickly learnt to conceal or subdue her inner feelings. Very early in her career as a parent, she imposed on herself a rigorous discipline which hid her emotions beneath an air of superficial calm. She refused to parade her feelings to satisfy the curiosity of those around her. When her fifth son, Ernest, was taken severely ill, and was thought to be dying, Charlotte's iron self-control amazed the curious Lady Mary Coke. 'I make no doubt of the queen's concern,' she confided to her journal, 'but I am surprised it does not appear more. The day I saw her, she did not seem as if anything gave her uneasiness.'[46] The preservation of a bland outward equanimity, gracious but impenetrable, did not allow much opportunity for the unguarded expression of strong affections.

Many aristocratic families of George and Charlotte's generation who were trying to raise their children in the modern style felt the pressures between their public and private roles. For the queen, the tensions between her two identities were acute. One observer noted that Charlotte was only free to act as a mother 'whenever those duties did not interfere with public duties, or any plans or wishes of the king'.[47] The close relationship that bound the king and queen together meant that George liked to have his wife by his side in every appropriate moment. She attended not just the twice-weekly Drawing Rooms, but also went with him on official trips, to military reviews and other ceremonial events. She was expected to be on duty for more pleasurable expeditions too, for visits to the theatre or to the musical concerts that formed such an important part of their lives. If George and Charlotte's marriage had been more typical of an arranged, royal alliance, the queen might have had more free time to deploy as she wished; but she and the king did not live the separate existences so common amongst those of their peers who were less happily married. This meant, as Charlotte herself so often wistfully declared, 'my time is not my own'. The primacy of her obligation to the king severely limited her ability to do anything else at all.

Rousseau and his followers offered a vision of motherhood as a kind of profession. It was one that Charlotte would surely have embraced, had she not already had a job, and one which she recognised, from her earliest days as a parent, would always prevent her from becoming a true model of modern motherhood. She could establish the principles by which her family would be raised; she could monitor their development, ensuring the most rigorous attention to their health and welfare; she could provide the moral compass by which their growing minds were to be steered; and whenever her other duties allowed, she could sweep into the nursery and see for herself how her prescriptions were working out in practice. But as she herself understood, Charlotte was essentially an overseer; the ideas were hers, but the detailed implementation of them would have to be managed by someone else. She needed someone who shared her vision, who understood her priorities, whom she could trust absolutely, and who had the authority and experience to implement her thinking. She needed, above all, someone who would offer the consistent, daily presence that she could not. In a world where her calling as a mother was constantly trumped by her duties as a wife and queen, she needed a proxy. In Lady Charlotte Finch, she found one.

CHAPTER 7

Private Lives

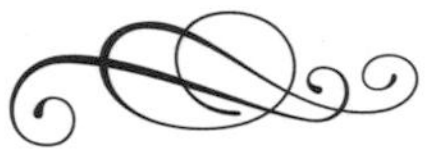

LADY CHARLOTTE FINCH WAS APPOINTED governess to the Prince of Wales only four days after his birth in August 1762. In addition to being well connected (she was the second daughter of the impecunious Earl of Pomfret), her intellectual qualifications were unimpeachable. Horace Walpole, whose standards were high, thought her 'a woman of remarkable sense and philosophy … the cleverest girl in the world'.[1] She had been painstakingly educated, her studies supplemented by travels across Europe with her rather rackety family. She was a voracious reader, consuming works of philosophy, history and theology in a formidable variety of languages. Walpole was impressed to discover she spoke 'the purest Tuscan, like any Florentine'.[2] In middle age, armed with only a dictionary and a great deal of determination, she taught herself to read Spanish. Her literary pursuits had not undermined her religious faith; she was a committed Christian, with a strong sense of moral purpose.

Charlotte Finch shared so many of the queen's interests and preoccupations that it was not surprising that Charlotte liked and admired her; she was the first of a long line of similarly minded, clever women invited into her household, and in many ways proved the most successful. She was exactly the kind of concerned, scholarly mother the queen would have chosen to be herself, if her rank had allowed it. When her own children were small, Lady Charlotte dedicated herself entirely to their upbringing, spending all her time with them. 'I rise at seven, and by eight have all my little ones about me in my dressing room … We read our Psalms and Chapter together, then at nine we go for breakfast, after which the children walk for an hour, then the three eldest come into my room and read to me the History of Scotland.'[3] The day progressed, taking in French, more history, some drawing and the reading of fairy tales together after dinner (which Rousseau, with his deep-seated distrust of all fiction, would never have countenanced).

But Lady Charlotte's apparently calm and contented family life had a bleaker side to it. Although her marriage to William Finch was for many years very happy – they had four children and he was an affectionate and engaged father – as he grew older, his behaviour grew increasingly erratic and violent. It was eventually rumoured that this once charming and likeable man had beaten his wife and attempted to throw her down the stairs, upon which the couple separated. As a result, Lady Charlotte was left to face the second tragedy in her life alone. In 1765, two of her adored daughters died young from tuberculosis, enduring long and painful periods of illness which their desperate mother could do nothing to assuage. 'It pleased Almighty God to take my dear child Frances to himself, this day a little before 5 o'clock in the evening,' she wrote bleakly in her diary.[4] Lady Charlotte knew from her own bitter experience how fragile was the happiness provided by children and family, and how quickly it could slip from one's grasp.

Despite all her difficulties, she proved a stable and loving presence in the lives of her royal charges. Child after child passed through her hands, all treated with the same 'constant, affectionate care' that she had brought to the raising of her own family. When they were young, she was probably the most important figure in the lives of George and Charlotte's children; long after they were grown up, they continued to speak of 'Lady Cha', as they all called her, with the warmest love and respect. When she was over fifty and living far away from home in Germany, the Princess Royal still kept Lady Cha's portrait in her room 'as my constant companion, and I never fail two or three times a day looking on that dear countenance I owe so much to'.[5] When Lady Charlotte died in 1813, Princess Mary declared simply that she was 'everything to me and all my dear brothers and sisters … my first friend, whose friendship I valued far beyond what I can describe'.[6]

Lady Cha worked hard to make a comfortable and secure home for the royal children. She oversaw all the practical tasks that non-royal mothers increasingly undertook themselves, but which the queen had not the time to do. She ordered their clothes, organised their games, bought their toys, and watched over their illnesses; she even put them to bed at night. Every aspect of their lives, great and small, came under her all-encompassing control. Her bond with the two eldest boys was particularly strong: she referred to them in her diary as 'my dear little princes', and cared for them tenderly when they were in the least unhappy or 'disordered' – including monitoring them with special attentiveness as they navigated the perils of inoculation.

George and Charlotte were enthusiastic advocates of this relatively new insurance against smallpox, and had all their children vaccinated. Before Edwin Jenner perfected the use of cowpox, the process was a lengthy and often dangerous one. Charlotte Papendiek, the young daughter of one of the queen's attendants, was inoculated alongside Prince William in 1768, and as an old woman remembered how painful it had been. A measured dose of infected material was introduced to the patient via 'two points in the arm ... made with the point of a lancet through which a thread was dragged several times under the skin and this on both arms'.[7] The child was then sent home to remain in bed for about ten days, preferably in the dark, until the disease showed itself. When the Prince of Wales and the Duke of York underwent the procedure, it was Lady Charlotte who undressed them and put them to bed. (Some days later, the Duchess of Northumberland heard that the prince had been asked if he was not bored with spending so much time in bed. 'He answered, "Not at all, I lie and make reflections." ... He was then only three years and seven months old, but the forwardest child in understanding I ever saw.'[8])

In the same year, Lady Charlotte began to instruct the prince and his brother Frederick in reading and writing. To engage the boys' attention, she used a set of alphabetical counters made of ivory, each with a letter on one side, and a picture of an object beginning with that letter on the other. She was clearly an able teacher; only a year later, the six-year-old Prince of Wales had made sufficient progress to write his first proper letter. In a large unformed hand, it was addressed to the queen. 'My dear Mama,' he wrote; 'Nothing could make me so happy as Your Majesty's letter, and I will always endeavour to follow the good advice you give me in it, being Your Majesty's most dutiful son, George P.'[9] It was the beginning of a lifetime of correspondence in which Charlotte urged her eldest son to live up to her standards of behaviour; few of his later replies were so innocently eager to please.

Lady Charlotte strove to replicate for the royal children the cheerful intimacy that had characterised the upbringing of her own family, creating in the nursery a private world that was as warm and informal as possible. In one respect, she was considered by some to have succeeded only too well. By the early 1770s, the behaviour of the princes had become a byword for boisterousness. In 1774, Lady Mary Coke heard that the queen's brother, Ernest, who was visiting from Mecklenburg, nearly lost an eye as a result of his nephews' uninhibited horseplay: 'Three of the younger ones were playing with him; one fell behind him, another was on one side of him, and a third he held by the hand.' When the youngest prince fell over, Ernest 'tried to prevent it, by which he lost his poise and could not recover himself, and finding that if he fell backwards he must fall upon the child, he threw himself forward and came down with his eye against a chair or a table'. Lady Mary was pleased to hear that 'providentially, the sight of his eye is saved', but for a while the hapless Ernest presented 'a terrible sight, from the blood having fallen down behind his eye'.[10] Years later, household attendants were still recalling with a shudder the 'loudness and … force' of the young princes' voices. One of the king's equerries stated that 'there was something in the violence of their animal spirits that would make him accept no post or pay to live with them'.[11]

The wildness of the princes' behaviour in private may have been a response to the formality of their lives in the public sphere. Lady Charlotte strove to build a safe space in which the children could experience as many of the unique pleasures of childhood as possible; but she could not prevent the outside world from making its presence powerfully felt. The contrast between the relaxed atmosphere of the nursery and the rigidity and pomp of the court could not have been greater, and from their earliest days, the children were expected to navigate it, shedding the carefree persona of the natural child and putting on the dignified bearing of a prince. This was particularly true of the Prince of Wales, who, as the heir, was on display from the very moment of his birth. Only a few hours after his delivery, he was 'brought out and shown to all'.[12] Some days later, placed in a grand state cradle, the lord mayor and a long line of City dignitaries filed past to pay their respects. These were the opening acts of a lifetime spent in the unflinching intensity of the public gaze.

Lady Charlotte did all she could to prepare her charges for the inevitability of their destiny, orchestrating little events to accustom them to the idea of being on show. In the summer of 1766, to mark the fourth birthday of the Prince of Wales, she staged a theatrical performance for the king and queen in which their three sons all took part. The eldest prince 'danced a hornpipe in a sailor's dress'; Frederick, aged three, accompanied him in a harlequin costume, whilst William, barely more than a baby, was dressed as 'a mademoiselle'. A year before, the infant George had held his first formal audience, when, under the watchful eye of his governess, he received a delegation from the Society of Ancient Britons. Lady Charlotte described in her diary how they arrived 'wearing three ostrich feathers in their hats', as a mark of respect to the Prince of Wales. They presented a formal address, after which the prince 'spoke a short answer to them' and 'gave them, from my hands, a purse with a hundred guineas'. Satisfied, the Ancient Britons 'kissed his hand, and marched away as they came, in procession, with music.'[13] When required to meet the Britons again, in 1768, Lady Charlotte was delighted to see the ease with which her young charge received his guests, exclaiming to her friend Lady Mary Coke that George had 'made his answer ... without so much as looking at her, and spoke as distinctly as if he had been twenty years of age'.[14]

Even when they were not on formal show, the royal children were rarely free from scrutiny. They lived in an atmosphere of intense and all-pervasive public curiosity; their looks, behaviour, tastes and conversation were constantly and minutely observed, described and commented upon. The Duchess of Northumberland and Lady Mary Coke, whose diaries give such rich accounts of court life in the period, were only two of a squadron of inquisitive courtiers who patrolled the periphery of the royal family's privacy, intrigued by any details they could discover. Even the nursery offered no sanctuary. Lady Mary was often invited to visit, and had no scruples about recording what she saw. She was an ardent royalist, almost fanatically devoted to the idea of monarchy, but she could be unsparing in her criticisms of the royals themselves, even the youngest members of the family. The hapless Princess Royal attracted her disapproving attention from her earliest days. 'I own I think her a very plain child,' she wrote dismissively in 1768, when the little girl was only two.[15] For Royal's eldest brother, however, Lady Mary had nothing but praise, painstakingly noting his every saying and observation. She thought him quite exceptional, charming, clever, polite and amusing. 'I see no fault in the Prince of Wales, thinking him one of the finest boys I ever knew.'[16]

It was no doubt easier to cope with this kind of attention if it was informed by admiration rather than disapproval, but the awareness of being on constant display was unlikely to nurture in the royal children a sense of carefree innocence. In this, as in many other ways, there were limits in the degree to which their upbringing could conform to fashionable contemporary models of child-rearing. The requirements of royalty too often trumped the desire for a more natural experience. Nothing could be more antithetical to the new ideas of childhood than the development of a formal image that they were obliged to adopt, an artificial dignity behind which the child's true identity was hidden or suppressed; but the royal children learnt very early that this was an essential part of their development.

In 1772, the Duchess of Northumberland saw the two eldest princes presented to their parents in full possession of their polished, polite, public identities. The boys, aged ten and nine, were 'both dressed exactly alike, their hair without curl or powder, otherwise they were full-dressed, had swords and crimson velvet, (without even a gold or silver button) dressed coats with plain gold tissue waistcoats'. Their behaviour matched the style of their clothes. 'They both accosted the king and queen in a most respectful manner. If anything,' added the duchess, 'I thought too formal.'[17] What troubled her was the incongruence between the boys' demeanour as children and as representatives of royalty. In a past world where formality was the touchstone of most elite behaviour, the gap between the princes' two roles would have been a small one; now it had widened into a great abyss, fraught with difficulties for those who had to negotiate its often confusing and contradictory demands. This was as true for the king and queen as it was for the young princes.

*

As they grew older, the demands of the formal, regulated life pressed hard on George and Charlotte's attempts to create a more intimate, relaxed space for themselves. On the same day that she watched the deferential presentation of the princes, the Duchess of Northumberland noted regretfully how much the behaviour of their parents too had changed. A decade after their marriage, the pressure of custom and tradition had squeezed out many of the small informalities that had been such an important feature of their early life together, and had defined their relationship, not just with each other, but also with those around them. 'Formerly, the queen had made the tea herself and the king carried it about to the ladies,' mused the duchess, but now, two pages performed the task. Etiquette had edged out easy simplicity. The duchess also noticed that the king no longer took off his formal clothes when he came into more friendly company: 'Another difference I remarked was that formerly, the moment the Drawing Room was over, the king used to strip into his frock, whereas this evening he appeared full-dressed.'[18]

Even in some of the most private areas of their life, George and Charlotte seem to have gradually given up the struggle to preserve the informality and homeliness they had once so prized. 'The king shaves his head and has put on a wig,' reported the duchess in 1772; 'he had always worn one till he was married, but after that, at the request of the queen, he let his hair grow, which became him extremely.'[19] The exchange of a natural look loved by his wife for an artificial style prescribed by custom could not say more about the slow encroachment of obligation and expectation on the optimism with which George and Charlotte had embarked on their life together.

It was surely not a coincidence that in the very year the duchess noted the alterations in the king and queen's way of life, the couple made a conscious attempt to preserve what remained of their original secluded intimacy. 'We are going to move this summer to Kew,' Charlotte told her brother in March; 'it will be better and more private.'[20] The move was made easier by the death, a month before, of the king's mother.

Augusta had lived an increasingly retired life since her son came to the throne, rarely attending court and making few public appearances. It had been clear for some time that she was seriously ill with cancer of the throat. As stubborn and secretive in sickness as she had been in health, Augusta would not acknowledge her condition, either to her children or her servants, and refused to consult a doctor. Walpole reported, with cruel detail, that 'she could swallow but with the greatest difficulty, and not enough to maintain life. At times, the disease oozed too plentifully from her mouth to be disguised. And her sufferings and her struggles to hide them, were so much beyond her strength that she frequently fainted and was thought dead.'[21] George and Charlotte were assiduous in visiting her every Saturday evening between six and eight. When it was clear she could not long survive, they arrived a day early, unannounced. 'Hearing they were come,' wrote Walpole, 'the princess rose, dressed herself, and attempted to walk to meet them, but was … [too] weak and unable.' The king and queen remained until ten, when Augusta 'signed to them to retire as usual'. They refused to leave, and stayed with her until six o'clock in the morning, when she died, with what Charlotte told her brother was 'the greatest possible ease'.[22] Even Walpole, who had been one of Augusta's fiercest critics and who had done more than anyone else to blacken her reputation, admired her bravery in her last days, declaring that 'her fortitude was invincible'.[23]

More than anyone else, except Lord Bute, Augusta had been responsible for shaping her son's character and destiny. It is impossible to know what George really felt about this complex woman, with her cool, undemonstrative character, her impenetrable reserve, and her iron determination concealed behind a mask of imperturbability. It is hard to see much evidence of warm affection in their relationship; but as long as she lived, he was tireless in defending her character against slurs and slander, and never treated her with anything less than the utmost respect and duty. Now she was gone, he felt able to sever a link with life as he had lived it for the decade since his marriage. His mother's death made it possible for him to establish a new home for his family away from a metropolitan existence he found increasingly uncongenial. It also offered a more direct opportunity. Augusta's house in Kew was now available; George quickly decided to take it over himself.

The king and queen had been regular visitors to Richmond since the earliest days of their marriage. Kew, just a few miles away, was in many ways an obvious destination for them. They liked the Thames-side scenery, and the relative isolation of the Surrey location: far enough from London to retain a whiff of the countryside, but sufficiently close to make communication with the capital straightforward. Augusta's old property was too plain and unpretentious to deserve the name of 'palace'; usually known simply as the White House, in 1772 it was full of furniture and objects which had been there for years, including statues, pictures and 'old tapestries'. Once these were cleared away, Charlotte had the house thoroughly redecorated in the modern style; under the eye of Mrs Tunstall, the housekeeper, the nursery was papered in red, white and green, and apartments fitted up for the king and queen.

The White House was not large enough to absorb all the royal children, so the boys were established in three separate residences clustered around Kew Green. Soon their attendants joined them; Lady Charlotte Finch was an early arrival, followed by a regiment of other household servants. Mrs Charlotte Papendiek, whose father was a royal page, was one of many who migrated out to Kew in George and Charlotte's footsteps. Her father was given a house that had been 'originally fitted out by the king for his mother, the Princess Dowager of Wales'. Mrs Papendiek remembered that 'the walls of the drawing room of this house were decorated with prints pasted on paper, collected and arranged by this fond son, with a print of Lord Bute in his robes of state over the fireplace'.[24]

Once it became clear that the royal family intended to make Kew a second home, a lively colony of artisans, entrepreneurs and courtiers moved there too. Painters, fashionable doctors, riding masters and dressmakers flocked into the village. Cottages were taken for the gardeners, stable staff and others whose labour supported what had quickly become a kind of extended royal compound. They formed a tightly knit community in which everyone knew their place, including the son of the local farmer, who 'lived upon housebreaking and footpad robberies', but had declared his intention to do nothing to disturb the tranquillity of Kew: 'Blows and murder belongs not to my gang, and if I am allowed to take my beer here on the green … I shall take care that no harm happens here. I know the bearings of the place.'[25]

For its comfortable inhabitants, Kew was a vision of life with all the unpleasantness and disorder excised from its calm and picturesque vistas, a bucolic contrast with harsher realities that held sway elsewhere. When Augusta was buried at Westminster Abbey, Walpole watched 'as the populace huzzaed for joy and treated her memory with much disrespect'. It was reported that the black silk hangings adorning her coffin were pulled down and thrown around by the London crowd. Such acts were unimaginable in the place Charlotte was later fondly to describe as 'loyal little Kew'. It was soon regarded by all the royal family as a haven from trouble, a retreat from their urban, court-based life. Inevitably, it attracted large numbers of genteel sightseers. The extensive gardens were opened to the public every Thursday, and Mrs Papendiek remembered Kew Green 'covered with carriages, more than £300 being often taken on the bridge on Sundays'. One of the major attractions for such prosperous visitors was the chance to catch a glimpse of their rulers. 'Their Majesties were to be seen at the windows, speaking to their friends and the royal children amusing themselves in their own gardens. Parties came up by water too, with bands of music.'[26]

In the midst of such crowds, life at Kew hardly constituted the secluded retreat that George and Charlotte had perhaps longed for, but the onlookers who surrounded them there were well mannered and polite, and the image of royalty they had come hoping to see was one of relaxed informality. As a result, it was at Kew that the family were most able to leave behind them the formal regality that dominated so much of their life in London. Fanny Burney, who lived there as part of the household from 1785, thought Kew the most private of all the royal residences: 'The royal family are here always in so very retired a way that they live like the simplest gentlefolks. The king has not even an equerry with him, nor the queen any lady to attend her when she goes in her airings.'[27] George and Charlotte lived there with as little ostentation as possible. The queen wore her plainest clothes, and spent the time released from her elaborate toilette in occupations she found more fulfilling. Her lifelong interest in botany was nurtured by her proximity to the famous gardens, established by her predecessor Queen Caroline, which flourished under her active patronage. She acquired many rare and exotic specimens, in whose progress she took an active and informed interest. Like other fashionable gardeners, she even tried to grow her own tea, and wrote to her obstetrician William Hunter in his role as a collector of natural curiosities, asking him to supply her with suitable plants.[28]

Above all, she was free to spend more time directly overseeing the wellbeing of her children. 'Every morning,' recalled Mrs Papendiek, 'they were expected at breakfast, from the eldest to the youngest, which the wet nurse herself took in.' Under Charlotte's supervision, 'the medical man saw them, and invariably directed the meals of the day, including those of the wet nurse'. There were two surgeons always on call 'to watch the constitutions of the royal children'.[29] Later in the day, parents and children reassembled to spend more time together. 'In the country at Kew, after their early dinner at four o'clock, the king and queen usually have their family about them in full liberty, and enjoying themselves with their attendants and often visitors suited to their different ages.' There were more organised pleasures too, such as 'birthday entertainments, dances and fireworks ... and a constant variety of amusements adapted to their several tastes, the elder princes and princesses attending the small evening parties of the queen at Kew on the same pattern as when at London.'[30]

For Charlotte in particular, Kew appeared to offer the prospect of genuine escape from the pressures of life at court. But the chance of establishing it as a settled alternative existence were compromised by two considerations: Kew was only ever a summer retreat – generally, the family decamped there in May and returned to winter in London; then, only four years after their arrival at the White House, the king turned his thoughts towards a potentially new base of operations.

Since boyhood, he had been fascinated by the decayed, ancient stronghold of Windsor Castle. Now he began to make active plans to restore it, with a view to making it inhabitable for himself and the queen. Besides its historic associations, it offered several opportunities which Kew did not: the surrounding countryside promised better riding and hunting, and the land around the castle seemed suitable for carrying out the large-scale agricultural projects in which George was increasingly interested. Like many husbands before and since, the king satisfied his own desires by projecting them on to his wife. 'The king has given me a house,' wrote Charlotte to her brother in May 1776, 'which we would very much like to furnish and stay in for a couple of days each week, and thus my life shall be very much in the country manner.'[31] The tone of faint resignation in her letter reflects Charlotte's very limited appetite for a fully rural existence. Although she was anything but an urban sophisticate, she did not share her husband's passion for the harsher realities of country life. The king loved being in the saddle, and would ride for hours, covering punishing distances and difficult terrain. Charlotte rarely, if ever, rode, preferring gentle 'airings' in her carriage. Unlike her husband and many of her daughters, neither was she a walker. She had no taste for bucolic authenticity in any form, always preferring what she described to her brother as 'that which is called COMFORT'.[32]

George was advised that renovating apartments in the castle itself would be both protracted and expensive. Instead he began work on two buildings adjacent to it. Queen Anne's Garden House, on the south side of the castle, was the first to be converted. It was renamed the Queen's Lodge when completed. In 1779, another property, the Lower Lodge, was acquired and remodelled specifically to house the royal couple's growing family. Obedient as ever to the strong feelings of the king, Charlotte did her best to share his enthusiasm for the new Windsor house. It stood just beyond the castle, and had originally been built for Queen Anne. The couple spent their first night there in July 1776. 'The house will be charming in the future, when the woodwork has taken on another face, which it has not done since Queen Anne put it there,' she told her brother bravely.[33] The king felt no such misgivings. He began a plan of building, designed to establish Windsor – which he once described as 'the place I love best in the world' – as the true home of his dynasty. He took a close interest in the progress of the refurbishments, and may even have drawn up some of the design plans himself, though none now survive. He had always been interested in architecture, which appealed to his exacting, meticulous nature, and the making of precise architectural drawings remained one of his chief pleasures throughout his life.

Charlotte's attitude to the Windsor project gradually warmed as their new base became less 'antique' and more in the modern taste.[34] 'Our house gets bigger every day,' she told her brother in 1779. 'Without being magnificent, it is elegant with a charming atmosphere of gaiety and cleanliness, next to the great castle which gives it great grandeur.' She was pleased to find that 'the inhabitants of this part of the world are extremely polite. They keep their distance without incommoding us, or continually meeting us.'[35] A few weeks later, she was even more positive: 'We have begun our little trip to Windsor, where we are always pleased to be if the Season and our affairs permit it.' There were friends to see in the neighbourhood, and interesting places to visit. 'And it is true that the air is so good and so clear that we are all cheered up, above all when the young ones are with us, which is what I like best.'[36]

Any sustained pleasure in her new surroundings was compromised from the very beginning, however, by the impossibility of enjoying it for very long. It was true that the situation of Windsor was unique, but 'the only thing that is not good is that we are not established there, consequently we are everywhere and nowhere.'[37] The family now had three homes in three locations, and the peripatetic life enforced on Charlotte by the constant commute between them soon began to exhaust and depress her. The route from London to Kew to Windsor became the pattern by which she mapped out her life; it was undertaken with great regularity and with striking speed. The haste with which the royal carriage chased up and down the roads of southern England was the subject of much comment. A newspaper article of 1779 reported: 'It is remarked of Their Majesties that when they travel, they go with the greatest speed imaginable.' A man who tried to keep pace with their coach on horseback 'says that the horses in the chaise galloped every step of the way, and that they could not have gone at a rate less than 14 miles an hour'. This was not necessarily considered a good thing. 'Several persons at different times have been thrown down and hurt through not being able to get out of the way soon enough.'[38] The wheels of a carriage in which the young princesses were travelling once caught fire, so fast were they turning. On one occasion the elderly Mrs Delany was travelling in a coach that was nearly forced off the road by the relentless, unstoppable passage of the king's carriage; a fellow passenger thought it evidence of incipient absolutism, arguing constitutional monarchs did not behave with such disregard for the welfare of other road users.

Although English roads were judged to be some of the best in Europe, the combination of speed, unmade surfaces and eighteenth-century suspension cannot have made such travelling a pleasant experience; and it was one which Charlotte sometimes endured many times a day. In 1776, only a few weeks after their first stay at Windsor, Charlotte described to her brother the frantic pace at which her life was now played out: 'Sunday, at six o'clock in the evening, we depart for Windsor, just the king and me, we leave in a carriage to go to the castle, see the beau monde on the terrace for an hour, then we sup. On Monday and Tuesday we stay there, leaving at nine to return at two, dining at three, leaving again at five, and returning at nine at night. On Wednesday, we return to Kew, only to change horses, then we go to London, and I dress, and in the evening we return to Kew. I stay there on Friday and Saturday to see my children. This is to show you,' she concluded ruefully, 'how little time I have to myself.'[39]

Charlotte's letters to her brother explode with frustration at the empty rush and purposeless bustle of her life: 'We are always on the move', 'We are often in three places in a week.' In such circumstances, it was impossible to have any kind of rational, regular life. Charlotte did not even know where her favourite books were, a major source of annoyance for such a tireless reader. 'Indeed, sometimes I think I have no books at all, for they are at Kew, or they are in town, or they are here; and I don't know which is which.'[40] The feeling of being 'everywhere and nowhere' became her dominant experience, leaving her with a profound sense of endless dislocation. Twenty years after the moves to Kew and Windsor, she was still railing against the restless existence the travel between them had imposed upon her: 'Our life, if you can call it life, is nothing but hurry.'[41]

It was not just the incessant travel between the family bases that weighed upon her spirits; even on arrival, she was not happy. This was not readily apparent to others. Charlotte was an expert and practised concealer of her feelings, and none of the eager diarists who watched her so carefully seems to have been aware of her true state of mind. To them as to everyone else – perhaps including even the king – she presented a façade of benign complaisance, willing to please and be pleased by everything that pleased others. The gloomier sentiments that lurked beneath that rigorously maintained exterior she confided to no one – with the single exception of her much-loved and much-missed younger brother Charles. She wrote to him in Mecklenburg with as much regularity as the posts and the many calls on her free time would allow.

While much of the correspondence concerns the shifting relationships between German princely families, with Charlotte offering advice and passing on news and gossip (in a way that rather undermines her own frequent claim to understand nothing of politics), the letters also reveal a voice that is heard nowhere else in any of her writings: devoid of all artifice, with no attempt to entertain or amuse; and one that is utterly candid in its descriptions of life as she lives it, and the effect it has on her state of mind. Across the years, she has some positive things to say: the pleasure she takes in the healthy development of her children is a constant, recurring joy, as is an unfailing interest in the wellbeing of her Mecklenburg relations, particularly that of Charles's hard-won brood. There are descriptions of enjoyable days, of occasional pleasurable outings and airings. But it is the bitter unhappiness of so many of her letters which shocks and surprises, a sense of resigned dissatisfaction with the entire tenor of her existence, confessed only to her brother.

In the letters, the 'private retreats' of Kew and Windsor are seen in a very different light. As early as 1773, just a year after the move to

Kew, Charlotte told her brother that she was sad to leave London, and that a solitary and retired life was not for her.[42] The boredom of her existence was a theme she returned to again and again. 'Your letters replace entertainment for me,' she wrote yearningly to Charles in January 1776; 'in fact, they are everything to me, because all other forms of entertainment are forbidden me.' She had begun to believe that, for her, 'real joy' was unattainable: 'I have not felt such a thing since I was fourteen or fifteen.' She knew she was wrong to indulge in such pessimistic thoughts, but her circumstances made it hard not to surrender to them. 'You will see that my continual confinement, or rather, my solitary life weighs heavy on my soul.'[43] As time passed, her feelings were unchanged. 'I can confirm that my solitary life is still increasing,' she reported in December 1776. 'We have very few resources when it comes to amusements,' she noted in April 1777. 'I hope your weather is better than ours,' she added two months later, 'and your amusements more varied than here.'[44]

Charlotte's life was hardly devoid of activity, but the obligations that crowded her days were not of her choosing and prevented her from doing what she really wanted. 'I would gladly ready myself for a trip to Germany,' she declared, 'a too happy thought for me.' She knew it would never happen. 'I cannot think of it without shedding tears.'[45] Her days were given up instead to activities she disliked. She resented the hours and hours she spent at court, describing it scathingly as 'that parade'. Even outings designed to entertain did not please her. 'I am getting ready to go to the theatre,' she told Charles in 1776, 'a trip I would gladly deprive myself of, since it bores and inconveniences me.'[46] Most of her official appearances gave her little pleasure, and even when they did – she was genuinely impressed at the sight of the fleet at anchor off Portsmouth at the height of the American War of Independence – none of this compensated for the miasma of tedium which enveloped her at most royal functions. At one military review, she complained, 'as to my own stay, I found it so stupid, as etiquette makes all the company men and the king was nearly always out all the time'. Charlotte found herself 'left with the company' of an unnamed lady 'who was as bored with my person as I was with hers'. Compelled to sit on the margins, Charlotte could only boil in silent frustration. 'It is in my opinion, infinitely preferable to stay in one's own lodging where one knows one can do nothing, than to be of a party where you have the temptation of good company without daring to profit by it.'[47]

If one cause of Charlotte's unhappiness was the boredom of her life, and her powerlessness to change it, there was another dimension of her experience over which she had no control, and which contributed overwhelmingly to her miserable spirits. Her long years of perpetual childbearing exhausted and depressed her. She made no public complaint, although in 1775, a rare year in which she was not pregnant, she noted with surprise that life could, perhaps, still hold some interest for a woman.[48] Usually, she sought to adopt the attitude of resignation regarded as an appropriate response to the perils of fertility. 'I tell myself, before being brought to bed, of the truth of the proverb, "Man proposes, but God disposes".'[49] But by 1780, after eighteen years of childbearing, and despite her best efforts to cultivate the required attitude of submission, she had simply had enough. 'I don't think a prisoner could wish more ardently for his liberty than I wish to be rid of my burden and see the end of my campaign. I would be happy if I knew this was the last time, at least I think so, because it is getting the better of me,' she told Charles.[50] In fact, she had two more pregnancies to endure before her 'campaign' was truly over.

Charlotte's fertility was in many ways a visible sign of the success of her marriage, proof that she had fulfilled her primary function as both wife and queen. In her public role, she had achieved all that could be required of her; but the private Charlotte perhaps suspected that her own happiness had been compromised by her long marathon of childbearing. If she had been pregnant less often, she might have had more time to pursue interests that genuinely engaged her intellect and provided a fulfilling alternative to the emptiness of her official duties. Above all, she could have devoted herself more thoroughly to the upbringing of her children; released from the tyranny of continual lyings-in, she could have had far more personal involvement with a smaller, more manageable family. But in this, as in so many other aspects of her life, the choice had not been hers. The seemingly unending cycle of pregnancy was yet another task imposed upon her, and one she found it increasingly difficult to bear. 'I have need of all my religion to support myself in this situation,' she confided to her brother. 'This has a strange effect on me, and prevents me from enjoying even the small amount of pleasure I have. For God knows, there is a small amount at present, and it gets less day by day.'[51] When unhappiness threatened to engulf her, Charlotte did all she could to pull herself out of her misery. Her most favoured technique was one of denial. Any form of sadness or frustration was best dealt with by simply refusing to acknowledge its existence. 'Although I am bored,' she wrote to Charles in 1780, 'I am following the old proverb which goes, "You must put on a good face in a bad game".'[52]

In an attempt to subdue and control her unquelled feelings, she called constantly upon the strict sense of duty which was such a defining aspect of her character. Happiness, she insistently told herself, was not and never could be the first objective of a responsible person. Duty must always come first; only when its claims were satisfied could any thought of personal contentment be considered. 'To a well-thinking mind, it is always pleasing to fulfil its duty,' she wrote. She admitted that, 'though I have frequently found that duty is very often connected with difficulties, it is frequently attended with a secret, inward satisfaction which *none* but those who act right can enjoy and of which no earthly power can deprive us.' True pleasure was to be found in the knowledge of an obligation discharged, real happiness in a duty fulfilled. 'Can we want any better approbation *than our own conscience*? I think not!'[53]

In practice, she often had to work hard to maintain her conviction that sacrifice was the key to all happiness, and that a refusal to recognise private desires was the key to overcoming them. 'God knows,' she admitted to Charles, 'I sometimes have regrets I think are justified, which I feel and know I must suppress.' Characteristically, she tried to deny these feelings. 'I reproach myself for these ideas, tell myself that God knows better than me. But alas, I admit I don't always think like that.'[54]

In one letter alone does Charlotte allow herself to analyse what she believes to be the source of her misery. It was not only the particular, daily circumstances of her life which drove her to despair; it was the dominating central fact of her existence, her role as queen, that was the real cause of her unhappiness. 'I confess I find myself day by day less suited to my position,' she wrote resignedly in 1778. '"Every rose has its thorn" says the proverb, ah, my dear brother, how many thorns a great rank has! There are many bitter pills to swallow; the very fact of being surrounded by people to whom one cannot become attached, even if one wanted to, is enough to repel a soul as sensitive as mine.' To be royal was to be isolated, as Charlotte had learnt through painful experience. The rigid emotional barriers which the king had insisted his young wife erect from the moment of her arrival, the studious maintenance of a proper distance, the knowledge that every aspect of her behaviour was watched and evaluated by an army of observers, had led to her 'forming a bad opinion of everybody. Perhaps this is taking things too far, but admit brother, that to always live, or rather, to weigh up every word, action or step that one makes is not really to live. At the very least, it is not the way to enjoy to the full the short life which providence has allotted us.'[55]

Nearly twenty years after becoming queen, Charlotte was not, she told her brother sadly, the woman he had once known. She had lost the cheerfulness she used to have, and which she regarded as 'a thing absolutely necessary to enable one to live in the world'.[56] It had been eroded by many difficulties, but had finally foundered on the realisation that those qualities increasingly thought vital to happiness – a measure of self-determination, the comfort of sustained family affection, some uncontested privacy – were, for the most part, incompatible with the requirements of royal life. For all the efforts she and the king had made to minimise and overcome them, the formal and the artificial were, it seemed, ineradicable qualities of royal life. Understanding this did not make Charlotte an advocate of change – like her husband, she had no desire to undermine the hierarchies of the traditional order – but nor did it make her happy. As her children grew up, she began to consider how their expectations could be shaped and tailored to equip them for the reality of the world they were to inhabit. Perhaps the right kind of education could prepare them for the rigours of the life that was to come?

CHAPTER 8

A Sentimental Education

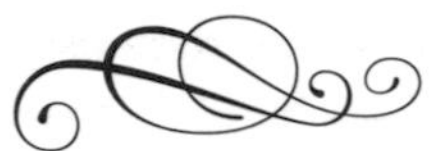

WHEN QUEEN CHARLOTTE'S LIBRARY WAS broken up and sold after her death, it was found to contain over a hundred works on education. Her collection included established classics of the genre, such as John Locke's seminal essay, *Some Thoughts Concerning Education*, which appears significantly close to Charlotte's maternal hand in Allan Ramsey's 1764 portrait of her and her toddler sons. Rousseau's *Emile* was there, as were a host of other books in German and French. Over the years, Charlotte also took a deep interest in the pamphlets produced by campaigning British female writers, who saw education as a vital first step in the moral regeneration of society. The writings of Sarah Trimmer, who founded some of the first Sunday schools for poor children, earned a place on the queen's shelves, as did those of Hannah More, the hugely influential and prolific propagandist whose work included *Hints Towards the Education of a Young Princess* and *The Influence on Society of the Manners of the Great*.

Ideas about education fascinated Charlotte to the very end of her life. Long after her children had grown up, she continued to buy a wide range of books on the subject, whether they offered practical advice, theoretical speculation or programmes for social change. On one level, Charlotte's eager consumption of these works was yet another manifestation of her robust intellectual curiosity; but they also informed the decisions she made about the education of her own children, ensuring that, when directly under her care, they experienced some of the newest and most exciting ideas about how best to equip the young for the adult world.

Although the queen was an instinctual conservative in almost every other aspect of life, in education, she was something of a progressive, keen to embrace the new thinking she had absorbed from her extensive reading. The appointment of Lady Charlotte Finch as governess was in itself a declaration of the modernity of her approach. Lady Charlotte was not just an accomplished intellectual in her own right; she was also connected, by ties of family and friendship, to a group of women who, through a potent combination of advocacy, influence and practical example, were both extremely active and remarkably effective in spreading the gospel of the latest educational theories.

Chief amongst them was an émigré Frenchwoman, Mme Jeanne-Marie Le Prince de Beaumont, who, as ideologue, teacher and entrepreneur, did more than almost any other of her female contemporaries to transform the landscape of upper-class education in mid-eighteenth-century Britain. Mme Beaumont arrived in London in 1748, and for the next fifteen years devoted her lively intelligence, formidable energy and shrewd eye for a commercial opportunity towards improving standards of teaching in Britain. She was horrified by the poor quality of educational provision she encountered everywhere, and was especially critical of the governesses who delivered it. Their 'crass ignorance' was, she declared, stunting the development of children in even the wealthiest homes.

For some years, Mme Beaumont ran a private school for girls in Covent Garden, where she sought to demonstrate what could be achieved when a curriculum that went beyond polite accomplishments was implemented by properly educated teachers; but this was not enough to keep her occupied, and she was soon involved in a wide range of educational enterprises. All of them reflected her central conviction that children learnt most effectively when the educational process was entertaining as well as informative. Pleasure was a far greater incentive to progress than the traditional combination of rote learning and physical punishment. To that end, she wrote a variety of books and magazines intended to entertain and inform young readers. Her *Magasin des enfants* featured a beguiling combination of fairy tales, fables and other stories which sat alongside nuggets of fact, designed to communicate more conventional knowledge. She had none of Rousseau's distrust for fiction, and actively aimed to excite the imagination of children.

Mme Beaumont's desire to stimulate children's minds through play also led to her involvement in the design and production of educational toys. It is not clear whether she actually invented 'dissected maps', an early form of jigsaw specially adapted for small hands, in which wooden pieces representing the component parts of nations could be joined together to form whole countries or continents; but they were always associated with her, and were known as 'Beaumont maps' for many years. Caroline Fox, who was exactly the kind of conscientious mother Mme Beaumont wanted to attract, as both convert and customer, used what she called 'the Beaumont wooden maps' to teach all her sons.

Most of Mme Beaumont's educational aids were intended for use not in schools but in private homes. Like Rousseau, she was convinced no teacher could instruct a child with the loving intensity of a mother, and believed that persuading women not to delegate this vital task but instead to glory in it as the crowning maternal virtue was the first step on the long road to educational reform. She also understood that to disseminate her principles, she would need to win the hearts and minds of key female opinion formers, and from the moment of her arrival in Britain, astutely targeted those she judged most susceptible to her message. 'I was looking out for mothers who were governesses to their children,' she wrote in 1764, 'that their examples might add weight to my efforts for engaging parents to take on themselves that duty.' She focused on rich, powerful and aristocratic women, heaping fulsome praise on those already aware of their responsibility to what she called 'that little rising generation', celebrating the commitment of those mothers who 'amidst all the avocations arising from your rank' devoted themselves to the education of their offspring: 'You are truly mothers to the children you have brought into the world.'[1]

She was soon invited to put her ideas into practice in a number of aristocratic families, including those of Lords North and Egremont. However, it was her role as governess to Sophia Carteret which brought her to the attention of the woman who would eventually translate her practices into the very grandest of schoolrooms. Sophia was the niece of Lady Charlotte Finch, and Lady Charlotte was sufficiently impressed by Mme Beaumont's work to ask her to assist in the instruction of her own eldest daughter. Lady Charlotte was clearly satisfied, and she became one of Mme Beaumont's most influential disciples. When she took up her role as governess to the royal children, it was the practical principles of Mme Beaumont, with their emphasis on pleasurable, creative enjoyment, which formed the basis of her plan for their education.

In this, she had the full support of the queen. Charlotte was a strong believer in the primacy of the maternal role in education, and was once reported to have delivered a stinging public rebuke to 'a celebrated duchess' who was unwise enough to admit that her children were not taught by her, but placed in the care 'of a most excellent governess and faithful servants'. Charlotte was said to have been outraged, declaring, 'it is impossible that servants, however true they may be, or however affectionate, can have the feelings of a parent ... There can be no apology for the neglect of the first duties.'[2]

The queen's words echoed the language of both Rousseau and Mme Beaumont, though her affronted response was disingenuous, coming from a woman whose public role compelled her to be more of a supervisor and less of a mother than she might have wished. Charlotte was well aware that she was herself entirely dependent on the services of others to educate her children; indeed, her inability to observe a principle in which she believed so profoundly may well explain her strident outburst.

Her endorsement of the other key foundation of Mme Beaumont's educational plan involved less of a gap between her principles and her practice, and perhaps, for that reason, allowed the queen to be uncharacteristically determined in its implementation. Charlotte was an early convert to the idea that education – at least, for the very young – was best delivered through play. Many years later, she assured her brother that 'the greatest merit' of a governess was in 'contriving that her pupils gain instruction without realising it, thinking themselves amused when they are in fact gainfully employed'.[3] Although Charlotte acknowledged this was a skill 'met with but rarely in education', it was one she valued very highly.

The queen's tenacious support of the pleasure principle in learning ensured that, during their earliest years, her children were the beneficiaries of one of the most benign and progressive educational theories of the time. Frederika Planta, one of Lady Charlotte Finch's teaching assistants, used it in the royal nursery to guide the young princesses gently through their first lessons. 'I believe they all love me,'

Frederika wrote to a friend, 'and I have gained their affection by making their learning as much play as possible.' To teach them history, she owned a set of cards illustrating important events of the past, which the girls were required to place in the right order. This, she explained, 'reduced the chronology of England to a game, by means of which the princesses are better chronologists than I was 3 years ago'.[4]

Alongside Miss Planta's historical flash cards, the royal children also made extensive use of Mme Beaumont's dissected maps. Sixteen of them were purchased, and kept in specially constructed cabinets.[5] For the older siblings, the schoolroom was supplied with imaginatively designed atlases, showing the countries of the world with their names written in letters which represented their physical shapes. Geography featured prominently in Lady Charlotte's curriculum. In the eighteenth century, it was a dynamic, exciting discipline, and one in which the king was especially interested. Although George showed little curiosity about his own kingdom, and never travelled further north than Worcester, he enjoyed poring over charts and maps of remote places. The king and queen were both well informed about the new discoveries, especially in the southern hemisphere, which were transforming ideas about the shape of the world and also the variety of human life within it. They wanted their children to share their enthusiasm, supplying them with globes and prints of foreign landscapes and even commissioning desks designed to display large-scale atlases.

To help her charges learn languages, Lady Charlotte used a series of 'Boards' on which Latin and French verb tables were laid out. She also owned some 'fishes and counters in a counter box, of Birmingham manufacture', which presumably aided first steps in arithmetic.[6] Twenty years later, having long outlived its originator, the Beaumont scheme was still in use in the royal nursery. The three youngest children were given a specially produced 'Set of Toys', three boxes that contained a variety of pictures and stories, for teaching spelling, grammar and 'figures'.[7]

Under this system, the young royals blossomed. Lady Mary Coke, on one of her regular patrols of the royal nursery, reported approvingly on their progress. 'Did I tell you that the Prince of Wales and Prince Frederick write amazingly well?' she asked her sister in 1768, when the princes were six and five respectively.[8] Both the eldest boys were 'the most charming children' and were 'much improved'. All the brothers had, in her opinion, something to recommend them. Prince Frederick was 'the most handsome', and Prince William, the third son, though 'not pretty', was nonetheless 'very good-humoured'. Prince Edward, dark and clever, learnt to speak at an amazingly early age: Lady Mary was astonished to hear him talking, 'although I believe he is but a year and half old'.[9]

For all their virtues, however, none could compare with Lady Mary's favourite, the Prince of Wales, the uncontested star of the schoolroom, who excelled in everything from his height ('I think I never saw a taller boy of his age'), to his charm ('he was extremely good company'), to his wit ('I can assure you he is the most comical child I ever saw').[10] Lady Mary was utterly smitten. She had no doubt that his early education had served him well, enabling a naturally agile mind to absorb knowledge far beyond what was usual for a child of his age. 'I forget to mention an anecdote of the Prince of Wales, much in his favour,' she told her sister in July 1771. The prince, not yet nine years old, had accompanied the king as he showed a deputation of French dignitaries around the treasures of Windsor Castle, 'the prince explaining to the ambassadors the paintings, etc. When they came into St George's Hall, he stopped short and said to the king, "I believe I had better not relate the history of this painting, as the French ambassador is present." You remember,' Lady Mary reminded her sister, "'tis the Black Prince leading captive the kings of France and Scotland.' Miss Planta's entertaining history lessons had clearly lodged in the mind of the Prince of Wales, enabling him to avoid – with characteristic elegance – a diplomatic faux pas. For someone of his age, 'so much thought, and so much delicacy of thought is very extraordinary', concluded Lady Mary, pleased as ever with the performance of her favourite.[11]

While the princesses would remain in the gentle, female atmosphere of the schoolroom for the whole of their childhood, their brothers were soon required to graduate into an altogether more rigorous environment. Even the most forward-looking Enlightenment thinkers agreed that the educational paths followed by boys and girls must eventually diverge. Male and female education was ultimately directed towards very different ends. Mme Beaumont too acknowledged this. She told her aristocratic female clients that their sons 'will tread in the steps of their fathers and fill, with applause, the principal offices of state'. Their daughters, in contrast, could expect only to oversee the development of the next generation, happily taking upon themselves 'the glorious appellation of governesses to their own children'.[12] Boys acquired knowledge to equip them to take their place in the world; girls learnt in order to make them suitable wives and mothers for the enlightened man. Female education stayed within the purview of women for its duration; boys quickly moved out of the control of women, and into the sphere of men.

*

In 1771, the nine-year-old Prince of Wales and his eight-year-old brother Frederick left behind the easy rule of Lady Charlotte, with its emphasis on the pleasure of instruction, and passed into a far more demanding regime of intellectual and physical exertion. It represented a huge change, not just for them, but also for the queen, who surrendered much of her personal control over their upbringing. From now on, their education would be overseen not by their mother, but by the king. He would appoint their instructors, approve their curriculum and lay down the rules that dictated the daily rhythm of their lives. The shift in their status was emphasised by their removal from the familiar life they had always known, and they left the crowded nursery to live in a separate establishment, with their own household around them. They had entered not only the world of 'manly learning', but an entirely masculine domain. Charlotte would never again exert the degree of influence over the young princes she had once enjoyed. Now they answered directly to their father.

The changes were immediate and radical, as the king implemented a far more orthodox approach to learning. A team of tutors was put in place, all men, under the nominal control of their governor, Robert, Earl of Holdernesse. Horace Walpole thought him 'a formal piece of dullness', but the king, who knew him well, perhaps hoped his stolid lack of flamboyance would act as a calming influence on his boisterous sons.[13] Holdernesse presided over a much more strenuous curriculum than that of Lady Cha: the princes worked for eight hours a day, studying French, German and Italian, as well as the inevitable Latin and Greek. Constitutional history featured prominently, as did geography, mathematics and music. The easy encouragements of the Beaumont plan were replaced by the harsher disciplines of an older tradition, which put more emphasis on punishment than pleasure.

Princess Augusta later recalled seeing her brothers 'held by their tutors to be flogged like dogs with a whip'.[14] As a grown man, Prince Frederick remembered the petty cruelty of one of his teachers, who 'used to have a silver pencil case in his hand while we were at our lessons, and he has frequently given us such knocks with it on our foreheads that the blood followed them'.[15]

None of the educational writers studied by the queen endorsed such measures; indeed, both Mme Beaumont and Rousseau specifically outlawed physical punishment. Nor did they approve of such an intense programme of formal learning for young children, who were, they considered, not yet ready to absorb so much factual knowledge. But Charlotte seems to have made no protest at the abandonment of the benign system which had governed the early lives of her sons. Her habitual deference to the will of the king would have made any active opposition to his decisions unthinkable, and her ability to distance herself emotionally from aspects of her life which she could not change made it impossible for her to contemplate any active disagreement. Perhaps she was able to quell any troublesome misgivings by concentrating on those aspects of educational purpose about which she and the king thought indivisibly as one.

George and Charlotte were united in their conviction that the ultimate aim of education was the instillation in a young mind of moral values that would guide and sustain a child throughout its life. Although both were bookish autodidacts with an ineradicable respect for learning, neither ever doubted that cleverness was of far less lasting value than goodness. For them, the point of all intellectual effort was to understand more clearly what God and the rank he had allotted you in the world required of you. Without that sense of responsibility, all learning was hollow, and all knowledge useless. 'Unless you are a good man,' the king later insisted to Prince William, 'you cannot be of utility to your country, nor of credit to your family. This may seem old-fashioned language, but experience will show you that it is most true.'[16]

Neither the king nor the queen ever questioned the way in which that goodness was best expressed. Some of the greatest thinkers of the eighteenth century grappled with the idea of what virtue looked like when defined by precepts other than those of religion. George and Charlotte were unmoved by their conclusions. For them, it was only through the prism of Christianity that true ideas of right and wrong could be understood. 'Moral philosophy,' George told his son Augustus, 'till a proper foundation has been made in the principles of religion, cannot be with utility pursued.'[17] The king was a devout Anglican with a faith that neither his father, grandfather nor great-grandfather had shared. He liked to attend religious services daily, and made his presence in church loudly felt, giving the responses in a forceful and enthusiastic voice. He believed profoundly in the idea of a personal God, who was concerned directly in the outcome of human affairs. George's letters frequently refer to the operations of 'Divine Providence', whose sometimes mystifying outcomes he struggled all his life to comprehend. He had no doubt his kingly role brought with it a special responsibility to preserve and foster religious faith. He firmly believed this was best expressed by the terms of his coronation oath, which bound him to uphold and defend the Anglican settlement. This led him to reject attempts to relax the restrictions under which Catholics and Protestant Dissenters lived, which effectively excluded them from participation in public life. On a personal level, however, George was more tolerant, visiting Catholics and Quakers in their homes and ignoring the criticism this provoked. He had little natural empathy with the Methodist movement, which made such an impact on many of his poorer subjects during his reign, distrusting its fervency and worrying about its potential to foment disorder. He had more sympathy with the aims of higher-class evangelical reformers such as Hannah More and William Wilberforce. The Proclamation Against Vice which George issued in 1787, to the immense amusement of the sophisticated world, urged better behaviour upon the nation in a way that strongly reflected evangelical concerns. However, George's heart would always be firmly rooted in the tradition of Anglican worship.

Charlotte, although brought up as a Lutheran, soon became as committed an Anglican as her husband. Their shared religious belief was one of the strongest bonds between them: it informed everything they thought and did, in their public and private roles. Both found religion a source of great personal solace and comfort. 'I am certain that without religion, none can be happy,' wrote Charlotte in reflective middle age, 'for it is the true and only support in every situation of life in prosperity, and it keeps us within bounds as it tells us that the hand who gives can also take from us, and in our adversity, it supports us in our distress.'[18]

Like her husband, she fervently hoped that their children would one day derive the sense of comfort and purpose that faith had delivered into her own life. It was never, in Charlotte's mind, too early to encourage that longed-for outcome. On the Prince of Wales's eighth birthday, she sent him a long, sober, distinctly uncelebratory letter, urging the little boy 'above all things, to fear God, a duty which must lead to all the rest with ease; as his assistance, properly implored, will be your guide through every action of life'. This would not only make him a better person; it would enable him to act as a model for the proper behaviour of others. 'Abhor all vice, in private as well as in public; look upon yourself as obliged to set a good example.'[19]

Conducting one's life with visible probity was a duty incumbent upon all Christians; but George and Charlotte believed it had particular force and meaning for royalty. Their strict public adherence to a code of conduct defined by duty, fidelity and family virtues reinforced those values in the minds of all who respected them and their office. Their behaviour, they believed, had the potential to influence their subjects in the most significant way imaginable. Instilling these ideas in the minds of their children was therefore of the very first importance, if they, in their turn, were to act as examples of moral leadership. It was for this reason that the king described as the most important aim of his children's education 'the making of them Christians and useful members of society'.[20]

Christian teaching on the value of humility was considered, by both king and queen, to be especially significant for those of high rank. It reminded princes that their status was not due to any innate superiority, but a gift from God, who expected great things from those on whom He had chosen to bestow it. 'For what is man to man?' wrote Charlotte to her eight-year-old son. 'We are all equal and become only of consequence by setting good examples to others.'[21] For the king, belief offered an astringent reminder that, before God, princely pretension and grandeur counted for nothing. In the Creator's eyes, 'all men are judged by their conduct, not their birth'.[22]

The levelling egalitarianism of religion was a powerful antidote to the sense of self-importance that George believed tainted the upbringing of so many royal children. Some time in the 1760s, as the nursery filled up with babies, he composed a short memorandum titled 'a Sketch of the education I mean to give my sons'. It was concerned less with the details of formal curricula than with the far more significant task of what Mme Beaumont had called 'the formation of the heart'; it was dominated by the king's conviction that 'the most severe trials a prince has to combat are those occasioned by his rank'.[23] Remembering perhaps the painful uncertainties of his own youth, the 'Sketch' shows George as hoping above all else to shield his children from the damaging consequences of court life. His particular obsession was flattery. He had clearly taken to heart the warnings contained in the 'Instructions' his own father had written for his benefit a generation ago, which had urged him to value the rarity of a candid friend above the crowds of smooth-tongued flatterers. Such people, unless checked or controlled, soon overpowered the natural modesty of a young mind, fostering instead unrealistic pride and ultimately placing their deluded victim firmly in the hands of his seducers. In this, as in so much else, the king was in complete agreement with his wife. 'Disdain all flattery,' Charlotte exhorted her eldest son. 'It will corrupt your manners and render you contemptible before the world.'[24]

Although a properly instilled Christian humility was, in the king's eyes, one of the most powerful defences against the flatterer's arts, he speculated whether even this would be enough to protect a vulnerable young prince. Perhaps more drastic measures might be necessary. He mused in the 'Sketch' if 'the most efficacious means of destroying this dangerous charm' would be to remove him altogether from the source of the contagion, 'keeping him perhaps distant from courts'. George even wondered if it might be possible 'to hide his rank from him, till he shall possess virtue enough to be frightened at being acquainted with it', although he was enough of a realist to concede that this most Rousseauian idea was unlikely to work in practice. 'Custom, that most powerful of tyrants, will never allow it to be adopted.'[25]

The 'Sketch', with its deep-seated anxiety about the malign nature of the wider world, its desire to protect innocence from the wiles of ill-disposed, self-interested parties, and its suspicion of the court, confirms the king as very much his mother's son. Like Augusta, he saw the best kind of royal upbringing as one which put as much distance as possible between royal children and direct experience of the life that was to be their eventual destiny. This meant that, in some respects, the regimen of his children echoed that of himself and his siblings – isolated, protected and very self-contained. It is true that, especially in the first years of their marriage, George and Charlotte were far more curious about the world than Augusta had ever been;

they read more, talked more and thought more, creating around themselves a far livelier atmosphere than the sombrely defensive gloom that had been the hallmark of so much of the king's youth. But for all their greater engagement with life beyond the narrow confines of the court, both king and queen shared something of Augusta's prime directive of protect and survive. Their deepest instincts were to shelter their children for as long as possible from the consequences of their birth, and to mould their characters to give them the most formidable armoury against the snares and wiles that would inevitably beset them.

Though their intentions were good, the heavy-handed, unbending severity with which they were so often delivered did not always encourage affectionate feelings between George and Charlotte and their children. This was particularly true of the king and his sons. The terms of the emotional engagement between the boys and their father were set by the king's firm intention to see them cultivate the moral character he believed was essential for their future public roles. No tender feelings were to be spared in achieving this end. His distrust of flattery coupled with his obsessive desire to nurture humility and self-knowledge in his sons meant that George proved implacable in acquainting each of them with what he called 'his own weakness, his own ignorance'. The memory of the misery he had himself endured as a boy, perpetually mired in doubt and fear, only too aware of the yawning gap between the reality and the ideal of what was expected of him, evaporated under the intensity of his conviction. Uncomfortable recollections of his own youthful failures were relegated to the past, and rarely informed the treatment of his sons. He was quick to condemn and slow to praise, unrelenting in his judgements, and insistent in his criticism. He had no doubt that strictness was in the best interests of the princes, believing that it was one of the principal duties of a father; but it is also true that he took a rather gloomy satisfaction in his severity, always finding it easier to complain than to celebrate. Once the princes had advanced out of the nursery and into the schoolroom, their father seemed to them a very different character from the cheerful man who had once romped with them on the carpet.

The king's intention to equip his sons with values more authentic than those of the fashionable world was expressed not only in the detached rigour that increasingly characterised his relationship with them, but also in the details of the grand project he devised for their education. In an attempt to counter the artificiality of court life, the princes were to spend a great deal of their time outside with their father. The king liked being outdoors, both on horseback and as an enthusiastic and resilient walker, and he hoped to inspire in his sons a similar love for rural pursuits. As soon as they were old enough, the princes accompanied the king on his more manageable rides, and soon became highly competent horsemen. They were also expected to take regular exercise in the gardens of the royal palaces, with no indulgence granted for bad weather. Lady Mary Coke recalled without pleasure the doleful walks she had made with the princes, 'round the garden in the rain', her formal court dress becoming more and more bedraggled in the wet.[26]

The family's regular retreat to Kew made it possible for the boys to follow an even wider programme of practical, outdoor education. Each of the princes was given a small plot of land which he was personally required to cultivate. They 'sewed it with wheat, attended the growth of their little crop, weeded, reaped and harvested solely by themselves'. As a boy, their father had farmed his own little garden under Frederick's watchful eye, and he was keen to see his sons follow in his footsteps. The project would have been enthusiastically endorsed by Rousseau, who argued that honest toil nurtured health and hardiness in the young, connected them to the natural world, and fostered understanding between the different social orders. This was considered particularly important for princes. 'They were brought to reflect from their own experience,' wrote a contemporary commentator approvingly, 'on the various labours and attentions of the husbandman and the farmer.' The boys ground the wheat themselves, 'and attended to the whole process of making it into bread'. The resulting loaf was served to the king and queen, 'who partook of this philosophical repast; and beheld with pleasure the very amusements of their children rendered the source of knowledge'.[27] In reality, agricultural pursuits were far more to the king's taste than to those of his sons. They hated their enforced engagement with the land, and never shared the passion for farming that George developed as he grew older.

Another way to make the princes hardy and fit was through their diet, the regulation of which the king took very seriously. George struggled to keep his own weight under control and, as soon as they were out of the nursery, he imposed a similarly careful regime on his sons, most of whom shared the family propensity to fatness. The Prince of Wales and his brothers began the day with milk 'and dry toast of the statute bread'. Lunch was a simple, single course of meat and vegetables. At dinner, the main meal of the day, they were allowed soup 'when not very strong or heavy' and 'any plain meat without fat'. Fish was served 'without butter, using the shrimps strained from the sauce, or oil and vinegar'. For pudding, 'they eat the fruit of the tart, without the crust'. On 'every other Monday', when the princes had their bath ('in a tub of tepid water'), there was no time for supper, which meant that they were allowed instead 'one glass of any sort of wine, which they chose, after dinner'.[28]

If not exactly a model of Rousseauian frugality, the princes' fare was far less extravagant and showy than that served at other royal and aristocratic tables. Some dishes were strictly forbidden: at a formal dinner, the young Prince of Wales once asked to be served a helping of roast beef, but in keeping with his father's orders, this was not permitted. Despite his bitter complaints, he was given instead 'some nasty veal' which he claimed to detest. As was so often the case, the king's apparent readiness to deny his children what they wanted arose from genuine concern for their welfare. He was keen to ensure they ate only the most wholesome food, and was active in seeking out anything he thought would do them good. When the Duke of Montagu told him that his own family had benefited from 'making a healthy breakfast of oatmeal porridge every day', George 'instantly requested the duke to order some for him'.[29] A steady supply of porridge, however, may not have compensated, in his sons' eyes at least, for the denial of more lavish treats. For unexpected pleasures the princes soon learnt to look elsewhere. A dependable supplier of the occasional good time was their elderly great-aunt, Princess Amelia, the last surviving daughter of George II. An unmarried, card-playing diner-out of independent mind, she delighted in offering the boys afternoons of games, music and edible delights, 'tables covered with all sorts of fruit, biscuits, etc.', which, unsurprisingly, they all 'ate very heartily'.[30]

Alongside their demanding programme of outdoor pursuits, the princes continued to follow the intensive course of formal study mapped out for them by the king. It left them little free time, especially when lessons in dancing and fencing were added to their evening schedule. As the eldest boys grew older, more subjects were added to an already exhaustive list, and new tutors employed to teach them. Dr Hurd, Bishop of Lichfield, took charge in 1776, teaching philosophy, law and the study of government. He was 'a stiff, cold but correct gentleman', with a manner 'that endeared him highly to devout old ladies'; but he was also perceptive in his assessment of his principal charge. He found the teenage Prince of Wales clever, but lazy; and glimpsed something slippery and elusive under his graceful façade. 'He will either turn out the most polished gentleman, or the most accomplished blackguard in Europe,' he commented on being asked to predict the prince's future. 'Or possibly,' he added presciently, 'an admixture of both.'[31]

Most observers would have agreed with Lady Mary's Coke's assessment that the prince was by some degree the most intelligent and self-assured of all the siblings. The Duchess of Northumberland watched him make a formal appearance at court when he was only ten. He had grown three inches in a year, she noted, and was now 'manly, well made, has a great air of his grandfather, holds up his head very straight, and with one hand on his sword, and the other in his bosom, stands in the exact attitude of George II'. It was true that he was still not as good-looking as his younger brother, but in every other respect he was universally regarded as the high-achiever of the family. 'Prince Frederick is tall and handsome,' reported the duchess, 'but has neither the dignity nor the grace of his brother.'[32] For those who liked him, and succumbed to his undoubted charm, the young George was regarded as a master of all the polite skills, well read, an excellent dancer, sharing the family passion for music and a proficient performer on the piano and cello. When the envoy from the newly independent American states met him at court, he was struck by the prince's easy command of European languages, and amazed to discover he also read Hebrew.[33]

Whilst some praised his accomplishments, however, his father remained resolutely unimpressed. By the time the prince had reached maturity, the king's disappointment and disapproval were fixed and irrevocable. In a long letter of reproach written to his eldest son two days after his eighteenth birthday, George had nothing to offer but criticism of what he considered the prince's lacklustre performance, both as a scholar and as a man. He had no doubt of his son's innate intellectual ability, but as he prepared to graduate from the schoolroom, his final assessment of his son's achievements was gloomy:

'Your own good sense must make you feel that you have not made that progress in your studies which, from the ability and assiduity of those placed about you, I might have had reason to expect.' His French and Latin were satisfactory, but in German, 'your proficiency is certainly very moderate'. He had read only 'cursorily' amongst ancient and modern historians, and had no 'comprehensive knowledge of the Constitutions, laws, finances, commerce etc. of these kingdoms, and of the relative situation as to those points of our rival neighbours, and of other European states'.

If the prince had failed to live up to his father's expectations intellectually, his shortcomings were even more apparent in the spiritual dimension of his education. 'I fear,' pronounced the king with dour accuracy, 'your religious duties are not viewed through that happiest of mediums, a gratitude to the Great Creator, and a resolution to the utmost of your power to obey His will as conveyed to us in the Scriptures.' The prince's private behaviour – his financial extravagance, his love of luxury, his burgeoning interest in drink, gambling and, above all, women – bore ample testimony to his wilful disregard for Christian principles. But what most concerned the king was his son's failure to grasp what his rank required of him, and why his moral shortcomings were of such significance. 'Everyone in this world has his peculiar duties to perform, and that good or bad example set by those in the higher stations must have some effect on the general conduct of those in inferior ones.' The prince's obstinate disregard of this essential truth boded ill for his future role, in his father's eyes.

As ever, the king insisted that his closely argued pages of criticism were intended only for his eldest son's good. 'Believe me, I wish to make you happy, but the father must, with that object in view, not forget that it is his duty to guide his child to the best of his ability through the rocks that cannot but naturally arise in the outset of youth.'[34] However, the recipient of the letter, which was but the latest in a lifetime of admonitory missives, ascribed it to a very different cause. A few years later, the prince assured his friend James Harris that the king 'hates me; he always did, from seven years old'.[35]

The prince was a volatile character, with a propensity for theatrical declarations and dramatic emotional gestures, but in this case there was a grain of truth in his assertion. By the time he was twenty, it had become impossible either to deny or ignore the fundamental lack of sympathy between father and son which, exacerbated by the prince's provocative behaviour, turned into mutual incomprehension and resentment. In 1781, the king was obliged to pay the huge sum of £5,000 to retrieve from the actress Mary Robinson a cache of embarrassing love letters written to her by the infatuated nineteen-year-old prince. This was a profound humiliation for a man whose own life was governed by unbending moral principle, as well as a very public declaration of his failure to pass on such values to his heir. The prince's association with leading figures from the political opposition was a further gesture of insult to his father, which added to the king's political difficulties. In both his private and public actions, his eldest son seemed determined to cause him pain. 'Your love of dissipation has for some months been with enough ill-nature trumpeted in the public papers,' complained the king, 'and there are those ready to wound me in the severest place by ripping up every error they may be able to find in you.'[36] By the time the prince had reached his majority, George's disappointment in his apparently feckless heir was bitter and undisguised.

The Prince of Wales must bear some of the responsibility for the bad-tempered collapse of the relationship between himself and his father. Much of what the king said about him was true. He was lazy and lacked application, he preferred his own pleasure to hard work, and his sense of honesty was fluid at best, usually shaped to serve his own ends. His behaviour often seemed calculated to enrage and disappoint in equal measure. However, if some of the fissures in their relationship were created by the prince, others were the responsibility of the king. George had never found a way to love his heir, as he had loved his other children when they were small. This coolness, the absence of paternal affection felt by the prince, was to set the tone of their dealings with each other for the rest of their lives. Lady Mary Coke heard in 1768, when the prince was five, that for all his winning ways he was 'not a favourite with the king and queen.'[37] That role was taken by Frederick, who could do no wrong in his father's eyes, and whom the king always described – with tactlessly wounding accuracy, and in words never used about his heir – as 'my dearest son.'[38] As a child, the king had seen his own younger brother Edward preferred at his expense by his parents, but had clearly learnt nothing from the experience. He made no secret of his devotion to Frederick, who was thought to resemble him closely in both looks and personality. The failings of the Prince of Wales were seen all the more clearly when contrasted with his brother's virtues. Where the young George was verbose and ineffectual, Frederick was stoic and unflappable; where the prince was mercurial, Frederick was measured; where the prince was clever and witty, Frederick was as plain-speaking, dogged and determined as the king himself.

George certainly saw little of himself in his eldest son. From the prince's earliest days, everyone who met him was struck by his graceful self-possession, easy assurance and confident bearing. He had none of the gauche self-consciousness that had been such a painful and disabling feature of his father's childhood and youth. 'He had an elegant person, engaging and distinguished manners,' recalled Mrs Papendiek, 'added to an affectionate disposition and the cheerfulness of youth.'[39] He was as much at ease beguiling the women of his mother's household as he was shepherding foreign ambassadors through the cultural minefields of patriotic artworks at Windsor. It is hard to imagine the king, so awkward and defensive when young, undertaking either task with the polished bravura demonstrated by his son.

From the first, the Prince of Wales engaged with the world in a way that had been impossible for his father. He anticipated life beyond the schoolroom, not with shrinking trepidation, but with a desperate desire to join it. He was pleased with himself, happy with his physical and intellectual attributes, which he surveyed with a relaxed contentment never enjoyed by the king. In a playful letter, written to one of his sisters' governesses when he was just seventeen, he described his looks and personality in terms that suggest few of the usual adolescent anxieties. Enumerating his qualities in the third person, he began with 'the features of his countenance', which he found 'strong and manly'. His mouth and teeth were good, his eyes, though grey, were 'passable'. He was especially pleased with his hair, of which 'he has more than usually falls to everyone's share', but less so with his figure, which, as he accurately foresaw, already showed 'too great a penchant to grow fat'. He regretted that the shape of his face was far too round to be judged really handsome, but on the whole, he was more than satisfied: 'Such are gifts nature has bestowed upon him, and which the world says she has bestowed upon him with a generous hand.' Deftly avoiding an air of too much smugness, he added a self-deprecating postscript: 'I forgot to add my ugly ears.'

He was equally at ease with 'his qualities of mind and of his heart'. He thought himself 'open and generous, above doing anything that is mean', although he suspected he was 'too susceptible, even to believing people his friends and placing too much confidence in them, from not having yet obtained a proper knowledge of the world and its practices'. 'His heart, he declared, 'is good and tender, if it is allowed to show its emotions.' He was not blind to his vices or, as he preferred to describe them, 'weaknesses'. It was true that he was too subject 'to passions of every kind', but maintained that he 'never bears malice or rancour in his heart'. He confessed that he swore too much, and was 'rather too fond of Wine and Women'. Summing up the balance sheet of his personality, his opinion of himself was extremely favourable: 'His character is open, free, generous, susceptible of good impressions.'[40]

For the young prince, with his quick mind, cheerful disposition and lively imagination, everything came easily. He was never accused of the lumpen, dull stupidity with which this father had been so often charged. His problem was laziness; not the terrified, almost catatonic inertia and inattentiveness that had paralysed the king when young, but the flighty indiscipline of a mind that found too little in the world around it to engage or direct it. Where the king had been oppressed by the scale of what lay before him, riven with self-doubt and suspicion that he was simply not up to the job, his son seemed untroubled by such concerns. The prince's good qualities were ones that his father had never himself enjoyed, whilst he was singularly lacking in those the king had developed with such effort, and had achieved only at the cost of the almost complete re-engineering of his character. It is hard not to see much of the frustration George felt for his heir as the unacknowledged resentment felt by a man for whom every step of his journey had been difficult, marked by sacrifice, submission and perseverance for a child whose experience was so very different – whose intelligence was considerable, whose charm was effortless, and whose lively personality had, from his earliest days, delighted those who knew him best.

The king complained, with some justification, that all these virtues meant nothing if they were squandered; but in a pattern that was to become depressingly familiar, drew no lessons from the experience of his own youth. Perhaps his most significant derogation in the management of the prince was his conspicuous failure to provide him with his own version of Lord Bute. Once emancipated from his influence, the king could never be brought to admit how the years spent under

Bute's tutelage had transformed him; and he was not eager to see established in his own household an alternative power base of the kind Bute had provided for him when he had been heir. Perhaps he assumed that as he was the living embodiment of Bute's prescriptions, he could himself fulfil the task Bute had once performed so powerfully; but this was not so. Although everyone – including George himself – insisted that the Prince of Wales regarded his father as his principal role model, the king was not well equipped for the task.

George had none of Bute's charismatic intensity. He was never able to inspire his heir, as Bute had once inspired him, with a sense of the particular mission of royalty, with the scale, not just of the obligation, but also of the excitement and possibility of power. For all his faults, Bute had been a galvaniser, an enthuser who had beguiled, fascinated and stimulated his pupil as much as he cajoled and even bullied him. There was no one in the prince's world of comparable energy and vision. His father offered him no shining outcome, no prize uniquely of his own making to be won at the end of his endeavours. He had nothing to recommend except hard work, duty and the selfless satisfaction of having fulfilled the purpose for which God had intended him. There was no model for kingship except that defined by the king's interpretation of it; and no forceful, inventive thinker to tailor this blueprint to the very different character of his son.

In place of the inspiration that was in such short supply, the prince was well provided with a steady diet of admonition. He was urged to regard his father as the perfect model for a moral life and regulate his actions accordingly. 'Try and imitate his virtues,' declared the queen, 'and look upon everything that is in opposition to that duty as destructive to yourself.'[41] There was no area of life, the prince was regularly assured, in which he could not learn something useful from the example of his father. Warning his young charge against 'the slow poison' of overeating, Lord Holdernesse loftily informed the prince that 'I cannot name one virtue which does not bring your royal father to mind. Abstinence is only one of the many that adorn His Majesty; equally master of his passion and appetites, he enjoys the greatest of blessings, *mens sana in corpore sano*. In this point, I wish the prince may rival the king.'[42]

The king himself saw it as one of his key responsibilities as a parent to ensure that all his sons – not just his heir – were aware of his displeasure and disappointment when he considered they had failed to live up to the high standards demanded of them. In his letters, his tone to them was often brusque, and sometimes one of ill-concealed annoyance. Even when he sought to show genuine affection, it was couched in terms which seldom failed to remind the boys that his love for them was conditional on their satisfactory conduct. On a rare trip away from home in 1778, worn down with anxiety about the progress of the war with America, he wrote to George and Frederick with uncharacteristic emotion. 'I know well I have a difficult time to steer the helm,' he declared, 'but the confidence I place in Divine Providence, the attachment I have for this my native country, and the love I bear my children are incentives enough to make me strain every nerve to do my duty to the best of my abilities.' He called the princes 'my dear sons' and signed himself 'your affectionate father', but he could not resist reminding them that the strength of his feelings was, even in this relatively tender moment, dependent on their future behaviour. 'Act uprightly, and show the anxious care I have had of you has not been misspent, and you will ever find me not only an affectionate father but a sincere friend.'[43] In their replies, both princes demonstrated how well they understood what was required of them. The young George hoped that he would be found 'hereafter worthy of your affection' whilst Frederick declared it his 'greatest ambition to deserve Your Majesty's and the queen's affections'.[44] Both boys knew that their father's love was something to be won rather than given freely.

*

The qualified nature of his attachment to his sons perhaps made it easier for George to implement the final stage of their education – sending them away from home. First to go was the third son, William. He was an affectionate, literal, no-nonsense boy, bluff and unpretentious, and much loved by his sisters. The king had always considered that his loud, blunt, unsophisticated nature made him specially suited to a career in the navy, and in 1779, at the age of fourteen, he joined HMS *Prince George* as midshipman. He was to be allowed no special privileges and treated exactly as the other young men on board: George commanded Admiral Samuel Hood that 'no marks of distinction are to be shown unto him: they would destroy my whole plan'. Charlotte was pleased to see that he went off very happily, 'and undertakes his profession with a great deal of zeal'.[45]

William's departure from the brotherhood made little impact on the Prince of Wales, who had always treated him as very much an outsider, not to be admitted to the closed senior partnership of himself and Frederick, the Duke of York. However, the king's decision the following year to send Frederick to live in Hanover was a devastating one for the prince. The queen explained to her brother Charles that Frederick's departure had been organised with great secrecy, 'so that all the difficulties that can be made here cannot harm this enterprise and nothing put back this affair that is so desirable for the good of the young man'. The plan, as publicly announced, was for Frederick to follow his military studies in Germany, but as Charlotte confessed to her brother, it was also a preventative measure, intended 'to make him see what a prince loses by cultivating bad company and bad ways'; for although her second son had 'a good heart, doesn't want spirit, has lots of liveliness and much sincerity', Charlotte admitted that 'prudence doesn't always guide him'. Despite all the care that had been taken with his moral education, the result had not been what she would have wished. 'As to religion, he has had the best instruction on this subject that could be had, better even than others in the Royal family have ever had, but with all the pains that have been taken with him, religion isn't treated in England as it is with you.'[46] In Hanover, it was hoped, the examples would be better. Moreover, he would be removed from what the king increasingly considered the most insidiously corrupting influence at work on the prince – that of his elder brother, who, George believed, had taught the younger to share in the pleasures of women and drink, which were becoming habitual for him.

It was a considerable sacrifice for the king to see his best-loved son leave home. The *Annual Register* reported that both he and the queen 'wept severely' on the day of his departure. But if his parents were upset, the Prince of Wales was heartbroken. He and Frederick had hardly been apart since they had shared their specially adapted cradle together as babies. The prince was 'so much affected with the misfortune of being deprived for so long a period of the sole companion of his youth', reported the *Register*, 'that he stood in a state of entire insensibility, totally unable to speak or to express the concern he felt so strongly'.[47] They would not meet again for over six years.

Where Frederick and William led the way, their remaining brothers soon followed. The king's dealings with his younger sons were never as intense as those with the elder two, and he seems to have parcelled them off abroad with few qualms. Certainly, they left home at ever-younger ages. In 1785, eighteen-year-old Edward was bound for Hanover. The following year, Ernest was sent to the University of Göttingen, aged fifteen, followed there by the thirteen-year-old Augustus and the twelve-year-old Adolphus. George viewed their loss with equanimity. He was a poor correspondent, ignoring his sons' regular pleas for more generous allowances and taking a dim view of requests for leave to visit their family. Like Frederick, most of the brothers were not to see home again for many years. Edward, who was later given the title of Duke of Kent, did not live in England again for thirteen years, returning only once, without permission, in 1790, when the king saw him for only ten minutes before ordering him away again. Ernest was absent for eight years; Adolphus for seven. Of all the adult brothers, only the Prince of Wales was kept at home, kicking his heels in frustration, and with nothing to do but drink, gamble and involve himself in political and sexual intrigue.

For all the modernity of George and Charlotte's early intentions, especially those of the queen, as the princes grew older, it was clear that they had been only partially successful in establishing a new kind of relationship with their sons. It had proved far harder than they had hoped to escape both the pull of the past and the limitations of their own personalities. The king, as had so many of his predecessors, failed to find a blueprint for the education of the Prince of Wales that captured his imagination and provided him with an apprenticeship appropriate to his future role. Suspicious and resentful of his heir's talents and his shortcomings, he had little to recommend to him but patience, restraint and good behaviour. Perennially unimpressed by the efforts of his other sons, who frequently complained that he was impossible to please, by the time they came to maturity, George had built around himself an image of fatherhood very different from the cheerful good nature that had marked his dealings with his children when they were small. Whilst all the boys paid lip service to the idea of their father as a model of rectitude, in practice their experience of him was very often one of dourness, irritation and sometimes even fear. When angry, George could be extremely intimidating – Lord Melbourne later told Queen Victoria that the Prince of Wales was 'monstrously afraid of him'. When disappointed, as he so often was, he was detached to the point of complete rejection, finding it easy to withdraw his affections, and consigned recalcitrant or simply uninspiring sons to an exile that was as emotionally chilly as it was physically distant. As the brothers grew older, their father seemed to grow colder, crosser and ever more remote. The queen rarely intervened. By the mid-1780s, the male part of the family was fragmented, dispersed across Europe, writing disgruntled, miserable letters home to an often unresponsive father. This was not the united, happy brotherhood of uncorrupted, contented probity that their education had been designed to produce. Perhaps, with their daughters, the king and queen might do better.

*

The question of how best to educate girls was one which perplexed many Enlightenment thinkers. Their learning could have no direct practical application: all academic institutions and other professions were closed to them, as were the informal centres of debate, discussion and enquiry that grew up around specialist clubs, societies and coffee-houses; these were male preserves, their sexual exclusivity protected as effectively by custom as the older bodies were by law. But did that mean women were to be denied all access to the transforming benefits of knowledge, excluded from participation in any life of the mind? Few progressive thinkers felt entirely comfortable with this position; yet even those who saw the perpetuation of female ignorance as a philosophical wrong, a denial of the potential they believed was there to be realised in all human beings, often felt uneasy when confronted with the consequences of their beliefs. Rousseau was not the only intellectual instinctually opposed to the idea of educated women playing a public role in society. For him, the learned female was useful only in her role as maternal educator; he envisaged no purpose for her beyond the confines of the nursery or schoolroom.

Even those more sympathetic to the principle of women's education rarely saw learning as a force designed to project women into the public sphere, transforming the existing relationships between the sexes. The scholarly woman was essentially an anomaly in the natural order of things, and she was strongly advised to wear her learning with tact and discretion. Too overt a demonstration of what she knew would only make her unhappy, undermining her in her traditional role whilst offering nothing meaningful in return.

The fate of a young female bluestocking could be a sad and lonely one, if not well managed by those around her. When the aristocratic Mary Hamilton confided to her usually indulgent uncle that she had begun to study Latin, that touchstone of masculine scholarship, he was horrified. He very much wished she had not started it, but now that she had, she should 'keep it a dead secret from your most intimate friends, as well as the rest of the world, as a lady's being learned is generally looked on as a great fault.'[48]

This was certainly the experience of Louisa Stuart, daughter of the king's mentor, Lord Bute. Even in the household of a man with such wide-ranging intellectual pursuits, her academic interests were seen as a deliberate provocation to her family, who 'daily snubbed and checked me … for reading books I had no business with, instead of minding my work as I should do. Whatever I wanted to learn, everybody was up in arms to oppose it, and represent that if indulged, I should become such a pedant nobody would be able to bear me.' She attributed the crippling shyness with which she was afflicted for the rest of her life to the campaign of attrition which she endured in her own home. 'Some of its effects have stuck faithfully by me … from the habit of dreading the ridicule which usually followed whenever I opened my lips and a constant apprehension, of being despised by men from having it dinned into me that if they suspected my pursuits and inclinations, they would spit in my face.'[49] Perhaps the most famously awkward bluestocking in all literature, subjected on her every appearance to dismissive ridicule of a kind Louisa Stuart would surely have recognised, was herself the creation of a brilliantly clever woman. Poor Mary Bennett, whose embarrassing attempts at intellectual assertion are ignored and whose accomplishments belittled by her indifferent family, is left at the end of *Pride and Prejudice* with only her books and piano for company. Her elder sister Elizabeth understands, as Mary does not, that wit is a more piquant attraction for even a clever man than insistent displays of acquired knowledge; as a result, she lands the eligible husband that eluded both the fictional Mary and the real-life Louisa Stuart.

Discouraged by law, custom and the disapproval of their peers from playing a meaningful role in the formal world of the mind, some aristocratic women sought other ways to satisfy their intellectual appetites. As the historian Clarissa Campbell Orr has shown, they attempted to bypass the public realm altogether, turning their grand houses into informal centres of learning, bringing into their homes the discursive enquiry and scholarly enterprise with which they could not engage in wider society. They used their wealth to fund not just their own academic interests, but also to support the work of scholars, for whom they found posts in their households as tutors, archivists or cataloguers. Around them, they attracted like-minded men and women of their own rank, amongst whom they shared books, artefacts and natural curiosities. In these informal salons, men and women met together to discuss the broadest possible range of subjects. They owed something to Rousseau in their self-contained desire to retreat from the world, but within the safe domestic world thus created, there was none of the intellectual separation of the sexes upon which the author of *Emile* so inflexibly insisted. In these aristocratic bolt-holes – a mansion of one's own – armed with the resources to fund their ambition, a few privileged women achieved a genuine degree of stimulating, scholarly independence.

Perhaps the most influential of these was Margaret Cavendish Bentinck, Duchess of Portland. She was an heiress to great fortunes from both her parents; but she was also far luckier in her father than poor, persecuted Louisa Stuart. The Earl of Oxford was a noted bibliophile and patron of the arts, and encouraged his intelligent, inquisitive daughter to follow her developing passions as a collector. She began by acquiring shells; by the time she was married, her natural history collection had expanded to encompass examples of almost every species, drawn from all over the world. Soon it was the largest and most comprehensive in Britain. The duchess was no hands-off dilettante; she was a conscientious cataloguer of her specimens, and employed a brigade of specialists to assist her in the task of identifying and recording her finds. Beyond her core natural history collection, she also acquired more conventional objects – fine art, historical artefacts (the famous Portland Vase belonged to her), fossils, medals, maps and drawings. All the objects were open to the inspection of visitors, and her house at Bulstrode Park in Buckinghamshire became a magnet for the philosophically inclined. She was also an eager collector of people, supporting needy scholars with grants from her private income, and taking those she found particularly sympathetic into her household. She was especially generous to women, recognising perhaps how few other opportunities were open to them; it was her assistance that allowed the intellectual Elizabeth Montagu to continue writing.[50] Mary Delany – the diarist and botanical artist whose delicate flower pictures made from cut paper were regarded as models of exquisitely accurate precision – lived for long periods at Bulstrode after her husband died, leaving her an elderly and impecunious widow.

For the king and queen, Bulstrode was an entrancing vision of the good life enjoyed as they would have chosen to live it: cultivated and private, retired and purposeful, where intellectual enquiry was in perfect harmony with the principles of received religion (the duchess, an observant Christian, was as interested in theology as in natural science). George and Charlotte, who rarely called on anyone, made an exception in the duchess's case. They took their two eldest sons and three daughters with them when they paid a grand visit to Bulstrode on the Prince of Wales's birthday in 1778. First they viewed the duchess's pictures, before moving on to the natural history collections, 'and with wondering and enquiring eyes, admired all her magnificent curiosities'. They 'admired all they saw, the young ones full of observations and proper questions, some skipping, some whistling, and delighted above measure'. Mrs Delany, who was present, had not expected to be noticed: 'I was below stairs in my own apartment, not dressed, and uncertain I should be thought of.' But Charlotte wanted to meet the famous botanical illustrator, and she was duly presented. Her latest book of flowers was placed on a table for the queen to examine. 'I kept my distance till the queen called me to answer some question about a flower, when I came, and the king brought a chair, and graciously took me by the hand and seated me in it, an honour I could not receive without some confusion and hesitation. "Sit down, sit down," said His Majesty, "it is not everybody has a chair brought them by a king."'[51]

Bulstrode brought out the best in both George and Charlotte. In its spacious rooms they were relaxed and charming, completely at ease in its atmosphere of calm domestic scholarship. They admired everything they found there, especially Mrs Delany, who was asked to visit the royal family at Windsor, and soon became a regular guest at royal evening parties and concerts. Charlotte particularly enjoyed her company, discussing with her every possible topic of joint interest, from chenille work to botany. In Mrs Delany – indeed, in Bulstrode and its expansively generous patroness – Charlotte saw not just a reflection of her own inquisitive mind, but also a vision of how female intellectual appetites might be satisfied in ways that did not threaten 'that tyrant, custom'. It was little wonder she spent so much time there.

As she entered her thirties, Charlotte's intelligence, always formidable, began to emerge from beneath the mask of discretion, where it had been judiciously concealed for so many years; gradually, it developed into one of the defining traits of her personality. Lady Elizabeth Harcourt, who later became the queen's closest friend, had no doubt that she was an extremely clever woman. 'Her understanding was of the first class; it was equally quick and solid.' She was ferociously well read, 'well acquainted with the best authors in the English, French and German languages; and her memory was so retentive, that she never forgot what she once knew'.[52] In the course of a single conversation with Fanny Burney, Charlotte referred confidently to the works of Milton, Wycliffe, Cranmer and Goethe, citing along the way a number of books in German which Burney did not recognise. She was, whilst the novelist knew her, never without a book in her hand, some of them acquired from very unexpected sources. Fanny was astonished to be told by Charlotte, as they discussed a recently acquired work, that 'she had picked it up on a stall'. The queen explained that she employed a servant who hunted down elusive titles for her among the second-hand volumes piled up on barrows in the streets of London. 'Oh, it is amazing what good books there are on stalls!'[53]

As Lady Harcourt observed, the queen loved to talk almost as much as she loved to read, although her enthusiasm was always tempered by a cautious self-censorship. 'She relished wit in others, but checked it in herself, from being aware that, dangerous as it was in all situations, it would be particularly so in hers.' Despite this, 'in the talent of conversing, she had few equals; whether the subject was serious or lively, she treated it in a manner that those must have been stupid indeed that did not listen to her with pleasure; no one narrated better than she did, and anecdotes that had little merit in themselves were made amusing by the way she told them'.[54]

It was a frequently expressed regret of Charlotte's that she could never get enough of the lively, interesting talk she loved; deference made everyone mute in her presence, the clammy hand of etiquette putting an end to the prospect of genuinely entertaining discourse. 'The queen often complains to me of the difficulty with which she can get any conversation,' Mrs Delany explained to her friend Fanny

Burney, when Fanny was about to meet Charlotte for the first time, 'as she not only always has to start the subjects, but commonly, entirely to support them.' She begged Fanny to speak up: 'Now I really do entreat you not to draw back from her, nor to stop conversation with only answering Yes and No.' It was all to no avail; as the queen approached, the writer was overwhelmed by shyness, and simply ran away and hid.[55]

Charlotte's appetite for knowledge expanded beyond the polite arts into science. She continued to nurture the passion for botany that had been a lifelong fascination for her, and was such a recurring feature of Hanoverian queenship. She followed her predecessors Caroline and Augusta in developing the gardens at Kew, as well as patronising scholarly studies in the same field. The great naturalist Linnaeus later dedicated one of his magisterial works of plant categorisation to her, as did Lord Bute, when he completed his *Botanical Tables*, the fruits of decades spent in the political wilderness after his ill-starred resignation from the premiership. She explored some of the newer thinking in geology, although she preferred works that did not contradict too forcefully the biblical version of the origins of Earth. In later years, she attended the lectures on science she had arranged for the instruction of her daughters, which included elements of physics and chemistry. Fanny Burney once watched her sitting with the princesses whilst Mr Bolton taught them geography: 'She was studying with him herself, as he stood before her, with a book in her hand.' The only teacher from whom the queen did not occasionally receive instruction was the dancing master, noted Fanny, 'so indefatigable and humble is her love of knowledge'.[56]

In other circumstances, Charlotte would probably have chosen to satisfy her intellectual needs rather as the Duchess of Portland had done at Bulstrode. However, she knew she could not retire from public duties as completely as had the duchess and her husband, who turned their backs on conventional expectations to pursue the pleasures of private scholarship. Charlotte did all she could, however, to adapt some elements of the Bulstrode model to her life at court. As she grew older, and exerted more control over the appointments made in her household, she chose to place around herself men and women who could be relied upon to deliver the kind of intellectual stimulation she so craved. Jean Andre Du Luc, for example, who was given the post of Reader to the Queen, was a geologist of European repute whose task was to keep his employer fully abreast of new developments in science, whilst deepening her existing knowledge of various scientific disciplines. Elizabeth de la Fite, another of the queen's readers, specialised in German literature, whilst the Reverend Charles de Guiffardière fulfilled the same role for works written in French.

The little salon which the queen created around herself from the late 1770s onwards was never intended to attract plaudits from other intellectuals. Its low-key tone was partly a reflection of the prevailing suspicion of female 'philosophers' and also a product of Charlotte's cautious, self-effacing character. Her ingrained sense of her own shortcomings meant that the queen had no great opinion of her own capacities. She insisted to Lady Harcourt that she was 'very sensible of my deficiencies in everything', and her correspondence is littered with references to 'my poor powers'.[57] This may say more about Charlotte's low self-esteem than it does about her real abilities, but her insistence on the modesty of her ambitions meant that she attracted very little of the opprobrium directed at more intellectually confident and assertive women. On the contrary, the range and seriousness of her interests were often regarded as highly desirable alternatives to the idle, empty obsessions assumed to preoccupy so many of her sex. The *Ladies' Poetical Magazine* urged its readers to regard their bookish queen as a role model:

> Happy for England, were each female mind,
> To science more, and less to pomp inclined,
> If parents, by example, prudence taught,
> And from their QUEEN the flame of virtue taught,
> Skilled in each art that serves to polish life,
> Behold in her a SCIENTIFICK wife![58]

On only one occasion did an expression escape Charlotte which suggested she may privately have harboured rather more radical views about the uses and abuses of female intellect. In 1779, she boldly assured her brother Charles that in her 'opinion, if women had the same opportunities as men, they could do just as well'.[59] This was not a view she was ever heard to repeat. It remained, as did so many other unsayable truths in Charlotte's life, repressed and unexpressed, a casualty of her iron self-control. For, despite all her commitment to learning, the queen usually valued female education not as a catalyst to transform women's traditional destiny, but as a way of making it more bearable. She loved knowledge for its own sake, and probably would have pursued it to the best of her abilities, whatever her circumstances.

No one appreciated more than Charlotte the secondary benefits delivered to women by a cultivated mind, the opportunities it offered to sustain and enrich the lives of those for whom independent choices were few and unavoidable obligations many. It was this resource – which alone made her own existence bearable – that she hoped to pass on to her daughters. 'The plan of this exemplary royal mother,' noted one perceptive observer, 'on which she was often heard to decant, was, in the education of her royal offspring to open as many resources to them as possible, in a variety of studies and pursuits; out of which they might subsequently make their own choice, and thus be independent of circumstance for occupation and amusement.'[60]

The queen hoped to achieve this in two ways. She was fully alive to the power of example. Her daughters, she hoped, would come to appreciate the value of a cultivated mind by being brought up in the company of clever people. They would see what learning looked like at first hand, through conversation, reading and discussion. They would also understand that education was not a single stage in life, to be abandoned on leaving the classroom, but a perpetually invigorating process, through which the intellect was constantly and fulfillingly refreshed. But before this could happen, they needed to be equipped with a solid foundation of useful knowledge. This could not begin too early; and every trouble should be taken to ensure that it was carried out by people of the very highest quality.

Charlotte laid out many of the principles on which she based the education of her daughters in a long letter that she wrote to her brother Charles after the death of his wife, offering him advice on how to raise his motherless girls. She began in her accustomed tone of self-deprecation – 'I have always more to learn than examples to give, in so important a matter as this' – but soon warmed to her task, laying out her ideas with an eager, confident assurance. Charles should not send the girls away to be educated, but should keep them 'under your eyes, and your protection, which I regard as the most important consideration.' He should appoint a governess, the best he can find, and ensure she reports only to him. Her responsibilities will go far beyond the academic: 'She will answer for the conduct of the princesses, will take care of their habits and arrange for their amusements when they are not with their teachers.' Charlotte laid great stress on the necessity of finding useful ways to fill all otherwise vacant hours. 'These moments of recreation are the foundation of laziness; where children do nothing, or worse than nothing, they get up to mischief.' Organised activities provided one answer to this problem; however, as Charlotte knew only too well from her own life, the best insurance against boredom came from within. 'The young people must also learn how to amuse themselves, for on nothing so depends the happiness of others than knowing how to use their time.' This was as true for grown women as for young girls, Charlotte insisted, declaring that 'I am almost certain that many fall into gallantry because they lack resources within themselves. It is thus that their laziness becomes the mother of all ills.' Charlotte added to the letter the 'plan of instruction which I followed with my own girls, which I believe has seen good effects' (though, sadly, this has not survived). Her final instruction directs the bereaved duke to further useful reading: 'I recommend to you most strongly the works of Mme de Genlis on education, as giving birth to a multitude of useful ideas.'[61]

Mme de Genlis was governor (she insisted on the more authoritative male title) to the children of the Duke of Orléans, and earlier that year had published her most influential work. *Adèle et Théodore* combined the thinking of Rousseau and Mme Beaumont with the practical experience of a mother, and her book proved immensely popular. Many of its recommendations would have been very familiar to George and Charlotte's sons, advocating as it did a simple diet, lots of exercise and physical labour in the open air. De Genlis added elements which would have been particularly attractive to the queen. Religious instruction, vetoed by Rousseau, was positively encouraged, and a more equal course of study for boys and girls was central to her thinking. So impressed was Charlotte with her ideas that she granted her an almost unheard-of private interview when she visited England. De Genlis's reputation had been much damaged by rumours that she had been the duke's mistress as well as his employee, but Charlotte was prepared, initially at least, to turn a blind eye to any such failings: 'She has, like everyone else, two characters. I neither do accuse her nor excuse her, but I own myself a great admirer of her works.'[62] Eventually, the queen's sense of rectitude triumphed over her intellectual curiosity, and she refused requests for another meeting. But long after she had despaired of Mme de Genlis's morals, she continued to remain interested in her educational theories.

In implementing a practical plan of education for her daughters, the queen had adhered very closely to the advice in the letter to her brother. In Lady Charlotte Finch she had found a governess of distinguished capacity, warm affections and unquestionable loyalty in whom she had absolute trust. Having discovered her, she did everything in her power to keep her, ensuring that the Finch family were well provided for with appointments in the royal household. As she had urged her brother to do, Charlotte maintained a powerful supervisory presence over all proceedings; her severely judgemental eye was keenly felt by both her daughters and their instructors. 'I have seen Her Majesty,' noted a chastened sub-governess in 1779; 'she is pleased that their Royal Highnesses have continued their writing, but does not think Princess Augusta's so well as what was done on Saturday, in either sense or handwriting, and she wishes M. Guiffidière [Guiffardière] would, when he corrects her false spellings, likewise correct, or rather, help her to style the phrases in a more correct manner or use her own words in better sense.'[63]

Charlotte had no compunction at all about the methods by which she acquired the best-qualified instructors. In 1768, Mlle Krohme was appointed as French teacher to the two-year-old Princess Royal. Lady Mary Coke heard that she had been seduced away from the Holdernesses, her previous employers, without the observation of the customary formalities. 'I imagined Lady Holdernesse had been applied to, and that it had been transacted with their approbation,' wrote Lady Mary, 'but the whole was transacted before any notice was taken to Lady or Lord Holdernesse … which does not please them.'[64] Unperturbed, the queen acquired another of her daughters' teachers in exactly the same way. Frederika Planta was lured away from Lady Hoskyns, who complained loudly about Charlotte's underhand methods, but to no avail. Miss Planta was delighted to be offered a place around the royal children, and stayed there until her early death in 1778. She came from a scholarly family: her father was a Swiss pastor of intellectual interests who produced a clutch of governess daughters; her brother was Keeper of Manuscripts and Medals at the British Museum. She undertook 'the instructive part of the education of the princesses', teaching them the rudiments of all the basic subjects, as well as reading and writing. Mrs Papendiek thought her 'quiet, patient, plodding, persevering disposition' was ideally suited to the job. After her death, her sister Margaret, always known as Peggy, inherited her post.

Alongside the Plantas, the queen appointed Martha Goldsworthy as sub-governess in 1774. She was, thought Lady Cowper, who knew her well, 'in every respect qualified for such a trust, by her manners, morals and accomplishments'. She was connected to the court through her brother, who was one of the king's favourite equerries. She was also known to Lady Charlotte Finch, who may have recommended her. Her family had once been rich: her mother, Lady Cowper noted, had had £10,000 but 'her father spent it all'.[65] As was the case for so many other unmarried women without resources, Martha Goldsworthy had no alternative but to hire herself out as a governess, albeit in the very grandest circumstances. Like Frederika Planta, her virtues seem to have been the dogged ones: she was loyal and honourable, hard-working and deeply committed to the wellbeing of her charges, but perhaps not the most inspiring presence. One of her colleagues recorded that she was 'most praiseworthy and indefatigable in the duties of her station, but she wants softness of temper and manner. Nor do I think her qualified, either by education or birth, to be sub-governess to the daughters of a monarch.'[66] There was always a hint of bitterness in 'Gooly', as the princesses called her. Mrs Papendiek heard that 'William Ramus, a page at court, had formed an attachment for Miss Goldsworthy, and proposed to her', but nothing came of it: 'On the queen saying that, in the event of her marriage, she must quit her situation, the idea was given up.'[67] She remained a spinster for the rest of her life, eventually retiring to live in the company of another unmarried royal instructress. Perhaps it was not surprising that her frustrations and disappointments sometimes overwhelmed her.

*

The pupils on whom so much care and thought devolved were bright little girls, with all the prodigious conscientiousness of their parents. The three eldest princesses, so close in age, spent all their time together. As a group, they sometimes seemed rather like a single organism, but in fact they had quite distinct characters.

The Princess Royal was eager to please, diligent and dignified. Frederika Planta thought her 'a noble child, very much the daughter of a king'. Her somewhat stately demeanour seems to have provoked the unwelcome attentions of the wilder princes; her essential good humour was, thought Lady Mary Coke, 'much tried by her brothers, who pulled her about most unreasonably'.[68] Perhaps aware of her deficiencies in looks – Lady Mary could never set eyes on her without remarking on her plainness – she sought to win approval by painfully correct conduct. 'She is remarkably sensible,' wrote Miss Planta, 'the propriety of her behaviour is very great.' Behind the façade of decorum, she was an anxious child, afflicted with the stammer that ran in the family. Her niece, Princess Charlotte, was to suffer from it. George himself displayed a much-commented-upon verbal tic, an insistently repeated 'What! what!' that punctuated his speech. Etiquette required the naturally shy king to begin all conversations and it was perhaps in response to this pressure that he developed this distinctive habit. Royal was said to resemble her father very closely, and certainly shared much of the shyness and timidity that had characterised his youth. She was more confident in the classroom than the Drawing Room, where her 'shining parts' showed to better advantage than her tentative and uncertain dancing skills. 'She speaks French very well,' enthused Miss Planta, 'is well versed in ancient *histoire*, and there is not an event of importance in English history with which she is not pretty well acquainted. She writes well, makes pertinent observations on what she reads, and has a competent knowledge of geography. Till next Michaelmas,' she reported proudly, 'she is not 8 years old.'[69]

Her younger sister Augusta had the inestimable advantage, in Lady Mary Coke's critical opinion, of natural good looks. She declared that the newborn Augusta was 'the most beautiful infant I ever saw', and never revised that opinion. She was the 'darkest of the family' and 'extremely pretty', slender and lively.[70] From her earliest days, Augusta was an engagingly responsive pupil with a particular taste for history. Miss Planta had encouraged her interest, tantalising her with 'some striking facts … in words adapted to her capacity, and then told them as diverting stories. This method has taken, and she tells them again in words of her own, with as much pleasure as she would a fairy tale.'[71]

Augusta was the most imaginative of the elder sisters, a trait which did not meet with everyone's approval. 'She tells long stories,' complained Lady Mary, 'which is not a good habit.'[72] In later life, Augusta was a writer of extremely entertaining letters, her correspondence marked by a laconic humour that implied a secret amusement with the world as she found it. Even as a very young girl, she seems to have written purely for her own pleasure. Two of her childhood 'stories' have survived, fragments transcribed in an immature, unformed hand. One concerns 'a lady and gentleman who married' and 'wished that they had children'. The husband is visited by a friend who promises to let him 'into a secret. Your wife told me she did not like children, and likewise, that she hated to be with a husband who plagued her all day.' When the husband expresses his shock – 'What lies are you saying!' – the friend confesses that 'I only said it to see what you would say.' The young author concluded blithely that 'they were friends ever after'. The mildly unsettling quality of these strange little pieces is even more evident in Augusta's other surviving composition. It is a 'Dialogue between Clare and Eloise' and takes place 'at Lambeth, Cornwall', suggesting that not all of Augusta's geography lessons had taken root. 'E: My dear friend, I had the pleasure of seeing your little brother last night, pray has not he got a wig, or something like one? C: He has, my dear, for he did tear the hair off his head, he is very sorry now that tore the hair off his head. E: He was very handsome before he had that trick. C: So he was, very pleasing.'[73] There was always something unknowable about the dark and elusive Augusta, a wryness and irony that did not quite suit the image of uncomplicated openness prescribed for princesses.

About Elizabeth at the age of four, Miss Planta had least to say: she thought she was sweet-natured, sensible, well behaved and, above all, rather large. From her earliest days, the unfortunate Elizabeth was always defined by her size. 'She was born fat,' declared Mrs Papendiek bluntly, 'and through all her illnesses she never lost flesh.'[74] As she grew older, the stolidly meticulous, purposeful toddler demonstrated that she too possessed 'the same surprising memory which runs through the family'.[75] She also acquired a robust and rather rollicking sense of humour, a taste for simple enjoyments, whether of the mind or the body, and a much-tried optimism that always sought to put the best possible complexion on events.

Alongside the grounding in academic basics provided by Miss Planta, the princesses studied a variety of more traditional feminine accomplishments. The queen was said to have 'a decided genius for drawing', which she felt had not been properly cultivated when she was young. She was determined her daughters would have the opportunity she had missed. The girls were taught all aspects of drawing and painting by a number of distinguished instructors, including, for a while, Thomas Gainsborough.

Like her husband, Charlotte was passionately fond of music, and sought to pass on to her daughters the shared pleasure they both took in it. The princesses were taught by Johann Christian Bach, who, by day, also gave lessons to the queen, and in the evenings accompanied the king on the pianoforte, whilst he played the flute. In a strongly musical family, only the Princess Royal derived no pleasure from it. She later confided to Fanny Burney that 'she heard it with almost pain'. Her inability to master instruments with the easy facility demonstrated by her brothers and sisters was perhaps another source of worry for a child already much pre-occupied with striving for recognition and acceptance.

There were no classical languages on the princesses' curriculum, but they did study other subjects often considered to be exclusively male preserves. The queen told her brother that 'my eldest daughters also took a little course in electricity and air to acquire some little idea of physics'.[76] Much of their early instruction in science came from M. de Luc, but, when older, they accompanied their mother to a series of lectures in botany given by the Reverend J. E. Smith, co-founder of the Linnean Society. The girls were also taken to see demonstrations of the most modern applications of science and technology. On one occasion, the king and queen went with the elder princesses to Wimbledon to witness a demonstration of fireproofing: Charlotte and her daughters watched a bedstead and its curtains set alight, whilst the floor, treated with chemicals, remained unscathed. They then proved their courage, 'in going upstairs and abiding in a room directly over that in which fire raged like a furnace beneath'.[77] Another visit took them to Samuel Whitbread's great new brewery at Southwark, where beer was manufactured on an epic, industrial scale. Such visits delighted the king, whose interest in works of technological and mechanical ingenuity was boundless: 'he explained the leading movements of the machinery in a way that clearly showed scientific knowledge', whilst his wife and daughters explored the giant cistern where thousands of gallons of beer would one day be stored. 'The queen and princesses would needs go into it,' it was reported, with some surprise, 'though with some difficulty, as the aperture was so small.'[78] Clambering with her girls through Mr Whitbread's massive machinery, Charlotte showed her commitment to education in its broadest form, as an aspect of life that went well beyond the confines of the schoolroom.

The princesses were also exposed to more conventionally practical skills. As their mother had done before them, they spent many hours at their sewing. Even though it was unlikely they would ever be required to make their own clothes, every woman was expected to have some mastery of this fundamental task, if only for the purposes of judging the work of others: 'You will be better able to know if it is well done for you,' as Mrs Delany explained.[79] More decorative needlework was an art cultivated by even the most aristocratic of women. It was a way of demonstrating wifely devotion; the making of shirts, cravats and other items of masculine clothing was a traditional expression of female affection and duty, and Lady Charlotte Finch was still embroidering waistcoats for her estranged husband long after she had formally separated from him. It also allowed women to display their feelings for favoured female friends and relatives, by presenting them with objects – purses, reticules, sewing cases – that were entirely of their own making and often the product of considerable time and skill. The expertise involved in their manufacture went far beyond basic needlework, requiring mastery of complex procedures of knotting and beading. Once acquired, these skills could also be applied to the creation of a wide variety of soft furnishings, cushions, chair covers and wall hangings. The queen was considered an extremely adept practitioner of these arts, and her own rooms at Windsor were copiously adorned with evidence of her work. She saw no contradiction between her passion for her needle and her appetite for learning; both offered different forms of stimulation and resort for the right-thinking female mind. From their earliest days, her daughters were trained to follow in her footsteps.

Unlike their brothers, the princesses were not subject to physical punishments. 'Your gentle, good-humoured dove must not be roughly opposed,' observed Mrs Delany, 'but led with a silk rein.' For girls, the discipline that came from within would always prove more effective than the threat of a whipping. 'The most essential ground is to teach them such a love of truth that on no account would they ever tell a lie.'[80] The queen was at one with Mrs Delany on the importance of inculcating in her daughters the strongest possible notions of right and wrong. Charlotte regarded the provision of their moral education as the most significant obligation incumbent upon her as their mother.

As young girls, they followed a course of religious study with her chaplain, Dr Schroeder, but the queen always considered the moral teaching of even the best professionals as secondary to her personal instruction, which she continued to practise with the princesses long after they had left the schoolroom. Fanny Burney once came upon them closeted with their mother, 'reading some religious books' together. She was glad of the opportunity to witness Charlotte's 'maternal piety' in action, and much impressed by the way in which 'she enforced, in voice and expression, every sentence that contained any lesson that might be useful to her royal daughters. She reads extremely well, with great force, clearness and meaning.'[81] Charlotte's efforts were not made in vain. In sharp contrast to their brothers, all her elder daughters grew up to share her piety; the Princess Royal mirrored the beliefs of her parents perfectly when she wrote, as a much older woman, that 'the making of her a good Christian' was the most important purpose of any girl's education.

The queen had much reason to be satisfied with her daughters' progress as they completed the first stages of their education. They were dutiful and conscientious, good learners who had benefited from the assiduous efforts of their carefully chosen teachers. But for Charlotte, this was not quite enough. Alongside their instruction, she also wanted to offer the princesses inspiration, placing them in the company of an intelligent, well-read young companion who would take their education to the next level by acting as both teaching assistant and role model. There is no doubt this had equal appeal for the queen herself, presenting the opportunity to bring a like-minded thinker into her small household circle, thus allowing her the kind of sociable intellectual stimulation she so craved.

In 1777, Charlotte considered that she had found exactly the right candidate for the job. Mary Hamilton was clever, young and well connected. She was twenty-five, the granddaughter of a duke, and the niece of William Hamilton, connoisseur, diplomat and, later, cuckolded husband to Lord Nelson's Emma. She was intellectually inquisitive and brimming with cheerful self-confidence; she kept up a lively correspondence with a wide circle of intellectual women. Her learning had made her neither solemn nor sombre; she was an entertaining and candid writer, with a slightly flirtatious tone, and was clearly an engaging presence. Everyone who met her liked her. Inevitably, she was known to that magnet for bright women, the Duchess of Portland, who seems first to have recommended her to the attention of the queen. Charlotte was impressed by an endorsement from so revered a source, and moved very fast to bring her into her household. When told that she was 'thought upon to fill a new place about the princesses', Mary Hamilton was astonished, and a little apprehensive: 'I had never in my life had the least desire to belong to a court, and to ask for such a thing would have been the last of my thoughts.' But the wheels were now turning and there was no going back. A few days later, she was seen and approved by Lady Charlotte Finch. She was then 'presented to Her Majesty, who received me in the most gracious manner', and, almost without knowing quite what had happened, found herself established in Prince Ernest's old apartments at Kew. 'The transaction was so sudden that I can hardly comprehend how it came about.'[82]

At first, Mary Hamilton found a great deal to enjoy in her unlooked-for new job. She went with the princesses to Kew where they walked in the parks, paraded around the village and sat in the gardens. At Windsor, she joined the family's regular, ceremonial procession across the public terraces, where anyone and everyone could watch them as they walked past. It was an exciting experience for a newcomer. 'Went on to the Terrace,' she wrote in her diary. 'There was much company – Nobility – Persons of Fashion – Pretty Women – Smart Girls – Handsome Men – Coxcombs – Officers – Misses and an Abundance of Clergy.' The king, clearly charmed by her, was kind and teasing, in his rather heavy-handed, bantering style. 'In his most amiable and good-humoured way, he charged me not to lose my heart to any of the old prebendaries.'[83]

She brought a great deal of energy and goodwill to her task, and did all she could to win the affections of her charges. A few months after her arrival, she organised a summer tea for the three eldest princesses in her rooms. Mary did not stand on her dignity, and seems to have had a more boisterous sense of fun than their other attendants. 'We went first into the garden, where we amused ourselves playing about. I say we, for I enjoyed it as much as them.' Later they played the card game Dumb Crambo, where 'there were a number of forfeits which gave rise to much amusement in framing punishments'. A good time was had by all, and 'their royal highnesses were quite rakes, as Lady Charlotte allowed them to stay till ten o'clock.'[84]

The queen was as delighted as her daughters with her new recruit. Mary Hamilton was exactly what had been missing from her cultivated domesticity, a witty, articulate addition to her entourage. Only two days after her arrival, Mary 'had the honour of sitting two hours with Her Majesty tête-à-tête. I read a manuscript of Glover's *Leonidas*. She praised my style of reading poetry, and was pleased to say she would take lessons from me.'[85] Soon, she was a favoured member of Charlotte's inner circle. The combination of Mary Hamilton's intellect and good-heartedness was a very attractive one, and completely overwhelmed Charlotte's usually impenetrable emotional armoury. The affection she felt for her was unprecedented, as was the freedom with which she came to express it. A few years after their first meeting, she was writing to Mary with a warmth and appreciation she extended to no one else. Theirs was, for Charlotte, a true and most welcome meeting of like minds. 'What can I have to say?' she enquired of Mary in 1780, 'Not much indeed! But to wish you a good morning in the pretty blue and white room where I had the pleasure to sit and read with you *The Hermit*, a poem which is such a favourite with me that I have read it twice this summer. Oh,' she enthused, 'what a blessing to keep good company. Very likely I would never have become acquainted with either poet or poem was it not for you.' With Mary, Charlotte revealed a sprightly playfulness that was usually kept well hidden. She even allowed herself to express some of the satiric attitude with which she privately regarded some of the more tedious requirements of her role. 'A droll idea started up in my head', she wrote teasingly to Mary, which she knew was 'dangerous to indulge'. It was 'comparing the Terrace – the Royal Terrace – with? … Patience … with a market! Oh fie upon the queen!' It is hard to imagine anyone else with whom Charlotte would have been so cheerful and so unguarded in declaring 'this wicked thought of mine. Promise to keep it to yourself.'[86]

The whole family shared something of the queen's strength of feeling for Miss Hamilton. When he was sixteen, the highly susceptible Prince of Wales noticed her, and immediately fell in love with her. She was ten years his senior, but that had no impact on his ardour. 'I not only esteem you, but love you more than words or ideas can express,' he wrote. Mary was flattered, but replied that, 'without injuring my honour', she could accept only his friendship. For all her restraint, it was a relationship of genuinely warm feeling, and the pair exchanged seventy-five letters between April and December 1779. In reply to his flowery declarations, Mary urged the prince to improve his behaviour, to give up swearing and drinking, and pay less attention to the purchase of expensive clothes; in reply, he insisted that he was encouraged to behave better merely by being in her company. Once, after she had left Windsor, he had searched her rooms hoping to find some memento of her; all he could discover was the remains of a bouquet he had given her. 'I seized it and kissed it with fervour,' he declared, 'and then, as you had worn it within your bosom … I placed it in mine, hoping it would confer some particular virtue in me.'[87]

But the most intense of all the relationships Mary Hamilton inspired within the royal family was with the small girls for whom she cared. From the moment of her arrival in the household, the princesses sought desperately to win her affection, by any means necessary. For both the elder girls, there seemed to be only one way by which they thought this could be achieved – by reminding her constantly of their impeccable behaviour. They had clearly imbibed the moral teachings of their mother very thoroughly, and were much preoccupied with goodness. Their earliest letters show them to be obsessively concerned with their ability to reach that pre-eminently desirable state, and often resemble a kind of moral barometer, alert to all the small shifts in the weather of their conduct. Writing to Mary Hamilton, Augusta was repeatedly determined to prove her worthiness in this most important respect: 'Upon my word, I will be very good to you, and everybody else that is around me in this house'; 'I will always be good, Madam'; 'I will be good all day.' The young Elizabeth was just as eager to fulfil the prime directive. 'I will be very good,' she assured Mary Hamilton, 'to please Mama, and make everybody happy and do my lessons well.' When Mary fell ill, for Elizabeth, there was only one way to make her better. 'I will be very good to please you, and make you well again.'[88]

Inevitably, the princesses sometimes fell short of the standards set for them. Although the sisters could not compete with the uncontrollable high spirits of their brothers, their behaviour was sometimes a challenge to those around them. Augusta seems to have been the main offender; Mary Hamilton kept a little cache of apologetic notes from her, a doleful catalogue of her transgressions. 'I am sorry that I behaved so ill to you this afternoon,' runs one sad little note, that reads as though punctuated by tears; 'I promise I won't do so any more, and assure you that I am ashamed of it, that I won't so any more. I beg you will believe me, for it is very true.' Sometimes her sins were the minor ones of 'impertinence' or 'meddling'. Others were more serious. 'I am very sorry for the blow I gave you last night, I am very sorry indeed … I have wrote to Gooly and she has forgiven me … I hope I have not hurt you, and was very sorry to find you with brown paper … upon your breast.' A few months later, the sins were again small ones. 'I beg you will ask Miss Goldsworthy to forgive me for being so foolish this morning about my rhubarb.'[89]

Augusta did everything she could to persuade Mary Hamilton of the depth and intensity of her affection. Sometimes she was commanding: 'I desire that you will love me', she once imperiously insisted. On other occasions she was more of a supplicant: 'Miss Hamilton is obliged to love Princess Augusta,' she begged plaintively, 'she is obliged to say so very often.'[90] In a way familiar to generations of teenage girls, she also sought to show the depth of her emotions by inflicting pain upon herself. When she was fourteen, and Mary Hamilton was no longer living at court, she sent her old governess a tiny card. On the back of it, Mary noted that she 'had pricked herself with a pin and wrote this in her blood to give to Miss H'.[91]

Augusta's devotion was more than matched by that of her elder sister. The awkward Princess Royal, anxious, tense and painfully self-aware, was desperate to come first in the affections of the glamorous, amusing, clever Miss Hamilton. Her campaign to attract and hold her attention was unrelenting. Shortly after her arrival, Mary found a note from Royal 'put into my work': 'Day and night I always think of you,' the eleven-year-old princess declared, 'for I love and esteem you.' Once their relationship was established, Royal was a demanding companion. 'The Princess Royal presents her compliments to Miss Hamilton, and begs to know why she would not kiss her last night.' There was no aspect of Mary Hamilton's daily life which Royal could not turn into a way of expressing her devotion. 'I am very sorry that you did not sleep well last night. I beg you will lay down and not think of anything but a flock of sheep … if you do what I desire, I shall love you very much.'[92] Her feelings grew stronger as she came to appreciate Mary's virtues. 'You do not know how much I love you, for you are so good natured and good to me, that I cannot help it.'[93] For Royal, as for her sister, only the really good deserved to be loved. But she hoped that genuine strength of feeling might be understood as a virtue in itself; surely she was entitled to affection, having given it so freely herself? 'Pray give me your love,' she urged, 'for I wish for your love so much that I think you must give it to me.' 'Pray love me,' she insisted, 'for I love you and it is but fair.'[94]

Royal's intense desire to extract from Mary Hamilton an unequivocal declaration of loving commitment perhaps reflected a deep emotional insecurity. Like Augusta, she had seen those close to her leave, in ways that were entirely beyond her control. When her French teacher Mlle Krohme died in 1777, she had been inconsolable. 'My daughter is incomparably upset,' the queen told her brother. 'She cries all the time.'[95] In the same year, her much-loved attendant Mary Dacres found a husband and left her service. Royal felt utterly betrayed. 'How could you be so sly as not to let anyone know you was to be married?' she demanded, drawing the sad conclusion: 'I do not think you love me as I love you.'[96]

If some of the hunger for affection displayed by the princesses can be attributed to their fear of abandonment, some responsibility for their neediness must also attach to the queen. The 'gravity of manner' and 'self-command' that she took such trouble to maintain did not encourage the warmest relations between mother and daughters. She shared the king's concern that her children might fall victim to the corrupting wiles of the court, as potent a fear for her girls as for the boys, despite all she had done to minimise the threat. 'Between you and me,' she confided to her brother, 'I think there is too much flattery mixed in with their education, and I need a lot of patience, faith and uprightness to prevent the bad effects that can result from this.'[97] But what looked like 'uprightness' to Charlotte could easily read as severity and detachment to her daughters. This was amplified by her inability to express the more openly affectionate emotions that they so desperately sought from others. Lady Harcourt, the queen's closest friend, did not think that Charlotte lacked deep sentiments, but agreed that she found them impossible to display. She was, she thought, 'very sensitive, but loved to restrain her feelings, from principle.'[98] The princesses were never less than respectful to their mother, and were always dutiful in delivering themselves of the conventional pieties. It is hard not to conclude, however, that in their childhood and youth, it was not from their mother that they expected to receive unqualified, demonstrative affection.

A decade later, in the eventful year of 1789, the Harcourt ladies were discussing with the queen the unfortunate fate of Marie Antoinette. Mrs Harcourt was struck by a remark of Charlotte's, criticising the chilly demeanour of the French queen's mother, Maria Theresa of Austria: 'The empress never made companions of her daughters,' she asserted, 'but kept them at the greatest distance.' Mrs Harcourt found this observation poignant in its lack of self-awareness. 'I could not but think, that in this account, the queen, without perceiving it, in part condemned her own conduct towards her daughters, for with the kindest intentions towards them, it certainly seems as though she kept them at too great a distance – preventing that confidence that would be of such advantage to them, and obliging them to find more pleasure in the society of friends than in their mother.'[99]

In fact, as the Harcourts well knew, the young princesses had few real friends except each other. Their lives were packed with occupation, but in the midst of their busyness, they were isolated, with only each other and their attendants for company. This was the darker side of Rousseauian retreat – a life populated by familiar faces and enlivened only rarely by anything exceptional or unexpected. For the women of the family, time could and often did hang heavy on their hands, with boredom an enervating backdrop to their days. Even the queen, so determined an advocate of time well spent, openly alluded to the creeping ennui that sometimes threatened to envelop the women of the household. 'Our amusements at Windsor are much the same as they were last year,' she told Mary Hamilton in 1780. The only difference she could see was that her drives were not quite as long as they had been then. 'For you know,' she wrote mournfully, 'we deal not much in variety.' This was not, she boldly declared, how she would prefer things to be. 'I am for some little change, why should it not be so in our society? We both agree and say yes! But when it must not be, what is to be done then? Why, to submit!'[100]

Until the king wanted a different style of life, everything would stay as it was. Three years later, as Charlotte had predicted, all was exactly as it always had been. 'There is never any news here,' one of her daughters' attendants wrote to Mary Hamilton, 'we are in faubourg of sameness.'[101] The unchanging routine weighed heavily on the whole female household. Their hours were long, with little time off, and their commitment was expected to be total. Even the indefatigable Lady Cha was eventually worn down by it. In 1774, after twelve years' service, during which the sickness and death of two of her own daughters had barely interrupted her duties in the royal nursery, she wrote to the queen and requested two days off each week in which she could see her friends. Charlotte reluctantly agreed, but asked her to increase the hours of her duties on her remaining days, in order to encourage the other attendants 'and make them look upon it less as a confinement'. Lady Charlotte was outraged, replying that she had 'ever made her own concerns … give way to the duties of my place, as everything belonging to me has experienced'. She was now forced to consider whether she must resign, as the queen 'must know what an uncommon stock of spirits and cheerfulness is required to go through the attendance of so many and such very young people in their amusements, as well as behaviour and instruction.'[102] Horrified at the prospect of losing her, the queen immediately capitulated.

Lady Charlotte was hardly alone in her expressions of unhappiness. The sub-governesses ranked beneath her shared all the grievances she described. They kept up a sad correspondence which reveals the depths of their common misery. Bored and exhausted by their long hours of service, they had, as they often assured one another, no real independent existence. Through the prism of their discontent, the daily round of the queen's household looked grim indeed. 'Our life here is not to be envied,' wrote Miss Goldsworthy to Mary Hamilton, as she arrived back from the Queen's House to Windsor. 'I return back to the *dungeon*, heated to death, and wishing, as I never have before in my life, for the hour of going to bed.'[103] Even activities that were supposed to entertain felt more like punishments. 'Yesterday we went a-hunting, I accompanied the princesses to see the stag hounds out of the park, we were *two hours and a half* going to see *that*.'[104] Much as she cared for them, the children tired her out, and she had no time to herself. 'The dear little angels are now asleep, their spirits beyond what you can imagine, I have not had a moment to myself during *twelve hours* that they are awake to do anything. I have tried various, but now I give it up.'[105]

After two years of such endurance, Mary Hamilton herself had had enough. Her days began at seven in the morning and did not end until she put the princesses to bed at midnight. Her hours of 'waiting' were too often exactly that – formless and pointless, without variation or purpose. Above all, she missed the company of her friends, for visitors were not encouraged and she was allowed only occasional leave. 'I continue in a situation for which I have neither inclination, strength of constitution or sufficient stock of spirits to support,' she wrote in 1779. For a while, she did her best to bear it. She endeavoured to do her duty; and 'had the satisfaction of being approved of'. She knew she was specially favoured by the queen, and tried to draw pleasure from her preferment, but it was all to no avail. 'I had not time to possess my own mind, my health and spirits suffered much from leading a life of constant restraint.' Nothing she experienced at court could compensate for what she had lost. 'I love independence and liberty,' she declared, 'and have no taste for a mere parade of life.'[106]

It was not until 1781 that she could summon up the courage to ask the queen for permission to resign. When she did so, she was refused. 'The contents of your letter I am inclined to treat as the effects of *low spirits*,' Charlotte replied, 'and therefore won't indulge you in an entire belief of what you have said.'[107] But Mary was determined. 'I wish a hundred times a day that I had never entered into this situation,' she confided to her diary. 'I am very unhappy.' It took her another year to persuade the queen to let her go.

She was very much missed. The faithful Augusta continued to write to her for some years; the Princess Royal, with whom relations had cooled as the princess grew older, passed on her rather more temperately expressed good wishes. The Prince of Wales, who had found far more complaisant mistresses since the days of their innocently playful correspondence, never entirely lost his feelings for her. In later years, one of his gentleman declared that Miss Hamilton was 'the only woman he ever heard the prince speak of with proper respect, except the queen.'[108]

Of all the family, though, it was probably the queen who missed her most. For Charlotte, Mary Hamilton's resignation was far more than simply the loss of a valued governess. Her inability to keep Mary as a happy member of her household undermined the entire vision of domesticated intellectual purpose that had meant so much to her. She had admired Mary's intellect and enjoyed her company, and clearly hoped she would stay as a companion for herself and an inspiration for her daughters. But women like Mary were precisely those who, like Charlotte, found the boredom and isolation of life at court impossible to bear. For all her efforts, Mary Hamilton's ineradicable unhappiness was a forceful reminder that Windsor was not – and never could be – the vision of fulfilled intellectual contentment the queen had glimpsed at Bulstrode.

As the education of George and Charlotte's sons drew to a close, they had been pushed away from their family with a haste that seemed designed to put as much distance as possible, both physical and emotional, between them and their erstwhile home. With the exception of the increasingly embittered Prince of Wales, the brothers were scattered around Europe, and were never to live again as full-time members of the domestic household. With their daughters, the opposite was the case. Their generous education had expanded their minds, but promised them no experience of life beyond the narrow confines of their family. Charlotte admitted this was not at all the kind of life she wanted for them. 'I regret more and more,' she wrote to her brother, 'by the day, very considerably not having any company except my children. We enjoy ourselves together, but all conversation cannot be animated conversation, and our life is too close and too good and too retired for us to know the world.' She confessed that she often found the rhythm of their days challenging, 'even with the aid of religion, which comes to my assistance'. How could such an arid existence benefit her girls, or prepare them for their futures? 'I fear for my daughters day after day,' she concluded sadly. 'It is necessary to know the world in order to judge it, and see how to behave.'[109] Charlotte was perceptive enough to understand the problem: her daughters were growing up denied the chance to engage with society, but it was unthinkable she would do anything about it. She had told Mary Hamilton that she considered herself '*totally* void of any wish or desire contrary to the opinions of those I live with.'[110] In this context, that meant the king, and until he was prepared to consider an alteration in his daughters' circumstances, it was inconceivable that anything would change.

CHAPTER 9

Numberless Trials

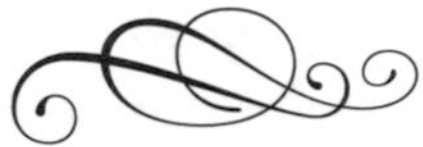

THROUGHOUT THE 1770S AND EARLY 1780S, as the queen struggled against the encroaching despondency she suspected was inseparable from her royal role, her husband was weighed down by a very different but equally heavy burden. If Charlotte felt thwarted by the isolation of her life, the confined existence imposed upon her by her rank, the king grappled with pressures in the public world that called upon all his powers of resilience and determination, and yet seemed impervious to solution. These were the years in which George faced a greater challenge to his authority than at any other time during his reign. The conflict between the American colonies and the government in London resulted in political and ideological turmoil of a kind not seen in British life since the Glorious Revolution of 1688. Cherished assumptions about the nature of liberty and the rights of Crown and Parliament were blown away as old alliances shifted, new relationships were formed and the constitutional landscape was reimagined in an entirely unexpected way. The crisis also struck a blow at George's carefully constructed vision of kingship, demonstrating the limitations of its effectiveness when faced with a direct confrontation. His inability to deliver an outcome that he believed was both right and just instilled in him an anger and unhappiness as acute as anything felt by his wife.

The sense of having failed in an endeavour which was central to his conception of himself as a man and a monarch was hard enough to bear; but George's frustration was made more acute by the prolonged misery of the experience itself. For nearly a decade he was involved on a daily, sometimes hourly, basis with the most intractable political problem of the time, dealing with issues and individuals for which he felt little intrinsic sympathy or understanding. Unlike his ministers, he could not look yearningly to the ultimate escape route provided by resignation; and his conscientious character meant he was never off duty. If Charlotte's discontents arose from too remote a relationship with the public world, the king suffered from never being allowed to escape its demands. 'The numberless trials and constant torments I meet with in public life must certainly affect any man,' he observed bitterly in 1780, 'and more poignantly me, as I have no wish but to fulfil my various duties.' Under the impact of his trials and torments, George's character, never naturally cheerful, hardened into a settled pessimism. He had no expectation that his situation would ever change or improve. 'The experience of now near twenty years has convinced me, that however long it may please the Almighty to extend my days, yet I have no reason to expect any diminution of my public anxiety.' Only one aspect of his life offered any respite from the perpetual harassments of a role from which, he had gloomily concluded, only death could eventually release him: 'Where am I therefore to turn for comfort but indeed to the bosom of my own family?'[1]

He had no doubt that Charlotte would not fail him. Whatever doubts about the meaning of her life assailed her in private, she remained loyal and devoted to George's interests. 'As to your mother,' he told his eldest son with patent satisfaction, 'I can truthfully say, that in nineteen years, I have never had the smallest reason but to thank heaven for having directed my choice among the princesses then for me to marry to her; indeed, I could not bear up if I did not find in her a feeling friend to whom I can unbosom my griefs.'[2]

One of his wife's chief virtues, in George's eyes, was that she never made trouble. The same could not be said for his sons. All the royal family were affected in different ways by the fallout from their father's unhappiness in these years, but it was in the king's relations with the princes that the collateral damage of his public frustrations was immediately apparent. The king once described his sons as 'the instruments I look for, in assistance in putting this country into any degree of prosperity'. George intended that the boys should one day act as dependable outriders of his will, taking from his shoulders some of the burdens of government under which he laboured so relentlessly. He was convinced this could only happen if they showed by their actions that they shared his vision of modern monarchy, of kingship characterised by duty, service and moral example. Their commitment to the professions he had chosen for them was regarded by him as a crucial indicator of their worthiness to assist him in that task. Did they apply themselves to their studies? Did they behave with propriety and moderation? Did they display a selfless dedication to improvement? Only by satisfying their father's high standards in all aspects of conduct would they be regarded as having deserved the right to be considered as potential confidants and apprentices. 'They must,' he insisted, 'by their behaviour convince me they are deserving of such trust.' Judged on these terms, their father decided that, with the possible exception of his favourite, Frederick, all his older sons had failed both him and the monarchy itself. He would struggle on alone.

It was unlucky for his sons – and indeed for their father – that so many of them grew into maturity in the years during which the king was under such intense political pressure. Under the strain of prolonged anxiety, the paternal affection that had been so visible a part of George's character when the boys were young evaporated with disconcerting speed. By the time the American War of Independence was over in 1783, George's sons were as alienated and distant from their parents as the Thirteen Colonies had been from the mother country in the midst of the conflict. The politics of the conflict mirrored the divisions that now ran through the heart of the king's family; but those politics had themselves helped create those rifts, by impacting so profoundly upon the king's state of mind.

From the earliest days of his reign, the practice of politics had not come easily to George III. As a young man plagued by chronic shyness, he had found many of his public responsibilities painful to perform. It was observed that at formal audiences he was often more uncomfortable than those lined up to meet him. He was even less at ease in private encounters; he was nervous with his first ministers, particularly those of forceful and blustering personality, such as George Grenville, whose bullying aggression in the early years of his reign the king never forgot nor forgave.[3] As he became more experienced, his confidence grew and he felt increasingly able to assert his views, though he never became an enthusiastic practitioner of the political arts. Other men might find pleasure and excitement in the drama and self-aggrandisement that was the defining tone of so much of eighteenth-century politics; George never did, and actively disapproved of those who pursued flamboyant, highly coloured careers.

He found it impossible to work with William Pitt. The architect of British victory in the Seven Years War, Pitt was a formidable strategist, an impassioned and dazzling orator, dubbed 'the Great Commoner' by an idolising populace which cheered and huzza'd him wherever he went. George thought Pitt unsound, disapproving of what he regarded as his demagoguery and his expensive foreign policy ambitions, and resented Pitt's attempts to 'manage' him. He retreated into the obstinate non-cooperation that was his response to all ministers with whom he disagreed, and Pitt's premiership was short-lived. It was not until 1770, nearly a decade after his accession, that George finally found a man with whom he felt he could do business: Frederick, Lord North.

North did not make a particularly good impression when first encountered. He was a large, dishevelled and not very attractive figure. 'Nothing could be more coarse or clumsy or ungracious than his outside,' recalled Horace Walpole. 'Two large prominent eyes that rolled about to no purpose (for he was utterly short-sighted), a wide mouth, thick lips, and an inflated visage gave him an air of a blind trumpeter.'[4] Somewhat woundingly for the king, North was considered to resemble him so closely in appearance that it was rumoured – without any foundation – that the politician was in fact George's illegitimate half-brother. But if North's looks did him no favours, his character charmed everyone who met him. He was clever, good-tempered, witty and, a rare attribute in a politician, entirely devoid of malice. He enjoyed a happy home life surrounded by a family famous for their entertaining repartee. 'It was impossible to experience dullness in his society,' wrote the diplomat Nathaniel Wraxall.[5] Everyone liked North, including the king. It helped that they had known each other since childhood, North's father having acted as a Lord of the Bedchamber to Prince Frederick. George also responded to North's quiet professional competence, his undoubted and unobtrusive mastery of political business. North's reputation is now so associated with the loss of America that it is hard to see him as master of anything, but in the judgement of the political historian John Cannon, he was 'ambitious, hard-working and efficient … a master of political tactics.'[6]

North had been in the House of Commons all his adult life, and understood its management better than any of his contemporaries. He was never a showy speaker, but he was a powerful debater, and his carefully marshalled arguments ushered many contentious bills through the chamber. He was associated with a number of projects close to the king's heart. He had led the government's attack on John Wilkes, and piloted the unpopular Royal Marriages Bill through an unsympathetic Commons. As a man of business, North's credentials were excellent, and George was delighted when he accepted the highest offices: he held, at the same time, the positions of first minister, Chancellor of the Exchequer and Leader of the House of Commons. Once established in power, the king never wavered in his support for him, making him a Knight of the Garter, the most prestigious chivalric order. More practically, in 1777, he paid off North's huge personal debts of over £20,000. 'I want no return,' George told him, 'but your being convinced that I love you as well as a man of worth, as I esteem you as a minister.'[7]

Like the king himself, North was a hard worker, and held down his demanding posts with a prodigious amount of effort. 'His labours are immense,' wrote one of his colleagues, 'and such as few constitutions could bear.'[8] But North's many virtues did not compensate for some ominous key failings. He was chronically indecisive, as he himself acknowledged. 'I never could, nor can decide between different opinions,' he confessed to the king in 1778. More worryingly, he suspected that he lacked the killer instinct that was required in an effective leader. He did not, he observed perceptively, possess 'the authority of character' that marked out a great premier. Above all, as even his supporters recognised, he was not a man to construct or deliver a grand, all-encompassing strategy. 'Your majesty's service', he later told the king, 'requires a man of great abilities, who can choose decisively, and carry his determination authoritatively into execution ... I am certainly not that man.'[9] The absence of these more forceful, driving qualities in North's character was, of course, one of the reasons why George found him so congenial. However, these weaknesses were to be ruthlessly exposed as the king and his minister were gradually overwhelmed by events neither of them was really qualified to control.

*

Trouble had been brewing in America for almost a decade when, in 1773, a group of discontented Boston citizens, dressed as Mohawk warriors, seized chest after chest of tea from the deck of the East Indiaman that had imported them, and hurled them into Boston Harbor. It was a dramatic gesture of a kind very common in the practice of popular politics in the English-speaking eighteenth-century world; but it was to have a significance that reached far beyond the theatricality of the event itself. Two years later, at Concord, Massachusetts, British military forces clashed directly with American colonists in the first engagement of what could soon be called nothing else but war. By July 1776, the Declaration of Independence had given the colonial opposition to British rule an intellectual coherence, a unifying principle, and a clearly articulated goal.

In 1778, the emergence of Britain's oldest adversary, France, as the key ally of the young republic brought a global dimension to the conflict. The French, joined by the Spanish in 1779, fought the British at sea as well as on land, opening up new spheres of operations in the West Indies, stretching already hard-pressed British resources, and immeasurably improving the prospects for American success. The defeat of the army commanded by General Cornwallis at Yorktown in 1781 effectively signified the end of British rule in what had once been the Thirteen Colonies and heralded the establishment of a new sovereign state. It had taken less than a decade for Britain's American empire, settled over a century and a half before, to be pulled apart.

The consequences were felt in every aspect of British life. The practices of diplomacy, trade, warfare and politics were all turned upside down and inside out by a shift in the balance of power that would have been thought inconceivable only twenty years previously. And its impact was felt with even greater force elsewhere, particularly in France, where Louis XVI's support for a war of independence abroad bankrupted the monarchy at home and led to the revolution that overthrew it. What happened in America between 1775 and 1783 genuinely changed the world. It also almost destroyed George III's kingship, and left him with a sense of failure from which he never fully recovered.

As with so many of the issues that bedevilled the first twenty years of George's reign, the roots of the crisis could be traced back to the 1763 Treaty of Paris which had ended both the Seven Years War and the political career of George's mentor, Lord Bute. The treaty's provisions determined that, as a consequence of British victories in Canada, the French surrendered all their North American territories. The cost of defending these new possessions thus devolved to the government in London, which took the view that, as the American colonies were the most direct beneficiaries of safer northern borders, they should bear some of the cost of maintaining them. To raise the necessary revenues, a series of taxes was imposed on luxury goods imported into the colonies.

Unsurprisingly, this was not a popular decision, and, faced with a chorus of colonial complaint, in the mid-1760s the government capitulated and withdrew all the levies, except the hugely profitable duty on tea. This was retained partly to protect the revenue stream it generated, but also to make a political point. The disgruntled Americans had asserted that new taxes could be imposed on them only with the direct agreement of their own representatives. The London government did not accept this principle, and held on to the tea duty as a symbolic demonstration of the right to tax Americans under the same rules that regulated the payment of taxes by Britons in the mother country. Many British taxpayers had no more direct representation in Parliament than their American counterparts. The unreformed House of Commons was infamously irrational in its definitions of what constituted representation. In populous places such as Westminster and Liverpool, relatively large numbers of men (women were, of course, excluded from the franchise) had the right to vote. In stark contrast, Manchester, an expanding town of comparatively recent growth, had no MPs at all, whilst run-down rural constituencies often boasted only a handful of voters whose loyalties could be bought by any rich purchaser with parliamentary ambitions. Defenders of the system argued that these anomalies were largely irrelevant; it did not really signify how individual Members were elected. What mattered was the status of the Commons as a united entity, for it was in the body of the House as a whole that true representation was to be found. The House of Commons did not derive its authority from a direct relationship with electors; it represented everyone, whether they had a vote or not. The British were, in constitutional terms, 'virtually represented'. For those who accepted this formula as justifying the absence of dedicated MPs for Manchester, it was hard to see why colonial America should be treated any differently.

In the early days of their opposition, some American campaigners hoped to circumvent what they saw as the intransigence of a parliament elected on such dubious grounds by appealing directly to the king to consider the natural justice of their case. Some were even prepared to contemplate a form of qualified direct rule, which placed colonial assemblies directly under George's protection. Other European rulers – the 'enlightened despots' of Prussia, Austria and Russia – might have jumped at the opportunity to oversee a modernising project which came with the tantalising prospect of concentrating more power in royal hands, but George was not interested. From the outset, he regarded American unrest as an attack on the sovereignty of Parliament, and advocated the adoption of the sternest possible response. 'The colonies must either submit or triumph,' he wrote. 'I do not wish to come to severer measures, but we must not retreat.' He hoped that a swift application of 'vigorous measures' would soon bring the Americans 'to a due submission to the mother country'.[10] In the early stages of the conflict, the king's view was shared by many of the political class. The historian Edward Gibbon reflected much of the national mood in his hostility to American claims and his support for firm action. 'I am more and more convinced that we have both right and power on our side,' he wrote; 'we are now arrived at the decisive moment of persevering or of losing forever both our trade and our empire.'[11]

However, as news of repeated military setbacks arrived with discouraging regularity from America, public enthusiasm for the war ebbed away. Defeats, such as that at Saratoga in 1777, when General Burgoyne was forced to surrender his entire army to colonial forces, were humiliating examples of British impotence; whilst victories, such as the taking of New York and Philadelphia, failed to deliver the longed-for knockout blow. In London, the political temperature steadily rose. Critics of the government attacked the ineffectual prosecution of the war, and railed at its escalating cost. Some also began to raise more worrying ideological questions. Was it right that Britain, justly proud of her own struggles to achieve liberty, was so busily (if unsuccessfully) engaged in attempting to extinguish similar efforts across the Atlantic?

The king was unmoved by such arguments. He never altered his conviction that it was the colonists who were attempting to subvert the delicate balance of powers which guaranteed Britain's unique constitutional settlement. This left his ministers very little room for manoeuvre. The skills which had served North so well in negotiating the passage of many a tricky parliamentary bill were useless in the face of the entrenched positions taken up by both George and the colonial powers. A powerful political force of nature like William Pitt, who possessed both grand vision and strength of will, might have managed it; but North, with his essentially compliant character, failed to evolve a strategy that offered any alternative to the highest possible stakes of total victory or total defeat. Even his attempts to appeal to the king, as one practical man of business to another, came to nothing. When North attempted to persuade George that the nation could not afford the cost of much more war, George, usually so attentive to financial considerations, was dismissive. 'I have heard Lord North frequently drop that the advantages to be gained from this contest could never repay the expense,' he observed coldly. He would not accept his first minister's timid attempts to sway him. It was, he believed, his sacred duty to uphold at all costs the principles he had sworn to protect in his coronation oath, and to make every human effort to preserve the integrity of his inheritance. To his critics, the king persevered in an obstinate denial to accept the reality of the situation. For George, his refusal to countenance defeat was a matter of personal honour, a manifestation of his deepest beliefs about his royal mission.

The uncompromising nature of the king's position was well known, and he was soon irrevocably associated with the aggressive prosecution of the war, both at home and abroad. In America he became a demonised figure, thought to bear a heavy personal responsibility for the death and destruction occurring in the colonies. The Declaration of Independence contains a lengthy recapitulation of his offences, not just as a head of state but as a malignly motivated individual, describing him as 'a prince whose character is marked by every act which may define a tyrant', and 'one who is unfit to rule a free people'.[12] Attacks of this kind must have been particularly painful to George, who saw himself as the defender of established liberties in the face of unjustified and potentially dangerous incursions. They hit him where it would hurt most, as they were intended to.

George increasingly saw himself as an isolated and persecuted figure, vilified abroad and left to carry much of the responsibility at home in driving forward the prosecution of the war. One of his principal tasks was shoring up the faltering commitment of his first minister. From the very beginning of the conflict, North had suspected that he was not qualified to be a wartime leader, and had made repeated requests to be allowed to resign. After the disaster at Saratoga, he declared to George that 'capital punishment itself is ... preferable to that constant anguish of mind which he feels from consideration that his continuance in office is ruining His Majesty's affairs'. Although persuaded by the king to reconsider and go back to work, North continued to insist that he was not up to the job. The workload overwhelmed him, and he could not cope with the constant anxiety and fear of failure. He was, he said, 'oppressed with a thousand griefs'. His desperate pleas to be released from office must surely have reminded George of similarly miserable requests made by Lord Bute in 1763. North maintained that 'his present distress of mind' was such 'that he would soon be unfit for the performance of any ministerial duty'.[13] The king, tougher than he had been nearly twenty years before, refused to contemplate North's resignation. 'No man has a right to talk of leaving me at this hour ... Are you resolved ... at the hour of danger to desert me?' North refused to rally, declaring that he could not understand, 'after so many proofs of his unfitness for his situation', why George was determined to keep him in office, 'though the almost certain consequence will be the ruin of his Majesty's affairs'.[14]

George would never have allowed himself to indulge in such obvious despair – his sense of responsibility would have made that seem a capitulation – but there can be no doubt that the burden of the conflict pressed heavily on him. This was not just in relation to the making of decisions, or coping with setbacks and criticism; the war also added hugely to the weight of bureaucratic, administrative tasks which fell upon his shoulders. From the first days of his reign, George had shown himself doggedly devoted to the unglamorous nuts and bolts of royal business. He was a tireless reader and writer of official letters, managing his vast correspondence without a secretary until his sight began to fail him in 1804. He tackled diligently the daily tide of documents which required his attention – diplomatic dispatches, reports of parliamentary proceedings, communications from government departments – annotating their margins with his comments and marking his usually terse replies with the exact time, to the minute, of their receipt. As the principal fount of official patronage, he was the subject of endless supplication for appointments and promotions, not just at court and in government, but also in the

Church, the universities and in all branches of the armed services. Over the years, he had built up considerable reserves of knowledge about the virtues and shortcomings of almost everyone in the public sphere, which he applied, not always without prejudice, in making his decisions.

Now this already prodigious workload was made even more demanding by the additional requirements of war. George was endlessly occupied, responding at all hours of the day and night not just to dramatic shifts in the political and military situation, but also to more prosaic issues of recruitment, supply and the provision of funds. In her letters to her brother Charles, the queen noted with concern the strain this extra work imposed upon her husband, the hours spent communing with ministers and listening to the gloomy reports of generals. She did what she could to support him, even attending reviews and military inspections at his side, although she disliked all such empty spectacles, and usually tried to avoid them if she could. The extraordinary nature of the times made all such selfish considerations irrelevant; everything, she told Charles, had been changed by the extremity of the situation. The atmosphere of general anxiety had become so all-pervasive that she confessed it had even driven her to abandon her prime directive of political non-engagement. 'Truthfully, my dear brother, I speak, I hear, I read and I dream only of war; thus do I believe that imperceptibly, I am becoming political, despite myself.'[15]

Charlotte's new-found preparedness to engage with politics did not, in fact, extend far beyond involving herself with renewed energy in projects undertaken by her immediate family. Alongside her active and public support for her husband's exertions, she was also able to rejoice in the bravery of her son William, who was the only one of the family to experience the American war at first hand. When, in 1779, the teenage prince joined the navy, the risk of his seeing action was already, as Charlotte recognised, quite high. She endeavoured to prepare herself for that possibility as best she could. 'I can only make myself behave like a Greek or Roman mother,' she wrote ruefully to her brother, although she confessed that her attempts to display severe classical resignation were only partly successful. 'I don't want to be distant from him, I don't want to see him put in a place where he could be killed or injured.' But if he had to fight, she hoped very much that he would acquit himself honourably. 'I confess to you, that

I would be well pleased, if in an action, my son did not fail to do his duty.'[16]

In January 1780, both Charlotte's hopes and fears were realised. The fourteen-year-old prince was present at a battle off the Portuguese coast at Cape St Vincent, in which a British fleet destroyed a number of Spanish warships. William witnessed a seventy-gun Spanish warship, with a crew of six hundred men, blow up under fire. 'I felt a horror all over me,' he admitted later.[17] His mother's response was less equivocal; she was, for once, able to express a rare, unqualified pride in the conduct of one of her boys. 'My son William was in the midst of fire,' she wrote excitedly to Charles, 'and the Admiral told me he behaved bravely and spiritedly.'[18] William was later stationed at British military headquarters in New York, and was thus the only British royal to visit the city whilst it was still under rule from London. He wrote to his father that he was greeted by 'an immense concourse of people who appeared very loyal, continually crying out "God bless King George!"'[19]

The cheering inhabitants of New York were not alone in their pro-British sympathies. Recent scholarship has estimated that between 15 and 20 per cent of Americans – about 500,000 people – thought of themselves as loyalists; but the tide of events had turned decisively against them. When General Cornwallis surrendered at Yorktown in October 1781, it was clear to almost everyone that the war was lost. The news reached England on 25 November, and Lord North reacted with a combination of horror and relief, declaring: 'Oh God! It is all over!'[20]

Even in the face of such an apparently decisive setback, the king, who shared none of his first minister's sense of release, was reluctant to concede final defeat. The consequences of surrender were, for him, still too momentous to contemplate. 'No consideration shall ever make me, in the smallest degree, an instrument that would annihilate the rank in which this British Empire stands among the European states, and would render my own situation in this country unsustainable.'[21] For a few months, George clung to the hope that something could be rescued from the ruins of his American policy, but in February 1782 the House of Commons passed a motion against 'the further prosecution of an offensive war on the continent of America.' With little political support for its continuance, the war was, as North had seen, effectively over, and the exhausted premier was at last allowed to resign. As he had always feared, his reputation would be forever overshadowed by the part he played in the loss of America; but the king was more generous to his fallen minister than posterity would be. When North finally departed to spend more time with his family, George thought of him with affection. During his illness in 1788, North was often in the king's disordered mind, as a correspondent explained to the retired politician. 'In his conversation, he often said he loved you, that you was his friend, that though you once deserted … he never could forget how you stood by him in the time of trouble.'[22]

George's trials did not, however, end with the cessation of hostilities. Although the guns were no longer firing, it proved almost impossible to manage an official closure to the conflict. The king struggled unsuccessfully to find an administration that was acceptable to him whilst also commanding sufficient political support to push a peace treaty through a discontented and restive Commons. A rickety government, led by the Marquess of Rockingham, proved as fragile as everyone had expected it to be, and collapsed in 1783. George, already pummelled and demoralised by military humiliation, was now confronted with a very bitter political pill to swallow. With few other options, he had turned to his old ally Lord North to rescue him from his difficulties. North, always happier dealing with parliamentary rather than global crises, was prepared to return to power, but only if he was allowed to do so as part of a most unlikely partnership. In North's opinion, the only viable administration was one built on the alliance of himself and Charles James Fox, the man who had hitherto been regarded as his great political opponent. North was convinced that only by acting alongside Fox, who had opposed the war from the outset, could a satisfactory peace be negotiated with the Americans. No one but North could possibly have persuaded George to accept the idea of such 'an unnatural and factious coalition'. Under his old friend's coaxing, he eventually agreed to accept the inevitable, though it was an arrangement he hated. He was not yet reconciled to the cessation of a conflict that Fox came into office determined to bring to an end. Fox had been one of the most influential critics of the war, and had not hesitated to blame the king for its unwise and unsuccessful prosecution. In having to accept such an unwelcome ally, George felt that he had been 'managed', an experience he loathed, and one that brought out his worst instincts. His dislike went far beyond political differences, however; he personally detested the man he was now required to accept as Secretary of State for Foreign Affairs.

*

Charles James Fox was one of the great presiding deities of eighteenth-century politics. He began his career as an orthodox Whig, an aristocratic defender of the liberties secured by the Glorious Revolution of 1688, and a vigilant, eagle-eyed exposer of any attempts by the Crown to exceed its prerogative and trample on the rights of free-born Englishmen. However, his politics, like those of so many of his generation, were transformed by the great revolutions of the century, in America and then in France. For men like Fox, these great upheavals changed for ever ideas of what liberty and freedom meant, expanding their reach and meaning far beyond that envisaged by the century-old constitutional settlement on which British politics rested. For many Whigs – especially those on the radical side of the party – these new revolutionary impulses seemed an exciting development that marked the next stage in the growth of freedom, and they embraced them with great fervour. Fox was a passionate advocate of the American cause, an eloquent champion of colonial rights, and a forceful objector to the British military mission. He even dressed in the buff and blue colours adopted by General Washington's army as he toasted its victories in rowdy and well-reported dinners of like-minded associates.

His political views alone would have been enough to make him unpalatable to the king; but there was a strong personal dimension to George's hatred of Fox. He was the son of Henry Fox, on whose unscrupulous mastery of the dark political arts the king had been forced to rely to achieve the peace treaty of 1763 which ended the Seven Years War, at much cost to his conscience and sense of himself as a moral agent in the business of government. Henry Fox had also played a subtle but influential role in George's youthful liaison with Sarah Lennox, about which the adult king harboured a complicated sense of denial and embarrassment that he preferred not to contemplate. The use of bribery to suborn Members of Parliament and his infatuation with an unsuitable young woman were humiliating examples of personal weakness and shame for the king, and Fox senior had been witness to both.

Fox's son, Charles, was, in the king's eyes, even worse. He was a libertine in every sense of the word, a man with no interest in the carefully regulated moral universe in which George was so thoroughly immersed. He was an obsessive gambler on a grand scale, playing sometimes for twenty-four hours at a time, losing huge sums with all the negligent panache expected of a louche, insouciant man of the world. On one occasion, he and his brother were said to have lost the truly enormous sum of £32,000 in one night.[23] Only the vastness of his father's dubiously acquired fortune prevented him following so many of his contemporaries into complete financial ruin. He was a hard drinker too, an uninhibited consumer of every kind of pleasure, the human cost of which was only too visible in his large, shabby, unkempt figure. The fastidious Horace Walpole noted with fascinated horror Fox's 'bristly black person', his dirty, untidy unshaven appearance, 'rarely purified by any ablutions', instantly recognisable in any caricature by his fleshy, stubbled face and huge, untrimmed black eyebrows, his shirt often hanging open to reveal the hairy chest beneath.[24] Despite his lack of physical appeal, he was an energetic and successful pursuer of women, who were entranced by his charisma and his seductive personal charm. He was prodigiously clever and effortlessly witty, and was proud of his ability to 'talk his looks away'. He deployed these gifts with equal effectiveness in the House of Commons, where he was a skilled and highly effective debater, and in salons and drawing rooms, where he captivated male and female alike. The glamorous and febrile Duchess of Devonshire, who was an intimate of his, described his conversation 'like a brilliant player of billiards, the strokes follow one another, piff, puff'.[25] His womanising proved less long-lasting than his devotion to gambling, however, and in 1795 he quietly married Mrs Elizabeth Armistead, who had served time as a mistress of the Prince of Wales, and was instantly recognisable amongst Fox's well-connected circle by the strong cockney accent she never lost.

George hated everything about Charles Fox – his beliefs, his behaviour and his paternity were all regarded with baleful disapproval by the resentful king – but it was Fox's relationship with his heir that completed George's enmity. The Prince of Wales idolised Fox, regarding him – in everything except his indifference to clothes and hygiene – as the model of rakish, gentlemanly sophistication. The king correctly believed that Fox encouraged his son to drink, to gamble, to spend recklessly and to share mistresses with him. The prince was a regular visitor to Fox's home in St James's and was regularly seen in his company at Brooks's club and at a host of other parties, dinners and entertainments.

But their alliance was, as the king suspected, based on more than a shared taste for pleasure. He also saw that Fox had recruited the prince into the informal political opposition of which Fox was the de facto leader. When George reached the age of twenty-one, Fox advised him on the complex and increasingly rancorous negotiations over the arrangements with his father for an independent income and separate establishment. In 1784, Fox fought the Westminster election, standing against a ministerial candidate in one of the liveliest pieces of political theatre of the entire decade, during which the Duchess of Devonshire famously kissed tradesmen whilst campaigning with a fox's brush in her hat. The prince wore Fox's colours of Washingtonian blue and buff, and threw dinners and fêtes to encourage his supporters, at which toasts hostile to the king's government – and sometimes to the king himself – were frequently drunk. At Brooks's club, Walpole reported that the king had been the subject of bets which even the diarist considered in dubious taste, as Fox and his circle 'proposed wagers on the duration of his reign'.[26] Elsewhere, Fox was said to have referred to the king as Satan, and, like the Americans, regarded him as personally responsible for the debacle of the War of Independence, observing that it was 'intolerable that it should be in the power of one block-head to do so much mischief'.[27]

The king did not decide to destroy the Fox–North coalition solely because he disliked Fox and resented his influence over his son, but his hatred undoubtedly contributed in some measure towards his appetite for its demise. Once the peace treaty with America had been finally concluded in September 1783, the king saw no further use for an administration he had only ever tolerated for reasons of temporary expediency. When Fox introduced an ambitious bill to reform the cumbersome East India Company – an unwieldy amalgam of business enterprise and political machine through which much of the ruling of the burgeoning empire in the East was conducted – the king saw his opportunity. George supported the bill's many critics, who feared Fox's plans were no more than 'a job' to place valuable imperial patronage in the hands of the Whigs, and declared that anyone supporting it would be regarded unfavourably by himself. The result was the defeat of the bill on its second reading in the Lords, and the subsequent collapse of the Fox–North coalition. Amidst furious complaints from its supporters that the king had acted unconstitutionally in declaring his opinions so openly, the twenty-four-year-old William Pitt was appointed to head the new government, a post he was to hold for seventeen years. Using the methods he had learnt from Henry Fox a generation before, George had engineered with Foxite efficiency the removal of Fox's son from power. (Charles Fox was not to hold the reins again until 1806, when he was a sick man nearing the end of his life, a pale shadow of the leader he might have been in 1784.) The king had no regrets over what had happened. 'I am perfectly composed,' he told Pitt, 'as I have the self-satisfaction of feeling I have done my duty.'[28]

He was, as yet, unable to summon up quite the same degree of equanimity towards events in America. Although he was a model of graceful resignation when he formally received John Adams as ambassador of the new American state in 1785, the king's formal politeness concealed a great deal of inner turmoil. Privately, George agonised over responsibility for the dismemberment of his patrimony. His continual insistence that it was not his fault – 'I should be miserable indeed if I did not feel that no blame on that account can be laid at my door' – suggests that he was, in reality, far from convinced by the strength of his own arguments in that respect.[29] He told himself that his attempts to do his duty had been frustrated at every turn by dilatory ministers, ineffectual generals and the duplicity of the colonists themselves, against whose collective failings no man could have prevailed. Yet beneath his bluster was a spirit-sapping conviction that he had been tried and found wanting. On at least two occasions during the conflict, his unhappiness had been so profound that he was driven to consider abdication as the only way out. In March 1783, faced with the prospect of defeat and the humiliation of negotiating an end to the war, he drafted a note to the Prince of Wales, informing him of his plans 'to resign the crown, my dear son, to you, quitting this my native country forever, and returning to the dominions of my forefathers'. Once established in Hanover, 'your mother, whose excellent qualities appear stronger to me every day, will certainly instantly prepare for joining me, with the rest of my children'.[30]

In the event, the proposed family exodus did not take place, and George hunkered down to endure what could be neither mended nor avoided; but the 'numberless trials' he endured during this most difficult decade tested his powers of personal resilience to the utmost, and reinforced his conviction that he would never find either peace or satisfaction in his life as a public man. It was only in the private world that fulfilment and tranquillity were to be looked for; from his family alone could he expect the solace of unconditional support. The difficulties of imposing his will on the national stage made him all the more determined to countenance no opposition to the vision of ordered happiness he envisaged for his wife and children at home. What had begun as a positive ideal of betterment increasingly evolved into an embattled refuge from the strain and pressure of a role that seemed sometimes beyond endurance. The dark years he spent coming to terms with the loss of America only increased the value George placed upon a well-regulated, harmonious family life; but, as he discovered, those qualities were as hard to find at Windsor and Kew as they were in Westminster and Washington.

*

The most punishing blows that fell upon the family in these years were not, in fact, delivered by politics, but by the operation of that malign chance to which all eighteenth-century parents were terrifyingly subject. In 1782, George and Charlotte had fourteen living children. Although they had suffered from the usual ailments, including such potentially serious illnesses as whooping cough, they were, in general, a robust and healthy brood. In defiance of the mournful attrition of the young and vulnerable witnessed in most other families, the king and queen had not lost a single child in twenty years. But with the birth of their last son, their incredible good fortune evaporated.

Alfred, born in 1780 when Charlotte was thirty-six, was a delicate baby from the start. He suffered from 'eruptions' on his face, and a persistent cough that defied all attempts to cure it. In the spring of 1782, when he was not quite two years old, the little prince's doctors recommended sea air and bathing as a potential restorative. Lady Charlotte Finch, still presiding over the royal nurseries two decades after her original appointment, accompanied the boy to Deal Castle on the Kent coast. She took with her a characteristic reading list of 'Antonio de Salis in Spanish' (complete with a dictionary 'without which I should not attempt it'), and Mme de Genlis's *Adèle et Théodore*.

She cared for Alfred with great tenderness, her fervent desire to nurse him back to health apparent in all the letters she sent to her friend Mary Hamilton back at court. 'I think there is no doubt of the sea-bathing agreeing with him,' she wrote hopefully in May. 'His nights are so much amended, and his appetite so good that he must gain ground.' He even seemed to enjoy the ceremonial firing of the great guns that so shook the castle that all the windows had to be opened beforehand: 'Prince Alfred is, upon that occasion, very courageous and seems to like it.'[31]

As spring turned to summer, Alfred appeared to improve. 'He now bathes two days out of three, which seems to agree with him,' wrote Lady Charlotte in early July, 'and he is certainly clearer in the face than I have seen him since we came here.'[32] But only two weeks later, her bulletins took on a more sombre tone. Alfred had again been troubled by fever, 'and he has a wan, dropping look'. He could no longer be persuaded to walk and she asked for 'the little chaise at the Queen's House' to be sent down for his use, as 'being constantly in arms, as he cannot walk, must be bad for him'.[33] It was soon clear that for all Lady Charlotte's tireless and devoted efforts, Alfred was growing steadily worse, and she and the little boy returned to Windsor. There, on 20 August, he died.

Lady Charlotte was desolated; but having seen two of her own young daughters sicken and die, she was more accustomed to resignation in the face of grief. Alfred, like her girls, was now in a far better place; 'the reflection on the happiness of the dear little object of all this sorrow must be our great consolation'.[34] She stayed with Alfred's body until the undertakers came to remove it, cutting locks of his hair to be sent to his mother and sisters. Finally, his tiny coffin was taken away, 'an office it was impossible to perform without feeling it tenderly, as indeed everybody seemed to do that was present at the scene. It closed with such endless happiness for him, that 'tis for ourselves only that we lament it.'[35]

The queen had not visited her ailing son during his stay at Deal. She may have felt her first duty lay with the king, who had so insistently declared his need for her presence at his side in such trying times. Perhaps she closed her eyes to the severity of Alfred's condition, hoping, as she had done with her son Ernest years before, that a refusal to countenance the worst outcome for a sick child would allow her to preserve the mask of regal self-possession, that she always adopted in times of trial. Whatever the reasons for her absence, she was certainly not indifferent to Alfred's death. She 'cried vastly' when he died, and sought, as Lady Charlotte had done, to assuage her misery with the conviction that at least his pain was now over. 'My fears and hopes are finished once and for all,' she told her brother Charles sadly; 'God being satisfied that this little angel should suffer no more in future days, he fell asleep with all possible tranquillity.' She would not allow herself to wish that his life had been longer, especially if that meant he would have endured more pain; therefore 'I must give thanks to Providence for having acted as it did.' Charles had himself lost two wives and many young children to early deaths. Charlotte acknowledged that 'as a family of fourteen children' they had been fortunate to have 'been struck' only once; 'thus I must submit without murmur.'[36]

At court, Miss Goldsworthy admired the queen's fortitude. She tried to imitate it, although she confessed to Mary Hamilton she did not find it easy. 'The certainty of the dear angel's happiness is certainly the greatest comfort, but to you I will own that this sad scene has taken deep root in my heart, and time alone will soften it.' All Miss Goldsworthy could do as she watched Alfred's parents grieve was to hope 'this is the only trial that they will experience' of such a deeply distressing kind.[37] Everyone around them was struck by the extent of George and Charlotte's grief; but the king, although moved and saddened, confessed that if it had been his son Octavius who had died, then he would have died too.

Octavius, as his name suggested, was George and Charlotte's eighth son. Born in 1779, he was a bright, lively and happy boy, with the family's distinctive fair hair and blue eyes. Mrs Papendiek thought him exceptionally attractive, 'a lovely child of sweet disposition, [who] showed every promise of future goodness'. The king was devoted to him, and spent a great deal of time in his company, playing with him on the floor, as he had done with his other children, and even seeking ways to involve him in more grown-up pleasures. On Easter Mondays, when the king always went stag hunting, 'this sweet little prince used to appear in the appropriate uniform with all the paraphernalia of long whip, etc., the king calling out, "Turn out the little huntsman also!"'[38] George had Octavius painted by Benjamin West holding a sword almost as long as the prince was tall; but even the smallest hint of future military ardour is utterly subverted by the boy's huge hat, short trousers and appealingly winning smile.

In April 1783, when he was four years old – and eights months after the death of little Alfred – Octavius was inoculated against smallpox alongside his young sisters. Louisa Cheveley, who worked with Mary Hamilton in the royal nursery, reported on the 23rd that all had gone as planned. 'You certainly would have heard if there has been any alteration in the health of the dear little royals – but they continue very well,' she assured her friend.[39] Three days later, she was still closely monitoring their progress, waiting for the spots to develop that denoted the successful preventative introduction of a mild form of the virus into the children's systems. 'Your dear little favourite Princess Sophia is in the finest way possible; Prince Octavius is in not so forward a state – I hope tomorrow it will make its appearance.'[40] A week later, Mary Hamilton was horrified to receive a shockingly unexpected note from one of the nursery assistants. 'I am sorry and much distressed to inform you that dear Prince Octavius, at twelve o'clock last night was released from this abode of sin and sorrow.'[41] A letter from Lady Charlotte Finch followed, confirming the terrible news: 'Prince Octavius died last night, and indeed, from the time he was taken ill, there was never any hope of his recovery.'[42]

Mrs Papendiek heard that 'this dear child and most interesting boy was supposed to have caught cold just when the eruption should have come out, the king having taken him into the gardens late in the evening towards sunset'. He died, she believed, 'apparently from suffocation, which nothing could relieve'.[43] However, Mrs Cheveley, who nursed Octavius, was adamant that his death was not a result of the inoculation. 'It is but right to tell you,' she wrote to Mary Hamilton, 'that the smallpox had nothing to do in the death of Prince Octavius.' He had, she insisted, recovered fully from its effects, and was perfectly well before being suddenly stricken. It was this which made his death so shockingly impossible to comprehend. 'Good God, when one thinks this misfortune was so entirely begun and ended in forty-eight hours – and that the dear child was as well and in as good spirits last Thursday as ever he was in his life – it appears to me a dream. I can scarcely believe the scenes I have been through.' It was, she concluded, 'such a blow as no language could describe, and could I do it, I would not, to you'.[44]

The other attendants who had loved and cared for Octavius were equally devastated. When his coffin was taken to Westminster Abbey to be buried, 'at the door stood His Royal Highness's wet nurse, who entreated to be allowed to enter, which was granted'. The king, in his grief, was much touched by hers, and made sure a letter was written to her saying how much he had felt 'her dutiful attentions'. Everyone was paralysed by the horror of suffering a second tragic loss in a year. Miss Planta told Mary Hamilton that 'my heart bleeds for the king and queen', and noted sadly that 'the princesses are all very much affected, indeed, the grief is universal'.[45] The Prince of Wales was as moved as his sisters by the tragedy, the warmth of his feelings for his young siblings being one of his more attractive traits. At the end of May, he wrote to Frederick in Germany, 'consoling with you for the loss of our poor, dear little brother'. Frederick had been gone so long that he could not have appreciated Ocatvius's virtues, but 'had you known what a sweet child he was, you would have felt his loss as severely as I did, and indeed, for that reason, I am glad you did not know him'.[46]

In the days after Octavius's death, Mrs Cheveley observed that both George and Charlotte had been 'afflicted beyond expression'. They had tried to temper their misery by 'a resignation and submission to the divine will that makes their grief as amiable as it is edifying'.[47] Christian fortitude, it seemed, had helped both king and queen past the initial pain, but whilst both may have done all they could to submit to what could not be changed, neither was as resigned as they appeared.

Charlotte's steely self-control hid a grief that was still woundingly raw years after the deaths of Alfred and Octavius. In 1785, she wrote a letter of condolence to Lady Pembroke, who had herself recently lost a child: 'I know that I need not add that I have and do now feel very strongly for your loss,' confided the queen, 'twice have I felt what you feel, the last time without the least preparation for the stroke, for in less than eight and forty hours, was my son Octavius, in perfect health, taken sick and struck with death immediately. Religion was my only support at this time, and I hope my dear Lady Pembroke found it likewise.' There was no comfort to be had in the face of such otherwise inexplicable loss except that provided by God. 'He is our strength, our only comforter, our friend and our father,' she insisted. Faith alone had given her the strength to endure. 'To him therefore it is owing that we are enabled to go through the difficulties of life with cheerfulness and bear our misfortunes with resignation.'[48]

The king tried his utmost to emulate his wife's heroic resignation, but with less success. 'There will be no Heaven for me if Octavius is not there,' he had declared bitterly at the time of the tragedy, and time proved no healer.[49] Some months later in that fateful year of 1783, and during the final stages of the American War of Independence, he told Lord Dartmouth that every day that passed 'only increases the chasm I do feel for that beloved object'.[50] Octavius's fate was, he told his son William, 'a subject that very much fills my mind, and I own it has strongly convinced me how very transitory all enjoyments are in this world, but it the stronger convinces me that fulfilling every duty is the only real comfort, and that our rewards must be looked for in another, not this world'.[51]

Some of the king's unquenchable misery was directed into constructing a suitable memorial for his lost sons. Only a week after Octavius's death, George and Charlotte, together with their older daughters, had dutifully attended the Royal Academy to witness the unveiling of Thomas Gainsborough's ambitious group portrait of the entire family, on which he had been at work for nearly two years. There among the fifteen figures depicting the king, queen and all their children (with the exception of the absent Frederick), was a sparkling miniature of the charming, sweet-natured Octavius. Alfred was there too, painted by Gainsborough from memory, a smiling toddler in a simple sash with short wispy hair. At the sight of their dead brothers, the princesses cried without restraint, and both their parents were visibly moved. Perhaps inspired by this unintended tribute, the king commissioned Benjamin West to paint a more allegorical commemoration. In his *Apotheosis of Prince Octavius*, the young prince is seen being welcomed to heaven by Alfred in an image of fraternal warmth and happiness which clearly gave great comfort to the family. Nothing, however, made any real impact on the submerged agony of the king's grief. Five years later, when illness had unhinged his mind, in his delusions it was Octavius for whom he constantly called, imagining that a bolster which he held in his arms was, in reality, his much-missed 'little huntsman'.

His early death guaranteed Octavius an especially privileged place in the king's heart. Fixed for ever in an eternal, sunny and complaisant childhood, he had never grown up to disappoint or frustrate his father. The comparison with his surviving brothers was, in George's mind, only too apparent. Announcing the news of Octavius's death to Prince William, the king informed him bleakly that 'it has pleased God to put an end very unexpectedly to the most amiable as well as the most attached child a parent could have. May I find those I have as warmly attached as he was,' he concluded meaningfully, 'and I cannot expect more.'[52]

*

There was little doubt in the king's mind which of his sons failed most profoundly to reach the high standard of affection and trust he believed he had enjoyed with Octavius. As the Prince of Wales approached adulthood, the king looked in vain for evidence of the mature deliberation in thought and behaviour that he expected from his heir. Instead, the prince seemed determined to provoke him. His costly affair with the actress Mary Robinson was followed by a succession of liaisons bound to invoke his father's disapproval. His relationship with the divorced Grace Elliot may have produced a daughter; others were briefer, more fleeting moments, generally with worldly, experienced women not averse to an indulgent flirtation with the heir to the throne. It soon became clear that the prince's love affairs tended to follow a familiar pattern. Most were with women older than himself, a preference that was to guide his choice of partners until the very end of his life. They began with an outburst of passionate intensity on his part, accompanied by extravagant and theatrical declarations. The thrill of pursuit, and the opportunities for extreme and self-dramatising emotion that went with it, was the aspect of an affair that the prince seems most to have enjoyed. Once he had won over the object of his desire, he quickly grew bored, and sought to disentangle himself as rapidly and surgically as possible. He had no compunction in allowing others – his friends, members of his household, his brothers – to act as bearers of the inevitable bad news to the superannuated loved one. Those around him were also expected to shield him from any adverse consequences of his actions; it was they, not the prince, by now usually involved with someone new, who negotiated with angry husbands and ex-lovers, many of whom often hoped for some material compensation as a result of their intimate connection with royalty.

The prince's affair with the wife of Count Hardenberg, a Hanoverian diplomat, was typical of the relationships he pursued as a young man. Mme Hardenberg was some years his senior, a polished veteran of European courts who caught his eye at St James's, where he spotted her playing cards with his sisters. He thought her 'divinely pretty' and when she did not reject his attentions, he was smitten with a desire that, in its early stages at least, was typically intense. 'From that moment,' he wrote to his brother Frederick in July 1781, 'the fateful though delightful passion arose in my bosom for her, which has made me since the most miserable and wretched of men.' Although he 'dropped every other connection of whatever sort and devoted myself entirely to this angelic little woman', she would not consent to become his lover. 'O, but did you but know how much I adore her, how I love her, how I would sacrifice every earthly thing to her. By heavens, I shall go distracted; my brain will split.' Showing the kind of application that his father found so lacking in all his other activities, the prince diligently persevered until, finally, he achieved his goal. 'O my beloved brother, I enjoyed beforehand the pleasures of Elysium.' All went well for a while, until, inevitably, her husband discovered the affair. The prince panicked, wrote to the count denying everything, and begged the king to give him leave to go abroad. The letter containing the king's firm refusal arrived at almost the same time as a note from Mme Hardenberg, 'saying she hoped I had not forgot my vows', and demanding that he 'run off with her that night'.

At that moment, the prince admitted to Frederick: 'I, in a manner lost my senses entirely.' He expected no sympathy from the king. 'You know our father's severe disposition,' he reminded his brother; 'everything that was shocking was to be expected from him.' Instead he threw himself upon the queen. 'My misery was such that I went under the promise of the greatest secrecy and confessed the whole truth to her. I fainted. She cried excessively, and felt for me very much.' In the midst of so much *Sturm und Drang*, Charlotte took control, sending one of the prince's entourage to tell Mme Hardenberg that 'an unforeseen accident' meant her lover would not now be joining her to elope. 'The queen only begged me to allow her to tell the king, on condition he took no part in it,' the prince told Frederick. He did not know whether she had kept her promise; probably not, since George immediately sent for Count Hardenberg and his wife, dismissed them from the court and sent them back to Germany.[53]

It was there, a few months later, that Frederick met Mme Hardenberg at a masquerade. She followed him around all evening 'in so striking a manner that everyone remarked on it', took his arm when he was talking to someone else, and after dancing with him, 'whispered me that if there was nobody in the next room, she would go with me there. Now,' Frederick told his brother, 'I think that is speaking in pretty plain terms.' The prince, he thought, should count himself lucky to be rid of her.[54]

The Hardenberg episode did little to improve relations between the king and his heir. George was deeply embarrassed by his son's conduct, angered by his refusal to reform it and frustrated by his total indifference to the impression he created. 'It is almost certain now that some unpleasant mention of you is daily to be found in the papers,' he had written to the prince in May 1781. This was very painful for him, but he was, he declared, prepared to overlook all if his son would agree to follow a different course of life. 'I wish to live with you as a friend, but then, by your behaviour you must deserve it. If I did not state these things, I should not fulfil my duty either to my God or to my country.' It was the prince's job to set a good example in the high rank that had been allotted him, as the king himself had endeavoured to do. The title of 'heir apparent' did not excuse its bearer from attention to the moral duties; on the contrary, it 'ought to be a means of restoring decency in this kingdom' and thus required especially upright conduct. He hoped that 'when you have read this over' the prince would acknowledge the honesty of his intentions. He was, he assured him, 'an affectionate father, trying to save his son from perdition.'[55]

The prince was unconvinced. In his father's attitude he saw not paternal concern but anger, irritation and a desire to thwart him at every opportunity. 'The king is excessively cross and ill-tempered and uncommonly grumpy,' he told Frederick in September 1781, 'snubbing everybody in everything. We are not upon the very best terms.'[56] Any feelings of gratitude he had felt for his mother in helping him wriggle out of his Hardenberg difficulties had evaporated by the autumn, when he found her as hard to deal with as his father. 'I am sorry to have to tell you,' he wrote to Frederick in October, 'that the unkind behaviour of Their Majesties, but in particular the queen, is such that is hardly bearable.' They had recently had a difficult conversation which had quickly spiralled into complaint and recrimination. 'She accused me of various high crimes and misdemeanours, all of which I answered, and, in the vulgar English phrase, gave her as good as she bought.' He thought she had been put up to it by the king, 'who wanted to try whether I could be intimidated or not, but when she found I was not so easily to be intimidated, she was silent.' Everything about his father annoyed him, including the king's parsimony, which he applied to himself with as much rigour as he did to his sons. He 'is grown so stingy with regard to himself', the prince added in a furious postscript, 'that he will hardly allow himself three coats in a year'.[57]

From Germany, Frederick urged his brother to tread carefully. 'For God's sake, do everything you can to keep well with him, at least upon decent terms; consider, he is vexed enough in public affairs. It is therefore your business not to make that still worse. He may possibly be cross, but still, it is not your business to take that too high.' Conscious that he perhaps crossed a line with his volatile brother, Frederick concluded by trying to conciliate. 'I hate preaching full as much as you do, and constraint if possible more, but still, for both your sakes, I entreat you to keep as well together as possible.'[58]

The prince did not reply for some time. He suspected, with some justification, that Frederick was being coached by their father to try to influence his behaviour. Frederick remained his father's favourite surviving son; safely removed from his eldest brother's influence, the king believed he was doing well. He discounted stories that trickled out of Germany hinting at drunkenness and womanising, and concentrated on the good reports he had of him, which said he was studying hard and staying – mostly – out of trouble. The king and Frederick were in regular correspondence, as the elder brother knew very well. 'Pray write to me soon,' the prince upbraided Frederick, 'or I shall begin to think you have forgotten me, especially as I hear of you writing frequent and long letters to the king. Indeed, I shall grow quite jealous of His Majesty if it goes on in this manner much longer.' He did not, he added, appreciate hearing the voice of his father through the words of his brother, and warned him not to offer him advice again. 'Write one of your facetious, giddy letters, and no more of your scolding ones.'[59]

In defiance of all Frederick's well-meant suggestions, the prince made no attempt to temper his behaviour to allow for the king's political difficulties and the anxieties they generated. When he failed to attend a formal levee reception at St James's Palace in 1782, without asking leave to be absent, his father made his disappointment at the prince's indifference very clear: 'At a time when I am so harassed by many disagreeable events, any improper behaviour of the Prince of Wales is doubly severe to me. He must know his conduct to me in general is so different to the plan I chalked out ... that I shall soon be obliged, if he does not amend it, to take steps that will certainly be disagreeable.'[60]

Shortly afterwards, negotiations began to agree on the terms for an independent establishment for the prince on his coming of age the following year. These opened a new theatre of opportunity for unpleasantness and disagreement between father and son that rumbled on for several years. The king was appalled when Fox's administration offered to grant the prince an income of £100,000 a year, a vast sum by any standards, but colossal for a single man with no dependants. It was, George complained, 'a shameful squandering of public money, besides an encouragement of extravagance'.[61] The king did all he could to fight it, drawing attention to the huge debts the prince had already incurred, which grew steadily larger once he had been given Carlton House as an independent residence in 1783. After long and rancorous argument, the prince's annual income was finally fixed at £50,000; the renovations of his new home quickly absorbed all of that and more.

The king's mother, Augusta, had been the last royal inhabitant of Carlton House, and the prince soon erased all trace of her mild and forgettable tenure in a programme of extension and improvement that lasted for over thirty years. The house, which became home to so many extraordinary and luxurious objects, was a great work of art in itself. The prince, who possessed a genuine and appreciative eye for beauty, matured into a connoisseur of taste and discernment. He bought widely and extravagantly, sending agents to China to buy fashionable pieces in the oriental taste to furnish his drawing room, a trip which cost more than £6,000. The most skilled – and expensive – craftsmen and decorators were employed in gilding and marbling every surface. He acquired pictures and tapestries, bronzes and china, as well as the best French furniture. In the gardens, fountains bubbled; in the basement, the kitchens and pantries were of the most modern design.[62] Horace Walpole thought the refurbished house was 'the most perfect palace in Europe'.

None of this was likely to appeal to the king, especially as he knew how little of it had been paid for. Although he was himself a buyer of beautiful things, his tastes ran to books, clocks and pictures rather than imported exotica – and his purchases never exceeded his income. 'With thirteen children, I can but with the greatest care make ends meet, and am not in a situation to be paying their debts, if they contract any,' he wrote to his son William, whom he also suspected of thoughtless extravagance. Indebtedness, he insisted, was not an excusable shortcoming habitual to inhabitants of the fashionable world; it was a shameful vice that any honourable man would seek to avoid. 'To anyone that has either the sentiments of common honesty or delicacy ... the situation of not paying what is due is a very unpleasant sensation.'[63] It is hard not to conclude that George had his eldest son in mind as he wrote those admonitory lines.

By 1784, the gulf between the king and the Prince of Wales seemed unbridgeable. In the celebrations that followed Fox's hard-fought victory at the Westminster election of that year, the prince's true allegiance could not have been made clearer. His prominent endorsement of an opposition victory would have been galling enough to his father; the news that, at the party which followed, his son 'was so far overcome with wine as to fall flat on his face in the middle of a dance, and, upon being raised from the floor, to throw the load from his stomach into the midst of the circle', must surely have added an extra dimension of distaste and humiliation to the king's bitterness.[64]

There was, however, another side to the prince, although it was one his father seldom witnessed. His appeal was legendary, when he could be bothered to exert it, and, like Fox, he had a winning, disarming smile. William Beckford thought that he was 'brighter than sunshine' and 'cast a brilliant gleam wherever he moved'.[65] Unlike many habitués of his father's court, he made people laugh. He was an accomplished mimic who possessed, the Duke of Wellington recalled in later years, 'a most extraordinary talent for imitating the manner, gestures and voices of other people, so much that he could give the most exact idea of anyone, no matter how unlike they were to him'.[66] He was well read, with a sophisticated appreciation of the fine arts, music and literature. The lawyer Henry Brougham, who was proud of his own intellect, and no friend of princes, conceded he was indeed 'a very clever person'. Charles Burney, father of the novelist Fanny, was equally impressed. 'I was astonished to find him, amidst such constant dissipation, possessed of so much learning, with knowledge of books in general, discrimination of character, as well as original humour.'[67] Almost everyone who met him speculated what he might have been if his abilities had been properly directed. 'He was a man occupied in trifles, because he had no opportunity of displaying his talents in the conduct of great concerns,' reflected one observer.[68]

The prince himself was said to have excused his obsessive interest in the minutiae of dress and manners, his late nights and long mornings spent idly in bed, by declaring that he found the days were 'long enough for doing nothing'.[69] He certainly did little to encourage his father to entrust him with any real responsibility; he was a talker rather than a doer, a starter not a finisher, someone who habitually avoided anything difficult or onerous. He was essentially a selfish man, his rather lazy good nature faltering at the first challenge to his own interest. The perpetual air of disapproval and disappointment in which he was so deeply immersed gave him no great incentive to rouse up his dormant powers. He had spent much of his youth and early twenties without a true friend or companion who might have acted either as a spur to his ambition or as a reminder of what disinterested affection looked like. His brother Frederick was by far the best candidate for the latter role, and their enforced separation continued to affect the Prince of Wales deeply for years afterwards. 'Good God, what would I give either to have you here with me, or to be with you for some little time,' he wrote plaintively in 1781; 'I literally ... lost half my self in being separated from you.'[70]

Whether Frederick, always calmer and more sensible than his tempestuous sibling, would have proved a steadying influence on the prince is debatable; certainly, when they were reunited after six years apart, the prince's dissipation quickly trumped Frederick's discipline, the elder brother introducing the younger to all his practised indulgences. But it is hard not to see the king's deliberate policy of isolating his heir as, in the end, counterproductive. Marooned at court whilst all his brothers went out into the world, the prince cut a lonely figure, vulnerable to the very flattery and seduction from which his father had been determined to protect him. That his personality was not in the end powerful or confident enough to withstand either was the prince's tragedy; but it was also in part the responsibility of his father. Neither the king nor his son could have been satisfied with their relationship, as described by the prince to Frederick in the summer of 1784: 'I think his behaviour is so excessively unkind that there are moments when I can hardly ever put up with it. Sometimes not speaking to me for three weeks together, and hardly ever at court, speaking to people on one side of me and then missing me, and then if he does honour me with a word, 'tis merely, "'Tis very cold, or very hot" ... and then sometimes, when I go to his house, never taking any notice of me at all, as if I was not there.'[71] The king had decided that the best way he could deal with the disappointments, insults and humiliations heaped upon his head by his delinquent eldest son in his time of greatest trial was simply to edit him out of his life.

If the Prince of Wales was regarded by his father as easily the most disappointing of his sons, none of the others, with the exception of the favoured Frederick, was treated with much greater consideration. Distance and denial were the hallmarks of his relationships with them. Having established the younger boys in Germany, the king kept them perennially short of cash – his sixth son, Augustus, was given just a guinea a week pocket money – with the result that all of them ran into debt, incurring his deep displeasure. Edward, who had been sent from Germany to study in Geneva, was especially unhappy. Geneva was, he wrote, 'a villainous dull place', and his minder, Colonel Wagenheim, gave him so little to live on that he could not afford 'to enjoy those indulgences, which not only princes, but private gentlemen expect at a certain age'. His father had surrounded him with men 'upon the footing of low-lived spies and pettifogging attorneys', whose only function was to ensure he stayed out of trouble. He was, he believed, 'losing the very best and most valuable part of my life and existence'. The king did not answer his letters, and, convinced he could stand it no longer ('I would rather join the fusiliers at Glasgow, for there at least the ground is British and one can manage to exist'), he fled back home. There his misery met with no sympathy. The king sent him off in disgrace to join the military garrison at Gibraltar. From there he was posted to Canada, without being allowed to visit England first. He was still in Quebec in 1791, after eight years' continual absence, wondering whether 'a further state of probation' would be required of him, or whether he soon might be allowed home.[72]

Even William, 'the naval prince' lauded in popular ballad as 'England's young but future pride', who had behaved very creditably under fire, rarely lived up to his father's expectations. He tried hard to tell his parents what he thought they wanted to hear, assuring them not long after he first went to sea that 'my moral conduct is not infected by the great deal of vice that I have seen, nor my manners made more impolite by the roughness particular to most seamen'.[73] When he arrived home after his first tour of duty, his father did not agree with his son's optimistic assessment of himself, finding him instead loud, boorish and crude. 'You know very well,' he told him, 'that after the first week, your behaviour on returning from America did not meet with my approbation.' He had forgotten completely what was required of him in terms of conduct. 'The station of a prince requires a behaviour very unlike that of a forecastle. You have', he concluded, in words by then exhaustingly familiar to his eldest brother, 'in Frederick an excellent example; follow it and you cannot fail of winning my good opinion and that of the public.'[74] Frederick himself admitted to the Prince of Wales that William was indeed sometimes 'so excessively rough and rude that there is no bearing it'. The king was not pleased to hear that on board ship, William's lack of decorum had extended to arguing with his fellow officers and that he had often manifested 'an unhappy disposition to resist control'. The prince was not alone in his tendency to talk back when given an order; the quarterdeck of an eighteenth-century warship could sometimes be a surprisingly disputatious place; but George felt that his son was diminished by such actions, and was determined to put a stop to them. When the American War was over, the king took action. William was temporarily removed from the navy and sent to Hanover to learn German, improve his manners and 'enable him to pursue his profession as an officer, not a mere sailor'.[75]

William was horrified: he loved service life, and hated Hanover, which he thought 'a dull place and much given to scandal'. He disliked the nobility, whom he found 'haughty and proud', and suspected they were equally unimpressed with him, especially 'my free tongue with English oaths'. For all his bravado, he seems to have been lonely there. He made no friends among 'the phlegmatic Germans' and was in trouble at home for flirting with one of his teenage Mecklenburg cousins. He asked the Prince of Wales to pity him, begging him to consider 'how disagreeably situated I am in this damned country ... Pretty qualifications for any young man like me, smoking, playing twopenny whist and wearing great thick boots. Oh! I wish I was returned. England, England forever, and the pretty girls of Westminster.'[76] Taken away from the profession he loved, and exiled to a country he disliked, William was not even allowed the consolation of a grand title. His attempts to persuade his father to make him a duke, like his brothers, fell on deaf ears. It was only when William threatened to stand for election to the House of Commons in order to bring his case before the public that the king relented, and granted him the dukedom of Clarence. William's long campaign for recognition – and the parliamentary grant that went with it – cannot have made him better disposed towards his father, or have improved his miserable mood. His attempts to gain a sympathetic hearing from his mother hardly fared better. 'I am sorry to find by another letter of yours that you continue talking of your disposition to melancholy,' she wrote. 'It is a thing so little known in your family that I cannot think it serious.' Charlotte blamed his unhappiness on his obstinate and wilful nature: 'You appear rather inclined to dislike everything that has been thought of as necessary towards your improvement. If such is your disposition, you deserve pity indeed.' If he continued to oppose 'every means the king has taken for your improvement, you will always be wretched yourself, and embitter the lives of those who have the misfortune to surround you.'[77]

Eight months later, in August 1785, when William was clearly no happier, the queen wrote in even stronger terms: 'Your reasons for liking and disliking are in general so trifling and frivolous that the best judgement one could form upon them would be youthful volubility.' Now that he was nearly twenty, that was no excuse and 'severer judgements must arise, which can be no less than want of a good heart, want of understanding, ambition, vanity, and wilfulness, and an uncommon share of caprice'. Unless he could master his failings, he would become 'a trifling character, which is the most despicable of all things in the world, and the higher the rank, the more it is observed'. His future was in his own hands. 'Cease, I beseech you, to be a great little man which is in reality, nothing at all.'[78]

William was pleased when he was at last allowed back into the navy that autumn, albeit not with the Mediterranean posting he had so coveted. Unlike the king and queen, he was a diligent correspondent, insisting that he 'wrote everything that is in my heart' to his parents, but by the following February he had still not had anything in reply. 'It appears to me strange that though I have written to them letters that require answers, I have not yet heard from either of them.' He was particularly troubled by the king's silence. Although not naturally a reflective man, his father's behaviour was so inexplicable that William devoted a great deal of effort to try to understand it, sharing his bemusement in his letters to his eldest brother. Why did the king seek to control every aspect of his sons' lives and yet show so little apparent interest in their wellbeing? 'What can be the use of his keeping us so close? Does he imagine he will make his sons his friends by this mode of conduct? If he does, he is sadly mistaken.' William did not deny his father thought he was acting in his sons' interests, and it could even be the case that beneath his apparent coolness, the king might actually love him; but it was, he concluded, impossible to tell. 'I cannot but regard him, and would do everything to please him, but he is so difficult to satisfy.'[79]

A year later, in 1786, having again received no answers to his many letters, William's attitude hardened. He was about to go home on leave, but viewed the prospect gloomily, 'with a certainty that my Christmas box will be a family lecture for immorality, vice, dissipation and expense'. He no longer felt in the least warmly disposed towards his critical and undemonstrative father. 'The conduct of late years that I have met with from a certain quarter has been so different from what I observe in other families that those tender sensations have been quite worn out.' His conclusion was a combination of puzzlement and resignation: 'I have never been able to find out the motives that have actuated him.'[80]

It was surely disappointment that explained much of the king's behaviour. During the greatest political crisis of his reign, he was convinced that, with the exception of Frederick, none of his sons had risen to the challenge of offering him genuine and heartfelt support. Not one had reformed his usual behaviour in an attempt to turn himself into the helpmeet he longed for: dutiful, obedient, attentive to his rules and a natural inheritor of his vision of kingship. He had not, of course, always made it particularly easy for them to live up to his ideal. Perpetually associated with admonition rather than encouragement, seemingly indifferent to their desires and feelings, capricious in his orders and unforgiving in his resentments, he was not an easy man to love. He was certainly much provoked by his sons, especially the Prince of Wales; but he was not generous in his dealings with any of the brothers, either financially or emotionally. In return, they closed their eyes to the rigours of his public role, ignoring the pressures under which he laboured, and the toll it took on his health and his temper.

The tragedies that stalked his private world made the difficulties of his public office even harder to bear. The death of Octavius inflicted a wound from which the king never recovered, whilst the memory of the little boy's innocent virtues threw the failings of his surviving sons into ever-darkening relief. By July 1783, two months after Prince

Octavius died, entangled in the morass of party politics and faced with negotiating the humiliating peace with America, the king's spirits sank to a new low. 'Every morning,' he declared, 'he wished himself eighty, or ninety or dead.'[81] It was only the refuge provided by his home, his wife and his daughters that enabled him to carry on at all.

CHAPTER 10

Great Expectations

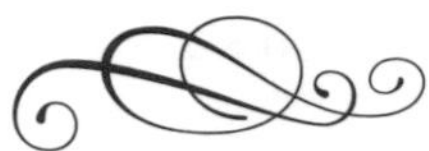

IN LATE 1783, THE ATMOSPHERE of lowering depression that had surrounded George and Charlotte for so many years began to lift a little. For good or ill, the military mission in America was over, and whilst the outcome was hardly to the king's liking, at least he was no longer required to endure regular news of humiliating and morale-sapping defeats. In the year that followed, he had recovered his energy sufficiently to pull off an astonishing act of political bravado, ridding himself of a minister he loathed, and replacing him with what was to prove one of the most stable administrations of his reign. Whilst the tempo of his life as a public man could hardly be called happy, it had at least become calm; and some of the stress that had been the dominating experience of the previous ten years began, slowly but surely, to ebb away.

The queen too had crossed a Rubicon, but of a far more personal kind. Her daughter Amelia, born in August 1783, was the queen's fifteenth child – and much to her relief, also her last. When she had found herself pregnant again in 1780, with the ill-fated Alfred, even Charlotte's formidable sense of resignation failed her and she had written bitterly to her brother that she had hoped to have no more children. Now, as must have soon become apparent to her, her formidable fertility had run its course. Charlotte was thirty-nine, and had been pregnant for two decades. With the arrival of this daughter, twenty-one years younger than her eldest brother, her long campaign of maternity was finally over.

For both the king and queen, there was a sense of a line being drawn under a demoralising period of protracted unhappiness; in the years that followed, they seem to have made an effort to lighten their spirits and find more entertainment in their lives. The couple allowed themselves greater opportunity to engage in the kind of sedate and dignified pleasures they both enjoyed, taking drives out to explore the countryside and, like other aristocratic eighteenth-century tourists, visiting grand houses, scrutinising the art, furniture and other collections of the owners. Perhaps more surprisingly, they even made some friends. Since the earliest days of their marriage they had been a profoundly self-contained pair; now, for the first time, they allowed people from outside the immediate family into the closed circle of their lives.

The Harcourt family had been courtiers for over fifty years. Simon, 1st Earl Harcourt, had fought with George II at Dettingen in 1743; the old king had later appointed him as governor to his grandson, in which post the earl's remote, elusive presence had quickly driven Augusta, the prince's mother, into agonies of angry frustration. His son George Simon (who inherited the earldom) was a far more thoughtful character than his remote, elusive father. Surprisingly for a man of his background, when young he had been a supporter of the radical John Wilkes. He lost his Wilkite sympathies as he grew older, but his devotion to the ideas of another radical energiser never wavered. Like so many of his generation, the earl was a passionate devotee of the works of Jean-Jacques Rousseau. The entrance to the gardens of his country house at Nuneham Courtenay in Oxfordshire was adorned with quotations from the works of the great philosopher; his bust occupied a place of honour among the lawns and flowers. The ideas Harcourt had imbibed from his reading of his hero changed for ever his attitude to his own wealth and the obligations that arose from it. The poor villagers who lived and worked on the Harcourt estates were, as the earl reflected, the chief beneficiaries. 'They have reason to bless Jean-Jacques,' he explained, 'for to him alone, not to me, have they any obligation, as, but for his writings, I might have left them in the misery and sickness they have for so many years been a prey to.' He established a model of philanthropic good practice at Nuneham, awarding prizes for industry and virtue, announcing the names of the winners in church, and emblazoning their cottages with an 'M' for merit. None of this, however, entirely assuaged the guilt he felt at the difference between their lives and his own: 'Whenever I return from their cottages, I feel ashamed and hurt at silver dishes and gilt ceilings.'[1]

Sentiments like these kept the thoughtful and reflective Harcourt away from the arena of conventional politics, towards which his background would otherwise have directed him. He was also subject to bouts of melancholy and depression, which led him to conclude, probably correctly, that he was temperamentally unsuited for the rough and tumble of Westminster life. Instead, he settled at Nuneham, married his cousin Elizabeth Vernon, and set out to live as philosophically and do as much good as his extensive means and rather tentative personality allowed. Although never as ferociously intellectual as the Duchess of Portland, the home Harcourt created for his family had something about it of the flavour of Bulstrode.

The dignified, uncontentious way of life adopted by the Harcourts was extremely attractive to George and Charlotte, who yearned to follow a similar plan for themselves. The Harcourts' determination to take no part in politics only added to their appeal. Lady Harcourt was intelligent and cultivated, just the kind of woman whose company Charlotte liked, whilst her husband's oft-declared lack of ambition helped the king feel at ease with him. Soon they were widely regarded as royal favourites. Inevitably, not everyone was quite as impressed with the Harcourts as the king and queen. Fanny Burney, who met the earl at court, wondered if he was quite as unworldly as he liked to appear, musing that no one who referred quite so often to the absence of any benefit he had received as a result of royal favour could be completely indifferent to it. The diarist Lord Glenbervie thought the earl's wife was similarly conscious of her privileged position, describing her as 'the lofty Lady Harcourt', noting that 'she sits and walks as if she had her coronet on her head, and were afraid of its falling off'.[2] If the Harcourts occasionally preened themselves on their royal relationship and the virtues that had promoted it, this had no effect on George and Charlotte. They felt free from either constraint or obligation in their company, and had no qualms in thinking of them as their friends.

The relationship became strong enough to include almost all the royal family. George and Charlotte's children all kept up a lively correspondence of their own with the Harcourts. The boys sent letters from Germany to pass on news about their progress, and the princesses, with less to occupy their time, wrote letters even more prolifically. Elizabeth, the third sister, surprised even Lady Harcourt, herself no slouch with a pen, by the sheer volume of what she wrote. 'Once, when I was ill and confined to my house for six weeks,' Lady Harcourt recalled, 'I received from her at that time 143 letters; for she often wrote twice and sometimes thrice in a day if the opportunity of sending a letter occurred.'[3]

For Elizabeth and her contemporaries, letter-writing came almost as easily as conversation. For those who could afford the time, paper and postage, keeping up one's correspondence was a crucial part of the daily round. This was especially true for women, who frequently took on the role of keeping their family's social network of friends and relations fully informed about domestic events. There was no state-sponsored postal service, but, nevertheless, letters circulated briskly from place to place with surprising speed and efficiency. In London, they were dropped off at named collection points, and carried by foot to the appropriate addresses, sometimes arriving only hours after they were sent. Even cross-country mail was delivered regularly, with only the very remotest destinations waiting for week after uncertain week for letters to turn up. The likelihood that their correspondence would arrive safely encouraged letter-writers to ever greater levels of epistolary output. It also changed the content of what they wrote. The ability to write a graceful, formal letter was considered the mark of an educated person, and collections of sample templates could be purchased for those uncertain of their compositional skills. But most letter-writing was far less practised and artificial than these coolly elegant pieces. Everyday letters were often written almost as a form of extended conversation, a link in a great chain of correspondence that went on for years. Others were dashed off in haste, in response to an event, a meeting, the inspiration of a casual thought. Eighteenth-century correspondents wrote with a freshness and immediacy that still leaps off the page, consigning their hopes, fears and joys to paper with a candour that buttonholes the reader after so many years. In a world with fewer diversions, the arrival of a letter was an event to be shared and celebrated or enjoyed as a private pleasure. In most households, there simply could not be too many of them.

Even by these formidable standards, Princess Elizabeth was an exceptionally prolific letter-writer, but, as she explained to Lord Harcourt, the volume of her correspondence demonstrated the strength of her feelings for him and his family. Nothing gave her so much pleasure as to see his handwriting on a note. 'You may believe with what joy I seized my letter,' she wrote to him in 1795, delighted 'that you had not forgot one who is most thoroughly attached to you. This friendship, or attachment, call it what you will, began at ten years old and has increased with my years.'[4]

Even the king, who rarely wrote an entirely personal letter to anyone outside his family, was an occasional contributor to the stream of correspondence that flowed between Windsor, Kew and Oxfordshire. The depth of his trust in the relationship was illustrated by his willingness to venture a most unlikely epistolary style. Twenty years before, Henry Fox had observed that 'the king is not much given to joke', and humour had not come much more easily to him in the intervening time. Nevertheless, confident of a sympathetic hearing from the Harcourts, George was prepared to try his hand at some mild and ponderous satire. Writing to Lord Harcourt in the guise of 'Timothy Trenchard', he posed as an antiquarian collector, offering the earl, who had a taste for ancient objects, 'invaluable relics of antiquity left to me by such an acknowledged virtuoso as Mr Sebastian Periwinkle … to whom they had been bequeathed by Mr Peregrine Pilkington'. He hoped the pieces might 'find a retreat in the magnificent museum I understand Your Lordship is about to erect'. A second letter followed, from 'Your Lordship's most obsequious, humble and devoted servant, Marmaduke Spooner'.[5] The date, 1 April 1796, is a clue that perhaps George thought everyone was entitled to a little amusement on April Fools' Day, even a king.

For the princesses, the Harcourts, who had no children of their own, came almost to occupy the role of surrogate parents, Lady Harcourt in particular often casting herself as a doughty defender of their interests. Only Lady Charlotte Finch enjoyed a similar level of unqualified and absolute affection in their minds. But the beating heart of the relationship was unquestionably the bond between Lady Harcourt and the queen. They would be intimates for nearly forty years, with only Charlotte's death putting an end to an attachment that other blows and misfortunes did nothing to erode. When they could not meet in person, they kept up a correspondence in which all the joys and miseries of their lives were reflected, rejoicing and consoling with one another, sharing news of pleasure and happiness alongside darker times of sickness, sadness and loss.

With no one else, except her much-loved brother Charles in Mecklenburg, was Charlotte as frank and unguarded as she was with

Lady Harcourt. In her, she found an intellect she respected, an aristocratic status which approached but did not threaten her own, and a disinterested, sustained affection which encouraged her to cast off the identity of queen and adopt the unfamiliar one of friend. 'I should like to tell you something,' Lady Harcourt once wrote to her, 'but pray, never let the *queen* know it.' 'Oh no,' replied Charlotte, '*she* can have no business with what passes between us in our private conversation.'[6]

None of her other letters captures so completely the flavour of the queen's life at this time, her enthusiastic devotion to self-improvement, her belittlement of her own 'poor abilities' and the easy intimacy of her shared interests with her husband. In a note of 1786, she thanked Lord Harcourt for a drawing he had sent her. She planned to copy it 'in my own humble way', although she had no hopes that it would turn out as well as his. 'The king says it is the shabbiest way of drawing in the world,' but she was not discouraged.[7] Her correspondence also illuminates the 'sportive wit' that was such a distinctive element of Charlotte's character when she was in good spirits, the 'innocent archness' that is so glaringly absent from the tone in which she wrote to her sons. In one letter, she describes at some length a visit she and the king made to Portland Island in Dorset, where the inhabitants had a rather free-and-easy attitude to matrimony. 'They never marry till the intended wife is a mother, and there is hardly any instance of their forsaking them; but if the man forsakes her, it is no disgrace for another to marry the lady in question. I am told in some parts of Oxfordshire it is the same; will you allow that my dear Lady Harcourt? I think I hear Lord H say, "Oh, that is too bad."'[8] One scribbled note reflects Charlotte at her most playful and engaging: 'Adieu, greatest haste for dinner is on the table. I am off to eat chicken to appear more beautiful when I see you next; but in case it does not, believe me, handsome as chicken can make me, or ugly as I am, yours.'[9]

It was Charlotte who managed and oversaw the relationship between the two families. She was a tireless issuer of invitations, regularly summoning the Harcourts into the royal presence in a whimsical tone. '*Odds bodikins*, Lord Harcourt, the king orders me to say he is of the opinion your presence in Windsor would be very agreeable to him and to us all.'[10] She also arranged the visits which the royals made to the Harcourts. As etiquette required, they invited themselves. 'We propose storming your castle at Nuneham on the 18th of this month,' wrote Charlotte in 1784. 'Don't be alarmed,' she insisted, 'for we are all good friends and well-wishers to the owners of the castle.'[11]

The young princes and princesses adored Nuneham, and were delighted by the prospect of time spent agreeably away from home. When, in 1785, the king agreed to Lord Harcourt's suggestion that they stay the night there, Princess Augusta was 'so completely happy when I found we did not go back till the next day that my spirits rose mountains high in half a second'.[12] She later wrote a long letter to Lady Harcourt, in an almost novelistic style, that captured some of the excitement she and her siblings felt at being allowed a rare change of scene. '"Dear Augustus," said Ernest, "think how amazing good it is of Lord Harcourt; he has promised that I shall sleep alone. I have seen my room, it has a yellow damask bed ... I suppose it is a great favour to let me have it. I fancy strangers in general are not allowed to sleep in it." "Say what you please," said Augustus, "Lord Harcourt has given me a much better room. I have a view out of the window; and what signifies a damask bed when one has not a fine view?" ... Adolphus said, "I suppose none of you has seen my room? I have got a tent bed in it. I should have you dare speak against a tent bed. It puts me in mind already that when I am an officer, and then I am encamped against the enemy, I shall have one just like it" ... And so,' concluded Augusta, 'we went on all day long; and I am sure we shall never hear the end of it, it was the most perfect thing ever known.'[13]

Their parents enjoyed themselves just as much. Thanking Lady Harcourt for 'the numberless civilities we received during our stay at Nuneham', Charlotte wrote that 'were I to say all I think upon that subject, my sincerity might perhaps be suspected, therefore I will in only a few words tell you *that you did contrive to make us all feel happy*, which', she admitted, 'is a thing but seldom attained'.[14] Her words might stand as a judgement, not just on a single visit, but on their attachment to the Harcourts as a whole.

This new confidence in venturing upon a friendship outside the family may have also reflected the growing sense of satisfaction the king and queen felt in their more settled domestic arrangements. The building programme which George had begun at Windsor in the late 1770s was now approaching the completion of its first phase. The Queen's Lodge was finished, and in 1781 her daughters and their household moved into the Lower Lodge, designed to accommodate all the younger sisters until they were considered mature enough to join their mother. Mrs Cheveley, who nursed the dying Octavius with such devotion, was cheerfully enthusiastic about their new quarters: 'Our house (you may say, how we apples swim) is charming – there is not a bad room in it.' She particularly appreciated its minimalist modernity: 'This house does not in the least resemble your old mansions, that have closets innumerable, and furniture that you cannot move for – there is perfect freedom in this respect, and nothing can obstruct your purpose but a few chairs and a very few tables.'[15]

Once fully established at Windsor, the king and queen asked the occasional, specially favoured guest to share what Charlotte called 'their sweet retreat'. The Harcourts were regular invitees, and in 1785 they seized the opportunity to add another sympathetic presence to their small list of friends. Mrs Mary Delany – whom they had met at Bulstrode, where she had lived for many years at the invitation of her friend the Duchess of Portland – had often been asked to join royal entertainments, concerts and suppers, usually in the company of the duchess. Both George and Charlotte felt great affection for the dignified and scholarly Mrs Delany, and when the duchess died suddenly in 1785, they decided to absorb her into their own household.

Charlotte gave her a small house in Windsor, a short walk away from the Queen's and Lower Lodges, and a pension of £300 per year. Seeking to deflect any suggestion of charity, she wrote with gentle persuasion, urging the proud, elderly lady to accept it: 'You may not possibly be aware that I am among the heirs of the duchess. She has left her well-beloved Delany to my charge and friendship; and I hope you will grant me the privilege of fulfilling this, the last part of her will, and settle in the house I have ordered and where I shall often be able to see you.'[16] George and Charlotte furnished her new home down to the very smallest items, instructing her 'to bring with her nothing but herself and her clothes, as they insisted on fixing up her habitation with everything themselves … even to sweetmeats, pickles, etc.'[17] On the day Mrs Delany took possession, the queen visited her to establish the terms under which she hoped their relationship would be conducted. 'She repeated in the strongest terms her wish, and the king's, that I should be as easy as they could possible make me, that they waived all ceremony, and desired to come to me like friends!'

They were as good as their word. In the space of a fortnight, reported Mrs Delany incredulously, 'their Majesties have now drunk tea with me five times!' Just as they had insisted they would be, their visits were 'paid in the most private manner, like those of the most consoling and interested friends'.[18] For the rest of her life, members of the royal family were rarely absent from her house, arriving without announcement or formality and eagerly entering into all her domestic pleasures. In return for allowing her royal patrons limitless access to her home, Mrs Delany was frequently invited to join them in theirs. More than any other friend – even more than the Harcourts – she was allowed into the intimate heartland of the family at its most relaxed and informal. 'I have been several evenings at the Queen's Lodge,' she wrote in 1785, 'with no other company but their own most lovely family. They sit around a large table, on which are books, work, pencils and paper. The queen has the goodness to make me sit down with her, and delights me with her conversation, which is informing elegant and pleasing beyond description; whilst the younger part of the family are drawing and working, etc., etc., the beautiful babe Princess Amelia bearing her part in the entertainment, sometimes in one of her sister's laps, sometimes playing with the king on the carpet.'[19]

These were scenes whose calm serenity owed something perhaps to the absence of George and Charlotte's eldest son, who rarely, if ever, appeared in them. As soon as he had an establishment of his own in the early 1780s, he avoided Windsor as much as he could. Years later, his younger brother Ernest echoed his feelings, declaring bleakly that 'nothing is so terrible in my eyes as a family party'.[20] But if the contentment chronicled so lovingly by Mrs Delany had been achieved only by the exclusion of those family members most likely, at least in the jaundiced opinion of their father, to disrupt it, that did not make it any the less delightful to those who witnessed it first hand. Mrs Delany had nothing but praise for the life she saw played out so engagingly at Windsor. Her genuine and unremitting admiration for the king and queen's attempts to create a private world based on rational pleasure was, however, to have an impact far beyond her own circle. It was to inform the writings of the woman whose portrait of that world, and of those who inhabited it, remains one of the most lively and influential pictures of George and Charlotte's court.

*

'I was led to think of Miss Burney first by her books,' the queen told Mrs Delany, 'then by seeing her, then by hearing how much she was loved by her friends; but chiefly by her friendship for you.'[21] Fanny Burney had met Mrs Delany in the wake of her career as a successful author. She had published her novel *Evelina* anonymously in 1778. Its tale of an orphan later revealed to be an heiress was told with wit and brio, and contained some lively satires of fashionable life. Dr Johnson thought it a better work than those of both Henry Fielding and Samuel Richardson, and his approval helped make it a bestseller. Once her identity was revealed, Fanny entered eagerly into bluestocking literary circles, where she met distinguished women including Elizabeth Montagu and Hannah More. Her second book, *Cecilia*, appeared in 1782, to equal acclaim. Like *Evelina*, it preserved beneath its surface gloss and polish a strongly moral message, contrasting the value of genuine feeling with the hollow fripperies of fashionable life, which no doubt commended it to Charlotte, who read it as soon as it was published.

In 1785, Charlotte expressed to Mrs Delany a wish to meet the author in person. Fanny thought this news was 'rather fidgeting intelligence', but it was an event which she knew could not be infinitely postponed. She was a regular visitor to Mrs Delany's Windsor house, and she knew it was likely she would eventually meet the queen there. For all her celebrity, Fanny was intensely shy – indeed, it was a quality she rather admired in herself. As some of her more critical friends observed, her somewhat 'showy retreats' from attention often attracted greater attention than more conventional behaviour might have done, and her attempts to avoid meeting the royal family illustrated her ability, whether conscious or not, to back into the limelight. She did all she could to avoid the encounter, on one occasion simply running away when she heard 'the thunder at the door' that signalled the king and queen's arrival. Even the saintly Mrs Delany 'was a little vexed' at this, but Fanny's elusiveness seems only to have whetted George and Charlotte's appetite to meet her. Next time there was no escape, and Fanny was duly introduced to them.

The king was kind to her, although he found her whispered answers hard to hear. He was undaunted by her hesitant manner, and when he and Charlotte met Fanny again, this time on the terrace at Windsor, George boldly leant in towards her bonnet to catch her hesitant words. For all her nervous apprehension, when she came to set down her account of the meeting, the writer in Fanny triumphed over the ingénue, and she captured exactly the distinctive staccato rhythms of the king's speech as he interrogated her about the origins of *Evelina*:

'But what – what? How was it?'

'Sir,' cried I, not well understanding him.

'How came you? – how happened it? – What? What?'

'I only wrote it, sir, for my own amusement – only in some idle hours.'

'But your publishing? Your printing – how was that?'

'That was only sir, because ...' The 'what' was repeated with so earnest a look that forced to say something, I stammeringly answered – 'I thought, sir, it would look well in print!'[22]

The queen's questioning was more delicate than the king's. Judging correctly that the best way to win Fanny's heart was to praise the moral purpose of her books, Charlotte did much to calm and soothe the apprehensive novelist, who concluded after their encounter that she had found the queen 'a most charming woman ... her manners have an easy dignity, with a most engaging simplicity'.[23]

Fanny met the queen several times after this, and seems not to have suspected that Charlotte's interest in her went beyond appreciation for her literary skills. The queen was in fact quietly assessing Fanny's suitability for a place in her household. She soon made up her mind, deciding that Fanny was exactly the kind of intelligent, bookish woman that she liked to have about her, a worthy successor to the much-missed Mary Hamilton. In the summer of 1786, Fanny was invited to take up the place of Second Keeper of the Robes, which carried with it a salary of £200 a year as well an obligation to live full time at court.

Fanny was horrified. For all her much-vaunted shyness, she enjoyed an active style of life that was neither retiring nor unrewarding. The Burneys came from solid, middle-class provincial stock, studded with clergymen and naval officers; there was also a strong musical tradition in the family which gave it a more expansive, intellectual, almost bohemian tone. Fanny's father, Dr Charles Burney, began life as a teacher of music and in later life he became a well-regarded writer, critic and musicologist. As a young girl, Fanny had worked alongside her father as his assistant whilst he laboured to produce his life's work, *A History of Music*. The family lived in Soho, not far from Leicester House, where the king had lived as Prince of Wales. There they moved with relish and enjoyment amongst cultural circles in which talent was always considered more important than social status or respectability.

As Fanny later explained to the queen, 'my acquaintance hitherto, I frankly told her, was not only very numerous, but very mixed, taking in … most stations in life'.[24]

Actors, musicians and opera singers were regular visitors to the Burney home, as were artists, writers and literary lions. She knew Samuel Johnson and James Boswell (whose obvious brash ambition she did not admire), as well as Richard Sheridan and Edmund Burke. David Garrick was a great family friend. It was a cosmopolitan world, in which Italian opera performers and French *philosophes* were all welcome. When her sailor brother returned from a voyage to the southern oceans with Captain James Cook, he brought with him the Tahitian islander Omai, whose stately bearing and winning personality made him a much-sought-after guest at London parties; he too was a favoured regular at the Burney dinner table. Fanny was also a happy member of a lively circle of female friends and relations, making extended visits to their homes; she enjoyed domestic life, and was particularly devoted to her sisters and their children, taking deep and unaffected pleasure in their company.

From the moment the offer of a place at court was made, she understood that the stimulating life she currently enjoyed was utterly incompatible with the demands of her potential new role. 'The attendance was to be incessant – the confinement to court continual – I was scarce ever to be spared for a single visit from the palaces, not to receive anybody but with permission – what a life for me, who have friends so dear to me, and to whom friendship is the balm, the comfort, the very support of existence!'[25] Her horror at the prospect was so apparent that Leonard Smelt, the court official who brought the news of the offer, was shocked by her unenthusiastic response: 'I saw in his own face the utmost astonishment and disappointment at this reception of his embassy.' He was 'equally sorry and surprised; he expatiated warmly upon the sweetness of character of the royal family', and asked Fanny to consider the honour done in preferring her 'to the thousands of offered candidates of high rank and birth' who were eagerly supplicating for places. He then played his trump card when he suggested that 'in such a situation … you have the opportunity of serving your particular friends, especially your father – such as scarce any other could afford you'.[26] Charles Burney had long hoped for royal recognition, and perhaps even an official post. He was enthusiastically in favour of the scheme, believing, as did Mr Smelt, that it promised great advancement, not just for Fanny, but for the whole Burney family. Fanny knew then that there was nothing to do but surrender to the inevitable. Only to her sister could she express the depth of her alarm at what awaited her. 'I am *married*, my dear Susan – I look upon it in that light – I was averse to forming the union and I endeavoured to escape it, but my friends interfered – they prevailed – and the knot is tied.'[27]

She could call on only one resource that might make this unwanted new life tolerable. When the doors of the court closed behind her in July 1786, she turned her author's eye on the world she now so reluctantly inhabited, capturing meticulously its habits, its tone, its preoccupations large and small, as well as the characters with whom she was now destined to spend all her waking hours. The five years she spent at court were very far from being the happiest of her life, but they did produce a literary work that has as much to say about friendship and happiness, about suffering and loss and the conflicting calls of duty and feeling, as any of her bestselling novels.

The letters and journals Fanny wrote whilst she was a member of Charlotte's household catch, better than any other account, the rhythms and requirements of court life: the exhausting journeys between Windsor, Kew and St James's, which both Fanny and the queen undertook armed for the formality of the Drawing Room with their hair already dressed and their elaborate clothes wrapped in paper, to protect them from the dust of the roads; the order of the days, which began with chapel and ended with a concert ('usually of Handel'), and which, for the queen, were interrupted by laborious changes of outfit to suit the occasion. In theory, the position to which Fanny had been appointed was little more than that of a dresser – she was not aristocratic enough to be given a more high-status role – and although the queen clearly wanted her for her company rather than her skills, her job required her to assist daily at the long and complicated process of the royal toilette. It was Mrs Thielky, a German woman, who did most of the actual work. 'She hands the things to me, and I put them on,' wrote Fanny in the earliest days of her attendance. ''Tis fortunate for me I have not the handing of them! I should never know which to take first, embarrassed as I am, and should run a prodigious risk of giving the gown before the hoop, and the fan before the neck-kerchief.'[28]

Both Charlotte and Fanny professed to find the business of dress tedious and time-consuming in equal measure. The queen, Fanny observed, 'equips herself for the Drawing Room with all the attention in her power … and is sensibly conscious that her high station makes her attire a matter of public business'. But Charlotte paid little attention to its details, reading the newspapers whilst her hair was being powdered, and 'never refusing herself the satisfaction of expressing her contentment to put on a quiet undress'.[29] She was particularly devoted to the greatcoat, an item of clothing which was not a coat at all, but an informal dress that buttoned down the front, and about which Fanny was persuaded by Charlotte to compose a very bad poem, hymning its comfortable virtues. Fanny was more direct than the queen in her dislike of 'my toilette – that eternal business – never ending and never profiting! I think to leave the second syllable out for the future.'[30]

The boredom of court life is a constant theme that runs throughout Fanny Burney's diaries. The requirements of her post, as she describes them, do not sound particularly onerous in themselves – a few hours in the morning, most of the afternoon free, back in waiting again in the evening, with a requirement to be present at the end of the day to undress the queen before bed, a process which took about half an hour to complete – but the days were long. Fanny rose at six, and Charlotte rarely retired before eleven or twelve o'clock at night. Fanny told her sister she was exhausted, falling asleep 'the moment I have put out my candle and laid down my head'.[31] The mental enervation she suffered was, however, far more distressing to her. 'I have a place of nothing really to do but attend.' Her days contained very little to stimulate or surprise. One of the tasks she was charged with was to prepare – or 'cook' – the queen's snuff. 'It is a very fine scented and mild snuff, but it is required to be moistened from time to time, to revive its smell.' Fanny was pleased to be told by the Princess Royal that she had managed it well – 'Mama says the snuff is extremely well mixed; and she has sent another box to be filled' – but the comparison with the life she had given up must have been particularly poignant at such moments.[32]

Even more uncongenial to her was the requirement to spend her free hours with people not of her choosing. Dinner was served each day at five, and it was made clear to Fanny that she was expected, without exception, to take that meal with Mrs Schwellenberg, the queen's favourite. By the time Fanny met her, she was an old woman in poor health with a bad temper and a high expectation of having all her wishes obeyed. She quickly reduced Fanny to a state of cowed, mute victimhood, bullying her and belittling her in company. 'In her presence,' Fanny wrote, 'little i as am one annihilated.'[33]

It may have been exactly such shrinking self-abnegation that Mrs Schwellenberg found so exasperating, and which provoked her to bait and taunt Fanny so relentlessly, although stronger personalities than hers were rebuffed by the force of her selfishness. On one memorable occasion, in a carriage crowded with courtiers, Mrs Schwellenberg insisted on having the window open, although dust was blowing into Fanny's eyes. Not even the forceful intercession of Mr Smelt could persuade Fanny's persecutor to draw up the window, and she sat suffering all the way to London. However, as writers will, Fanny had her revenge, crafting so successful a portrait of Juliana Schwellenberg as a comic grotesque that it overshadowed every other description of her, and became the defining picture of who she was. Fanny portrays her as an eccentric, insensitive bore, her German accent emphasising her indifference to the finer feelings of those in her company, a woman of strange tastes and ridiculous foibles. Mrs Schwellenberg kept a number of frogs as pets in a box – perhaps a sign of her own loneliness and boredom – which, as Fanny reported, she presented guilelessly to the inspection of the king's equerries, blind to the suave irony with which they greeted her unlikely passion. '"I can make them croak when I will … When I only go to my snuffbox, knock, knock, they croak all what I want." "Very pretty indeed," exclaimed Colonel Goldsworthy.'[34]

For Fanny, it was the company of the equerries, of whom Colonel Goldsworthy was the most senior member, which made the empty hours of confinement in Mrs Schwellenberg's parlour just about tolerable. These male attendants, usually military men, joined her at the tea table every day, and their bantering liveliness brought some much-needed cheerfulness and colour into her life. Colonel Goldsworthy was the brother of Miss Martha Goldsworthy, the much-tried sub-governess of the princesses' household. His loyalty and attachment to the royal family was, Fanny thought, equalled only by his laconic accounts of the misery he liked to pretend he endured in serving them. He was a favourite of the king's, which ensured he was always included on the punishing daily rides George enjoyed in the countryside around Windsor. The king's indifference to the weather, combined with the austerity of his tastes, made them rather challenging experiences. As the colonel explained to Fanny, rainy days were particularly unrewarding. '"Here Goldsworthy," cries His Majesty; so up I comes to him, bowing profoundly, and my hair dripping down to my shoes … "Here, Goldsworthy, I say," he cries, "will you have a little barley water?" Barley water in such a plight as that! Barley water! I never heard of such a thing in my life! Barley water after a hard day's hunting!'[35]

For all the pleasure Fanny took in delineating their characters, both Mrs Schwellenberg and the equerries were only supporting actors in the unfolding drama of court life. The central character, on whom so much of Fanny's concentration focussed, was, without doubt, the queen. The two women, as they may perhaps have recognised, had much in common. Both were small and slender, and neither was regarded as conventionally good-looking. They were quite close in age, Charlotte being only eight years older than Fanny, although the queen's regal title, dignified air and status as wife and mother made her seem much more mature than the unmarried, acutely self-conscious novelist.

At their first encounter, Fanny had been struck first by the queen's accent, which she found 'a little foreign, and very prettily so', and then by her manners, which she thought had 'all the fine high breeding, which the mind, not the station gives'.[36] As she grew to know her better, it was the breadth and penetration of Charlotte's intellect which formed the basis of the admiration Fanny felt for her, and which she never ceased to respect. She had known the queen was learned, but had not expected her to be quite so acute. 'For the excellency of her mind, I was fully prepared,' Fanny wrote shortly after her arrival at court, 'but the depth and soundness of her understanding surprised me.' She had hoped to find 'good sense' in the queen, but was unprepared for the power of her curiosity about aspects of the world from which her royal role would always exclude her. Charlotte had applied her intelligence to fill in the gaps left by the secluded nature of her life, and Fanny paid unqualified tribute to what she had achieved. 'In the course of this month, I spent much time quite alone with her, and never once quitted her presence without fresh admiration of her talents.'[37]

A scholarly woman herself, Fanny recognised a like-minded spirit in the queen, and it is in her depiction of Charlotte as literary enthusiast that she comes most alive. 'The queen, when in my room, looked over my books,' wrote Fanny, 'a thing pretty briefly done as I have scarce any of my own, but a few dictionaries and such works as have been given by their authors … I believe she was a little disappointed, for I could see by her manner of turning them over that she expected to discover my own choice and taste in the little collection I possessed.'[38] The queen loved to discuss her literary preferences, offering her opinions with a freedom she rarely ventured elsewhere. She was surprised to hear that Fanny had not read Goethe's *The Sorrows of Young Werther*, although it was not a book Charlotte could recommend. For her, its equivocal moral message – it was alleged by its critics to sanction suicide – negated all the undoubted beauties of its style, concluding: 'It is done by a bad man for revenge.'[39]

Alongside her avid consumption of books, the queen also enjoyed literary gossip, asking the well-informed Fanny if it was true that 'Boswell is going to publish a life of your friend Dr Johnson', or if a character she had noticed in the *Observer* was based on the bluestocking Mrs Montagu.[40] Fanny, who came to believe that the queen's real intention in employing her was to have her act as her informal 'English Reader', was often asked to assess books and advise on their suitability. She had no hesitation in blacklisting Horace Walpole's *The Mysterious Mother*, which the queen had borrowed from Lord Harcourt. Fanny was appalled to discover that the plot revolved around incest between mother and son. 'Dreadful was the whole! Truly dreadful! A story of so much horror, from atrocious and voluntary guilt never did I hear!' She would never be able to read Walpole's books in the same way again, and was only thankful she had prevented the queen undergoing the same ordeal.[41]

In their shared love of literature, grounded in respect for books and their authors, Fanny understood that her status was equal, if not superior, to Charlotte's. Indeed, she had access to knowledge and experiences which the queen could never enjoy. As a result, there were moments when Charlotte deferred to her, acknowledging her primacy in a world where she could never be more than a distant spectator. This was not the case in other aspects of their relationship, and in these a sense of unease and discomfort on Fanny's part is much more apparent. She hated the element of 'service' that was inseparable from her role, and much resented its outward manifestations. More than anything, she detested being summoned to the queen by a bell.

'A bell! It seemed so mortifying a mark of servitude. I always felt myself blush, though alone, with conscious shame at my degradation.'[42]

Life at court often seemed to her a series of small humiliations, all of which combined to infantilise her and reduce her freedom of action. On the first occasion when she was obliged to ask the queen for permission to visit a friend, she found it 'inexpressibly awkward'. A little later, when Mme de Genlis, whose reputation was now so tarnished, had expressed a wish to open a correspondence with her, Fanny felt obliged to seek the queen's advice on what to do. Charlotte, assuring her that she had been right to speak to her, advised her not to write. Fanny had no real quarrel with the queen's judgement, but was inwardly furious at the suspension of her right to decide for herself. 'I got behind her chair,' she told her sister, 'that she might not see a distress she might wonder at; for it was not this application itself that affected me, it was the novelty of my own situation, the new power I was calling forth over my proceedings and the all that I was changing from – relinquishing – of the past – and hazarding for the future.'[43]

Fanny was particularly angry with her own collusion in the abdication of her independence. She understood the value of what she was surrendering, yet she seemed compelled to ask Charlotte to take more and more control over every aspect of her life. She desperately sought the queen's approval, even at the cost of losing the small freedoms that were left to her. She was eventually driven to ask Charlotte for absolute clarity on the subject of who was permitted to visit her at court, although she must have known what the answer would be. Shortly afterwards she was called on by Mr Smelt, with a list of restrictions and directives: 'That I should see nobody at all, but by appointment … That I should see no fresh person whatsoever, without an immediate permission from the queen … That I should never go out without an immediate application to her,' and, most significantly, that with the exception of her father and brothers, 'to have *no men – none*!'[44]

Fanny's response to this progressive extension of control rarely extended to direct criticism of the queen. Only once did she acknowledge real anger. Thinking she was not needed, she arrived late and flustered for her attendance upon Charlotte, who was not amused. 'The queen, a little dryly said, "Where have you been, Miss Burney?"' When informed she had been walking in Richmond Gardens with Mr Smelt, Charlotte looked even more displeased. Despite herself,

Fanny bridled. 'What republican feelings were rising in my breast,' she admitted, 'until she softened them down again' by asking her in a more normal voice 'to look at Lady Frances Howard's gown and see if it was not pretty'. Soon she was 'all smiles and sweetness' again.[45]

In general, it was these smoothly benign qualities, the cheerful graciousness of the queen, that Fanny preferred to emphasise. 'O sweet queen!' she once declared, in an epiphany of feeling. Throughout Fanny's journals, Charlotte is repeatedly praised for her gentle concern, her unaffected kindness, but, above all, for the unalloyed 'sweetness' of her character. She is a 'sweet woman', 'unremittingly sweet and gracious', who 'converses with the sweetest grace imaginable'. This was not simple self-deception on Fanny's part; Charlotte was indeed capable of very winning behaviour. Like her eldest son, the queen could be extremely charming, understanding exactly what would please and exerting herself to win over susceptible hearts and minds. When she presented Fanny with a bunch 'of the most beautiful double violets I ever saw', she knew it was the kind of simple, personal gesture that would delight her, as indeed it did. Fanny declared that she valued the bouquet far more than an earlier present of an expensive gown, which had been delivered through the tactless hands of Mrs Schwellenberg, and which, with its humiliating suggestion of poverty, had wounded Fanny's pride.[46] When left to herself, Charlotte handled these matters much better.

Charm and sweetness had their place in the queen's character, but they were only one aspect of a much tougher, more complicated personality. Fanny, who lived with her in such close proximity for so many years, must have known this, and she did not lack the literary skill to create a more rounded identity for the queen. Something of a believable Charlotte occasionally bursts through her descriptions; the general image, however, is calm, rational and beneficent – a vision of female royalty very close to the model at the heart of the king's family project, but somehow not entirely convincing as a depiction of a real woman. This was a portrait from which the sharper edges had been purposefully and skilfully softened. In doing so, Fanny may have been motivated by discretion; she considered herself bound by a bond of trust not to reveal aspects of royal life which would have been painful to the family; the good relationship she enjoyed with Charlotte and her daughters long after she left her employment at court is testimony to the rigour with which she observed that rule. But there may also have been less conscious motives involved. Perhaps the shame of her subservient position – 'I have always and uniformly had a horror of a life of attendance and dependence' – did not seem as difficult to bear if the submission was made to a person of exceptional moral worth.[47] It was easier to serve an idealised paragon than a woman with the human mix of good and indifferent qualities that make for a flawed but ultimately more credible character.

Fanny saw Charlotte's daughters through a similarly rose-tinted prism; like their mother, their true characters struggle to escape from the limitations of the framework Fanny imposed upon them. They are first and foremost illustrations of the new idea of royalty, rightly conscious of their status but with their moral compass securely in place, modest, unaffected and with an easy, simple dignity that equally disarms and impresses the candid observer. For Fanny, this was to be seen even in the behaviour of the junior princesses, two of whom she encountered for the first time in August 1786, when Princess Mary was ten years old and Sophia a year younger. 'I met the Princess Mary just arrived from the Lower Lodge; she was capering upstairs to her elder sisters, but instantly stopped at the sight of me, and coming up to me, inquired how I did with all the elegant composure of a woman of maturest years.' This happy combination of the uninhibited behaviour that marked out the natural, unforced child with the polite requirements of rank greatly impressed Fanny. 'Amazingly well are these children brought up. The readiness and grace of their civilities, even in the midst of their happiest wildnesses and freedom are at once a surprise and charm to all who see them.'[48] Later that day, she was equally pleased by Princess Sophia, who came to collect a basket belonging to Badine, the queen's latest dog. '"Miss Burney," cried she, curtseying and colouring, "Mamma has sent me for the little dog's basket." I begged permission to carry it to the queen's room; but she would not suffer me, and insisted on taking it, with a mingled modesty and good breeding extremely striking in one so young.'[49] Sophia's shyness and self-consciousness are entirely to her credit in Fanny's mind, far preferable to the pride or arrogant lack of consideration which might have been the result of a less careful upbringing.

Even Amelia, the youngest princess, displayed a similarly pleasing blend of authentic feeling and gracious good manners. 'She is a most lovely little thing, just three years old, and full of sense, spirit and playful prettiness; yet decorous and dignified when called upon to act *en princesse* to any strangers, as if conscious of her high rank, and the importance of condescendingly sustaining it. This little princess,' concluded Fanny approvingly, 'thus in infancy, by practice and example taught her own consequence, conducts herself on all proper occasions with an air of dignity that is quite astonishing, though her natural character seems all sport and humour.'[50] Fanny, who liked the company of children, was soon established as a particular favourite with Amelia. The little girl occupied a special place in her father's affections too; she had been born weeks after Octavius's death, and although no one could replace the boy in the king's mind, her company seems to have eased his grief, and he spent a great deal of time with her. When Amelia burnt her fingers by 'playing with some wax given her by Princess Mary', it was her father and Fanny whom she wanted near her. 'She wanted to come to you,' said the king, 'very much – would not be denied; Miss Burney is first in favour with her now.'[51]

Perhaps Amelia appreciated not just Fanny's tenderness, but also her ready willingness to indulge in some boisterous fun. Along with Mr Smelt, Fanny and Amelia once played a game in which the young princess pretended to drive around the room in a carriage. Soon things had become 'rather noisy, by Mr Smelt's choosing to represent a restive horse'. Then, without warning, the king entered the room. Immediately the entertainment came to an end. Amelia's efforts to make Fanny resume the game were all in vain. When Fanny explained that they must not disturb the king, Amelia insisted that her father should leave: 'Papa, go!' 'What!' cried the king. 'Go Papa – you must go!' repeated Amelia. The king refused to oblige. 'He took her up in his arms, and began kissing and playing with her,' ignoring his daughter's loud, indignant protests.[52] It was a scene redolent with symbolism for Amelia's future experience, suggesting as it did that even the most loving father was capable of looking in the other direction when his daughter's desires did not coincide with his own.

The older princesses were rarely as forceful in pursuit of what they wanted as their youngest sister. In Fanny's accounts, they were always well behaved; but she was also keen to portray them as neither solemn nor pompous. The Princess Royal and Elizabeth once cornered her in their mother's dressing room to interrogate her about her recent poor health. 'Pray, is it really true that in your illness last year you coughed so violently you broke the whalebone of your stays in two?' They were delighted to hear that it was 'as nearly true as possible'.[53] The sisters loved to talk, and did not stand on ceremony in pursuit of a good gossip. Fanny was proud of having often been in 'easy and delightful chattery with Princess Elizabeth', who was not above asking her advice on style when writing a letter and in general showed 'truly amiable modesty and humility'.[54] She recognised similarly relaxed virtues in Elizabeth's elder sisters, Royal and Augusta, who 'both came up to me and began conversing in the most easy, unaffected, cheerful and obliging manner that can be conceived'.[55] When Royal chatted freely, whilst she held the queen's snuffbox for Fanny to fill – and insisted that Fanny should sit in her presence – and when she took leave of the author, 'with as elegant a civility of manner as if parting with another king's daughter', these were examples of Royal's good taste and graciousness. 'I am quite charmed by the Princess Royal,' wrote Fanny approvingly; 'open, unaffected condescension and native dignity are so happily blended in her whole deportment.'[56]

Fanny understood that theirs was not, nor ever could be, a relationship between equals; but it could be conducted on terms of mutual respect, in which the feelings of the junior partner were given proper consideration by her social superior. This was what was meant by 'condescension', a word which, in the eighteenth century, had none of the pejorative connotations it has today. The condescension shown by Charlotte and her daughters to all who deserved it was, in Fanny's opinion, one of their most attractive traits.

There is little in Fanny's picture of the Princess Royal that recalls the angry, needy teenager who had made the lives of her governesses so miserable. Her portrait of Royal – and indeed of all the sisters – does not at all attempt to capture the genuine reality of their lives. For all its apparent intimacy, it is an idealised image designed to show the princesses with all the petty disfigurements and difficulties of life expertly removed. It is very skilfully done, and it is not exactly untruthful in what it says. The characters of the sisters, as Fanny delineates them, are recognisably their own, but they are seen through a warm glow, a transformative mirror of goodwill that makes them both more and less than the people they really were.

In one sense, Fanny's portrait is a literary version of the great painting made of the three eldest princesses by Thomas Gainsborough in 1784, two years before she arrived at court. The three sisters, then aged eighteen, sixteen and fourteen, are shown posed close together, arms entwined. They are fashionably dressed, with hair up-swept and powdered, their gauzy dresses rendered in subtle shades of gold, pink and turquoise. When working on the group of single family portraits which he had completed a few years earlier, it was said that Gainsborough 'was all but raving mad with ecstasy in beholding such a constellation of youthful beauty'; none of that ecstatic moment is evident in this work.[57] Its defining qualities are precisely those that Fanny celebrates: grace, restraint and easy dignity. The sisters are models of self-possession, gazing calmly out of the canvas; only Royal's sideways glance catches the viewer's eye. Behind their cool stares, however, there simmers a powerful sense of emotional control; for all their apparently relaxed manner, their eyes give nothing away. They are gracious but guarded, elegant yet remote. Gainsborough said the picture had been painted 'in a very tender light', and it is indeed an image of fragile, delicate beauty, albeit with a suggestion of steeliness glinting below its luminous surface. Like Fanny Burney's writings, it takes the sisters' characters and turns them into art, creating an image of royal majesty in which the qualities that make them human are both celebrated and denied.

Elizabeth in particular had become a far more imposing character, in both looks and behaviour, than her mild depiction in both painting and Fanny's writings suggests. She was large in presence and in figure, an unapologetic lover of good humour, good food and drink, with a bold turn of phrase that matched her hunger for enjoyment and fun. In later life, she sometimes sounds like a character from the novels of Henry Fielding: loud, emphatic and with not a hint of prim gentility about her. 'Anything so disgusting as the breakfast at Woodgate's Inn on the way from Weymouth, thank God, I never saw before, and I never wish to see again,' she declared to Lady Harcourt. It was fortunate that she had stored in her carriage 'a large plum cake put up as stowage for the stomach'.[58] She was sensitive about her size and, as a young woman, was acutely embarrassed when her mother, still slender after so many pregnancies, insisted she try on a new pair of stays in front of Mrs Delany. 'When Her Majesty came in, she felt them here and there and said, "Elizabeth, they are too tight." "Indeed Mama, they are not,"' insisted the princess plaintively.[59] But for all her protestations, nothing really interfered with her pursuit of a good dinner, which no unforeseen consequences could persuade her to forgo. 'I was taken exceedingly ill in the night,' she once explained to the

Prince of Wales, a fellow trencherman, 'violently sick and so swelled that they think I must have been poisoned, owing to the remarkably large lobster which I ate at supper.'[60]

Determinedly cheerful, Elizabeth was proud of her own sense of fun. She was an avid collector of jokes and squibs, passing them on to the Harcourts with great relish, even those she knew she was not supposed to enjoy. 'I have just got some good lines upon the new peers, very good,' she told Lord Harcourt, 'in my next you shall have them, but remember, that as king's daughters are among honourable women, I must not be named as the person that wrote them to you.'[61] Alongside her taste for sharp witticism, Elizabeth took great pride in her love of plain-speaking and dislike of elaborate *politesse*. 'Though brought up at court,' she reflected in old age, 'I could never form my mouth to make compliments.' She sometimes referred to herself as 'Sally Blunt': 'I just say what I feel and think ... and cannot make fine speeches. I could as well spit.' Indeed, she declared, 'I had rather be spit at than anybody make me a head and shoulders compliment, which is detestable and not to be stood.'[62] Like so many of her family, she believed she would have much preferred a simpler life. 'It is a mistake, my living at court,' she confided to Lady Harcourt; 'It was certainly intended I should have lived in the country and been a younger brother's wife.'[63]

Her older sister, Augusta, was much harder to read than the forthright Elizabeth. Mrs Harcourt, Lady Harcourt's sister-in-law, thought her 'a less marked character' in every way, finding it hard to sum up her somewhat elusive personality.[64] Her family thought her very shy. She surveyed the world with a watchful air of amused irony which those who recognised it found extremely attractive. 'Augusta looks very well,' commented her brother William on a visit home from sea in 1789; 'she looks as if she knew more than she would say, and I like that.'[65] Fanny Burney, who regarded her own shyness as a form of heightened sensibility, saw something similar in Augusta. She was very fond of her, with the appreciation of one quiet satiric eye for another, and Augusta eventually became Fanny's favourite among the sisterhood. 'She has a gaiety and humour about her that is resistless,' she declared, 'and much of true, genuine and original humour.'[66] Fanny and Augusta once amused themselves 'saying comical things about royal personages in plays,' and Augusta 'very gravely asserted that she thought some of those princes on the stage looked really quite as well as some she knew off it.'[67] Writing to Lord Harcourt on a wet day, she observed that 'steady quiet rain puts me in mind of what I should think a Quaker's grief must appear to persons of a more lively disposition.'[68]

Augusta was the only one of the sisters with a sustained interest in the active, wider world beyond the bounds of court and family. Although her own politics were conventional – 'I was always proud of being born a Briton … No people can boast of such a heart as dear John Bull'[69] – she was curious about new ideas, even those at the wilder edges of radical thinking. In 1798, when popular unrest and political agitation was at its height, Augusta and Fanny Burney sat down to discuss 'loyalty and then its contrast, democracy'. Fanny was understandably surprised to hear Augusta quote at length 'from a lecture of Thelwall's … which was very curious from her mouth'. John Thelwall was a popular Jacobin orator who had stood trial for high treason in 1794, and narrowly escaped the death penalty. His speeches were uncompromising in their criticism of the established system, arguing that 'one order of society has no right to pillage, to plunder and oppress the other parts of the community'.[70] Fanny does not give any further details of what must have been a most unusual conversation, except to declare that Augusta, with her generous, candid character, was capable 'of abstracting rays of light from the darkest shades. So she did, even from Thelwall.'[71]

Less surprisingly, Augusta was also a great partisan of the Royal Navy, and seized the opportunity to visit the thirty-two-gun frigate HMS *Southampton* when on a visit to Weymouth in 1789. She was not at all deterred by the precarious business of being 'whipped' into the ship, which, as she described, involved being drawn up the steep sides of the vessel 'in a chair by two cables'.[72] Her naval passion may have been related to the strong bond she felt with her sailor brother William. The relationship between the wild and unpolished third brother and the most reserved and introspective of the sisters was surprising, but built on a lifetime of genuine affection. 'We had been each other's early friends,' Augusta explained, 'and I had known every secret of his heart, the same when he was quite a lad, that I could believe and pity all his worries, real and imaginary.' As they grew older, their love for one another grew stronger. 'He was like my second self,' said Augusta.[73] Her admiration both for her brother and his way of life is enthusiastically apparent in a letter she wrote to her young brother, Augustus, in 1787. 'I believe him to be, as I always did, a very hearty good English tar, liking a hammock better than a bed, and plain salt beef than all the fine dishes and luxury that townspeople fare upon.' She was as insistent as Elizabeth in indicating where her own sympathies lay: with the plain over the pompous, the authentic over the falsely genteel. 'He always wears his uniform and no curls, and yet looks as well dressed and more of a man than the fashionable powder monkeys. He talks', she concluded with obvious approval, 'of affectation in a man as the thing that has the same effect upon him as an emetic.'[74]

Augusta showed little interest in her own appearance, although she was reckoned to be the most attractive of the elder princesses. Fanny Burney thought her 'exquisite'. She once watched Augusta prepare for a night at the theatre, utterly indifferent to the suggestions offered by the hairdresser working so assiduously on her complicated toilette. Asked what ornaments she wanted placed on her head, she had nothing to say: 'You understand all that best, Mr Robinson, I'm sure. There are the things, so just take what you please.' Fanny was impressed by 'a mind so disengaged from vanity, so superior to personal appearance'. Augusta put it more simply: 'Oh, I hate myself when so fine … I cannot bear it, but there is no help – the people at the play always expect it.'[75]

The Princess Royal was generally agreed to possess the most complex character of the three elder sisters. As she entered her twenties, and despite the unaffected dignity to which Fanny Burney often alluded, she was in some ways still as painfully self-conscious as she had been when a teenager. Mrs Harcourt noticed 'the extreme quickness of her feelings, which show themselves in her perpetual blushes'.[76] She seemed awkward and uncertain, combining 'a great sense of her own situation' with an 'excessive sensibility'. She was not well understood or always appreciated by those around her. 'She is unjustly considered proud,' thought Mrs Harcourt, 'and a peculiarity in her temper is mistaken for a less sweetness than it deserves.' She was particularly devoted to her father, whom she was thought 'in many points of character' to resemble.[77] Like him, she was literal, hard-working, prone to unsparing, critical self-examination, and inclined to censoriousness. She was the daughter he had longed for after a succession of sons, and she never lost a high place in his affections. She was, according to one observer, 'his comfort and his darling', and fully returned his love, declaring him in 1786 'the best of kings and fathers'.[78]

For her mother, her feelings were less straightforward. She was never less than dutiful in her attentions to her, but theirs was not an easy relationship. 'She was always shy and under restraint with the queen,' asserted Mrs Papendiek. 'Timidity, with want of affectionate confidence in the queen's commands and wishes always brought her forward as ill at ease; while out of the queen's presence, she was a different being.'[79] Her exacting character meant that she was often conscious of falling short of the high standards expected from her as the senior princess, and of incurring her mother's formidable disappointment as a result. She knew that she did not always conform to the image of sophisticated composure with which Gainsborough had credited her in his shimmering triple portrait. 'She was never elegant in exhibition,' recalled Mrs Papendiek, 'though her figure was good and imposing.'[80] She rarely managed the sartorial style achieved by her mother, who, for all her protestations about the waste of time involved in her lengthy toilette, was always scrupulously turned out. Royal 'did not take notice whether your gown was a new or an old one', remembered Louisa Stuart, unlike her sisters and the queen, 'who took an exact account of everyone's wardrobe and trinket box'.[81] She was a nervous dancer, her anxiety perhaps increased by a well-founded suspicion that she had no sense of rhythm. She felt isolated by her inability to share a passion which united every other member of the family. 'I am not more partial to music than I was when you left us,' she wrote sadly to her young brother Augustus on the eve of her twenty-second birthday. The occasion was to be marked by a concert which she knew she would not enjoy. 'I am afraid you will not have a very good opinion of me from this confession, as a love of music to distraction runs through this family, of which I alone am deprived. Pray,' she concluded, 'do not love me any less for my want of ear.'[82]

The contrast with the easy musical assurance of her younger sisters must have been additionally painful. Mrs Delany's niece, Marianne Port, was treated in 1786 to a private performance on the piano by the ten-year-old Princess Mary. She dashed off 'a lesson by Handel' and, 'with all the sweetness in the world, played it twice'. When she had finished, 'Princess Sophia said, "Now I will play to you if you like," and immediately played the Hallelujah Chorus in the Messiah; and Princess Mary sung it.'[83]

Royal sought other ways to please. She threw herself into the pursuit of a variety of accomplishments and skills, devoting all her time and considerable powers of application to mastering them. She worked diligently at her academic studies, tackling challenging volumes of history and theology. Fanny Burney had observed that 'she writes German with as much facility as I do English'; in that language, too, her preferred authors were of a distinctly serious tone. Like her mother, her grandmother and her great-grandmother before her, Royal was also fascinated by the study of botany. When the queen decided to embark on a botanical work of her own, classifying and illustrating different kinds of herbs, she chose Royal over her other daughters to assist her: 'Her natural steadiness never makes her shun labour or difficulty,' observed Charlotte, paying a rare tribute to her eldest daughter's meticulous and painstaking nature.[84]

Royal displayed a similarly intense commitment to her pursuit of artistic activities. All the royal women were enthusiastic amateur artists, and the princesses explored a wide range of what would now be called mixed media, painting on velvet, decorating furniture, stencilling walls, and even illustrating their own fans. They also undertook the more traditional forms of drawing and painting. The copying of great works was thought a useful training for artistically minded girls, and Royal spent many hours making her own versions of old masters from the royal art collection. Influenced by her own studies of plants, and by the extraordinarily beautiful illustrations she had seen made at first hand by Mrs Delany, she was equally interested in the painting of flowers. Many of her drawings demonstrate considerable skill and accomplishment. But whatever pleasure she took in creative works seems to have been overpowered by the sense of relentless, punishing self-improvement with which she undertook them. She was terrified by any interruptions to the demanding schedule she imposed on herself, obsessed with the idea that she would fall behind and be found wanting. When the queen hired 'Miss Mee, a flower painter' to give her extra lessons in technique, it only added to her self-lacerating sense of inadequacy: 'If I do not come on, I must be wanting in capacity; for I have every advantage, and therefore no excuse but my own stupidity if I do not improve.'[85]

Royal's frantic desire to leave no moment unfilled in her pursuit of 'improvement' was encouraged by the attitude of her mother.

Charlotte was obsessed with time and the proper use of it. At her first meeting with Fanny Burney, she had made her views very clear: 'Oh, for me, I am always quarrelling with time! It is so short to do something, and so long to do nothing.' There was little that made her so angry, she declared, 'as to hear people know not what to do! For me, I never have half time enough for things.' The perennial solution to any complaint of boredom was obvious to her: 'Why, employ yourselves!'[86] It was a brisk injunction that must have been very familiar to her daughters.

Royal did all she could to follow her mother's directive, and make rational use of her time. She accompanied her parents on visits to gardens and houses; when they were in London, she went with them to their favourite concerts of ancient music – which tried her patience – and to the theatre, which she enjoyed only if the underlying message of the drama made the expedition worthwhile. (Unlike her father, she had no taste for simple, knockabout comedy.) Sometimes great actors were invited to give private readings to the family, but she found these stilted affairs. Fanny Burney was once asked to read a play in front of the queen and princesses, and found it a depressing experience. 'It went off pretty flat – nobody is to comment – nobody is to interrupt – such is the settled etiquette.' She thought 'the annihilation of all nature and pleasantry' all the more dispiriting as she knew how much the queen and her daughters loved lively conversation.[87] When David Garrick was invited, he made the mistake of choosing to read a comedy. Nobody laughed. 'It was as if they had thrown a wet blanket over me,' he commented gloomily.[88]

Royal probably gained most pleasure from her role in educating her younger sisters. The queen had never devoted as much attention to the intellectual upbringing of the three younger princesses as she had done to the elder three, and Royal gratefully grasped the opportunity to fill the gap. She became both teacher and mentor to the girls, spending many hours in their company and proving an effective and imaginative teacher, especially with the young Princess Amelia, whom Charlotte Papendiek thought 'had much improved under her tuition'. Royal was in her early twenties when she took on the role of 'governess to her three younger sisters'. It must have occurred to her, as she watched them stumble over their German verbs, that at her age the queen had been mother to a growing tribe of children. In contrast, Royal was marking time, held in an ever-extended girlhood which could not satisfy her, however earnestly she sought to force purpose and activity into its empty hours.

Princess Elizabeth once declared that she and her sisters were certain of having all the amusements their parents could devise for them. Her elder sister would no doubt have agreed with such a dutiful pronouncement; but she might also silently have observed that they were not necessarily the amusements she would have chosen for herself. As a daughter, even when loved and indulged, she was not, as her life daily reminded her, a free agent. She existed in a world of good-natured dependency in which every aspect of her existence was subject to the wishes of others. Even her clothes, made in colours designed to complement those of the queen, were not of her own choosing.

There was, as Royal well understood, only one answer to her growing sense of impotence. She was ready to graduate from the life of a daughter into that of a wife. The time had come for her to marry.

*

George and Charlotte's children had from their earliest days understood that royal marriages were not like others. They knew that they could expect relatively little freedom in the choice of a spouse, and that dynastic or political considerations were more significant than their own preferences. With far less opportunity than their brothers to investigate possible partners during their travels abroad, the princesses were resigned to marrying men they barely knew before leaving their home and family for ever, with little prospect of ever returning. This had been their mother's experience, and it was a destiny they imagined they would one day share. Both sons and daughters were equally aware of the primacy of their father's intentions in managing their marital prospects. Royal children were expected to do their duty, and marry – or not – as their sovereign directed. In the past, the monarch's ability to proscribe and prevent had been enforced largely by tradition, through fear of reprisals and the sheer force of royal personality; but the actions of George III changed all that. When, as he saw it, his right to influence who married whom in the heart of his own family was ignored and defied, he took decisive action to ensure it would never happen again. The Royal Marriages Act enshrined in law the king's ability to veto alliances he did not like. As a piece of legislation, it was to impact directly on the lives of three of his daughters and one of his sons; as a demonstration of his desire to exert emotional control over even those he loved, it was the basis from which so much of the future unhappiness of his children flowed.

The Act was a response to the behaviour of the king's youngest brother. Henry, Duke of Cumberland, was a man of pleasure in the classic Hanoverian mode: a drinker, a gambler and a serial taker of mistresses. In 1770, much to the king's shame, Cumberland had been named in a divorce suit brought against him by Lord Grosvenor, and, in a trial that attracted enormous public attention, his love letters to Lady Grosvenor were read out in court. Beneath their conventional declarations, these revealed a rather sad and lonely man hidden behind the brittle persona of the rake; but this had no effect on the outcome, which resulted in damages being awarded against the duke for the vast sum of £13,000. As he had no assets, this was paid by a reluctant and angry king. However, it was the shocking news that Cumberland had married without George's permission which finally destroyed any lingering affection the king felt for his brother.

Cumberland had not informed George of his intention to take a wife because he knew he would never have agreed to his choice. The new Duchess of Cumberland was Anne Horton, a daughter of Simon Luttrell, who later became the Earl of Carhampton. For the king, she had many objectionable qualities, the first of which was that she was British. George had given up Sarah Lennox because he had been persuaded by Bute that any alliance between royalty and the local aristocracy was fraught with political risk. Anne Horton's relations were, if possible, even less attractive to the king than the Foxes had been in 1760. The bride's four brothers and her father all sat in the Commons, where their behaviour was as unpalatable to the king as their morals. Simon Luttrell's dissolute activities led to his being dubbed 'the King of Hell'. He and his sons were all hard-drinking, hard-living men of the kind George despised, and his new sister-in-law had an equally raffish air. She was extremely attractive, reported Horace Walpole, 'with the most amorous eyes in the world, and eyelashes a yard long'. She had, he admitted, 'more of the air of a woman of pleasure than woman of quality', with a gift for dancing 'and a great deal of wit, but of the satiric kind'.[89]

When Cumberland told the king what he had done, George was first horrified and then furious, though, characteristically, he sought to control his anger. 'After walking some time to smother my feelings,' he told the Duke of Gloucester, his other surviving brother, 'I, without passion, spoke to him to the following effect – that I could not believe he had taken the step ... to which he answered me he would never tell me an untruth.' Once forced to accept the veracity of Cumberland's confession, the king was implacable. 'I told him, as the step was taken, I could give him no advice, for he had irretrievably ruined himself.'[90]

Almost immediately, George moved to introduce legislation to prevent an event of this kind happening again. The Royal Marriages Bill sought to prevent any of the king's close family from marrying without his permission until they were twenty-five; even then, they would be obliged to inform Parliament and the Privy Council of any proposed alliance. Objections could be made for up to a year following such a declaration. Any marriage contracted in defiance of these provisions would be deemed null and void, and any children produced regarded as illegitimate. It was not a popular bill, due to the considerable unease felt at the idea that a universal human right – the freedom of a competent adult to marry whom they wished – could be compromised by royal decree. Lord North had a difficult time shepherding its passage through Parliament; but the king would not be deflected, instructing North to drive the bill on 'with a becoming firmness'. George's public declaration to Members sitting in the ministerial interest, that 'I have a right to expect a hearty support from everyone in my service and I shall remember defaulters', carried the day.[91] 'The king grew dictatorial and his creatures kissed the earth,' commented Walpole. In 1772, the bill became an Act of Parliament on receiving royal assent.

The progress of the bill must have given the Duke of Gloucester much uncomfortable pause for thought. As early as 1766, it had been rumoured that he too was concealing a secret wife. Lady Mary Coke recorded that when he walked into the royal chapel at St James's, the lady beside her 'bent forward and said to me "Married"'. Lady Mary replied that she did not believe it, 'upon which she repeated, "Married, I assure you it is true"'.[92] Later, Lady Mary also heard that every night at Windsor, on the stroke of twelve, a rocket was let off in the Great Walk, a signal to 'a certain royal duke' that the coast was clear for him to join his lover in her lodgings. Eventually, the rocket 'became such a ridicule at Windsor that he was obliged to leave it off', but his nightly visits continued, rocket or no rocket.

The woman with whom the duke spent his nights was Maria, Lady Waldegrave. As a young woman, she had married Lord Waldegrave, who had been George's governor when he was Prince of Wales; she was also the niece of Horace Walpole, which meant that the diarist had unusually full access to the details of her story, at least as it appeared from her point of view. Walpole argued that the relationship between Lady Waldegrave and the duke was not 'a dissolute connexion': she and the duke were 'remarkably religious'. He was sure they were married, and thought the king and queen suspected it too. Certainly, George and Charlotte extended to Lady Waldegrave – who was nowhere near as objectionable to them as Anne Horton – 'a sort of equivocal acknowledgment of what she was'.[93] Two events made it impossible for a situation of such carefully calibrated discretion to continue: the introduction of the Royal Marriages Act and the discovery that Lady Waldegrave was pregnant. The Duke of Gloucester now had no choice but to admit to the king that he, too, was married. If his coming child was not to be declared illegitimate, he would also have to prove that the wedding had taken place before the Act was passed.

In the autumn of 1772, the duke summoned up his courage, and confessed to the king that he had been married since September 1766. Whatever George may have privately suspected, the shock of Gloucester's admission was devastating. He had expected such behaviour from the rackety Cumberland, but not from Gloucester. 'Reserved, pious, of the most sober and decent disposition,' Walpole believed that Gloucester 'was of all the family, the king's favourite.'[94] The knowledge that he had said nothing, whilst the king confided in him all his misgivings about the Cumberland marriage, added to George's distress. Walpole heard that 'he cried, and protested he had not slept all night' after the fateful meeting with Gloucester. 'He talked of not seeing the duke again, though he said it should not be forever, that he should be miserable not to see again the brother whom he loved.'[95] Smarting from a sense of betrayal, the king grew vindictive, subjecting his brother and his heavily pregnant wife to the ordeal of formal investigation into the legality of their marriage. Only when it was at last proved valid, if unsanctioned, was Lady Waldegrave acknowledged as Duchess of Gloucester, and her newborn child, Sophia Matilda, safely legitimate, given the title of princess.

The king, his resolve stiffened by the queen, who disliked both her sisters-in-law, remained fixed in his disapproval of his brothers' marriages. Neither duchess was received at court. The Cumberlands, indifferent to their exclusion, filled up their house with gamblers and reprobates, and indulged in heavy-handed ridicule of George and Charlotte. 'A mighty scope for satire was afforded by the queen's wide mouth and occasionally imperfect English, as well as by the king's trick of saying What! What!, his ill-made coats and general antipathy to fashion.'[96] Nothing like this was permitted in Gloucester's more decorous household: 'the duke respected himself and his brother too much to permit it'. But in terms of lasting happiness, it was the partnership of the louche Cumberlands which proved most resilient. The duke never looked at another woman until he died in 1790, as devoted to his flamboyant duchess as he had been when they married nearly twenty years before. By 1781, in contrast, the marriage of the sober Gloucesters was falling apart. The duke blamed the duchess's 'very unfortunate turn of mind and temper'; when their daughter was only a year old, she had, he said, threatened to leave him. He confessed to the king, with whom he was partially reconciled, that he had made a terrible mistake and that his heart was 'very full. I am indeed punished for my juvenile indiscretions by the very ungrateful return I receive at home.'[97]

Chastened and penitent, the Duke of Gloucester was gradually admitted back into the family circle, but never again to the uniquely privileged position he had once occupied in the king's heart. Beneath his habitual good nature, George nurtured a steely resentment for those he considered had flouted his authority; a dutiful man himself, he expected a similar display of respectful obligation from others. The Royal Marriages Act translated that conviction into a legal requirement. It had its origins in the uncontrolled behaviour of his brothers, but it reached far beyond and into the lives of the next generation, as George had intended that it should. 'I have children who must know what they are to expect if they follow so infamous an example,' he had written with cold determination in 1771. It would take a great deal of courage to suggest to the king that any judgement, any opinion, any feelings other than his own had a role to play in securing their future happiness.

Whilst he could veto their choice of a wife, there was little the king could do to prevent his sons taking lovers, as he was repeatedly forced to acknowledge throughout the 1780s: as soon as they emerged from the schoolroom, the princes found themselves mistresses. Amongst aristocratic sophisticates, there was some sympathy for their plight. 'Consider what a sad dog a prince of the blood is,' exclaimed Lord Temple to the diarist Joseph Farrington, 'who cannot by law amuse himself with any women except some damned German princess with a nose as long as my arm, and as ugly as the devil. In my opinion, a prince of the blood is the most miserable being on Earth.'[98]

The lives of the princesses were far more susceptible to parental control. The sisters saw few people beyond the royal household, and their strongest bonds of friendship were often with women much older than themselves: Mrs Delany, Lady Cha and Lady Harcourt were all either middle-aged or elderly. Elizabeth and Royal had a small circle of female friends nearer their own age, with whom they enjoyed occasional gossipy encounters, but there were few opportunities for unsupervised, unregulated intimacy. The exacting restrictions placed by the queen on Fanny Burney's freedom to entertain male guests suggested how carefully access to the royal palaces was monitored. There were certainly few opportunities for the princesses to meet men, other than those appointed by the king and queen to carry out court business. Three of the sisters were later to form relationships with their father's equerries. When a serious illness removed Princess Elizabeth from public view for much of 1785–86, it was rumoured that she had given birth in secret to two illegitimate babies. The supposed father was the page William Ramus, who had once been mentioned as a possible husband for Miss Goldsworthy, the princesses' sub-governess. There was no truth in the story, but it demonstrated the narrowness of the circles in which the sisters moved. Even gossip could not imagine for Elizabeth a partner other than one employed by her parents. The salacious tale did demonstrate, however, that even the youngest of the three elder princesses was now considered mature enough to have an affair. It would surely not be long before the king began to make plans for more honourable arrangements. Could marriage, for each of his eldest daughters, be very far away?

Yet the years went by, and no treaties were drawn up, no dowries negotiated and no announcements made. There had been some interest in the princesses when they first made their debuts into public life; as early as 1781, the Emperor of Austria was said to have enquired about Royal as a possible consort, although his advanced age was thought to have ruled him out as a husband for the fifteen-year-old girl. A more persistent enthusiast for a marital alliance was the king's eldest sister, Augusta, Duchess of Brunswick, now established in Germany with a clutch of children for whom she was eager to find suitable matches. The Duke of Gloucester told Mrs Harcourt that 'the duchess had long and ardently desired to see her son married to the Princess Royal, but the king always disliked the idea.' George had never entirely trusted Augusta, whom he thought tactless, indiscreet and prone to trouble-making. 'He had a strong prejudice against the alliance,' continued Gloucester, 'and against his sister. He even said one of her last letters was the best he had ever received from her, because there was no scheme in it.'[99]

The queen entirely shared her husband's lukewarm response to the Brunswick proposal. She and the duchess had disliked each other from the moment of Charlotte's arrival; indeed, the duchess blamed the queen for alienating her brother's affections, describing her bitterly as 'an envious and intriguing spirit.'[100] Unsurprisingly, Charlotte was determined to put an end to thc wholc idea. 'I would rather keep all my daughters at home forever,' she declared to her brother, 'than let them marry there.'[101] When the king wrote to his sister rejecting her offer, her reply was tart and to the point: 'Your daughters must be very different from all other girls, if they did not feel themselves unfortunate not to be established.'[102] Ten years later, when the bleak truth of her observation was apparent, even to their father, George was in more conciliatory mood. In 1794, the duchess said that the king had 'offered her a princess for her son, if he would come over and be seen,' but it was too late, and she would not reconsider. 'Charles was certainly a very good-humoured, harmless boy, and would certainly make a good husband, but she would not send him over, as she was quite sure if he was to show himself, none of the princesses would have him.'[103]

Other marital prospects also came to nothing. Gloucester told Mrs Harcourt that on a visit to England the Duke of Saxe-Gotha, 'a very good man,' had 'fallen in love with the Princess Royal, his own wife being then supposed dying. In which case, he could have married her'; but his wife recovered, and, as Gloucester bluntly observed, 'though afflicted with fits, there was no prospect of a vacancy.'[104] Gloucester later discussed the matter with the sickly duchess herself, who confirmed the story. In a poignant illustration of the sad reality of loveless royal marriages, she told him 'she believed her being alive was a disappointment to her husband, for he had expected her illness to end fatally, and she knew he had set his heart on marrying the Princess Royal'.[105] Gloucester heard that, frustrated in his plan to marry her himself, Saxe-Gotha 'would now try and get her for his son', but that plan also went nowhere.

Writing in 1789, Gloucester thought Royal's remaining options were limited. 'He doubted the Prince of Prussia being disposed to any such alliance. He thought the Prince of Denmark a very desirable match, but doubted his disposition to marry.'[106] As the brevity of Gloucester's list suggested, the number of princes with qualifications that entitled them to be considered as potential husband material was not long; Royal's contemporaries, however, seemed to enjoy more success than she did in finding candidates who were available, Protestant and willing to marry. Her Mecklenburg cousins, daughters of Charlotte's favourite brother Charles, were quickly and advantageously settled, as was one of the Duchess of Brunswick's daughters, who was snapped up although aged only fifteen. Royal was now well into her twenties, and, humiliatingly, no nearer marriage at the end of the decade than she had been at its beginning.

This was not how anyone, least of all Royal and her sisters, could reasonably have expected things to turn out. George III was one of the most powerful monarchs in Europe, ruling the continent's wealthiest nation, a vibrant, expansionist power with which many smaller Protestant principalities might have hoped to secure a profitable alliance sealed by marriage. None of the princesses suffered from disabling deformities of mind or body; none had reputations for difficult tempers of the kind that had led their father to reject several potential spouses nearly thirty years before. Yet the flood of proposals that the sisters must surely have anticipated never materialised. There was little serious interest in securing their hands, and the small trickle of offers that had drifted in uncertainly when they first graduated from the schoolroom slowly but steadily dried up. Perhaps this was because from the earliest days of their entry into the marriage market, the sisters had been dogged by a sense that, for all their apparent readiness for matrimony, they were not properly available; princes in serious pursuit of a wife looked elsewhere, convinced by experience that the king would never agree to any proposal that took his daughters away from him.

By any standards of eighteenth-century behaviour, George's failure to promote and secure the marriages of his daughters was a significant dereliction of paternal duty. Finding and vetting a possible husband, and negotiating the settlement that sealed the match, was the crowning act of a father's career, perhaps the greatest service he owed to his daughters. This was a responsibility incumbent on all fathers, not only royal ones; in Jane Austen's *Pride and Prejudice*, Mr Bennett's lazy indifference to the marital prospects of his daughters, his inability to rouse himself to manage their interests, almost brings ruin on the whole family. Unlike Mr Bennett, the king was no indolent ironist; no one was more committed to the meticulous fulfilment of all moral and familial duties. Why, then, did he fail his daughters so profoundly in the execution of an obligation so crucial to their future happiness?

The Duke of Gloucester, who had clearly reflected a great deal on his brother's complex attitude to marriage, thought that the princesses would never have been allowed to choose British husbands. His own experience, and that of the Duke of Cumberland, had demonstrated the king's bitter and unwavering opposition to any such idea. Thus, their only option was to marry away from home. This, too, the duke thought, their father would never contemplate. The king had often stated his belief to Gloucester 'that he had not looked out for Continental alliances for them from a notion that they would be unwilling to leave England'.[107] There was, in fact, nothing to suggest that this was indeed how the princesses felt; whilst the prospect of permanent separation from their family may have filled them with sadness, they understood this was the price to be paid for moving into the next stage of life. In Royal's view, it was a painful sacrifice, but a necessary one: despite all the grief that accompanied it, leaving home was a choice any sensible girl would make in order to secure for herself a degree of independence. Writing in 1823, when she was approaching the age of sixty, she made her feelings very clear, insisting that any woman 'will lead a pleasanter life in a proper establishment of her own, than if she was to continue for years unmarried. No one can speak more feelingly than myself on this subject, as certainly, my home life was far from being comfortable.'[108]

For the king, however, the prospect of his daughters' departure was unbearable. It was alleged that 'he positively howled' whenever the subject of their marrying was raised.[109] This sounds out of character for a man who exerted such strenuous control over his emotions, but, if true, the intensity of his reaction was not entirely the result of his selfishness. In many ways his concerns for his daughters' welfare were legitimate; he feared that once removed from his supervision, they would fall prey to a host of malign possibilities from which he would be powerless to protect them. He knew only too well from the experience of so many of his own female relations that arranged royal marriages only rarely had truly happy endings.

George's youngest sister Caroline Matilda – a posthumous child, born after the death of her father Frederick – was only fifteen years old when she was married in 1766 to Christian VII of Denmark. She was a very reluctant bride. Prior to the ceremony, the Duchess of Northumberland watched her brought into the royal Drawing Room in tears: she 'cried so much … she was nearly falling into fits.'[110] Once married, she set out for Denmark, separated from everyone she had ever known. Her British ladies left her at the Danish border; 'not a chambermaid belonging to this country is to go with her into Denmark', observed Lady Mary Coke.[111] When she arrived at Copenhagen, she discovered that her new husband was a deeply unhappy and disturbed man. Years of systematic bullying as a child by a brutal governor had left him scarred, physically and mentally; his grasp on reality was fragile, and he was dominated by his powerful and manipulative mother. In the midst of this dark, Gothic drama, the seductive personality of the court doctor, Johann van Struensee – clever, charming and charismatic – was very attractive to the isolated young queen. Soon the couple were lovers; together, they took effective control of the kingdom, ruling in Christian's name, until toppled in 1772 by a coup d'état organised by Christian's mother. In the chaos that followed, Struensee was executed, being messily beheaded. Caroline was forcibly divorced from her unresisting husband, and, in response to pressure from Britain, allowed to leave Denmark and retreat to the remote castle of Celle in her brother's Hanoverian possessions. Like her unfortunate great-grandmother before her, she was not allowed to take her two children with her. On hearing her crying, an attendant once came into her room and found her talking to the miniature of her son that hung by her bed.[112] She was never resigned to her exile, and hoped one day to return to Denmark. However, in 1775, she died of scarlet fever, at the age of only twenty-three. With tragic, if probably unintended, symbolism, she was buried next to Sophia Dorothea, the repudiated wife of George I, another unhappy woman who died in exile.

The king had no doubt that it was his sister's unfortunate marriage that was the cause of all her misery; it had thrown her, unprotected, into a world of intrigue and horror where her hitherto 'amiable character' had been 'perverted by a wicked and contemptible court'.[113] It was a deeply depressing story, and one which weighed heavily on George's mind for many years. He had been concerned from the outset that Caroline was neither experienced nor robust enough to cope with such a sudden exposure to the realities of the world, brooding gloomily on the eve of her departure on 'the precipices into which she may probably fall'; but once she was gone, there was little he could do to help her. When, years after these shattering events, an offer was received from the Danish court proposing Caroline's son Frederick as a possible husband for Augusta, the king was determined not to see history repeat itself. 'After the treatment my late sister received there,' he wrote with chilly finality in reply, 'no one in my house can be desirous of the alliance.'[114]

The marital experiences of George's eldest sister Augusta were less dramatic than Caroline's, but no one could doubt thc humiliation and unhappiness of her position. Augusta had been married in 1764 to Charles William, the Hereditary Prince of Brunswick. He was handsome and cultured, a military hero who had fought bravely as an ally of Britain in the Seven Years War. At first, the couple seemed well matched, and she told her family that she 'never knew anybody with more real good heart. In short, he is monstrously fond of me, and I am a happy woman.' But Augusta's protestations did not convince her brother. When she arrived in London to comfort their mother as she lay dying, George wrote to Gloucester that 'she seems by her manner to be much graver than before, and I should think that it goes on but coldly between her and the Hereditary Prince, though she has not dropped the most distant hint of it'. To her younger sister Caroline Matilda, Augusta was more frank. 'She says', Caroline told her brother, 'that the prince's humour grows worse every day … She finds a great alteration in him.'[115] He had always had affairs, but had recently moved his new mistress into the palace and allowed her to usurp Augusta's position there. Rejected by her husband, she found little consolation in her children. Their wellbeing was a continual anxiety to her: one was blind, and another had developmental disabilities. She wished for nothing now except to retreat into seclusion where she could find some peace. Even her old enemy,

Queen Charlotte, was aware of the depth of her misery. 'She is not happy, so Lady Gower tells me. To the king, she has written just once, and in this letter, she said, Home is Home. Yet when she was there, she was just as unhappy.'[116]

Escape from one form of unsatisfactory life did not, as Augusta sadly discovered, guarantee the discovery of a happier one elsewhere. The arranged marriages that were the destiny of most royal women rarely promised the possibility of much genuine fulfilment. Perhaps the bleakest commentary on their limitations was delivered, with cruelly unrelenting precision, by Augusta's unwilling partner, the Duke of Brunswick. His words are a reminder that husbands, as well as wives, suffered when trapped within them. 'Only private people can live happily married,' he wrote, 'for they can choose their mates. Royalty must make marriages of convenience, which seldom result in happiness. Love does not prompt these alliances, and these marriages not only embitter the lives of the parties to them, but all too frequently have a disastrous effect upon the children who are often unhealthy in mind and body.'[117] It was a sad comment on his and Augusta's wasted years together.

'What unhappy wretches are princesses!' Mrs Delany had written, years before she lived among them. 'How they are sacrificed! It is to be hoped that they all have not the tender affections of their happier subjects.'[118] The king knew better than anyone that his daughters were fully supplied with the 'tender affections', and he had no desire to see these trampled underfoot by alliances that offered little protection for the women obliged to endure their unpredictable outcomes. George was not prepared to make sacrifices of his daughters, and his instinct to protect them from the possible consequences of arranged marriages was sincerely felt. But these honourable motives do not entirely explain his antipathy to their leaving home. There was also a strong element of unacknowledged self-interest in his refusal to allow them their independence. They were, he told Gloucester, 'the comfort of his life'; their presence was a solace so powerful and affirming that he did not intend to give it up. The princesses were everything their unsatisfactory brothers were not: uncomplicated in their affections, untainted by ambitions that did not match his own. They were neither unruly nor unpredictable. They did not contradict, embarrass or disappoint; they were deferential and attentive, and willingly subjugated their needs to his. As his sons became adults, with inconvenient personalities and desires, George's feelings for them cooled; by keeping their sisters unmarried, they would remain forever suspended between childhood and maturity, frozen in a condition of permanent emotional dependency. In neglecting to find them husbands, the king ensured that they would remain as dutiful, loving daughters for the rest of their lives.

George did not think of himself as a domestic tyrant; he would have been extremely uncomfortable with the idea that he had deliberately thwarted his daughters' happiness. Instead, he simply persuaded himself that he and they thought as one on the subject. He made no attempt to discover their real feelings, and they did not seem willing to enlighten him. Gloucester, who was aware of the true state of the princesses' minds, 'thought that His Majesty should be apprised of their real sentiments', but made no attempt to do so himself. Nor, more significantly, did their mother. Charlotte knew that her daughters longed to enjoy the benefits of homes and families of their own, but she did nothing to persuade her husband to acknowledge the unfairness of their situation. Mrs Harcourt attributed her inaction to 'a timidity', which her daughters shared. 'Lest they offend him, they keep their wishes too generally unknown to him, though it seems as if, when laid before him, he has no greater pleasure than in obliging them.'[119] The queen understood her husband better than that. She recognised that this was an issue on which he would not be moved, and retreated to her habitual position of saying nothing that would challenge his authority. 'I have so many things I could say,' she once told Lady Harcourt, 'but prudence imposes silence; and that dear little word has so often stood my friend in necessity that I make it my constant companion.'[120] The interests of her daughters were sacrificed to her iron determination never to contradict the expressed desires of her husband. In the face of the king's resolve to keep them at home, the three eldest princesses seemed doomed to mark time, with little to fill their days but the increasingly desperate pursuit of personal accomplishments.

Then, against all expectations, the king suddenly changed his mind. In November 1788, Royal and Augusta were driving in a carriage, taking the air with their father, when he made an announcement that startled them with both its implications and its candour. 'He expressed his concern that he had not secured proper matches for them, but alleged as reason the pain the idea of parting from them always gave him.' Now, he insisted, everything would be different: he would travel to Hanover the following spring, 'and make his court there as gay as possible to draw all the young princes of Germany to it. He told the Princess Royal in particular that if it was not a misalliance, he would consent to her marrying any one of them who was likely to make her happy; for the happiness of his daughters was of more consequence to him than the extent of their husband's dominions.'

It was everything the sisters must have hoped to hear for many years; but they could not bring themselves to exult in their good fortune. The king, usually so healthy, had been ill throughout the summer, his actions and speech becoming unpredictable and erratic. Although 'he behaved to them in the kindest manner' as George delivered his plan, his voice was hoarse, he was extremely agitated, and 'he spoke with a degree of eagerness and rapidity that was distressing to the princesses.'[121] As they travelled back in their carriage, it was plain to both of them that he was a very sick man.

CHAPTER 11

An Intellectual Malady

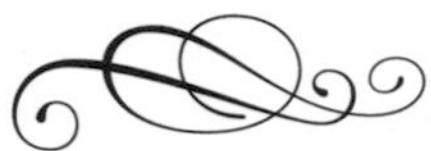

LIKE LORD HERVEY BEFORE HER, Fanny Burney thought the royal family had little true understanding of what it was like to be ill. 'The fatigues of a court attendance are so little understood by them,' she confided to her journal in 1788, 'that persons known to be able to quit their rooms and their bed are instantly concluded to be qualified for all the duties of office.'[1] Her own frequent indispositions were, she thought, greeted with a wounding lack of sympathy by those around her – especially the queen. Charlotte did indeed find the many ailments that beset the female members of her household frustrating. Determinedly healthy herself, she found their continual parade of fevers, headaches and 'lowness of spirits' extremely trying. Fanny, who took her health very seriously, was most offended at any implication of self-indulgence she sensed in the queen's remarks. 'Illness here ... has been so unknown, that it is commonly supposed it must be wilful and therefore meets little notice till accompanied by danger or incapacity of duty,' she wrote tartly, before adding her own explanation for behaviour that so contradicted her usual vision of the natural condescension of her employers. 'This is by no means from hardness of heart – far otherwise – there is no hardness of heart in any one of them; but it is prejudice and want of personal experience.'[2]

Like the queen, George was rarely unwell. He had quickly recovered from a bout of chickenpox in 1761. Four years later, he had been ill with chest pains and a recurring fever which, for a few months, refused to respond to treatment. Tuberculosis was suspected, and his condition had been sufficiently threatening to trigger plans for a regency if he did not rally. Since his recovery he had been as healthy as it was possible for a middle-aged man to be in the eighteenth century. Now aged fifty, he attributed his wellbeing to his ascetic life-style, telling an observer who commented on his careful diet that he simply preferred eating and drinking sparingly to 'growing feeble and diseased' through overindulgence.

His sudden sickness in the summer of 1788, therefore, took every-one – including the king – by surprise. On 12 June, George told his first minister, William Pitt, that he was too ill to leave Kew and come to town, having suffered 'a pretty smart bilious attack' that had caused him severe pain. Writing some weeks later to her brother Augustus in Göttingen, Royal stressed 'how ill our dear Papa has been. His complaint was very disagreeable and indeed alarming for the time that it lasted; the spasm beginning at three in the morning and contin-uing till eight in the evening.'[3] Sir George Baker, the royal doctor, had been summoned – a measure in itself of how ill the king felt, for, as he told Fanny Burney, he 'had a detestation of all physicians' and was extremely averse to consulting them.

No one, least of all Sir George, had any idea what had caused the king's sudden indisposition. 'It is supposed,' wrote the queen, 'that the dryness and the heat of the season has occasioned these violent attacks, for everybody has been troubled with this complaint.'[4] Once the initial spasm had subsided, Baker had little to offer, either as cure or preventative. The best he could suggest was a trip to Cheltenham to take the waters there, which were thought to be particularly effec-tive in curing bilious complaints. The king was persuaded and, with his usual economy, borrowed a house from Lord Fauconberg, and on 12 July set off for the first real holiday he had taken in nearly thirty years. He had no doubt that 'the efficacy of the waters, the salubrity of the air … and above all the exercise of riding and good mutton will do what may at present be wanting.'[5]

'A smaller party for a royal excursion cannot be imagined,' wrote Fanny Burney as she packed for the trip. The queen and her three eldest daughters were to accompany the king. Fanny and Miss Planta travelled with them; few other members of the household were invited. Even so, their departure was not achieved without the upheaval that was inseparable from all royal journeys. 'We were all up at five o'clock,' wrote Fanny, 'and the noise and confusion reigning through the house and resounding all around it, from the quantities of people stirring, boxes nailing, horses neighing and dogs barking, was prodigious.'[6] Once begun, the route westward was an adventure in itself. News of the excursion generated great interest amongst those living on its route, and Fanny noted that the crowd 'waiting for the king and queen to pass was immense and almost unbroken, from Oxford to Cheltenham'. The many spectators were, she observed approvingly, remarkably well behaved: 'So quiet, so decent, so silent … How unlike a London mob!' In more populated places, the curiosity of eager sightseers was even more intense. 'All the towns through which we passed were filled with people as closely fastened to one another as they appear in the pit of a playhouse. Every town seemed all face.' Fanny's goodwill did not, however, extend to the spontaneous musical tributes that accompanied the travellers, and which owed more to enthusiasm than skill. As the sister and daughter of musicians, her judgement was merciless. 'All the way upon the road, we rarely proceeded five miles without encountering a band of most horrid fiddlers, scraping "God Save the King" with all their might, out of tune, and all in the rain.'[7]

When the royal party finally arrived at Cheltenham, Fanny was astonished to discover that Lord Fauconberg's house was really very small for such grand occupants. The queen was unperturbed, showing Fanny to her room 'in excellent spirits'. When Fanny commented on its lack of space, Charlotte assured her that she had seen nothing yet. '"Oh, stay," cried she, laughing, "till you have seen your own before you call it little!"'[8] Once squeezed into their accommodation, the family soon established the orderly routine the king and queen enjoyed. At six in the morning, the king and Royal went to the wells to drink the famous waters (Fanny tried them only once, finding that more than enough). Afterwards, George and Charlotte, together with the three princesses, promenaded together on the gravelled public walks that were at the heart of the town's sedate social life. The king then took a morning walk, which he followed with a lengthy ride in the surrounding countryside. At four, he sat down to dinner and then 'strolled out, like a citizen, with his wife and daughters, on the public walks after seven; and by eleven at night, everything was as completely hushed at Fauconberg Lodge than as at any farmhouse'.[9] Sometimes the royal family stayed up late enough to attend Cheltenham's small playhouse, much to the gratification of the locals. One night, the royal couple saw Mrs Jordan, the celebrated comic actress, perform; the king enjoyed it so much that he sent a present backstage to thank her for the pleasure she had given him. They did not know then that one day, through her long liaison with their third son William, she would provide them with ten illegitimate grandchildren.[10]

Venturing beyond Cheltenham, George and Charlotte saw, for the first time in their lives, something of the country over which they reigned. The king's travels had previously been very circumscribed, taking him mainly across the southern English counties, for naval business at Portsmouth and the Nore (a base in the Thames estuary) and for military reviews on the southern plains. He visited Oxford twice, perhaps because it was so close to the home of the Harcourts in Nuneham Courtenay. The roads he knew best were those that linked Windsor, Kew and London. He never reached the north, Wales, Ireland or Scotland. But now George sought to extend his limited experience, exploring Worcester, where he and Charlotte attended the Three Choirs Festival, and Tewkesbury and Gloucester, where they inspected the cathedral. Not all their trips were to seek out culture or visit antiquities; George was equally keen to observe at first-hand evidence of industrial prosperity. 'I am this instant returned from seeing the most beautiful sight I ever saw,' he wrote eagerly to Pitt, 'namely, the clothing country near Stroud; above 40,000 people were assembled and they all confess the trade is now brisker than the oldest person remembers.'[11] So unusual were these royal journeys that the press covered the king's movements with unprecedented and enthusiastic detail. 'There is nothing, however minute and unimportant, that His Majesty does at Cheltenham but what the newspapers report to us daily,' observed Anthony Storer, a politician of Whiggish sympathies, 'so that we now know more about how he passes his time than if he were living at Buckingham House. He eats cherries, it is found out, like other men, but walks further than most.'[12] Readers could also discover that George ordered bats and balls sent down to Cheltenham so that his servants could play cricket and keep themselves fit. The first royal holiday had, it seems, ushered into being the first royal news reporting.

The king told Sir George Baker that he felt better for his visit. 'The waters certainly agree, they only give good spirits and appetite.' They also delivered a more intimate outcome. 'He finds,' George confided to his doctor – his use of the regal third person contrasting with the personal nature of the information – 'that a pint and a half of the water is the proper quantity to give him two openings … he finds himself in better spirits and has never been obliged to take the rhubarb pills.'[13] A few weeks into the trip, everyone around him thought the king completely recovered from his brief episode of illness. Fanny Burney noticed he had 'a flow of spirits quite unequalled' during his stay. She thought his decision to construct 'a portable wooden house', designed to accommodate his visiting son Frederick, for whom there was no room within Fauconberg Lodge, seemed eccentric and noted that it was pushed forward by the king with an almost manic intensity. But whatever was to be asserted in retrospect, Lady Harcourt was firm that she had seen nothing untoward in the king's behaviour at Cheltenham. 'Living with him as I did, in the most unreserved intimacy from six in the morning to eleven at night … I can most solemnly affirm that I never saw the least symptom of mental derangement, and that the king was invariably good-humoured, and often declared that from the beginning of his reign, he had never known such happiness as he then experienced, from the conviction of being loved by his people.'[14]

When the time came to leave, none of the party wanted to go home. 'Melancholy, most melancholy was the return to Windsor,' declared Fanny Burney on 16 August. She had enjoyed herself and did not look forward to the resumption of the old routine, 'destitute of all that could solace, console or delight; replete with whatever could fatigue harass and depress!'[15] The queen, too, was sad to depart, telling Augustus ruefully that 'we are now returned from Cheltenham after a stay of nearly five weeks, and never did schoolboys enjoy their holidays equal to what we have done our little excursion.'[16]

Once back at Windsor, it was soon obvious that whatever good had been done for the king at Cheltenham was quickly ebbing away. In September, he confessed to Pitt that he did not feel himself and was again under the care of the doctors. He was well enough to celebrate Royal's twenty-second birthday on 29 September with a concert and supper, which went off, Lady Harcourt loyally maintained, very cheerfully; but soon she too had heard that the king was ill again, this time complaining of a stubborn rash. Lady Harcourt recounted that on 12 October, after a day's hunting, 'he told Princess Elizabeth, from whom I had these particulars, that the rash upon his body was gone in, but that were some remains of it on his arm, which he showed her.

She told me it looked very red, and in great weals, as if it had been scourged with cords. She advised him to take some care, but he disregarded the caution.'[17] Against all advice, on 15 October, the king went to London to hold the levee at St James's Palace. 'He ate no dinner, as was frequently his custom on levee days,' noted Lady Harcourt, 'and having had no nourishment but a cup of coffee and a dry biscuit (his common breakfast) at nine in the morning, he went in the evening to the Hanoverian ambassador's … there he ate several pears but nothing solid.' The next day, the king was even more neglectful of himself. 'Early in the morning when the dew was very strong upon the ground, His Majesty walked round Kew and Richmond gardens, and being afraid when he returned that he should hardly be in town time enough for the queen and princesses to be dressed for the Drawing Room, he only pulled off his boots, which were so wet that the water ran out of them, and without changing his stockings, got into the coach.' The consequence of such thoughtlessness was, to eighteenth-century eyes, entirely predictable. 'That night he was seized with spasms in his stomach and bowels which gave him the most excruciating pain.'[18]

The opposition Whig politician Sir Gilbert Elliot heard a similar account of the king's illness, which he reported to his wife in terms far less respectful than those of Lady Harcourt. He too knew the story of the pears, the dew and the wet stockings, but he described what happened next in far greater detail. On returning from the levee, the queen 'wished him to take some cordial, but Georgy boy liked his own way' and refused:

> He was unwell all evening, and went to bed at his usual hour. About one in the morning, he was seized violently with a cramp or some other violent thing in the stomach, which rendered him speechless, and in a word, was 'all but'. The queen ran out in great alarm, in her shift, or with very little clothes, among the pages, who were at first retiring out of respect, but the queen stopped them and sent them instantly for the apothecary at Richmond, who arrived in about forty minutes, during which the king continued in the fit, and speechless.

Like the queen before him, the apothecary 'tried to make him swallow something strong, but the king … still liked a bit of his own way, and rejected, by signs, everything of that sort. They contrived, however, to cheat him, and got some cordial down in the shape of medicine, and the fit went off.'[19]

Sir George Baker, who arrived the following morning, transcribed his own impressions into his diary: 'I found the king sitting up in his bed, his body being bent forward. He complained of a very acute pain in the pit of the stomach, shooting to the back and sides and making respiration difficult.' The king told Sir George that he had 'of late been much troubled in the night by cramp in the muscles of his legs' and that 'he was lame, especially on first going out in the morning'. Baker did what any of his contemporaries would have done faced with a case such as this, and administered a purgative, a copious amount of castor oil and senna. But 'the effect of this being too much', he then gave him laudanum to counteract it. Baker noticed that there was also 'some yellowness in the eyes, and urine bilious'.[20] The king was now considered too ill to travel and the household's planned departure from Kew to Windsor was postponed.

Fanny Burney had heard that the king was ill, but could get no clear information about his condition. She could see that the queen was uneasy, 'but she talks not of it'. As the days passed and the stay at Kew was extended again and again, life there became increasingly uncomfortable. The attendants' clothes had been sent to Windsor against their expected arrival and, as Fanny remarked, 'as to books, there are not three among us'. In such miserable circumstances, Fanny could think of only one thing to occupy her increasingly anxious thoughts. 'I have just begun a tragedy. We are now in so spiritless a situation that my mind will bend to nothing less sad, even in fiction.'[21]

The king himself was aware that he was not improving, and found his official duties increasingly beyond his strength. 'I must admit,' he told Pitt, 'I have been so thoroughly fatigued by the medicines that continued active all night that it has required several hours for my reading my papers.'[22] He still hoped for the best, but on 22 October his condition took a new and alarming turn. Sir George Baker attended him and prescribed his usual purgative. He was completely unprepared for what came next.

A few hours later, the king sent for Baker 'to scold him, as he said, for giving him a medicine that always disagreed with him. His Majesty spoke with so much more warmth and displeasure than usual' that Baker was completely taken aback.[23] He confided to his diary how shocked he was by the king's 'very unusual manner', of which 'I had not the least expectation. The look of his eyes, the tone of his voice, every gesture and his whole deportment, represented a person in the most furious passion of anger. One medicine had been too powerful; another had only teased him without effect. The importation of senna ought to be prohibited, and he would give orders that in future it shall never be given to any of the royal family.' Angrily repeating his complaints over and over again, the king kept Baker for nearly three hours and sent him away so concerned that the doctor wrote immediately to Pitt, 'and informed him that I had just left the king in agitation of spirits bordering on a delirium.'[24]

The next day, the king seemed calmer; but the queen was now very worried about her husband's condition. She asked Baker to urge him not to travel up to London for the levee as she knew he intended, but to stay and rest at Kew. George ignored the doctor's advice. 'I shall go to St James's to show I am not as ill as some have thought,' he wrote on the 24th.[25] If it was intended 'to quiet the fears of the people', the king's appearance in London was not a success. 'It was remarked that he looked ill,' reported Lady Harcourt, 'and that his skin appeared muddled, as if there was an eruption under it that wanted to come out.'[26] His dress was untidy, his speech hurried and agitated. The first minister was among those shocked by his looks, as the king did not fail to notice. He admitted that he no longer felt capable of attending to public business and instructed Pitt not to send him the usual dispatches for a week. He hoped to feel better soon.

Few shared his optimism. William Grenville, a member of Pitt's administration, confessed to his brother that he and his Cabinet colleagues were now seriously worried by the king's worsening condition. 'We put as good a face as we can upon it; but I cannot but own to you that I think there is still ground for a good deal of alarm.' His failure to rally so long after the original attack did not, in Grenville's opinion, bode well. The physical symptoms were bad enough; but other aspects of his behaviour gave even more cause for alarm. 'Part of the king's disorder is an agitation and hurry of spirits which gives him hardly any rest ... independently of the king's great dislike of its being known that he is ill, we have the strongest reasons of policy ... to wish that idea not to prevail.'[27]

Any serious hopes the government entertained of keeping the more unsettling aspects of the king's illness secret were doomed. Throughout October, anyone who had dealings with him could not fail to notice a significant alteration in his behaviour. He was peevish and irritable. He had also become unstoppably voluble. 'He now talked so much more than usual, and spoke to everybody on strange varieties of subjects. His incessant talking became at last so remarkable that it was thought necessary to recommend His Majesty to be a little more silent,' wrote an observer.[28]

One night during this period, he waylaid Fanny Burney in a corridor at Kew. There she 'had a sort of conference with His Majesty, or rather, I was the object to whom he spoke, with a manner so uncommon, that high fever alone could account for it; a rapidity, a hoarseness of voice, a volubility, an earnestness – a vehemence rather – it startled me inexpressibly'. She was at pains to stress that he was not a threatening figure: he behaved 'with a graciousness exceeding all I have ever met with before – it was almost kindness!', but the speed and eccentricity of his conversation puzzled her. She met him again the next day, and found him no better. 'He stopped me and conversed upon his health for near half an hour with that extreme quickness of speech and manner that belongs to fever.' He told her that he hardly slept 'one minute all night'. He was desperate to convince Fanny that he was not really ill. 'Nobody speaks of his illness,' she noted, 'nor what they think of it.'[29] Although his physical symptoms had subsided, and he seemed well enough to undertake the journey to Windsor, nothing could dent his worrying loquacity.

In the midst of this climate of foreboding, 'the queen grows more and more uneasy'. Fanny was not sure what to make of Charlotte's oscillations between anxiety and glacial composure. 'She alarms me, sometimes for herself, at other times has a sedateness that wonders me still more.'[30] In the week to come, all Charlotte's formidable powers of self-control would be tested to the utmost, but, as no one seemed to know what was wrong with her husband, or what to do about it, the long-delayed return to Windsor finally took place on 25 October. When the royal party arrived, all those who had assembled to greet the king were horrified by his disturbed state. 'As the coach drew up to the door,' wrote Lady Harcourt, 'the king saw his four youngest daughters waiting to receive him, and was so overcome that he had a hysteric fit.' The sight of their father, usually so assured and so dignified, in a state of extreme agitation was not what they, or any of those around them, had been expecting. 'His children and attendants were all struck with the alteration in his looks, and he said to Colonel

Goldsworthy, one of the equerries who had always had a great share of his confidence and favour, "I return to you a poor old man, weak in body and mind."'[31] This was the first occasion that the king acknowledged that his illness went beyond the purely physical, and 'from this time', wrote Lady Harcourt, 'he allowed that his disorder was nervous'.[32]

This confession was especially hard for a man who, as Lady Harcourt recalled, 'had always laughed at the idea of nervous disorders'. She herself had 'often been the object of his pleasantry upon this subject'; Lady Harcourt's mother had suffered from 'nervousness', a term which the king dismissed, telling Lady Harcourt that '"You may talk of them as you please, but the complaints you call nervous appear to me to be only to a greater or lesser degree, insanity." Of what really deserved that name, he had a greater horror than any person I have ever conversed with.' He had, Lady Harcourt recalled, 'almost expressed a wish for the death of persons for whom he has had a regard, from the apprehension that such a dreadful calamity was hereditary in their family'.[33] This deep-seated revulsion at the very idea of insanity can only have made the king's next few days even more terrifying to him, as his inability to control his actions became increasingly pronounced. On Sunday the 26th, he went with his family to the service at the chapel at Windsor. 'Just before the sermon started, he seemed to have lost all power over himself, embraced the queen and the princesses and then burst into tears.' The royal pew was an enclosed one, and no one outside it could see the king's distress; but his daughters were, as usual, witnesses to his disturbed and desperate behaviour. The king said to Princess Elizabeth: 'You know what it is to be nervous, but was you ever as bad as this?' When she was fifteen, Elizabeth had endured a series of debilitating 'spasms' which had laid her low for many months. She had made a full recovery, and her symptoms had been very different from those her father displayed, but she knew what was expected of her. 'With great presence of mind,' observed Lady Harcourt approvingly, 'she answered, "Yes,"' and gradually the king calmed down.[34]

The queen was now worried enough to ask Sir George Baker to attend the king without having sought his permission to do so, a considerable step for a woman in whom deference to her husband's wishes was so deeply ingrained. The doctor watched George closely during a concert, and observed that 'he talked continually, making frequent and sudden transitions from one subject to another', but he noted there was 'no incoherence in what he said, nor any mark of false perception'.[35] Clinging on to this sliver of good news, the queen tried hard to keep up some semblance of normal life. On the 28th, she went with the king to visit their old friend Lady Effingham. During their stay, Charlotte thought she had observed 'particular agitation' in his behaviour, and his talking continued at the same frantic pace as ever. On the 29th, Baker arrived to take another look at his patient, discovering him again at a concert, but enjoying it far less than he had on the previous occasion. Music was no longer the pleasure it had always been for him: 'It seems to affect my head; it is with some difficulty I hear it.' He now confessed to Baker 'that his vision was confused, that whenever he attempted to read, a red mist floated before his eyes, and intercepted the objects'.[36]

In the face of such confusing symptoms, Baker had little to say. He was sure the king was no longer feverish, although he continued to attribute his distracted behaviour to delirium. His lameness and general physical debility were, he hoped, the consequences of 'an unformed gout', which had yet to reveal itself and settle recognisably in a distinct part of the body. A diagnosis of gout would, at this stage, have been regarded as a great relief, but Baker looked for its familiar presentation in vain. He was uncertain but still emollient, assuring the worried queen that 'the king was certainly very ill, but that there was nothing that alarmed him'.[37]

The king, however, was not convinced; he kicked his foot against his heel, arguing that 'they make me believe I have the gout, but if it was gout, how could I kick the part without any pain?'[38] Lady Harcourt thought he had drawn his own conclusions about what was happening to him, 'for much of his conversation seemed as if he intended to prepare the queen and princesses for some fatal event'.[39] He made a new will, and began to set his papers in order. The queen urged him to take courage, declaring that 'she thought everybody ought to bear up under their afflictions, and that she had a confidence in God not inflicting more than we are able to bear'. In response, 'he took her round the waist and said, "Then you are prepared for the worst."'[40]

The queen's spirits must have been cast down by the king's pessimistic sense of what was to come. She was also made increasingly anxious by the central role she had begun to play in her husband's disordered mind. On their first return to Windsor, the king had told

Lady Effingham that although he took all the medicines prescribed for him, it was to his wife that he looked for real improvement. 'The queen is my physician, and no man need have a better; she is my friend, and no man can have a better.' Fanny Burney, who witnessed this passionate affirmation, found it very moving; but an avowal that Fanny found 'touching', expressed as it was 'in his hoarse voice and altered countenance', might just as easily have seemed unsettling in its single-minded intensity. The queen's misgivings about her husband's behaviour could only have been made worse by the events of the night of 1 November. When Fanny arrived at Charlotte's bedroom to undress her, the king was already there, as insistent and anxious as ever. 'He was begging her not to speak to him when he got to his own room, that he might fall asleep, as he felt great want of that refreshment. He repeated this desire, I believe, at least a hundred times, though far from needing it, the poor queen never uttered one syllable!' The 'kindness and benevolence of his manner' made no difference at all to the queen's frozen, mute response; nor did his declaration that he 'had no wish but to set the queen at rest'.[41] Charlotte now seemed paralysed with shock at the man her husband had become.

On 2 November, the king went out for an airing in his carriage with Royal and Augusta. It was at this moment, in this distracted condition, that he explained why he had not sought husbands for them and promised to make amends by taking them to Hanover as soon as he was better, where they could choose any princely partners they wished for themselves. 'There was nothing improper in what he said,' maintained Lady Harcourt, implying that perhaps improper things had been said before now, 'yet he spoke with a degree of eagerness that was very disturbing to the princesses.'[42]

An atmosphere of heightened tension engulfed the entire household. 'We are all here in a most uneasy state,' wrote Fanny Burney. The king had given up any pretence at keeping 'the punctuality he used to observe in respect of hours'. Meals went uneaten on the table; 'the drinking coffee and the concert were deferred beyond their usual time, nor could he be prevailed upon to go to bed before two o'clock in the morning'. On eventually retiring, his attention always focussed on Charlotte. 'When he went to the queen's room, he was particularly anxious to see that all the doors were locked,' wrote Lady Harcourt, who added obliquely that 'precautions had however been taken, and two pages attended in the passage to go in if necessary'.[43]

The following day, 3 November, was Princess Sophia's eleventh birthday, but her mother was in no state to celebrate anything. 'The queen is almost overpowered with some secret terror,' wrote Fanny, appalled to see Charlotte's much-tried self-control slipping away from her. 'I am affected beyond all expression in her presence, to see what struggles she makes to support serenity. Today, she gave up the conflict when I was with her, and broke into a violent fit of tears. It was very, very terrible to see.'[44] Hour after hour the queen walked up and down her room, without uttering a single word. The king's very appearance had become a source of horror to her. She told Lady Harcourt that 'his eyes she could compare to nothing but blackcurrant jelly; the veins in his face were swelled, the sound of his voice was dreadful; he often spoke till he was exhausted, and the moment he could recover his breath, began again, while the foam ran out of his mouth.'[45]

It was on 5 November – 'O dreadful day!', as Fanny Burney called it – that the storm which had been brewing since mid-October finally broke over the family's heads. At noon, the king went out in a carriage with the Princess Royal. Fanny watched him leave from her window. He seemed cheerful and smiling; 'but he gave so many orders to the postillions, and got in and out of the carriage twice with such agitation' that she grew more worried. When she arrived at the queen's rooms, she found her spirits 'worse and worse'. Charlotte had been 'greatly offended by some anecdote in a newspaper – the *Morning Herald* – relative to the king's indisposition. She bid me burn the paper,' and ruminated on who could be sent to tell the editor how close to treason he approached.[46]

In the evening, Fanny dined alone with Miss Planta. Neither had much to say. 'A stillness most uncommon reigned over the whole house. Nobody stirred, not a voice was heard, not a motion.' Then, at seven o'clock, Fanny's servant came to tell them that 'the music was all forbid, and the musicians ordered away! … I could not understand this prohibition; all seemed stranger and stranger.' Finally, Mr Digby – Fanny's favourite equerry – came in and asked her if she knew what had happened, 'whether I was yet acquainted how bad all was become, and how ill the king … Oh, my dear friends,' wrote Fanny, 'what a history!'[47]

Gradually she pieced together an account of what had taken place while she and Miss Planta had eaten in anxious silence. Earlier that evening, the royal family had gathered for dinner. The Prince of Wales and Frederick, Duke of York, had come down from London to join them, perhaps hoping to assess their father's condition at first hand. Lady Harcourt heard that the king had raised the emotional temperature from the outset by telling the duke with great feeling 'that he loved him so well it was not in his power to refuse him anything except where the Prince of Wales was concerned; and that though he had been ill used by him, he was his son and should always love him'. As the king's loud and uncomfortable declarations rolled on and on, his wife and children sat horrified around the table, with no idea what to do next. The Prince of Wales, Lady Harcourt said, was so upset 'that he was almost convulsed, and Princess Elizabeth was obliged to rub his temples with Hungary water; but neither this, nor the whole party being drowned in tears appeared to have the least affect upon the king'.[48] From Digby, Fanny Burney heard even more distressing details that Lady Harcourt had perhaps tactfully omitted from her story. 'The king, at dinner had broken forth into positive delirium, which had long been menacing all who saw him most closely; and the queen was so overpowered as to fall into violent hysterics; all the princesses were in misery, and the Prince of Wales had burst into tears.'[49] The prince later told Lord Jersey that his father had thrown him against the wall in a paroxysm of rage.

The queen's tribulations had not stopped with dinner. Lady Harcourt described how she had left the ghastly dining table, 'having put a constraint on herself beyond what she had the strength to support', and when she reached the privacy of her room, she collapsed. Soon the king arrived in pursuit of her. Her lady-in-waiting attempted to tell him that she was ill and could not see him, but George would not be deterred, declaring that he would take care of her himself. 'Presently,' reported Lady Harcourt,

> the king proposed moving Her Majesty into the drawing room where he made a sort of bed upon one of the sofas, and placed her upon it; he then fixed where each of the princesses should sit, and ordered all candles, except two to be put out. Sometimes he hung over the queen with the kindest solicitude, at others he talked to his children with the most paternal fondness, yet in all he said and did, the strongest marks of a deranged mind were visible … it was not until past twelve that he could be prevailed upon to let the queen retire to her apartment.[50]

Allowed at last to go to bed, the queen summoned Fanny Burney, who had been waiting over two hours for the call. 'My poor royal mistress! Never can I forget her countenance – pale, ghastly pale she looked.' Charlotte sat unmoving and silent, waiting to be undressed. Fanny was herself so nervous that she could do little to help, 'my shaking hands and blinded eyes could scarce be of any use'. Eventually the queen spoke. '"How cold I am," she cried, and put her hand on mine; marble it felt! And went to my heart's core!'[51] The ladies could hear the king talking in the bedroom adjoining Charlotte's. 'He would not be further removed.' Fanny was now dismissed, with Miss Goldsworthy, 'by the king's direction', appointed to stay with the queen.

An hour later, the king returned. 'About one o'clock,' reported Lady Harcourt, 'he came into her room; he had not been in bed; he shut the door, and going to the chimney, he took up the light, and then went to the bedside; he held the light to the queen's face and said, "Yes I am not deceived. I thought she would not leave me."' He then turned to Miss Goldsworthy, who was lying on the bed next to the queen, and added, '"Gooly, you are honest, I can depend on you, you will take care of her. They said the king was ill, he was not ill; but now the queen is ill, he is ill too." He then put down the light and walked fast round the room.' Finding her voice at last, 'Her Majesty entreated him to take some rest; and he left her, shutting the door with violence, and locking it.'[52] Fanny Burney heard the next day – perhaps from the queen herself – that the king had 'stayed a full half-hour' watching her in bed. 'The depth of terror during that time no words can paint. The fear of another such entrance was now so strongly upon the nerves of the queen that she could hardly support herself.'[53] In fact, this was the last time Charlotte would see her husband for six weeks.

*

In the early dawn of 6 November, Fanny 'dressed in haste by candle-light, and … stole along the passage in the dark' to go to the queen. Miss Goldsworthy ushered her inside. As soon as she saw Charlotte, Fanny burst into tears, overcome by the queen's misery. 'She looked like death, colourless and wan; but nature is infectious; the tears gushed from her own eyes, and a perfect agony of weeping ensued, which, once begun, she could not stop … when it subsided, and she wiped her eyes, she said "I thank you Miss Burney for making me cry; it is a great relief to me – I had not been able to cry before, all this night long."'[54] Despite her prostrate condition, there was no question of the queen moving to a less exposed location – she had been advised by the doctors not to do so 'lest the king be offended that she did not go to him' – so she, Fanny Burney and Miss Goldsworthy sat immured in her dressing room, forced to listen to the king next door. 'He kept talking incessantly; his voice was so lost in hoarseness and weakness that it was rendered almost inarticulate.' Its tone was, Fanny insisted, 'all benevolence – all kindness – all touching graciousness', but that did nothing to calm Charlotte. 'She would not let me leave her now; she made me remain in the room and ordered me to sit down. I was too trembling to refuse.' Together, the women heard the king repeatedly berating his doctors. 'I am nervous,' he cried, 'I am not ill, but I am nervous; if you would know what is the matter with me, I am nervous.'[55] The princesses asked permission to come and join their mother, but she refused. 'She burst into tears and declared she could neither see them, nor pray while in this dreadful situation, expecting every moment to be broken in upon, and quite uncertain in what manner.' Fear of what the king might do next had filled her with alarm. 'Who could tell to what height the delirium might rise? There was no constraint, no power; all feared the worst, yet none dared take any measures for security.'[56]

Gossip circulating beyond Windsor suggested an even darker explanation for Charlotte's frightened hysteria. Writing in late November, James Bland Burges, a politician with connections to the royal household, reported a disturbing story he had heard: 'The first symptom of the king's madness was his running naked into the queen's room, he insisted upon throwing her on the bed and that the women in the room should stand by to see whether he did well.' A few days later, Burges recorded that the king 'seized the Princess Royal, and attempted to ravish her. She was rescued from him with great difficulty, and he was at such a rage at his disappointment as to strike the queen.' Burges claimed as authority for the account Dr Majendie, an habitué of the royal household, 'who was at Windsor when the affair happened.'[57] It is impossible now to establish the truth of Burges's allegations, but if nothing else, they illustrate the atmosphere of panic that had gripped Windsor, transforming it into a place where anything might be said to have happened.

It was at this point that Sir George Baker's nerve failed him. Faced with a visibly deteriorating patient whose sickness seemed to follow no recognisable pattern, he declared he was not equal to managing the king alone. In the vacuum of all other authority, the twenty-six-year-old Prince of Wales took the decision to call in another physician, and summoned Dr Richard Warren. 'From this fatal step,' Lady Harcourt believed, 'many of the evils that followed resulted.'[58]

In 1788, Richard Warren was considered to be at the very top of the medical profession. Even Lady Harcourt, who disliked him, did not deny that he was a clever man of undoubted skill; but she also thought him supercilious and arrogant, with 'that sort of inflexible firmness that is rarely found in a feeling heart'. When it suited him to do so, he could be charming. He was especially skilled at dealing with wealthy female patients, to whom he judiciously recommended the kind of treatment they would have chosen for themselves, 'dissipation in winter ... and a spell at the watering place they liked best in summer'. In the light of such accommodating prescriptions, he had built himself a fashionable and very lucrative practice. He was extremely rich, and Lady Harcourt heard that he sometimes lent his patients money. When he looked at his own tongue in the mirror each morning, he was reputed to transfer a guinea from one pocket to another. But all of this paled into insignificance before Warren's real besetting sin in the eyes of the king's friends. His patients were drawn almost entirely from among the great Whig aristocrats, the Dukes of Devonshire and Portland, Lord Fitzwilliam and Charles James Fox. These men formed the opposition to the administration of William Pitt, the government party endorsed by the king. 'Through their protection,' wrote Lady Harcourt, 'Dr Warren came to know the Prince of Wales and Carlton House [the prince's London home] soon afforded him an ample field for the display of his talents in political intrigue.'[59]

None of Warren's qualities, personal or political, was such as to commend him to the king, and when he arrived later that day, George refused point blank to see him. Undaunted, Warren eavesdropped on the king from outside his room, where he could hear all that he said. The queen had not been consulted about the summoning of Warren, 'and would never have consented to the calling in of a physician for whom the king had a particular objection', but now he was there, she was desperate to know what he thought about her husband's condition. She waited 'in dread incessant' but 'he neither came nor sent'. A message to Sir George Baker begging him for news was rebuffed: 'he would not speak alone'. Eventually, Charlotte sent one of her ladies to find the recalcitrant doctor, but she returned with the appalling news that Warren had already left the house. 'Run! Stop him!' she said. 'Let me but know what I am to do!'[60]

Charlotte was devastated to discover that rather than calling on her, Warren had instead gone straight to report to the Prince of Wales. There could have been no clearer demonstration of the speed with which her world was collapsing. As her husband's authority fell away, that of her son grew by the hour. In a single day, the internal balance of the family had been completely overturned, and her position rendered entirely provisional.

Fifteen minutes later, Colonel Goldsworthy arrived in her room to bring the message which none of the physicians had been prepared to deliver themselves: 'Her Majesty should remove to a more distant apartment, since the king would undoubtedly be worse from the agitation of seeing her.'[61] Privately, Warren told the prince he believed 'the king's life to be in the utmost danger, and declared that the seizure upon the brain was so violent that, if he did live, there was little reason to hope that his intellects would be restored'.[62] If this was what the queen suspected, no one discussed it with her.

Taken to her new room, which Fanny Burney noticed had only a single door, making it easier perhaps to secure against intrusion, she entirely lost control of her feelings. 'The poor wretched queen once more gave way to a perfect agony of grief and affliction, while the words "What will become of me! What will become of me!" uttered in the most piercing lamentation struck deep and hard into all our hearts.' After nearly thirty years of marriage, a life beyond the all-encompassing presence and authority of her husband was unthinkable to Charlotte; the raw incomprehension of her cries suggests she could imagine no other way of being. 'Never can I forget their desponding sound,' wrote Fanny with a heavy heart; 'they implied such complicated apprehensions.' In her extremity, she at last agreed to see her daughters. 'The three elder hastened down. Oh, what a meeting! They all, from a habit that is become second nature, struggled to repress all outward grief, though the queen herself, wholly overcome, wept even aloud.'[63] For the princesses, the obligation to support their mother took precedence over the anguish they themselves must have felt. Even in the worst of times, their emotions did not come first.

In his part of the house, the king continually asked for the queen and his daughters, but 'they were not allowed to go to him, under the pretence', as Lady Harcourt asserted, 'that they would agitate him'. But if that was indeed the doctors' policy, it was a very ineffective one. The king's enforced isolation did nothing to calm him; on the contrary, Sir Gilbert Elliot heard that the king 'was extremely impatient under this separation, and was indeed violent and outrageous in his attempts to get to [the queen's] apartments. He once forced his way to her door, and finding the outer door made fast, he was near crying and said, "Surely they might have thought one door enough to stop me?"'[64]

By the next day, 7 November, he was so agitated that 'four men were obliged to be constantly by his bed to prevent his jumping out of it'.[65] The well-informed Cabinet member William Grenville wrote to his brother that 'the king has now been two days entirely delirious, and during part of that time, has been thought to be in the most imminent danger'. The doctors seemed helpless, unable to say whether recovery or death was the most likely outcome. 'The other alternative is one to which one cannot look without horror – that of a continuance of the present derangement of his faculties.'[66]

Now Pitt himself came hurrying down to Windsor to confer with the Prince of Wales. He returned to London in a bleak frame of mind, penning a memorandum that concluded, in the light of all he had heard, 'that on the whole, there was more ground to fear than to hope, and more reason to apprehend durable insanity than death'.[67] To others, death itself looked pretty close. Jack Payne, the comptroller of the Prince of Wales's household, heard late that night 'that all articulation even seems to be at an end with the poor king'. The Archbishop of Canterbury was ready to attend him, 'but he is not required to come down, it being thought too late'.[68] 'His recovery is hopeless,' echoed Elliot, 'but he may linger a few days … The queen', he added, almost as an afterthought, 'does not now see him; the state of his head probably rendering the scene too painful to her.'[69]

Isolated, desperate and with no idea what to do next, Charlotte effectively gave up. 'She lived entirely in her two rooms, and spent the days in patient sorrow and retirement with her daughters.' Fanny Burney felt helpless to comfort her. There seemed nothing to do but sit and wait. 'Even my melancholy resource, my tragedy, was now thrown aside. Misery so actual, so living and present, was knit too closely around me to allow my depressed imagination to fancy any woe beyond what my heart felt.'[70]

On 9 November, it was widely reported that the king had died. 'The belief was universal throughout the metropolis,' maintained a contemporary pamphlet, 'that His Majesty was no more, and that the awful event was withheld from publication.' Even Lady Harcourt found it impossible to discover whether the rumours she too had heard were true, so hard was it to 'procure authentic information'. The doctors issued no bulletins. Gilbert Elliot was convinced that this was a deliberate policy, intended to hide the reality of the king's illness from the public. 'The physicians … talk of fever, but I am inclined to believe he has never yet had any fever, in the common acceptance of the word, and that they avail themselves of some occasional quickness of the pulse to avoid the true nature of his distemper.'[71] On 12 November, Dr Warren wrote to Lady Spencer, one of his Whig grandee friends, offering the diagnosis that many had begun to fear was both accurate and inevitable: '*Rex noster insanit; nulla adsunt febris signa; nulla mortis venturae indicia*.' Cloaked in the deliberate obscurity of Latin, Warren stated his opinion that the king was mad, that there was no sign of fever, and no danger to life.

What had caused the king's sudden descent into madness the doctors did not know. In mid-November, Warren told Pitt that they had ruled out 'the idea of its proceeding from some local cause … such as water on the brain, or by some change in the texture of the brain itself, by induration or ossification'. Shortly afterwards, Pitt passed on to his Cabinet colleague Grenville the doctors' first, tentative explanation for the king's condition. 'The cause to which they all agree to ascribe it, is the force of a humour which was beginning to show itself in his legs, when the king's imprudence drove it from thence into his bowels; and the medicines they were then obliged to use for the preservation of his life, have repelled it upon the brain. The physicians are now endeavouring by warm baths and by great warmth of covering, to bring it down again into the legs, which nature had originally pointed out as the best mode of discharge.'[72]

From this diagnosis derived virtually all the medical treatment which the king received over the next five months. Some of the procedures were benign, if useless, such as the 'prescribing of carded wool and woollen bootikins applied to the king's feet'; other, more invasive techniques were positively dangerous. Throughout his illness, the doctors sought to raise blisters on the king's legs as a method of drawing out the malign humour that had settled on his brain. To do so, they used an irritant made from Spanish fly applied as a mustard plaster. This caused eruptions on the skin, which, when infected, discharged pus. Contained in this pus, the doctors believed, were the humours which had caused the sickness, and though unpleasant, blistering was therefore vital in effecting a cure. In practice, the discharging pustules were not only extremely painful, but potentially very harmful. In an age before antibiotics, any infection could, and often did, result in very serious consequences for the patient; to introduce one deliberately was, in retrospect, an act of astonishing recklessness. Blistering also added hugely to the discomfort and misery of the invalid; in every case, it would have been better to have done nothing at all than to have subjected sick and anxious patients to a procedure which could only weaken and distress them.

Yet none of the king's doctors were deliberately cruel, or indeed, by the standards of their day, uninformed. Sir George Baker was president of the Royal College of Physicians, and highly regarded for his application of rational scientific method to medical investigation. He had made his reputation by proving that 'the endemic colic of his native Devonshire' had been caused by the contamination of cider with lead.[73] For all his fashionable manner and titanic self-regard, Richard Warren too was a serious physician who would not have risen to the top of his profession without significant medical skill. They were unable either to diagnose or treat the king's illness not because they were ignorant or wilful, but because it was probably caused by a physiological condition unknown – and indeed unknowable – to them.

It was not until the 1930s that porphyria was eventually identified as an illness. It is a metabolic disorder caused by a genetic malfunction that alters the body's chemistry, resulting in the overproduction of toxins which impact severely on the operation of the nervous system. Porphyrins are the purple-red pigments that give blood its colour. When too many of them are produced, they effectively poison the patient, causing pain and weakness in the limbs, impeding the automatic activities of digestive and respiratory functions, and sometimes affecting the brain, interfering with vision and producing sleeplessness, excitement and confusion.

In 1969, Ida Macalpine and Richard Hunter, a mother and son team, both psychiatrists with an interest in the history of mental illness, first linked the disease – which they termed 'acute intermittent porphyria' – to George III's malady. Their highly influential book *George III and the Mad-Business* swept away years of conflicting interpretations of what ailed the king, replacing them with a diagnosis still accepted by many historians as the most convincing explanation. They identified a number of the king's symptoms, particularly his discoloured, purple-hued urine, as indications that he was suffering from porphyria. Noting that it was an inherited disorder, they examined the medical histories of several of George's ancestors, including Mary Queen of Scots, her son James I and grandson Henry, Prince of Wales, who died young, and concluded that they too had been affected by the condition. They speculated on whether some of the king's more immediate relatives, including his youngest sister Caroline, might also have died from it.

However, more recent research has questioned many of their findings, arguing that 'the porphyria diagnosis was based on weak foundations, bolstered by indiscriminate aggregation of symptoms and suppression of contrary indicators'. In a scholarly article written in 2010, T. J. Peters and D. Wilkinson conclude that 'it remains very unlikely that the king was suffering from porphyria'. Peters and Wilkinson dispute many of the connections made by Macalpine and Hunter between the symptoms presented by the king and porphyria. They suggest that the hoarseness from which he suffered was more likely to be caused by incessant talking than by the disease, as loss of voice in a porphyric case indicated that the condition was so advanced and severe that, in the eighteenth century, it would 'almost certainly be a prelude to death'. They argue that the lameness and limb pains from which the king suffered were spasmodic, and at other times he was capable of great strength and energy. They even dispute the well-known linkage between the discoloured urine produced by the king and the diagnosis, claiming that the relatively few examples cited by Macalpine and Hunter of this occurrence were subject to other interpretations, and that there were simply not enough of them to confirm a conclusion. The urine of a genuinely porphyric patient would have been noticeably and more consistently discoloured, evident to all the doctors treating the king. In rejecting the diagnosis of porphyria, Peters and Wilkinson were initially cautious about offering an alternative explanation: 'It appears very unlikely that the king was suffering from porphyria, and therefore the causes of his "madness" remain an unsolved mystery.'[74]

In a further article, Timothy Peters and co-author Allan Beveridge moved towards a different interpretation of the illness. Examining some of the early material collected by Sir George Baker, they concluded that the king had probably suffered initially from 'recurrent episodes of obstructive jaundice'.[75] This may have triggered some of his initial agitation, but for Peters and Beveridge, George's later behaviour is best understood as primarily a mental condition. They attribute it to late-onset 'bipolar disorder with recurrent manic episodes', arguing that the king's successive bouts of illness were often linked to periods of extreme stress in his public life.[76] In this reading, the 'royal malady' was indeed, as was widely maintained at the time, a psychiatric rather than physiological disorder.

If, even now, there is such disagreement about the causes of the king's condition, it is hardly surprising that George's doctors were baffled and confused by his wildly fluctuating state. If the disease was porphyria, they could have done very little to control it. It still has no cure, and is treated by careful management of lifestyle; significantly, avoidance of stress is seen as an important contributor to the well-being of patients. In the late eighteenth century, there was nothing that could have been done for the king, except perhaps to leave him alone and hope for spontaneous recovery, as the severity of the attack receded. If his illness was a recurring psychiatric disorder, given the state of contemporary understanding of mental health, a do-nothing approach might also have been the best prescription for George's care. Instead, as they sought to make sense of a sickness that seemed to respond to none of their remedies, the king's doctors subjected him to months of painful and humiliating treatment that could deliver no effective result.

At Windsor, the Prince of Wales was now in charge. 'Nothing was done but by his orders,' noted Fanny Burney mournfully. Almost his first action was to place the house under a kind of informal exclusion zone. To avoid the spread of damaging speculation and gossip, he directed that no one was to be allowed entry who was not already in residence. No exceptions were made. Even Lady Harcourt, one of George and Charlotte's oldest and most trusted friends, was denied admission. When Leonard Smelt, another of the king's inner circle and once the prince's tutor, was also turned away, he was so angry that he went straight back home to Yorkshire. 'From this time commenced a total banishment from all intercourse out of the house,' recorded Fanny, 'and an unremitting confinement within its walls.'[77] She herself was one of the confined, and barely went outdoors.

Kept away from his family, and denied the opportunity to see his friends, George's world too had become much smaller since 5 November. The doctors visited regularly, but more as perplexed observers than to offer coherent advice. The daily management of the king was left in the hands of his pages and his equerries: Mr Digby, Colonel Goldsworthy, General Harcourt (the brother-in-law of Lady Harcourt) and the soldier and former MP Robert Fulke Greville.

Greville, unusually for a man entirely free of literary pretension, kept a detailed diary during the gruelling months of his attendance on the king. He spent more time with him than anyone else during the worst of his disorder, and his journal consistently provides the most illuminating insights into George's shifting state of mind and body. Greville was a straightforward, unpretentious character of the kind the king liked best. He was an aristocrat, the third son of the Earl of Warwick (in her journals, Fanny Burney called him 'Colonel Wellbred'). He was passionately fond of horses and riding and, like the king, took an informed interest in agriculture. He probably would have described himself – approvingly – as a simple man, but his diary reveals a thoughtful, independent and subtle mind. He knew the king better than any of the medical attendants now around him, and consequently understood how profound had been the change in the very essence of his personality. He was often sceptical of the value of the treatment he saw George endure, but appreciated more than most how wild and unmanageable he could be, and how necessary it was to take some measures to control him. Like everyone else, he was puzzled by the vertiginous speed of the king's decline, and by the extreme swings in his mood; but even in the blackest moments, he never lost a sense of affection for a man whom, in happier times, he had clearly liked, and who had clearly liked him.

In its very first pages, Greville's diary captures with stark clarity just how disturbed the king had become. He slept very badly, rarely more than two or three hours at a time, and never stopped talking. He had occasional moments of clarity, but these were inevitably succeeded by acute confusion. 'I saw him this night sit up and eat his posset, and afterwards take his draught,' he wrote on 11 November. 'The former he ate well, and seemed as composed as ever, but the ramblings continued and were more wild than ever, amounting, alas, to an almost total suspension of reason – No sleep tonight – The talking incessant throughout.'[78] On the 12th, the king was quiet in the morning, but by eleven o'clock, 'he became more loud and his voice more exerted than I had ever heard it, and he became much agitated and the subjects changed. He now talked much of Eton College, of the boys rowing, etc., but everything he mentioned was with great hurry and exertion.' This lasted for two hours, at the end of which, 'in a violent perspiration, he called to have the windows opened and complained of burning.'[79]

Later in the day, lying on his bed, he seems to have suffered convulsions: 'HM had a violent struggle, jerking very strongly with his arms and legs, but made no attempt to rise.' Afterwards, Greville noticed he was almost himself for a while, 'asking if he might have clean linen ... and on one of his pages offering to assist him in putting on his flannel waistcoat, he said, "No, sir, I can do that myself when I have the use of my own hands."'[80]

On the 13th, encouraged by such episodes of lucidity, even the cautious Greville began to wonder if the king was indeed improving. 'He awoke with more composure and recollection than he had obtained since his illness and remained for a longer time so. He drank his tea and ate his bread and butter with appetite – he knew everybody and conversed rationally with all. He arranged his watches and seemed more cheerful and more like himself, and we all entertained hopes of much good and amendment.' But as the night came on, his delirium returned. The king woke at two in the morning, 'and alas, at waking, his ramblings returned, and dampened our eager hopes'.[81]

Even the slenderest grounds for optimism were earnestly seized on by Fanny Burney when they filtered back to her apartments at the other end of the house. When yet another doctor was added to the 'medical tribe' in attendance, Fanny lost no time in buttonholing him. The new man, Sir Lucas Pepys, was what Fanny called 'a hoper'. He gave her 'such unequivocal assurances of the king's recovery' that she ran immediately to the queen's rooms to pass on the good news. She found few takers for her encouraging information. 'I waited in the passage where I met Lady Charlotte Finch, and tried what I could to instil in her mind the hopes I entertained; this however, was not possible; a general despondency prevailed throughout the house, and Lady Charlotte was infected with it very deeply.' When at last she saw the queen, she could do nothing to lighten her mood. Her positive account 'was received most meekly by the most patient of sorrowers'.[82]

The queen was right to be cautious. On the 15th, George's condition was worse again. Greville no longer believed he was getting any better, partly because the king now insisted he was fully restored to health. 'He has spoke much of his recovery, observing (poor man) that he has been very ill, but that he is well now, and says that he has been light-headed.' But his behaviour contradicted his words. He spent the day issuing hollow and confusing orders, in a parody of his usual regal role, telling Colonel Goldsworthy 'to go to Eton to order the boys a holiday on account of his recovery – To prepare the queen for the firing of the guns at twelve o'clock on the same occasion, and ordering the Dettingen *Te Deum* to be sung in church, etc., etc.'[83] Later in the evening, 'sensible (without prompting) that he was talking very fast', in an attempt to slow himself down, he decided to make use of the royal third person. '"The king did so" – "the king thinks so" – etc. This correction he thus explained, "I speak in the third person as I am getting into Mr Burke's eloquence, saying too much on little things."'[84] General Harcourt told his wife that the king 'spoke without ceasing from one o'clock this morning, and when Warren told him he ought not to do so, he said, "I know that as well as you, it is my complaint, cure me of that and I shall be well."'[85] By 18 November, his voice was rasping and he had developed 'a catch in his throat', but still his conversation rolled unstoppably on, 'one subject succeeded by another before the one begun was finished'.[86]

Robert Greville observed that, despite all his difficulties, the king had not yet become an abject or broken figure. He was used to being obeyed, and did not easily surrender the ability to exert his will. 'I think I foresee from late occurrences that HM will ere long give more trouble to his attendants than hitherto,' wrote Greville gloomily. He thought a struggle for mastery was inevitable. 'HM, from being somewhat recovered in bodily strength, believes himself to be almost well, and in consequence, now tries to command, and struggles hard for obedience.' Even getting the king to take a bath turned into a process of negotiation: 'he proposed terms if he took it'.[87] He attempted to regulate every last detail of Greville's dress and behaviour. 'He has ordered how I shall be dressed and where stationed in my next watch – I am ordered to be in the room adjoining his own apartment, to be dressed in a plain coat and to be very neat.' More ominously, 'he has asked for the Master Key of the Queen's Lodge and he battles hard and very often to prevail in having it delivered to him.'[88]

Attempts to shave the king proved equally difficult. The king insisted he would not be shaved; after much argument he finally consented, 'but when half shaved, he refused to let the other half be finished, unless certain indulgences were granted'. More argument took place, during which the king 'remained half shaved, a singular appearance as he had not been shaved for upwards of a fortnight'. Eventually the king was persuaded to allow one of his pages, Mrs Papendiek's husband, to finish the job, though it took him 'above two hours'.[89] In this phase of his illness, as Greville knew better than anybody, managing the king was no easy task.

This was especially so when he was in the grip of the powerful delusions which clouded his mind. In a lucid spell, he described 'some of the phantoms of his delusion during his delirium – Said he thought there had been a deluge – That he could see Hanover through Herschel's telescope – That he had thought himself inspired, etc.'[90] 'Sometimes,' noted Greville, 'he doubted his own accuracy in what he was saying, and would ask me if such and such things had been so, as, said he, "I have been very much out of order."'[91] On other occasions, he was quietly melancholy. 'In one of his soliloquies he said, "I hate nobody, why should anyone hate me?" Recollecting a little, he said, "I beg pardon, I do hate the Marquis of Buckingham."'[92] He could also be completely ungovernable, especially towards his doctors. He was said to have flung Sir George Baker's wig in his face, thrown him on his back, 'and told him he might star gaze'.[93] When Warren once annoyed him, 'the king advanced up to him and pushed him'. Greville and another equerry stepped in and rescued the doctor, leaving the king furious 'and foaming with rage'.[94]

The king's relations with his physicians now reached a new low. He told Greville that they 'had been forced upon him, and dwelt on the treatment he had received from the doctors with much sensibility'. Greville attempted to pacify him, explaining that they were acting for his own good, his recovery was dependent on his remaining quiet and calm, 'and that the trifles that had been withheld from him, and the occasional restraints he had experienced had been measures which had been adopted solely to this point, and they would cease in a very short time.'[95]

Behind Greville's careful use of the word 'restraints' lurks a multitude of possible interpretations. The MP George Selwyn had heard that on 20 November Warren had been deputed 'in some set of fine phrases to tell His Majesty that he is mad and must have a strait waistcoat'. None of the diarists close at hand – Fanny Burney, Lady Harcourt or Greville himself – mentions the king being placed in one at this point. This could arise from delicacy – nowhere in her extensive account of the king's illness does Fanny use the words 'madness' or 'insanity' – but it is more likely that George had been subjected to the less symbolically significant process of 'sheeting' as a method of controlling his agitation. This involved the patient being 'swaddled with fine linen', their limbs confined and controlled. It was not likely to have increased the king's goodwill towards his doctors, who were faced with an impossibly difficult task in attempting to subdue a man who was also their monarch. As Selwyn commented tartly, 'If it should please God to restore His Majesty to his senses … I should not like to stand in the place of that man who has moved such an address to the Crown.'[96]

Greville certainly believed that the physicians were inhibited by the king's status in their dealings with him: 'They appear to shrink from responsibility, and to this time, have not established their authority, though pressed to by every attendant.' The doctors had failed to take command. Without their leadership and guidance, the attendants were rudderless, subject to every changing order. 'From those thus appointed,' complained Greville, clearly stung by the equerries' mounting sense of inadequacy into uncharacteristic forcefulness, 'we should have plain and positive directions in an anxious and difficult charge. We ought not to be embarrassed by fluctuating decisions, nor puzzled with a multitude of directions from other quarters … All of us are desirous to do our best for the good and comfort of our dear king, but we must be plainly and properly directed in our course.'[97]

Nowhere was the disruptive effect of the 'fluctuating decisions' – so deprecated by Greville – so apparent as in the management of George's desire to see his children. The king, who had been visited by none of his family since the terrible night of 5 November, told Greville that he wanted very much to see his daughters, 'and desired I would look across the garden to the Lower Lodge to see if I could observe any of his children at the windows, expressing at the same time a great anxiety to see them and desired an attendant might be sent to them, to request that they might show themselves before the Lower Lodge, if only for a few minutes'. When the doctors were consulted, they advised against it. Greville thought the decision wrong, 'but acquiescence to it rested not with me'.[98]

Then the doctors changed their minds. On 24 November, 'they thought they would try what effect the letting him see his children in the garden would have', wrote Mrs Harcourt, the general's wife. 'When he was told he was to do so, he at first seemed pleased, but as the time approached, he grew distressed and said – "No, I cannot bear it; no, let it be put off till evening, I shall be more able to see them then."' The doctors were told of the king's sudden reluctance, but decided to let the experiment go ahead anyway. 'So, instead of stopping the royal family, who were just going into the garden, they let them go on.'

What followed was a psychological disaster. 'The king seemed to struggle with himself to bear it, but ran to open the windows, which were screwed down. They made a great bustle about his having appeared to wish to break the window to speak to his children,' continued Mrs Harcourt; 'surely if he did, nothing could be more natural.' The king urged one of his gentlemen to 'go down and beg them to come near; they did so, and he called to them all through the window'. The last time the princesses had seen their father he had been in a state of excited confusion. Now, if anything, he seemed worse – frantic and alarmed. 'Poor souls, they were all so much affected, and Princess Elizabeth was so near fainting, that they were obliged to go in immediately, but I hope he did not see how much they were agitated; the Princess Royal was quite overcome, and so was Princess Mary; and in truth, they all seemed more dead than alive when they got in the house. Unluckily,' added Mrs Harcourt, 'the king had his nightcap and gown on, which, with his appearance being very pale, made a change in his appearance that could not fail to shock them.'[99] She had no doubt who was to blame for the debacle. 'I know not what the physicians mean by their conduct; they seem to be amusing themselves, as they would with any other singular character, and feel no more for him than they would a dog or a cat.'[100]

It was hard to find any relief from the oppressive atmosphere that hung so heavily on everyone at Windsor. On 25 November, Fanny met Robert Greville in a corridor. The two diarists 'condoled on the state of things. I found him wholly destitute of all hope, and persuaded the malady was a seizure for life. How happy for me that I am made of more sanguine materials! I could not think as they think, and be able to wade through the labours of my office.'[101] She acknowledged, sadly, that few shared her optimism. Lady Charlotte Finch 'is no hoper; she sees nothing before us but despair and horror'. Even Colonel Digby 'now leans to the darker side, though he avoids saying so'.[102] All news was bad news. General Harcourt told his wife, 'I fear we have gone from bad to worse. The whole of yesterday, and particularly in the evening, the king was more agitated and unmanageable than ever; so much so that it was not without difficulty that he could be controlled, and several of the gentlemen in attendance were more than once obliged to be called in.'[103] On the same day, the king 'gave one of his pages a sharp slap on the face, with a violence by no means usual to his natural dispositions'. He was profoundly sorry afterwards, and on going to bed, 'called for the same page, took him by the hand, and asked his pardon twenty times'.[104] Then, in the midst of all this unhappiness and despair, the Prince of Wales decided the time had come to move the king to Kew.

By 26 November, Sir Gilbert Elliot knew all about the prince's plan. 'He is, I believe, pretty sick of his long confinement at Windsor, and it is very natural that he should be so, for besides the scene before him, he has been under greater restraint in his behaviour and way of life than he has ever known since he was his own master.'[105] It was said the doctors had agreed to it as they hoped, once returned nearer to London, to resume some of their regular practices there. In fact, the move was, on one level at least, designed to improve conditions for the king. At Kew, where the gardens were extensive and enclosed, he could take more exercise than was possible in the exposed terraces and parks of Windsor. But, as the prince himself explained to the king's attendants, greater privacy would also permit the adoption of more punitive measures: 'sad necessity ... obliged the faculty to declare that they found that lenient measures increased the malady, and that they had determined among more coercive ones'.[106]

For some weeks, even those most sympathetic to the king's predicament had been asking for the implementation of a firmer regime; at Kew, such a policy would be far less visible. Everyone knew there was little chance that George would go willingly. He was deeply attached to the life he had built for himself at Windsor, regarding the place as a symbol of everything he had striven to create over the years; a manifestation of both dynastic continuity and family stability. It was where he felt most rooted and at ease; it was, more than anywhere else, his home. Although he had been happy at Kew, it did not have for him the deeper meaning and resonance of Windsor. His extreme reluctance to be taken there also owed as much to the way the decision was made as to the destination itself. George had spent all his adult life in absolute charge of his personal destiny. It had been nearly thirty years since anyone had overruled or contradicted his wishes. Now, all his accustomed self-determination had been peremptorily removed. He was not consulted about his removal, and his known hostility to the idea was disregarded. There could have been no clearer demonstration of the degree to which power had deserted him. It was hardly surprising that the first coercive measures used against the king would be those employed to ensure that he went at all.

When Colonel Digby told Fanny Burney what was intended, her immediate response was that the king 'will never consent to quit Windsor', though she suspected that, in the end, the alliance between the doctors and the Prince of Wales would be too powerful to be resisted.[107] The queen, too, was deeply apprehensive about the scheme. She knew the king did not want to go, and agreed to it only 'with the extremest reluctance'.[108] The prince had persuaded Pitt, the Lord Chancellor and the Cabinet that the move to Kew was a necessary one. Despite her misgivings, Charlotte did not resist what now seemed inevitable. It was unthinkable, however, that she would not accompany her husband. Mrs Harcourt, who wondered if she should not have shown a little more backbone, believed she would stand firm on that, at least. 'I shall be surprised if she does not insist on going with him; if she suffers herself to be parted from him, he is lost forever, but at such an important moment I hope she will act with spirit.'[109] When the prince did indeed suggest that his mother remain at Windsor while her husband went to Kew, the queen gathered up enough remnants of her dignity to refuse point-blank: 'Prince of Wales, do it at your peril; where the king is, there shall I be.'[110]

On the day appointed for the move – 29 November – the queen's courage faltered. 'Her mind now quite misgave her about Kew; the king's dislike was terrible to think of, and she could not foresee in what way it might end.' The plan was that she and her daughters should leave Windsor first, 'and then the king should be told that they were gone, which was the sole method they could devise to prevail with him to follow. He was then to be allured by the promise of seeing them at Kew.'[111] The queen and the princesses did as they were ordered, although in tears and with a mounting sense of disquiet. Once at Kew, 'the suspense with which the king was awaited [was] truly dreadful'. The queen had decided to return that night if he did not appear, and, as a result, no one was allowed to unpack. Meanwhile, back at Windsor, 'in what confusion was the house! Princes, equerries, physicians, pages – all conferring, whispering, plotting and caballing how to get the king to set off.'[112]

Things went quite as badly on the journey as Greville had expected. 'The king most stoutly objected to every hint for his removal, and would not get up.'[113] In the face of his refusal to cooperate, it was eventually decided to send for the first minister. 'Accordingly, Mr Pitt went in and, telling the king that it was a fine day, asked him if he would not get up and set off to Kew where the queen had gone.' Just as Charlotte had feared, the king did not take this news well. 'The king objected, and said the queen had gone without leave, and that she should return to supplicate his pardon.' George was resistant to all inducements, attempting, as he always did, 'to make terms', agreeing to go only if he could travel in his own coach or with the Princess Royal. 'Mr Pitt, baffled in his endeavours, left the apartment and the king continued in bed.' When Greville and General Harcourt came to talk to him, 'he became very angry, and hastily closed the bed-curtains and hid himself from us'. Later, he showed the equerries letters which they thought he had written to request a military force to rescue him. Finally, the physicians marched into his room in a phalanx, told him he must go and that 'if he continued his refusal longer, he would be forced'. Eventually, he asked if Greville and General Harcourt would accompany him, and on their agreeing, 'he rose and dressed'.[114]

Having at last got on their way, at Datchet Bridge on the Thames 'twenty loyal tradesmen appeared. As the king's carriage drove by them, they bowed respectfully and took a melancholy leave.' Seeing them, the king 'felt the greatest emotion' which Greville had seen him display so far. 'The "big tear" started in his eye, and putting his hand before his face, he said with much feeling, "These good people are too fond of me," and then added with an affecting sensibility, "Why am I taken from the place I like best in the world?"' When they passed through Brentford, 'a drunken man halloed out as the carriage passed.

The king mistook this, and thinking the shout was intended against him, said that they often hissed him as he passed this town.'[115] Soon the gates of Kew appeared; once inside, the king was not to be seen again for four months.

*

If George's condition had been bad at Windsor, at Kew it soon became far worse. During his confinement there, the extremity of the king's behaviour exposed all the fracture lines in his family that decorum, discipline and distance usually concealed. Without the iron certainty of his will, the centre did not – perhaps could not – hold. Relations between mother and son, husband and wife, daughters and parents, all were subjected to excruciating and unprecedented strain; and none of them, including the king himself, ended the period quite as they had begun it.

The king's arrival at Kew was even more disturbing than his departure from Windsor. He left his carriage with his usual dignity, but on entering the house, 'making a run, he attempted to go into the suite of apartments on the left. His intentions were baffled on finding the door locked, and he evidently showed much disappointment. He had expected to find the queen and his family at dinner in those apartments.'[116] Instead he was ushered into a series of rooms on the right. The king considered, with some justification, he had been tricked. He had been told that if he went to Kew, he would see his family, but they were no more visible here than they had been at Windsor. He blamed the queen, declaring that she had betrayed him. Perhaps as a result, Greville thought the king had become, if possible, even more manic in his behaviour. 'He told us that though a bed had been prepared for him, he would not go to bed, and dwelt on his firm intention to tire out his attendants. He remarked that he was very strong and active, and in proof of this, he danced and hopped with more agility than I suspected could have been in him.' Greville could hardly bear to watch. 'The light of such an exhibition in our dear king, and so much unlike himself, affected me most painfully.'[117]

On 1 December, he was no better. Greville also noticed a new and worrying addition to the king's repertoire of problems. 'In his conversation, oaths, which had never yet been heard from his lips, now for the first time were blended not infrequently with indecencies.'[118] On the following day, he descended to a new depth of misery. 'So much was he depressed in thought, that he even gave hints of being tired of his existence, and actually entreated his pages to despatch him.' There was still the occasional lucid interval. 'When more composed, the king resorted to an occupation not uninteresting to him in settled days. He drew plans of the house, and sketched alterations in it; this he did with tolerable accuracy.' In moments like this, Greville was sure the king was aware of his situation. 'An observation dropped from him this morning, which marked the sense he had of his misfortune pretty strongly. Having drawn a line pretty firmly and straight, he approved, by saying to a page, "Pretty well for a man who is mad."' But later in the same day, 'he was mischievously jocose, and at which time, burnt two wigs belonging to his pages. At another, he was childishly playful, begging romps and making his pages wheel him around the room.' All talk of lasting 'amendment' had long disappeared.[119]

Elsewhere in the house, silent misery prevailed. The queen, princesses and their attendants were established in a suite on the first floor, where Princess Augusta camped out on a small bed placed in her mother's room. Clearly Charlotte was still terrified of being 'broken in upon' again. The other princesses and their much-reduced household were distributed along a maze of dark passages, their names chalked on the doors by the Prince of Wales, who had personally allocated everyone's rooms. They were not immediately above the king – everything there had been shut up lest he 'be tantalised by footsteps overhead' – but near enough to be aware of what went on downstairs. On the first night at Kew, Fanny Burney could not sleep. 'I thought I heard the poor king … his indignant disappointment haunts me. The queen too was very angry at having had promises made in her name which could not be kept.'[120] Like her husband, Charlotte 'had passed a wretched night and already lamented leaving Windsor'.

The house itself was extremely uncomfortable. It was rarely used as a winter residence, and was cold, draughty and not very clean. 'The parlours were without fires and washing,' noted Fanny as she crept along the frozen corridors. Colonel Digby ordered carpets to be installed in the princesses' rooms, at his own expense, so cheerless did their surroundings appear. Without Digby's initiative, nothing would have been done. 'So miserable is the house at present that no general orders to the proper people are ever given or thought about … everyone is absorbed in the calamity.' Digby also planned to supply the princesses 'with sandbags for windows and doors, which he intended to bring and place himself. The wind which blew against these lovely princesses, he declared, was enough to destroy them.'[121]

The queen's spirits, low enough already, can hardly have been improved by such oppressively spartan conditions. As her husband grew worse, she knew a decision had to be made about his treatment, which she could neither avoid nor devolve to anyone else. Fanny wrote that 'The length of the malady so uncertain, the steps which now seemed requisite so shocking; for new advice, and such as only suited disorders that physicians in general relinquish, was now proposed, and compliance or refusal were almost equally tremendous.'[122] Hidden in Fanny's deliberately elusive prose is a reluctant acknowledgement that the king's illness was now considered by all those around him to be madness – and that the summoning of specialist help could not much longer be avoided.

It came in the form of seventy-year-old Francis Willis, a clergyman who had qualified as a physician, together with his sons John, Thomas and Robert Darling Willis. Early in his medical career, Francis had decided to devote himself to the treatment of madness and, with the help of his sons, established a highly regarded private asylum at Greatford in his native Lincolnshire. He had treated Lady Harcourt's mother, and it was probably on her recommendation that he was invited to attend the king. Almost from the moment they arrived, the Willises and their methods created controversy. Dr Willis 'is considered by some as not much better than a mountebank,' sniffed Lord Sheffield, 'and not far different from those who are confined in his house. That such a man should be called in … has caused some jealousy; but the opinions of the physicians are not much respected.'[123]

Certainly Francis Willis did not inspire much regard among 'the medical tribe' already established around the king. He was an unpolished, unsophisticated man, with no experience of courts. Unlike the other doctors, he was not a member of the Royal College of Physicians. Warren declared that he did not consider him 'in the light of a physician' at all, although he quickly delegated to Willis the difficult and exhausting task of the daily management of the king. 'I took the liberty of speaking to him with some degree of authority,' Warren admitted; he clearly thought of Willis as a man of little intellectual or professional expertise, to be kept totally under his command. When, in response to the clamour for information about the king's state, regular medical bulletins were at last issued by the physicians, Warren ensured that Willis was not allowed to sign them until instructed by the Lord Chancellor to let him add his name to the others. Teased and patronised by everyone around him, including his patient, Willis was an outsider, never treated as a medical or a social equal by those compelled to act as his colleagues. None of this seems to have mattered much to him. He was sure that he could cure the king where everyone else had failed, and it was this unshakeable certainty that kept him buoyant in the face of all disappointments.

The queen had initially been very reluctant to agree to the summoning of Willis, as it was 'a measure which seemed to fix the nature of the king's attack in the face of the world; but necessity and strong advice had prevailed over her repugnance.'[124] George shared his wife's sense of shame, telling one of his pages that, 'as Dr Willis was now come, he could never more show his face again in this country and that he would leave it forever and retire to Hanover'. His first meeting with Willis, on 5 December, had not gone well. Although George received him 'with composure … and seemed very anxious to state to him that he had been ill but was now quite well again', his dislike of doctors soon triumphed over his initial politeness. He observed that Willis's dress 'bespeaks you of the Church, do you belong to it?' Willis said that he 'did formerly, but lately I have attended chiefly to physic'. 'I am sorry for it,' answered the king, 'for you have quitted a profession I have always loved, and you have embraced one I most heartily detest. Alter your line of life, ask what preferment you want and make me your friend. I recommend you Worcester.'[125] Willis had gamely attempted to defend himself. 'Sir, our saviour himself went about healing the sick.' 'Yes, yes,' replied the king, 'but he had not £700 a year for it.'[126]

In the evening of his first day at Kew, Willis returned to the king's room and demonstrated the techniques he was to employ in treating his patient. He later explained to Greville that 'he "broke in" patients, "like horses in a manège", as his expression was.'[127] Like his colleagues, Willis believed that the king would only improve when he was able to control himself and act calmly; but Willis was convinced measured behaviour did not just emerge from within – it could be imposed from without. A patient could be compelled into calmness by the authority of another – especially if that other was himself. Willis took pride in his ability to quell all forms of dissension by the sheer force of his gaze. For all his apparent simplicity, he was not easily intimidated. When he was examined by a parliamentary committee investigating the king's condition, he made short work of the celebrated politician and fiery orator Edmund Burke – by any standards no flinching spirit. Willis told Lady Harcourt that Burke had asked him 'what methods he used to subdue the king when he was outrageous. Willis answered, "I do it by my eye", and at the same time, darted such a look at his antagonist as made him shrink into himself and stopped his questions for that time.'[128]

The king began their meeting with 'much inconsistency and too much eagerness. He again launched out in strong invective against his physicians, and abused the profession.' Willis was unperturbed, raising his voice when the king raised his, never wavering or retreating. 'The king became violently enraged, rushed in great agitation against Dr Willis, with both hands, intending to push him away but not to strike him.' Unmoved, Willis told him 'he must control himself, or he would put him in a strait waistcoat. On this hint, Dr Willis went out of the room and returned with one in his hand … It was in a paper and he held it directly under his arm. The king eyed it attentively, and, alarmed at the doctor's firmness of voice and procedure, began to submit. He promised to go to bed, and with difficulty, went to the next apartment and undressed.' For Greville, this was the moment he had long hoped for. 'It was immediately necessary to have this struggle. He seized the opportunity with judgement and conducted himself throughout the interview with wonderful management and force.' For the first time, Greville allowed himself a glimpse of hope: 'This seems to have been the first solid step leading to permanent recovery that has taken place as yet.'[129]

Although in reality the king's condition continued pretty much unchanged, Willis introduced order, direction and, above all, a glint of optimism into the darkness that prevailed at Kew. 'I have great hopes of His Majesty's recovery,' he maintained determinedly. Given the particular stresses to which the king's situation exposed him, he was reluctant to predict precisely when this might occur, but that it would eventually take place, he had no doubt. Willis's indefatigable conviction gave encouragement where there had been none before, and he was treated like a hero by the king's friends. Fanny Burney thought him 'a man in ten thousand: open, honest, dauntless, light-hearted, innocent and high-minded'. The queen was equally impressed. She quickly came to regard Willis, whose arrival she had so dreaded, as an unlikely ally in her ordeal. She was, she said, 'very much dissatisfied with Sir George Baker and Dr Warren, and very well satisfied ... with Dr Willis', whom she wished 'could be left to care for the king without the interference of the other physicians'.[130] However, the queen's increasing reliance on Dr Willis was to usher in a host of fresh complications.

The king had been unable to attend to any public business for over a month by this time, and whatever small improvements 'hopers' like Willis and Fanny Burney discerned, it was impossible to imagine him doing so in the immediate future. This situation could not be allowed to continue indefinitely. George's role in the political process was far from nominal. His assent was required for all legislation, and the absence of the king meant that there was a vacuum – and potentially a very destabilising one – at the heart of politics. Although the government was chosen from and depended on the support of an active, engaged political class that was extremely protective of its role, a stable administration was all but impossible without the approval of the king. A substantial number of office holders sitting in the House of Commons were heavily dependent on the Crown for their income, and their support could be marshalled to come to its aid when necessary. Harnessing the power of these 'placemen' gave the king considerable weight in Parliament, when he chose to use it: as has been seen, George had deployed them to dispatch at least one administration he disliked. The role of the monarch in the business of government was a real and vital one; indeed, it was impossible to imagine the culture of contemporary politics without it.

There was a possible solution, of course – although it was one the king's friends could hardly bear to contemplate. It was not until the end of November that Fanny Burney could bring herself even to mention the term 'regency', a word she admitted 'I have not yet been able to articulate'.[131] The Prince of Wales had had no such qualms, having compiled the first list of ministers he intended to place in office as early as 10 November.[132] He was not alone in seeing a regency as inevitable. It was the obvious implication of the memorandum on the king's health that Pitt had drawn up on 8 November, and his Cabinet colleague Lord Thurlow, the Lord Chancellor, was said to have declared on the 12th that 'there must be a regent, and that regent is the Prince of Wales'.[133]

However, as everyone knew, if the prince did come into power, he would not retain any of his father's ministers; Pitt's name certainly did not feature on any of the lists that occupied the prince in his speculative spare moments. It had been one of the many causes of friction between father and son that the prince had thrown in his lot with men whom the king disliked, both for their morals and their Whiggish politics. Like every other Hanoverian Prince of Wales before him, he had added opposition politics to the heady mix of provocation designed to outrage his father. If the prince became regent, a change of administration would inevitably follow.

Faced with the prospect of political obliteration, Pitt played for time. There was little else he could do, as events seemed to be moving irrevocably in the prince's favour. Charles Fox, who had been travelling in Italy and was unaware of the king's illness until a messenger turned up in Bologna begging him to return, arrived back in London after an exhausting nine-day journey across Europe. Alongside Richard Sheridan and the Duke of Devonshire, he met the prince on 26 November and began to plan for their transition into government. Meanwhile, Pitt had Parliament adjourned in order that precedents for the establishment of a regency might be investigated. He also arranged to have the physicians interviewed by the Privy Council, to try to establish more clearly the king's current condition. From Pitt's perspective, the meeting, which took place on 3 December, was hardly encouraging. The doctors agreed that the king was 'at present totally incapable of attending to public business'. They thought it not impossible that he might, at some later stage, recover, but they could not say when this might happen. During the proceedings, Warren was reprimanded for 'mentioning the word insane; and when he was advised not to, and another expression was dictated to him, he answered it was the same thing'.[134] Supporters of the prince – and Warren was his physician before he was engaged to be the king's – were keen to stress the seriousness of his condition, whilst Pitt's followers and the king's friends found themselves compelled into optimism. Willis, with his bullish assessment of the likelihood of the king's recovery, soon found himself, not unwillingly, pressed into the political service of Pitt. The war between the politicians was fought by proxy amongst the king's physicians, and with just as much venom and guile. The sickroom at Kew was soon as highly politicised as the chamber of the House of Commons.

A powerful combination of diffidence, depression and the deeply ingrained instinct of a lifetime impelled the queen to do all she could to avoid being sucked into this volatile brew of argument. Shortly after the king had been moved to Kew, the Lord Chancellor had asked her to take nominal responsibility for the king's person. Fearing the consequences of such an ill-defined obligation, and desperate to obey the king's much-repeated directive never to involve herself in domestic politics, she had refused to accept the task. But as the prospect of a regency grew ever more real, she was forced into more direct action by what seemed to her the manipulation of the king's illness for political advantage. Yet, in attempting to defend the interests of her husband, she found herself opposed to those of her son. The result was a rift between Charlotte and her eldest child which would take years to heal, and was, perhaps, never entirely forgotten nor forgiven by either of them.

At the beginning of December, Pitt revealed his proposals for filling the political vacuum with a plan of staggering boldness aimed to stop the opposition in their tracks. Its provisions would also sour even further relations between the queen and her eldest son. Pitt argued that, as the doctors agreed that the king might at some stage recover, his authority should be considered not as terminated, but merely 'interrupted'. In such delicate circumstances, the appointment of a regent could not be a simple matter of succession. The hereditary principle was, in this unprecedented case, subordinate to the will of the people: Parliament would decide on the most appropriate person to take up the office. Even more provocatively, Pitt added that Parliament would also determine the nature and extent of a regent's powers, subjecting the issue to debate in both Houses. This was an audacious and brilliant move, transforming at a stroke the fortunes of Pitt's party. It forced Fox, who had built his career on a defence of British liberty against the encroachments of the Crown, into arguing in favour of the prince's entitlement to exercise his hereditary right without the interference of or curb by Parliament, a position that was as uncomfortable for him intellectually as it was politically. The widespread unpopularity of the Prince of Wales did nothing to help the beleaguered Fox. The possibility of his accession to power was greeted with no enthusiasm beyond the circle of his political intimates. His reputation as a spendthrift and a reprobate impressed the serious men of the City no more than they did his father. 'The stocks are already fallen 2 per cent,' wrote one observer, 'and the alarms of the people of London are very little flattering to the prince.'[135]

When Pitt's proposals were debated by the Commons on 10 December, they were passed by 286 votes to 204. A few weeks later, Pitt sent the prince the terms on which the regency would, if circumstances did not change, be offered to him. He was to have no power to bestow titles on anyone except members of the royal family; he was not to be allowed to sell or make use of any of the king's personal property; and he was to have no power to grant any other offices or pensions. By denying him the lifeblood of eighteenth-century politics – the exercise of patronage – Pitt sought to tie the prince's hands as tightly as he could. 'It was clear that they intended to put the strait waistcoat on the Prince of Wales,' wrote one onlooker, wryly.[136]

The prince told the Duke of Devonshire that he must crush Pitt or Pitt would crush him, adding ominously that he thought 'the queen had been playing a very underhand part'. Opposition politicians were convinced that Pitt's political boldness was rooted in his certainty that if the prince refused the regency in the restricted form on offer, the queen would be persuaded to take it. Lady Elizabeth Foster, a passionate advocate of the prince's cause, had heard as early as 5 December that Pitt meant to offer the queen at least a share in the regency. Some weeks later, Gilbert Elliot was even more convinced of Charlotte's duplicity: 'She is playing the devil, and has been all this time at the bottom of the cabals and intrigues against the prince.' Significantly, he identified Willis – whom he described as 'a quack' – as a key player in such schemes. 'One principal engine of the intriguers is the opinion that they contrive to maintain in public that the king's recovery is to be expected with certainty, and very speedily. Dr Willis was brought about the king for that purpose, the other physicians not being sufficiently subservient.' He too had no doubt that if the prince felt himself unable to accept the regency, the queen 'was ready to accept it'.[137] It became an article of faith amongst the prince's friends that the position and power that should have been his by right had been deliberately and calculatedly denied him by the machinations of his mother.

It certainly suited Pitt for his opponents to believe that he had another royal card up his sleeve, as it were, ready to play if the prince proved recalcitrant. Even William Grenville, his astute colleague, thought it possible that Charlotte might be induced to take the job, though it seems unlikely that the queen ever seriously considered the possibility. Her deep-seated fear of incurring the king's displeasure by any act of self-assertion was probably enough to have prevented her; and worn down by anxiety and depression, she was unlikely to have chosen this moment to reverse the emotional subservience instilled over a lifetime. Yet, for all her accustomed timidity, she was prepared to adopt a more bullish stance in defence of what she identified as the king's interests. It is certainly true that during December she emerged a little from her seclusion to play a pivotal part in the war between the physicians that had begun with Willis's arrival on the 5th.

Most of the battles took place over the bulletins on the state of the king's health which the physicians issued jointly each day. As the only form of regular official information on his condition available to the public, they were extremely sensitive documents, made more so by the prevailing belief that madness was a shameful condition to be concealed and hidden from view wherever possible. The queen strove hard to ensure that the bulletins contained as little as possible that could embarrass or humiliate the king. She was deeply distressed at the inclusion of the words 'much disturbed' in one of the reports, and succeeded in having them altered. As the crisis over the regency continued, the official description of the king's condition took on even greater significance. On 16 December, for example, the king had had six hours' sleep during the night, far more than usual, and potentially an encouraging sign. Willis accordingly argued the bulletin should state that he had had a very good night. But his colleagues disagreed, arguing that the hours of sleep had not in fact been consecutive, but 'composed of three different sleeps'. Willis refused to retreat and 'would only sign to a very good night'. The other physicians remonstrated and complained, but Willis was adamant; in the face of his immovability, his colleagues backed down.

Dr Warren – who, significantly, was not present on that occasion – was made of sterner stuff. Throughout December and January, Warren opposed all efforts by Willis to turn the bulletins into what he considered unrealistically upbeat assessments of the king's state. In doing so, he saw himself as defending the interests of the Prince of Wales, his patron. If the queen had come to rely entirely upon Willis, her son invested his faith just as explicitly in Warren's judgement. These simmering grievances came to a head early in January, when the determined optimism of Willis and the queen clashed directly with Warren's refusal to endorse it. On the morning of the 2nd,

Warren and the other doctors compiled their bulletin, which was sent to the queen for inspection. She returned it immediately. It did not, she felt, adequately reflect the many lucid intervals that the king had enjoyed. Greville, who was present, 'found that she had wished an alteration and that the physicians would insert "that the king continued mending"'. This Warren refused to do. In his opinion, episodes of occasional lucidity were not the same as steady, progressive recovery. 'On being further pressed, Dr Warren said that he had often, in such cases, heard many sensible remarks made by a patient, but these did not prove that the person was well, but improper remarks always were decisive, and proved that the person was still deranged.'[138]

When the queen heard that Warren was still refusing to agree to the inclusion of the disputed words, she sent for him, clearly intending to have it out with him herself. Gilbert Elliot, who probably heard the story direct from Warren, reported that he found her 'white with rage'. Lady Harcourt, who was also present during the interview, recalled that when Warren was asked to explain why he would not sign the contested bulletin, he repeated the argument he had used with Willis. 'If a man was perfectly reasonable for 23 hours and deranged during the other hour of the 24, then he considered him in the same light as if he had no lucid intervals.'[139] He added in support of his opinion 'that the king had cried very much'. 'If you call that being disturbed,' said the queen, 'then the whole house is disturbed.'[140]

Warren was undeterred, arguing that anyone who had heard the king's conversation that day could have no doubt of his true state. When the queen demanded to know what he had said, Warren refused to repeat it, 'on the grounds of the impossibility of relating such discourse to her'.[141] He said she might speak to another of the physicians, who had been there when the crucial words were uttered. When the doctor arrived to be interrogated, Warren set the tone for what followed by observing: 'I believe you will not think it proper to repeat to these ladies what the king said.' 'Certainly not,' agreed the doctor.[142] Charlotte must eventually have discovered exactly what her husband had said. Certainly his alleged comments were soon common currency amongst the social and political elite. Lady Elizabeth Foster heard that, referring to Willis, the king had 'wondered the queen would allow that ugly, fumbling old fellow to go to bed with her'.[143] The realisation that these hurtful words had, as one writer put it, 'amused the town much' can only have added to Charlotte's distress.

The knowledge that Warren had witnessed these humiliations – and the suspicion that he had discussed them with his Whig friends – did not dispose the queen in his favour. 'I should be glad never to see him again,' wrote Lady Harcourt, 'and the queen has told me she never will.'[144] For ever after, he remained fixed in Charlotte's personal demonology as 'that black spirit Dr Warren'.[145]

In the midst of such contradictory reports, it was hard to know what to believe about the king's true state. Greville, who saw more of him than almost anyone else and was unencumbered by political prejudice or family relationship, did not think him much improved. In fact, though no supporter of the prince, like Warren he thought that Willis often allowed his loyalties to sway his judgement. A few days before the row with the queen, he had noted that 'Dr Willis gave to Mr Pitt this night the most flattering accounts, assuring the minister that His Majesty was ... so well that he was sure he was at that moment as capable of transacting any business of state as ever he had been in his life.' Greville, who was far too much the gentleman to accuse anyone of lying, confined himself to the observation that 'I was not a little surprised at Dr Willis's hazarding thus, and un-pressed, such very strong assertions.'[146] He had long suspected that Willis was as much driven by politics as Warren. On 19 December, he wrote that Willis was 'unguarded and imprudent' for a man in such a conspicuous and responsible situation. Not only did he lean 'strongly to a political party', he also did 'not appear to confine his politics to the approbation of present measures or to the admiration of Mr Pitt, but he attacks Mr Fox and the Opposition with as much zeal as any partisan I know'. Greville was increasingly disillusioned, writing morosely in his diary that 'less triumph on short successes and more check on the eagerness of politics are the two most desirable essentials wanting'.[147] Neither was much in evidence at Kew during December and January.

*

The king had probably been at his worst around mid-December 1788, when any beneficial effects delivered by the quinine and opiates originally prescribed by Willis had worn off. The physicians continued to dose him with emetics, which made him vomit, and with castor oil in an attempt to move his costive bowels. As none of this had any effect on his behaviour, except perhaps to render him increasingly agitated, the strait waistcoat was brought into ever more frequent use. Even Greville, who had once been in favour of a firmer regime, was horrified by what he witnessed. Arriving at the king's rooms at noon on 20 December, he discovered that 'recourse to the strait waistcoat' had been necessary during the night and that the king was still to be found 'in the same melancholy situation … His legs were tied, and he was secured across the breast.'[148] Willis recorded that, whilst pinioned to his bed, throughout the night the king had called despairingly on his five-year-old favourite daughter Amelia to help him. 'Oh Emily, why won't you save your father? Why must a king lie in this damned confined condition?'[149] The king was kept 'under coercion' till two in the afternoon, noted Greville, but became 'agitated and disturbed' again later in the evening. 'He was checked at this time by Dr Willis, who recommended him to be more calm or that he would certainly talk himself into a strait jacket.'[150]

On 23 December, he was given a couch to rest his blistered legs upon, 'but was too riotously inclined to stay long on it', and was again tied down. Once confined, Greville noted that he was not violent, and 'as he lay stretched on his bed, he sang'. On Christmas Day, he was again 'very troublesome and turbulent'. Greville heard that 'among his extravagances of the moment, he had at this time … taken off his nightcap, and got a pillowcase round his head and the pillow in bed with him, which he called Prince Octavius, who he said was to be new born this day'.[151] There were occasional episodes of calmness. On the 26th, he managed to play backgammon with Dr Willis, 'very much in his usual style'. To the watching Greville, 'it appeared … singular that he should play the game with tolerable correctness … and yet at the same time, his conversation should continue so wrong and incorrect'.[152] Greville was concerned by the frequent 'indecency and incorrectness' of the king's speech. Its continuance, even in his quieter phases, only confirmed his opinion of the grim reality of George's true condition. The king's health was, he believed, 'in a more precarious state than it has yet been since the attacks commenced'.[153]

Given the king's volatile condition, it seems extraordinary that two weeks earlier, Willis had agreed to George's repeated request to see the queen and their youngest daughter. Only her faith in Willis's judgement could have persuaded the apprehensive Charlotte to meet her husband again for the first time since the traumatising events of early

November. Lady Harcourt's account of what happened when the meeting took place on Saturday the 13th was tellingly brief. 'The scene was a most affecting one; he showed strong marks of tenderness, he parted from them with the greatest reluctance.'[154] From within the heart of the opposition camp, Lady Elizabeth Foster recounted a fuller version of events. She too had heard that the scene between the king and queen was 'most affecting. He kissed her hand passionately and said he held what was dearest to him in the world. The queen pressed his hand but could not speak. The king let the queen go, on Willis saying he had promised to do so – he pressed the Princess Amelia in his arms, who cried very much and was frightened.'[155] Gilbert Elliot's version was much bleaker. He had been told that as soon as the king's youngest daughter was within his reach, 'he caught her up in arms and swore that no power on earth should ever separate them again. The girl was terrified, and so were the bystanders; and they could not get the child away until they promised to bring the queen. She was brought accordingly, and the king behaved in exactly the same way – catching fast hold of her, and swearing that nothing should ever part them again. The king fell into fits and they were obliged to separate them by main force.'[156]

There seems little doubt that, whichever of the accounts was true, the meeting with her father was distressing for Amelia. She had not seen him since his arrival at Windsor at the end of October, when he had collapsed into hysterics upon climbing out of the carriage to meet her and three of his younger daughters. At best, he must have appeared to her as a much-diminished figure: thin, uncertain, with none of the authority he had always displayed so confidently in her presence. At worst, he was violent, angry and uncontrolled.

For her mother, however, the meeting was, if possible, even more troubling. Charlotte's response to it was not recorded by any of the diarists, perhaps because she chose not to reveal her feelings publicly; but her husband was unable to act with similar discretion. As the king's every action was witnessed by others, it was soon apparent how disturbing he had found her visit. During the night that followed, even Lady Harcourt conceded he had been 'extremely turbulent, as much as any night since his illness.'[157] Significantly, when Greville returned from a short break away from attendance, he found a new obsession preoccupying the king, one which seems to have been provoked by his brief meeting with his wife.

On 18 December, George spoke for the first time 'of a Windsor Castle duchess'. A few days later Greville observed that 'the queen was now in no favour'. Since the clear onset of the king's illness in October, Charlotte had been threatened, abused and isolated. She had been drawn into party politics in a way that frightened and worried her. Her sons had allied themselves with the king's professed opponents and schemed, as she saw it, to remove him from power. She had sought at every turn to do the best she could to protect his interests and promote his welfare in the face of a terrifying malady that no one could either diagnose or cure. Now she was to undergo what was surely her greatest trial – a public humiliation of the most wounding kind, as her husband declared that he did not and had never loved her; that he preferred another and would marry her if he could.

'In his more disturbed hours,' Greville confided to his diary, 'the king has for some time spoke much of Lady Pembroke.' Elizabeth Herbert, Countess of Pembroke, was one of the queen's ladies-in-waiting and a close friend of the royal family. She had endured a difficult marriage to a serially unfaithful husband, and was nearly fifty – the same age as the king – at the time of his illness. In his clearer moments, George suspected that he had spoken about her in an unguarded manner, using phrases of which he would normally be ashamed. On 27 December, Greville noted that 'he had said very feelingly to one of his pages that he hoped no one knew what wrong ideas he had, and what wrong things he had said respecting her. He observed ... that in his delirium he must have said many very improper things and that much must have escaped him then which ought not to, and that he must try and find out what had slipped from him.'[158]

For all his good intentions, his behaviour, once his grasp on reality given way, was very different. The next day, Greville was surprised to meet Willis as the doctor made his way upstairs to invite the queen to visit her husband. Greville doubted this was a good idea, but Willis was adamant it would do no harm. On his assuring an anxious Charlotte that 'he was sure HM would receive her well', she was eventually persuaded to come down. The visit was planned to last no more than a quarter of an hour, and on these terms, the queen went in, accompanied by Willis. Greville and the others standing outside in the anteroom could hear the king's voice, 'but without hearing his conversation – and at times he appeared to us to be crying'. The meeting lasted nearly an hour, and was brought to an end only when two of Willis's men went into the room, 'and the queen was released, not quite without difficulty'. Willis later insisted to Greville that 'the king received the queen with much kindness. He sat down by her while he spoke to her and often kissed her hand and he cried very frequently.' Greville was sceptical, noting that most of what passed 'was in German, not a word of which does Dr Willis understand'. He watched with sympathy Charlotte's valiant attempt to make a dignified exit from what had clearly been a difficult encounter. 'It was painful to see the poor queen coming out of the king's apartment unattended, through the anteroom where there were many attendants. As she passed, Her Majesty seemed to make an effort to look up and by her countenance show us that she was not overcome.' She needed all of her courage to do so. The king soon eagerly recounted his own version of what had been said to his doctors and attendants. 'It was such as was improper for her to have heard,' wrote Greville sadly. 'In substance, it was that he did not like her, that he preferred another, that she was mad and had been so these three years, that he would not on any account admit her to his bed till the year 1793 for reasons he then improperly explained and such-like extravagant and wild conversation.'[159]

It is hard to know exactly what triggered the king's impassioned declaration of dislike for his wife. It was true he blamed the queen for many of the most painful aspects of his situation. He believed she had been complicit in the plot to bring him to Kew, and still resented her leaving Windsor without his permission. He was convinced, with some justification, that the pre-eminence of Willis, and the free hand he enjoyed in placing him under painful and humiliating restraint, was due to Charlotte's unwavering support of the physician. Greville thought she did not know much of what was done to the king in the name of treatment; but knowledge of her ignorance would probably not have lessened her husband's anger against her. Most woundingly, George considered she had deserted him, left him to suffer alone when she should have been loyally at his side. His isolation from his family weighed heavily upon him; by the end of December, he had seen his wife only twice in eight weeks.

Whatever the causes, he continued to rail against the queen in terms increasingly bitter and forceful. He pulled off the wall a painting by Zoffany she had commissioned for him. When in January she sent him 'a fine bunch of grapes from the hothouse', the king's first question on receiving them was to enquire who they were from. 'He was told by the queen. He asked what queen, and if it was Queen Esther who had sent them.' Esther was his name for Lady Pembroke, whom he now described as his true wife. 'The page answered that it was Her Majesty the Queen, upon which he said that he would not receive them and ordered them away.' Although he later relented and ate the grapes, 'he talked much of Lady Pembroke as usual – much against the queen – and dwelt on a great variety of subjects with great inconsistency and incoherence.'[160]

Greville thought his antipathy towards Charlotte proved how far he still remained away from recovery. 'Since this illness has been upon him, he has in general spoke unkindly of the queen, and nothing proves him less like himself than this. He said this evening that he never liked her, that she had a bad temper and that all her children were afraid of her.'[161] Greville was sure that 'when such expressions are let loose, he knows not what he says', but it is impossible not to consider that the campaign of insult and rejection directed by George against Charlotte represented something more than random, delirious ravings. Could the voicing of thoughts usually so strictly and determinedly policed suggest a deeply suppressed resentment against the narrowness of his emotional experience? No one was more committed than the king to the principle that by doing his duty he had obliterated at a stroke all his other desires. Since he renounced Sarah Lennox in his early twenties, he had never allowed himself to consider the possibility that he might have acted differently, that he might have had other women besides his wife. Significantly, in the last days of his illness he confessed to the Lord Chancellor that he had been thinking a great deal of 'an attachment he had had in his youth'. Thurlow advised him that it was far too late, at the age of fifty, to be thinking about such things, and the king never mentioned it again. But perhaps his tirades against Charlotte were an expression of his unacknowledged frustration with the consequences of choices he had made when very young and had never reneged upon in twenty-seven years of meticulously faithful marriage.

On 12 January, he told Greville that he was planning to visit Lady Pembroke, and had 'filled his pockets strangely, with two or three pairs of stockings, a couple of nightcaps and a pair of drawers'.[162] When he played cards with Willis he referred to her as the Queen of

Hearts and declared, 'Oh, if the queen should fall to the king.' On the back of his cards he wrote: 'Oh dear Eliza ever love thy prince, who had rather suffer death than leave thee.' He sang love songs which Greville was sure referred 'to the history of Eliza'.

On the 16th, Greville arrived in the middle of the morning at the king's apartments. It had been a difficult night, with the king 'very angry and abusive to those with him, and at whom he was swearing much.'[163] 'The violence was not abated' at eleven o'clock, when Greville took a short break. When he returned, he was astonished to discover 'that the queen and two of the princesses were actually with the king in his apartment. Never was information more unexpected than this was to me at this time.' Greville knew that 'both in the early as well as in the latter part of the morning he had been speaking improperly of the queen', and he dreaded to think what had occurred in his absence. The king, Greville discovered, had received a letter from his son Adolphus and had asked that the queen and his daughters be allowed to read it with him. 'Upon this, Willis agreed to the suggestion and the interview took place.' Just as he had on the occasion of the queen's disastrous last visit, Willis maintained 'that the king had behaved with the greatest propriety and affection to the whole party and that the queen had, by the king's desire, played a game at piquet'. 'I was not doomed to be long cheered by this welcome report,' wrote Greville resignedly. The king had gleefully explained to one of his pages what had really happened. 'He told him that the queen had consented that Lady Pembroke should come to him, and that this he had promised before his daughters.' The queen's humiliation was now complete. Her husband had repudiated her in front of her children. A few hours later, George asked Greville to find a book for him. 'He desired me to go and look for Paley's Philosophy, in which I should find, he told me, that though the law said that a man might have but one wife, yet that Nature allowed more.'[164]

The female diarists made no comment about the king's outspoken and lacerating attacks on his wife. Fanny Burney simply noted on 10 January: 'my poor royal mistress now droops.'[165] On the 15th, Lady Harcourt wrote that the queen 'has been very low and very far from well', and thought her so ill that she begged her to seek medical advice, to no avail.[166] Despite all she had to bear, Charlotte did not buckle. 'She has a strong mind and a strong judgement,' commented Lord Harcourt approvingly; and she did not shrink from continuing to perform what she thought was her duty. It was on her official birthday, 18 January, that the king insisted on seeing her, with three of the princesses – but, as Fanny Burney laconically observed, 'it was not a good day'.[167] Even the ever-hopeful Willis admitted that throughout the morning, 'the king was never more disturbed in his life'. By evening, when the queen and her daughters arrived, he was a little calmer, although his behaviour was still excited. In a cruel echo of the musical evenings that had occupied much of the family's time when he was well, 'the king proposed catch singing. The queen, Princess Augusta and Princess Elizabeth were pressed to take part, and Dr Willis was obliged to join in.'[168]

As the king's behaviour continued to be so unpredictable, on 24 January Willis found it expedient to introduce a new form of coercion, 'a chair fixed to the floor that cannot be thrown down. When shown it,' Greville reported, 'the king eyed it with some degree of apprehension.' The next day, he showed off the contraption, 'which he called his Coronation Chair', to one of the doctors. The King of Spain, George said, had been mad but kept his state; 'only in England could a king be confined in a strait waistcoat'. On the 28th, Willis had him placed in it 'and gave him a severe lecture on his improper conversation, Eliza, etc.'.[169] When the king became 'loud and impatient under this lecture, Dr Willis ordered a handkerchief to be held before his mouth' until he became quiet.

By the end of January, with the king having been ill for more than three months, it seemed as though the queen was finally broken. Her eyes were inflamed, wrote Lady Harcourt, and she spent her days in a darkened room. 'She is very low, very thin and eats nothing.'[170] The princesses were all worried about her. But just as she seemed about to give up, out of nowhere the first signs appeared that the king might at last have begun to recover. Both his vision and his powers of concentration improved enough for him to be able to read again. 'Shakespeare is what he generally prefers,' stated Lady Harcourt, 'and he particularly likes to read *King Lear*.' On one of their visits, he told his daughters that although the experience of his illness meant he had some things in common with Lear, 'in other respects he was not like him, for he had no Goneril, nor Regan, but three Cordelias. Judge how this affected them all.'[171]

He had also started to draw again, applying himself to calmly making meticulous architectural plans of buildings, which had been one of his favourite occupations when well. Encouraged by these indications, Charlotte was persuaded to see him again. On 31 January, she brought twelve-year-old Princess Mary to visit her father. Mother and daughter played cards together, whilst the king read aloud to them from the *Life of Handel*. 'He then sung parts of some of the choruses, and commented upon their different advantages of composition. He became afterwards jocose,' noted Greville, and at that point 'it was thought proper to end this visit.'[172] He was still, Greville thought, subject 'to flight and hurry', but 'on the whole he behaved as well as he has done at any time since his illness to the queen'. The next night, Charlotte took their daughter Sophia to see him; a few days later, Augusta came too. Greville believed these were some of the best days the king had enjoyed since his arrival at Kew.

On 2 February, Fanny Burney met him by accident as she walked in Kew Gardens. Catching sight of the king and his party in the distance, she 'ran off with all my might!' but the king pursued her, 'loudly and hoarsely calling after me "Miss Burney, Miss Burney!"' At first, not knowing 'in what state he might be', she continued to run away, until Dr Willis called out that it hurt the king to run. She came to a reluctant halt and 'forced myself forward to meet him', thinking this by far 'the greatest act of personal courage I ever made'. When they spoke, she was surprised to find him so much improved. In his face she saw 'all his wonted benignity of countenance, though still something of wildness in his eyes'. She was very shocked when 'he put both his hands round my two shoulders' and kissed her cheek. 'Involuntarily, I thought he meant to crush me'; but gradually she realised his intentions were friendly. 'What a conversation followed! What did he not say!' The king commiserated with Fanny on her difficulties with Mrs Schwellenberg, insisting she ignore the old woman's bullying and consider him a friend and protector. He talked about her father, about Handel, about Mrs Delany and, most uncharacteristically, about politics, declaring 'he was very much dissatisfied with his state officers and that he meant to form an entire new establishment'. Fanny could not deny that his manner was both intense and indiscreet, 'but upon the whole how inexpressibly thankful I was to see him so nearly himself – so little removed from recovery'.[173]

The king's behaviour continued to fluctuate wildly. On the 3rd, Greville overheard 'very high words' between Willis and the king which he discovered arose from 'his having spoke improperly of the queen and having refused to see her'. Nevertheless, Charlotte arrived in her husband's apartments as arranged, this time accompanied by the Princesses Augusta and Elizabeth. They found their father 'high in spirits' and talking incessantly. 'Piquet was attempted but did not go very smoothly. Afterwards, HM proposed singing ... The king on this occasion himself joined in heartily in "Rule Britannia" and "Come Cheer Up My Lads".'[174]

The following day, the visitors were the queen and Princesses Mary and Sophia. Their father 'behaved with more calmness and propriety than he had on the preceding night'.[175] Lady Harcourt found the queen that evening 'more delighted than I have ever seen her after any of her visits ... Twice she believed he was going to say something wrong, but he put his hand upon his mouth said "Hush", and then in a moment spoke properly ... Our spirits and hopes are very much revived.'[176] Two days later ('a day of indulgence') the king was allowed to use a knife and fork and to shave himself, which he did very carefully, shaving his head as well as his face, to prepare himself for wearing a wig again.[177]

*

In the world beyond Kew, the political process had ground steadily onwards. Pitt's delaying tactics had been very effective; but for all his political dexterity, he was aware that for him, and for his administration, time was running out. On 30 December, advised by Fox, the Prince of Wales had stated his intention to accept the regency even in its restricted form. Much of January had been spent in further interrogation of the physicians, instigated by the opposition, who still hoped to engineer a declaration of the continuing seriousness of the king's state. The Regency Bill was finally published on 6 February.

The parliamentary process duly began, but Fox had left it all too late. In the second week of February, the king's health began to improve with a speed no one could have predicted. His constipation was finally cured, and even his familiar patterns of speech returned. An evening spent with his wife and Princess Amelia passed off, Greville noted, extremely well, the king serenading his family on his flute as they arrived in his apartments. Willis was overjoyed, telling Greville how good it was 'to hear the king repeat his usual singular expression (so usual to him on all occasions formerly) of "What!

What! What!"', which he had heard the previous day. Everyone had noticed the absence of the king's familiar verbal tic during his illness, and though even the loyal Greville could hardly regard it as 'a grace in language', he too was glad to hear it again, 'as it may be presumed a forerunner of returning reason and as such should be hailed with welcome'.[178]

Even the sceptical Dr Warren was impressed by the obvious improvement, telling Greville on the 11th that he had just come from the king and that 'not the least impropriety had escaped him during the interview'. Greville, who seems always to have harboured a well-concealed sympathy for Warren, thought his attitude more generous than that of Willis, who was 'sneeringly triumphant on the excellent bulletin of the day'.[179] Nothing now could deflate the buoyant sense of hope that had at last taken hold at Kew. 'The old doctor is jumping around the house and cannot command his joy,' Lady Harcourt told her husband, 'we are all in high spirits.' The queen too dared to display a little cheerfulness: 'Oh, I never saw the king so well since his illness began, as he is this evening.' This, Lady Harcourt enthused, 'was the queen's joyous exclamation as she entered the room after her visit last night, to which she added, "There has not been a look or a word unlike himself." The princesses spoke of him in the same manner.'[180]

On the 12th, the Regency Bill passed the Commons, although it appeared increasingly redundant day by day. The following week the king was well enough to see the Lord Chancellor, who, in the course of a lengthy interview, found him 'rational and collected'. He spoke of 'foreign politics in a hurried sort of way', but not, Thurlow thought, with sufficient agitation to suggest he was still ill. As a result, the Lord Chancellor made a very significant decision. Two days later, as the Regency Bill was about to begin its final reading in the Lords, Thurlow brought proceedings to a halt, declaring the king's recovery made them 'wholly unnecessary'.[181] This effectively put an end to his long confinement.

George's doctors could not explain the sudden improvement in his condition, any more than they could account for its mysterious onset. If his complaint was porphyria, his return to better health marked the end of a particularly severe episode of the disease, but it did not mean that he was cured. If the problem was purely psychological, his recovery signified his emergence from a prolonged manic phase; that too, however, offered no guarantee that it would not recur. With either diagnosis, George's improvement would be best understood as the regressive phase of a deep underlying condition, rather than permanent freedom from sickness. For now, his subjects, with a mix of puzzlement and relief, concentrated only on the good news – especially as the speed of his improvement seemed to accelerate every day.

On 19 February, for the first time since his arrival at Kew, the king left his rooms of his own accord, and went upstairs to take tea with his wife and daughters. Princess Augusta wrote to Miss Goldsworthy that he had stayed two hours with them. 'I am so happy that I could hardly believe my eyes when I saw him; he was so exactly what you and all our friends could wish.'[182] On the 24th, he met his first minister for the first time since Pitt had attempted to persuade him to leave Windsor for Kew. Perhaps neither of them had expected to see each other again, at least not as king and minister. Pitt observed that the king 'spoke of his disorder as a thing of the past, which had left no other impression on his mind other than that of gratitude and a sense of what he owed to those who had stood by him'.[183] On the 25th, the physicians' bulletin declared the king entirely free from complaint. The following day, in his first public act since November, George put an end to the issuing of bulletins. His illness was now officially over.

In practice and in private, however, the king's recovery was altogether more gradual. He was still being regularly dosed with a tartar emetic, thus preventing, so Willis believed, the accumulation of any remaining malign humours. The metallic-tasting substance was put in his food and drink, in his milk and even in his bread and butter. It was hardly surprising that George did not yet feel ready to resume his duties fully. He told Greville 'it was his wish to keep quiet, as things were going on so well, and he was recovering so fast'. He knew, he said, that 'I have no child's play before me.'[184] The king was as good as his word. In his first letter to Pitt since October, he laid out his plans for a complete alteration in behaviour that he believed was vital to preserve his health: 'I must decline entering into a pressure of business, and indeed, for the rest of my days, shall expect others to fulfil the duties of their employments and only keep that superintending eye which can be effected without labour or fatigue.'[185]

Gradually, George began to show himself outside the apartment in which he had been confined for so long. He met Colonel Digby in the library, and greeted him affably, even demonstratively. 'He quitted his papers, leaned himself back, extending his arms, and came forward with great glee, and said, "Ah Digby!" and took me by the hand and kissed me.'[186] By the third week of February, the king had seen his watchmaker, his astronomer, and the gardener who looked after his exotic plants, from whom he was horrified to hear that all the labourers at Kew had been laid off during his illness and had not been paid. And there remained one interview that promised to be far less pleasant, but which could not much longer be delayed. At some point, he would have to meet his eldest sons.

*

The Prince of Wales and Frederick, Duke of York, had been attempting fruitlessly to see their father for some time. They had 'gone repeatedly to Kew', wrote Gilbert Elliot, 'desiring to see the king; but were constantly refused on one pretence or another, although the Chancellor and many other strangers were admitted'.[187] Finally the prince wrote to the queen demanding that he and his brother be given access to their father, or supplied with documents from the physicians explaining why this was impossible. Faced with such a direct challenge, the queen capitulated and a meeting was arranged for 23 February. Willis said that 'he was not anxious, having prepared the king's mind'. He had told him 'of the intended regency, and what day it was finally to have been passed'. The king maintained that he was satisfied and was ready to bear anything 'vexatious' that he might now need to be told; but his political instincts had not entirely deserted him – in the same conversation, he told Willis that he fully understood how difficult 'had been the struggle' and added 'had they crushed you, Doctor, they would have crushed me – we must have fallen together'.[188]

Almost the first question the king asked, on emerging from his confusion, had been about the conduct of the princes – 'what his sons had done' – but he had 'acquiesced in the propriety of not dwelling on such subjects at present'. As he recovered, the full extent of their actions was revealed to him only gradually; Charlotte once hurried him out of a room to prevent him seeing the newspapers and pamphlets that covered her tables.[189] Yet he could not have been unaware of the queen's bitter, pent-up anger towards both her eldest sons, nor have been totally ignorant of its cause. He had probably not yet heard some of the worst gossip about their behaviour, but as such stories were avidly exchanged around the court, it would have been surprising if none of the rumours had reached his ears. Although they had demanded the meeting, it seems unlikely that the princes looked forward to it with anything but apprehension. Perhaps it was a combination of fear and shame that made them, in defiance of all etiquette and decent consideration, arrive over two hours late for it.

The king had tried hard to compose himself ahead of what he knew would be a difficult encounter: 'he made a pause, and after being silent for a few seconds, he took his handkerchief from his pocket, and wiping his eyes with it, said, "it was a maxim of his ancestors of the House of Brunswick never to shed a tear"'.[190] Mrs Harcourt heard that whatever had been the king's intentions, weeping was certainly in evidence once he was face to face with his sons. 'He caught the princes in his arms with great affection. Both shed tears. He said he always loved them, and should always love them.' Somewhat unconvincingly, the Prince of Wales declared it 'the happiest day of his life'. The king, however, was careful not to venture into sensitive territories, and made no mention of any specific actions taken during his enforced absence from public life. The prince confirmed the tactful blandness of the meeting, telling Greville that their talk had been general. The brothers stayed only half an hour; Mrs Harcourt thought 'they were evidently surprised at the king's perfect self-possession'.[191] Other, more hostile observers thought they were not pleased by their father's apparent recovery. 'They went off,' reported one commentator, 'quite desperate … and endeavouring to drown their care, disappointment and internal chagrin in wine and dissipation.'[192]

Nothing illustrates quite so clearly the limitations of George and Charlotte's earnest intentions to rewrite the pattern of Hanoverian family history as the behaviour of their eldest sons during the king's illness. For all their efforts, the crisis revealed a family split along the fault lines of inheritance and succession, exactly as it had been for generations. George and Frederick were seen at their best during the onset of the king's illness in October the previous year. Gilbert Elliot, admittedly a friendly witness, described the prince's actions at that point as 'exemplary'. The prince and his brother both visited Windsor to see their stricken father; the king himself acknowledged that his eldest son had wept on seeing him so ill.[193] Frederick wrote regularly to his brother, sending bulletins on the king's condition that suggest genuine concern for his welfare. Yet both seemed unable to resist the temptation of sharing the most distressing and intimate details of the king's behaviour with their friends and political allies. 'The prince and the duke came with this account,' concluded the Duchess of Devonshire, having listed a catalogue of the king's bizarre and violent actions, which opened with the declaration that 'the king is as mad as ever'.[194] Having helped feed the hunger for gossip and speculation, it was unsurprising that the princes soon became the targets of it themselves. Lurid stories circulated, asserting that the Prince of Wales had smuggled his friends into the king's sickroom to hear his ravings, or that he had spied on him through a hole in the wall.[195] The brothers were said to have regaled their drinking companions at Brooks's club with anecdotes of their father's illness, the prince making full use of his talent for mimicry to imitate his delirium. 'If we were together,' wrote William Grenville to one of his correspondents, 'I could tell you some particulars of the Prince of Wales's behaviour towards the king and queen within these few days that would make your blood run cold.'[196]

It seems undeniable that once the prospect of a regency loomed, the attitude of the princes towards their father did indeed shift. They veered away from solicitude and towards grasping a political prize that would, they believed, wipe out both their huge debts and their sense of powerlessness. Their ambition and self-interest trumped any emotional obligation they felt towards their father. But if both were on this occasion deficient in filial loyalty, that was perhaps a reflection of the king's inability to show paternal warmth and affection towards his adult children. There may also have been an element of horrified gleefulness in the brothers' response. For their entire lives, the king had been presented to his sons as the living embodiment of the high moral standards to which it was their duty to aspire. From their shared cradle, he had been held up to them, particularly by the queen, as a model of integrity against which they were to measure their own attempts to live a proper and useful existence. The sons' defects, they were insistently assured, were all the more apparent when contrasted with the king's peerless sense of duty and purpose. Having endured a lifetime of lectures on his virtues, it would have required the selflessness of saints not to have experienced some secret satisfaction when his much-vaunted self-control so publicly and spectacularly deserted him. Their father, it turned out, could swear, curse and fight like other men. Like his sons, he too lusted after women, some of them unsuitable, unavailable and inappropriate. Like his sons, he was also revealed to have ambivalent feelings about the queen. His moral superiority had once made him impregnable; his sickness revealed to his eldest sons a vulnerability in which they were neither sufficiently generous nor sympathetic enough to see anything but their own advantage.

Although the king was disappointed by the response of his eldest son to his troubles, he was probably not surprised. His expectations of the Prince of Wales were already low, and sank steadily by the year. In return, it seems unlikely that the prince felt much genuine or consistent affection for the king. A sentimental romantic, he liked the idea of loving his father; the actual practice of it he found almost impossible. George surely hoped for a better return from his much-loved second son. Frederick was the only one of the princes for whom he asked during his illness – with the exception of the dead Octavius. Yet even his favourite seemed to preserve an emotional distance from his suffering father. Whilst in Germany, Frederick had often acted as the king's advocate, urging better behaviour on the Prince of Wales. Once back in England he had given up all attempts to act as his brother's keeper, often outdoing him in excess, particularly at the gambling table. As his conduct became more dissolute, Frederick's attitude towards his father hardened. Perhaps he was ashamed he had failed to live up to the king's high opinion of him; perhaps, like his brother, he was seduced by the vision of a life no longer dominated by the long shadow of that difficult, disappointed man. Certainly Frederick responded very coolly to the king's predicament, writing with calm dispassion to his brother Adolphus that their father was 'a complete lunatic'.[197] The king told Francis Willis that he would rather have been obliged 'to his Frederick than to any other individual' during his illness, but the possibility of throwing in his lot with his beleaguered parents never seems to have occurred to the Duke of York. His lifelong position as the best-loved son did nothing to stop him allying himself with the Prince of Wales when sides came to be taken. The bonds between the two eldest brothers were, in 1789 at least, stronger than those that linked York to the king.

It was some time before even the semblance of good relations between the princes and their parents was restored. Charlotte was widely reported to be more resentful than the king towards their sons. During the meeting on 23 February, whilst the king embraced the princes, Elliot described the queen's behaviour as far less conciliatory. She was observed to be very angry, 'walking to and fro in the room with a countenance and a manner of great dissatisfaction; and the king, every now and then went to her in a submissive and soothing sort of a tone'.[198] In March, the situation deteriorated even further. Elliot heard that the Prince of Wales 'had had a smart tussle with the queen, in which they came to strong and open displays of hostility'. In what was clearly a fraught exchange, all the repressed resentment of the last few months came pouring out. The prince told his mother that she had 'connected herself with his enemies, and entered into plans for destroying and disgracing him and all her children and that she had countenanced misrepresentations of his behaviour to the king'. Stung into a rebuke, Charlotte 'was violent, lost her temper, and the conversation ended, I believe, by her saying that she would not be the channel of anything that either he or the Duke of York had to say to the king, and that the king did not mind what either he or the Duke of York either did or said or thought'.[199]

A few days later, clearly still angry, the queen summoned Frederick to announce that a concert was to be held at Windsor to celebrate the king's recovery. Both he and his brother were formally invited: 'But it is right to tell you that it is to be given to those who have supported us during the late business, and therefore, you may not possibly choose to be present.' The duke 'tried to laugh the thing off', protesting that everyone would be welcome, as all had acted as they thought best. The queen was having none of it. 'No, no, I don't choose to be misunderstood. I mean expressly that we have asked ministers and those persons who have voted in Parliament for the king and me.' Frederick was outraged. Elliot thought it 'tells one a great deal and shows something of the queen. You see that the princes are represented in the king's family by the queen herself as enemies of their father, and are denied any opportunity to justify themselves to the king.'[200] Certainly the king did not seem in any hurry to meet his sons again. Perhaps, as Elliot suspected, what the queen had told him about their behaviour made him less ready than he had been to forgive and forget all. As late as December 1789, Princess Augusta was working hard to persuade her mother to do either, 'endeavouring to obtain her favour' for her two eldest brothers. The princess was fighting a losing battle: 'there were some parts of the princes' conduct she could never forget', Charlotte insisted; and by now, her husband felt much the same. 'The king looked to amendment of conduct, not declarations.'[201] George's health recovered far more quickly than did either his or Charlotte's feelings for their eldest sons.

*

The queen was never the same again after the long ordeal of the king's illness. Always slender, she was now 'dreadfully reduced', thought Mrs Harcourt. In a graphic demonstration of her loss of weight, Charlotte 'showed me her stays, which would wrap twice over'.[202] The king too was painfully thin. He had lost over three stone, and when he appeared at the service of thanksgiving held at St Paul's in April, his face was observed to be 'as sharp as a knife'. Both now looked old. Charlotte was only forty-four at the time of the service, but, as Mrs Papendiek recorded, her lustrous hair, one of her best features, was 'now quite grey'. This was perhaps not the best time to sit for a portrait, but in September her daughters persuaded the queen to be painted by the rising young artist Thomas Lawrence. Perhaps they hoped the process would occupy her mind, and calm her nerves; if so, it was not a success. 'Her Majesty was rather averse to sitting for him,' noted Mrs Papendiek, 'saying that she had not yet recovered sufficiently from all the trouble and anxiety she had gone through to give so young an artist a chance.'[203]

Nothing went right from the beginning. Charlotte chose to be painted in a dove-coloured dress, which did not suit her sallow complexion and was 'most unbecoming'. Unable to decide what to wear on her head, she gave up and wore nothing at all. 'When the king came to look at the portrait,' wrote Mrs Papendiek, 'this disgusted him, as Her Majesty had never been so seen.' Lawrence suggested that a scarf might be an appropriate ornament, but the queen refused to discuss it. 'The manner in which Her Majesty treated him was not with her usual kind consideration,' noted Mrs Papendiek primly. Impatient with the whole affair, the queen declared she would allow no further sittings. Mrs Papendiek found herself propelled into the limelight, required to serve as a stand-in for the queen, modelling a scarf pinned with her jewels. After all this trouble, no one liked the picture. The king declined to buy it, and it lingered for years in Lawrence's studio, unsold until after the painter's death. Only Mrs Papendiek admired it. 'To my mind,' she declared, 'the likeness is stronger than any I recollect, and it is very interesting.'[204]

Mrs Papendiek's judgement may perhaps have been swayed by Lawrence's obvious interest in her; he went on to paint a portrait of her in her own right, and later made an exquisite and tender drawing of her with her young son. His depiction of Charlotte is far less obviously attractive. The queen looks out from the canvas with a wary, guarded expression. There is defeat in her gaze; she looks exhausted and subdued. In Lawrence's picture, the reality of what she had suffered was subtly but powerfully captured. No wonder the king had little desire to see it on his walls.

It was not only Charlotte's outward appearance that had changed. She never recovered the cheerfulness that she had embraced so eagerly when her 'long campaign' of childbearing came to an end, and which had so endeared her to her new-found friends. The betrayal and alienation of her eldest sons hardened her heart, and the humiliations heaped upon her by her husband helped consolidate the very character traits he had deplored during his ravings. Her personality darkened and her temper grew worse. She became resentful and suspicious. The king did what he could to make amends. Lady Charlotte Finch had told Mrs Harcourt, on 23 February, that 'the king showed the greatest affection to the queen. It was the attention of a lover. He seemed to delight in making her presents – kissed her hand and showed every mark of tenderness.'[205] But she could not forget the cruel things he had said during his illness and never felt the same uncomplicated confidence in her husband's fidelity that she had enjoyed for the past twenty-seven years. At the celebration concert held in April, Elliot heard that 'the king showed very marked attention to Lady Pembroke; that the queen often seemed uneasy and tried to prevent it as often as she could; but that the queen being at last engaged with somebody in conversation, the king slipped away from her, and got to the end of the room where Lady Pembroke was, and there was extremely gallant and that Lady Pembroke seemed distressed, and behaved with a becoming and maidenish modesty'.[206] Knowing how eagerly such episodes were watched for, and with what relish they were recorded, can only have added to Charlotte's acute sense of public embarrassment.

In an attempt to clear the air, the king had written to Lady Pembroke about his behaviour whilst ill, and she had replied in terms of delicately distancing forgiveness: 'Your Majesty has always acted by me as the kindest brother, as well as the most gracious of sovereigns.' Since he had asked for her friendship, 'I give it most sincerely, and if I might presume to say, that I felt like the most affectionate sister towards an indulgent brother, it would exactly express my sentiments.'[207] Eventually Lady Pembroke became again what she had been before the events of the winter of 1788/89: a valued friend of both king and queen. But for Charlotte, there could never be a return to the way things were before. For her, as much as for her sons, the king's 'intellectual malady' changed everything. The queen was never again the woman she once was, and never became the woman she might have been if her husband had not fallen ill.

The effects of the king's illness upon his daughters were harder to gauge. The brothers spent the crisis travelling up and down from London to Kew, plotting and politicking in clubs and fashionable drawing rooms; for them, there was a whiff of horrified exhilaration about the whole affair. The experience of their sisters was very different. They spent the entire period of the king's illness closeted in seclusion, seeing no one beyond the embattled redoubt of their reduced and chilly household. They bore without complaint week after week of anxious confinement – Fanny Burney described it as 'the terrible Kew campaign' – long, emotionally exhausting days succeeding one after another in dreary monotony. They lived entirely with their mother, spending all day in her room, and often all night too, attempting to protect her from the fear she never lost of being once more intruded upon by her deranged husband. Although they were constantly exposed to the misery, fear and dejection that coloured Charlotte's days, the daughters were, almost without exception, mute witnesses. Though they doubtless discussed their parents and their predicament among themselves, virtually nothing remains that describes how they felt. Fanny Burney reported approvingly that they 'behaved like angels, they seem content to remain in this gloomy solitude forever, if it prove comfort to their mother, or mark their duteous affections to their father.'[208] Had any of the sisters left first-hand accounts of their experience, it is doubtful that they would have added much to Fanny's perception of their state; as she had herself observed, they were well schooled in concealing their emotions, and were trained to present an imperturbable face to the world. What they really thought when confronted with the reality of their shambling, agitated and incoherent father; how they responded when he told their mother, in their presence, that he no longer loved her and preferred Lady Pembroke; from what horrors they imagined they were protecting their mother as they slept in her room each night to deny her husband access to her; with what hidden feelings they struggled through another painful evening of manic choral singing – no one will ever really know.

There was one last cruel disappointment for them to endure. Back in November 1788, with a rare flash of insight into the loneliness of their single state, the king had assured his elder daughters, Royal and Augusta, that in the spring he would take them to Germany and find husbands for them all. If the sisters had clung on to this sliver of hope through all the dark days at Kew, they might have been even more encouraged as he began to recover. He told Greville in February that he did indeed intend to go to Hanover, and on the 24th George wrote to his son Augustus in Germany, giving him 'a little hint, not yet known to your brothers ... that you must not be surprised if you have a call to Hanover, and find me accompanied by the queen and your three eldest sisters'.[209]

But, for all the king's enthusiasm, the expedition came to nothing. No one but George himself – and perhaps his hopeful daughters – thought it a good idea. 'One can hardly conceive anything so strong as sending the king abroad in his current condition,' declared Elliot.[210] Greville was equally opposed to the project, not just on grounds of its impracticality, but because all talk of Hanover was, he believed, irrevocably linked with the worst of the king's delusions. 'None have been more constant than the expression of his desire to go to Hanover, against which visit I do most earnestly pray.'[211] Everyone around him conspired to dissuade the king from making the journey; little by little the prospect of the trip faded away, and eventually, it was totally abandoned.

George would never see the flat landscapes of his dynasty's homeland, and there would be no parties and balls at German courts designed to attract husbands for his daughters. It was the onset of their father's madness that had first held out the prospect of marriage to the princesses, in his hurried declaration that they should all be found partners. Now, the apparent irrationality of the scheme had fatally tainted it, ensuring it would *never* happen. The sisters would accompany their convalescent father on a trip to recover his health; not to Hanover and the Continental courts beyond, but to sedate and respectable Weymouth, in Dorset, where husbands suitable for princesses were unlikely to be found.

CHAPTER 12

Three Weddings

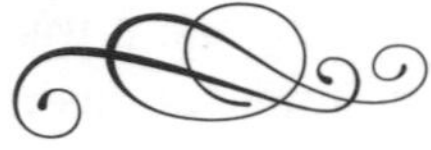

ALMOST A YEAR AFTER FANNY Burney had accompanied the king and queen on their ill-starred holiday to Cheltenham, she found herself on the road again as part of the royal entourage, travelling to the seaside resort of Weymouth. If the crowds that had marked their progress on that first journey had been vocal in their appreciation for their monarch, in the summer of 1789 they seemed even more delighted to see him. 'His popularity is greater than ever,' thought Fanny. 'Compassion for his late sufferings seems to have endeared him to all conditions of men.'[1] As the party travelled through Hampshire, they passed under floral arches festooned with mottoes celebrating 'the king restored', to the ever-present sound of the national anthem played by what Fanny called 'the *crackiest* of bands'. At Lyndhurst in the New Forest, where the royal family stayed for a few days, they were greeted by 'the delighted mob' singing 'God Save the King' with great gusto. When George and his family sat down to dine, the villagers were allowed to watch the spectacle from the grounds of the house, looking in at the window. 'They crowded so excessively,' noted Fanny 'that this can be permitted them no more, for they broke down the all the paling, much of the hedges and some of the windows.' They had, she hastened to add, meant no harm; it was only their eagerness to catch a glimpse of the king that had led them on, 'for they were perfectly civil and well behaved'.[2]

It was a small royal group that eventually arrived in Weymouth. The three youngest princesses had been left behind at home with their governesses, but even so it proved a tight fit to squeeze everyone into the accommodation arranged for them. Just as he had in Cheltenham, the king borrowed a house, Gloucester Lodge, to stay in, this time from his brother William. Again, there was not much space for the attendants. Fanny Burney was lodged in the attic, and although she enjoyed the views of the sea and the sands from her lofty perch, these did not, she felt, compensate for the pokiness of her room. 'Nothing like living at a court for exaltation,' she observed dryly.[3] She was luckier than her male colleagues, who were obliged to find lodgings where they could; even the grand Colonel Goldsworthy, the king's senior equerry, boarded at the house of a local farmer.

What Weymouth lacked in luxury, it made up for in loyalty. 'Not a child could be seen that had not a bandeau round its head, cap or hat of "God Save the King",' noted Fanny. The town's principal business was selling the curative powers of sea-bathing to sick or convalescent visitors, and it lost little time in attaching the king's name, as prominently as possible, to the source of its prosperity. 'It is printed in golden letters on most of the bathing machines, and in various scrolls and devices it adorns every shop and almost every house in town.'[4] The phrase also adorned the women known as 'dippers' whose job it was to immerse their clients in the water. 'The bathing women had it in large coarse girdles round their waists,' wrote Fanny. They 'wear it in bandeaux on their bonnets, to go into the sea; and have it again, in large letters round their waists to encounter the waves'. Fanny was not sure it was a good idea to allow one's loyalty to so decisively overwhelm one's sense of taste. 'Flannel dresses tucked up, and no shoes nor stockings, with bandeaux and girdles, have a most singular appearance; and when I first surveyed these local nymphs, it was with some difficulty I kept my features in order.'[5]

It was Dr Willis who had suggested Weymouth as a place for the king to convalesce. In keeping with contemporary medical opinion, Willis considered sea-bathing a stimulant to sluggish bodily function. Bathing, for Willis and his patients, did not mean swimming, but immersion, or 'dipping', below the waves, aided by professional attendants. Men could take the plunge naked; women were always fully clothed. Charlotte, who disliked the whole idea of watery immersion, was content to spend her time quietly, in a spacious bathing-machine where she could read and pursue her needlework uninterrupted. The king, in contrast, was a dutiful bather, arriving early in the morning to take his cure. However, at Weymouth, not even a royal wade into the sea could be attempted without due ceremony. 'Think of the surprise of His Majesty,' exclaimed Fanny, 'when, the first time of his bathing, he had no sooner popped his royal head under the water than a band of music, concealed in a neighbouring machine struck up "God Save Great George Our King".'[6] In the face of such a relentless barrage of enthusiasm, even Fanny decided shortly after her arrival that 'The loyalty of this place is excessive.' But the king was undeterred, convinced that the sea air and the healthy regime of the little resort would do him nothing but good.

The king enjoyed himself so much on his first visit to Weymouth that the family returned again, this time with all six daughters, plus Prince Ernest, in 1794, 1798 and then on an almost annual basis for as long as his health allowed. Gradually, as the town became accustomed to its royal guests, it became less fervent in its demonstrations of loyalty, allowing them to spend time there with a minimum of ceremony and fuss. At Weymouth, and in the countryside that surrounded it, George came closest to living the life he so often declared he would have chosen for himself – 'that of a Berkshire gentleman and no king.'[7] Robert Greville went with the family on their 1794 trip, and accompanied the king on the bucolic, low-key activities he most enjoyed. Both George and Greville particularly relished the lengthy daily rides they took meandering over the rolling Downs that ran down to the coast. Even though he was now middle-aged and not in perfect health, the king still spent hour after hour in the saddle in the open air, devoting whole days to the pursuit of stags and hare. As late as 1801, when he was sixty-three, he spent from nine in the morning till four in the afternoon on horseback, hunting deer.[8] As his equerry Colonel Goldsworthy had once mournfully complained to Fanny Burney, bad weather did nothing to diminish the king's enthusiasm. He actively sought out punishing rides, sometimes covering thirty or forty miles at a time. For him, these demanding journeys were an escape from the pressures of office, a physical and emotional release from the confinement of his daily routine. They were also a vital form of exercise, an indispensable tool in his lifelong battle against corpulence.

The king's rides also allowed him to indulge one of his great sustaining passions – investigating local farming practices. Nothing pleased him more than detailed, technical conversation with knowledgeable farmers. He was passionately interested in agricultural improvement, particularly in the breeding of sheep. He had converted some of the deer park at Richmond into grazing land, and later carved out three model farms from the parkland at Windsor. He was the first to import the merino breed from Spain into Britain, and reared them with more success than many of his competitors, making a real contribution to the improvement of the British wool stock. Although he showed little interest in the processes of mass production that were beginning to transform the industrial landscape of Britain, George was a keen and informed advocate of the new practices in agriculture whose effects were just as significant. Under the pseudonym Ralph Robinson – borrowing the name of one of the shepherds on the Windsor estates – the king contributed two letters to the influential periodical *Annals of Agriculture*, edited by Arthur Young, the campaigning proselytiser for the radical farming techniques that were so rapidly enhancing the productivity of the eighteenth-century countryside. He invited the great agriculturalist to inspect his farms at Windsor, giving him a personal guided tour. He was delighted to be told that all was 'in admirable order, and the crops all clean and fine'. In return, George told Young: 'I consider myself more obliged to you than any other man in my dominions.'[9]

The king's stays at Weymouth, so close to the fertile sheep runs of the Dorset Downs, placed him in the ideal position – both intellectually and geographically – to indulge his interests to the full. 'On the Esplanade, the king met Mr Bridge, the eminent farmer and breeder of Wenford Eagle in this county,' recorded Greville. 'Talked much with him on the management of his farm and his sheep and promised to come and look at them.'[10] The king's reputation for buttonholing those who worked the land, with scant regard for ceremony, was well enough known for it to become the subject of one of James Gillray's best-known caricatures of him. In *Affability*, produced in 1797, George peers closely into the face of a startled peasant farmer, rather lower down the social scale than the eminent Mr Bridge, and subjects him to a barrage of questions that mimics George's idiosyncratic patterns of speech: 'Well friend, where a'you going, hay? What's your name, hay? Where d'ye live, hay, hay?'

In August 1794, on one of their rides across the Downs, Greville and the king met 'an intelligent young Somersetshire farmer'. So impressed was the king by the enthusiasm and ingenuity with which he cared for his flocks that he invited himself to Farmer Ham's home, and soon became a regular visitor and confidant of his entire family. Ham's niece Elizabeth recalled that the king would send

> one of his equerries to my father to enquire if his brother were at home, as it was the king's intention to visit his farm that day. The king was so well pleased that this continued an annual event until his mind began to fail. As my father always received notice of this intended visit, he took it for granted that he was always to accompany His Majesty, and in consequence they became quite gossiping acquaintances. The king was scarcely ever in Weymouth a day before he took my father by the button to learn all the news.[11]

The young Elizabeth Ham was an interested, if sceptical, witness to her farming family's dealings with the king. Unlike almost everyone else in Weymouth, she was defiantly resistant to the tide of loyalty that had engulfed the little town. She secretly wore a locket containing a picture of Napoleon Bonaparte, and, given those sympathies, her recollections inject a more astringent tone into the vision of royal life at the sedate resort. She refused to be beguiled into rose-coloured pictures of any kind, even when applied to her own close family. Thus, in her account, her uncle, 'the intelligent young farmer' of Greville's description, is 'a shrewd, hard-headed man' whose machinations are driven by greed and rarely bode well for his naive brother, her father. She adds a similarly barbed footnote to Greville's story of the king's professional interest in Farmer Ham's livestock. 'The king admired some sheep of my uncle's, and commissioned him to procure a flock of the same sort for his farm in Windsor. This was accordingly done through a cousin who resided in Somersetshire, and who sent his own shepherds with the flock to Windsor. Neither the sheep nor the expenses attending to them were ever paid for.'[12] In Elizabeth Ham's world, idylls – whether rural or royal – did not have much of a place.

Unconscious of the beady-eyed disapproval of this unimpressed young observer, the king was probably as happy on the Downs above Weymouth as he was anywhere else in his world. There he could surround himself with men whose work he respected and understood, with whom he felt naturally and unselfconsciously at home. He was as at ease in their houses as he was in their fields. His conversation was of ewes and rams rather than Cabinets and treaties. It was surely this enticing image of the life he might have enjoyed as a private man that lured him back year after year to this unexceptionable small town. Nothing else Weymouth had to offer could compete with the compelling vision of an alternative existence that destiny, inheritance and duty had combined to deny him.

There were other attractions, of course, although some found them more pleasurable than others. When the royal family was in residence, Weymouth Bay was patrolled by the Royal Navy, and the king made full personal use of the warships, organising excursions up and down the coast, standing out to sea to catch a sight of the Channel fleet in full sail, or crossing over to Portland, where 'their Majesties, with their family, dined at the Portland Arms at the small romantic village of Chesilton'. Whether the promise of such treats was enough to compensate the queen and her daughters for numerous, less successful trips – such as the one to Lulworth Cove when they endured hours of hard sailing and were forced to beat back towards Weymouth in the teeth of a hostile wind – seems doubtful. With the exception of Augusta, who never lost her love for all things nautical, any pleasure the queen and her other daughters took in maritime expeditions did not long survive their repeated experiences of seaborne misery at Weymouth. Greville, who delicately absented himself from the king's boating projects, witnessed one unhappy ending to 'a party of pleasure', which 'had not exactly answered its expectations'. Conditions that day were so bad that 'the coming on board and leaving the ships was by no means an easy ceremony, and Her Majesty and the princesses were a great deal alarmed in rowing in and from the frigate'.[13] Some of them were seasick; all of them were distressed; and the queen was so badly shaken by the first part of her journey that she had to be persuaded to leave the frigate at all when it was time to get back in the boats and head for the shore. She was so terrified of these excursions that eventually the king put a reluctant stop to them.

The royal women were happier with land-based entertainments, especially visits to the theatre. Although Fanny Burney, who took a semi-professional interest in the stage, viewed Weymouth's theatrical offerings with faintly patronising disdain (''Tis a pretty little theatre, but its entertainment is quite in the barn style; a mere medley – songs, dance, imitations – and all very bad'), the king and queen, whose tastes were less exacting, were regular attendees.[14] Greville saw *She Stoops to Conquer* there, as well as lesser works such as *Animal*

Magnetism and *Ways and Means*, which he thought 'very tolerably acted'. There were, however, 'no actors of any note' until the arrival of Sarah Siddons, the most highly regarded female performer of her generation. Like the king, she was in Weymouth for her health – Fanny Burney spotted her walking purposefully with her family on the sands, 'a lady of very majestic port and demeanour' – but she was soon enticed to take to the stage for George and Charlotte. In Fanny's view it was not a great success; Mrs Siddons specialised in the epic tragic roles, and was not well suited to the type of comedies the king enjoyed. Fanny noted: 'Gaiety does not sit naturally on her – it seems like disguised gravity.' Comic actors fared much better at the seaside, the best winning over even the hard-to-please Fanny, who admitted that 'the burlesque of Quick and Mrs Wells made me laugh immoderately'.[15]

When the theatre palled, other gatherings filled up the time. 'On Sunday evenings,' recalled Elizabeth Ham, 'the Assembly Rooms were opened for tea and promenade. This the king never missed.' A cord was drawn across the room to distinguish 'those who had the entrée' from those who did not, and the royal family were conducted beyond it by the Master of Ceremonies, 'with a candle in each hand, who walked backwards before them, up the stairs and into the ballroom'. Curious Weymouth-ites could also attend public breakfasts where, before the dancing began, they were permitted to gaze through an open marquee and watch the king enjoying his favourite simple meals. 'His loving subjects could enjoy the satisfaction of seeing their beloved monarch draw a drumstick through his teeth, in which he seemed to delight,' wrote Elizabeth Ham tartly, 'and hearing him call for "Buttered Peas" and "Moneymusk" to set the dancers in motion.' These were the tunes that accompanied the country dances that were then 'the only ones in vogue'; but Elizabeth Ham noticed 'the princesses never joined in … on these occasions'.[16]

Like the king, Charlotte and her daughters appreciated Weymouth's lack of formality. 'The princesses enjoy the ease they have here,' noted Mrs Harcourt, observing that 'even the queen goes about with only one lady and goes into the shops'.[17] The favoured shopping destination was Delamotte's, which opened at half past five in the morning to accommodate the early hours kept by the king. When they had made their purchases, the princesses accompanied their father on his lengthy walks along the Esplanade, on one occasion waiting patiently while the king 'stopped and talked to all the children he met'.[18] For other occupation, the princesses had their needlework, which they undertook with their mother, sitting in covered chairs on the lawns in front of Gloucester Lodge. Sometimes their quiet days were enlivened by the arrival of unexpected visitors. In August 1794, a caravan drew up near Gloucester Lodge which turned out to be 'the conveyance of two brothers called the Albinos from the mountains of Chamonix'. Everyone – the king, the queen, the princesses and of course the ever-inquisitive Greville – 'honoured them with a visit inside their caravan, and were surprised at these extraordinary-looking people. They have strong milk-white hair, their eyebrows, eyelashes and beards white. The skin of their heads was of a pinkish colour, and their eyes also inclined to pink.' Despite their unusual appearance, 'they spoke very tolerable French, were affable in their manner and well bred in their behaviour'.[19]

In the evenings, there were cards, played with a determined regularity that even news of the death of the queen's elder sister Christiane – who died a spinster, Charlotte's marriage having made her own planned union with the Duke of Roxburghe impossible – did not interrupt, somewhat to the surprise of onlookers. Sometimes there were 'parties at home', but, as Mrs Harcourt noted, these did not include any company from outside the inner household, and especially no new male guests: 'Lord Chesterfield and the other gentlemen in attendance are the only men who are invited; they do not wish to encourage people to pursue them here.'[20]

There were occasional visits from the princes and their friends, who descended on the sedate surroundings of Gloucester Lodge bringing with them the unmistakeable whiff of dissolute bad behaviour. The Prince of Wales, Ernest and Lord Clermont arrived back from a trip on HMS *Minotaur*, where they had 'taken so liberal a potation that they were much animated, and poor Lord Walsingham totally overcome by it. They left him, stripped and laid out on a couch aboard the *Minotaur* under the care and protection of Admiral McBride, who promises to return him safe on shore tomorrow.'[21] The brothers rarely stayed very long in Weymouth, unless compelled to do so. They had no appetite for its quiet pleasures, preferring the gamier appeal of the Prince of Wales's house along the coast at Brighton.

It was not just the princes who found that time at the king's favourite little town dragged out slowly. 'Nothing but the sea affords

Weymouth any life or spirit,' confessed Fanny Burney. Infected perhaps by the same sense of ennui, the queen's dislike of the town grew stronger with every visit. She described it to Lady Harcourt as 'this unenjoyable place', and was convinced that, in spite of its alleged health-giving properties, it actually made her ill. 'The heat, when we first arrived did not agree with me,' she wrote in 1800, 'and according to old custom, brought on my complaint in my bowels and rendered me so stupefied that I could not employ myself, which is, I do assure you, the strongest proof of my being disordered.'[22]

The most passionate denunciation of the resort's limitations came from the queen's fourth daughter, Mary, who, beneath a polite demeanour, boiled in frustration. 'This place is more dull and stupid than I can find words to express,' she fumed on her second visit to Weymouth in 1798, 'a perfect standstill of everything and everybody, except every ten days a long review, that I am told is very fine, but being perfectly unknowing in these things, come home less amused than before I left home.'[23] She was resentful at the isolated existence she and her sisters led there, surrounded by elderly courtiers. 'I do not know one soul except Sir William and Lady Pitt, the Pouletts and that poor little duet, Lord and Lady Sudeley.' The tedium of it all provoked her beyond measure. 'George Pitt's stupid old father is now at Weymouth. He looks as if he died three months ago, and was taken out of his coffin to come and show that he was alive to the king.'[24] Her older sisters, as was their custom, were more discreet; but it is hard to imagine Mary was alone in her condemnation of their somnolent visits.

The king, for whom Weymouth was a welcome interlude of peace in otherwise crowded days, found it a soothing balm for his frazzled spirits. In the more circumscribed lives of the queen and her daughters, their sojourns at Weymouth served less as breaks from daily routine than as amplifications of it. If the princesses had nursed hopes that their lives might change following the terrible catalyst of their father's illness, the limitations of their experiences at Weymouth soon extinguished them. Whatever the landscape, their role in it seemed destined to remain the same: dutiful deliverers of support and comfort to their parents.

The queen had her own disappointments. Any optimism she may have cherished that things could return to the way they had been before her husband's illness ebbed away during the early 1790s.

Sea-bathing and fresh air could do nothing to help her recover the playful pleasure in life that had briefly emerged as such an attractive aspect of her character. Now the best of which she felt herself capable was a detached resignation, a disciplined withdrawal from any greater expectations. 'I am … of the opinion that the best thing is to enjoy what I have and not to make myself uneasy about things in which no human power can direct,' she wrote to her son Augustus in 1791. 'The real wants in life are few; sufficient for myself, and if possible, a little more for the relief of neighbours, is perfect happiness for me.'[25]

It was not at Weymouth but at Frogmore, the little house she owned in Windsor Park, that Charlotte came closest to achieving this ideal. There she sought to create for herself a calm retreat where the stresses of the public world were kept firmly at bay and only those she truly loved were welcome. 'A life of constant hurry and bustle is not reasonable,' she mused, as she surveyed her small domain. 'A country life is to be preferred, but we must not forget the society of which we are part. My own taste is for a few select friends, whose cheerfulness of temper and instructive conversation will pass the time away without leaving any time for remorse.'[26]

Regretful feelings were kept at bay by filling her days with the mild, rational enjoyments she loved. Botany remained her favourite pursuit, and exotic plants arrived at Frogmore from collectors around the world; they were sketched, dried and duly classified, her daughters acting as her assistants in her studies. 'Mama sits in a very small green room which she is fond of,' wrote Elizabeth, 'reads, writes and botanises. Augusta and me remain in the room next to hers across a passage and employ ourselves in much the same way.'[27] Soon Charlotte was keen to translate what she had learnt into an ambitious programme of practical gardening. She had a greenhouse erected, 'by all connoisseurs allowed to be very fine', and employed a horticulturally inclined clergyman to help her plan the planting. 'It is at present in the midst of a kitchen garden, where there is no garden stuff except a few old cabbages,' noted Princess Elizabeth, although she was certain it would, with a little work, emerge as 'a perfect bijou'.[28]

As the garden flourished, Charlotte extended her ambitions to the landscape around it, erecting a number of decorative buildings to adorn the view. Elizabeth, the most artistically gifted of the sisters, was encouraged to design many of them. The intention was to create an elegant retreat, which was to be simple, but certainly not austere.

The grounds soon included a thatched hermitage, an octagonal Temple of Solitude and a barn big enough to be used as a ballroom. There was also a lake backed by artificial hills and a specially constructed Gothic ruin, where Charlotte and her daughters had their breakfast when the weather allowed. In her comfortably appointed and, above all, very private home (visitors were strictly by invitation only) the queen was as happy as she was anywhere. To Fanny Burney she spoke 'with delight of its quiet and ease, and her enjoyment of its complete retirement'.[29] It was not for nothing that she described Frogmore as 'my little paradise'.[30]

But however hard Charlotte tried to keep the real world at a distance, some events proved impossible to ignore. The royal family had been at Weymouth in 1789 when the first accounts of the Revolution in France began to break. On 17 July – three days after the storming of the Bastille – 'Mr Parish, a brother-in-law of Miss Planta's came in the evening, just arrived from France', and horrified Fanny Burney with his account of the 'confusion, commotion and impending revolution' he had witnessed there.[31] At Gloucester Lodge the news was received with apprehension and concern. But for some, the fall of a monarchy that had ruled without offering voice or influence to those who lived under its government was an occasion to be celebrated. 'How much the greatest event this is that ever happened in the world!' declared the Whig Charles Fox. 'And how much the best!' Now, optimists declared, there was the opportunity to bring about the establishment of the first genuinely modern state, founded on rational and equable principles rather than sclerotic and unjust customary right.

Not surprisingly, neither George nor Charlotte shared any of this enthusiasm. Both realised the magnitude of what was unfolding across the Channel, and saw that it struck at everything they represented and believed. As an assiduous reader of Rousseau, the queen understood that the Revolution was the crucible in which a war of ideas was being fought out, a conflict in which the new thinking of the Enlightenment was poised to do battle with older traditions of hierarchy, duty and obligation. 'God knows, the want of principle and the forgetting of all duties towards God and man, and the want of religion are regarded as the causes of the unhappiness of our neighbours,' she wrote to her brother Charles at the end of 1789. Charlotte struggled to understand God's purpose in allowing it to happen at all. 'Perhaps

Providence has sent these unhappy events to bring man back to right.'[32]

Most of her thoughts were directed not at the high politics of the Revolution but towards the horrible predicament of Louis XVI and his family. As a fellow queen, she felt a special sympathy for Marie Antoinette, whose earlier peccadilloes – which Charlotte herself had been quick to condemn – counted as nothing compared to the trials of her current situation. 'Whatever faults she had,' Charlotte told Mrs Harcourt, 'she could but pity her – she had more than paid in suffering for them. She thought her present conduct had much merit, and her former errors much excuse.'[33] Throughout the early months of the Revolution, Charlotte hoped fervently that somehow the French queen and her family would escape their dark destiny. 'I pity both the king and her, and anxiously wish that they may meet with some well-disposed people to extricate them hourly out of their great, horrible distress.'[34]

The king, whilst he recognised his wife's sympathies, was reluctant to intervene, sharing the opinion of his government that it was impossible for Britain to involve itself in the internal politics of another nation. Month by month, the position of the French royal family grew progressively worse. In October 1789, hungry Parisian crowds marched on Versailles, demanding bread and storming the palace. The desperate violence of the mob moved Charlotte to appalled astonishment: 'I often think this cannot be the eighteenth century in which we live at present, for ancient history can hardly produce anything more barbarous and cruel than our neighbours in France.'[35] She was not alone in the strength of her reaction.

Both Charlotte and Fanny Burney found much to admire in Edmund Burke's *Reflections on the Revolution in France*, published in 1790, the most influential British refutation of revolutionary principles and practices, and one of the foundations of modern conservative thought. 'It is truly beautiful,' wrote Fanny, 'alike in nobleness of sentiment and animation of language.' It was also marked by a profound feeling for the personal sufferings of the French royals, arguing that Marie Antoinette in particular deserved the sympathy, if not the more active support, of any honourable, chivalric man. Burke's florid and emotional style earned him a good deal of ridicule from his erstwhile Whig colleagues, but Fanny, whose father knew Edmund Burke well, was not among them: 'How happy does it make me to see this old favourite once more on the side of right and reason!' With a faint echo of the occasional spasms of liberalism that had surfaced since she entered the royal service, she did ask herself whether, 'I call it the right side only because it is my own?' But in truth, Fanny was in little doubt where her loyalties lay. In 1792, she was present at a private dinner with Burke, in which he treated the other diners to a passionate diatribe on the threats posed by the French Revolution, 'even to English liberty and property from the contagion of havoc and novelty'. 'I tacitly assented to his doctrines,' confided Fanny to her journal. She had little difficulty in agreeing with Burke on the importance of monarchy, and the absolute necessity of protecting the persons of kings. 'Kings are necessary,' Burke insisted, 'and if we would preserve our peace and prosperity, we must preserve THEM! We must put all our shoulders to the work, and aye, stoutly too.'[36]

All Burke's persuasive powers had done nothing, however, to deliver any practical assistance to the beleaguered Louis XVI. In the summer of 1791, he and his family had failed in a last-ditch attempt to flee France. They were caught at Varennes, just miles from the Belgian border, spotted by a man who recognised the king's familiar profile from the coinage. Both George and Charlotte were said to be 'much affected' by the news. It was hard to see what hope now remained for their stricken French counterparts. In August 1792, the Tuileries Palace was attacked, Louis's Swiss Guards were massacred and he and his family taken into custody. 'Nothing can be so dreadful as the affairs of that unfortunate country,' wrote the Princess Royal, who was as shocked by the extremity of events as her parents. 'I think they must defeat their own plans by pushing them on with such violence, as it opens everyone's eyes.'[37]

Royal's hopes were unfounded – in fact, the establishment of a European military coalition to restore order in France had probably already sealed Louis's fate. In a pre-emptive action, France declared war on Austria in April 1792, instigating over two decades of worldwide hostilities that ended only with the defeat of Napoleon in 1815. The unexpected defeat of Austria's Prussian allies, routed by French forces at the village of Valmy as they attempted to march on Paris, transformed the prospects of the revolutionary government. Buoyed up by the extraordinary and unexpected success of their armies, the French briskly abolished the monarchy on 21 September 1792 and proclaimed the First Republic. In December, Louis – or 'Citizen Capet' as he was now known – was brought to trial. He was allowed no legal representation, and on 21 January 1793, he was executed. Marie Antoinette followed him to the guillotine in October. Their children were imprisoned in the Conciergerie fortress where they were abused and humiliated, treated with such systematic cruelty and neglect that the dauphin, Louis's ten-year-old heir, died in 1795. His older sister survived the ordeal, but was so traumatised by her experiences that she did not speak for years.

This horrifying sense in which the personal was now irrevocably linked to the political – where no indulgence was extended on grounds of age or complicity, when it was no longer what you had done, but what you had been born that made you a target for popular hatred – must have introduced a new level of anxiety into the lives of George III and his family. The execution in Paris of Louis and Marie Antoinette could not have been contemplated by their counterparts in London without some apprehension that, if events in Britain followed the revolutionary pattern of those in France – a circumstance closer in the 1790s than at any time since the English Civil War – then they too might share the fate of the French monarchy.

The prospect of sudden and unexpected public death was not of course an entirely unfamiliar prospect for any member of the royal family, but before 1789, it seemed more likely to come about through the act of a madman than a revolutionary tribunal. George's family had always lived with the knowledge that their role exposed them to the unwelcome attentions of the disturbed and the obsessed. 'As soon as a man is mad,' wrote Anthony Storer to his friend Lord Auckland, 'he is sure to fall in love with someone of the royal family, or, as love and hatred are very near akin, to wish to assassinate some of them.'[38] The principal target was, almost without exception, the king. One of the best-documented attempts on his life had occurred in 1786, as he arrived at St James's Palace. As George told the story to Fanny Burney, he had just alighted from his carriage, 'when a decently dressed woman who had been waiting for him for some time approached him with a petition'. As he bent forward to take it, she drew a knife 'which she aimed straight at his heart!' When the king started back, the woman made a second thrust 'which touched his waistcoat before he had time to prevent her'. It was just as well she had not pushed harder or had a sharper knife, the king maintained, 'for there was nothing for her to go through but a thin linen and fat'. Immediately, 'the assassin was seized by the populace', who were carrying her away when the king, 'the only calm and moderate person there present', came forward and said, 'The poor creature is mad! Do not hurt her! She has not hurt me!' Once he was satisfied that his assailant was safe, he 'gave positive orders that she should be taken care of, and went into the palace and had his levee'.[39]

George was always remarkably phlegmatic about the ever-present danger of meeting a violent end. Responding to an earlier threat to kill him as he rode to the theatre in 1778, he observed that 'as to my own feelings, they always incline me to put trust where it alone can avail – in the Almighty ruler of the Universe, who knows best what suits his all wise purposes'.[40] When, in 1794 – at the height of the Terror in France – the London Corresponding Society, one of the most influential organisations of radical protest, was alleged to have concocted a plot to murder him with a poisoned arrow fired from an air gun, he took a similarly philosophical view.[41] 'I have ever had but one opinion,' he maintained. 'We are all with the utmost caution open to events of the most fatal kind if men will at any hazard prosecute their plans, therefore anyone would be ever miserable if, not trusting in his own honest endeavours to act uprightly, and trusting in the protection of Providence, he did not banish the thought that men will be found to harbour such wicked intentions.'[42]

The king's wife and daughters, however, did not share his sangfroid. When Fanny Burney first heard of the 1786 assassination attempt, she 'was almost petrified with horror at the intelligence'. The queen took the news even worse, although the king did not perhaps break it to her in the most considerate manner. 'He hastened up to her with a countenance of striking vivacity, and said, "Here I am! – safe and well – as you see! But I have very narrowly escaped being stabbed!"' The two ladies-in-waiting immediately burst into floods of tears, and the Princesses Royal and Augusta 'wept even with a violence', while Charlotte sat stupefied, unable to speak at all. 'After a most painful silence, the first words she could articulate were … "I envy you! I can't cry!"' The king, 'with the gayest good humour did his best to comfort them', and related the whole story in great detail, 'with a calmness and unconcern' that Fanny thought wholly admirable. He also insisted that the regular routine of walking on the terrace should not be postponed. Pale and silent, the queen dutifully accompanied him. The atmosphere of barely suppressed anxiety had still not lifted when the nightly concert performance was held as usual at their father's insistence. 'It was an evening of grief and horror to his family,' wrote Fanny. 'Nothing was listened to, scarce a word was spoken; the princesses wept continually and the queen, still more deeply struck, could only, from time to time, hold out her hand to the king and say, "I have you yet."'[43]

The queen, thought Fanny, was convinced 'some latent conspiracy' lay behind the attempt, and 'this dreadful suggestion prays upon [her] mind, though she struggles to conquer or conceal it'. In fact, the king's would-be assassin at St James's was, as he had instantly recognised, motivated by insanity rather than political malevolence. Margaret Nicholson was an impoverished seamstress who lived alone after the failure of an unhappy affair. Neighbours in her lodging house later testified that she was often to be heard muttering to herself; in her room were found many letters to the king, asserting her claim to the throne. She had perhaps sewn for herself the stylish black silk cloak and fashionable hat that proved such a gift to the illustrators and caricaturists who rushed to picture the almost-fatal scene; but she had no other assets, her entire resources amounting to no more than one sixpence and three halfpennies. When the case was investigated, she was declared to be mad, and confined for the rest of her long life in Bethlem Hospital for the insane at Moorfields.

In 1795, a very different kind of attack was made upon the king, which had as its cause exactly the kind of political purpose the queen had so feared a decade earlier. Britain had by then been at war with revolutionary France for nearly three years; taxes were high, a succession of poor harvests had raised the price of food beyond what the poor could afford, and political ideas advocating a more equal distribution of wealth and power were proving unsurprisingly attractive to those suffering most acutely in such desperately hard times. 'Everyone is in great trouble about the scarceness of provisions,' wrote Charlotte to Lady Harcourt in July. Things were so bad that she had heard several families 'are come to a determination not to use pastry or white bread and to furnish all the family with brown bread'.[44] It was not long before the royal household followed their example. The queen sent the Prince of Wales a recipe 'for the making of potato bread which proves to be remarkably good, and we have had it baked with great success at Windsor'. It is hard to imagine such a homely dish making an appearance in the studied elegance of Carlton House;

but George and Charlotte, naturally economical and abstemious, had not needed the grim example of Marie Antoinette to remind them of the political inexpediency of eating cake when others went hungry. 'The king has given orders to have no other bread served to the household but brown bread,' Charlotte told her eldest son with satisfaction, 'and it is to be hoped this will encourage others to do the same.'[45] But the queen was not convinced that, even if other wealthy families did follow their lead, it would have the necessary calming effect. 'Whether the poor will be brought to that submission is a question,' she admitted to Lady Harcourt. 'The proverb says necessity has no law, who knows but that this distress may serve those who are unfriendly as a foundation for many unpleasant scenes.'[46]

At the end of October 1795, just such an 'unpleasant scene' erupted in central London, with the king at its heart. The mood of the capital was volatile in the extreme, the tension increased by the knowledge that legislation was about to be introduced which would curtail severely traditional rights and liberties. The Treasonable Practices Act outlawed serious criticism of the king, the government or the constitution, whilst the Seditious Meetings Act banned mass political meetings. The previous year, George had supported the suspension of habeas corpus, effectively sanctioning imprisonment without trial in certain cases. For all his genuinely paternalist sympathies for the sufferings of the poor, George had no doubt that mass disorder was to be suppressed at all costs. His candid advocacy of measures he described as 'highly right and salutary' made him as unpopular amongst reformers as he had once been amongst American rebels. In response, radical balladeers composed songs which contrasted strongly with the loyal declarations of the populace in Weymouth.

May we but live to see the day,
The crown from George's head shall fall,
The people's voice will then bear sway,
We'll humble tyrants one and all.[47]

All this contributed to the hostile reception the king met with as he travelled to open Parliament. Along the route, an angry crowd surrounded the royal carriage shouting, 'Peace and bread! No war! Down with George!' Lord Onslow, who was sitting alongside the king, was appalled at what happened next: 'a small ball, either of lead or marble, passed through the window glass on the king's right hand, and perforating it, passed through the coach out of the other door … We all instantly exclaimed "This is a shot!"' The king displayed his customary self-control, which was more than some of the other passengers could manage. 'Sit still, my lord,' he rebuked one of his companions who was fidgeting in alarm, 'we must not betray fear whatever happens.' The shaken entourage eventually forced its way through to Westminster, where George delivered his speech.

The journey home was worse. The crowd had grown bigger and far more restive, and threw so many stones at the royal carriage that all its windows were shattered. 'Several stones hit the king, which he bore with signal patience, but not without sensible marks of indignation … at the indignities offered to his person and his office.' At the end of the fraught journey, Onslow recorded that the king 'took one of the stones out of the cuff of his coat, where it had lodged, and gave it to me saying, "I make you a present of this as a mark of the civilities we have met with today."'[48]

The queen and the princesses, waiting for the king's return at St James's, were greatly unnerved by the events of the day, which they had seen and heard from within the palace. 'It is impossible to paint to you in any degree what we have gone through,' wrote Elizabeth to Lady Harcourt. The possibility that a bullet had been fired at her father was clearly 'a most shocking thought'; but it was the hostility of the crowd that upset her most, the behaviour of 'the Mob, who followed the coach in an insolent fashion, moaning and screaming "peace, no war", "give us bread", "down with Pitt" and "off with your guards"'.[49] The princess was unable to get the images out of her mind. 'I trust in God never to be again in the agonies I felt the whole of that day. It was indeed very horrid; and my poor ears I believe will never get the better of the groans I heard that Thursday in the Park, and my eyes the sight of that mob.'[50] As she listened, transfixed, to 'the hootings, the screams', did the experiences of Louis XVI pass through her mind?

She did not feel properly safe until back in Windsor, where, considering the circumstances, she thought 'my sisters and myself are surprisingly well; but it has had such an extraordinary effect on me that I, who naturally cry a great deal, have scarcely shed a tear'. In contrast, her mother, as traumatised as her daughters by what she had seen and heard, finally gave way to her feelings. 'I am much more comfortable about Mama,' Elizabeth wrote, 'as she cried yesterday, which she has never done while she remained in Town; for she always said that did she let herself once go she could never conduct herself as she ought.'[51]

Charlotte had embarked on the new decade of the 1790s with a renewed determination to keep her feelings firmly under control. Bruised, insulted and undermined by her husband's illness, she fought hard not to give in to grief and despair. As a result, even her small domestic pleasures often seem undertaken as much in the spirit of 'banishing remorse' as in pursuit of genuine enjoyment. Anxiety dominated her existence. In the public sphere, a new threat, both political and personal, far-reaching and yet horribly immediate, had been introduced by the French Revolution, and given a cruel pertinence by the sad fates of Louis XVI and his family. In her private world, things were, if anything, worse. The king's health remained a subject about which everyone worried and nobody spoke. The 1794 trip to Weymouth had been undertaken in an attempt to head off what had seemed like an ominous return of his old disorder. Princess Elizabeth told Lady Harcourt she thought the holiday 'absolutely necessary' in the light of 'much hurry of mind' and sleeplessness that everyone had noticed in her father although it was not openly discussed. 'Never write to me on the subject, nor own to the family that I have mentioned it,' she warned Lady Harcourt; 'but the truth will out to you. We never talk on the subject.'[52]

But amongst all Charlotte's trials, it was the behaviour of her children that caused her most distress. This was the decade in which the first serious challenges appeared from within the family to the emotional authority established by the king decades earlier. As the struggles grew more prolonged and unpleasant. Charlotte's attempts to carve out a quiet space for herself, where she could retreat into a somewhat chilly and isolated calm, became ever less successful.

*

Relations between the queen and her eldest daughter had not been good for some time. Alongside Augusta and Elizabeth, the Princess Royal had endured her father's illness as a member of the suffering sisterhood who rarely left their mother's side. But as the king recovered, it became clear that Royal did not entirely approve of her mother's conduct during those difficult months. Like her eldest brother, her political sympathies lay with the opposition Whigs, and she was said to object strongly to the queen's passionate identification with the king's ministers. Soon her disapproval was reported to have tipped over into something much stronger. 'Her Royal Highness now averred that she had never liked the queen, from her excessive severity, that she doubted her judgement on many points, and went so far as to say that she was a silly woman.'[53] It seems unlikely that the painstaking and punctilious Royal would ever have described her mother in terms of such dismissive disrespect, certainly not in any place where she might be overheard; but there is little doubt that as the new decade opened, the twenty-four-year-old princess was plumbing new depths of unhappiness. Her principal complaint was boredom. Whether at Weymouth, Windsor or Frogmore, there was little to break the monotony of royal routine. Sometimes even the resilient Elizabeth's spirits wilted when she was forced to contemplate the emptiness of their lives, in which nothing marked one day out from another except the playing of a little cards followed by the prospect of some cursory squabbling.

For the princesses, the lowering effects of this life were made harder to bear by their mother's increasingly bad temper. The misery that Charlotte fought so hard to conceal under a veneer of disciplined resignation too often exploded into angry words, 'sour looks' and bitter recrimination. Her daughters, who spent nearly all their time in her company, bore the brunt of it. 'I am sorry to hear the behaviour of a certain person continues so bad,' wrote the queen's youngest son Adolphus to his eldest brother. He could not understand why their mother chose to be 'so odd, and why make her life so wretched when she could be just the reverse'.[54] James Bland Burges – junior minister, poet and friend of the princesses' lady-in-waiting, Lady Elgin – had heard similar stories of Charlotte's irascibility: 'I understand that the smiles and graces worn at court are generally laid aside with the full-dressed gown and jewels.'[55] Burges thought the Princess Royal was particularly susceptible to the peevish moodiness of the queen, 'before whom she is under the utmost constraint, and who maintains a very strict discipline and the most formal etiquette even in her moments of relaxation'.[56] By 1791, this combination of isolation, aimlessness and squabbling had exhausted even Royal's much-practised powers of endurance. Driven to desperation, she approached the one member of her family who she hoped would not only take her plight seriously, but might also help her change it: the Prince of Wales.

In the eyes of his sisters, their eldest brother could do no – or very little – wrong. To them, he was not only the very model of aristocratic elegance and refined modern taste, he was also generous, charming and indulgently kind. Even his more disreputable behaviour, of which they were not unaware, did little to affect their rosy view of him. He brought excitement and a touch of glamour into their otherwise monochrome days. They enjoyed his immersion in the life of high society, seeing him as an emissary from a raffish and exotic world which they knew they could never themselves enter. In return, the prince made a genuine attempt to live up to the standards set by the unconditional admiration of his sisters. More than anyone else, they penetrated the armour of his monumental self-regard; he made time to write to them, visit them and send them presents. He remained a part of their lives when it would have been only too easy for him to have drifted away into the louche world that was his accustomed habitat.

There was, of course, another dimension to both the princesses' desire to confide in the prince and his willingness to listen to their problems. All knew that a time would come when he might have the power to change their situations. The prospect of his succeeding their father was never openly discussed, but it was the unspoken undercurrent to all the conversations the prince was to have with his sisters for over two decades. The extraordinary exchanges he had with the Princess Royal in 1791, when, for the first time, she openly declared the depth of her unhappiness and called upon her brother to help her find a way out of it, was the first of many appeals to come.

In May, the Prince of Wales had gone to the Queen's House to sit with his mother on the occasion of her birthday. As he wrote in a letter to Frederick, Duke of York, their eldest sister was there too, 'with whom I joked much in a good-humoured way about herself in the presence of my mother'. This was quite clearly family business as usual for the prince, and he had not at all expected what happened next. 'Soon afterwards I took my leave and went upstairs to sit with my other sisters, when the eldest followed me and begged to speak two minutes in private with me, to which I immediately assented. She then told me how much obliged she would be if I would never joke with her respecting the smallest trifle in the presence of her mother, as I did not know how she suffered from it afterwards, how she was treated, etc., etc.' Clearly somewhat bemused, the prince promised that he 'would do as she asked, and had I known it sooner, she never should have suffered a single moment's uneasiness by my means, as it ever was the principal object of my life to do everything in my power to render every individual of my family as happy as possible'. Royal seems to have taken her brother's polite apology as an invitation to further confidences. She asked to see him again, and when the prince agreed to do so, described with passion how miserable she felt:

> She said that the evident partiality which was shown on every occasion and in every trifle by her parents to all her other sisters in preference to her, the manner in which she was treated on all occasions, particularly by her mother, the constant restraint she was kept under, just like an infant, the perpetual and tiresome and confined life she was obliged to lead, no attempt being made at settling her abroad, or giving her a species of establishment at home, but what was worse than all, the violence and caprice of her mother's temper, which hourly grows worse, to which she is not only obliged to submit, but to be absolutely a slave – in short, these circumstances combined were such as had led her to speak her mind.[57]

Having stated her grievances so powerfully, Royal expected something more from her brother than just sympathy. As the prince described it to the Duke of York, she had made it clear that 'Nothing should make her undergo another year of what she had for some years past … anything was preferable to the misery she was slave to at present.' All the prince's attempts to calm her down were brushed aside; she was not to be fobbed off.

Both Royal and her brother knew there was only one way to extricate her from the sad life she had described with such loathing, and that was marriage. She begged her brothers to 'endeavour to form some sort of alliance for her abroad, or in case that did not succeed, to press for some sort of establishment being formed for her here … If we would not, both of us, enter into these views cordially and engage to do the most we could for her, she gave me to understand she was determined to pursue her own plans and schemes.' This was fighting talk indeed for the dutiful daughter of a dutiful queen, educated to believe that submission to the requirements of the family must always take precedence over her own happiness. Made reckless perhaps by the exhilaration of her defiance, Royal went even further, making it pathetically clear to her brother with whom she hoped her happiness might be found. 'She then entered into an argument with me about what the propriety would be, supposing no attachment could take place abroad for her, were an alliance to be thought of with our friend the Duke of Bedford, and to tell you the truth, my dearest Frederick, I think she seems more anxious about this than for any foreign match in the world. She says she is come to a time of life that will not admit of any scheme of this sort being any longer postponed.' The prince found this such an extraordinary idea 'that to tell you the truth I could hardly forbear laughing'.

He knew such a marriage would never take place. Bedford was one of the greatest of the great Whig grandees, and therefore effectively an hereditary member of the opposition. The king's hostility to seeing his daughters marry British peers would only have been intensified by the knowledge that it was Bedford whom Royal had chosen. The prince told his sister bluntly that such a match was impossible. 'I told her I thought if I knew my father, which I thought I did pretty well, that he would never think of giving his consent to anything of this kind.' He considered a foreign alliance was a far more realistic prospect, and promised her that both he and the Duke of York would consult 'mutually what was best for her interests, and to endeavour … to alleviate those distresses which seem to press so much upon her mind'. In the meantime, 'she must take a little patience'.[58]

However, when he responded to his brother's long letter, the Duke of York was pessimistic whether much could be done. 'Nobody pities her more than I do,' he wrote, 'or wishes to see her married sooner, knowing what a dreadful life she must lead,' but he thought there were no opportunities in Prussia, where he was then living. 'I cannot think that she can expect to marry the Prince Royal here because she is now five and twenty and he is only one and twenty. Besides, though I know that it is his great plan to marry one of our sisters, yet I believe he looks forward to Mary, who is certainly in every respect more suited to him in age. Tell Princess Royal however from me that I will give her my opinion very full how to proceed.'[59]

In the end, nothing came of Royal's attempt to force the issue of her unhappy situation. No more was said about the Duke of Bedford, who died young and unmarried. The only union that came out of Germany in 1791 was that of the Duke of York himself, who married the woman he called his 'old flame', his cousin, the King of Prussia's eldest daughter, Frederica. 'I do not say that she is the handsomest girl ever formed,' wrote Frederick contentedly to his elder brother, 'but she is full enough so for me, and in disposition she is an angel.'[60] When she arrived in England, the stylish and sweet-natured Duchess of York soon became one of the Princess Royal's closest friends and confidantes; but she was no substitute for the husband and independence that she had so desperately desired. As time passed and her hopes ebbed away, Royal's only resource was the patience her brothers so insistently urged upon her, to sustain a life she found unendurable.

It is possible that Royal's parents were not even aware of her abortive bid for freedom. Her failed attempt was followed, however, by a far more direct challenge from within the family, both to the legal authority the king had established for himself in the Royal Marriages Act of 1772 and the desire for emotional control that lay behind it. No one saw it coming, perhaps because it was mounted by one of the least flamboyant of the princes.

Augustus was the second youngest of George and Charlotte's surviving sons, a bookish and thoughtful boy. He was originally destined for the navy, but suffered from asthmatic attacks so severe that he was often unable to lie down to sleep at night, and was forced to try to rest sitting up in a chair. The king therefore decided that, after he had finished his studies at Göttingen, a career in the Church would suit him better than the sea. In the meantime, he sent him off to Rome, where it was hoped the climate might improve his health. Augustus was at first a reluctant traveller, disliking the attendants his father had chosen for him, and soon exhausting the pleasures of the tourist sights. Things looked up outside the church of San Giacomo when he met Lady Dunmore and her daughter Lady Augusta Murray. Noticing that Lady Augusta's shoelace was untied, he knelt down and tied it for her. Soon they were reading *The Tempest* together; next they exchanged love letters, full of passionate references to 'Goosey' and 'Gussy'; and not long after that, on 4 April 1793, in defiance of the Royal Marriages Act, they were married by an English clergyman at Lady Dunmore's hotel. Augustus was only twenty; his new wife was some years older, and as a result was generally regarded as a cradle-snatcher. Augusta was clearly more experienced in the ways of the world than the rather innocent Augustus. Lady Harcourt thought she 'had the address to conceal or gloss over some of the earlier transactions of her life'.[61] The diarist Joseph Farrington, no stranger to worldliness himself, thought Lady Augusta 'coarse and confident-looking', concluding that the prince 'is generally considered as having been drawn into it'.[62]

Rumours about the affair must have reached the king by the spring of 1793, as he ordered Augustus to return home. The prince took his time and did not arrive in London until the autumn. As soon as she met him, his mother suspected, 'by the agitation Augustus is in', that the gossip was right, but she surely cannot have suspected just how far matters had gone. Lady Augusta was now pregnant, and, at Augustus's urging, the couple underwent a second marriage ceremony. On 5 December at St George's, Hanover Square, in the very early morning, a man calling himself Mr Augustus Frederick, in a greatcoat pulled up to hide his face, married Miss Augusta Murray, who was eight months pregnant, the bride maintaining 'she had married Mr Frederick in Italy when he was under age and so she decided to be re-married'.[63]

If Augustus hoped this second wedding in Britain would give some extra degree of security to his wife, he was wrong; neither ceremony had any validity in English law, as both contravened the terms of the Royal Marriages Act. He later described his marriage as 'a misunderstanding', but it is hard to imagine he was not aware of the provisions of an Act that loomed so large in the lives of all his siblings. In January 1794, a few days before his son was born, Augustus wrote to his eldest brother in frantic anxiety. 'My situation I believe to be one of the most unpleasant in the world, from various reasons I cannot mention ... Many times has my mind been so overcome with despair that I have been almost distracted.'[64] He must have known by then that the king had ordered him back to Italy. He left a few days later, having said nothing to his father about his wife and child, leaving them in London to face the consequences alone.

The king was officially informed of his son's illegal actions at the end of January, and coolly instructed the Lord Chancellor to 'proceed in this unpleasant business as the law directs'.[65] It took just over six months for the inevitable verdict to be reached. On 14 July 1794, the Arches Court of Canterbury pronounced the marriage between Prince Augustus and Lady Augusta Murray null and void. The King's first grandson – another Augustus – was by this action declared illegitimate. Lady Augusta was established quietly in the country with her son, on a small pension, but warned not to try to join her erstwhile husband abroad.

Meanwhile, the prince brooded on his situation in Rome. Cut off from all contact with the princesses – he was convinced there was 'an order existing which forbids any correspondence betwixt my sisters and me' – he relied on his brothers to keep any link with home alive. As many of his exiled forebears had done before him, he began to assemble a picture gallery of his closest relatives. He wrote to Ernest in October asking him to 'sit for a miniature for me and send it by the first opportunity'. He had already managed to gather together images of almost everyone else. 'The Prince [of Wales]'s and Adolphus's are the only ones missing as the Princess Royal has promised me hers, and the queen that of Amelia. Pray put the Prince of Wales in mind of it. In my solitary and unhappy moments, the sight of these pictures affords me great comfort.'[66]

Despite his miserable state, he insisted to the Prince of Wales that he would not capitulate; but the king was implacable, and as the months passed, Augustus's loneliness gnawed away at his resolve and a more conciliatory tone crept into his letters. He begged the king to understand the difficulty of his situation: 'Can a man of feeling who, through involuntary error, has become a father, forsake his child because the law is ignorant of his birth? Who is to protect the unfortunate companion of my misfortunes and my helpless infant if I do not stand forward?'[67] Throughout 1795, Augustus tried to persuade his father to accept that he could not repudiate his wife and child, 'those who have suffered on my account and whom I love'. He repeatedly begged him 'to find some efficacious remedy' for his impossible position, but to no avail. In the end the king refused to respond at all to his pleas, and gradually it became clear to Augustus that there was nothing to be done.

Kept away from both his families, new and old, this inoffensive and affectionate man began to sink into a deep depression. 'I want nothing but to be left alone. My whole disposition is altered, that I hate society, and only feel less uncomfortable when alone.'[68] For the next four years, Augustus cut a sad and solitary figure among the classical ruins of Rome. It was not only George and Charlotte's daughters whose lives were blighted by the king's cold determination to command emotional obedience from his children. As Augustus's story suggests, a sensitive son could suffer as profoundly as any of his sisters.

By 1794, it seemed as though the misery engendered by Augustus's exile and Royal's disappointment threatened to overwhelm the entire household. 'I assure you, from what I have lately heard,' wrote James Bland Burges in December, 'that royalty, when closely inspected, has few charms for reasonable people. I do not believe there is a more unhappy family in the kingdom than that of our good king. They have lately passed whole hours together in tears; and often do not meet for half a day, but each remains alone, separately brooding over their misfortunes.' Burges cited a long list of reasons for the atmosphere of despair, all of them related to the behaviour of the princes. There was 'the bad conduct' of Augustus; 'the ill-success and disgrace' of the Duke of York, who had been removed from his role as commander-in-chief of British forces after a series of defeats fighting the French in the Low Countries; and inevitably, 'the strange caprices and obstinacies of the Prince of Wales'. All these causes, Burges believed, 'are perpetually preying on them and make them miserable'. Hunkered down behind her impenetrable façade of detachment, it seemed to Burges as if 'the queen seems to suffer and feel the least'. Other members of the family were less constrained in expressing their distress. 'The king sometimes bursts into tears – rises up and walks about the room – then kisses his daughters and thanks God for having given them him to comfort him – whilst the princesses are variously agitated, and sometimes so much as to go into fits.'

This atmosphere of hysterical distress weighed heavily on the already wilting spirits of the princesses. Burges thought 'the effect of this kind of life' upon them

> has been very different according to their constitutions. Princess Augusta, soft and tender-hearted, vents her sorrows at her eyes and cries until she becomes composed and resigned. Princess Elizabeth feels very strongly, but soon recovers her spirits, and observes that, thank God, she does no harm herself and that she will not be such a fool as to make herself more unhappy than she is obliged to be; and therefore, she will be merry if she can, and drive away all the care, which she is strong enough to keep at a distance.

As Burges saw, the eldest of the princesses lacked either Elizabeth's robust refusal to succumb to unhappiness or Augusta's ability to cry the misery out of herself. 'The effect of all this on the poor Princess

Royal is very different. She is naturally nervous, and susceptible of strong impressions. Convinced she now has little chance of altering her condition; afraid of receiving any impressions of tenderness or affection; reserved and studious; tenderly loving her brothers and feeling strongly every unpleasant circumstance attending them, she is fallen into a kind of quiet desperate state, without hope and open to every fear; in other words, what is called broken-hearted.' Sunk in sadness, Royal's mute dejection was so severe that she had been seen by the doctor Sir Lucas Pepys, who was shocked by her depression, whilst correctly diagnosing its cause. Burges reported that he 'expresses considerable apprehension for her and even privately hints that he thinks her in great danger, as from her particular situation, there is no chance of her being able to marry, which, he pretty plainly says, is the only probability he can see of saving her life or her understanding.'[69]

The knowledge that there was nothing she could do for herself to change her prospects was undoubtedly a factor in Royal's decline. Her one attempt to take the initiative had ended in failure, illustrating forcefully her total dependence on the intervention of others to bring about any change in her life for the better. Her elder brothers were not indifferent to her fate; but when there proved no easy solution to her problem, it gradually slipped down the list of their priorities, emerging as an issue only when other women achieved the 'settlement' Royal so craved. 'I suppose I was as much vexed as you,' wrote Frederick to the Prince of Wales in 1793, 'that my two brothers-in-law [the princes of Prussia] are engaged to marry the two Princesses of Mecklenburg-Strelitz.' These were the daughters of the queen's beloved brother Charles, on whose education she had been so eager to advise years before. 'I had hoped they would have married two of our sisters,' commented Frederick ruefully. 'However that cannot be now.'[70]

There was, the brothers concluded, little that they could do for Royal. Besides, her eldest brother had other things on his mind. With a freedom to make his own choices that was denied to her, the Prince of Wales had decided to have for himself the very thing his eldest sister wanted most in the world. It was, he considered, time for him to marry.

His decision came as a surprise to everybody. The prince had always insisted that he had no wish to take a wife, and declared himself perfectly happy to see the royal line continue through the children of his brothers. In 1791, in the course of an interview in which he sought the king's approval for the marriage of the Duke of York, who was absent in Prussia, he explained in detail exactly why he believed marriage for himself was not a likely option: 'I was come to a time of life when I thought I had tolerably weighed all my own sentiments and prospects, that it was not everyone who could expect to be as lucky as His Majesty had been to meet with a person whose disposition suited so perfectly with his own as the queen's did, if one might presume to judge by the unanimity that appeared to reign between them.' Dropping the circumlocutory politeness that characterised most of the prince's exchanges with his parents, he then spoke more plainly: 'That as to us princes particularly, the choice of a wife was indeed a lottery, and one in which I did not at present intend to draw a ticket. There were very few prizes compared with the number of blanks.' It was possible, he admitted, that his feelings on the subject might one day change, but at present he thought them unconquerable. 'I did not mean to bind myself not to marry at all, but thought it most likely I should not, as the sentiments I had expressed were prejudices I could not get the better of.'[71]

There is little doubt that the prince meant what he said; but with his usual ability to convince not just others but also himself that a partial truth represented the whole of a story, he had omitted one important detail from his explanation.

He was, in fact, already married.

*

The Prince of Wales had met Maria Fitzherbert in 1784 through his Whig friends. Twice widowed, like so many of his mistresses, she was older than him, by six years. Her deceased husbands had left her comfortably provided for, and she surveyed the churning metropolitan social scene with an air of quiet confidence in her own value. She was handsome rather than beautiful, with a good bosom, striking eyes, fair hair and a clear complexion. Her critics considered her 'perhaps too much inclined to fullness of figure', but the prince was always drawn to amply proportioned women.[72] She was thought good-natured, if a little proud; and beneath her calm exterior, she shared some of the hair-trigger temper and unpredictable mood swings of her royal lover. She was not a sparkling conversationalist, but was a kind and patient listener, which appealed to the loquacious and needy prince.

When they met, he was twenty-two and already the veteran of a string of affairs with women of every conceivable background. His lovers had included grand ladies of the court, opera singers, Maids of Honour, the wife of the Hanoverian ambassador, actresses and a number of semi-professional courtesans, many of whom he inherited or poached from his closest friends. Despite her affection for him, Maria was made of sterner stuff than most of George's conquests, and refused to become his mistress. This only served to fan the flames of George's desire. With his usual theatricality, George declared that he would die if she did not surrender, and attempted – somewhat half-heartedly – to stab himself. Seriously alarmed, Maria ran away to France. Whilst there, the prince bombarded her with letters, some over forty pages long, declaring that he could not live without her, that he would 'ever remain unto the last moments of his existence unalterably thine'. He declared that he considered himself married to her in spirit, and insisted that the king could be persuaded to 'connive' at their union, although his rational mind must have known this was impossible. He called her 'his dearest wife', 'his beloved wife' and urged her to return to him. 'Come then, oh! Come then, dearest of wives, best and most adored of women, and forever crown with bliss him who will through life endeavour to convince you by his love and attention of his wishes to be the best of husbands.'[73] Mrs Armistead, Charles Fox's mistress, was horrified by the violence of the prince's behaviour, 'rolling on the floor, striking his forehead, tearing his hair'. He repeatedly declared that he would 'abandon the country, forgo the crown, sell his jewels and plate and scrape together a competence to fly with the object of his affections to America'.[74] The prince was clearly in a state of hysterical distress. He'd always had a volatile personality, but beneath the drama lurked a hint of real feeling, a kernel of perception that, more than any of his other transient relationships, his love for Maria Fitzherbert offered the prospect of something genuinely transformative in his life. 'Save me, save me,' he urged her repeatedly, 'save me on my knees, I conjure you, from myself.'[75]

Eventually, Mrs Fitzherbert capitulated, came back to London, and on 15 December 1785, she and the prince were married. It took the prince's aides some time to find a clergyman who was willing to perform the ceremony; finally a curate, currently imprisoned for debt, agreed to conduct it in return for the payment of creditors and the promise of future preferment. The wedding took place in Mrs Fitzherbert's drawing room, behind securely locked doors.

As the prince must have known, the marriage was invalid, as it breached every provision of the Royal Marriages Act. But it did more than that. Maria Fitzherbert was a Catholic, and the 1689 Act of Settlement required succession to the throne to be forfeited if the heir married a Catholic. The prince, focussed as ever on achieving his short-term desires, paid no attention to all to the possible consequences of his actions. The couple did not actually live together, but Mrs Fitzherbert was soon established in a house in Brighton, close to George's retreat at the Royal Pavilion. In London, she lived in St James's, not far from Carlton House. The marriage could never be formally acknowledged, but the pair were often seen together in society. The prince made it known that she was to be invited to all events he was expected to attend, and required that she was always to be placed at his table.[76] The exact nature of their relationship was the subject of much speculation. Only months after the supposedly secret ceremony, the Catholic aristocrat Lady Jerningham was certain, from all she had heard, that the prince and Mrs Fitzherbert were indeed married. Seemingly better aware of the laws he had flouted than the prince himself, she thought it 'a very hazardous undertaking … God knows how it will turn out'.[77] The rumours finally surfaced in the House of Commons in 1787, and were put directly to Charles Fox, the leader of the Whig opposition and the prince's close friend. Fox assured the House that the stories were false: the marriage 'not only never could have happened legally, but never did happen in any way whatever'.[78] He claimed 'the immediate authority of the Prince of Wales' for his assertion. This was indeed the case. Fox had been against the union from the beginning, recognising the dangers it posed to the prince's future, and had done all he could to dissuade him from taking so potentially dangerous a step. In response to his warnings, the prince had assured his old friend that he had no plans to marry Mrs Fitzherbert, telling him that 'there not only is, but never was, any ground for these reports which have of late been so malevolently circulated'.[79] Fox told the truth as he believed, or wanted to believe, he knew it; but Mrs Fitzherbert was furious, declaring that Fox had 'rolled her in the kennel like a streetwalker', and never spoke to him again.[80]

For a while, it seemed as though Mrs Fitzherbert had succeeded where so many others had failed, and had indeed saved the prince from himself, enticing him into the enjoyment of a more domestic life. Certainly his family thought so, and considered this more settled relationship as a great improvement on its ramshackle predecessors. They did not know – or chose not to know – that it was based on a double illegality. But as the years went by, the partnership began to founder, partly on George's duplicity. He took other lovers – his pledges of lifelong fidelity had not proved long-lasting – and justified himself to his friends by arguing that he knew his marriage had no real meaning, although his wife persisted in believing in it.[81] Painfully anxious about her ambiguous status, wife and yet no wife, Mrs Fitzherbert grew resentful. The couple argued over the prince's affairs, his drinking, his habitual and wounding dishonesty, and his recklessness with money.

Soon it was well known that their romantic idyll was over; one popular caricature showed Mrs Fitzherbert throwing a cup of tea in the prince's face. Then, in the summer of 1794, the prince met someone new, the elegant and manipulative Lady Jersey, who was as experienced as he was in the conduct of extramarital affairs. Mrs Fitzherbert was brutally dismissed, the separation announced by a curt letter which, she insisted, 'was preceded by no quarrel, or even coolness and came upon her quite unexpectedly', whilst she was sitting down to dinner with William, Duke of Clarence.[82] George was unrepentant. Should his letter 'not meet with the success which the good intentions with which it is written merit and entitle it to, I have nothing further to say or reproach myself with'. He wrote to Frederick in Germany that though 'we are finally parted … you will not lay the fault, whatever it may have been, at my door'.[83]

The ink was hardly dry on the prince's letter ending almost ten years of life with Mrs Fitzherbert, than he was on the road to Weymouth to announce to his father his plans to marry. The prince's complete volte-face on the subject of matrimony produced a rich crop of speculation about his motives, but it seems likely that three different factors had brought him to act so swiftly. Firstly, he saw marriage as a way of paying off his huge debts, which by this time approached £630,000. As a married man, he would be entitled to a greater payment from the Civil List, which would secure him more credit, even if it did not wipe out all his indebtedness. Secondly, Lady Jersey, now fully established as his principal mistress, was said to have encouraged him in the scheme as a way of preventing any resurgence of feelings for Mrs Fitzherbert. And finally, and in some ways most significantly, the judgement declaring his brother Augustus's marriage invalid in July must have reassured him that his own union would not be held binding if brought to a court of law. Having effortlessly shrugged off any sense of moral obligation, he could now plan a marriage in the reasonable assumption that he was also legally free to do so.

It is often asserted that it was the king who selected the Prince of Wales's wife for him, but that was not the case. The prince made the decision himself, declaring his choice to the king in the same conversation in which he had announced his intention to marry. Exactly why he chose his cousin, Princess Caroline, the Duke of Brunswick's daughter, will probably never be known. Contemporary gossip attributed it to the malign influence of Lady Jersey, who hoped 'that disgust for the wife would secure constancy to the mistress'.[84] It was even suggested that the prince had been swayed by admiration for her father, a military hero of some renown. It seems more likely, however, that the prince pursued the project with a characteristic lack of reflection, intent only on considering the immediate benefits of the alliance, without giving any serious consideration to the life-changing implications of his choice. Back in 1791, he had told the king that he would never take a wife 'unless at the moment I did, I thought I preferred the woman I was going to marry to every other creature existing in the world'. The thrill of a passion immediately and intensely indulged was everything to him. He was a romantic, of a particularly narcissistic and indulgent kind. He sought out sensation and extremity of emotion, perhaps in an attempt to deliver into an otherwise purposeless existence a sense of meaning and excitement. All this made him a particularly bad candidate to cope with the requirements of an arranged marriage. He had none of the traits which had served his father so well in a similar situation: a dogged determination to make the relationship work combined with an iron resolution not to indulge the lure of passion. Nor was he prepared to take precautions, as the king had done thirty years before, to ensure he did not find himself yoked to a woman who did not suit him. He maintained that he would never marry unless 'I knew enough of the disposition of my wife to think it would form the happiness and not the misery of my future days.'[85] Now he disregarded entirely his own advice, making no enquiries at all about the character of his future bride. This was, perhaps, the biggest mistake of his life. A little more care in making his choice might have spared all of those concerned the years of grief, bitterness and recrimination which made it the unhappiest royal marriage in modern times, and in whose throes the royal family was engulfed, divided and almost destroyed.

The king told the prince that he was entirely satisfied with his choice of bride. She was the daughter of his older sister, Augusta, and it was therefore not surprising that he thought it 'the only proper alliance'. The queen, on the other hand, was horrified. Neither her son nor her husband had thought it worth seeking her opinion before the decision was made, although if they had done so, they would not have liked what she had to say. Charlotte was an assiduous collector of Continental gossip with an almost encyclopedic knowledge of the reputations of female German royalty, and what she had heard about her niece Caroline was far from good. Coincidentally, Caroline had been the subject of a conversation between Charlotte and the king only weeks before the prince's surprise announcement. 'A fortnight ago I went into the king and found him busy sealing some letters, and he gave me one to show me it was for you,' explained the queen to her brother Charles. In it, the king offered his recently widowed brother-in-law advice on finding another wife, and suggested as a possibility his niece, Caroline of Brunswick. 'I was stupefied by these words; fortunately he did not notice; and said, "What do you think of it?" I said, "Perhaps Your Majesty is in more of a hurry over this event than my brother," and that said, I shall take care not to reopen the conversation.' Had the queen broken her usual self-denying ordinance, and ventured to offer her husband her true opinion, a great deal of misery could have been avoided. Instead, she confided only to her brother everything she knew about Caroline of Brunswick's many and alarming shortcomings. 'They say her passions are so strong that the duke himself said she was not to go from one room to another without a governess, that when she dances, this lady is obliged to follow her for the whole of the dance to prevent her from making an exhibition of herself by indecent conversation with men.' Charlotte had also been told that 'all amusements have been forbidden her because of her indecent conduct on account of which her father and mother have spoken with pain'. Breathless with indignation, the queen rested her case. 'There, dear brother, is a woman I do not recommend at all.'[86]

Having successfully warned off her brother, Charlotte must have been appalled to have the unsuitable Caroline now produced as a potential wife for her son. In desperation she seems to have made at least one attempt to persuade the king to veto the idea, even to the extraordinary extent of disagreeing with him. 'Something is in agitation, God knows what,' wrote Prince Ernest at the end of August to his eldest brother, 'but the honoured authors of our days have had yesterday a very long conversation tête-à-tête which seemed to be very boisterous, for though the wind made a horrible noise, one could perfectly well hear them talking.' Ernest was not sure what was at the heart of their argument, 'but I suppose you was. The king was in remarkable spirits, but his counterpart the very reverse.'[87]

However forceful their discussions, nothing the queen said made any difference, and the preparations for the wedding went on. Unable to halt the inevitable, Charlotte retreated back to her customary position of mute, self-consuming anger. 'She said that she had resolved never to talk, no never to open her lips about your marriage,' reported Ernest to the prince, 'so that no one should say she had a hand in anything.' She promised she would treat the princess well; more than that she would not say. 'Her opinions she could not give, as she never intended to speak about it. She hoped you would be happy, and all this she said with tears in her eyes. God knows what is the matter with her, but she is sullen.'[88] When the Prince of Wales wrote to his mother to try to discover why she was so upset, she refused to engage with him on the subject at all. She no longer hoped to prevent the marriage, but was determined to absolve herself from any responsibility for it. 'When a person keeps silent upon every subject as I do and have done,' she replied, 'I cannot plead guilty.'[89]

In November 1794, the prince's envoy arrived in Brunswick to escort the princess to London. James Harris, later created Earl of Malmesbury, was an experienced and sophisticated diplomat who knew the prince and his tastes well. His first impressions of Caroline's physical appearance were not, on the whole, very favourable. 'Pretty face – not expressive of softness – her figure not graceful – fine eyes – good hand – tolerable teeth, but going – fair hair and light eyebrows, good bust – short, with what the French call *des épaules impertinantes*.'[90] Although he bravely listed the princess's best features, Malmesbury was clearly uneasy. He knew that the prince was accustomed to select his mistresses from among the most elegant and sophisticated women of the fashionable world. It was true that his preference was often for women who were both larger and older than convention dictated, but he considered himself an appreciative connoisseur of female beauty and his standards were high. Malmesbury suspected he would not respond well to Caroline's unexceptionable and slightly overblown looks; nor was he reassured by what he had begun to discover about her character.

His first conversation with Caroline's father did nothing to calm his mounting sense of disquiet. The Duke of Brunswick confessed that he was very worried about how his daughter might behave once she arrived in England. 'He was extremely anxious about her doing right … He wished to make her feel that the high situation in which she was going to be placed was not simply one of amusement and enjoyment; that it had its duties and those perhaps difficult and hard to fulfil.' Confirming what Queen Charlotte had heard, the duke admitted that anxiety about Caroline's flightiness had indeed led to her having been raised 'very severely'. He hinted that the 'free and easy unreserved manners' of his wife, George III's sister Augusta, had not provided his daughter with a very satisfactory model for correct regal behaviour. The duchess, who had already regaled Malmesbury with her dislike of Queen Charlotte and told him an indiscreet story about her eldest brother's bedwetting habits as a child, was, as Malmesbury diplomatically concluded, 'at times … certainly apt to forget her audience'. The duke was even more worried when he considered what he knew about the behaviour of his future son-in-law, who, he correctly deduced, was unlikely to act as a stabilising influence on his daughter's uncertain grasp of correct behaviour. He told Malmesbury that 'he dreaded the prince's habits'. He had already urged Caroline never to appear jealous, and 'not to notice' any of his affairs. In conclusion, he begged a clearly shaken Malmesbury 'to be her adviser, not to neglect her when in England'.[91]

Malmesbury soon saw for himself why her father was so apprehensive. Sitting beside the princess for the first time at dinner, whilst he noted approvingly that Caroline was 'cheerful and loves laughing',[92] he was less satisfied with other aspects of her personality. She was loud, impulsive and unrestrained, with little of the dignity he knew she would be required to demonstrate in her new life. The more he got to know her, the more his concern grew. She was gushing and indiscreet, lavishing endearments upon relative strangers, 'making miss-ish friendships that last twenty-four hours'. She would talk to anyone who amused her, and say anything to anyone. 'I find her inclined,' he confided to his diary, 'to give way too much to the temper of the entertainment, and to get *over cheerful and too mixing*.'[93] She prided herself on her ability to discover the secrets of those around her, and eagerly passed them on. She was, Malmesbury concluded, an even more inveterate gossip than her mother. At twenty-six, she still behaved as if she were a naive and impressionable teenager. He was dismayed to hear her make 'improper remarks' about the supposed affairs of her friends, and was even more unhappy to hear rumours of her own flirtations, of over-familiarity with dancing partners, of tokens allegedly given to handsome young officers and of romantic feelings harboured – indeed openly admitted – for unsuitable men.

But for all her obvious shortcomings, Malmesbury gradually warmed to Caroline. Although it was only too clear to him that she had 'no fixed character, a light and flighty mind',[94] he thought she meant well, and came to believe that beneath her obvious failings was concealed an essentially good heart. Declaring encouragingly that 'she improves very much on closer acquaintance',[95] he decided it was worthwhile doing all he could to improve her prospects for success in her life to come. Casting himself as her unofficial mentor, he sought to tone down those aspects of her personality he knew would not serve her well, whilst attempting to instil in her a more realistic sense of what her new role would require. Above all, Malmesbury tried to persuade her of the importance of adopting a dignified bearing, encouraging her to become less dependent on the noisily solicited approval of those around her.

To this end, the earl prescribed a plan of action strikingly similar to the guidance George III had given the young Charlotte a generation before. He was horrified by Caroline's repeated insistence 'that she wished to be popular' in her new home,[96] and urged her instead to place herself above all considerations of liking and disliking. 'I recommend perfect silence on *all* subjects for six months after her arrival,'[97] he advised. After that, he instructed her 'to avoid familiarity, to have no confidantes, to avoid giving any opinions; to approve, but not to admire excessively; to be perfectly silent on politics and party'.[98] When she complained that he 'recommended too much reserve',[99] he merely repeated his advice with even greater force. Again and again he begged her 'to think always before she speaks'.[100] He was unsure how much, if any, of his advice she heeded. She listened to his lectures with good-humoured patience, but, as Malmesbury noted with a sinking heart, they did little to depress her ebulliently high spirits. She was still 'vastly happy with her future expectations', undaunted by his attempts to make her reflect more soberly on her future. Even her future husband's reputation as a womaniser did not dismay her. She was naively confident that she could manage him, telling Malmesbury that she 'was determined never to be jealous … and was prepared on this point'.[101] Malmesbury, suspecting that her avowed resolution would be pretty quickly tested, urged her to do all she could to stay true to it, maintaining that 'reproaches and sourness never gained anybody … and that the surest way of reviving a tottering affection was softness, enduring and caresses'.[102]

After two months in Brunswick, Malmesbury and the princess set out in freezing weather on the long journey through war-torn Germany to reach the North Sea coast, from where they would embark for England. The journey was slow, and during it Malmesbury had plenty of time to reflect on his feelings for his complex and often contradictory charge. He remained impressed by her resilient good nature. Few things made her angry; she had submitted to his many admonitions with good, if not always very attentive, grace. She was, he thought, no fool; Malmesbury believed she had 'quick parts', though 'without a sound or distinguishing understanding'. It was her lack of mental discipline which Malmesbury believed undermined all her more positive qualities. She was 'caught by first impressions, led away by the first impulse; turned away by appearances or enjoyment'. Nor did she seem to possess any real ideas of right or wrong. She had, Malmesbury concluded, 'some natural, but no acquired morality, and no strong innate notions of its value and necessity'. With a better upbringing, he thought she might have been a very different person. 'If her education had been what it ought, she might have turned out excellent, but it was that very nonsensical one that most women receive – one of privation, injunction and menace, to believe no man and never to express what they feel or say what they think.'[103]

If Malmesbury was concerned about the shortcomings of Caroline's inner life, he was even more anxious about the image she presented to the world. For all his efforts, her manners remained crude and unpolished. He explained to her repeatedly that she must learn to be less blunt in her language as the 'English were more nice than foreigners. Never to talk about being sick, etc.'[104] He was horrified when she sent a bloody tooth she had just had extracted down from her room for him to inspect. And he was genuinely shocked by her lack of personal delicacy. Despite his embarrassment, he felt it necessary to have a very explicit conversation with her on the subject of hygiene and general cleanliness. 'On these points, I endeavoured, as far as was possible for a man, to inculcate the necessity of great and nice attention, as well as to what was hid as to what was seen.' She was, Malmesbury maintained, often 'offensive' from lack of attention in this regard. He knew she wore coarse petticoats and shifts 'and these [were] never well washed nor changed enough'. Nor was she very particular about her toilette, preferring to wash quickly rather than properly. For this, as for so many of her other failings, Malmesbury blamed the Duchess of Brunswick. 'It is remarkable how on this point her education has been neglected, and how much her mother, though an Englishwoman, was inattentive to it.'[105] Cheerfully impervious to shame, Caroline obediently followed Malmesbury's advice and, for a while at least, appeared each morning properly scrubbed and tidied; but none of this promised well for her eventual reception in London by a prince of famously fastidious temperament.

Whilst Malmesbury strenuously applied himself to preparing the princess for her uncertain future, back at Windsor, Charlotte and her daughters diligently assembled her trousseau. There too Caroline's mother was found wanting. 'I received yesterday the pattern of the princess's nightdress,' wrote the queen, but 'what to do about shoes I do not know, and feel very sorry for it, particularly as I thought to have expressed myself circumstantially enough on every subject for the duchess.'[106] Nothing could prevent Charlotte making peevish remarks about her Brunswick sister-in-law, but her daughters were heroically optimistic about the approaching wedding. Who could not be delighted at the prospect of marriage with their brother? 'Were I the princess,' wrote Elizabeth to the prince, 'I should certainly sing when I came to St James's. Oh! Had I the wings of a dove, I'd fly away and be at rest, and by what one has heard, she must thank God to have let her take flight and that to you. I trust in God that neither of you will ever know what it is to have an uneasy moment.'[107]

Little of this anxious optimism survived the first meeting of the prince and princess in April 1795. Already disconcerted to discover that Lady Jersey – whose exact relationship with her husband-to-be had been communicated to Caroline by an anonymous letter sent to her whilst still in Germany – was to be her lady-in-waiting, the princess arrived in London flustered and ill at ease. She tried to behave well, kneeling to the prince as Malmesbury had instructed, but he was unmoved. 'He raised her (gracefully enough) and embraced her, said barely one word, turned round, retired to a distant part of the apartment and calling me to him, said, "Harris [i.e. Malmesbury], I am not well; pray get me a glass of brandy."'[108] The princess, shocked by his behaviour, commented with typical bluntness that she thought him very fat and nowhere near as handsome as his portrait.

From a bad start, things only got worse. A formal dinner held later that night was a disaster. Caroline forgot everything she had been told about the value of regal discretion; her behaviour, 'flippant, rattling, affecting raillery and wit, and throwing out coarse vulgar hints' about Lady Jersey, embarrassed everyone present, and in Malmesbury's opinion fixed for ever the prince's dislike of her.[109] The marriage ceremony, which took place a few days later, was a painful harbinger of the couple's future relationship. The prince arrived drunk, did not look at his bride, but gazed instead at Lady Jersey. When the archbishop asked whether there were any lawful impediments to the marriage, 'he laid down the book and looked earnestly at the king, as well as at the bridegroom, giving unequivocal proof of his apprehension that some previous marriage had taken place'. With equally heavy-handed significance, the archbishop twice repeated the passage requiring the husband to be faithful to his wife. 'The prince was much affected, and shed tears.'[110]

The couple's brief honeymoon was spent in the unpromising company of some of her new husband's more disreputable friends at Kempshott in Hampshire, who were, Caroline later asserted, 'constantly drunk and filthy, sleeping and snoring in boots on the sofas'. Their wedding night was an ordeal for both of them; in their very different accounts of what went wrong, each blamed its failure on the other, in a pattern that was to recur throughout their partnership. The prince told Malmesbury that Caroline had gasped, '*Ah, mon Dieu, qu'il est gros*', when they finally got to bed and she saw how he was endowed, but far from finding this encouraging, it had convinced him that 'her manners were not those of a novice'.[111] He maintained he slept with her only three times, disgusted 'by such marks of filth both in the fore and hind part of her … that she turned my stomach, and from that moment I made a vow never to touch her again.'[112]

Caroline told a rather different story of what had happened on those fateful Kempshott nights. 'If I can spell out her hums and haws,' wrote Lord Minto, to whom she confided the tale years later, 'I take it that the ground of his antipathy was his own *incapacity*, and the distaste which a man feels for a woman who *knows* his defeats and humiliations.'[113]

After only a few weeks of marriage, George ceased to appear in public at all with his wife. The king was obliged to give Caroline his arm as the family walked on the terrace without the Prince of Wales. It was obvious to all that something was seriously wrong, but his sisters nevertheless bravely attempted to seek out reasons to be cheerful about this increasingly ill-starred union. Writing to her brother, Elizabeth praised the 'open character' of 'my sister' the Princess of Wales. 'I flatter myself you will have her turn out to be a very comfortable little wife,' she insisted optimistically. The news that the princess was pregnant briefly inspired the family to invest new hope in the tottering relationship, and when, in July, the couple retreated to the country for a brief stay, every letter received was scrutinised for phrases that might suggest a better understanding between them. 'Mama is … happier than words can express at your ending your letter with the words "we are all very happy and comfortable here",' wrote Elizabeth. 'It has not only made Mama happy, but all of us who love you in every sense of the word, and could the wishes of your poor sisters have been of any use, you certainly had them from the first to last … I am commissioned with loves, loves, loves on all sides to you as well as the princess to whom I beg to be very kindly remembered.'[114]

But, as time went by and the prince showed no real signs of softening in his harsh and unrelenting attitude, the queen gave in to despair. She told Lady Harcourt in August that she was 'so low and dejected that I had every difficulty in the world to muster up some degree of cheerfulness for the evening. The situation is truly deplorable, for what to say I do not know.' She grew increasingly disenchanted with her daughter-in-law, whom, for all Charlotte's protestations that she would treat her fairly, she had never learnt to like. 'The utmost we can do,' she concluded wearily, 'is to keep out of the scrap ourselves.'[115]

The princess's baby was born on 6 January 1796, after what the prince described as 'a terrible hard labour for above twelve hours.' She had given birth to 'an immense girl' whom her father greeted 'with all affection possible … notwithstanding we might have wished for a boy'. The king declared himself delighted – 'indeed I always wished it should be of that sex'. ('You know Papa loves little girls,' commented Princess Mary.) The king hoped parenthood would bring them closer together, as it had done for himself and Charlotte. 'I trust they will have many more children, and this newcomer will be a bond of additional union.'[116]

In fact, the birth of his child drove the prince into an even greater frenzy of hatred for his wife. A few days later, in a state of nervous collapse, he convinced himself he was dying and rewrote his will. As ever when he was in desperate straits, his thoughts turned to Maria Fitzherbert, and it was to her, 'the wife of my heart and soul', that he bequeathed all his property. 'To she who is called the Princess of Wales' he left only a shilling. For all its empty posturing, it was a gesture that indicated the depth of his repulsion for Caroline, with whom he never lived again.

In April, for the first time, he suggested a formal separation which, he informed his wife, he would not infringe 'by proposing at any period a connection of a more particular nature', even if their daughter – now baptised Charlotte after her grandmother – were to die. The queen sympathised with her son's unhappiness, but thought there was little chance of his father agreeing to a separation of any kind; indeed, the king was not prepared to countenance any open acknowledgement of the couple's incompatibility. 'You seem to look upon your disunion as merely of private nature,' he wrote to his son. He had 'totally put of sight' the fact that as heir apparent, the prince's marriage was a public act, and one which could not simply be set aside by everyone agreeing it had been a regrettable mistake: 'a separation cannot be brought forward by the mere interference of relations'. The king advised him instead to think of his daughter, and do all he could 'to make your home agreeable'.[117]

Although his decision correctly reflected the political realities of their position, the king's refusal to allow the ill-matched couple a separation effectively consigned them to years of mutually aggravated misery. Most blamed the prince for the unhappy situation. Everyone – with the possible exception of his sisters, for whom he could do no wrong – agreed that he had treated Caroline in an insulting and brutal manner from the very moment of her arrival. He paraded his mistress

Lady Jersey before her, and appointed her as one of the ladies of her household, compelling his wife to spend most of her days with her preening rival. He gave Lady Jersey jewellery that had originally been presented to the princess, which his mistress wore as ostentatiously as possible. On the rare occasions the princess visited the Royal Pavilion at Brighton, she was sure to find Lady Jersey already in confident residence. So many and so public were the humiliations heaped upon his wife by the prince that his ill-treatment of her was common knowledge. 'If a twentieth part of them have any foundation,' commented Lord Glenbervie, 'that is sufficient to fix the highest degree of blame on his conduct.'[118]

It was true that Caroline's behaviour was, as Malmesbury had observed in Germany, sometimes unpredictable. She did not always seem to understand the distinctions between what could and could not be said or done – as the prince saw, and trumpeted to anyone who would listen, there was something odd about her, and she was to grow progressively stranger as she grew older – but in the early days of her marriage she was never malicious, although she had a great deal to bear; and she was a conscientious and affectionate mother to her baby daughter. The extremity of the prince's behaviour was a puzzle, even to those closest to him. 'My brother has behaved very foolishly,' Prince William was reported to have said in 1796. 'To be sure, he has married a foolish, disagreeable woman, but he should not have treated her as he has done, but made the best of a bad bargain as my father has done.'[119]

It was not until 1797 that the king was finally persuaded to concede that the warring prince and princess might live apart, although it was hoped the separation would be a temporary one. Caroline eventually settled at Montague House in Blackheath, a few miles south-east of London. She furnished it with none of her husband's famous good taste; instead, it was a triumph of exuberance over style. Lady Charlotte Bury, who became Caroline's lady-in-waiting, described it as 'an incongruous piece of patchwork; it may dazzle for a moment when lifted up at night, but it is all glitter and trick and everything is tinsel and trumpery about it; it is altogether like a bad dream.'[120] The princess was delighted by her new home. 'I was free,' she later declared to Charlotte Bury, who sought, somewhat laboriously, in all her reminiscences to capture Caroline's strong German accent: 'Oh, how happy I was! Everybody blamed me, but I never repented of dis step. Oh mine god, what I have suffered! Lucky I had a spirit, or I never would have outlived it!'[121]

The Prince of Wales, in contrast, could summon up no comparable sense of cheerful detachment. His sense of revulsion for Caroline remained raw and visceral. 'My abhorrence of her is such,' he wrote, 'and the rooted aversion and detestation that I feel towards her, that I shudder at the very thoughts of sitting at the same table with her, or even of being under the same roof with her.' 'Never, dearest and best of mothers,' he begged the queen, 'propose to me to humiliate myself before the vilest wretch this world was cursed with, who I cannot feel more disgust for from her personal nastiness than I do from her entire want of all principle.'[122] His passionate rejection of his wife was, as he so often and so vituperatively declared, a reaction to who she was, to a personality he despised and a body that repulsed him; but it may also be possible that the fervency of his hatred owed at least some of its intensity to what Caroline represented – that his overwrought reaction to her was an unconscious revolt against the very idea of an arranged marriage, even one that he had arranged himself.

The campaign of spite and persecution that the prince waged against Caroline makes it hard to feel much sympathy for his predicament – in the matter of his marriage, as in so many other aspects of his life, George was his own worst enemy; but perhaps behind his blustering venom was concealed a deep sense of shame and humiliation at the position in which he found himself. On his wedding day, a rare sympathetic witness, looking beyond the drunkenness and tears, caught a glimpse of a desperately unhappy man, 'who looked like death and full of confusion, as if he wished to hide himself from the looks of the whole world.'[123] Even George's first biographer, writing in the year he died and in a tone deeply critical of his many moral and political failings, thought his marital position pitiable. 'That the heir apparent to the throne of a free country should be compelled, against his inclinations, to unite his destiny with an individual he did not love is a circumstance which the statesman, the moralist, and the philanthropist must deplore.'[124] Everything in his character and his chequered amatory history suggested that, despite all the earnest hopes of his sisters, George would never have found it easy to adapt himself to the demands of a calm, companionable marriage. Asked by a fellow diplomat before he left Germany how he thought Caroline would cope, Malmesbury had warily reflected that 'with a steady man, she

George III: a confident, unpretentious image of kingship that was much to George's taste and considered 'very like' (oil on canvas, by Johann Zoffany, 1771).

Queen Charlotte: the queen stands before her tribe of healthy children – her great dynastic achievement (oil on canvas, by Benjamin West, 1779).

Frances (Fanny) Burney: reluctant courtier, astute diarist (oil on canvas, by Edward Burney, c. 1785).

Mary Delany: model of cultured femininity and much-admired royal family friend (oil on canvas, by John Opie, 1782).

Charlotte, Princess Royal: 'Always shy and under restraint with the queen' (watercolour on ivory, attributed to Mrs Joseph Mee, possibly 1790).

Princess Augusta: 'She looks as if she knew more than she would say' (watercolour on ivory, unknown artist, c. 1798).

Princess Elizabeth: 'Though brought up at court, I could never form my mouth to make compliments' (oil on canvas, by William Beechey, 1797).

George, Prince of Wales: in his own words, 'too fond of Wine and Women', with 'too great a penchant to grow fat' (oil on canvas, by John Russell, 1791).

Princess Augusta, Princess Charlotte and Princess Elizabeth: the three eldest sisters depicted in a very tender light (oil on canvas, by Thomas Gainsborough, 1784).

Princess Mary: the most elegant of the sisterhood, with a surprisingly tart wit (oil on canvas, by William Beechey, 1797).

Princess Sophia: 'If a sinner, [she] has the demeanour of a very humble and repentant one' (oil on canvas, by William Beechey, 1797).

Prince Octavius: 'There will be no Heaven for me if Octavius is not there' (oil on canvas, by Benjamin West, 1783).

Princess Amelia: 'an air of modest candour and a gentleness so caressingly inviting' (oil on canvas, by William Beechey, 1797).

Caroline, Princess of Wales: 'If her education had been what it ought, she might have turned out excellent' (oil on canvas, by Thomas Lawrence, 1804).

Princess Charlotte of Wales: 'There is a tone of romance in her character, which will only serve to mislead her' (watercolour, by Thomas Heaphy, c. 1815).

Queen Charlotte: painted immediately after the king's first illness, the horror of the experience shows clearly on the queen's strained face (oil on canvas, by Thomas Lawrence, 1789).

George III: the king during his last illness, a Lear-like figure, isolated and alone (mezzotint, by Samuel Reynolds, c. 1820).

would do vastly well, but with one of a different description, there are great risks.'[125] Much the same might have been said about the prince. He might never have been a particularly satisfactory husband, but the uninformed and unreflecting alliance he entered into with a complete stranger cauterised something deep in his soul, destroyed his always shaky moral compass, and introduced into his character a sense of bitterness that he carried with him until the day of his death. He was not a very attractive victim, it is true, but in his own self-regarding and theatrical way, the Prince of Wales suffered too from the unpredictable iron dictates of the royal marriage market.

The prince was not, however, one to keep his sufferings to himself, seeking to draw all his family into the tense atmosphere of accusation and blame he created around himself. His mother was soon exhausted, both by her proximity to so much misery and her inability to do anything about it. 'How many unpleasant things have passed since we last saw each other,' she wrote sadly to Lady Harcourt in the spring of 1796. 'To know them and not to have the power of soothing and assisting the sufferer is real martyrdom. I hear all sides and know so many things which must not be revealed that I am most truly worn down with it; and my dislike of the world in general gets the better of me.' Everyone involved, 'all say most cutting things.'[126] Her daughters were equally in thrall to their brother's unhappiness. 'We are all truly miserable about you, and the first question in the morning and the last at night is, have you heard anything from London?'[127]

By the beginning of 1797, the queen had simply had enough. The prince had worried and harassed her throughout the autumn, demanding that she admit his mistress Lady Jersey to court. Bolstered perhaps by her deep-seated dislike of her daughter-in-law, and her desire to please her son, Charlotte did so, and found herself at the centre of a whirlwind of criticism as a result. It was the final straw. In January, she took the unusual step of writing to the king, putting down on paper the long list of her many grievances, and stating her intention effectively to withdraw from public life. 'Your Majesty saying on Friday last at dinner that you supposed I would shut up shop until the town filled, induces me to beg leave of you to shut up shop entirely as far as relates to assemblies.' This was not, she explained to her husband, solely the result of recent difficult events. 'Before anything unpleasant happened last year, I found the fatigue almost too much for me.' Fortified by a doctor's prescription, she had managed to keep going, 'though not without great exertion, and Your Majesty will I am sure be sensible that as from Monday to Saturday, we live in a constant bustle, either upon the road or in public, I may now begin to feel the consequences of that life.' But it was the disintegration of her son's marriage, and the pain attendant upon it, that had stiffened her resolve to remove herself from the spotlight. 'Since the unpleasant affair of the Prince and Princess of Wales began, I will fairly own to Your Majesty that my dislike of everything public is greatly increased, and I have given full proof of that by appearing but three times on the Terrace last year, and not oftener at the Esplanade at Weymouth.' The widespread criticism of her reception of Lady Jersey had increased her habitual suspicion of the press: 'I found every word I spoke in the papers, and thereby was convinced that spies were sent to watch me.' Her inability 'to clear my character when things were at their worst in London' had been the final straw. 'I then determined never to appear but where my duty called me. I have been so thoroughly wounded at this time that nothing can ever make it up to me, and my dislike to mankind is so general that I distrust every soul and everybody that surrounds me.' She concluded by asking the king to consider moving the time of dinner from four to five, as 'this would certainly make the evening less long for the females of the family', and reduce the opportunity for depressing gossip. 'The encouragement for me,' she observed in the closing lines of her long letter, 'is not great in doing anything but what is merely my duty.'[128]

If, at the beginning of the 1790s, the queen had hoped that she and her family might end the decade in better shape than they had begun it, she was miserably disappointed. The public world had grown infinitely more threatening, whilst the carefully nurtured calm of her private life had foundered on the disastrous attempts made by two of her sons to establish their independence through marriage. Her daughters, she knew, were restive and anxious; even her once-dependable husband had become a source of terrible anxiety, to be treated with trepidation, lest his terrifying and inexplicable illness return with the same speed and severity with which it had descended from nowhere in 1788. Charlotte's response was, as ever, one of retreat, fleeing not just from the glare of her public role, but from any honest and open emotional engagement with her family and their seemingly insuperable problems. Ignored when she had attempted to offer advice, and recruited into recriminatory contests she was powerless to resolve, the queen effectively abdicated all responsibility for any further role in shaping the destinies of her children. Intent instead on preserving her own sense of self-righteousness – as she had declared when she failed to persuade either her husband or her son to listen to her misgivings about Caroline's character, 'no one should say she had any hand in anything' – she left them to shape their own futures as best they could. For her daughters, dependent as they were on the advocacy of others to promote their interests, this was a dark development in lives already shadowed by disappointment. If their mother would not fight for them, who would?

*

Almost the only unalloyed pleasure the princesses enjoyed during the 1790s had been the birth of their baby niece Charlotte in January 1796. 'God grant every blessing and happiness may attend my (already) dear little niece,' wrote Elizabeth as soon as she had heard all was well, 'and may she resemble in everything (what is most affectionately loved by me), her dear father.'[129] The excitement with which the news was received contrasted starkly with the chilling disregard shown by the king for the welfare of his other grandchild, Augustus, born in such difficult circumstances two years earlier. For the baby Charlotte, things were very different. 'The king could talk of nothing but his pretty little grandchild,' Elizabeth assured the prince. 'He said there was never so perfect a little creature, and everybody here was delighted to see him in such ecstasies of joy.'[130] The happiness the princesses took from the safe arrival of their brother's child was genuine, generous and strongly felt; but it also focussed their minds on their own unchanging state, still at home, still single and with no immediate prospect of motherhood looming for any of them. Telling the prince once again that 'my sisters are quite enchanted', Elizabeth added a telling postscript: 'Old one rather anxious to follow your example.'[131]

The Princess Royal lost no opportunity to tell anyone how desperately she still wanted to be married; but for all their concern over the depressed state into which they knew their eldest daughter had fallen, her parents made no attempt to help her out of it. It was left to others to do what they could to further her interests. The Harcourt women were particularly active on her behalf. Mrs Harcourt, living alongside her soldier husband, who was fighting in the Low Countries, was constantly looking out for suitable candidates for Royal's hand. In 1795, she had been much impressed by the widowed thirty-nine-year-old Duke of Oldenburg, with whom she had spent a very agreeable evening. Mrs Harcourt worked on him as hard as she could, telling him that 'he was much considered and esteemed by our royal family', how much 'his virtues must naturally be the object of their attention', and that 'I was sure they would be glad to see him.' Surely, she exclaimed, this 'must suggest to him that an alliance might take place?'[132] In the midst of all his marital difficulties, even the Prince of Wales found time to advance his sister's case, writing to the queen's younger brother Ernest, and asking him to help in bringing about the Oldenburg marriage. Royal was effusively grateful and was, she maintained, 'perfectly convinced that the Duke of Oldenburg's character is such that could this be brought about, it would be the properest situation.'[133] Princess Elizabeth was soon teasing her sister by calling her 'the Duchess of Oldenburg', noting 'that her maiden-blush cheek is turned to a damask rose whenever the duke's name is mentioned.'[134] But, as with so many of Royal's hopes for change, nothing happened. No more was heard about it, and the Duke of Oldenburg, who never remarried, drifted gently but permanently away from the royal family's ambit.

On this occasion, however, the Princess Royal was not left to nurse her disappointment for long. In December 1795, Frederick, Hereditary Prince of the Duchy of Württemberg, wrote to the king asking to marry his eldest daughter. As usual, George's initial response was to refuse, but this time he did so on the basis of something other than his wish not to see a daughter go abroad. 'Knowing the brutal and other unpleasant qualities of this prince,' he told his Foreign Secretary, 'I could not give an encouragement to this proposal.'[135] Frederick of Württemberg had been the subject of dark speculation in Europe for some years. He had been married to Augusta of Brunswick – the sister of the new Princess of Wales – and had taken her to Russia whilst he served in the army there. The couple lived in Russia for six years, and had three children. In 1786, Frederick and the children returned home, but without his wife. No one seemed to know exactly what had precipitated their separation; there were rumours of an affair, but these were never substantiated. Others said Augusta had simply chosen to stay at the behest of her then great friend, the Empress Catherine the Great. At some point, Augusta fell out of favour with the empress, and was sent to live at the remote castle of Lhode. There she died, of unknown causes and in circumstances sufficiently inexplicable to ensure that gossip about her possible fate continued to circulate around the courts of Europe for years afterwards. It was never spelt out exactly how Frederick was considered accountable for his first wife's death, but it was an unhappy story that did not make the king eager to consider a marital alliance with him. 'I shall not consent to his request,' he declared, 'and if he will not take a gentle hint, I have no objection to adding that after the very unhappy life my niece led with him, I cannot as a father bequeath any daughter of mine on him.'[136]

Frederick proved impervious to all attempts, gentle and otherwise, to reject him. Württemberg was poor and surrounded by bigger and hostile principalities; the prospect of an alliance with the wealthiest and most powerful state in Europe was not one to be easily surrendered. For months, Frederick's envoy, Count Zeppelin, laboured in London, 'going door to door' to remove 'the ridiculous prejudices' harboured against his master. With the help of John Coxe Hippesley, a barrister who had worked for the East India Company and who had experience of investigating tricky questions of law, a body of evidence was assembled that appeared to exonerate Frederick from any complicity in his wife's fate by placing the blame on her alone. A picture was gradually assembled in which Augusta was depicted as an irresponsible woman, swayed by strong emotions, without much self-discipline or restraint, a character, indeed, not unlike that of her younger sister, the hapless Princess of Wales. It was also implied that she had added infidelity to this catalogue of faults, which may, or may not, have resulted in the birth of an illegitimate child.

Augusta's parents had been 'lately undeceived' by learning details such as these, which Frederick claimed he had been too delicate to reveal to them at the time.[137] The Empress of Russia too had stood forward to declare the hereditary prince's innocence. 'Can it be supposed,' exclaimed Hippesley, 'that the Duke and Duchess of Brunswick, the Emperor and Empress Queen of Russia would all enter in a conspiracy to impose upon His Majesty, and sacrifice the Princess Royal to a prince so undeserving of Her Royal Highness?'[138] The king, outflanked by the negotiators, and aware of his eldest daughter's overpowering desire to see herself 'settled', capitulated, and on 15 June 1796, he wrote to Frederick giving his formal consent to the match.

There is no written account of how Royal responded when she at last achieved the object she had wished for all her adult life, but soon she was seen wearing a medallion with a portrait of the prince hanging from it, tangible proof that against all her expectations, she had been claimed at last, and would not now live out her days in her mother's increasingly dismal shadow. Fanny Burney, who knew her so well, did not doubt that the translation from dutiful daughter to independent duchess would do more than provide Royal with the happy prospect of a husband and family; it would also satisfy a deeply rooted desire in her to exercise authority, rather than be perpetually subject to it. 'She is born to preside,' mused Fanny, 'and that with an equal softness and dignity; but she was here in utter subjection, for which she had neither spirits nor inclination. She adored the king, honoured the queen and loved her sisters and had much kindness for her brothers; but her style of life was not adapted to the royalty of her nature, any more than of her birth; and though she only wished for power to do good and confer favours, she thought herself out of place in not possessing it.'[139]

Royal had bought her freedom at what some considered a fairly high price. When Frederick arrived in London, the newspapers were explicit about his physical failings. 'His Serene Highness is in truth a most excessively corpulent man,' commented *The Times*, 'so much so that his servants, in assisting him to put on his pelisse [cloak], are obliged to walk quite around him to put it on from one shoulder over the other.'[140] Napoleon, who thought him 'a man of talent', commented that nature had created the prince to see how far human skin could be stretched without bursting. His size was an undoubted gift to the caricaturists, who drew him waddling into St James's like a great moustachioed whale. When presented at court, the sisterhood loyally looked past the prince's shortcomings, tactfully commending his manly looks and strength of character. When finally brought face to face with her husband-to-be, however, the Princess Royal's nerve failed her; she was 'almost dead with terror and agitation and affright ... She could not utter a word. The queen was obliged to speak all her answers. The prince said he hoped this would be the last disturbance his presence would ever occasion her.'[141]

A few weeks later, on 18 May 1797, the couple were married. Royal wore a dress of white and silver, every inch of which she had painstakingly embroidered, knowing, as her sister Augusta told Fanny Burney, 'that three stitches done by any other would make it instantly said it was none of it by herself'. The result had been far more elegant than anything the princess usually wore. ''Twas the queen herself that dressed her! You know what a figure she used to make of herself with her odd manner of dressing herself; but Mama said, "Now really, Princess Royal, this one time is the last, and I cannot suffer you to make such a quiz of yourself; so I really will have you dressed properly." And indeed the queen was right, for everybody said she never looked so well in her life.' ('The word *quiz*, you may depend on it,' observed Fanny, 'was never the queen's.'[142])

On 2 June, the new Duchess of Württemberg set off with her husband for Germany. Everyone in the family knew it was unlikely they would see her again. Princess Amelia, the youngest of the sisters, reflected the complicated mix of emotions that marked her departure: pleasure at seeing Royal achieve the matrimonial status for which she had so long and desperately pined, tinged with sadness at her loss. 'My heart is so full with parting with my dear sister, I can hardly write … I am rejoiced to see how much she feels the going, but to be sure it makes me much more a fool.'[143] The queen's response was more circumspect. She wished the princess well, but regarded her future with a distinctly sombre eye. 'I have just separated from my daughter Royal,' she wrote to her brother. 'It has cost us much, God hopes she will be happy. The prince has esprit, worldliness, and knows how to get what he wants. They are both of an age when they must know how to discern what true contentment consists of, and first youth being past, they must endeavour to make themselves mutually happy.'[144]

The duke and his duchess seemed determined to do the best they could to achieve that mutual happiness as they travelled towards their new home in Germany. After a crossing of the North Sea that made her Weymouth excursions seem very tame – 'I have been most miserably sick, not being able to leave my bed the whole time' – the couple arrived eventually in Hanover, where they were met by the princess's young brother Adolphus. He had not seen his sister for some years, and 'must own I find her charming and I am convinced that with her excellent understanding and goodness of heart she will be very happy with the prince; he is extremely fond of her'. The duke had described his wife 'as a blessing from heaven', and, Adolphus told the king, 'I really do believe he thinks so. It would be very unnatural if he did not, for it is impossible to behave in a better manner towards a husband than she does to him.'[145]

The contrast with the first weeks of her elder brother's marriage could not have been more striking. In July, now established at her new home at Ludwigsburg in the heart of the duchy, Royal assured the family that 'my dear prince is unwearied in his attentions and love, doing everything that he can imagine which will give me pleasure; in which he so totally succeeds that I am never so happy as when we are at home, and am always anxious for the moment when I can return.'[146] Over the next months, she often described him as 'the best of husbands', and although in later life the couple's relationship was to be tested to the extreme by the experience of war, occupation and personal grief, she never departed from that conviction.

Not everyone shared Royal's determinedly positive assessment of her marriage and her husband. There was, as had been earlier suspected, a less genial side to Frederick's character. Queen Charlotte declared in 1802 that she had never liked him, that 'he had a vanity that made him detested in England', that he had not known 'how to govern his bad humour in the presence of the women of my daughter's suite', and that 'he displeased us totally and his departure was not regretted'.[147] It is possible that Charlotte's openly critical attitude towards her son-in-law – which she had not expressed in 1795 – was in part explained by his devious political manoeuvring. Desperate to hold on to his duchy when so many of his German counterparts had lost theirs to the French, he was as persistent a supplicant as he had been a suitor, nagging the king for expressions of support, both financial and diplomatic. In a letter his wife wrote to her father on the very day of her departure from England, she added a postscript, clearly written at the behest of her husband, hoping that the king 'will be so gracious as to join your influence to that of the two Imperial courts in support of the interest of his family'.[148] It was the first of a lifetime of such requests. Frederick was an astute opportunist: by 1805, he had thrown in his lot with Napoleon, to the extent that the emperor's brother married Frederick's daughter (news that was not well received at Windsor). Frederick had no illusions that his marriage was not based on political necessity, but he never treated his wife with the callous and insulting hostility that Royal's brother had meted out to Caroline, and for this she was sincerely and lastingly grateful. In later life, his temper worsened, and he was sometimes seen to bully and harangue his increasingly long-suffering duchess, but she never uttered a word of criticism of him, and reacted severely to those who did.

In 1817, she scolded the Prince of Wales for listening to 'idle reports of those whose only object must have been to do mischief' in suggesting all was not always well between herself 'and my adored husband … Believe me, dearest brother, never could I have been as happy with him as I was had not our minds been congenial.'[149] In 1823, when the duke had been dead for seven years, Royal delivered to Lady Harcourt her verdict on their life together which, in its calm admission of the importance of compromise in marriage, might be allowed to stand as the final word on its success. 'I believe that in my married life, I enjoyed as much reasonable happiness as falls to the lot of most mortals. Perfect happiness is not to be sought for on this earth; but affection enables us to counter even disagreeables with courage; and the great mainspring of leading a comfortable married life is confidence in each other, and the making it the rule to bear and forbear.' If, in later life, most of the forbearing had been done by Royal, who, it was said, was 'always puffing up the conjugal fidelity of her husband', she would never have swapped the risks and challenges of marriage for the dreary certainties of spinsterhood. 'Many people laugh at me for being such a great advocate of matrimony,' she admitted, 'but I am every day convinced that few single women are happy.'[150]

Although, from the moment of her arrival in her new husband's home, Royal was determined to find everything about it good, she missed her family, especially her father, whom, as she must have known, she was never to see again. As she wrote sadly to the king, her arrival at her new home had been a forceful reminder of what she had left behind. At a dinner given to welcome her to Ludwigsburg, 'the duke had "God Save the King" performed by both vocal and instrumental music, and Your Majesty's health drunk with a royal salute. I own that I required all the strength in my power not to burst into tears. However, I fought with my feelings and behaved pretty well.'[151] She had new relations to meet, especially her husband's children by his first marriage, among whom was a teenage daughter, Catherine. Frederick had written rather brusquely to his daughter, as he and his second wife travelled through Germany, instructing her to behave well 'to her new Mama'; but Royal was very far from being the harsh stepmother of fairy tale. At their first meeting, Royal had been delighted by Trinette, as she was known. 'She is really very handsome, being the image of her father,' she commented approvingly, and had soon won the girl's affections. She was pleased that her stepdaughter seemed to like her: 'from the beginning she took to me very much, and her age being the same as my dearest Amelia's makes her doubly interesting to me.'[152]

Her happiness was crowned with the discovery, in August 1797, that she was pregnant. Throughout the summer, she wrote constantly to the Prince of Wales, hungry for news of the young Princess Charlotte – 'all the letters I receive from home are full of her praises' – and anticipating the imminence of her own motherhood. 'I look forwards with great anxiety to the moment when I shall be equally blest.'[153] She was still waiting by the middle of April 1798, and did not go into labour until the 27th; then, after a long and difficult delivery, she gave birth to a stillborn daughter, 'a big and beautiful child'. The English minister at Stuttgart reported to the Prince of Wales that the duchess 'suffered very greatly in her lying-in, and so much fever ensued, that for a short time, the physicians were very apprehensive of her safety'.[154] She was not told for some days that her longed-for child was dead. Her first letter was to her father, to whom she wrote in an uncertain hand on 4 May: 'Do not think me ungrateful to Providence for the many blessings with which I am surrounded when I say that the loss of the dear child has deeply affected me.' She was, she assured the king, doing all she could to 'submit to the will of the Almighty; but nature must ever make me regret the loss of the little thing I had built such happiness on.'[155]

A few days later, she was 'much better and stronger', but still sunk in grief. 'I can with truth assure you that at the moment, I feel the most deeply the loss of my little angel.' She sought to find some comfort in religion. 'Though I shall long and silently mourn my child, I am so convinced of the wisdom of the Almighty, and of her happiness, that were it in my power to recall her to life, I would not do it. These times are not those to make one pity children it pleases God to save from the miseries of this life.'[156] On the same day she wrote to the Prince of Wales, confessing that, although 'I gain strength every day, I am very low,' adding despondently, 'you who have the blessing of so charming a little girl as Charlotte will feel for my loss.'[157] There would be no other children. The 'two sets of children's clothes, supposed to last the first three years, one for a boy and one for a girl', which Royal had brought with her as part of her trousseau, 'were never needed and were sold at her death.'[158]

For the rest of her life, Royal would take a compassionate interest in the welfare of young girls, devotedly fulfilling her thwarted maternal affection through her loving care of other people's daughters. If she felt any sense of injustice when she compared her situation to that of her prolifically fertile mother, she kept such thoughts to herself. Though she never forgot her lost baby, Royal was long schooled in dutiful submission to events beyond her control. Replying to a letter from her father which had given her 'great comfort', full as it was with 'motives for resignation', she bravely summoned up those aspects of her life that kept her from despair: 'Parents that I so justly love and respect, to whom I owe the principles which at all times are the only source of happiness, and can in times of affliction be the only true comfort ... a husband whose affectionate tenderness has attached me to him in the strongest manner, sisters I dearly love, and friends that are kind to me. Ought I then to repine or murmur when it pleases God to afflict me?' Despite the rawness of a grief she rightly expected would never completely fade, Royal refused to rail against her fate. 'The Almighty has granted me blessings which he has refused to most women, and still more to the greatest number of princesses.'[159]

Of the three weddings which took place in the royal family during the 1790s, that of the Princess Royal was by far the most successful. It was not always characterised by 'the inexpressible bliss' that the queen had felt radiating from the letters she sent home in its earliest days; but for Royal, it delivered a degree of satisfaction enjoyed neither by Augustus, unwillingly separated from his wife and son and living in crushed and lonely exile abroad, nor by the Prince of Wales, consumed by an all-pervasive hatred for a partner from whom he knew he could never be free. Of all the family, only Royal ended the decade in a happier situation than she began it; only she, contrary to all her own expectations, salvaged something positive from a period in which all other attempts by her siblings to create more settled lives for themselves ended in disaster.

Her brothers must bear some of the blame for what went wrong for them: Augustus was reckless, and the Prince of Wales gave no thought at all either to the character of the woman he chose or the demands married life would make upon him. Yet the miserable situation of their two sons was also partly of George and Charlotte's making. The king rigidly enforced his legal right to control the formal relationships of his children, but, during ten years, made not a single effort to help any of them find a partner of whom he could approve. At the same time the queen withdrew from further involvement in the emotional difficulties of her children, hiding her bitterness behind an air of resentful disapproval.

The resulting unhappiness affected everyone in the family. 'The world never appeared to me so bad as this year,' wrote Elizabeth in September 1796, in a heartfelt response to the plight of her idolised eldest brother. But whilst she sympathised with his sufferings – 'I cannot conceive how anybody can treat you ill in any way whatever' – they had done nothing to dampen her own desire to be married. On the contrary, she was now more eager than ever. 'I trust that the Princess Royal's lot being determined upon, it may open the way for others,' she declared, 'for times are much changed, and every young woman who has been brought up as we have, by the goodness of Mama, must look forward to settlement.'[160] Royal's example proved to Elizabeth that a husband and establishment, and perhaps even love, were still within the sisters' grasp. Not all the experience of marital misery she had witnessed at such close hand would deter her from seeking a similar opportunity for herself.

CHAPTER 13

The Wrong Lovers

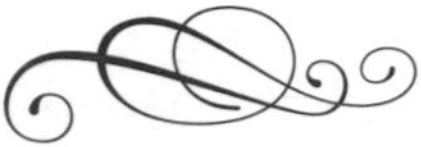

GEORGE AND CHARLOTTE'S THREE YOUNGEST daughters grew up in an atmosphere very different from that which had shaped the characters of their elder sisters. As with so many other aspects of family life, it was the king's illness which changed everything. When, in 1788, both doctors and politicians insisted that the queen must in future devote all her energies to her husband, Charlotte's first thought had been to lament the effect it would have on the upbringing of the junior princesses: 'I pity my three younger daughters,' she observed, 'whose education I can no longer attend to.'[1] The king's eventual recovery did nothing to alter this seismic shift in her responsibilities and, as a result, Mary, Sophia and Amelia rarely found themselves exposed to the sustained, demanding programme of academic and moral instruction that had been the daily experience of the senior princesses. Charlotte's expectations were reluctantly tailored to accommodate her new burdens, and the education of the youngest girls was competent rather than outstanding. They were mainly instructed by governesses, with whom they lived in sometimes uneasy proximity at the Lower Lodge at Windsor. They were physically and emotionally more detached from their mother than the older princesses, less dependent on the ebb and flow of her restrained but powerful personality.

The impact on their development was marked. Removed from the glaring intensity of the queen's ambition, not one of the girls grew up to share the breadth of their mother's intellectual tastes, nor the rigour with which she pursued them. But if they lacked the hard-won accomplishments of their more studious sisters, they were also far less consumed with their anxious desire to excel. They displayed none of the punishing obsession with self-improvement that characterised the Princess Royal, desperate to prove her worth by the quality of her painting and the range of her reading; they were untouched by the collecting mania which drove Elizabeth to accumulate china and porcelain she could not afford, and to cultivate ferociously an ever-expanding list of new skills, from japanning to woodcuts to etching. On the surface at least, the younger princesses seemed calmer, blander personalities than their intense and striving elder sisters.

Yet, beneath their polite demeanours, each of the younger princesses nurtured, as the older princesses had not, a small but resilient core of rebellion, which would have major consequences for the family as they grew into adulthood. Two of these younger daughters would challenge more powerfully than any of their elder sisters the moral framework of the world their parents had created for them. Their attempts to follow the promptings of their emotions led them into extreme and unexpected situations, and both, in their different ways, would eventually be overwhelmed by the consequences of the choices they made. Without the accident of their father's illness and the resulting degree of separation from their mother's dominating presence, it is hard to imagine any of Charlotte's daughters seizing the opportunity to follow their own inclinations in defiance of the principles of sacrifice and submission their parents valued so highly. The queen may have suspected that turning her attention away from her younger daughters would have untoward results, but even she could not have predicted quite how far-reaching and disruptive to the family those results would be.

Of all the sisters, it was Princess Mary, the fourth daughter, born in 1776, who presented the least troubled face to the world. The most classically beautiful of the princesses, her slim figure, fair hair and blue eyes gave her an almost doll-like prettiness. Mrs Papendiek remembered her as 'exquisite, both in figure and grace'.[2] The diarist Sylvester Glenbervie sat next to her once at dinner when she was in her mid-twenties, and found her 'perfect, a very pretty small face, full of sense and sweetness'.[3] The Earl of Malmesbury – who, as a much-travelled diplomat, had had plenty of opportunities to survey the physical attractions of female royalty across Europe – was equally captivated, declaring her 'all good humour and pleasantness, her manners perfect ... [I] never saw anyone so exactly what she should be'.[4] Mary enhanced her natural advantages by dressing with particular care and attention. She was seriously interested in clothes and spent a great deal of time honing and developing her taste. The result was a pared-down, minimal elegance that made her immediately identifiable among her sisters. Mary would never have allowed herself to be painted, as was her youngest sister Amelia, in a curious and fussy confection of ruff and cap that muffled up her youth in a frumpish and unflattering form of fancy dress. In 1802, Mary took matters directly in hand, remodelling Amelia's eccentric fashion choices to reflect her own more worldly tastes. 'I flatter myself Amelia will look in great beauty,' she told her eldest brother, 'as I have given her a dress in my own style to make her look less like an old woman than usual.'[5] Everyone commented on her warmth and the frequency of her smile. The miniaturist Andrew Robertson, who painted her in 1807, found her beguiling: 'Beautiful creature – most difficult to paint, fidgets about, nor sits steady one moment – affable and laughs.'[6]

Although she shared with almost all her family a well-developed musical talent, Mary was not an intellectual. References to books and other literature are rare in her correspondence, in stark contrast to the stream of comments, reviews and recommendations that pepper the letters of her mother, elder sisters and, much later, her niece. Once she had finished her formal education, she seems to have given up books for ever. She had few pretensions to cleverness, but nurtured an acute observer's eye for the foibles of the world around her. She was a lively and entertaining writer, whose letters are characterised by an Austen-like directness that often leaves behind it a surprisingly tart sting. No one described the boredom of the lives she and her sisters led with more economy or more bite than Mary. And no one was safe from her brusque and unforgiving judgements, not even her much-admired older brothers. 'Frederick left us on Monday,' she wrote to the Prince of Wales from Weymouth in 1798; 'he is grown very fat, but looks well in the face. He does not like to hear that he is fatter, but it is so very visible that I could not help making the remark.'[7] Even her father, regarded by her sisters as beyond even the lightest criticism, was not immune. 'We go two or three times a week to the play,' she reported to the prince during the same trip. 'It was pleasant enough, but one may have too much of a good thing, and that is my case in going so often to see a set of very bad actors; however, it amuses the king, and we have nothing to do but submit and admire his being so easily pleased.'[8]

For a woman whose beauty was so celebrated, Mary attracted surprisingly little attention from male admirers. She was never the subject of any scandal, and her name was seriously linked with no one except her cousin, the Duke of Gloucester, who was said to have yearned fruitlessly after her since his teens. Others suitors – both legitimate and unsuitable – kept their distance. For all her easy charm, there was a quality in Mary that did not encourage approaches. Her sister Elizabeth once described the natural condition of king's daughters as '*noli me tangere*' ('touch me not'), and it was a prescription Mary seems to have internalised very early in life. Her closest relationships were conducted safely within the confines of the family circle. Like all her sisters, she preserved a special place in her heart for her eldest brother. He was her '*eau de miel*', whose letters gave her intense and lasting pleasure. 'Anything from you can create that sensation in my heart, as no one loves you more than she who is now addressing you.'[9] He fully reciprocated her admiration. Mary was often regarded as the prince's favourite sister. He appreciated her beauty and equally admired her sensible, grounded character. 'Oh, what an angel she is,' he wrote in 1799, 'how gifted she is in body and mind by Providence, and what a blessing she is to us all.'[10]

As the younger princesses had grown up it was clear that Mary's deepest bond was with her youngest sister Amelia. Seven years Amelia's elder, there had always been a hint of the maternal in Mary's protective affection for the last, and most indulged, of George and Charlotte's children. Mary's family nickname – Miny – was a result of Amelia's toddler attempts to say her sister's name, and by the time they were adults the pair formed one of the sisterhood's most resilient and mutually supportive partnerships. Once, when the two women quarrelled, both were bereft. 'After the number of years we have loved each other, you could not be so blinded or so led away,' reproached Mary. 'The more I think of it, the more it hurts me … No one will feel the more mortified to hurt you than I should.'[11] The row had arisen from Amelia's suspicion that Mary had been too accommodating to the queen, too ready to reveal confidences; that she was, in short, 'Mama's tool'. Others shared her misgivings in this regard. Princess Elizabeth was reluctant to confess a secret with her sister, 'for fear of it coming out elsewhere';[12] and Mary's niece, Princess Charlotte, later described her as 'too great a repeater' and 'the carrier of everything back to the Prince [of Wales] whose great favourite she is'.[13] But these criticisms also perhaps reflect Mary's powerful desire to act as an emollient negotiator between the increasingly bitter factions that divided her family. Not suffering great peaks and troughs of emotion herself, she felt ideally placed to smooth away, as best she could, the disturbing results of intense feelings in others. She once told her eldest brother that it was the object of all the sisters 'to keep the peace, and when they can do no good, they will do no harm'.[14] It was as good a description as any of her own sense of her role within the complicated and shifting family dynamic.

If the defining tone of Mary's outward character was one of calm self-possession, her youngest sister was a far more volatile and forceful personality. As a teenager, the passionate intensity that was to distinguish all Amelia's actions in later life was largely hidden, shrouded beneath a lazy-eyed, sweet-natured voluptuousness that beguiled those susceptible to her rather ripe appeal. 'Lovely creature, fine features, melting eyes,' noted the painter Andrew Robertson, 'charming figure, dignified, finest hair imaginable.'[15] She had none of her sister's discreet elegance; Amelia was majestic rather than slender, and, thought Mary, 'promised … to be very large indeed in time'. Fanny Burney, who remembered the toddler Amelia as her father's indulged favourite, met her again when she visited Windsor in 1798. 'She is now as tall as Princess Royal,' she wrote, 'and as much formed; she looks seventeen, though only fourteen, but has an air of innocence, a Hebe blush, an air of modest candour and a gentleness so caressingly inviting, of voice and eye, that I have seldom seen a more captivating young creature.'[16] Neither had Fanny's four-year-old son Alexander, who had been brought along on the visit and had so far proved embarrassingly resistant to the appeals of the older princesses to play with them. When Amelia entered, it was quite a different story. 'The child was instantly delighted with her! … She stooped down to take his unresisting hands, and exclaiming "Dear little thing!" took him in her arms, to his own as obvious content as hers. "He likes her!" cried Princess Augusta, "the little rogue! See how he likes her!"'[17]

When Fanny met Amelia again, later that year, it was in far less happy circumstances. Amelia had been 'extremely ill … of some complaint upon the knee, which caused spasms and was most dreadfully painful'. She had been sent to Worthing to try the effects of sea-bathing as a potential cure, and was now on her way home. Fanny, who lived near to where Amelia had broken her journey back to Windsor, visited her. 'The princess was seated on a sofa in a grey French riding dress, with pink lapels, her beautiful and richly flowing and shining fair locks unornamented.' She received Fanny 'with her brightest smile', but Fanny, who had not forgotten the manners she had learnt at court, at first refused the invitation 'to come and sit by her' and 'drew a chair at a distance'. Only when the princess insisted did Fanny finally agree to come closer, and spent a happy hour exchanging family news. At the end of their meeting, it was very clear that the Worthing cure had not worked. Amelia was unable either to get up or walk, and had to be 'painfully lifted from her seat' and carried out. Though she did so 'with a dignity and self-command extremely striking', it was plain to the shocked Fanny that she was far from well.[18]

Amelia had been a boisterous and healthy child. It was not until 1798, when she was fifteen, that she had the first hints of serious illness. Although it started with an acute pain in her knee, other worrying symptoms soon emerged. She was always tired, and lost her appetite. She was, she wrote to the Prince of Wales from Worthing in August, 'suffering a great deal'. The strengthening diet that had been prescribed made her 'very sick, and I confess it was I think owing to eating and drinking the porter, for I could hardly lose the taste of it'.[19] In September, the prince was sufficiently worried to travel along the coast from Brighton to visit her. He was not reassured by what he saw there. 'Her appetite', he told the queen, 'is shocking and if she goes to force it at all, her stomach throws up in a short time what she has swallowed.' As well as the troublesome knee, 'the smallest touch' of which gave her 'the most dreadful agonies', he was concerned to see that she now had 'a most dreadful cough'.[20]

When she grew no better, more rigorous solutions, aimed at addressing her manifestly deteriorating physical condition, were tried. 'Since I last had the pleasure of seeing you,' wrote Amelia to her eldest brother, 'I have taken two emetics, but I cannot say as yet I find my appetite improved. I have been electrified, which I hope I shall find shall do me a great deal of good, but as yet there is no judging, it is so short a time since I first began it.'[21] Dr Thomas Keate, who attended Amelia during her stay at Worthing, hoped that passing an electrical current through her inflamed knee might diminish the pain. When Mary went to visit her sister in October, she saw no improvement. Amelia herself knew she was no better. 'As to my own sufferings, I find them the same; every little exertion adds a great deal to my pain.'[22] In fact, none of the treatments prescribed by Keate could have made the slightest difference to Amelia's condition. She was suffering from the early stages of tuberculosis, and the pain in her knee resulted from an inflammation of the joint caused by the disease.

She remained weak and ill throughout 1799, and in the summer was again taken to the sea for the benefit of her health, this time accompanying the rest of the family to Weymouth. There, in August, she at last seemed to improve. This was not, as was later to become so painfully apparent, the complete cure for which everyone had so fervently hoped; the progress of her tuberculosis had been held in check, but the disease had not been eradicated. It would later reappear, with symptoms so sadly familiar to Georgian doctors that there was little doubt about the probable outcome. Yet, for some years, Amelia seemed to recover some of her health, and a good deal of her cheerfulness. She felt well enough to trade gossip again with her eldest brother, the acerbic wit she shared with her sister Mary reappearing along with her health. Her own sufferings had not given her much compassion for her eldest sister, the Princess Royal, whose situation in far-off Württemberg she mercilessly lampooned: 'Don't tell, but I hear she is so prodigiously large she can scarcely walk up or downstairs. This is out of compliment, I suppose, to her duke; very romantic, but if I was her, I would not, if I could help it, show my affection in this manner.'[23] To the Prince of Wales, she showed a far sweeter, more affectionate face. When, after repeated promptings, he sent her a new dress, which she had insisted 'I am in great want of', she was touchingly grateful: 'The beautiful gown … arrived this morning; it made me particularly happy, since it showed you sometimes thought of me, even when I was not with you.'[24]

Throughout her illness, Amelia's affection for her generous and entertaining eldest brother grew more and more heartfelt. During her long stay at Worthing, she had little direct contact with her parents; it was the Prince of Wales who visited her, and kept her cheerful with 'perfect and kind' letters that raised her spirits and made her laugh. Gradually, the prince came to dominate the landscape of Amelia's emotions, edging out other, more distant familial figures. He was twenty-one years older than Amelia, and increasingly seemed more like a father to her than her real, much-respected but increasingly remote parent. She made her own reading of their relationship very clear, signing one of her letters to the prince as 'your own child (meaning myself)'.[25] A year later she again assured the prince, 'you know, I have always been so vain as to consider myself as your child'.[26] For the rest of her life, this was the signature with which she concluded all her correspondence with George. He was the only one of her male relations she really trusted, and to him alone she poured out all the feelings for which she found no expression elsewhere.

Sometimes, the strength of her affection for her eldest brother was expressed in terms that mirrored in their intensity the language of romantic love. 'No words can express half how dearly I love you,' she assured him in 1801, 'or how vain I am of the place I have in your heart. If you ever changed towards me, it would break my heart.'[27] Her love for her parents, whilst always dutifully observed, was described in far cooler terms. 'I think dearest Mama pretty well,' she wrote on Christmas Day, 1799. 'How great has been her affection and kindness for me, and indeed, how grateful I ought to be, and indeed, am, in having always such a model before my eyes.'[28] Her mother and father were examples to be admired; but for unconditional affection and liveliness she had learnt to look elsewhere. Amelia's little world had long since ceased to revolve around her parents.

The queen was not unaware of this. She recognised that with her younger daughters she had never quite achieved the emotional ascendancy she still preserved with the senior princesses. She also suspected that, of all her girls, it was Amelia who had travelled furthest from her influence. She was later to attribute this to 'the indulgence you have met with through a long series of ill health, which both affection and humanity led myself and those about you to yield to at that time, and which none of your sisters were ever allowed to enjoy'.[29] Charlotte saw correctly that there was a steeliness in Amelia, fostered in those years when she was freer than any of her other daughters to shape the world around her to suit her own tastes. But it was not from Amelia that the first challenge to the precarious status quo of royal respectability was to come; it was from her older sister, Sophia.

*

With the possible exception of Augusta, who as a grown woman seems deliberately to have turned as blank a face as possible to the world, Sophia was the most elusive of the sisterhood. As she grew older she had become increasingly withdrawn. The fifth daughter, she sat almost invisibly between the classically perfect Mary and the statuesque Amelia. At first glance, she lacked in every way the immediacy of their impact. She was small, delicate and extremely short-sighted, 'as to be almost blind'.[30] The queen had given Sophia permission to wear spectacles in public, but the princess, as self-conscious and embarrassed about her sight as Elizabeth was about her weight, refused to do so. She would not even put them on to go to the theatre 'for fear of some paragraph in the paper'. Her sister Augusta was airily dismissive. 'Well, I ask her, what can they say? That the Princess Sophia wears spectacles. Well, and what harm can that do her? Would it not be better they should say it than she should lose all sight of the performers?'[31] Sophia was never one to relish bravura displays of defiance; shy and uncomfortable in the glare of public attention, she much preferred the privacy of her own rooms.

In less exposed situations, her muted virtues became far more visible. As a child, she had been the favourite of nearly all her teachers, who responded with pleasure to her quiet concentration, 'her attentive sensible countenance'. Clever and perceptive, she was adored by her governess Mlle Moula, who maintained that 'she had more sensibility, more energy and more imagination than all the others put together'.[32] She shared a gift for mimicry with the Prince of Wales, and in private she occasionally revealed a sharp tongue. But her wide eyes, set in a small, pale face, gave her a vulnerable, fragile look that reflected her shrinking, anxious character. Mlle Moula had, when she was very young, identified Sophia's tendency to 'nervous irritation', and thought her cruelly 'subject to low spirits'. She was to suffer from these complaints all her life, coupled with an imperfectly described and undiagnosed physical debility that saw her endlessly confined to her room or to her bed. She was not without admirers in the family – her brother Edward, Duke of Kent, referred to her as 'that clever little thing and my first favourite, Sophy' – but her cleverness and sensibility were generally less apparent to those around her than the many physical difficulties she endured. Eventually, these problems came to define her, and she was almost always referred to in terms that accentuated her weakness and fragility. She was 'poor Sophy' or 'little Sophy' or 'Madam Little'.

Sophia's health problems seem to have started in her teenage years. In 1793, when she was sixteen, she began to experience problems in her throat with what she called her 'swallow'; she also suffered from fainting fits that attacked her many times a day. Later that year, having made no improvement, she was sent to take the waters at Tunbridge Wells, but with little tangible benefit. It was hardly surprising that she was so often depressed. 'Things are so-so here,' she wrote to her eldest brother from Tunbridge, coining a phrase she was to use throughout her life, and which perfectly sums up her assessment of her low-key unhappiness. Some of her misery resulted from her lack of sympathy for those around her. Far less gregarious than her sisters, she often found herself out of step with their moods and puzzled by their shifting alliances. She did not always find their company congenial. When her eldest sister was still at home, Sophia thought her dominating and managing. 'Many unpleasant things have passed since we have last met,' she told the Prince of Wales in 1793. 'Princess Royal and Lady Cathcart I strongly suspect are at the bottom of everything. I should not say this unless I was quite sure. My reasons I will give you when we meet.'[33] A year later, she was still oppressed by 'the ups and downs of life', telling Lady Harcourt that 'my spirits are weak. I am easily overset, however I struggle as much as possible.'[34]

Her poor health contributed greatly to her weakness of spirit. Her recoveries were only ever temporary, mere gaps in a catalogue of cramps, fits and spasms that went on for year after year. In 1797, she collapsed at a review at Weymouth. 'She was so ill that she could not be taken home for some time,' and had to be undressed by her ladies, 'for the violence of the pain swelled her so much that she could not bear her clothes on, and she was purple in the face.'[35] It is not at all clear what caused Sophia's attacks, which are too imprecisely described to suggest any real diagnosis, but it has been suggested in recent years that they may have been a result of porphyria, which she may have inherited from her father.

The sad regularity of Sophia's bouts of sickness meant that, at first, little attention was paid to the news that she been again taken ill in the summer of 1800. She had apparently recovered by August, when the queen wrote to Lady Harcourt, noting that 'my dear Sophia, on whose account we prolong our stay', was by now 'so much amended in her health that the physician thinks she may, without any risk, give up the warm sea-bathing'.[36] But by the following spring, gossip had begun to circulate that the princess's indisposition had not been quite what it seemed. The diarist Lord Glenbervie was one of the first to hear the stories. 'I heard yesterday a recapitulation of Princess Sophia's extraordinary illness last autumn at Weymouth, from the most authentic information.' With uncharacteristic circumspection, he chose at that point not to transcribe the rumours: 'They are of too delicate a nature for me to choose to commit them (at least according to my present feelings) even to this safe repository. But they are such as to scarce leave a doubt in my mind.'[37] In the same year Thomas Willis, who had assisted his father in treating the king in 1788/89, was in correspondence with Princess Elizabeth over the state of her father's health. He was shocked to hear from Elizabeth herself news of 'the cruelty of a most scandalous and base report concerning P.S.'. He was deeply indignant on behalf of the whole family: 'Such a report must be in its nature false, as those who are acquainted with the interior of the royal houses must testify.'[38] But Glenbervie was right and Willis wrong. The rumour – that Sophia had given birth to a child in or around Weymouth in late July or early August 1800 – was, it seems, the truth.

It was widely believed in Weymouth that something scandalous had taken place there during the summer. Elizabeth Ham – the teenage girl whose farmer uncle was so often visited by the king to discuss agricultural matters when the royals were in residence – was dimly aware of the stories circulating around the resort's tea tables:

> It was about a fortnight after the royal family had come for the season, and so, according to custom, there were aunts and other visitors staying at our house. I was listening to all these discussions going on, and of course, saying nothing. When the conversation ceased for a minute, I looked up from my work and said, 'I wonder what is the reason that the Princess Sophia has never been seen out since the family came?' Upon this, the whole party burst into a laugh, for it was very evident that everybody had been thinking the same thing, but had deemed it high treason to give it utterance.[39]

Elizabeth Ham soon knew all the details of the gossip that had so entertained the female members of her family. The 'delightful story' centred on a wealthy tailor by the name of Sharland, whose wife had just given birth. During Mrs Sharland's confinement, the doctor attending her found an excuse to send the midwife away; when she returned, 'she found two babies where there had been only one'. Under pressure from the inquisitive midwife, Mrs Sharland revealed that 'a few minutes after she was sent away, a carriage stopped at the door. The doctor had brought a newborn infant and placed it by her side, with a purse of money, and told her that she must say that it was her own.' This she clearly did not do, for it was soon known to all the town that the child was not hers. Mrs Sharland admitted as much to Elizabeth, who went to investigate a few weeks later. 'Seeing an infant in its cradle, and stopping to kiss it, I asked if this were her own child or the little foundling and she told me it was the latter. I gazed upon it with great interest, for I was sure it would turn out a hero.'[40] The baby, a boy, was given the name Thomas Ward and baptised on 11 August.

A few years later, Glenbervie reported that 'the foundling, which was left at the tailor's at Weymouth … is now in a manner admitted by the people about the court to be Princess Sophia's'. How the birth had been managed, or where it had taken place, he did not know; but he was confident he knew the identity of the father, naming him as 'General Garth, one of the king's equerries, and a very plain man with an ugly claret mark on his face.'[41]

Major General Thomas Garth was a career soldier, like all the royal equerries, and had served in Germany, the West Indies and Flanders. He was thirty years older than Sophia, closer to her father's age than to her own. There clung about him something not quite of the modern world, one observer describing him as 'a fine gentleman of the old school, in powder and pigtails'. He was hardly a conventionally handsome man, his appearance dominated by the birthmark that was the first thing anyone noticed about him. Captain Landmann, another soldier, who met him in Weymouth, described him as 'a little man with good features, but whose face was much disfigured by a considerable purple mark on the skin, extending over part of his forehead and one eye'.[42] Elizabeth Ham, still young enough to have rather naive ideas about the unpredictable wellsprings of mutual attraction, thought it impossible that 'a fair young princess' could possibly have chosen for a lover 'a little old man with a clarety countenance'.[43]

But there was more to Garth than his unprepossessing looks. Fanny Burney had known him at Windsor and he more than satisfied her very exacting standards for what constituted good company and gentlemanly behaviour. When he left court, she declared she had been 'very sorry to lose ... a man of real worth, religious principles and unaffected honour, with a strong share of wit and a great deal of literature'.[44] He had a cultivated appreciation of art, and could lay claim to having recognised the raw talent of one of the greatest artistic talents of the day: he discovered the young Thomas Lawrence drawing the customers at his father's tavern at Devizes, and kick-started his career as a portraitist by introducing him to wealthy aristocratic patrons. He was a generous and considerate host, known for his excellent dinners. When the sickly Princess Amelia was making her slow and painful journey to Weymouth in 1809, he opened his comfortable, if old-fashioned house to her, diligently scouring the countryside for the asses' milk he was told might help her condition.

Perhaps his best qualities were displayed in the unswerving love and pride he showed for the child left at Weymouth. Garth took the boy – named Thomas, like himself – into his own home, bought him horses and sent him to expensive schools, first at Datchet, then to Harrow. He introduced him to all his visitors, even the grandest. 'He tells me he dotes on him beyond anything,' reported an incredulous Princess Charlotte, daughter of the Prince of Wales, who visited General Garth in 1814, and was shocked to find herself in the presence of a child whom she clearly believed to be her illegitimate cousin. Garth proudly confessed to Charlotte the strength of his feelings for the child. 'He is afraid that he spoils him ... He thinks of nothing else, morning, noon and night.'[45] It was not unknown for eighteenth-century fathers to recognise their responsibilities to their illegitimate children. In acknowledging the boy and making him his heir, Garth had behaved well, if not exceptionally, by the standards of the time; but the lifetime of affection lavished by the general on young Tom Garth, whom he always treated as a much-loved son, blithely indifferent to the disapproval of others, illuminated his most attractive qualities, and perhaps explains what drew Sophia to him in the first place. Proud as he was of his paternity, Garth remained silent on the subject of the boy's maternal origins. 'He now acknowledges himself to be the father,' noted Glenbervie, 'but does not say who is or was the mother. His niece, Miss Garth ... has often thrown out hints to him ... but he has always given the subject the go-bye, by saying, I perceive what you mean, but you are mistaken.'[46]

For all Garth's delicacy, there seems little doubt that Princess Sophia was the mother of young Thomas Garth, and that she and the general had conceived him in the autumn of 1799, when Sophia was twenty-two. Glenbervie attributed their unlikely pairing to the whim of a moment, 'in which opportunity had, with HRH, proved too strong for reason, principle and good taste'.[47] The diarist Charles Greville also thought that the couple's relationship could only be explained as the momentary product of an overwhelming and irrational desire. Unlike other scandalmongers, Greville did not think that Garth's unimpressive looks made the liaison unlikely, 'for women fall in love with anything, and opportunity and the accidents of passion are of more importance than any positive merit, either of mind or body'.[48] Sophia's susceptibility to 'accidents of passion' had been intensified, Greville believed, by the seclusion in which she and her sisters had been brought up, 'mixing with few people, their passions boiling over and ready to fall into the hands of the first man whom circumstances enabled to get at them'.[49]

It never occurred to either man that Sophia might have chosen for herself the man who became her lover, nor that their relationship was anything more than a momentary impulse of gratification. A single line in a letter written by Princess Mary as early as 1798 suggests that Garth's name already had some romantic significance among the sisters. 'As for General Garth, the purple light of love, *toujours la même*'.[50] The general was obviously a figure of sufficient familiarity to be worthy of a somewhat patronising dismissal by the sharp-tongued Mary. The existence of a more established understanding between the couple has recently been further confirmed by the biographer Flora Fraser. An undated letter, written by Sophia to 'my very dear, dear general', suggests, in tone and content, that the princess and the soldier were more than just good friends. Certainly, they were close enough to have exchanged tokens of affection. 'Your ring has given me tremendous pinches,' wrote Sophia, in an uncharacteristically playful and flirtatious style, 'but I have bore them like a heroine. If you looked at your little finger when you were naughty, I believe a certain little ring would have been impertinent enough to give you a pinch. I think you deserve it. And now my dearest general, do not forget that when you are neglecting your own health, you are the cause of giving many unhappy moments to those who love you.' The letter closes with a declaration that leaves little doubt of the strength of her feelings: 'I shall never forget you, my dear general, to whom I owe so much. Your kind remembrance of me is a cordial. Your calling me your S makes me proud as Lucifer ... I love you more and more every day.'[51]

Charles Greville, whose source of information was Lady Caroline Thynne, daughter of Queen Charlotte's Mistress of the Robes, believed the affair had been consummated at Windsor: 'The princesses lived at the Lower Lodge. Princess Sophia, however, was unwell, and was removed to the Upper Lodge, and a few days after, the king and queen went to town, leaving the princess there. Garth ... remained also, and his bedroom at the lodge was just over hers. Nine months from that time she was brought to bed.'[52] It is impossible to say why the couple were prepared to take such a risk. Caroline, Princess of Wales, thought Sophia was too naive and inexperienced to have understood what she had done, arguing that she 'was so ignorant and innocent as really not to know until the last moment that she was with child'. Yet, as Glenbervie commented dryly, 'everybody says the Princess S is very clever'. He asked the Princess of Wales if she really thought Sophia 'did not perceive something particular had passed, and if she could think it a matter as indifferent as blowing her nose'.[53]

Despite his scepticism, Glenbervie transcribed into his diary a lengthy account given to his wife by 'a person of unquestionable veracity', which confirmed the idea of Sophia's naivety. Lady Glenbervie's source was sitting 'tête-à-tête with the princess [when] the latter mentioned to her the continued motions, and as she called them, convulsions in her inside, and bid her put her hand on her belly that she might feel them. The lady did so, and having had many children, was so certain of the nature of the motion that she was quite panic stricken. But neither on that, or any other occasion, ever spoke or looked as if she thought or suspected that others might think she was pregnant.'[54]

If Sophia did not know what was happening to her, it is hard to imagine that her mother, a woman with twenty years' experience of childbearing behind her, would not have recognised the signs of pregnancy in her daughter. Perhaps Charlotte knew more than she ever disclosed. An undated letter from the queen to Lady Harcourt, perhaps written in the summer of 1800, appears to refer, albeit obliquely, to the events of that time. Charlotte is pleased to report 'a most unexpected though long wished-for change in dear Sophia's health. Not without much suffering and pain, but as I am sensible that our wishes could not properly be obtained without it, I was prepared for it, and thank God that I can say she goes on as well as circumstances allow.'[55] There is nothing else in Charlotte's surviving correspondence that hints she was aware that her daughter gave birth to a son during these months, nor is there any report of any comment made by her on the stories that began to circulate so soon after the event. Yet again, it seems she trusted in 'that little word, silence' which had so often seen her through difficult times.

For all her refusal to confirm or deny the facts, however, Charlotte was believed to be in full possession of them a few years later. 'It is now said,' wrote Glenbervie in 1804, 'that the queen knows the child to be Princess Sophia's, but the king does not.'[56] Greville too thought that George's ignorance had been successfully maintained by being kept away from his daughter during the crucial months: 'The old king never knew it, for the court was at Weymouth when she was big with child. She was said to be dropsical, and then suddenly recovered. They told the old king she had been cured by eating roast beef, and this he swallowed, and used to tell it to people, all of whom knew the truth, as a very extraordinary thing.'[57]

In the immediate aftermath of the birth, Sophia herself made no comment on her situation. In December 1800, she wrote an ambiguous letter to Lady Harcourt, assuring her that 'our private conversation has often occurred to my mind' and 'how happy I was that I had the courage to begin it', as the outcome 'has greatly soothed my distressed days and unhappy hours'. Without declaring the subject of her thoughts, she concludes that 'no doubt that I was originally to blame, therefore I must bear patiently the reports, however unjust they are, as I have partially myself to thank for them'. Sophia's extreme discretion makes it impossible to know whether she is, in the most guarded manner, referring to her pregnancy. Her next sentence is no easier to interpret: 'It is grievous to think what a little trifle will slur a young woman's character for ever. I do not complain. I submit patiently, and promise to strive to regain mine, which, however imprudent I have been, has, I assure you, been injured unjustly.'[58] It is hard to think of any woman at any time describing the birth of a child as 'a little trifle'; perhaps Sophia was attempting to deny the reality of what had happened to her; perhaps, only a few months after the event, she still hoped it might somehow be concealed or forgotten, and that she could start life again.

In the event, neither proved possible, not least because the boy's proud father insisted on displaying his son to the fascinated gaze of the public at every opportunity. The general's country house was not far from Weymouth, and young Tom Garth was frequently to be seen playing on the sands there, even when the royal family were visiting the resort. This was very painful for Sophia, as she confessed in a letter of 1805. Writing to her friend Mrs Villiers, she lamented the general's insensitivity in placing her son so visibly before her. It would, she said, be 'very desirable' if 'some check could be put to the odd conduct of a certain person', but admitted that 'that person is very difficult to manage, and thus I have more than once endeavoured to point out to him how ill-judged it was … allowing the younger object to be with him'. It is apparent from the tone of the letter that Sophia's affair with Garth was now over. It also contains the clearest possible acknowledgement that she was indeed the mother of 'the younger object', even though she was powerless to admit to the relationship publicly. 'All my entreaties proved useless, and I merely received a cold answer that it was selfish, and that I could not pretend affection as I had never expressed a desire of seeing what God knows was out of my power. This wounded me beyond measure, for my conduct too plainly showed that I am not selfish.'

It was possible for a bachelor general to brave the stares of the curious and raise his son with pride, but it was inconceivable for an unmarried princess to do the same. Whatever her feelings, Sophia could never behave as if she was the child's mother; this made the situation Garth had so thoughtlessly created intolerable to her. 'I own to you that what hurt me more was the indelicacy this year of knowing it so near me, and that I could never go through the town without the dread of meeting what would have half killed me, had I met it.' Compelled to be near a son whom she could never recognise, to catch sight of a child in whose life she could have no part, there was nothing she could do but 'try in my poor way, to serve what I must ever feel an instinct and an affection for'.[59]

It is hard to imagine a sadder predicament than the one in which Sophia found herself. She knew now that all hopes of future settlement for her were at an end: 'I never could answer it to myself to marry without candidly avowing all that has passed.' She later confessed to Mrs Villiers that there was 'one love to whom I am not indifferent' and with whom she thought she could have been happy, but she knew that such an outcome was now impossible. 'I feel that, did he but know the full content of this story, he might think me very unworthy of him; and how could I blame him? For I know too well that I have lost myself in the world by my conduct, and, alas, have felt it humbly, for many, many have changed towards me.'[60] Weighed down by unhappiness, Sophia retreated into her rooms and saw no company. 'I live away from everybody,' she wrote in 1805; 'I find silence in the situation in which I am placed the best thing, for as to one person who does understand me, hundreds don't, and to a feeling heart, it chills and kills you.'[61] She wished she could take upon herself the sorrows that she saw afflict her friends. Unlike them, she now had nothing to lose. 'For me, it would be of no consequence, having no home, nor no blessings of husband and family.'[62]

In her miserable state, the best Sophia could hope for was to achieve a resigned acceptance of her fate; and there were times when it looked as though she had done so. When Glenbervie sat next to her at dinner in 1810, he was impressed by her air of self-effacement. 'The Princess Sophia, if a sinner, has the demeanour of a very humble and repentant one. She has something very attentive, kind and even affectionate in her demeanour.'[63] But his fleeting sympathy did nothing to quell his appetite for gossip about her, and he soon had something extraordinary to record in his diary: 'The Duke of Kent tells the Princess [of Wales] that the father is not Garth, but the Duke of Cumberland. How horrid.'[64] (Ernest, the king and queen's fifth son, was created Duke of Cumberland in 1799.) In fact, Glenbervie had heard this story before, as early as 1804. It was the Princess of Wales, Glenbervie records, who 'told Lady Sheffield the other day that there is great reason to suspect the father to be the Duke of Cumberland. How strange and how disgusting. But it is a very strange family, at least the children – sons and daughters.'[65]

The rumour that Sophia's brother Ernest was the true father of her child was to haunt both of them for the rest of their lives. Over thirty years after the disputed event, gossip which had simmered away for years, whispered behind hands at dinners and card parties, finally exploded into a public scandal. With the general long dead, Tom Garth was encouraged to put pressure on the royal family, in an attempt to recover his 'rights'. He wanted an income sufficient to pay his extensive gambling debts, and hinted at the possibility of exposure if no cash was forthcoming. His inept and ineffective attempts at blackmail succeeded only in reviving rumours that he was not the general's son at all. The newspapers fell on the story with hungry enthusiasm, and Sophia found herself once again the focus of crude speculation about the paternity of her unacknowledged son.

Glenbervie – who, over the years, eagerly chronicled every version of the scandal that came his way – summarised the essence of the rumour with brisk economy. The Duke of Cumberland 'called upon her when she was in bed with a cold, took advantage of the family temperament in her, and without her having a very precise idea what had happened, got her with child'.[66] The narrative was identical to that which had been used to explain Sophia's liaison with Garth. It was a story of opportunity seized, of ignorance exploited, and repressed passion overwhelming prudence.

Most of those who gave credence to the accusation probably responded much as Glenbervie did, with a mixture of horror and curiosity. Incest was clearly and unequivocally a sin, but it was one which exerted a particular power of fascination in eighteenth-century culture. It featured prominently in the immensely popular Gothic novels of the period, where it operated both to drive plots and provide a frisson of shock amongst readers. Horace Walpole's *The Mysterious Mother*, which had so repulsed Fanny Burney when she was asked to assess its suitability as royal reading matter, was entirely typical of its genre in allowing the forbidden liaison to develop as a result of hidden or disguised identities, which meant neither protagonist was aware of their genuine relationship to the other. Some romantic observers justified the rumoured connection between Ernest and Sophia by passing it through exactly such a fictional prism.

Elizabeth Ham, who wrote her memoirs after 'the shocking story' of the royal brother and sister had become the subject of public speculation, was sure she had seen evidence of their closeness back in Weymouth in the fateful year of 1800. Elizabeth – along with all her female friends and relations – was certain Sophia had been delivered of a child during the summer, and had at first concluded that the princess must have been secretly married before the birth. Then, she later asserted, doubts arose in her mind once the Duke of Cumberland arrived in the resort. She noticed that the princess was often to be seen leaning on his arm. She saw the couple visit the Sharland family together, and watched as the contested baby boy was shown to them at the door. 'Her brother must know of the marriage and is a good friend of the husband, thought I.' But as she herself tellingly noted, Elizabeth was 'soon obliged to weave another framework for my romance'. She was watching when the Duke of Cumberland met his sister as she disembarked from the royal yacht; he 'seized on the Princess Sophia, and kissed her, then drew his arm through hers and conducted her on shore'. Elizabeth was sure there could be only one explanation for such behaviour. She concluded, as the plot of so many novels had encouraged her to do, that the duke 'was not really the son of the king and queen, but of some foreign potentate, who, for political reasons, they had brought up as their own'.[67]

It helped that Sophia seemed, in many ways, the very image of the Gothic heroine: fragile, innocent and abused. It was far less disturbing to consider her as the victim of male passion, rather than a willing partner in love. General Garth was past middle age and plain, with no hint of mystery or intrigue about him; the relationship which genuinely resulted in the birth of Tom Garth was, to many observers, so much less exciting than rumours of an incestuous union.

The resilience of the story linking Sophia and Ernest did not solely stem from the dark appeal of a transgressive scandal, however. It was also actively disseminated from within the royal family itself, giving it a credibility it would otherwise have lacked. Many of the stories about the duke and princess can be traced back to the extravagantly imaginative Caroline, Princess of Wales. Lady Glenbervie was a member of her household, and a great deal of Lord Glenbervie's scurrilous gossip was based on what he heard at the princess's table at Blackheath. Not everything Caroline said was wrong; but as she found herself marginalised by the hostility of the Prince of Wales, her desire to shock the narrow sensibilities of his female relations became increasingly marked. Wildly inventive about her own emotional life – which had by then become baroque in its complications – she was always ready to seek out the shameful secrets of others. If she did not create the rumours, she certainly seems to have made sure they were well circulated.

Finally, there was the issue of Ernest himself. By the time stories of an incestuous connection with his sister began to be murmured abroad, the prince's reputation was so black that any accusation levelled at seemed felt credible. From his earliest days, George and Charlotte's fifth son was always to be found in close connection to trouble. Even as a small boy, he was considered the most intemperate of the royal children – noisy, boisterous and uninhibited. He was much loved by his governess, the redoubtable Mrs Cheveley, who admired his high spirits, referred to him indulgently as 'my boy', and stoutly defended him against the disapproval of the other staff; but his parents were less sympathetic and, like his younger brothers, he was shipped across to Germany at an early age to have his high spirits quashed and to learn to become a soldier. He was eventually commissioned into the Hussars, where he cut a good figure on a horse; he was over six feet tall and, unlike most of his family, slim and taciturn, with brooding good looks. He loved the army life, and fought bravely in the early days of the French revolutionary wars. He was involved in hand-to-hand combat, writing to his father that in one encounter, he had been forced to kill a man. Later, his face was injured by a cannonball, which resulted in a severe and lasting disfigurement. His left eye was 'shockingly sunk and has an amazing film grown over it', reported the Prince of Wales to the queen.[68]

As well as his bravery, in other respects he was a typical soldier, swearing and drinking to excess. Mrs Harcourt, the wife of his commander, and sister-in-law to the queen's best friend, tried to see the best in the young man, but even she found her affection for him tested by his uncontrolled conduct. On campaign with her husband in northern France, she and Ernest visited a convent together. It was not a success. 'I had some difficulty in endeavouring to make him behave well. He would kiss the abbess and talk nonsense to the poor nuns. I know a thousand good traits of his heart,' she wrote sadly, but now even she reluctantly concluded that he was 'too wild for England'.[69]

Ernest was desperate to come home to recuperate after his injury. He petitioned the king for years before he was finally granted grudging permission to return. As Mrs Harcourt had foreseen, Ernest did not fit into the decorous life of his parents' court, and was soon bored and resentful. In 1797, Fanny Burney encountered him haunting the corridors of St James's with a disconcerting intensity. Fanny was chatting to Princess Augusta whilst she dressed to go to the theatre, when she noticed Ernest's silent arrival at the door of the apartment. 'A tall, thin young man appeared at it, peeping and staring, but not entering. "How do you do Ernest?" cried the princess. "I hope you are well; only pray do shut the door." He did not obey, nor move, either forward or backward, but kept peeping and peering. She called to him again, beseeching him to shut the door; but he was determined first to gratify his curiosity, and when he had looked for as long as he thought pleasant he entered the apartment.' By then Augusta had lost patience and told Ernest that she would see him at the play that night. 'He then marched out, finding himself so little desired, and only said, "No you won't, I hate the play."'[70]

It was this sort of unsettling behaviour that made people talk, and made the princesses treat him with wariness. In 1794, Sophia had written to Lady Harcourt about 'dear Ernest', whom she insisted was 'as kind to me as is possible, rather a little imprudent at times, but when told of it, never takes it ill'.[71] What form his 'imprudence' took is not alluded to. Over a decade later, Amelia assured the Prince of Wales that she would not receive Ernest in her rooms without company. 'I am grieved to think there should be a necessity for avoiding being left alone, but I fully understand and you may depend on my remembering your kind injunctions on this subject.'[72] The prince was at that point engaged in one of his periodic quarrels with Ernest, so it is possible that his real concern was to prevent Amelia being dragged into their disagreement; but he argued with most of his brothers at one time or another, and never sought to stop them seeing any of his sisters in private. Clearly, Ernest was considered to pose a different kind of threat. The prince's daughter, Charlotte, certainly found him a sinister figure. She had nothing but contempt for her uncle, whom she described as 'pest to all society', 'a bird of the most fatal omen', and 'at the bottom of all evil'. She disliked 'his indecent jokes' and deplored his language as 'not of the choicest kind'. He was, she said, hated by her aunts, who dreaded his periodic visits to Windsor. 'I must say, he has no heart nor honour,' she concluded, 'but a deep, dark, vindictive and malicious mind, brooding over mischief and always active in pursuit of everything that is bad.'[73]

In later life, Ernest was involved in fiercely contested adultery cases and accusations of physical assault. In 1810, he was badly injured in what appeared to be an attempt by his valet to murder him in his bed; the motives suggested for the attack ranged from jealousy at an affair Ernest was alleged to be having with the valet's wife, through to the man's angry rejection of the prince's homosexual advances. Ernest was a character around whom a whiff of violence and deceit persistently hovered, and the sheer scale of his alleged misdeeds made it easy to believe the worst about him. However, it seems that in the case of young Tom Garth's parentage, Ernest was almost certainly innocent of the charges levelled against him. Sophia's own testimony suggests that she was both Garth's lover and the mother of his child, and that the general's proudly declared paternity was in fact wholly justified.

*

Whilst Amelia and Sophia spent months in the sickroom, and the Prince of Wales was frequently felled by disabling attacks of gout or stomach pain, their father, who turned sixty in June 1798, seemed to march stoically onwards. For almost a decade he had enjoyed better health than many of the younger members of his family. He had been a prominent actor in what he called 'the active theatre of the world' for over forty years, and had seen his reputation shift profoundly during that time.

For the first half of his reign, he had enjoyed only sporadic periods of popularity. His early connection with the much-disliked Bute, his eager support of the governmental attacks on the radical John Wilkes, and his unsuccessful prosecution of the war with America meant that for many years George struggled to win the hearts and minds of many of his subjects. All this had changed in 1788/89, when there was a genuine upsurge in affection for him at the time of his recovery from his disabling illness. He was by then a familiar figure, having been on the throne for nearly three decades; the brief possibility of his being replaced by his unsatisfactory son no doubt helped make his solid if unexciting virtues seem even more appealing. These warmer feelings had been intensified by the opening scenes of the French Revolution, which made many of the liberal, propertied classes reconsider where their loyalties lay, as the foundations of the old order were overturned throughout Europe. Edmund Burke was not alone in deciding he preferred to live with the shortcomings of a constitutional monarchy rather than expose himself to the unpredictable and violent upheavals of early republican government.

But for those who held on to their beliefs in the revolutionary origins of English liberty, and especially for those encouraged by events in France to claim new rights for themselves, George appeared a far less benevolent figure. He was opposed to all calls for constitutional change for which political reformers campaigned, and had no desire to see the franchise either rationalised or extended. He keenly supported the measures William Pitt introduced to combat the looming threat of popular disorder, provoked by a succession of bad harvests and the expensive and ineffective prosecution of a war in which it seemed impossible to land a decisive, knockout blow. In 1797, a serious naval mutiny at the bases of Spithead and the Nore seemed, albeit briefly, to compromise the military effectiveness of the nation's most important fighting force. In the same year, a financial crisis led to the collapse of the gold standard, and the introduction of a paper currency. In 1799, income tax was introduced for the first time, in the face of great discontent from those obliged to pay it. These were perhaps some of the most dangerous and unsettling years of George's reign. Whilst he benefited from the support of those who preferred the stability of the old order to the challenges of the new, the nature and character of politics changed hugely during these years.

Opposition to the king's administration moved out of Parliament and onto the streets, where working men, inspired by events in France, formed societies to challenge the entire basis of the constitutional settlement. These radical movements were often underpinned by an ideological opposition to the very existence of kingship. For their most extreme members, it was not only the institution of monarchy that came under attack, but the person of the king himself. In his pamphlet *King Killing*, published in 1795, the radical bookseller Richard Lee argued that the assassination of kings was not murder, but 'a patriotic duty'. There was nothing sacred or untouchable about the person of a prince; his murder was, Lee declared, entirely justified as 'the infliction of terrible justice by the people'.[74] This was the same year in which George's carriage had been attacked as he went to open Parliament. Two years later, a former British Army officer, Edward Despard, and a small number of conspirators were charged with plotting to assassinate the king en route to Parliament; their group was infiltrated by informers, and Despard was tried and hanged.

George's response to the challenges – both personal and political – he faced in the final decade of the century was constant: he never wavered in his conviction that firm and decisive action was as necessary in the war against political radicalism at home as it was against the revolutionary armies abroad. He was personally courageous in the face of genuine threats to his own safety, and was also tireless in his attempts to rally the propertied and the anxious to the loyalist cause. He showed himself to the public – in the south of England at least –

attending reviews of troops and inspecting local yeomanry exercises. He personally congratulated the commanders of successful naval actions, rewarding admirals on their quarterdecks and ensuring enterprising officers were duly promoted. He led the procession of Naval Thanksgiving held in St Paul's in 1797, receiving a better reception from the London crowds than he had two years before. He took a deep interest not only in the strategic prosecution of the war, but also in the administration of military matters, commenting on issues as abstruse as the proposed reform of the dockyards or the commissioning of captains in the West Indies stations.[75]

As a result, at least amongst those who felt they had a stake in the existing order, the tide of opinion turned steadily in George's favour. The monarchy was increasingly seen as a totem of order and continuity, a counterbalance to the insecurities and chaos of France exemplified by the horrors of Robespierre's Reign of Terror. The rise of Napoleon Bonaparte, who became First Consul in 1799, and was crowned emperor five years later, also shifted the nature of the conflict in Europe, making it less a battle of ideologies and more a struggle of national powers in which it was easier for most Britons to decide where their loyalties ultimately lay. The transformation is nowhere better demonstrated than in a comparison between two satirical prints made by the master of the form, James Gillray. In 1795, Gillray had drawn the king, sitting unmoved in his coach, assailed on all sides by missiles, including a dead cat, whilst his coachman Pitt drives over the shattered figure of Britannia; the crowd waves a French flag inscribed 'Peace and Bread'. The image could be read as one of royal imperturbability in the face of danger; but it also suggests an indifference to the plight of suffering subjects, and a willingness to trample over traditional rights in the service of self-preservation. In 1803, George appears very differently. Gillray portrays him as Jonathan Swift's King of Brobdingnag, a giant image of benign authority, holding a tiny Napoleon in his hand, inspecting him with a spyglass. George, uniformed, grizzled and hefty, regards the newly crowned emperor with relaxed contempt. The king is now the embodiment of all the virtues that will eventually ensure a British victory: immovable, stoic; dismissive of the gimcrack, gaudy pretensions of a strutting enemy.

The consolidation of George's role as the personification of British patriotism did not arise from his own exertions alone; he was the beneficiary of a shift in attitudes brought about by political forces operating far beyond his power. He had never been an original philosophical thinker, nor a strikingly imaginative politician; but his exacting, solid qualities now appeared far more attractive than they had done at any time in the previous three decades. His sense of endurance and application, his limitless capacity for detailed, bureaucratic work, his willingness to identify with the hopes and aspirations of the unsophisticated heartland of the nation he ruled all earned for him a degree of general approbation.

But then, just as his reputation was thrown into positive relief by changing times, he stumbled, reviving for his family terrifying memories of the ordeal that had threatened to overwhelm them in 1788, and which they had prayed never to have to endure again.

It began, as it had done before, with a chill. On 15 February 1801, George was visited by the new first minister, Henry Addington, who found him 'with a severe cold upon him, and almost total loss of voice'; a few days later, Addington called again and found the king 'wrapped up in a long black velvet cloak'. He also noticed that 'his manner was more hurried, and his countenance more heated than usual'.[76] By the 19th, he was worse. 'Bad accounts from the Queen's House,' commented Lord Malmesbury. 'The answer at the door is, the king is better but it is not so – he took a strong emetic on Thursday and was requested to take another today, which he resisted.' Malmesbury was worried. 'God forbid he should be ill!'[77] No one wanted to put a name to their fears, but everyone felt them, especially those closest to the sufferer himself. 'The prince yesterday, after seeing the king, said to the queen he was heated and feverish; the queen, with warmth, hastily said, "He is not. He has not been feverish."' Glenbervie thought everyone was in a state of wilful denial. 'Not a hint of his state of mind, of his ever being mad in his life, or the Catholic question having ever existed.'[78]

In fact, as suggested by Glenbervie's reference to 'the Catholic question' in the same breath as the king's madness, everyone in the political world knew the king had spent the previous few months in a condition of extreme and all-consuming anxiety. He had been horrified by the declared intention of his then first minister William Pitt to remove, at the earliest possible opportunity, historic restrictions imposed on Catholics that prevented their holding major public office in Britain. The recent Act of Union with the Parliament of Ireland made it impossible, Pitt believed, to sustain a policy that excluded so many British subjects from full participation in political life. The king, however, was implacably opposed to the measure, believing that it violated his coronation oath to uphold and protect the Established Church of England. Pitt would not back down and, in the midst of a ferocious controversy, offered his resignation on 3 February 1801, which two days later the king felt obliged to accept. It was the end of a political partnership that dated back to 1784. Without his valued first minister, George was utterly bereft. Pitt left office on 5 February; the king's illness began a few days later. For most observers, the two events were closely linked. 'Fatal consequence of Pitt's hasty resignation,' noted Malmesbury gloomily.[79]

By 22 February, the king had deteriorated even further. The true extent of his illness could no longer be denied, and Thomas Willis was again summoned. He found the king in a very bad state, 'in the height of frenzy fever, as bad as at the worse period when he attended him in 1788'.[80] 'It is now known that the king is deranged,' wrote Glenbervie in his journal. On the same day, at a private concert, the Prince of Wales was overheard declaring that 'my father is as mad as ever'. His brother William took a similar view. 'Well, we shall have it all our own way now,' he assured a shocked courtier, 'for he is not only mad but dying.'[81]

At the end of the month, death indeed appeared the most likely outcome of the king's worsening condition. Malmesbury did not think a Regency Bill would need to be drawn up, as 'the case was different' from that of 1788. 'There was no room to fear a lasting derangement of intellects; he would either recover or sink under the illness; and the physicians said that at his time of life, the probability of one of these events happening much sooner than in 1788 was very great.'[82] On the evening of 3 March, it looked as if it was all over. The king's fever increased and he fell into a coma, with his teeth clenched, unable to swallow. The doctors were so certain he was dying that the queen, the Prince of Wales and the princesses were summoned to take their leave of him.

Then, in the midst of the crisis, he started to rally. Thomas Willis had given him 'a strong dose of musk' to stimulate his nerves; the politician Henry Addington, who had replaced Pitt as first minister, had recommended the use of a pillow stuffed with hops to bring on sleep, a favourite remedy of his father, a country doctor of the old school. Both claimed success for their own remedy. By 5 March, the king could sit up and even feed himself.

The news of his recovery was greeted with spontaneous relief. Glenbervie watched with astonishment 'the crowds on foot, on horseback and in carriages who press through all the avenues to see the bulletin' that announced the king's improvement. 'They are prompted by various motives, but I really believe love, affection and pity for the king predominate.' He recounted a story that poignantly illustrated what the king had endured in his two weeks of confinement. On the very morning of the celebrations, 'when the king was dressing ... and the page had laid his ordinary dress by him, he turned to Willis and said, "Must I put on the [strait] waistcoat?" and Willis replied, "I trust in God, sir, that it will not be necessary." What can be so affecting?'[83] A year later, Glenbervie was to hear darker accounts of the king's treatment at the hands of the Willises. 'The king cannot bear the name of any of the family, and he ascribes the weakness which he now complains of in his limbs to their severity during his illness.' Their 'only medicine was the strait waistcoat and they generally employ that improperly'; it was also said that they beat him 'most violently'.[84] But no one – not least the king himself – wanted to cast a shadow across the apparently rosy prospect of his steady progress to complete recovery.

On 6 March, the king wrote to senior members of the Cabinet declaring himself entirely well again. He received in reply, Malmesbury reported, a letter from Pitt, 'which was dutiful, humble and contrite and said he would give up the Catholic Question'. 'Now my mind will be at ease,' responded the king. The next day he met the Duke of York, who found him 'looking pale and ill, but perfectly collected'. The king, who had determinedly forgiven his second son for his behaviour at the time of his previous illness, was sufficiently in control of himself to tease the duke about his obvious apprehension. 'Frederick, you are more nervous than I am; I really feel quite well, and I know full well how ill I have been.' He went on to enquire about the queen's health, 'and expressed great solicitude lest she and the princesses should have suffered a great deal of uneasiness on his account. "They certainly did, sir," replied the duke, "but the only uneasiness now remaining on their minds ... [is] lest Your Majesty should, as you get well, not take sufficient care of yourself." Much affected, the king declared, "You may depend upon it ... Be assured, I will be more careful for the future."'[85]

Sadly the duke's cheerful vision of the welcome awaiting the king as he prepared to re-enter family life could not have been further from the truth. The reappearance of her husband's mania had awoken all the fears Charlotte had suppressed for nearly thirteen years, and she now dreaded his return to her presence. As in 1788, she was terrified of being left alone with him. When Thomas Willis met her on 12 March, she was in a desperate state, 'greatly distressed' and adamant that 'she wished not to remain so long with the king. It was more than she could sustain,' she told Willis, who recorded in his notes that 'she appeared to despair'.[86] But now that the king was officially cured – he had resumed state business some days before – she had no choice but to take her place by his side.

She did so with extreme reluctance. When the royal couple, together with Princesses Mary and Amelia, went on an excursion to Battersea, it was a difficult experience for them all. The king was irritable and excited. Princess Elizabeth told Willis that the queen endured 'a hard time of it' in the coach whilst the king vented his anger on everyone around him. On her return, Charlotte told Willis that if she was obliged to accompany her husband in the coach again, she would not see him in the evening.[87] Willis conceded that the king was very voluble, and that he concentrated his attentions on his wife, which Willis accepted she might find 'irksome and distressing'; but he could offer her no respite. The king was much offended by Charlotte's obvious anxiety in his presence, 'talked much of German coldness' and deeply resented any attempt she made to avoid his company.[88] The doctors did all they could to encourage her to spend more time with her husband, but she would not be persuaded, and in early April Glenbervie heard that 'the queen is sometimes two days without seeing him'.[89]

However, on 16 April, all Charlotte's attempts to put some distance between herself and her husband were overturned when, with the tacit approval of his doctors, the king 'crept upstairs to the queen'. He was now so well, Willis declared, that 'there was no objection to his sleeping above stairs in the queen's apartment'.[90] Charlotte never told anyone what took place when the king joined her in the privacy of her rooms – she confessed to Willis that the king 'had sworn never to forgive her if she relates anything that passes in the night' – but whatever happened, it was clearly too much for her to bear. Three days later, acting on her mother's wishes, Princess Elizabeth wrote to Thomas Willis asking him and his brothers to return and take the king under their care again. Willis did not need to be invited twice;

but he sought to legitimise his actions by appealing to Addington. The first minister refused to accept responsibility for the king's possible detention, and referred Willis back to the queen. It was a measure of Charlotte's desperation that she, usually so cautious and tentative in pursuing any course not sanctioned by her husband, was willing to authorise Willis's actions, 'only requesting that she might not be named or be supposed to know anything that was intended'.[91]

On 20 April, the Willises entered the house in Kew where the king was staying and effectively took him into custody. 'I spoke to him at once of his situation, and the necessity there was that he should be immediately under control again,' wrote Willis; 'His Majesty sat down and ... looking very sternly at me, exclaimed, "Sir, I will never forgive you while I live."'[92] The queen told Willis she was 'very thankful' for what he had done, telling him 'it is not to be conceived what I have endured for the last five nights'.[93]

If her own experiences had not been enough to convince Charlotte that all was far from well with the king, his attitude to their errant daughter-in-law confirmed her worst fears. The Princess of Wales, living in increasingly eccentric isolation in Blackheath, was still the object of the prince's passionate detestation. She had, as a result, few friends among her female relations, who mostly took his side in the destructive battles that erupted periodically between them; and her imprudent friendships with unsuitable men had not endeared her to the king. She was, therefore, as she told Glenbervie, 'very much surprised' to find her father-in-law arrive without warning at her villa on 18 April. She assumed he had come to visit his five-year-old granddaughter but, as he explained, it was she and not Princess Charlotte he had come to see. He began by declaring 'his entire approbation of her conduct and his affection for her', adding that he had thought about her a great deal during his illness. He had resolved to visit her as soon as he was well, to assure her 'that she would in future find the greatest kindness from all his family, with the exception of one, he was sorry to say'.[94] In a final flourish, he assured the bemused princess: 'I shall always regard you as a sixth daughter'. (The Princess Royal, lost to marriage in far-off Germany, perhaps no longer qualified as a proper daughter in the king's mind.)

The king knew his visit would cause disquiet among his wife and daughters. On his return, he 'bid them guess where he had been'. Everyone imagined he had gone to see his granddaughter; but the king soon put them right. 'I have been to see the Princess of Wales and I was determined none of you should know till I had been there.'[95] The queen saw clearly that the king's sudden embracing of the princess's cause could only make his already sour relations with their eldest son even worse. But she was also fearful that his new-found interest in his daughter-in-law might conceal a more predatory intent. Princess Elizabeth confided to Willis that the king was 'most extraordinary about the princess – you do not know how he torments and plagues Mama about it'. He 'was very full of taking the Princess of Wales over to Hanover', saying 'he would take her away by stealth'. Caroline herself, who relished anything dramatic or exciting, added to the family's sense of foreboding by telling Elizabeth 'she would never reveal what had passed' when the king came to Blackheath. It was hardly to be wondered at that, as a result, the queen was 'frightened to death', and welcomed her husband's renewed confinement at Kew.[96]

Even when he was securely under Thomas Willis's eye, Charlotte tried to regulate the degree of intimacy she was expected to extend to her husband. If she and her daughters agreed to walk with him, she said they should not be required to attend him in his rooms as well, and was 'extraordinarily angry' when Willis failed to enforce this. She complained when the king smuggled letters out to her, and Princess Elizabeth was instructed to write to Willis, telling him 'not to suffer' any more such missives to leave his apartments. For nearly a month the king made the best of it, bizarrely conducting public business from inside his informal place of detention, but, by 19 May, he had had enough. He informed the Lord Chancellor that 'unless he were, that day, allowed to go over to the house where the queen and his family were, no earthly consideration should induce him to sign his name to any paper, or do one act of government whatever'.[97] Faced with the imminent implosion of the entire machinery of government, Willis and the queen capitulated. The king left the apartments where he had been closeted for a month and went to rejoin his family. It was Charlotte's fifty-seventh birthday.

In June, the king took his wife and daughters to recuperate at Weymouth. None of the royal women had wanted to go, terrified that his behaviour would be subject to unwelcome public scrutiny. Elizabeth had written to Willis in despair at the very idea. 'Oh, consider the precipice we stand upon … here we can keep a secret … but at a public water-drinking place, the thing's impossible, and was he to expose himself there, I firmly believe we should die of it, for what we go through now is almost more than we can stand.'[98] In fact, the king behaved perfectly well during his time by the sea. Glenbervie saw him in July, and although he thought him 'very much altered indeed, with ... an emaciated face and his clothes hanging about him', also saw that he took care to avoid 'any unnecessary hurry' and 'every thing of fatigue' so that he felt himself 'gradually gaining ground'.[99] 'I have been a very unhappy man for the last four months,' the king assured a concerned courtier calmly; 'however, it is all over now.'[100]

A year later, Glenbervie saw him again at Weymouth, 'in the hottest of dog days, at a very crowded play, where two tolerable female performers danced a sort of dumb show duet to the tune of "God Save the King", the audience standing up and humming in chorus. The king remained seated, attentive to his own applause, but not unbecomingly so.'[101] It may have seemed as though the equilibrium of royal life, disturbed yet again by the jolt of the king's illness, had been restored to a kind of order – but this was not the case.

At the beginning of January 1804, the king was attacked by painful symptoms of gout. At a party held for the queen, 'He was too lame to walk without a cane,' observed Lord Malmesbury, a guest at the event, 'and his manner struck me as so unusual and incoherent I could not help remarking on it to Lord Pelham.' Pelham, who was playing cards with the queen, noticed that her attention was not on the game: 'her anxiety was manifest, since she never kept her eyes off the king, during the whole time the party lasted'. By the end of the month, 'it could no longer be concealed that the king had a return of his old illness'.[102]

For a fortnight, the royal physicians attempted to cope with the king's relapse. By mid-February, when it was apparent that his mind was as impaired as his body, Addington sent for the Willises. However, when they arrived at the Queen's House, they were refused entry by the Dukes of Kent and Cumberland. The dukes explained to Addington that their father had, after his last illness, extracted 'a solemn promise and engagement' from them both, by which they undertook 'to use every means in our power to prevent anyone of the Willis family from being placed about him'. Forcing them upon him would, they thought, 'be productive of an irritation of mind from which the worst consequences might be apprehended'; but significantly, it was not only their father's health which they feared would suffer from the return of the Willises. 'We are fully convinced that if it were persisted in, another evil of the greatest magnitude would in all probability ensue – no less a one than His Majesty taking up a rooted prejudice against the queen.' The dukes believed no argument would ever persuade the king that Charlotte had not agreed to the Willises' presence during his previous illness. The king was right – it was indeed at Charlotte's behest that he had spent an extra month confined at Kew under the humiliating supervision of the detested doctors. He was determined this should never happen again, and extracted a binding commitment from his sons to prevent it. As a result, the dukes were resolved to avoid 'the consequences to be apprehended from such a calamity' in which 'the destruction of the peace of the whole family would be involved, more especially the female part of it.'[103] Reluctantly, Addington capitulated, and Dr Simmons, physician to St Luke's Hospital for Lunatics, was appointed in place of the Willises.

The king's illness followed a pattern similar to the attack in 1801. For forty-eight hours he seemed close to death, and for some weeks afterwards remained in an extremely unsettled state. As ever, his condition pressed hardest on his wife and daughters; the princesses felt very severely the burden of supporting their mother, whilst also comforting their disturbed father. 'The king never left us till half past seven,' wrote Mary to her eldest brother on 13 February, 'and such a day I never went through in my life.' Amelia had been sent away, as 'she had not been strong enough to bear such scenes of misery.'[104] The queen's nerves were 'shot to pieces', confided Elizabeth to Lady Harcourt, adding that she herself had 'never quitted my mother's room morning, noon, nor night ... I am told I am very much altered, look twenty years older ... [but] if my father gets well, what care I for my looks?'[105]

By May, he was no better. Edward, Duke of Kent, noted that his father was hurried and restless, and that 'a great coolness of manner towards our mother is predominant, and a general asperity towards the whole family on the subject of his confinement frequently shown.'[106] Mrs Harcourt, now back in England with her soldier husband, confirmed Edward's bleak assessment. She observed that 'the king was apparently quite well when speaking to his ministers or those who kept him in a little awe; but that towards his family and dependants, his language was incoherent and harsh, quite unlike his usual character'. Dr Simmons, she thought, could not control him, unlike the Willises, 'who had this facility to a wonderful degree and were men of the world'. With no one to discipline his actions, the king turned the household upside down: 'he had dismissed and turned away and made capricious changes everywhere, from the Lord Chamberlain to the grooms and footmen'. All this 'had afflicted the royal family beyond measure; the queen was ill and cross and the princesses low, depressed and quite sinking under it'.[107] Most unlike his normal abstemious self, the king developed a voracious appetite. He had also begun once more to draw up extravagant architectural designs, planning building after building to replace existing royal homes with no consideration for the expense involved. His unpredictable whims and manic energy reduced his wife and daughters to exhaustion. 'God knows, I am more wretched than I can express,' confessed Amelia to the Prince of Wales, 'and I can see no end to it. Could an extinguisher fall upon the whole family, I think, as things are, it would be a mercy.'[108]

George was in no condition to undertake his usual summer sojourn in Weymouth, but he was determined to go; it is a measure of the collective inability to defy him that he got his way, despite the well-placed misgivings of his family. From the minute of their arrival, the king's behaviour attracted curious and increasingly disapproving attention. Sir Robert Wilson, a visitor to the resort, kept a critical account of the king's actions, describing them with a combination of prurience and relish. He noted that the king vacillated between 'being sometimes very intelligent and communicative, at other times sullen or childishly trifling'. He was particularly shocked to observe that 'his original propriety is a fugitive quality'.[109]

George's new-found willingness to engage in suggestive sexual banter came as a great shock to those around him. On 1 October, he went on an excursion on the royal yacht with three of his daughters and one of their ladies, a Mrs Drax. Wilson heard that the king had 'commenced the conversation … by observing, "Mrs Drax, you look very well, very well indeed dear lovely Mrs Drax, how I should love to stroke you."' As everyone on board the *Royal Charlotte* knew, 'stroke' was then a colloquial term for sexual intercourse. 'The officers of the ship and many of the sailors who heard the speech, which was attended with particular emphasis and strength of voice, could scarcely contain themselves.' Sir Robert, clearly something of a prude, was shocked to find that 'the speech of the king was not misunderstood by any even of the youngest of the ladies', including, presumably, the three princesses.[110]

From the beginning, the king's illness had been characterised by what his son Edward called 'a variety of shades, some of these highly unpleasant'.[111] The courtier George Villiers told William Pitt that he had personally witnessed 'what is quite wrong, particularly at the stables yesterday before the grooms, indecent and obscene beyond description'.[112] Colonel Macmahon, a friend of the Prince of Wales's, said he had been told by the princes themselves that their father 'gives loose to every improper expression, and is so violent in his family, that all dread him'.[113] As in 1788, the king certainly seemed to be in the grip of a strong sexual impulse. He again wrote love letters to Lady Pembroke, the object of his obsession in his first bout of madness. She was now, like him, approaching old age, but still as dignified as ever. 'In favour of his taste, she is the handsomest woman of seventy I ever saw,' admitted Lady Bessborough.[114] Colonel Macmahon heard that the king wished 'to take Lady Pembroke into keeping ... but that if Lady P declines his offer (which he has made through Dundas his apothecary) he will then make it to the Duchess of Rutland'.[115] An ever-growing number of aristocratic female courtiers were cited as having attracted his less than honourable attentions. 'The king frequently threatens to keep a mistress,' wrote Sir Robert Wilson, 'and several times has declared that since he finds Lady Yarmouth will not yield to his solicitations, he will make love elsewhere.'[116] Lord Essex reported in November that George had now set his sights upon a woman closer to his daughter's age than his own. 'I hear Lady Georgiana Bulkeley is supposed to be a favourite, for in this subject he still continues to be absurd and to talk as much nonsense as ever ... he calls Lady Georgiana Venus, and I find there is a party of the princesses against her.'[117]

The king also sought satisfaction rather closer to home. Glenbervie recorded that George rode out two or three times a week to call upon the Princess of Wales in her exile at Blackheath. She told Lady Glenbervie that she dreaded his visits, claiming that her father-in-law persistently tried to seduce her, that 'the freedoms he took with her were of the grossest nature'.[118] On one occasion 'he made such a violent attempt on her person that it was with the greatest difficulty she escaped being ravished by him'. He had thrown her down 'on one of the sofas, and would certainly have ravished her, if, happening to be without a back, she had not contrived to get over it on the other side.'[119]

The Princess of Wales was not always the most reliable of witnesses, but during his illness the king had clearly lost all sense of which women were legitimate objects of desire, and which were not. Glenbervie heard rumours that the king could not always be trusted to behave appropriately even with the closest female members of his family. For a while, he had not been allowed to travel alone in a coach with the queen 'or any other of the ladies, a circumstance which seems to confirm the very many well-authenticated reports concerning one particular symptom attending his disorder'.[120] The Marquess of Buckingham heard that whenever the king went out on an airing in a coach, he was only ever accompanied by one of his sons, 'the queen and princesses following in another carriage, having found it impossible to control the king to any propriety of conduct in their coach'.[121] The Duke of Kent saw it as evidence of his father's improving state of health that by June he again possessed enough self-control to ensure that 'to all my sisters, [he was] particularly kind, but in a proper and not in an outré way'.[122] But as late as December 1804, Sophia admitted all was still far from well, confiding in her friend Mrs Villiers that her father was 'all affection and kindness to me, but sometimes an over-kindness if you can understand that, which greatly alarms me'.[123] At the very time when it was first rumoured she had been impregnated by her brother, Sophia was fending off the unwelcome attentions of her sick and delusional father. No wonder she described herself as 'wretched'.

As his illness drew him into ever darker places, the king turned on his wife with the same passionate rejection that had marked his behaviour to her in 1788. He abused her to the Princess of Wales, explaining that he had determined to part from her 'and had made arrangements accordingly'.[124] He declared 'before his sons and the princesses that … he'll never have connexion more with her'. In fact, it was the queen who seems to have put an end to whatever sexual relations had survived the king's sickness in 1801. Now she was implacable. 'I have never been able to ascertain the cause of the queen's great disgust for the king since his last illness,' mused Sir Robert Wilson, 'for disgust it amounts to, but no doubt she must have very good reasons to resist nature, her duty, the advice of physicians and the entreaties of ministers, for all have interested themselves in the matter.'[125] Even on the night of their wedding anniversary, in September, 'when it had been presumed that the king would be allowed to sleep with the queen, which hitherto had not been the case', she refused to allow him into her rooms. 'The precautions are, first the occupation of the bedchamber by the two German ladies at an early hour. When the queen retires, two or three of the princesses constantly attend her, and stay until the king leaves the apartment.'[126] Malmesbury heard the same story. In his account, Charlotte 'never says ... a word; piques herself on this discreet silence; and ... locks the door of her white room against him'.[127] Sophia, called upon to undertake the uncomfortable task of acting as the queen's chaperone, hated the horror of the situation – and resented her mother deeply for involving her in it. From a position of limitless reverence for her father, whose behaviour to her seems to have done nothing to diminish him in her eyes, Sophia had no doubt the queen should have done her duty and submitted to her husband's demands. She could not bear to sit in her mother's bedroom and hear the king dismissed. 'Will you believe she keeps us there and at last says, "Now sir, you must go for it is time to go to bed" – My God ... how can she refuse him anything?'[128] Her mother's heart, she thought, must be 'as hard as stone'. It was not, she insisted, that 'I am insensible to [the king's] faults, but I know what he was. And how can I love him less when I reflect that this sad change arises from the will of God?'[129]

By the autumn of 1804, it was clear that much of the warmth and affection that had sustained the king and queen's marriage for over forty years had withered away. The old habits of intimacy that had withstood so many pressures and difficulties finally shrivelled into nothing under the impact of George's illness. It seems unlikely that they ever slept together again; soon it was apparent that they no longer wished even to share each other's company. 'Nothing can be worse than he is with the queen,' wrote Lord Essex ruefully. 'That breach is, I believe, never to be healed, beyond the outside appearances.'[130]

Even after his slow recovery, the king showed no desire for the old, uxorious way of life. He decided not to return to the Queen's Lodge at Windsor, where he and Charlotte had lived before his illness, and began to restore the castle itself, creating apartments where 'he could select his own society'. 'He sees the queen now but in company,' recorded Glenbervie, spending most of his time with the Princesses Sophia and Amelia, avoiding the other members of the family, 'all of whom he suspects of caballing against him'.[131] Lord Auckland too had heard that 'within the family there are strange schisms and cabals and divisions amongst the sons and daughters'. Auckland acknowledged that the king never mentioned the queen with overt disrespect, 'but he marks unequivocally, and by many facts that he is dissatisfied with her and is come to a decided system of checking her knowledge of what is going forward'. He clearly regarded the new arrangements as permanent, and ordered his library to be sent down to Windsor from the Queen's House in London. 'The discontinuance of all residence at the town house' seemed to Auckland to indicate 'another mark of separation'. 'It is a melancholy circumstance to see a family that had lived so well together for such a number of years completely broken up,' lamented one of Auckland's correspondents.[132]

Charlotte herself made only an opaque comment on her new situation. 'We are now returned to the castle in our new habitation,' she wrote to Lady Harcourt, 'and I will only tell you that I have changed from a really comfortable and warm habitation to the coldest house, rooms and passages that ever existed, and that all idea of comfort is vanished with it.' Did she refer solely to the underheated rooms she occupied, or was there a nod to the chillier emotional landscape that now surrounded her? 'I tell myself every moment – *il faut s'y faire* – but oh! Stubborn heart!' It was hard, she acknowledged sadly, not to give way to 'melancholy reflections'.[133]

It must have been a dispiriting task to survey the bleak outcome of so many years of devotion to the shared ideal of rational, affectionate, family harmony, to see the relationship which she had tended so assiduously, for so long and at the cost of so many other thwarted desires, founder so completely on the unfathomable mystery of her husband's illness. In the spring of 1805, when the new life had become more familiar to her, Charlotte wrote again to Lady Harcourt, attempting to summon up her accustomed attitude of resignation. It was fortunate, she concluded bitterly, that it was impossible to predict the future, for it was best not to know what unhappiness it would bring. 'I acknowledge fairly that I have every day more reason to adore Providence for keeping us in ignorance of what is to come, as I am perfectly sure that with our best endeavours to prepare for it, we should miss our aim. For our walk within this twelve month has been in a maze, but *n'importe*, I will go on, do my duty and endeavour not to forfeit the good opinion of those I love and also the world, for I am not above that.'[134] As she so often said, she would put a good face on what could not be changed, and endure, because she could do nothing else.

What the king thought, as he surveyed the troubled landscape of his family life, riven by dissension, scarred by unhappiness and dragged down by a powerful undertow of unacknowledged frustration, must remain conjecture, as he confided his feelings on the subject to no one. Perhaps he did not allow himself to contemplate the ever-widening gulf between the optimism of his early hopes for a new kind of domestic happiness, and the bleak reality of more recent experience. George had never been a particularly reflective man; he was not given to fluent articulation on big subjects, especially where they touched upon ideas and emotions. The grand family mission had always been for him a project to be lived rather than talked about, and, as it began to founder, he showed no willingness to examine – publicly at least – what had gone wrong. To do so would have involved asking some very uncomfortable questions about his own role in its collapse, and nothing in his character suggests that he would willingly have undertaken such a potentially painful form of self-examination. Instead, like the queen, he sought to put the best possible construction on what had been achieved, concentrating on those aspects of his private world that still offered fulfilment and pleasure, and carefully turning his gaze away from more challenging issues.

*

By the beginning of 1805, much of the work on the new apartments at Windsor was done, and the new living arrangements were in place. Charlotte was not impressed. When the king asked her to inspect the alterations with him, she declined, declaring herself 'not an enthusiast'. Only one tantalising prospect raised her spirits. At the end of 1804, her brother Charles had written from Mecklenburg suggesting that one of her daughters might marry George, his eldest son. The queen was delighted; there was nothing she wanted more than to cement her lifelong affection for her brother with an alliance of this kind.

She did not feel it right to approach the king with the idea until the spring, when he seemed at last to have recovered from the worst effects of his illness. The letter she wrote to him advocating the match was unusually bold in its tone, reflecting both her love for her brother and a determination to forward his proposal. For the first time in any of her correspondence, she suggested to the king that he might put the wishes of his daughters above his own and agree to what Charlotte knew they wanted. In the past, she said, 'I have made it a rule to avoid a subject in which I know their opinions differ with those of Your Majesty's. For every one of them have at different times assured me that, happy as they are, they should like to settle if they could, and I feel I cannot blame them.'[135] The king replied with polite good nature that 'after having had the happiness of possessing such a treasure from Strelitz', he would not hesitate to say 'that if my daughters are disposed to marry, I should prefer an alliance with this family than any other in Germany'. He went on to add perhaps the clearest explanation he ever gave for his failure to find suitable husbands for the princesses: 'I cannot deny that I have never wished to see any of them marry: I am happy in their company and do not in the least want a separation.'

He was quite unembarrassed by a confession of such frank self-interest, and does not seem to have thought it made him appear either selfish or heartless. For George, this simple assertion of the primacy of his feelings merely reflected the natural order of things. His needs ranked higher than those of his daughters, and it was he who would determine whether or not they should be fulfilled. He was not an intentionally cruel man, but he found it very difficult to distinguish between his own interests and those of the princesses. He was entirely satisfied with things as they were and could not understand why his daughters were not. If he was content, how could they be unhappy? He never appreciated their desire for a life that did not have him at its centre. However, perhaps age and illness had mellowed him, for on this occasion he decided not to stand in the way, telling Charlotte that if she considered this 'a serious offer', he would put his own feelings aside: 'I should certainly not want to oppose what they feel will add to their happiness.'[136]

The queen told her brother that she was 'full of joy and impatience' at this unexpectedly positive response, although she advised the hereditary prince not to come to England immediately, but to wait until after the summer trip to Weymouth. She was still exuberantly happy in May, telling her brother that she could not express all she felt, 'especially when I picture one of my daughters in the home where I was so happy'.[137] But the months went past, the family returned from Weymouth, and still the hereditary prince did not come, Finally, in

1806, Charlotte received a letter from Charles announcing that his son had decided not to marry yet.

It was a bitter blow. There seemed little now to engage the queen's hopes for the future. Wherever she looked amongst her close family, she saw nothing but unhappiness. Relations between her eldest son and his wife had deteriorated to new levels of acrimony. The prince, who told his sisters that the princess was 'a perfect streetwalker', had accumulated extensive written evidence of her numerous alleged adulteries. He had presented the incriminating documents to the Cabinet and demanded they take action against her. Reluctantly, the ministers had agreed to appoint a commission to investigate. It was hard to see what good could possibly result from such a public display of private misery, and the queen despaired.

The king's physical health was another source of anxiety. For many years, he had been troubled by cataracts in one eye; now the other was attacked, leaving him virtually sightless. Even though their relations were cooler now, Charlotte was still deeply affected by this disabling blow to her once robust husband, and although George showed 'an exemplary fortitude ... under this heavy calamity', she admitted to Lady Harcourt that she found his dependency hard to bear. 'The necessity of keeping up before him is such a strain on both body and mind that all idea of amusement, excepting what is necessary to enliven him, vanishes.'[138] Her life at Windsor became even more restricted; one day followed another with little to distinguish them. Even the steady flow of correspondence to her loyal confidante began to dry up. 'I thought it just as well not to increase the number of letters from a place like this,' she told Lady Harcourt mournfully at the end of 1808. 'Where nothing occurs to entertain, [they] must soon become very stupid.'[139] After enduring two years of an existence she found exhausting and enervating in equal measure, Charlotte sent Lord Harcourt a verse couplet which she believed summed up 'our style of living':

> They Eat, they Drank, they Slept – what then?
> They Slept, they Eat, they Drank – again.

She added ruefully that she and her daughters could no longer be described as '*la bande joyeux*'. Those days seemed long past. The best they could aspire to now was to be considered '*la bande contente*'.[140] That would be enough to satisfy her diminished expectations.

Charlotte must have known that even this was an optimistic assessment of the princesses' shared state of mind. Sophia was angry, resentful and increasingly withdrawn; Mary and Augusta concealed depths of frustration beneath superficially calm exteriors; Amelia was fragile in health and emotionally volatile.

Even Elizabeth, her mother's most active supporter and the most determinedly upbeat of the sisters, had been ground down by the challenges of the past few years. She had turned thirty in 1800, and knew that every year that passed made the likelihood of her becoming a wife and mother more remote. In the absence of any credible marriage prospect, she did everything she could to offset the boredom of her life. She engraved, she painted, she embroidered – and still the empty hours yawned before her. That was especially true at Weymouth, where time dragged even more slowly. 'I amuse myself with an hour's German, then write, and draw and dress for dinner, read to the queen the while till cards, when I play at whist till my eyes know not hearts from diamonds and spades from clubs.' The conversation was as dull as the amusements. 'News there is none, but who bathes and who can't,' she wrote in 1802, 'and who won't and who will, and whether warm bathing is better than cold, who likes wind and who don't, and all these silly questions and answers.'[141] Six years later, nothing had changed: 'We go on as we have for the last twenty years of our lives'; life continues 'much as usual, as you know, vegetating.'[142]

No one worked harder than Elizabeth at the business of being cheerful. She said she always preferred being happy to being sad, and could not understand why others did not feel the same. Life did not have to be so dull or so depressing, but those around her, she felt, had fallen into the habit of misery: 'It is astonishing to me that they can have happiness within their grasp, but not trouble to put out their hand.'[143] In spite of all reverses, she did her utmost to see the best in her situation. 'Trials we must have, and they would not be trials if they were not felt. I therefore rejoice in the good, try to go on mildly with the bad, and bear all good-humouredly.'[144] She worked hard to keep up 'that great flow of spirits' which alone enabled her to get through the long days, and gamely sought to bury her own discontents. However, there were some frustrations which overwhelmed even her relentless cheerfulness.

As she grew older, she became increasingly impatient with her royal status. On the one hand, she was proud of her high social standing; on the other, she was painfully aware of the limitations that accompanied it. She referred more than once to her royal identity as 'the canister at my tail' and felt its weight upon her keenly, declaring that she was not at all suited to the world into which she had been born. The world of the court was hateful to her, 'a hotbed of insincerity, jealousy and a thousand other stings of uncomfortable littleness belonging to human nature'. She liked to think of herself as a plain dealer, unimpressed by pretension, and impatient of hollow ceremony. 'Though born at court,' she declared to Lady Harcourt, 'I have no court cant, and love my friends as truly as any plebeian in this or any other country.'[145] She longed to escape from the false, artificial and purposeless life she felt closing in on her: 'I wish I could cut through that fence, maybe a rabbit hole would let me through, though my size comes in my way. Modern dress might let me squeeze out, we live in strange times, I will not give up.'[146] What she needed was a way out, an escape route to a different existence. Like her mother with her Frogmore retreat, Elizabeth found it in the shape of a private place she could truly call home.

With a loan from the Prince of Wales, she leased a small cottage, 'The Garden House', in Old Windsor. Here she planted a garden and ran a model farm, of which she was very proud. She had inherited, as none of his sons had done, the king's passion for agriculture. 'You are perfectly right in thinking that I feel and think all most perfect at the Cottage for eggs, butter, cream and milk,' she wrote in 1808. 'I am unworthy of pigs, though I watch them with a hawk's eye and my broods of chickens and ducks are beyond everything my delight.'[147] A cottage of her own offered Elizabeth the sliver of privacy and independence that enabled her to survive the grim years of the early 1800s. Yet, for all the pleasure she took in her rural retreat, something was missing. 'Between friends,' she confessed to her eldest brother, 'a mate not being there (though I hope will make an appearance, though time flies)', she was still lonely and unfulfilled.[148]

None of her sisters was as frank or as unashamed in declaring the urgency of their desire to marry as Elizabeth. 'I continue my prayer,' she had told Lady Harcourt in 1802, 'of, Oh how I long to be married, be married, before that my beauty decays.'[149] News of a wedding always made her think of her own stark marital prospects. When her friend Augusta Compton announced her engagement, Elizabeth was heartfelt in her congratulations, although the disdain she felt for her own single state tinged her goodwill with bitterness. 'Thank God again and again that you have determined to quit that vile class, you know what I mean ... You have set me a good example, and I will follow it whenever I can.' The desire to put behind her the shame and humiliation, as she saw it, of spinsterhood was one important aspect of Elizabeth's desperate desire to find a husband. But she was also aware that she was missing out on other pleasures. Her vision of the married state was never fey or over-romanticised. She anticipated the physical side of wedlock with the same gusto with which she applied herself to the large meals she so enjoyed. She offered Augusta Compton her cottage as 'the place where you will pass your HONEYMOON', and signed off her letter, in words an inch high, 'Amen and A-Man'.[150]

As the years passed and there was still no prospect of a husband in view, it grew harder to keep her hopes alive. 'Time is a vile old gentleman, for though I court him as much as anybody, he, like all other gentlemen, gives me the slip.'[151] Neither she nor her sisters had known of the Mecklenburg proposal in 1805, as the queen had not told them of it; and in any event, it was extremely unlikely that Elizabeth would have been selected as the suitable candidate for the hereditary prince, as she was nine years older than him. But then in 1808, when she was thirty-eight and after so many years of fruitless anticipation, she at last received a proposal of marriage, from a completely unexpected quarter.

When his name was first linked with hers, Louis Philippe, the exiled Duke of Orléans (and cousin of the executed Louis XVI), was living a modest life at Twickenham. Since the Terror, during which his father was guillotined despite actively supporting the Revolution, his family had scattered across continents, and he had pursued a variety of careers. For a while he had been a schoolmaster in America; and it was probably during his travels in Canada in the late 1790s that he met Edward, Duke of Kent, after which he came to settle in England. The two men became firm friends and remained close – Edward had lent the needy Orléans money, and kept a bedroom available for him to use at Kensington Palace – and it may have been at Kent's prompting that Orléans came to consider Elizabeth as a potential wife. It is not known whether Louis Philippe and Elizabeth ever met, although it seems probable that they carried on some form of private correspondence. Certainly they seem quickly to have developed favourable opinions of each other. Orléans was confident enough of his position to write to the Prince of Wales in 1808, declaring that he wished to marry Elizabeth, and suggesting that she was likely to accept him. Elizabeth confirmed this, telling her brother that 'I own that this has been the wish of my heart for so long … and that my esteem has been gaining ground for so long that it has truly been my prayer.'[152]

In late September, the queen discovered the existence of the Orléans letter, and confronted her daughter, demanding to know if she had been aware of it. Elizabeth was deeply hurt at the implication she had sought to conceal the proposal from Charlotte. 'I had flattered myself that from my constant attendance upon my mother, with my natural openness of character, I had hoped she would have gained confidence in me at my time of life.' She was grieved to find that this was not the case, but was not prepared to be cowed into submission. 'I let her know that I was not ignorant of what had passed, with my sentiments and feelings on it.' She begged the Prince of Wales to help bring the match about, pleading 'that you will not dash the cup of happiness from my lips.'[153]

Perhaps emboldened by the princess's enthusiasm, Louis Philippe now made an open declaration of his intentions, writing directly to the queen to ask her to speak to the king. Charlotte replied with an uncompromising negative, as she informed her unhappy daughter. 'My mother … though kind to me, has assured me it can never be, and that she never will hear of it again.'[154] Orléans was an impoverished refugee, living on the charity of others, with no prospects before him. He was also a Catholic. This did not concern Elizabeth – 'being firm to my own faith, I shall not plague them on theirs' – but as the queen knew, the king would never allow his daughter to marry a man who was not a Protestant. Still Elizabeth refused to give up, and she was encouraged by the Prince of Wales, who urged her not to despair. Her resolve had been further stiffened by the support of her sisters, and by secrets that had come to light in the upheavals following the proposal. 'Many things I will tell you which determined me at once to say I would NEVER GIVE IT UP, for, it was hinted, many things had been brought forward and rejected without a word from us, and therefore we all felt the sun of our days was set.'[155] Elizabeth and her sisters now learnt, probably for the first time, of offers and refusals made for their hands going back over many years. It was unlikely to have made any of them more resigned to their fates.

It may have been these revelations which spurred Elizabeth to explore every possibility rather than see this offer too pass away from her. After the queen delivered her refusal, Elizabeth claimed that what she hoped for was not an immediate union – she seems to have accepted that her father would never agree to it – but some form of engagement, which would allow her to marry the duke after the king's death. She was confident Louis Philippe would agree to these terms, which 'may be very unfortunate to us, but which will make everything *couleur de rose* afterwards by considering my father before myself'. These, she declared, were the only terms on which she would consider proceeding, 'for without being a perfect good daughter, I can never make a good wife.'[156]

However, despite her protestations that she would never abandon that 'degree of submission' that she believed was the particular burden of 'an HRH', there are indications that Elizabeth may have considered defying her parents and making a private marriage with the duke. Her correspondence suggests she and Orléans had discussed the terms on which this might be brought about. In November, she wrote to the Prince of Wales seemingly on the duke's behalf, asking her brother to confirm that when he became king, he would regularise the position of any children they might have. 'He wishes, in justice to himself, as well as out of delicacy to me, that you would merely ensure the legitimacy of children, should there be any, for that subject once clearly decided upon, his mind will be at ease.' An undertaking of this kind would only have been necessary if the couple planned to marry before the death of the king. 'I must now only make one request to you,' asked Elizabeth of her brother, 'from myself, which is that you would send for him before he goes, and not feel shy in talking the subject over with him, for it must be an ease to his mind as well as to mine to hear what you have said to me from your own mouth, and that he would swear never to reveal what passes.'[157]

For all the hope that radiates from Elizabeth's letter, it was the last she wrote on the subject of marriage to Louis Philippe. The duke, it seems, lacked Elizabeth's perseverance. Perhaps he was reluctant to agree to such a potentially open-ended and uncertain engagement; perhaps the complications involved in navigating the provisions of the Royal Marriages Act put him off. Whatever his reasons, he drifted out of Elizabeth's life with the same vagueness with which he had apparently drifted in. Just over a year after Elizabeth had written to her brother about the legitimacy of any children she might have had with him, in November 1809, the Duke of Orléans married Maria Amalia, the unencumbered daughter of the King of Naples and Sicily. When, against all expectations, Louis became King of France in 1830, it was she and not Elizabeth who became queen.

Elizabeth had promised her mother that if her marriage plans came to nothing, 'you shall never see a wry face, and believe me, she never shall, for I have gone on just the same.'[158] If she was bitter, she did not show it (she was too well trained for that); but whatever demeanour she felt obliged to adopt publicly, she perhaps drew some private comfort from a relationship which had far deeper roots than the cruelly tantalising encounter with the Duke of Orléans. While the duke was a pragmatic if ultimately flawed marriage prospect, Lord St Helens was the man whom, if she had been free to do so, she would have chosen for a husband.

Alleyne Fitzherbert, Lord St Helens, was an experienced, highly regarded diplomat who had served in France, Spain and Russia, and a friend of writers, politicians and travellers. Mount St Helens in Washington State was named after him. The king liked him and made him a privy councillor and a Lord of the Bedchamber. Glenbervie, who knew him well, described him as being 'for several years of the select society at Windsor and the Queen's House.' He was a rather reluctant courtier, complaining to Glenbervie that he had 'been in a manner forced to become a Lord of the Bedchamber, which adds nothing to his income.'[159] He was a self-contained, sharp-witted man, and an undiplomatic diplomat who was 'apt to say very blunt things to the different royal personages of the court.' Princess Sophia once asked him to 'say something to the king which she thought would gratify him.' St Helens stubbornly refused to do so, adding that 'you know very well he never would hear, and never will hear the truth from anybody.'[160] He was said to have treated the Empress of Russia with similar abruptness. She asked him once how well she played whist. 'Like everyone else,' he answered. She protested that people had told her that she played rather well. 'They flatter you,' he said.[161]

His disdain for court life and the directness of his manner must have appealed strongly to Elizabeth, who prized those qualities in herself. He was a man of the world, seventeen years her senior, admired by everyone around her, including her father. It was hardly surprising she found him so attractive. She called him her saint. 'You know, it is always holiday with me when he is near, for I love him to my heart and must say it,' she told Lady Harcourt in a long letter. 'There is no man of my acquaintance I love so well, and his tenderness to me has never varied, and that is a thing I never forget.' For all her superficial bravado on the subject of men and marriage, Elizabeth was in reality far from confident in her powers of attraction. 'I am sure I was never, from my earliest days, a person to please men in general, and ... if ever I was such a fool and tried to be agreeable, I have often gone to bed thoroughly dissatisfied and displeased with myself.' With her saint it was different. Secure in his regard, she was able to be herself, shrugging off the part she usually felt obliged by her position in life to adopt. She yearned to see him 'at all times, hours, minutes, days, nights, etc.'. She was old enough now to appreciate how rare it was to find a man like him: 'God knows, they are not found often, they are diamonds without flaws.'[162]

Elizabeth wrote this at the end of 1808, when she was still hoping that she might marry Orléans. This made no difference at all to what she felt for St Helens, even though she knew it would never end in marriage. Whether she followed her heart or her head, it must have seemed as though the result was always the same – hers were always the wrong lovers.

Writing to the Prince of Wales in 1810, she tried to be philosophical. 'The good times not coming, and yet time going on, I fear all my bright castles in the air (which have so entirely failed in this world, and left, I fear, a deep scar not to be effaced, though smothered in my breast) are nearly at an end.' She hoped she would learn to bear her disappointments with 'good humour', and was determined to approach middle age with dignified resignation. If love, marriage and a family were denied to her, she would attempt to find comfort in smaller pleasures. 'I have been well tried in my spring and summer of life; I expect my autumn and winter to be free from chilling cold and whilst I have kind and good friends, a great chair, a pinch of snuff, a book and a fireside with a kind brother, I think I shall in the end rest very quietly.'[163]

*

Such stoic renunciation would never be Amelia's way. Beneath her rather dreamy, voluptuous exterior, the youngest of all George and Charlotte's children concealed a will stronger than any of her sisters, perhaps because she had less experience than they did of being thwarted in her wishes. When she fell in love, she pursued the object of her desire with an intensity that was in the end to consume her.

She first met Charles Fitzroy in 1800, when she was seventeen. He shared many of the characteristics of the men to whom her sisters were attracted. Like General Garth and Lord St Helens, he occupied a trusted place in the royal household. He too was an equerry and was liked by the king, who seems to have felt at ease in his undemanding company. He was twenty-one years older than Amelia, making him exactly the same age as her idolised eldest brother. But unlike the 'hard-favoured Garth', Fitzroy was extremely good-looking. As a young soldier in Germany, he had caught the eye of the susceptible Frederick the Great, who enjoyed the company of attractive young men and 'the attentions of the veteran monarch to the handsome youth were especially marked'.[164] Fitzroy was unmoved by Frederick's appreciation, or indeed, it seems, by anything very much. He was a decent, good-natured man – 'we love him for his good affectionate heart and his attachment to his parents', wrote the Duchess of Brunswick, the king's sister, who knew him in Germany in 1786 – but he was placid rather than passionate, with a sedate self-containment that revealed little to the world. He was of respectably aristocratic parentage, the second son of Lord Southampton, though allegedly also descended through an illegitimate line from Charles II, which may have added a whiff of the exotic to his otherwise straightforward appeal.

In 1801, during the regular retreat to Weymouth, Amelia's health had been poor. When the rest of the family returned to Windsor, it was decided she should stay by the sea to benefit from the fresh air. Miss Gomme, her elderly governess, remained with her, as did Fitzroy, who was charged with overseeing her daily rides. It was perhaps here that their relationship began. When Amelia went back to Windsor in the winter, Fitzroy came too; their rides continued, and it was noticed that he was always her partner at cards. The Princess of Wales, that energetic transmitter of scandal, told Glenbervie that once, when she was at Frogmore, she had seen Amelia and one of her ladies 'in one of the retired walks'; the lady 'took a piece of paper from her pocket, wrote something on it and threw it into a hedge or bush near the walk'.

After they had gone, the princess picked up the paper, saw the number twelve written on it 'in large Roman letters' and put it back. 'Soon afterwards, General Fitzroy came into that walk, and looking with apparent eagerness on each side, when he came up to the same place, perceived the note and put it in his pocket.' At supper that night, Amelia insisted that she had a headache and wanted to go to her room, but the princess deliberately kept her talking 'till considerably past XII o'clock.'[165]

By 1803, the attraction between Fitzroy and Amelia was so apparent that Miss Gomme grew alarmed, and begged Amelia to behave more prudently. When this had no effect, the governess went to the queen, urging her to act to put an end to a relationship she considered damaging to the princess. Amelia was furious, and demanded that her mother dismiss Miss Gomme. In response, Charlotte wrote her daughter a lengthy and circuitous letter, whose principal object seems to have been the avoidance of any further discussion of such a difficult subject. In it, she revealed that she was aware of Amelia's behaviour, and had already issued warnings intended to put a stop to some of its more obvious public manifestations. There was to be no more dawdling along next to Fitzroy whilst out on horseback, but beyond these remarks, she had little more to say. She refused to consider her daughter's appeal to send the governess away; Miss Gomme's 'motive did her honour, as it was meant to make you sensible of the necessity to watch every step in your conduct'. Nor would she respond to Amelia's rather petulant demand to cancel her rides if Fitzroy was no longer allowed to accompany her. 'I am sorry that the request about the riding must also meet with a refusal. This must be done for your health.' The queen was aware that the sudden discontinuance of her outings would probably give rise to more gossip. She was firmest of all in declaring that no mention of the affair was to reach her father, to whom Amelia had clearly threatened to appeal. 'To say anything on this subject to the king would expose you more than anything – make him unhappy, and make our home unhappy, and as there is sufficient distress to be found out of doors, there can be no good reason why it should be unnecessarily increased indoors.'[166]

At no point did Charlotte mention Fitzroy's name, or specifically instruct her daughter to stop seeing him. To do so would have been to acknowledge the reality of a relationship she hoped could be wished away. 'Let it from this moment be buried in oblivion,' she instructed

Amelia forcefully, but her commands did not have the effect that they might have had on her more pliant elder daughters. Amelia's response, as she told Mary, was uncompromising. 'I cannot but say I am no longer a child, and though ready to take advice, yet I cannot ... submit to government at my age.'[167] She was now twenty years old and had no intention of ending her affair with Fitzroy, in whom she was certain she had found the love of her life.

From the earliest days of their relationship, Amelia was all but overpowered by the strength of her feelings for him. 'O God, how I do love you! ... I live but for you. I love you with the purest affection, the greatest gratitude; I owe you everything. All my happiness and comfort I derive is through you.'[168] It was Amelia, always unswerving in her determination to achieve what she wanted, who had begun the affair. 'I have liked you from the first I sought you,' she reminded Fitzroy in one letter to him, 'and Blessed be God – I gained you.'[169] None of his letters to her survive, so it is not known how he responded to this avalanche of passion. He did not run away, as he might have done if the situation had been truly intolerable to him; his staying at court, where Amelia's very visible obsession placed him in a difficult position for the better part of a decade, suggests that he felt something for her in return. Yet nothing about his passive character implies that he could match the fervency of her devotion. His undemonstrativeness sometimes drove her into agonies of anxiety. 'Don't be angry, but tell me the truth, I felt as if your manner towards me today still as if you had doubts about me ... I think something I did annoyed you last night.' To be happy, she required repeated proofs of his affection. 'If you can, give me a kind word or look tonight ... look for me tomorrow morning riding ... I go to Chapel tomorrow ... do sit where I may see you, not as you did last Sunday morning, good God, what I then suffered. Do have your dear hair cut and keep it for me.'[170]

She was strongly attracted to Fitzroy, and clearly longed for their relationship to go beyond clandestine meetings in midnight gardens. 'Oh God, I am almost mad for you, my blessed and most beloved Charles ... Oh God, that dear soft face, that blessed sweet breath.' She promised him that once they were married, she would keep him in bed for a week, 'the joy would be so great.'[171] Yet, for all the undoubted power of Amelia's feelings, it seems unlikely that they consummated their relationship. 'Her amours with Fitzroy have long been notorious to the courtiers,' wrote Glenbervie, 'but whether carried to the furthest extent seems uncertain.'[172] Amelia herself told her friend Mrs Villiers that 'General Fitzroy was the most noble and honourable of men ... and that she never did anything to be ashamed of.'[173]

Her lack of shame was in other ways quite remarkable. She wrote to Fitzroy with a candour extraordinary for a woman of her background. With him, there was nothing she would not discuss; even her most intimate bodily difficulties were considered suitable subjects on which to seek his reassurance. In a revealing letter discovered by Flora Fraser, Amelia opened her heart to him about gynaecological problems which were clearly the source of great distress to her. After so much sickness in her teens, she was perhaps used to the close observation of her body, and had become concerned about symptoms in her genitalia. 'Don't be angry or shocked, but do you think my spot being out is likely to prevent my having children if I was married to you? And what is its being out owing to? I ask you anything, I say anything to you so don't be angry.' She did not want to disgust him, 'but from all I have suffered in those parts, I have often thought and dreaded having a cancer in my womb.'[174] The Princess of Wales told Glenbervie that Amelia's later illnesses could be traced back to a venereal disease she had contracted whilst convalescing in Worthing in 1798, with the complaint on her knee, where the nephew of her surgeon Keate 'communicated the infection to her'.[175] It seems unlikely that Amelia, who had a high sense of her own status, would have engaged in a sexual relationship with a provincial surgeon's assistant (and the fact that the Princess of Wales was involved in passing on the story is noteworthy); but the episode may reflect a history of gynaecological difficulties that were not discussed publicly by her doctors.

Amelia's frankness, so untypical of the time, was perhaps the result of her conviction that she and Fitzroy were linked by ties so profound that they were not subject to conventional niceties of behaviour. As she assured him, 'no two ever loved or was as tried as we are, and instead of separating us – which in all others it would – it has bound us tighter and more sacredly together'.[176] She was convinced that the strength of their devotion meant that they were married in all but name, insisting that 'for years I have considered myself his lawful wife'.[177] But despite her confidence that their relationship was sanctioned in the eyes of God, she nevertheless yearned for the conventional recognition of the relationship: 'Marry you, my own dear Angel, I really must and will.' Sometimes she sought to persuade herself that the formalities of marriage did not matter to her, but this was overshadowed by what she thought was their destiny: 'O God, why not be together? I pine after my dear Charles more and more every instant … I really must marry you, and though inwardly united, and in reality that is much more than the ceremony, yet that ceremony would be a protection … would to God my own husband and best friend and guardian was here to protect me and assist, as I am sure was destined in heaven, I should have nothing to fear.'[178]

Precisely what Amelia had to fear became evident at the end of 1807. Miss Gomme, whose efforts to regulate Amelia's behaviour towards Fitzroy in 1803 had been so unsuccessful, received a series of anonymous letters accusing her of deliberately ignoring the intimacy between the princess and Fitzroy, which had now become a public scandal. (These letters were eventually revealed to have been written by Lady Georgiana Bulkeley, the 'Venus' the king had found so attractive during his illness in 1804.) Panicked, Miss Gomme demanded to see Princess Elizabeth, always regarded as the queen's de facto secretary, and poured out to her a torrent of pent-up hysteria in which rumour, anxiety and accusation were fairly equally mixed. 'That there was still time to save Princess Amelia who was all but ruined – all the world talked of Gen FR and Princess Amelia's behaviour – the queen [had] connived at it, and had sanctioned the promise of marriage the moment the king was dead – that the queen was equally ruined.' When Elizabeth refused to carry such a scandalous account to her mother, Miss Gomme declared that if she would not do so, she would feel it her duty to speak to the king. Shaken, Elizabeth took the story to Charlotte, whose response was 'outrageous … She thought it the height of infamy to be accused of deceiving the king and ruining her child.'[179]

Amelia was horrified when told what had happened by her brother, Frederick, Duke of York; but she was also perhaps secretly relieved at having matters in the open at last. When Amelia told him that she considered herself married to Fitzroy, the duke replied that he thought 'a time will come when you may do as you please, and the queen will be your friend, but don't say so, all this has offended her very much, her being said to have deceived the king.'[180] In fact, Frederick's assessment of his mother's state of mind was far too optimistic. If Charlotte had ever been prepared to turn a blind eye to Amelia's affair until the king's death made marriage a possibility, she would have done so only if it were conducted with sufficient discretion to allow her to maintain a studious public ignorance of the true facts. The anonymous letters sent to Miss Gomme, together with her terrified and outspoken response to them, made such tactical unknowing on Charlotte's part unsustainable.

A bright light had been shone on to things best kept hidden, and the queen was forced into action. She wrote a letter to Amelia intended to put an end to any glimmers of hope she might have mistakenly entertained about future possibilities. 'You are now beginning to enter into the years of discretion and will, I do not doubt, see how necessary it is to SUBDUE every passion in the beginning, and to consider the impropriety of indulging any impression which must make you miserable and be a disgrace to yourself and a misery to all who love you.' Had the king known of what had passed, 'he would have been rendered miserable for all his life and I fear it would create a breach in the whole family'.[181] It was a bleak message, but a clear one. Whilst the king lived, Amelia must give up all thoughts of marriage to Fitzroy and abandon any idea of an informally acknowledged engagement.

Yet again, the wishes of the daughters had been weighed against the king's peace of mind, with no doubt as to who would be required to make the necessary sacrifice. Charlotte had tactfully stressed only the unhappiness that would result from George's discovery of Amelia's defiance, but others were more explicit in the pressure they exerted on the recalcitrant princess. When Amelia told her friend Mrs Villiers that she was 'making up her mind to leave the castle with General Fitzroy and take her chance of forgiveness', Mrs Villiers did not hesitate to invoke the spectre of the king's precarious health as a means of bringing Amelia to her senses. 'What would be her feelings of remorse if, as more than probable, such a shock as this would be to the king brought on a return of insanity? She was the most devoted of daughters to him, and this touched her.'[182] Even her doctor resorted to similar methods of emotional blackmail. When, weighed down by depression, Amelia's health began to fail, she asked her physician Sir Francis Milman to explain to the king that her sickness was aggravated by the misery of her situation. He refused to do so, 'saying that for the king's sake, she must sacrifice herself and patiently bear all the hardships that were imposed upon her'.[183]

Suffering with new symptoms from the tuberculosis which had first appeared in her knee, prostrated by anxiety, and lectured and criticised by so many of those around her, still Amelia refused to give up her dream of marriage to Fitzroy. In April 1808, when she thought she was dying, she wrote a long letter to be given to her lover after her death. 'I feel our wishes are known and sanctioned in heaven,' she wrote, 'and there we shall meet to part no more. I solemnly declare the truth that you are the only person who ever suited me, for whom I could ever find the same confidence and affection.' He was, she declared, 'my husband! Though from situation, the rights I have not enjoyed.'[184]

She had no doubt now whom she blamed for her intolerable situation. Her mother had let her down when she most needed her support; and close examination of the Royal Marriages Act had proved to her the degree to which her father was the architect of the laws from which her unhappiness flowed. From 1808 onwards, a new harshness towards her parents was evident in all Amelia's letters. 'You know how little reason I have to love my family,' she wrote to Fitzroy, 'or esteem them in any way, and though I never hurt any of them, they God knows, have me – in many ways, various and cruel.'[185]

Amelia turned twenty-five in August 1808, and as she knew from her study of the Act, she could now apply to the Privy Council for the right to marry without the king's permission. She drew up a formal letter to the Prince of Wales announcing her intention to do so; but throughout it, she referred to the king as 'my late father', suggesting that she could not bring herself to begin the process during his lifetime. The resentment towards her family so evident in her letter to Fitzroy was now focussed upon the king, as she bleakly recapitulated 'the trials I have gone through, on account of not offending my late father, which cause has so long made me submit to them … You must know,' she admonished her brother, 'how cruel our situation has long been, and I may say, how unjust.'[186] A year later she repeated her complaint, with an even greater sense of anger directed towards 'the laws made by the king respecting the marriage of the royal family' which had prevented her from becoming Fitzroy's wife, 'which I consider I am in my heart.'[187] Alone of the sisters, Amelia was prepared to declare that it was the actions of her father – both past and present – which had so effectively denied her the only form of happiness she sought for herself.

This sobering realisation did nothing to improve Amelia's state of mind or body. By the spring of 1809, she was again seriously ill.

Mrs Villiers found her 'bled and blistered' and extremely unhappy in April, concentrating much of her anger on her parents. 'She says herself, poor thing, that she must die for the ill-treatment she receives,' wrote Mrs Villiers, adept at stoking up Amelia's resentment. 'It really makes me boil with rage! And then one hears of the king and queen being patterns of conjugal fidelity and parental affection! I am sure the queen never had one grain of the latter quality in her composition – the former I daresay she may boast of, for I don't believe there is one person in the kingdom who would ever have had bad taste enough to propose to her to be otherwise.'[188] It was remarks of that kind which resulted in the effective dismissal of Mrs Villiers from Amelia's company. As she grew weaker, Amelia's world shrank in on itself. 'As to myself, I have nothing new to say, but I am sadly plagued with a cough,' she wrote to the Prince of Wales in July. 'I go out in the garden but am tired of myself, and believe I shall never recover. None but your dear self know what human feelings are; none of my family do.'[189] Only her sister Mary was exempt from the bitterness that now consumed her. Mary's calm presence soothed her mind, whilst her practical helpfulness sought to relieve her physical sufferings.

There was little however anyone could do to improve Amelia's worsening condition. She had a persistent pain in her side which no medicine helped. Eventually it was decided to insert a seaton, a skein of silk placed inside a surgically created wound, intended to act as a form of primitive drainage tube. She already had one in her chest, and now submitted 'to this very severe remedy' again. But the seatons made no lasting difference to her state, and her doctors, with nothing else to suggest, recommended she retreat to Weymouth. She was quite willing to go. 'My only wish is to get well, and God knows I long to feel I am no longer a burden to my family.' Her only request was 'that Miny [Mary] might go with me.'[190]

The journey from Windsor was a hard one; 'obliged to rest at every place we stopped to change horses … in one constant fainting from the fatigue and violence of the pain in the side'. The sisters spent the night at General Garth's Dorset house, where he treated them with his customary generosity, despite being lame with gout. He had arranged their apartments at Weymouth, and had 'secured good milk and butter for our breakfast and fruit of all sorts, particularly grapes for Amelia; indeed he has forgot nothing, and thought of everything'. At the resort, Amelia made little progress. Taken into a bathing machine 'to breathe the sea airs, she lay a quarter of an hour on a couch we contrived to place in the machine'; but, reported Mary, she remained 'faint and low'.[191] Soon she was too weak to walk down the seven steps of the pier to get into a boat. 'She now finds great comfort in sitting quiet all day and not speaking,' reported Mary sadly.[192]

At the end of September, she was worse, 'thoroughly good for nothing … sickish all day and the pain in my side continues very much the same … For the last three days I have looked very yellow, they tell me. I feel it all swimming about me.'[193] A letter from the Prince of Wales cheered her up, and she particularly enjoyed the fun it poked at their mother. 'Your account of your interview with the queen amused me very much, and did not astonish me, for I see her snuffing and her so-ing you with all her might.'[194] Throughout the autumn, the misdeeds of the queen and Amelia's sister Elizabeth – or Fatima, as she called her, with cruel reference to her weight – occupied her mind. Elizabeth was regarded as the queen's ally, and, as such, became the object of much of Amelia's frustration and anger. 'I shan't mind the queen's ill and cross looks now, or Fatima's; her letters are such that they surpass one another in hypocrisy.' It was impossible, she told her brother, 'for me to say what I wish or what I ought; silence sometimes says most, and does so in this case'. She was convinced her mother had no appreciation of the true state of her health. 'I must tell you that in one of her last letters to Miny, she don't name me, but in a post script says "I am glad Amelia is better, and hope very soon to hear she is perfectly well." This has provoked Miny … though she has always tried to make me think the queen's letters are not unkind.'[195]

Amelia's belief that her mother lacked 'feeling or pity' and was indifferent to her suffering was painful, as she knew her health was failing fast. 'I can't boast much of myself,' she told her brother. Mary heard her moaning in her sleep and noted that 'she complains of constantly dreaming that she is in pain.'[196] The seatons, which were badly inflamed, had to be treated with caustic, which was 'a sad trial', wrote Mary. 'I never remember her in all this long illness suffering more pain.'[197] By the beginning of November, it was clear that the stay in Weymouth had done nothing to improve her health and that she would have to go home to Windsor for the winter.

Amelia was prepared to return, but only if she was not required to spend time in close company with her mother. Mary agreed that it would be disastrous for her sister to live with the queen again.

Charlotte had objected strongly to Mary's accompanying her sister on the extended stay in Weymouth. She had disliked her prolonged absence from home, 'which is not thought right, and is considered selfish of Amelia'. Mary dreaded any of this being said to Amelia; as she told her father, 'you must understand, it will half kill her, who really, poor soul, never thinks of herself, and only wishes to give as little trouble as possible'.[198] The king was touched by his daughter's plight and agreed that a place must be found for Amelia where she could enjoy some respite from her mother's bad temper, and avoid 'unpleasant situations'. Now that he was 'aware of the real object in view, nothing shall be wanting on my part to facilitate it'. An old house belonging to one of the king's physicians, Dr Heberden, which was comfortable and at a safe distance from the castle, was fitted up for her. Amelia and Mary began the slow, painful journey home.

The cause of the queen's lack of sympathy for her suffering daughter is not easy to understand, but it may have been an aspect of her descent into an increasingly depressed state of mind which was remarked upon by everyone around her. The pressures of her position had often driven Charlotte into melancholy sadness, as her letters to her brother during the early years of her marriage attested; but since the king's first illness, her low spirits were often accompanied by anger and frustration, usually directed at those closest to her. After George's 1804 bout of sickness, her moods grew even worse. 'The queen's temper is become intolerable,' Glenbervie observed, 'and the princesses are rendered miserable by it.' [199] It is also possible that Charlotte considered her youngest daughter had brought some of her miseries upon herself.Amelia had refused to give up a relationship which had no future and could only end in pain for all concerned. She had paid no attention to her mother's warnings, nor had she obeyed her direct instruction to 'subdue every passion', as Charlotte herself had sought to do throughout her life. Instead, she had abandoned herself to irrational emotions which could never be gratified in the way she sought. It was hardly surprising that her health had suffered as a result. If these were her thoughts, Charlotte would not have been alone in holding them. Mary, who was closer to Amelia than anyone, and ministered to her with a truly selfless devotion, was equally convinced that her sister's misplaced love for Fitzroy was the cause of her illness. She talked of it later as 'that most unfortunate attachment, which destroyed her health by degrees ... As far as I am concerned upon the subject that I look upon as having killed her, I have nothing to reproach myself with, as I never encouraged what could not be for her happiness.'[200]

Once she was back at Windsor, Amelia's attitude to her father grew warmer, as she saw for herself how worried he was about her; but for her mother, she continued to feel nothing but cold fury. 'As for the queen,' she wrote to the Prince of Wales in December 1809, 'to describe her feelings, her manner and her visit to me yesterday, all I can say till we meet is that it was the STRONGEST CONTRAST to the dear king POSSIBLE, but I am too used to it to feel hurt, but I pity her.'[201] Her mother visited her every day, but 'never names my health.'[202]

Amelia had not seen Fitzroy since she had been sent to Weymouth some four months earlier. She was now too weak to venture out alone, and their secret meetings, so avidly awaited and planned for, had come to an end. Her illness had achieved what nothing else in over a decade had done, and made the secret prosecution of their affair impossible. Amelia no longer had the strength to enjoy anyone's company beyond the narrow circle of her sister Mary, her maid Mary Anne Gaskoin and her doctors. By May 1810, she could no longer hold a pen and the tirelessly loyal Mary Anne was obliged to act as secretary for her. Sir Henry Halford, a new doctor brought in to consult on her case, was pessimistic about her prospects: 'I cannot persuade myself that HRH is better,' he informed the king. 'I think her weaker, and I do not find that any one of the symptoms … has disappeared. They are all to be found distressing in their turn, and HRH has less power to bear up against them.'[203] A spasm in her bowels added 'a violent sickness' to her long litany of medical problems; by June she could keep down only beef tea, hock and laudanum. But in all her pain, she had not lost sight of the aim that had been her most cherished ambition for so long: in the last months of her life, when she could hardly move or eat solid food, she made a final effort to bring about her much-desired marriage to Charles Fitzroy.

In July, she wrote to the Prince of Wales, appointing him her executor and sending him a copy of her will. In the same letter, she urged him to speak to Halford, who 'is now become so good a courtier that he does not venture to oppose anything the king and queen like, though it may be very contrary to my wishes.' She begged her brother to 'impress upon him how greatly you know the unhappiness of my mind increases my bodily sufferings.'[204] The prince was, in effect, to prepare the ground for an approach Amelia intended to make herself upon Halford, whom she believed was uniquely positioned to persuade the king to change his mind on the subject of her marriage. Through him, she would exert the same emotional blackmail on her father that had been used on her all her adult life, and planned a last-ditch attempt to convince the king that by removing the principal cause of her unhappiness, he could improve her chances of recovery. The king had assured her that 'there is no object dearer to my heart, no blessing for which I pray more fervently than that you may be restored to me'.[205] Amelia wanted to test the truth of those assurances.

She wrote to Halford, asking him to explain to her father that her condition was greatly impaired by her reduced emotional state, and that marriage was the only solution to her misery. Halford – whose slippery disingenuousness later earned him the nickname of 'the eel-backed baronet' – refused point-blank to entertain the idea. He did not believe her father would agree to her request, and it was his opinion that merely raising the subject might fatally endanger the king's fragile state of health. His message to Amelia was both uncompromising and sadly familiar: in the scale of both public and private importance, her wellbeing would always be secondary to that of her father.

Matthew Baillie, a colleague to whom Halford had shown the letter he wrote to Amelia, commented that it would be 'perhaps not much to her taste'. Amelia was appalled by it and drew on all her feeble resources of energy to deliver the response she thought it deserved. Mary watched her working on it, spending 'all day writing and erasing'. The result was a chilly dismissal of Halford's egregiousness, coupled with an unsparingly accurate depiction of the reasoning that lay behind it. Although Halford had himself told her that he was 'thoroughly convinced that my disease is more of the mind than the body and that affliction is shortening my days, you have nothing to offer but an exhortation to filial duty and respect to my parents'.[206] She was sorry that he should 'think so meanly of me as to believe me deficient in either, or that my conduct is likely to be such as to become the object of impertinent remark at every street in every town in this island'. Amelia was convinced she knew where to place the blame for his refusal to help: 'I cannot but apprehend that the sentiments contained in your letter are the suggestion of some part of my family.'[207] Baillie doubted that would be end of it: 'Probably in the course of two or three months, she will make an application through some other channel.'[208] But that was not to happen.

Everyone, including Amelia herself, knew there was little hope now. A skin infection that 'erupted in her face and is now nearly all over her body' caused her pain 'far beyond anything I can describe', wrote the devoted Mary in September. Knowing that her sister had not long to live, Princess Augusta broke through the cordon of propriety that surrounded Amelia and arranged a final secret meeting between her and Fitzroy. After he had gone, Mary Anne Gaskoin wrote on Amelia's behalf her last letter to the man she had loved with passionate intensity since she was seventeen years old. 'The princess had desired me to tell General Fitzroy how very happy his visit of this evening has made her, so much that all words must fail in description. HRH wished me to say how much she had to say, but that it was impossible for her, being so short a time with you.'[209] As a leave-taking, it was as poignant in its simplicity as anything else she wrote to her lover, a sparely forceful comment on the 'cruel situation' which had blighted her youth and ruined her chances of happiness.

On 25 October, the Prince of Wales wrote to the Duke of York, asking him 'to come directly here, as well as William and Edward, as Amelia is anxious to see all you three … Pray bring them (if you can find them) with you as quick as possible.'[210] Certain that she was dying, Amelia prepared to say goodbye to her family. When she saw the king, beside himself with grief and 'weeping … all day long', she gave him a ring which contained a small lock of her hair set under a crystal tablet, engraved 'Remember me'. She asked him to 'wear this for my sake and I hope you will not forget me'. The king replied, 'that I can never do, you are engraven on my heart', and then burst into tears.[211] He was said to be 'much distressed that she gave nothing to the queen'. Finally, *in extremis*, Amelia relented and, putting aside the bitterness that had dominated her relations with her mother in her last years, 'she did at last give the queen a locket'.[212]

Princess Mary, Amelia's companion and support during all her suffering, was with her when she died on 2 November. Sir Henry Halford felt her pulse, held a candle to her mouth and told her sister it was all over. Mary kissed her and then went upstairs to tell her parents.[213] The king, already in the grip of the relapse of madness that was shortly to overwhelm him, refused to believe she was dead, declaring: 'I know very well she can be brought to life again.' Lady

Cranley, a courtier, noticed the queen standing, alone and unregarded, in the passage outside Amelia's room, 'looking half distracted'. She took her hand and led her away.[214] Mary had already gone to write a note to Fitzroy. 'Our beloved Amelia is no more, but her last words to me were, "Tell Charles I die blessing him." Before I leave the house, I obey her last wishes.'[215] Fitzroy acknowledged her death with grave dignity. 'To the memory and transcendent purity of the adored and departed angel, I owe every self-value I possess.'[216] A few months later, Mary Anne Gaskoin, Amelia's companion through so many years of sickness and adversity, died herself, probably of the same tuberculosis that had killed her mistress. The king, who was moved by her death, had her buried 'as near as might be' to 'his beloved daughter'.[217] In her own way, Mary Anne was the final victim of a complex web of unhappiness that had tainted the lives of everyone caught up in it – and which, as the queen had predicted, had in the end produced nothing but misery for all concerned.

*

In the last months of her life, Amelia had occupied herself reading Samuel Richardson's *Clarissa*, which she had not altogether enjoyed. It is not surprising that the novel, with its unforgiving moral message, did not entirely please her, for Amelia was at heart a romantic. The intensity of her emotional life was far closer to the dramas later to be imagined by the Brontës, in which passions too profound and powerful to be contained by the ordered world of everyday life end up consuming the lovers themselves. It was her sister, Sophia, whose experience was far closer to the tragic heroines of Richardson's severe mould, in which a single departure from moral rectitude, whether willed or not, results in a lifetime of bitter atonement. Elizabeth's thwarted attempts to find happiness might be seen as a dark inversion of the plots of Jane Austen – presented with two men who offered different visions of rational happiness, she would have been content to accept either, but was denied both. It had been powerfully demonstrated to the sisters that each of them had, in their different ways, chosen very much the wrong lovers; but there was no suggestion at all as to what might constitute a more acceptable solution, and they prepared to enter the next decade no more advanced in the pursuit of happiness than they had been ten years before.

CHAPTER 14

Established

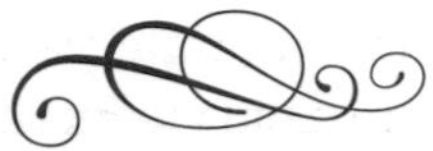

ON 25 OCTOBER 1810, SHORTLY before the death of Princess Amelia, the king had made a halting, tentative appearance at court. It was the fiftieth anniversary of his accession. George was seventy-two years old, and had now been on the throne for longer than any monarch since Henry III in the thirteenth century. It was a remarkable tribute both to his personal powers of endurance and to the stability of the institution of kingship itself. Despite the forebodings of many of his subjects, fears which George himself had sometimes shared, the British crown had survived not just the loss of the American colonies; it had also weathered the storms of twenty years of political upheaval that had seen dynasty after dynasty fall across Europe in the face of the seemingly unstoppable advance of Napoleon and the ideas he represented.

As the war against the French dragged on, George was now well established as a symbol of the values for which many Britons believed they were fighting. In the toasts raised at formal dinners, in the fulsome language of loyal addresses composed in cities, towns and villages, in the banners of processions that marched through the streets, the king was praised as the defender of a mild and beneficent constitution and the guarantor of traditional liberties. Observing the outpouring of affection, the radical politician Samuel Romilly commented with some bemusement that George had gone from being 'one of the most unpopular princes that ever sat upon the throne ... to one of the most popular'. He had little doubt that it was the horrors of the French Revolution which had prompted such a decisive shift, arguing that it had 'added tenfold strength to every motive of endearment to the king'.[1] In London, crowds turned out in huge numbers and in uncharacteristically respectful demeanour to show their appreciation. 'All most perfectly quiet and civil,' noted one witness, 'not an offensive word or insulting gesture.' He could not recall ever before seeing 'such perfect order and decorum in any great assemblage of the middling and lower orders'.[2]

At Windsor, the tone was very different. The mood was sombre, darkened by both the final stages of Amelia's illness and the parlous state of the king's own health. His sight had completely failed him, and he walked unsteadily. A small family party was arranged as most appropriate for the subdued circumstances. The king was led into a circle of sympathetic friends and specially favoured courtiers, leaning on the arm of the queen. Cornelia Knight, the last in the long line of Charlotte's literary-minded lady companions, watched him hobble into the room. 'As he could not distinguish persons,' she recalled, 'it was the custom to speak to him as he approached.' His responses were disconcerting. 'He said to me, "You are not uneasy I am sure, about Amelia." At the same time, he squeezed my hand with such force that I could scarcely help crying out … As he went round the circle as usual, it was easy to perceive the dreadful excitement in his countenance.'[3] Everyone could see something was wrong; but few could have predicted the scale of what was to come. This was the last time the king was seen in public by anyone other than his ministers, his family and his doctors.

The king had suspected that his health was again about to fail. George Canning, the Tory disciple of Pitt, reported that 'he was conscious that the complaint was coming on some days before it actually seized him … He said on Thursday or Friday last, "I am sure I am going to be ill – for I had the same dream last night that I have had every night before my illness." Accordingly, on Friday night he was taken decidedly ill.'[4]

His friends and family were certain it was anxiety about Amelia that had triggered the attack. 'Aggravating subjects have been the cause of his former illnesses,' wrote Princess Elizabeth to Lady Harcourt, 'this one's owing to the overflowing of his heart for the youngest and dearest of his children; a child who never caused him a pang, and whom he literally doted upon.'[5]

His early symptoms were horribly familiar. When Spencer Perceval, who had been first minister for just over a year, saw him on 29 October, he found 'his conversation was prodigiously hurried, and … extremely diffuse, explicit and indiscreet'.[6] His mind was agitated, and he did not sleep. 'The truth is,' Canning told his wife, 'poor old Knobbs is as mad as ever he was in his life … The hearing of him … was most dreadful – a sort of wailing, most heart-rending to hear.'[7] Whilst he remained docile, the king's case was managed by his physicians, Matthew Baillie, Henry Halford and William Heberden. But when he became more violent – on 4 November, he was put into a strait waistcoat – ministers insisted that more specialist expertise was required, and, inevitably, sent for Dr Robert Willis, who was later joined by his brother John. Thomas, the third Willis brother, did not attend; the king regarded him as principally responsible for his humiliating confinement in 1801, and his absence may have been an acknowledgement of the scale of the king's hostility towards him. However, if Thomas was singled out for particular resentment, none of the Willises was regarded by George with anything but dislike. The queen protested at their appointment, saying she had promised the king he should never again be left in the care of the Willis family, but her objections were overruled and Robert Willis arrived on the 6th. For a few days, the king appeared to improve. He was lucid enough on 11 November to ask how long he had been confined, saying that he remembered nothing at all of the last few weeks and that 'this was the fourth blank in his life'; but he grew worse as the month went on.[8] Princess Mary wrote that she held out little hope for the future. 'I have had no heart or spirit to write since Dr John Willis came … My heart has been quite broke, for he is decided he can be of no use, as he finds no mind to work upon.'[9]

Willis's assessment was more circumspect when he and the other physicians were called before a parliamentary committee in mid-December. The king, they said, had recovered before, and might do so again, although they saw no evidence that this was imminent. It was true he had rational moments, which might – or might not – become more frequent. His age and general 'bodily infirmity' counted much against him, but they would not rule out the possibility of an eventual return to health. The queen, refusing to succumb to despair, placed the most optimistic gloss on the doctors' evasions. 'Our beloved king's illness leaves us still under some anxiety,' she wrote to Lady Harcourt, 'but thank God, there is not the smallest doubt of his perfect recovery, of which the physicians give us all the greatest assurance ... and if we go on, improving by degrees, great hopes may be entertained of some unpleasing events not taking place, *comprenez-vous*?'[10]

The 'unpleasing event' Charlotte hoped to avoid was a regency, which would declare to everyone the nature and severity of the king's illness, and which had, through a combination of luck and political manoeuvring, been avoided during all his previous attacks. But Perceval, with none of the queen's emotional investment in her husband's predicament, could see that there was now no alternative. On 20 December, he wrote to the Prince of Wales, telling him he planned to introduce a Regency Bill into Parliament without delay. The prince would be offered the job with a number of limitations, which echoed those devised by Pitt in 1788. He would not have the power to create peers, to appoint or dismiss office holders, or to grant pensions. At the end of a year, if the king's condition had not improved, the regency would be made permanent, and the restrictive clauses dropped. The queen, meanwhile, was to be given the task of looking after the king, and a council appointed to help her do so.

As he had done a generation ago, the Prince of Wales argued that the regency should come to him with no restrictions; but in the face of the first minister's refusal to negotiate, he capitulated and accepted Perceval's terms. The politics surrounding the appointment were very different from those of 1788/89. Now the king was an old man with a melancholy history of repeated illness; the political world had, on three earlier occasions, been forced to contemplate the prospect of his replacement by his eldest son, and, as a result, the idea had lost much of its power to shock. The prince, a middle-aged man, was a diminished political figure, a far less attractive figurehead for the Whig opposition than he had been twenty years before. His accession no longer seemed to presage the complete overturning of the balance of established party politics; and in the event, the bill progressed through Parliament relatively smoothly. On 6 February 1811, the prince took the oath of office as regent.

The king was not unaware of what was happening. On 29 January 1811, Perceval went down to Windsor to explain to him the measures that had been put in place. The king offered no dissent, but observed that at the age of seventy-two, perhaps 'it was time for him to think of retirement'. Hoping to encourage him towards the idea of voluntary abdication, Perceval highlighted how onerous his life would be if he returned, stressing the hard work that would await him, but the king refused to rise to the bait. 'He listened with some unwillingness, and said "He should always be at hand to come forward if wanted."'[11]

In the early months of 1811, he enjoyed a number of rational intervals. He was lucid enough to have the contents of Amelia's will read to him, with the frequent and potentially embarrassing references to General Fitzroy explained delicately away by Henry Halford in terms that successfully deflected any further enquiry about the exact nature of their relationship. He was able to signal his approval of the conduct of the regent, for whom, in his illness, he now seemed to feel an affection that had not been apparent when he was well. 'The dear king … spoke in the handsomest terms of you,' gushed Elizabeth to her eldest brother in February 1811, 'and told my mother how right she had always been about you … His heart overflows at your amiable and affectionate manner concerning everything about him … he cried fit to break his heart.'[12]

But for most of the time, even when seemingly calm, George's mind was clouded and confused. The Duke of Clarence went to visit him in early 1811, arriving just as dinner was served. Although the king ate 'with appetite roast mutton, took his broth with turnips and bread and cheese with pleasure' and William thought his father looked quite well, 'his thoughts flew from one subject to another'. He was full of eccentric schemes, planning visits to Kew, Weymouth and St James's, and brimming with ideas for the redecoration of individual rooms and the deployment of servants. The duke had thought himself prepared for what he might find, but was deeply shocked. 'Halford, in going over to the castle, told me this was a good day; if so, I do not understand what a bad one can be; in short the mind appeared to be amused by absolute trifles. There was not any obscurity or any tendency to it, but an absolute vacuum of mind.'[13]

By March, the king's obsessions had come to the notice of the queen's council, a committee under the nominal headship of the queen that was charged with overseeing the king's welfare, who instructed the physicians to 'point out to His Majesty that the various plans and projects which he dwells upon are considered as inconsistent with his complete recovery'. His preoccupation with inventing new knightly fellowships and designing ribbons and medals to accompany them did not, they thought, bode well. The councillors were particularly distressed to discover his plan to establish 'a new Female Order ... which is altogether novel and inconsistent with the dictates of a sound and deliberate judgement ... and does not correspond to His Majesty's manly character'.[14]

His delusions had already taken on a familiar alarming tone. General Garth accompanied him on an uncomfortable walk on the terrace, telling Henry Halford on their return that the king's speech had been 'very incorrect indeed'. When the Duke of York visited the family in May, he too was shocked by his father's comments, made 'without the least regard to decency', despite the presence of the queen and 'all our attempts to change the conversation'. The main topic of his discourse was Lady Pembroke, who loomed just as large in the king's disordered mind in 1811 as she had done in 1788. 'Is it not a strange thing, Adolphus,' the king declared to his son the Duke of Cambridge, 'that they refuse to let me go to Lady Pembroke, although everyone knows I am married to her; but what is worst of all, that infamous scoundrel Halford was by at the marriage, and has now the effrontery to deny it to my face.'[15]

The doctors were divided about the best way to manage the king. The Willises advocated more of what they had offered in the past – physical restraint coupled with extreme seclusion, a regime in which George was deliberately isolated from all sources of stimulation, any of which, they asserted, would agitate him and hinder a cure. William Heberden, a general physician and not a professional 'mad doctor', took a different view. He was a passionate advocate of greater freedom for the king, arguing that some participation in normal life would keep his mind engaged and distract him from 'incorrect ideas'. With nothing to occupy his thoughts, was it any surprise he did not improve? 'We must study to place him in a situation that may call forth the energies of his mind, and divert the wanderings of his fancy, not by vain expostulation, but by objects of natural interest.'[16]

For a while Heberden got his way. The king was allowed to ride out with his gentlemen occasionally, and to see his family to drink tea, but the experiment came to an abrupt end in the summer when the king's illness took a new and more sinister turn. His physical symptoms were severe: nausea, abdominal pain, constipation, sweating; his pulse raced and he could not sleep. By 15 July, the doctors were convinced he was dying. It was not until the end of the month that they felt he was out of immediate danger. Although his bodily health gradually improved, his mind seemed permanently damaged. At the height of the attack, he had been 'so violent and unruly as to render restraint absolutely necessary ... displayed bursts of passion, gross and indecent allusions, loud and continual talking'.[17] When the violence of the 'paroxysms' subsided, there was no accompanying return of even occasional lucidity. The Duke of York reported that the king was still 'under restraint' on 31 July, and that 'every delusion, even of the wildest kind, which had appeared at the height of his delirium, still continues in force'.[18] The king now lived for the most part in a universe entirely of his own making. 'His conversations for a fortnight now are with imaginary beings, or rather, with those that are dead,' observed Lady Albinia Cumberland, who had known him at court. He spoke often to the long-dead Prince Octavius, 'forming a plan for his marriage and supposing him 17 years of age'. He believed Princess Amelia was alive and living in Hanover. 'He fancied that he had the power of raising persons that are dead, and making them 17 again and that an interview with the Almighty caused this power.'[19] He referred to himself as 'the late king'; on other occasions, he refused to answer any questions about his health on the grounds that he was immortal. He would wear only white clothes. 'Bed-gown and drawers – no stockings, only gaiters. All his ideas on purity. He would drink only water and milk, and not eat. Sometimes he thought himself in heaven and that it was the day of judgement, and that he spoke for the wicked.'[20] His tenuous connection with reality gradually ebbed away. 'The patient has two or three times asked about his family,' the doctors noted, 'generally however he has an impression that his sons are dead or sent away to distant parts of the globe.' Heberden concluded that George now much preferred the company of the imaginary dead to that of real people. 'He actually described the dress, the conduct, and the conversations of different persons who are thus recalled to life. In short, he appears to be living ... in another world, and has lost almost all interest in the contents of this.'[21]

The queen, deep in despair, blamed Heberden and his short-lived liberal dispensation for all that had happened, and, in the absence of any credible alternative, reluctantly placed Dr Robert Willis in sole control of her husband's welfare. Halford and the physicians were downgraded and stripped of much of their authority, the council stipulating that they were never to have any communication with the king except in the presence of the Willis brothers. Under their prescription of isolation and inaction, the king disappeared from public and private life. He occupied his own suite of rooms in one of the lower levels of Windsor Castle, furnished with a number of harpsichords, which he played with great gusto. To attend him, he had the Willises and their keepers – and, of course, the company of the dead. In October 1811, he complained to Halford 'of the noises made by the people of his imagination standing about him, and endeavoured to close his ears against such seeming disturbance'. The doctors were allowed occasional encounters with their nominal patient; once the indefatigable Heberden attempted to read him a newspaper, in the face of Willis's scornful disapproval. The king paid little attention, but still Heberden held to his conviction that 'the present medical treatment and management applied to His Majesty's case are fundamentally and practically wrong'.[22]

Heberden's protests made no difference. By the end of 1811, detached physically and mentally from the world, George III's active life was effectively over; not just as king and a public man, but also as a husband, as a father, and as a self-determining individual. As Princess Augusta wrote sadly to Lady Harcourt, not even his family could reach him now. 'In all his other illnesses, he was rejoiced to see us and vexed beyond measure when we left him … But this time, he had just the same satisfaction of pouring out his complaints or telling his schemes to us or anyone else.' He made no distinction now between his loving daughters and strangers, 'not caring in the least for the individual to whom he was speaking, and wished us good-bye without the smallest unconcern'. She had not seen him 'but at a distance' for three months, 'and now probably I shall never see him again, for under his present melancholy state, I would not see him for worlds; as I cannot serve him, I could do him no good, and he would not know me'.[23]

The sisters attempted to keep up their spirits, but in such dark days this was difficult. They diligently passed on accounts of the king's health to their brothers and trusted friends, chronicling the quiet and the bad times, the latter marked by 'a great deal of very unpleasant laughing', or 'a great deal of violent action in stamping with feet upon the floor'.[24] Sometimes, Elizabeth confessed, there seemed nothing to hope for but the king's release. 'I live in agony and dread its ending suddenly with my father; though his is, I believe the only instance that would not cause me horror; for when well, no man's life was ever more perfect than his.' She thought of little else. 'My head is so full, and my whole thoughts absorbed in this one subject, that it quite kills me.'[25]

The queen found it almost impossible either to rest or to come to terms with what was happening. 'My mother is in a constant state of anxiety,' wrote Elizabeth, 'very, very nervous and full of fidget in wishing to do her duty in every way.'[26] Charlotte attempted to do as she had always done and submit to the unpredictable, sometimes inexplicable dictates of Providence, 'which alone directs all for the best.'[27] She did all she could to overcome the revulsion at her husband's state that had haunted her since his first illness. In July 1812, she agreed to visit him in his secluded quarters. He had just recovered from 'a very alarming storm' of disturbed behaviour and she had no idea what to expect. 'I found him very quiet in appearance, thoughtful, but excepting asking for his shoes, no other word passed his lips.'[28] Even when he was calm, George was unreachable. The sight of him sent Charlotte into despair. 'I think my mother very much altered,' Elizabeth noted, 'at times very low and often complains in her bowels.'[29]

Depressed and fearful, the queen's sense of duty, which had seen her through so many difficult years, now faltered; she could not bring herself to behave with understanding to her disturbed and unfathomable husband. 'I went down to visit the king with the queen,' Princess Mary told the regent; 'it was shocking to hear the poor king run on so.' Charlotte's 'unfortunate manner' often made things far worse:[30] 'An unguarded word by the queen may bring on a thousand unpleasant things,' observed Mary. After one particularly agonising encounter, Elizabeth asked Halford to speak to Charlotte and, as a medical man, urge her to be 'more gracious and soothing to the king when he is reasonable.'[31] This had no effect; Mary believed her mother was simply incapable of showing the generous, affectionate behaviour which might help 'the king to make up his mind to his long confinement'. Part of the problem was 'her extreme timidity', but Mary also identified a more powerful character trait: the emotional detachment that had resulted in an inborn deficiency in her mother for 'warmth, tenderness, affection'. She thought that Charlotte would always honour her obligations, but she could not do so with any real loving kindness. In that respect, 'she always contrives to fail, not only by the king, but, if I may say so, by us all'. This was, as Mary knew, a harsh judgement, but one which had to be faced. If their mother was incapable of supplying the tenderness their stricken father needed, the princesses must provide it instead. And it might be better if they did so alone, releasing the king from encounters both he and the queen found painful.

Mary suggested that she and her sisters 'might go down two at a time, we might do both the king and queen good and save the queen much fatigue, and it would enable us to speak kindly of her to the king, and agreeably so of the king to the queen, repeating all that could do good, and give comfort to both'. By such means, Mary hoped the princesses might keep something of their parents' shattered partnership alive. 'I fear we can never make them a real comfort to each other again, as all confidence has long gone, but I am sure they have a great respect for each other; and the queen loves him as much as she can love anything in the world. I am clear that it is in the power of their daughters, if they are allowed to act, to keep them tolerably together, so far as to make no complete separation, which I own I dread now, if great care is not taken.'[32]

Mary's scheme was approved by the queen's council. Charlotte made no protest; her visits to the king grew increasingly rare, whilst her daughters shouldered the burden of keeping him calm and content. Their actions may have removed one cause of emotional tension; but in doing so, they inadvertently gave rise to another. Charlotte cannot have been unaware that the princesses had displayed a sense of duty and affection far more powerful than her own. They had risen to the challenge where she had stumbled. An unwelcome sense that she had been tried and found wanting nurtured in Charlotte a volatile mix of guilt and humiliation, a prickly sense of aggrieved virtue that did not put her in the best state of mind to deal with the events that were to follow.

In January 1812, the physicians were again asked to give evidence to a parliamentary committee on the king's condition. All were far less hopeful now than they had been at the beginning of the attack. Baillie thought a recovery 'highly improbable', Willis 'all but impossible'. As a result, the temporary regency, its probationary year now expired, was made permanent, and the prince, after a lifetime of expectation, was confirmed in the exercise of all his father's powers. At nearly fifty, he was king now in all but name. For the regent, the severity of his father's illness clarified his position, releasing him from years of uncertainty and impatience. For his sisters, there was no such resolution. Halford had commented in October 1811, that 'there was not the smallest chance of the king's recovering his reason,' but that he might live for a long time'. In such a situation, what were his daughters to do? Were their obligations to their sick father absolute? Did the future hold nothing for them but perpetual half-mourning, the rest of their lives spent in an ever-deepening seclusion? Or did his incapacity offer them at last, as it had done their eldest brother, a sad kind of emancipation? If the king did not know them, how could they be essential to his comfort? After so many years of denial, might they not discreetly seek out slightly richer, more varied lives for themselves?

In the shadow of the 'great calamity' of what would prove to be their father's final illness, the princesses sought to redefine the nature of their lives, to grasp a measure of independence that had hitherto been denied them. In this, they were bitterly opposed by their mother, acutely conscious of her own humiliation, and terrified by the implications of her daughters' determination to free themselves from her control. Where they might have been united in grief, mother and daughters instead found themselves at war.

*

It was an argument about money that precipitated the rift between the queen and the princesses. At the end of 1811, the regent turned his thoughts to practical matters. His precarious financial situation was, as ever, uppermost in his mind. He hoped to increase his allowance from the Civil List, and wrote to the first minister, Perceval, demanding that £150,000 be found to recompense him 'for regency services'. This was a quite staggering misreading of the political situation. After almost twenty years of global warfare, the economy was stagnant. Trade was paralysed by the difficulties of exporting goods abroad, to markets that were either inaccessible or impoverished. In Britain, desperate men formed 'combinations', early trade unions, to protect their skills from new technologies that threatened what few employment opportunities remained. In the manufacturing towns of the Midlands, machinery designed to speed up the process of spinning was destroyed by those whose jobs it displaced. Violence, real and imagined, was in the air. The first minister himself would fall victim to the discontent: in May 1812, Spencer Perceval was assassinated in the lobby of the House of Commons by John Bellingham, a merchant with an obsessive grievance against the government.

The response of the regent and the queen to the febrile atmosphere of the times could not have been more different. Like many of the worried wealthy, Charlotte suspected that the riots and other political disturbances were motivated by 'French principles and money', but, unlike her eldest son, she displayed, as she had in bitter 1790, some sympathy for the suffering of the poor. Like the king, she was a paternalist of a very traditional kind. Naturally thrifty, she prescribed economy and restraint as the best response to economic difficulties, but was horrified by the high price of bread, which she understood was the staple food of the hard-pressed population. She sought out pamphlets and other publications which suggested ways to alleviate their plight, especially those that offered practical solutions to the high price of foodstuffs. She told Lady Harcourt she was 'most desirous to obtain true information' about the use of rice flour, which she had heard might offer a cheap alternative to wheat, 'which would be an excellent introduction for many poor families'.[33] It is impossible to imagine her eldest son demonstrating a similar interest in the well-being of the very poor. His ill-timed request for more money showed no sensitivity to the straitened circumstances of a population severely tried by war and hunger, and did his already tarnished reputation a great deal of harm. His well-publicised extravagance, which was frequently and damagingly contrasted with the frugal lifestyle of his parents, ensured that his demands met with a hostile response. Perceval told the regent there was no chance at all that the money he wanted would be granted, and added that in the present difficulties he would not advise asking even for a much smaller sum.

Perceval soon made it clear that he had even tougher measures in mind. He believed the severe economic difficulties under which the country laboured meant that sacrifices were required in all aspects of public expenditure. The king's situation was very unfortunate, but his enforced withdrawal from many of his royal duties meant that reductions could be made in the cost of running his household. The family were horrified, maintaining that a king was a king, even when his mind was gone. Elizabeth argued that the external trappings of royalty were indispensable, securing its place in the public imagination, and contributing to the respect in which it was held. Perceval was unmoved. The size of the king's establishment must reflect his diminished role, and economies must and would be implemented.

There was only one request made by the regent which Perceval was prepared to entertain. If the king could no longer act as a king, he was equally unable to do his duty as a husband and father; this meant that Charlotte and the princesses were no longer provided for, 'deprived of the supplies afforded them hitherto by His Majesty'. The regent suggested an allowance for the queen of £50,000 per annum, with £9,000 each for his sisters. Perceval was sympathetic to these ideas, but the queen was not, and declared herself passionately opposed to the whole project. She wrote a long and angry letter to the minister, rejecting the very idea of retrenchment, decrying 'the principle of extreme economy which seems to pervade the proposed plan' and 'the inadequacy of the proposed provision'. She was horrified at the consequences she believed would result for royal employees, especially for 'the oldest servants, those who are encumbered with families ... thrown upon the world without bread for themselves or their families'.[34]

Charlotte's concern for her servants was doubtless genuinely felt; but her strongest objections to the changes were rooted in the plans made for herself and her daughters. She was particularly unhappy at the suggestion that her allowance would not be given to her personally, but would be included in the sums put aside for the king. She feared 'accusations of encroachment' if she was thought to take too much for herself from their joint fund, and was furious that the princesses were not subject to any such restrictions and would be granted their incomes individually. As she explained to Perceval in her grandest third-person voice, the distinction thus made between herself and her daughters could not be justified. 'She conceives that the adoption of the principle by which the princesses are set upon an independent footing, furnishes a strong ground for her own claim to a separate and distinct Establishment at the present period.'[35] The princesses' allowances and her own soon became an obsession with her; but, as quickly became clear to everyone, and especially to her daughters, the queen's resentment was only partly attributable to the way in which the payments were to be made. At the heart of her hostility was the principle of paying the princesses at all. With an income came the prospect of an establishment; and with an establishment came the promise of independence.

The term 'establishment' contained within itself a multitude of meanings. On one level, it related to tangible, practical things: access to an adequate income, occupation of an appropriate home. It also implied something about the social and, indeed, moral status of the possessor. To be 'established' was to have taken up a settled position in life, to have fulfilled one's personal destiny. It was a mark of maturity and brought with it a degree of respect and self-determination. For women, it was nearly always marriage that delivered them an establishment, in the traditional forms of a husband, a family and a household to run. It was occasionally possible for a single woman to enjoy some of the privileges usually granted by the more conventional route of married life. Wealthy widows, protected by an inheritance, were perhaps the most free of all propertied women, their position secured by both law and social position. Occasionally, a spinster might acquire for herself some of the trappings of independence, if cushioned by wealth and in possession of the kind of forceful personality that refused to bow to conventional niceties. A generation earlier, Princess Amelia, George II's formidable unmarried daughter, had carved out an agreeable life for herself, dominated by card playing and the taking of an occasional lover. But for most unmarried women, even those from aristocratic families, their fate was not unlike that of George and Charlotte's daughters: a life spent in the family home, ministering to ageing relations, with little status and no self-determination, rarely treated as an adult, whatever their age. An income and an establishment changed all that. It offered the prospect of emancipation from a life of extended infantilism, from the restrictions imposed by fathers, brothers, mothers. To be established was to be allowed to make choices: to choose who to see, where to go and what to do, to live as a mature and thinking person. It was, as the queen recognised, an implicit declaration of independence. Her daughters understood that, and for the first time in their lives refused to buckle under the weight of their mother's passionate displeasure. If they could not emancipate themselves through marriage, they would do so with the help of their eldest brother and an income of £9,000 a year.

In the face of their mother's anger, the sisters did all they could to stand firm. This was not always easy, especially when they felt they were adding to the burdens of their much-loved elder brother. They worried that the proposals would exacerbate his political difficulties. They knew that the queen had been relentless in her campaign to prevent him approving the plans for the allowances, haranguing the prince on every possible occasion, pursuing him even on his sickbed when he was taken seriously ill. His sisters hated to see him tormented in this way. 'For God's sake, don't let us be the cause of any mischief or distress,' Mary told her brother. 'We have so long submitted to a thousand disagreeables, and are so used to our situation, that we are all quite prepared, I assure you, not to be disappointed.' His peace of mind must come first. 'We shall be miserable if we hear that you have been vexing yourself, and making yourself ill.'[36] Sophia too was sufficiently concerned to write to the regent. In a letter she addressed as coming 'From the Nunnery', she shared her sister's anxiety not to cause him any further trouble: 'My heart overflows with gratitude for all your noble and generous intentions towards us which, should you succeed or not, our gratitude is much the same. The only thing that frets and worries me, is that your kindness to four old cats may cause you any *désagréments* with the ministers. I could forfeit anything sooner than we should be the cause of this.' As the bitterness of her language suggests, Sophia viewed the situation of herself and her sisters in a very poor light indeed. She was unsparing in both her despair and self-hatred: 'Poor old wretches as we are, a dead weight upon you, old lumber to the country, like old clothes, I wonder you do not vote for putting us in a sack and drowning us in the Thames. Two of us would be fine food for fishes, and as for Miny and me, we will take our chances together.'[37]

In the end, the measures implementing the princesses' new allowances passed through Parliament relatively smoothly. The queen, however, remained unreconciled, both to the fact of the new arrangements and to the principles underlying them. When Perceval sent letters for her daughters to sign, confirming their acceptance of the money, she was furious that no communication had been addressed to her about it. Augusta explained that all the proper procedures had been followed, but Charlotte would not be mollified. 'She looked very steadily at me,' Augusta told her brother, 'and said with a kind of suppressed anger, "That may be so, but still I think I ought to have been addressed straight to myself." These were her words.'[38]

The queen's temper was made worse by the implementation, in February 1812, of the economising measures which she had opposed so fruitlessly earlier in the year. As Charlotte had expected, it was a harrowing experience. Old servants were dismissed or left, and everyone was sadly aware that this was the end of an era. 'It was Miss Planta's last day,' wrote Elizabeth to Lady Harcourt, 'and she was the picture of misery and breaking her heart, which of course affected us much.' The sisters and their old governess had had their differences, but all was forgotten now 'and only the good was recalled. Then came a servant, he was a porter … to tell us he was going, there was another scene and so it goes on all day, grief and vexation of spirits, every hour something springs up to end our hearts, letters from other servants etc., etc., by the present melancholy change.'[39]

If her daughters found the process of dissolution heartbreaking, how much harder was it for their mother, who watched as so much of the life she had made for herself over half a century was dismantled before her eyes? The king's horses, no longer ridden, were sold, as was his prized flock of merino sheep. The queen's German band was dismissed. None of this made any impression on her husband, who, in his secluded part of the castle, sat silent, 'employed in arranging, tying and untying his handkerchiefs and nightcaps, and unbuttoning his waistcoat.'[40] But it was a painful reminder to Charlotte of her new and indeterminate status, no longer a real wife, yet denied the dignity of widowhood. What the future held for her was anything but certain as she watched her old existence crated, packed and carried away. It was perhaps not surprising that as a result, she clung so tenaciously to any security and support offered by her daughters, and could not see in the dawning of a new life for them anything other than a narrowing and darkening of her own.

The princesses were adamant they intended to make very few alterations to their daily routines. They certainly had no plans to abandon their parents; they had already arranged matters to ensure they would never all be absent from Windsor at the same time so that the king should never be left alone. There were, however, some changes they did want to make. They were determined to spend more time away from the gloom of Windsor and to enjoy a greater variety of company, especially that of their brothers, whose occasional invitations to dinners and parties illuminated their otherwise monotonous days.

This was exactly what the queen feared; and when the princesses were asked to stay with the regent at Oatlands, the Duke of York's house, she took it as a test case of her authority over them, and refused to let them go. Perhaps realising the larger implications of so apparently insignificant an event, Augusta and Elizabeth would not back down. Mary, always the queen's most vigorous opponent, described to the regent how she had instilled a little backbone into her siblings. 'I took this opportunity of giving my mind strongly to my two elder sisters, that this time must prove to them how decided we must be.' They carried the point, and made the visit, although at the cost of the queen declaring she should go too.

These petty demonstrations of their mother's displeasure were, as Mary put it, 'very provoking', and formed the constant backdrop to their days. The barrage of complaint and frustration to which they were subjected affected the sisters very deeply, eventually emboldening them, as nothing had done before, to abandon their lifelong policy of capitulation and containment and confront the queen directly. In April, Augusta wrote frankly to her mother, stating her intention, and that of her sisters, to venture out occasionally into society. She was confident this would have no impact on the duty they owed to the king, which they would continue to perform with the same good heart. Elizabeth echoed her sentiments in a letter she wrote to the queen at the same time. 'The melancholy situation in which we are placed, Augusta has explained with so much delicacy and feeling that … I trust you will see she was right in doing.' She added that the obligations the sisters owed to their mother were no less important to them than those due to the king. 'I must assure you that all perfectly agree that you ought to be considered in everything, and never left alone.'[41]

Far from reassuring her, these notes drove the queen to even greater levels of outrage. She wrote her daughters a letter that Augusta felt she could not show the regent because it was written in such fury. It was certainly an exclamation of pent-up rage; but it was also a fervent repudiation of the new freedoms her daughters claimed for themselves, an uncompromising statement of the retired life Charlotte considered appropriate for them in light of their father's condition. 'As this may be the last time any of you may be inclined to take a mother's advice, let me beseech you to consider that your situation is very different to that of your brothers.' The princes had public duties to perform that necessarily took them into the world, 'but in your sex, and under the present melancholy situation of your father, the going to public amusements, except where duty calls you, would be the highest mark of indecency possible'. She had nothing further to add and would not meet the princesses as usual at breakfast. 'I do not think I ever felt as shattered in my life as I did by reading your letter … The stroke is given and nothing can mend it.'[42]

This was too much for even the long-suffering sisterhood to bear. 'I certainly expected a storm when we made known our decided wishes and ideas as to our future plans,' wrote Mary to the regent, but even she had not expected the queen to react with such anger. 'Great allowances must be made for a woman who has had her own way for many years, and who we all have reason to know has not a good temper.'[43] Mary was clear things could not remain as they were, and there was only one member of the family with any influence over the queen. The regent would have to speak to her. 'We must freely own,' the princesses declared to him, 'that we have neither health nor spirits to support for any time the life which we have led for the last two years.' In the face of a full-scale revolt by the sisters, the prince exerted himself, hurried down to Windsor, charmed and cajoled his mother as only he could, and bought the princesses a moment of respite. In May, they went to London without the queen, although they thought it wise not to provoke her by accepting the regent's invitation to Carlton House, 'not because we saw the smallest impropriety in it (which is the queen's reason)', explained Mary, but because 'the great object is to break the ice'. Their sacrifice made little difference. They still lived 'upon very cross words and sour looks'.[44]

For much of the rest of the year, the queen and her daughters rubbed along in a state of subdued unhappiness; but their brother had not forgotten their plight. In the autumn of 1812, the regent came up with a plan. The princesses should be asked to accompany his sixteen-year-old daughter Charlotte on some of her first forays into London society. In doing so, they could take the place of her mother, the Princess of Wales, whose behaviour the regent considered made her an impossible companion for a young girl, and who was allowed to see her daughter only under strict supervision. The Duke of York was duly sent to Windsor to break the news to the queen. 'Her Majesty seemed to view in a right light the necessity of Charlotte enjoying more liberty and passing a part of her time in London,' he reported to the regent, 'but there was a very visible alteration in her manner when I stated to her the wish that our sisters should accompany her. She said however but little.' The duke thought all would be well if the regent himself raised the subject. 'I have no doubt if you speak to her with gentleness and firmness, and can make her sensible of our sisters' situation, she will easily be got the better of. All our sisters … are determined to be stout and trust that you will support them.'[45]

Shortly afterwards, the regent wrote formally to the princesses, requesting that they take Charlotte to the House of Lords, where she could see for the first time the state opening of Parliament. Augusta and Elizabeth agreed immediately to attend; a few days later, Mary decided to join them. When the queen discovered their plans on the night before they left Windsor, a furious row erupted. For Charlotte, this scheme amounted to more than just a lapse in taste and decency; it implied the princesses believed there was no point in remaining at home, since there was no prospect of any improvement in their father's health. It was, she argued, 'a full declaration that the king can never recover, and which you know not even any of the physicians have ventured to declare'.

The accusation of indifference to their father's plight was too much for Elizabeth. She was infuriated by her mother's words, and 'in defending her own conduct, struck upon a book, saying she had done all in her power to please'. Elizabeth, usually the most cheerfully devoted of the sisters, was so enraged that the queen said she would not have been surprised to have received 'a box on the ears' from her. Elizabeth admitted she had been so affected by her mother's criticism that she thought she was about to have a seizure. 'I own the blow of being thought unfeeling and wanting in my duty to the king really haunts me.'[46] Augusta thought Elizabeth was right to be so angry. 'Never was there a daughter more faithfully attached than Eliza to the queen,' she wrote, adding that their mother 'won't allow that any of us feel for the king's unhappy state of mind'.[47]

This latest breach with their mother marked a major shift in the princesses' attitudes. Afterwards, none of them felt able to summon up so uncomplainingly the posture of disciplined submission that had marked their behaviour until then. Elizabeth now pondered whether she should leave the castle and live permanently in her cottage. For Mary, the episode served to confirm her bleak assessment of Charlotte's character. 'It was the object of the dear king's life to keep from the world all he suffered and went through with her temper. He brought his daughters up with a most anxious wish we should assist him in that most unfortunate point, and her conduct in all this business has been such that by her own imprudence (excuse me the expression) she has destroyed the poor king's honest labours of the last fifty years past.'[48] Even Augusta, who could still declare that 'I love the queen with all my heart', felt her affection severely qualified by the experience. 'I feel the injustice most deeply with which she treats us all four. It is undeserved. And our lives have not been too happy, but we have never complained, nor should we if we were but quiet and comfortable with the queen.'[49] She too had begun to think the previously unthinkable, and consider whether it might not be better for her to find a home of her own.

Faced with the unappetising prospect of a permanent rupture between his mother and his sisters, the regent sent a letter to the queen with which he intended to put an end to the whole affair. He wrote in tones of icy courtesy, quite unlike the effusive and elaborate style in which he usually addressed his mother, suggesting that he expected his words to be taken seriously. He had been 'deeply afflicted at hearing from my sisters the strong objections which you have made to their coming to town for the purpose of going to the House of Lords'. He reminded her that the idea had been his own, 'and not taken up by me without the most thorough consideration'. He did not want to hear of any more opposition to it. 'I rely with confidence that you will not throw any further obstacles in the way of a plan which I feel so essential to the comfort and happiness of our family.' He concluded by stressing the importance 'of showing to the world that the greater number of our family are united in sentiment and affection'.[50]

At first Charlotte bridled, and sent the regent a long letter of self-justification and complaint; but he was having none of it. 'I am particularly grieved at the feelings of dissatisfaction which you have manifested towards my sisters,' George replied, 'whose general conduct has been so truly proper and affectionate.'[51] Having sufficiently applied the stick, he now brandished a carrot in the shape of an invitation to dine at Carlton House. Once she arrived, he did all he could to persuade her that she would survive the occasional absences of his sisters from home. His charm offensive worked. At last, the queen began to thaw and her mood lifted.

Although it was not the end of the sisters' difficulties – much of their time was still spent in the cloistered dullness of Windsor, reading, sewing and waiting for something to happen – there was no return to the life of almost total seclusion that had been their lot for the two years after the onset of their father's final illness. The great battles of 1812 won them some degree of independence. They bought new carriages, decorated their apartments, visited their brothers' houses, and went more often to London, to dinners and even the occasional ball. Their new freedom did not please everyone – the young Princess Charlotte was horrified to discover that she was 'to be seen out with a parcel of old maids' – but for the sisters, their victory made all the difference between a quiet life and an unbearable one.[52] They were too dutiful not to be aware that their partial release had been made possible by unhappy circumstances. 'My heart is full, not elated by what has happened,' confessed Elizabeth, 'for when I think what has caused it, this is so affecting to my feelings that I cry when I think of it, and when do I not think of it?'[53] But they had emerged from the ordeal with as much liberty as they had perhaps ever enjoyed in their lives. As single women past their first youth, and in their 'very particular situations', that was, as they acknowledged, something to be thankful for.

*

For one of the sisters, however, the prospect of better relations with her mother and the occasional trip to London fell far short of what she had hoped 1812 would bring. Not long after her brother's regency had been made permanent, Princess Augusta wrote to him describing a predicament 'from which you alone can relieve me'. She hoped that, in his new role, he would grant her what she knew her father would never have allowed – permission to marry the man she loved. 'If it is in your power to make us happy, I know you will. I am sensible that, should you agree to our union, it can only proceed from your affection for me, and your desire of promoting my happiness and that of a worthy man.'[54]

Augusta had grown into a guarded, inward-looking woman in whom it was difficult to discern any traces of the lively wit she had been known for when she was younger. At twenty-five, she had playfully assured the Prince of Wales, 'I intend for the rest of my life to be very despotic till I have a lord and master and then … I shall give myself up to his whims.'[55] In 1812, Augusta was forty-four, and had lost her taste for whimsy. She knew now that, for princesses, love was a serious business, fraught with problems, and marriage anything but the inevitable state she had once assumed it to be. Perhaps as a result, she conducted her life's one love affair with the same mute discretion that had become the watchword of her character. 'Our sentiments,' she told her brother, 'were of too delicate a nature to make them known, unless at a moment when we might hope to have our sufferings relieved.' Over time she had learnt to keep to herself feelings which could not be gratified. 'This was my own secret,' she declared. She denied that in hiding her love she 'had not acted with candour' towards her family; like her mother, she believed that 'there is no duplicity in silence'.[56]

Augusta and her lover had sustained their carefully concealed devotion for many years. The regent was, as she reminded him, one of the very few people who knew about it as she had first broached the subject with him in 1808. She would not have broken her vow of silence if her lover had not been away, fighting abroad on active service. 'My heart was full of care and I knew you would feel for me, and the idea cheered me!'[57] Nowhere in her letter does Augusta name the man himself, but it is now known that the man she loved was Sir Brent Spencer, a career soldier, and – like many of the men with whom the princesses fell in love – an equerry to the king.

Born in Ireland, Spencer had entered the army as a young man. He had fought alongside the Duke of York in 1799, attached to the duke's forces as part of the disastrous Anglo-Russian invasion of Holland, in which the army commanded by the duke suffered a humiliating defeat at the hands of the Dutch and French at the Battle of Bergen. The duke, who enjoyed his company, mentioned him in dispatches and Spencer went with him when he returned to England. It may have been as a friend of her brother's that Augusta first met Spencer in 1800. He spent much of the next decade fighting across the world in some of the major battles of the Napoleonic Wars, serving in the West Indies, Egypt, Denmark and Portugal. He was an active, energetic commander, engaged in numerous hard-fought actions. Although regarded as perhaps not the brightest of men, his bravery was never questioned, and he was seen at his very best in action on the battlefield. An old colleague remembered him as 'a zealous, gallant officer, without any great military genius; anxious and fidgety when there was nothing to do, but once under fire, like a philosopher solving a problem.'[58] The Duke of Wellington, with whom he fought in the Peninsular War, admired his courage and recommended him for some mark of royal favour: 'There never was a braver officer, or one who deserved it better.'[59] Spencer had none of the Iron Duke's laconic wit, and his somewhat literal, ponderous character seems to have been a source of amusement to his more sophisticated colleagues; but none of this was likely to have qualified Augusta's admiration for him. A life spent at court had made her wary of over-polished articulacy. Her own mind was sharp, but in others she prized the simpler virtues of honesty, loyalty and bravery, all of which Spencer possessed to a degree that made him for her the model of what a man should be.

Augusta told the regent that her relationship with Spencer had been 'mutually acknowledged' some time in 1803. Spencer was then stationed in England, spending much of his time at court, where the couple could occasionally contrive meetings together. In 1807 he was posted to Denmark, in command of a brigade given the task of preventing the Danish fleet from falling under French control. Augusta, anxious for his safety, was delighted to hear that the operation had been a success. 'Judge what my happiness must have been when we were stopped going up Henley Hill with the intelligence that Copenhagen had really surrendered.' But, as she confessed to Lady Harcourt, who knew all about the affair, 'my heart was very ill at ease until I came home and found that all my friends were safe.'[60] Spencer was then sent almost immediately to Spain. It is not known whether he and Augusta corresponded during his absence, but the princess devotedly followed his progress in the Peninsular War. The Duke of York, who seems to have been aware of the couple's affection for each other, was a reliable source of military information, supplying accounts of Spencer's exploits to his eager sister. 'We have good reports from Spain,' she told Lady Harcourt in September, happily recounting accounts of General Spencer's bravery. He was, she assured her, 'one of my elite friends in the bunch with you.'[61]

Augusta knew that the king, whilst he certainly admired Spencer as a soldier, would never have considered him suitable as a son-in-law. Conscious that their mutual attraction could not culminate in marriage, for years the couple had attempted to suppress their feelings for each other. Augusta told the regent that Spencer had offered to 'give up his situation around the king, or at least to plead his being on the Staff, that he might not come too often where we must meet in circumstances he was aware were most painful to both of us'. Augusta had thought this too extreme; she did not want him to damage his career, and felt that total withdrawal would undermine his 'private worth'. Instead, she suggested he should come to court 'as seldom as he could do consistent with that gratitude which he must feel for the king's marked favour towards him ... and he had never deviated from this plan of conduct'. It had been a very severe sacrifice for her not to be in the company of the man she loved; but, as she explained, 'it was my duty to exert every effort not to express my feelings, both for his own sake and my own.'[62]

Thus the thwarted couple had gone on, separated sometimes by war and distance, sometimes by propriety, but never apparently varying in their silent, secret devotion. Finally, in the events of 1812, over a decade since their first meeting, Augusta thought she saw an opportunity to transform their circumstances. With her brother regent, she hoped he would agree to an arrangement her father would never have countenanced. That was the purpose of her long, confessional letter. 'To you we look up, for our comfort and peace of mind. Your sanction is what we aspire to.' As she was well over twenty-five, in principle, under the terms of the Royal Marriages Act, Augusta could have applied to Parliament to approve her union with Spencer, but like Amelia before her, she seems to have been incapable of defying the known wishes of her father. Instead, she begged the regent, acting in the king's place, to give his permission for what Augusta called 'quite a private marriage'. She wished this to be done with the greatest discretion, and may have hoped that the partnership could be properly acknowledged after the king's death. If the regent was prepared to gratify the couple's desire, she implored him to inform the queen. Augusta did not seek her mother's consent, as she knew it was 'not necessary'; but she did want her blessing. She hoped against hope that it would be given. If Charlotte could be persuaded to look beyond considerations of rank, 'when she considers the character of the man, the faithfulness and length of our attachment, and the struggles I have been compelled to make, never retracting from any of my duties, though suffering martyrdom from anxiety of mind, and deprivation of happiness, I am sure she will say, long and great has been my trial, and correct has been my conduct'.[63]

Augusta's affair had none of the emotional flamboyance of her sister Amelia's relationship with Charles Fitzroy. Where Amelia had been angrily defiant, Augusta was silently resigned; where Amelia railed against her fate, Augusta did all she could to conceal her frustration. But the single letter in which she sought to explain and justify her love for Spencer is one of the most touching documents in all the sisters' correspondence. 'I confess I am proud of possessing the affection and good opinion of an honest man, and highly distinguished character,' she told her brother simply, 'and I am sure that what you can do to make us happy, you will not leave undone.'[64]

It is not known whether the regent agreed to grant Augusta her 'heart's wish'. There is no further reference in her correspondence or in that of any of her siblings to the proposed marriage. Gossip circulating in the German courts a few years later maintained that one of the princesses had been recently married, but no evidence survives to confirm or disprove the rumour. After his retirement from the army, Spencer bought an estate at Great Missenden, not far away from Windsor, and became a regular visitor there, in contrast to his tactful absences of earlier times. He was made a Knight of the Bath by the regent in July 1812 – quite a distinction for the son of a country gentleman – and was present at his coronation as George IV. He was certainly regarded with sufficient favour to have accompanied Augusta, Elizabeth and the queen to Bath in 1817, where they had gone to take the waters for Charlotte's health. It was said that when he died in 1828, he was wearing round his neck a locket with Augusta's picture in it. But whilst these details suggest a continuance of the devotion he and Augusta had shared for so many years, and perhaps even an informal acknowledgement of it by her family, they do not necessarily imply that a marriage had taken place. If it had, it would have been a partnership of a very unusual kind, for Augusta did not move out of Windsor Castle until after her father's death in 1820. Whilst she was able to enjoy more of Spencer's company in the years after 1812, it seems unlikely that Augusta achieved the principal objective of the dignified and moving letter she wrote to her brother in that year – that of becoming Sir Brent's wife.

Whilst Augusta brooded over the difficulties of her love for Spencer, in another Windsor apartment, her sister Sophia was, if possible, even more unhappy. The illness of her father, to whom she was devoted, had pushed her fragile spirits into the deepest of depressions. Her niece, Princess Charlotte, who knew herself what it felt like to be alone and unloved, was horrified by Sophia's misery. 'It is melancholy and very distressing to see how she suffers, and the very visible decline of her health.' The life she led at Windsor was, Charlotte thought, a major cause of Sophia's distress. She did not sleep, and was subject to more or less continuous physically disabling 'spasms'. Her relations with her sisters, in whose company she was obliged to spend her time, were not easy. 'She is not a favourite with the elder ones,' noted

Charlotte. 'There is nothing they have not said against her.'[65] Sophia herself admitted that she was not, 'at any time, inclined to be very intimate with females, as they are not always true to each other, and this house abounding with them, all I can do is to steer clear of any intimacy'.[66]

By 1813, her niece thought Sophia so reduced and unhappy that she wondered if she would survive. 'I have gradually prepared my mind for her not being long lived, both from her tender and dwindling state, besides which, her sensitive mind and exquisite feeling must have had too many death blows to her spirits or her health ever to recover.'[67] Twelve months later she seemed even weaker, and Charlotte was horrified to be told by Dr Baillie that he saw frightening similarities between Sophia's complaint and the illness which had killed Amelia just four years before. She retreated into a narrow world of her own making, bounded by the privacy of her rooms, from which she rarely ventured. 'Real misfortune, I am afraid, has given me a degree of suspicion and dread of people in general,' she confessed, 'which I am ready to admit I may carry too far.'[68] Between 1812 and 1814, she lived a life of total seclusion at Windsor so severe that it mirrored that of her father.

There were, however, some advantages to Sophia's retired life. Chief among them was that it excused her from spending time in the unwelcome company of her mother. Although the queen sometimes expressed pity for her daughter's pathetic condition, her attitude to Sophia's mysterious illness was generally one of impatience. 'My odious low spirits is always a bone of contention,' Sophia observed ruefully, 'though God knows I cannot help it.'[69] Her mother's attitude was noticed by others in the family, who were saddened by it but not surprised. 'I perfectly understand all you say about the difficulty of making a certain quarter understand the real state of things,' wrote the Duke of Kent to Henry Halford, who was treating Sophia, 'but where there is a natural want of warmth, it is difficult in the extreme to make a proper impression.'[70]

Isolating herself at Windsor also removed Sophia from scenes even more distressing than the familiar manifestations of her mother's disapproval. In the world beyond her rooms, the presence of her son, born in 1800 as a result of the affair with General Garth, was becoming harder and harder to ignore. Young Tom's father had always done all he could to make the boy visible to both the royal family and the curious, fashionable world. When Sophia's niece, Charlotte, visited Weymouth in the summer of 1814 – where the Garths were also staying – she noted that the general's son crossed her path 'fifty times a day'. She saw Tom Garth all the time, riding up and down the sands, passing her carriage, patting the horses in the old general's stable while the servants and officers 'look at him and then talk to themselves'. Increasingly embarrassed by the father's insouciance and the boy's proximity, Charlotte began to wonder if there was not some plan behind Garth's behaviour. Brooding over what it all meant, she concluded that General Garth's shameless promotion of their son was driven by spite and recrimination – his chief purpose to make Sophia unhappy. 'That not being able to torment her now any longer with the sight, he will continue it upon the relative she loves best in the world – which is me – a sort of diabolical revenge that one cannot understand.'[71]

It seems unlikely that Garth's intentions were as complex as Charlotte imagined. He may have hoped the princess would find young Tom as winning and attractive as he did; he was certainly never ashamed of showing the world how much he cherished him. By placing the boy so insistently and conspicuously in the company of one of his royal relations, he may also have hoped for an informal, tacit acknowledgement of his true identity. But whatever his motives, Charlotte was right in thinking that, for Sophia, even the knowledge of such encounters would be unbearably painful. Hidden away in Windsor, Sophia increasingly concentrated her feelings on the few people who penetrated the solitude of her apartment: her brothers, her sister Mary, her niece Charlotte – and her doctor, Henry Halford.

Over the years, Sir Henry had become of far greater importance to the royal family than his title of physician-extraordinary to the king would suggest. During Amelia's long illness, he had often been asked to manage difficult conversations and broker delicate arrangements, involving himself in matters that went far beyond the usual duties of a medical practitioner. He became a kind of informal family fixer, called upon whenever sensitive subjects required careful handling. When added to the authority he displayed as a trusted doctor, these qualities made him extremely attractive to a woman like Sophia, who was always drawn to older, masterful men. His famously emollient manner – charming, sympathetic and endlessly patient – could not have formed a greater contrast with that of Sophia's unsatisfactory mother; and, of course, he was one of the very few men entitled to visit her on a regular basis. In the depths of her unhappiest years, Halford became for Sophia something much more than just her doctor. He was her adviser, her confidant, an endless source of consolation and support – and also a man on whom she could lavish a great deal of otherwise undirected affection. In her own eyes at least, Halford was the closest thing Sophia possessed to a lover.

By 1811, their relationship had already gone far beyond that of doctor and patient. In that year she wrote Halford a letter in which all her strongest feelings for him were laid bare. Significantly, she began it just before her mother was due to arrive in her rooms for one of her regular visits. 'Now it is just past five. I am trying to recover myself before a Great Personage makes her appearance, and to find comfort, I shall write to you, my dear good soul.' Sophia spent the rest of the evening working on her letter, pouring out her heart in her crabbed, tiny handwriting. When finished it ran to over 1,500 words, a stream of consciousness that captured her thoughts in no order other than the moment at which they occurred to her. It began with the banal – 'I had my dinner at three. Tried to eat the chicken but it went down very so' – but soon moved on to her governing preoccupation: the condition of her inner emotional life. Its fragmented observations illuminate some of the strongest traits of her character, from her tendency to self-pity ('no one ever makes allowances for my feelings') to her deep sense of isolation ('I told you how friendless I am … and now I solemnly declare that except for my dear brother, you are the only creature to whom I could open my heart'). She assured Halford it was he who had rescued her from the despair into which she had sunk. 'How much the difference since I have known you, all my dormant feelings have been roused and I have gained your affection and kindness.' There is also a hint of the physical desire she felt for this authoritative, attentive man. 'Your feelings do so consist with my own, and your attentions are so kind and gentle that they half kill me.' If Sophia sometimes enjoyed seeing herself as a victim, it was often as one overwhelmed by passion. 'Remember,' she told him, 'I can love and not by halves, so pity and forgive me.'

It is hard to know to what extent Sophia's feelings were reciprocated. She maintained that her affection had grown in response to Halford's fondness. 'You gain upon me every hour,' she told him, 'and how can it be otherwise, for such kindness I never before experienced.

It is so different to everything I have been accustomed to.' But as with every one of her relationships, she knew nothing could come of it. Halford had a wife and children living in London, and he was far too politic to risk serious entanglement with a vulnerable princess whose reputation was already tainted by sexual misadventure. And yet Sophia's heart refused to submit to rational objections. 'I have thought of you a great, great deal. I think till I make myself miserable, and then I know you will scold me. No, I hope not, for I am sure you cannot blame my trying to struggle against impossibilities.' Perhaps, for all his worldliness, Halford shared some of Sophia's conviction that they were 'necessary to each other's happiness'. He kept her letter till the day he died, when it was found carefully preserved among his papers.[72]

*

As the sisters passed into middle age, still only partially resigned to their uninspiring futures, it cannot have been easy for them to contemplate the arrival into the public world of the sole legitimate representative of the family's next generation. Princess Charlotte, the daughter of the warring Prince and Princess of Wales, had just turned fifteen when her father became regent, and it was not long before the question of her future marital prospects very speedily eclipsed those of her aunts. Her youthful eligibility was a visible enough reminder of their humiliating unmarried state; and Charlotte rarely passed up an opportunity to refer to it herself. The sisters were 'the old girls', 'a parcel of old maids', 'a brace of very ugly daughters'. Charlotte's slightingly dismissive references to her aunts' enforced spinsterhood perhaps reflected her confidence that she was unlikely to follow in their footsteps.

Her expectations were, as she was already aware, very different. As heir presumptive to the throne, the question was not whether she would marry, but only when and to whom. As she was to discover, however, it was more of a struggle than she imagined for a princess to take control of her destiny. Despite her great expectations, she too was to face many of the same struggles for freedom and self-determination that had blighted the lives of her aunts. But Charlotte fought her battles with a very different spirit. As she pitted her will against her father in a way they never would have attempted with theirs, the princesses watched from the sidelines with a mixture of horror, sympathy and perhaps envy; Charlotte was capable of asserting her wishes in a way that, with the possible exception of Amelia, they had never done in the past and could not imagine doing in the future.

Charlotte had been a lively, intelligent child who escaped having the wilfulness educated out of her by the peculiar situation of the Prince and Princess of Wales. Her eldest aunt, the Princess Royal, ascribed much of her later behaviour to 'the many disadvantages of her education, and from not being constantly under the eye of a parent'. This fateful conjunction meant that 'she has from infancy, been a little too accustomed to act for herself'.[73] After her parents separated, Charlotte lived at first in apartments in Carlton House, under the supervision of her governess, Lady Elgin; but the findings of a 'Delicate Investigation' of 1806 changed everything.

The inquiry 'into the Conduct of Her Majesty Highness the Princess of Wales' was carried out at the behest of the Prince of Wales into allegations that his wife was guilty of adultery with a number of men; it also enquired into rumours that William Austin, a young boy whom the princess raised at her house at Blackheath, was in fact her illegitimate son. The ministers who conducted the procedure eventually concluded that William Austin was not the princess's child, but that her behaviour was in all other respects far from satisfactory. One of her footmen told the investigators succinctly that 'the princess was very fond of fucking'.[74] Among the men named as her possible lovers were the politician George Canning, the artist Thomas Lawrence (who painted the most flattering of all Caroline's portraits, showing her resplendent in a red velvet dress) and the naval hero Sir Sydney Smith.

None of this proved enough to secure for the Prince of Wales the divorce he longed for, but it did empower him to limit the princess's access to their young daughter to once a week. As her father rarely visited, Charlotte's closest relationships were with her governess Lady Elgin and her dresser, Mrs Gagarin, for whom her affection was said to be 'like that of a child for its mother'.[75] The Princess Royal wrote regularly to Lady Elgin from Germany, offering lengthy, well-intentioned advice on Charlotte's upbringing. Inevitably, her moral development was at the forefront of Royal's concern. She was convinced the chief objective of her education must be the eradication of any tendencies to vanity, 'which is a little in her blood, as you know full well'.[76] She suggested as a corrective 'a selection of interesting stories in which humility and goodness of heart' prevailed.[77] Perhaps to add a little pleasure to this rather starchy diet, she also recommended Mme de Beaumont's *Magasin des enfants*, which she recalled having read under her mother's direction when she was small.

In the schoolroom, Charlotte displayed a quick and energetic mind. Although she never really acquired the habit of concentrated study, she learnt to read early and, like her father, displayed a natural aptitude for both music and languages (although to the disappointment of her grandmother, she never really mastered German). In common with most of her female relations, she was a voracious reader of novels. She shared her father's and aunt Sophia's gift for mimicry, but like so many of the Brunswick family, suffered from a painful stammer which grew worse when she was nervous or excited. Her spelling was very poor, littered with errors 'a common servant would have blushed to commit'. She was very well informed about British history – at least as seen through the prism of the Whig Party, the Prince of Wales having taken pains to 'instil into the mind and heart of my daughter the knowledge and love of the true principles of the British Constitution', using as a 'model for study, the political conduct of my most revered and lamented friend, Mr Fox'.[78] Her mathematics, like her spelling, was undistinguished.

The patchy nature of Charlotte's education reflected the lack of steady supervision in her early life. As a child, she rarely encountered a will of equal determination to her own. Lady Charlotte Campbell, one of the Princess of Wales's long-suffering ladies, acknowledged that Charlotte 'has quickness, both of fancy and penetration' and that she was 'kind-hearted, clever and enthusiastic'; but, she added, 'I fear that she is capricious, self-willed and obstinate. Her faults have evidently never been checked, nor her virtues fostered.'[79] George Keppel, the 6th Earl of Albemarle, knew her very well when they were growing up. His grandmother, Lady de Clifford, was appointed as Charlotte's second governess, and on Saturdays Charlotte was allowed to visit the Keppel mansion in Earls Court, where she seemed to Keppel 'like a bird released from a cage'. Her spirits were always boisterously high. As soon as she arrived she would dash to the kitchens; once she persuaded the cook to let her prepare a mutton chop for the duchess's lunch. It was not a success, 'so ill-dressed and so peppered as to be uneatable'.[80] In the gardens, she would entice Keppel's younger sisters to the top of a grassy mound 'in order to roll them down into a bed of nettles below'. If they were brave enough not to cry, she would reward each of them with a doll.[81] Charlotte was generous to Keppel – she gave him his first pony, and sent him back to school at Westminster each term with extra pocket money, which made him her devoted admirer for years. But for all his appreciation of her kindness, he thought his friend was often too uncontrolled and 'free in her deportment'. She was also sometimes 'excessively violent in her disposition', once beating him with her riding whip. She was a fearless rider, happier in the stables than in a drawing room, enjoying the company of her grooms. She liked male company, and had acquired some masculine habits. 'One of her fancies', Keppel recalled, 'was to ape the manners of a man. On these occasions, she would double her fist and assume a defence that would have done credit to a professional pugilist.'[82] Hers was not a delicate or conventionally feminine character. She was said to walk with a determined and forceful stride, and she spoke more loudly and directly than was considered polite for an aristocratic young woman.

Charlotte was too much of a Hanoverian to be considered classically beautiful. Like her father and grandfather, she struggled with her weight. At fifteen, Lady Charlotte Campbell thought her 'extremely full for her age' and worried that her 'voluptuous' looks would be lost to 'fat and clumsiness' unless she took a great deal of exercise.[83] In her bluntness, as well as in her size, she somewhat resembled her aunt Elizabeth – although no girl brought up under the queen's unforgiving eye would have been allowed to behave as Charlotte did. Lady Glenbervie, meeting her one night, found her 'forward, dogmatical on all subjects, buckish about horses and full of exclamations very like swearing. She was sitting with her legs stretched out after dinner, and showing her drawers, which it seems she and most young women wear.'[84]

Across the North Sea, the Princess Royal fretted about her niece, wondering anxiously how this clever, perceptive child would react when old enough to understand how much her parents hated each other. Royal was right to be concerned. Charlotte was soon only too aware of the hostility which blazed so rancorously between the prince and princess. Much of the 'nervousness' which observers commented upon as one of the defining attributes of her character arose from conflicted loyalties towards her mother and father that troubled her for the rest of her life. As each placed the worst possible interpretation on the actions of the other, it was not surprising that their daughter responded to any perceived slight in the same painfully hysterical way. When she was only nine years old, the Princess of Wales passed by her daughter in her carriage without acknowledging her. Charlotte rushed home and wrote a furious letter in which she declared her mother was 'a monster', and 'struck her pen a great many times against the paper, saying, "This I do to show how many devils there were that took hold of her!"'[85] When she was older, she tried to extend to her mother a sympathy that neither of her parents, absorbed in their mutual hatred, ever troubled to offer their daughter. On the whole, she thought the princess was more sinned against than sinning, although she conceded she was no saint. 'My mother was wicked,' Charlotte famously concluded, 'but she would not have turned out so wicked if my father had not been much more wicked still.'[86] 'The truth is,' she later reflected, 'I believe her to be both a very unhappy and a very unfortunate woman, who has great errors, great faults, but really is oppressed and cruelly used.'[87]

However, as she grew older, Caroline's increasingly irrational and outrageous behaviour made it harder and harder for her daughter to hold on to the respect she longed to feel for her. Caroline's house was full of raffish men, the nature of whose relationship with her was the subject of scandalous public speculation. Her attitude to her husband was one of extravagant, even baroque, disdain. One of her ladies described how, after dinner, it was the princess's custom to make a wax figure of the prince 'and give it the amiable addition of three horns; then take three pins out of her garment, and stick them through, and then put the figure to roast in the fire.'[88] (The horns were the traditional emblem of the cuckold.) Her father hardly set a better example of parental responsibility. Perhaps unsurprisingly, he refused to allow Charlotte to live with her mother, and, once she was out of the schoolroom, established her in Warwick House, a rather gloomy building adjacent to his own London base at Carlton House. But close proximity did not mean he saw very much of her. He did not invite Charlotte to any of the social events he held there, and when he was away barely found time to write to her. When he did pick up his pen, his daughter knew him well enough to distrust what she accurately described as his 'sugary' style. It was, she said, 'all but *des phrases* without any meaning'. On his rare visits, he spent most of the time regaling her with denunciations of her mother's behaviour. His unpredictable moods disturbed her. Sometimes his mere presence was enough to bring on the stutter that plagued her. 'His visits strike a damp and create fears long after they are over,' she confessed, 'and I fancy evils that do not exist.'[89] Even the queen, who noticed how Charlotte 'seems very strongly to feel any apparent neglect', was aware how badly the Prince of Wales managed his daughter, and begged him to reconsider the way he treated her. He should call upon her more frequently, and take the trouble to display more of his famous charm when he did so. 'From the bottom of my heart, do I wish that she should connect with her filial duty a sincere friendship for you, which may be gained by seeing a little more of her, and by making her look upon you as the source of every amusement and pleasure granted to her,' she told him.[90]

The prince ignored his mother's good advice. He still declined to invite Charlotte to dinners and balls at Carlton House – she had to have them described to her by others – and snubbed her in public when he thought she had shown too much favour to her mother, refusing to speak to her or turning his back upon her. It was difficult for him to see in his daughter anything but ammunition to fuel the war he waged against his wife. He once complained to the author Cornelia Knight, who for a time was the queen's literary adviser, of 'the little regard the Princess of Wales had shown for the Princess Charlotte when she was a child, and how by her negligence, there was a mark of the smallpox on her nose, having left her hands at liberty; whereas he used to watch continually by her cradle'.[91] Not surprisingly, Charlotte came to distrust all manifestations of her parents' erratic and self-interested demonstrations of feeling towards her, telling Miss Knight that their 'unfortunate quarrels with each other rendered their testimonies of affection to her at all times precarious'.[92]

Against such a background, it had proved impossible to instil in Charlotte the powerful combination of awe and respect for her parents that had acted so significantly upon the minds of her aunts. The first major clash with her family took place in 1812, and was triggered by the political manoeuvrings of her father. When the restrictions on the prince's regency were lifted, it was assumed that he would dismiss the Tory ministers appointed by his father before his final illness and call into office the Whigs who had been his friends and supporters all his life. To everyone's surprise – including the ministers themselves, who had fully expected to be turned out – he decided instead to retain the existing administration. It was said that he had been persuaded to do so by Halford, who told him the knowledge of a change of government would probably kill the king, if he were ever to recover. The regent's decision caused outrage amongst his erstwhile supporters, who considered he had betrayed a lifetime's political principles. Few disapproved of his actions more than his daughter. 'Is it not too clear,' she wrote indignantly, 'that he has given up friends, party, promises, professions and everything? … All these things must make good Whigs tremble – but not give up, as the motto must be perseverance.'[93] Charlotte was indeed as good a Whig as the regent had been himself in his youth. 'God knows,' she wrote, 'I hope we shall never sink into a tyrannical government such as in the time of Henry 8th and the unfortunate but misguided and grossly blinded Charles the 1st.' At another point she called herself 'a decided Jacobin.'[94] Fearing that his daughter's very obvious disavowal of an already controversial action could only make his position more exposed, in the spring of 1812 the regent sent her to spend six months at Windsor, where he hoped she would repent of her unfortunately expressed opinions.

He also forbade her to see her closest friend, whom he suspected – with some justification – of encouraging Charlotte's opposition sympathies. Mercer Elphinstone was indeed an outspoken and committed Whig. A wealthy heiress in her own right and the daughter of a highly regarded admiral, she was twenty-three and the princess fifteen when they became friends. For the next five years, theirs was the single most important relationship in Charlotte's life. Mercer provided her with the unconditional affection she craved and which was so painfully unforthcoming from anyone else in her family. She was also highly intelligent, and offered Charlotte a great deal of thoughtful advice as she sought to navigate her way through the various 'difficulties and tracasseries' that lay in her way. Charlotte's dependence on Mercer was soon as absolute as her grandfather's had been on Lord Bute a lifetime ago. In her language to Mercer, Charlotte echoed the willingness with which the king had once gladly submitted to Bute's guidance, almost celebratory in its deference to a more active, controlling intelligence. Everything she did that turned out well was attributed by Charlotte to the excellence of Mercer's counsel. 'May I ever follow those precepts, and may I be able to convince you of that gratitude and affection with which my heart is bound to you.' Mercer was her guide and mentor in everything she did. 'I shall regularly transmit to my commander-in-chief my plan of operations, my manoeuvres, my skirmishes, etc. If I win the battle and obtain the flag, I will lay it at your feet, for you gave me yourself my armour.'[95]

To be deprived of Mercer's emotional support was punishment enough for Charlotte; but to be consigned to the tedium of Windsor, with no company but her grandmother and aunts, was worse. Charlotte had always disliked her visits to the castle – 'heavens, how dull!' – perhaps because she knew it was used by her father as a form of punishment. Certainly, that was how it felt. 'I assure you, I hate going there', she told Mercer. 'It will be dreadful to be shut up in the evening in the royal menagerie, for the evenings are so short that there is no going out after dinner. So they work without a word being uttered.' She urged her 'dearest Mercer' to 'take pity on me and write to me whilst *au grand couvent*'.[96]

Exiled to the convent, she was happiest in the company of Sophia, who made great efforts to please her niece. Charlotte found Mary just about bearable, but had no sympathy for 'the old girls' – the two eldest princesses still at Windsor – whom she thought 'very much altered' for the worse. Augusta was cross, and Elizabeth 'false and artful'. Elizabeth fully returned her dislike. 'I am not sorry her visit is over,' she told Lady Harcourt in October 1811; 'I do not think her at all improved. Self-opinionated to a great degree and holding every soul as cheap as dirt.' It was obvious to Elizabeth that her niece 'in her heart hates being here and she confessed it yesterday saying three days was enough'.[97]

Charlotte had few illusions about the miserable and divided state of her family. A short stay at Windsor was enough to make that plain. 'No family', she told Mercer, 'was ever composed of such odd people, I believe, as they all draw their different ways, and there have happened such extraordinary things, that in any other family, either public or private, are never heard of before.' Just as it had done for the king before her, first-hand experience of acute disharmony persuaded Charlotte that there had to be a better way to manage these things. 'In so large a family as there happens to be, it is of great consequence to be well together; it is impossible that one can like all the same, or have the same opinion of them all indiscriminately; but yet to keep up appearances and have no wide breaches is what is required.'[98]

It is impossible to know what the mature Charlotte might have done with such ideas if she had survived to inherit the crown, but as a teenage girl, sequestered at Windsor for month after uneventful month, Charlotte's good intentions crumbled away. She was soon as deeply mired in family conflict as any of her more combative relations. Her anger was most frequently directed at the queen and her daughters, whom she regarded as her gaolers, and whom she thought were determined to belittle and insult her. 'I have causes every day of being shocked with some fresh proof of bitterness, meanness or ill humour. I am treated very cheaply by them, and they look upon me as but to obey.' As she complained to Mercer, she had now fallen out with Mary, 'who is the most violent person I ever saw, as well as Princess Elizabeth. There is but one difference, that the former, being a fool, cannot contrive things so well as the other, who has cleverness and deepness both.'[99]

Charlotte was not allowed to leave Windsor until the end of October. The end of her six months of confinement in 'that infernal dwelling' was welcomed by all the women of the family, none of whom had found her stay congenial. But the lesson Charlotte drew from her experience was not one that her father would have been pleased to hear. 'This cannot go on for very long I think,' she wrote to Mercer. 'Emancipation cannot be very far away, I trust. It is to that desired point that I look.'[100] Soon she would be seventeen. She was convinced that the imminence of adulthood must bring with it 'my own power, my own account and deed, independent of everyone'. Her father, however, had other ideas. Cornelia Knight, who had recently joined Charlotte's household, was tapped on the shoulder one night by the regent with a message for his strong-minded daughter. 'Remember,' he told her, 'that Charlotte must lay aside the idle nonsense of believing she has a will of her own; while I live, she must be subject to me, as she is at present, if she were thirty or forty or five and forty.'[101] There was, as both Charlotte and Cornelia Knight knew, only one form of release from the authority of a father: replacing it with that of a husband.

Charlotte had understood from her earliest days what marriage meant for someone in her position: 'In our high situation, we do not marry as others.' Her eventual partnership would be a pragmatic alliance rather than a love match. But what her mind had long been schooled to accept, her heart often refused to acknowledge. 'There is a tone of romance in her character, which will only serve to mislead her,' predicted Charlotte Campbell gloomily.[102] It was true that Charlotte was an avid consumer of novels and verse. Like so many other women of her generation, she was mesmerised by poetry, particularly that of the quintessential Romantic bad boy, Lord Byron. Charlotte read everything he wrote. '*The Corsair* was out yesterday, and I had the first that was issued, and devoured it twice in the course of the day.'[103] She had fallen upon *The Bride of Abydos* with the same enthusiasm. When a new portrait of the brooding poet was made available as a print, she immediately bought a copy, and spent a lot of time gazing at it. 'I admire it so very much, and think it so very beautiful. I try to trace the man and his mind in it, but cannot; it belies what he is, for it looks so loving and so loveable and something so very much above the common sort of beauty or what is regularly handsome.'[104] Dark, dramatic heroes attracted her; and so too did romantic heroines governed by passion rather than propriety. '*Sense and Sensibility* I have just finished reading,' she enthused to Mercer, 'I think Marianne and me are very alike in disposition.'[105] Neither her father nor grandmother would have been very gratified to hear Charlotte liken herself to a character led astray by her love for an unsuitable man, but the desire to follow her affections rather than the dictates of prudence ran very deep in her. It was to shape her life profoundly over the next few years as she attempted to balance two apparently contradictory visions of her future. On the one hand, she knew that marriage offered what she wanted most – emancipation from the petty tyrannies and destructive self-interest of her parents – but she found it hard to contemplate a partnership in which love and attraction played no part; and all but impossible to accept that she would have little or no role to play in selecting the man with whom she would spend the rest of her life.

Charlotte felt this all the more acutely as she already had some experience of how exciting a love affair could be. Her name had been linked with that of the handsome Captain George Fitzclarence, an illegitimate son of her uncle, William, Duke of Clarence, who was often seen riding alongside her carriage in the park. She was later attracted by the fabulously wealthy Whig peer the Duke of Devonshire, though when taxed on it by her father, denied vehemently that she had ever written him a letter addressed to 'my dear, dear Duke'. She was first flattered and then irritated by the attentions of Augustus

D'Este, the son of another of her uncles, Augustus, and the unfortunate Lady Augusta Murray. He stood pining beneath her windows, and hid behind pillars at church in an attempt to catch a glimpse of her. When D'Este wrote her 'a formal declaration of the most violent passion possible sealed with a royal crest, that was too far', and she complained to his father. Her most serious attachment was with yet another of her many illegitimate cousins. Captain Charles Hesse was the son of the Duke of York and a German lady. Charlotte met him when she was sixteen, and he was serving with the 8th Hussars. They took rides together; there were flirtations and, later, private assignations. More worryingly, there was also correspondence. Charlotte told Mercer that 'on first setting out' she and Hesse had agreed 'to burn all letters, which I did most strictly, for certainly they were much too full of protestations and nonsense not to have got him into a most desperate scrape if ever seen'. But it was Charlotte who ran by far the greater risk – especially as she suspected Hesse had not kept his part of the bargain. 'I suppose he has kept them,' she wrote glumly. She asked Mercer to try to get the letters back, but Hesse was fighting abroad and did not reply to requests. Hesse was, as Charlotte fully understood, a very bad choice for an affair, and she referred to him guiltily – he was 'this unfortunate folly of mine', 'my weakness … the most wrong thing possible'.[106]

Conscious of having made a mistake she might regret with one man, Charlotte was unresponsive when she was first approached with the suggestion that she marry another. It was in the summer of 1813 that the Hereditary Prince of Orange, the heir of the Dutch royal family, was suggested as a husband for her. The proposal, which would unite the interests of two Protestant dynasties, was favoured by the government and also by the regent, who was now convinced that if his daughter was not settled soon, she might find herself in serious trouble. He knew nothing as yet about Hesse; but he had heard the rumours about Fitzclarence, and returned continually to the subject of the Duke of Devonshire. Throughout the autumn, Charlotte was badgered and hectored by almost every member of the family to accept the Orange match. She continued to resist, explaining that she had 'not the smallest inclination to marry at present as I have seen so little and I may add, nothing of the world as yet, and I have so much before me in prospects that for a year or two it would not come into my head'.[107]

Parcelled off as ever to Windsor when her will was to be worked on, she was resistant to all her aunts' protestations of the hereditary prince's many sterling qualities. 'It is very unpleasant being exposed to the observations of a set of ill-natured spinsters who only regret not being young enough to seize upon him themselves.'[108] When the regent arrived to add his arguments to those of his mother and sisters, Charlotte was still unmoved. He father was furious, complaining she was subject to 'a constitutional perversity in temper and nature which nothing can now correct or eradicate' – which was, he supposed, hardly surprising 'when we reflect and recollect that part of the stock from whence this has sprouted forth'.[109] Finally, the ubiquitous Sir Henry Halford was pressed into action, to offer Charlotte a medical perspective on her suitor. 'That with regard to looks, he was not at all of the Dutch make; that if he was too thin, he would fill out, if he had bad teeth, that might be remedied; and that as to his being fair, that had nothing to do with manliness of character, for though he might look delicate, yet there was quite as much character as in a dark man. He then added language, which, I do assure you, I never heard from anyone, and certainly never expected to hear but in a book,' an incredulous Charlotte told Mercer. 'When he saw I looked severe, he turned it off with a laugh.'[110]

Then, quite suddenly, a week after her encounter with Halford, Charlotte changed her mind and agreed to see the prince. Perhaps she had been worn down by the arguments directed at her for the better part of a year. Perhaps she was encouraged by reports that the prince was 'very manly, shy but not awkward or forward, but master of the subjects you talk to him upon'. She had also been told that 'he is lively and likes fun and amusement'.[111] They were to meet at a dinner held at Carlton House on 12 December 1813. Just before the event began, she was cornered by her father, who bullied her into making an extraordinary commitment. He 'extracted a promise from me to give him my fair and undisguised opinion of him after dinner, for that my answer must be given that night one way or another with no hesitation'. Filled with trepidation at the prospect of having to make a decision on a potential husband in the course of a single dinner, Charlotte spent an anxious evening trying to assess the character of the man sitting next to her. She did all she could to be generous. He was undoubtedly very plain, but he 'presented himself gracefully' and was 'so animated and lively that it quite went off'. At the end of the meal, the regent took Charlotte into an anteroom to find out what she thought. 'I certainly hesitated for a moment, but he was so alarmed that he cried out, "Then it will not do!" But when I said he was mistaken, and that I approved what I had seen, he exclaimed in the greatest agitation, "You make me the happiest person in the world!"' Inviting the Prince of Orange into the room, the regent took the hands of the nonplussed couple in his and 'affianced them' on the spot.[112]

Initially, Charlotte seemed content, if somewhat uncertainly so, with her decision. Further meetings with the prince had confirmed his essential decency and his regard for her. 'Our tempers and minds will, I think, perfectly suit,' she told Mercer on 16 December. She liked his frankness and affectionate nature, and was especially touched by his desire 'to be on a good footing with all my family, to keep out of their quarrels and disputes among themselves'.[113] She wrote again a few days later. 'To say I am in love with him would be untrue and ridiculous,' she acknowledged, 'but I have a very great regard and opinion of him, which is perhaps better to begin with, and more likely to last than love.'[114] On the 20th, she was more sombre, describing her forthcoming marriage as 'at least a change for the better, as I shall no longer be confined, or obliged to submit to every caprice of the prince or his family'. It would also keep her 'out of a thousand scrapes and *désagréments*'; beyond that, her expectations were moderate. She hoped that 'we shall be very good friends always, but as to love that can never have any share at all'. It was, she told Mercer, 'much wiser to crush at once all wishes or hopes and feelings which never could have ended in anything'. Was she thinking of Hesse, perhaps? Or the Duke of Devonshire, who had featured so frequently in her letters that year? 'At least the one I wished to have married, the prince [i.e. her father] would never have consented to.'[115]

As the months passed, and the formal negotiations ground slowly on, Charlotte's mood became more and more troubled. She was convinced her father 'had used me ill and deceived me through the whole affair'.[116] The Princess of Wales did nothing to assuage her daughter's misgivings. She opposed the marriage, insisting that the Orange family were all violent intriguers of the worse kind. The hereditary prince himself had returned to Holland, and was no longer present to remind Charlotte of the qualities she had admired in him. And above all, she had been horrified to discover that she would be required to spend at least part of every year in her husband's territories.

Her fiancé had attempted to reconcile her to the idea with promises of travel, 'to Berlin, or anywhere I might like in Germany'; but she grew increasingly determined that she would not leave Britain. As heir presumptive, she protested it could not be right for her to absent herself from the country she might one day rule. She asked to see a copy of the marriage contract, and demanded that a clause be inserted guaranteeing her right not to be forced to live in Holland. The Dutch government reluctantly agreed; but Charlotte was too far gone now to recover any of the initial enthusiasm she had felt either for Orange himself or the marriage. On 16 June 1814, she met the hapless prince and announced to him that she considered the engagement over. 'I am of the opinion,' she explained 'that the duties and affection that naturally binds us to our respective countries render our marriage incompatible ... I must consider that our engagement from this moment to be entirely and totally at an end.'[117]

Charlotte could not have chosen a more humiliating moment to announce that she had scuppered her father's cherished marriage project. Representatives of every major European power had arrived in London to celebrate the signing of the Treaty of Fontainebleau that marked the victory of the Allied powers over Napoleon. The regent had looked forward to presiding confidently over a glittering parade of elaborate and status-enhancing dinners, balls and fêtes. Instead, he was defied by his eighteen-year-old daughter, and forced to endure the amused condescension of an army of crowned heads, most of whom were also his relations. His state of mind was not improved by learning that Charlotte had been receiving regular, and, if rumour was to be believed, unsupervised visits from one of the more attractive delegates, the sophisticated, worldly and untrustworthy Prince Augustus Frederick of Prussia.

The regent determined to take control of a situation he could no longer endure. On 12 July, he arrived in person at Charlotte's Warwick House home. Announcing that 'all was over', he dismissed Cornelia Knight and all Charlotte's servants. His told his daughter she was to stay the night at Carlton House, after which she would be sent to Windsor, to a small house where she would live under the direct supervision of the queen; new and more responsible ladies would be appointed to attend her. 'God almighty, grant me patience!' expostulated Charlotte. Whilst her father was turning away her household, Charlotte, acting on the spur of the moment, seized the opportunity to slip away. She ran outside, found a hackney carriage and drove immediately to Connaught Place, where her mother was staying. 'I have just run off!' she told the incredulous inhabitants.[118]

Once she arrived, no one knew quite what to do with her. The Princess of Wales summoned Henry Brougham, her legal adviser; Augustus, the Duke of Sussex – whose early experiences had given him some understanding for those whose emotional lives came into hard collision with the royal will – was also asked to come and help. But whilst they listened to her complaints and sympathised with her predicament, both Brougham and Sussex offered the same advice: Charlotte must return to Carlton House. She could not, they assured her, be forced into marriage; but it was impossible for her to defy the authority of her father, who had the right to tell her where she must live. Whatever argument Charlotte advanced, their answer was the same. In the end, tired and tearful, there was nothing for Charlotte to do but submit. At five in the morning, the Duke of York arrived and took her back to Carlton House. From there, circumventing measures designed to stop her communicating with outsiders, she managed to write a note to Mercer. 'No ink or paper in my room. I stole these few sheets.' Yesterday had been 'such a dreadful day as no one can conceive'. She told her friend she was to be sent down to Cranbourne House, in a remote part of Windsor Great Park, the next day. She was allowed no books and the ladies put about her were 'stupider and duller than anything'. She did not know what would happen next. She was adamant that she would not, under any circumstances, be persuaded to change her mind about the marriage. She prepared herself for a campaign of emotional attrition of a kind she had experienced many times before. But this time, things at Windsor were not to turn out quite as she expected.[119]

At first, she was anxious and fidgety, convinced 'they will force down my throat that nasty, ugly, spider-legged little Dutchman when I will not have him'. She was shocked beyond measure to be told by the regent shortly after her arrival, with evident satisfaction, that her mother had decided to leave the country and live abroad. The Princess of Wales declared she had endured enough of her husband's persecution, and was resolved to live a freer and, as it turned out, even more eccentric life abroad. She did not seem to have given much consideration to her daughter's plight. Charlotte, who had always tried valiantly to see the best in her mother, was bitterly disappointed. The princess had not even taken the trouble to arrange to see her before she left. 'She decidedly deserts me,' concluded Charlotte. 'I must say, what goes most to my heart (for after all, she is my mother, and she does share it) is the indifferent manner of her taking leave of me.'[120]

Charlotte was very miserable. Her marriage prospects had evaporated, her mother had abandoned her, her father regarded her with ill-disguised hostility, and she was again confined amongst people she thought disliked her. Then, against all expectations, her female relations began to treat her quite differently. Mary called upon her, and listened quite calmly to Charlotte's version of the ending of her blighted engagement. She told her niece that she regretted things 'having gone so far as they did, but if I could not be happy and we did not suit, it was much better that it should be over, for she did not see why I was to be unhappy, or more so than any other person, because I was a princess.'[121] Even her grandmother, usually so unbending, was 'remarkably good-humoured and gracious to her'. Charlotte suspected the Princess of Wales's departure had something to do with it. The queen 'begins to have her eyes opened … and to see that the regent only used her as a catspaw. Her oracle Princess Elizabeth says the same thing, so I hope she will continue as she has begun.'[122]

It was certainly true that her grandmother's attitude changed considerably when her aggravating daughter-in-law was removed from the scene. The queen seemed able to see Charlotte more clearly, to appreciate her as a personality distinct from her overbearing and often alarming mother. In these new circumstances, Charlotte's virtues became more and more apparent. 'You do not see Charlotte at all to advantage,' the queen told the regent in September. 'She is quite different with us, I assure you.' Her son disagreed: 'she appears to be half in the sulks'. The princess's standing with the sisterhood was also transformed. She was, she told Mercer, now 'a great favourite'.[123] The queen's main objective was to see her son and granddaughter on better terms; harmony was not to be obtained, however, at the price of resuscitating the Orange engagement, for which the 'female council' at Windsor had lost all enthusiasm. It had always been the prince's project; he had not consulted his mother about it before pushing it forward and, now that it had failed, the queen wanted to hear no more about it, telling her son that 'she would take no more orders, or directions, or have anything to do with his arrangements'.[124] Soon, she declined to discuss it all, and reassured Charlotte that she would do nothing to promote it. 'There are things that one cannot talk of, and the more one does, the worse they are ... Now, let us be done with that foolish subject.'[125]

Despite the conciliatory atmosphere that prevailed at Windsor, Charlotte still did not feel able to confess the source of her unhappiness to the queen and her aunts. As only Mercer knew, it arose, in part at least, from unrequited love: she was still passionately attached to the feckless Prussian, Augustus Frederick. 'I think and think and think about how it will all turn out till my head gets quite bewildered.'[126] When he returned to Germany, they corresponded, with Mercer acting as courier. His letters kept hope alive in Charlotte's heart: 'A man must mean something by writing as he does.' She wondered if she should propose to him, although she acknowledged it would be very difficult, 'shy as I am, to confess my partiality or my sentiments to him.' She thought of him continuously, but disclosed nothing of her feelings to any of her family: 'I begin now to have my feelings under perfect control. Adversity has taught me that necessary lesson. I can go down now and appear as calm as possible, with a smile even on my face when often I have been low and crying or sighing above.'[127] In fact, when she did decide to make a grand confession, it was not about Augustus Frederick at all – it was about Captain Hesse.

On Boxing Day 1814, driven perhaps by a combination of remorse, anger at her mother's selfishness, and gratitude for the kind treatment she had received from her relations at Windsor, Charlotte related to the regent and Princess Mary a story which horrified them. So disturbed were they by her account that the regent asked his sister to make a record of the conversation, which she did the next day. Charlotte began by admitting that 'she had witnessed many things in her mother's rooms which she could not repeat'. She went on to tell them about her relationship with her cousin, Captain Hesse, and to describe in detail her mother's strange role in it, somewhere between that of an indulgent go-between and a pimp. Charlotte had met Hesse at her mother's house, 'and had had interviews with him there with the Princess of Wales's knowledge and connivance, as the princess used to let him into her apartment'. The princess had done more than allow the young couple a place to meet. She actively encouraged them to take advantage of it. 'She then left them together in her own bedroom and turned the key on them saying "*A present, je vous laisse, amusez vous.*"' ('There, I leave you to it, have fun.') Charlotte was appalled at the very recollection of it. 'God knows what would have become of me if he had not behaved with so much respect to me.' The regent was convinced his wife had intended to disgrace Charlotte in order to embarrass him. Charlotte found her mother's motives impenetrable, observing poignantly 'that she never could make out whether Captain Hesse was her own lover or her mother's.'[128]

Although Charlotte told Mary that 'her mind was greatly relieved once she had told all she had on her mind to her father', she knew there would be consequences. Perhaps hoping to pre-empt any decision from the regent, she had come to her own conclusions about what to do next. She had decided that the only way to escape from the unpleasant situation in which she found herself was to marry. Plagued and harassed by unsuitable men, and disappointed by the apparent indifference of the one man she cared for, she now saw an arranged alliance as the best way out of her difficulties. As she anticipated, her father had come to a similar decision, but Charlotte was horrified to discover that he was considering a revival of the Orange engagement. Panicked, she wrote to him begging for it not to be thought of again. 'I think I cannot be too plain in humbly stating my strong and fixed aversion to match with a man for whom I can never feel those sentiments of regard which are surely so necessary to a matrimonial connexion.'[129] The regent's reply was a chilly statement of the foundations upon which royal marriages were traditionally based and an admonition that she resign herself to them. 'We cannot marry like the rest of the world, for both our elevated rank and our religion limit our choice to few indeed ... matrimonial connexions must be guided by a superior sense of the duty we owe to the country, and if we are so far fortunate as to be allied to virtue, it is proved by experience that the comfort of a matrimonial union will follow in a reasonable degree, as to render life comfortable.'[130] Ignoring the example of his own unconsidered and disastrous match, which displayed none of the compensating qualities he now urged his daughter to fix her eyes upon, he advised her to 'conquer her prejudices' against the Orange marriage, as it was the only respectable choice open to her now.

A few days later, the queen asked Charlotte what response she had received from the regent to her letter. 'When I told her it was not quite what I could have wished or hoped for, she instantly said, "That is very bad indeed," and there followed a silence of ten minutes.' But no one could have anticipated the queen's reaction when Charlotte read to her what her father had written. 'She was deeply overcome, and she wept, which is very uncommon for her. She was very affectionate to me, implored me on her knees not to marry ever a man I did not like, that it would be endless misery, that she was not going to encourage me in disobeying my father's wishes, but in what so wholly concerned my earthly happiness and wellbeing, I had a right to have my own opinion, and by it to be firm.' It was an extraordinary outburst. In a few sentences, the queen repudiated almost all the principles by which she had conducted her entire adult life. It was a plea for the primacy of affection over duty, for the value of happiness over resignation and for the rights of daughters over the authority of fathers. It was a defence of her granddaughter which she had never mounted for her own daughters. 'She wished me well out of it, that I might be assured that her opinion was from the first against its ever being urged again, that such it was and such, I might depend, it would remain, and that if the Prince Regent gave her any opportunity to speak, she would stand up for me.'[131]

In fact Charlotte had already decided on a different method of combating her father's last-ditch attempt to force the Prince of Orange on her. She had found another candidate as a husband.

*

She had met Leopold of Saxe-Coburg when he was in London in 1814 for the victory celebrations. He had very little to recommend him in terms of power and money – his family's territories were small, he was virtually penniless, and he was not even the eldest son – but he was tall, handsome ('extremely prepossessing in his figure', Charlotte observed) and, unlike Augustus Frederick, eminently respectable and not entangled with other women. She had been brooding on him as a possible partner since November, when she first named him to Mercer. She was, she said, looking 'for a good-tempered man with good sense with whom I could have reasonable chance of being less unhappy and comfortless than I have been in a single state. That man, I can repeat is the Prince of Saxe-Coburg.' This was an entirely pragmatic decision and made no impact on the strength of her feelings for the absent Augustus Frederick. 'This appears very odd, does it not? What odd mortals we are, and how little likely to be understood or faithfully represented by those who don't know us. That I should be as wholly occupied and devoted as I am to one, and yet think, talk and even provide for another would appear unnatural to the highest degree if it were written in a novel and yet it is true.'[132]

Throughout the next few months Charlotte struggled to subdue the Marianne in her character – the romantic swept away by unregulated feeling – and replace her untrammelled sensibility with a dose of practical sense. She mentioned Leopold to Mary, who, delighted with the idea, 'launched forth vehemently in his praises, said no one's character stood higher, and that he was of a very old house'.[133] By January 1815, she had 'decidedly fixed' upon him. She did so with no great expectations. 'Nobody was less warm or eager about it than myself, for I don't at all pretend to have one feeling in the world for Prince Leopold.' Her affections were still directed elsewhere – 'I continue to be attached (to my shame, be it said) to another who is quite unworthy of any consideration' – but she knew there was little to hope for there. Augustus Frederick's letters had dried up, and he had even returned her portrait. There was nothing to prevent her connecting herself to the Prince of Coburg 'with the most calm and perfect indifference'. She was resigned to the inevitable, 'and I don't see at all why in the end, once tacked to him, that I should not be very comfortable and comparatively happy'.[134]

With the energetic support of the queen, the regent was persuaded to accept the Prince of Coburg as a potential son-in-law; and for the second time in eighteen months, a new contract of marriage was drawn up. When the prince arrived in England, Charlotte met him at her father's house in Brighton, and, for the first time in over a year, her black mood lifted. Brought face to face with the handsome reality of her husband-to-be, Charlotte was enthralled. 'We have had a delightful evening together,' she enthused to Mercer, 'full of long conversations on different subjects interesting to our future plans in life. As far as he is concerned, I have not one anxious thought left, as I am thoroughly persuaded he will do all and everything he can to make me happy.' He had even delighted the queen, who assured Charlotte, 'it is a match she most highly approved of, and had long wished'.[135]

Over the next few days, everything she learnt about Coburg made Charlotte like him more. 'I think him very much talented with a thousand resources – music, singing, drawing, agriculture and botany – besides, he is a capital Italian scholar so I have almost all I could wish and desire collected in one.' She was particularly pleased to discover that he was 'vastly fond of his family, who are exceedingly united'. He promised Charlotte that 'he will never act as a tyrant' but nevertheless very quickly persuaded her to give up her beloved horses as 'he does not much like a lady's riding, he thinks it violent an exercise'. She was glad to surrender them in return for the intimate companionship she had always longed for. 'He says we shall walk together, and be a great deal together, and that he intends to have me a great deal and for very long, and if there are parties he could go to and that I could not, why, that he should decline them, preferring to stay with me and not leaving me alone.' After a lifetime of conditional affection, here was a man who promised to make her the treasured heart of a happy, settled partnership in which consideration of her wishes would always be paramount. It was hardly surprising that Charlotte could not believe her good luck. 'I am certainly the most fortunate creature, and have to bless God. A princess never, I believe, set out in life (or married) with such prospects of happiness, real domestic ones like other people.' Even the regent told her that 'it would be my own fault if I was not happy'.[136]

Leopold and Charlotte were married on 2 May 1816. They spent their honeymoon at the Duchess of York's house at Oatlands. It was possibly the first time they had been alone together. Two days later, Charlotte wrote to Mercer from her honeymoon retreat, clearly much affected by the huge changes that had been so quickly wrought in her life. 'You ask me about Leo. He is very amiable and affectionate and kind to me, the perfection of a lover (which I still view him as).' She could not say she was 'much at my ease, or quite comfortable yet in his society, but it will wear away, I dare say, this sort of awkwardness'.[137] A week later, she was cautiously expressing her hopes for the future: 'the foundation is very reasonable, and therefore there is less chance of its ever being otherwise than with most others; indeed, on the contrary, I am more inclined to think that it will improve'. She had decided not to interrogate her emotions overly. 'Sometimes I believe it is best not to analyse one's feelings too much or probe them too deeply.'[138]

By August, all her misgivings had disappeared and she was entirely captivated. As Leopold had promised, the couple did everything together. They walked, they read, they enjoyed their music, Leopold sitting beside his wife as she played the piano. Charlotte loved to comb his dark hair; in the evening, she contentedly folded his cravats.[139] They lived at Claremont near Esher in Surrey, just the right distance from Windsor – close enough for visits, but far enough away for privacy. In choosing it they had followed the advice of the queen, who, continuing to surprise, had implored the young couple to make an independent life for themselves. 'She was sure it was a bad thing to see too much of one's family, or be too intimate with them soon after marrying.'[140] Soon Charlotte could declare to Mercer that she was completely content. 'I am so perfectly happy ... What makes it more delightful is that our mutual affection has grown by degrees, and with the more intimate acquaintance and knowledge of each other's dispositions and characters; which will ensure us perfect domestic comfort, as our attachment has founded itself upon too firm and rational a basis for it to be overthrown.'[141]

There was a price to be paid for such devotion. Charlotte had always made it clear that one of the principal attractions of marriage was that it would free her from the power her father had over her. She had once assured the Princess of Wales that she would marry 'only in order to enjoy my liberty'. When her mother commented that her husband would one day become a king and 'you will give him a power over you', Charlotte was airily dismissive. 'Never! He will be only my first subject – never my king!'[142] That was before she met Leopold. Now she had little to say about the independence she had once been so determined to achieve for herself. Leopold achieved by the exercise of affection what her father had never managed by argument and force; in a few months, unmanned by love, Charlotte submitted to her husband's will in almost everything he required of her.

Perhaps the greatest casualty of Charlotte's capitulation was her friendship with Mercer. Leopold did not like what he had heard about her. It was rumoured she planned to marry the Count de Flahault, who had fought for Napoleon, and whose political principles Leopold found as disagreeable as his reputation as a womaniser. The letter Charlotte wrote to her friend immediately after her first meeting with Leopold contained a warning of things to come. 'I must not forget I am desired by him to scold you for your intimacy with Flahault. He knows him personally and disapproves highly of him, and thinks his acquaintance is likely to do you no good.'[143] Mercer's lover was the first to feel the strength of Leopold's dislike; Mercer herself soon followed. Leopold was determined to put a stop to the intimate relationship that she had enjoyed with his wife; he wanted no competition for her affection and no challenges to his influence. Gradually, the friendship that had lasted for so many years, that had sustained Charlotte throughout her greatest times of trial, went the way of the horses she had once loved – banished under the kind but firm direction of her husband. The correspondence between the friends that had once been daily slowly stuttered to a halt; and Mercer became to Charlotte little more than an acquaintance with whom she exchanged coolly polite notes.

Charlotte seems hardly to have noticed as Mercer drifted out of her life, so absorbed was she in the amazed contemplation of her own good fortune. Against all expectations, she had achieved that most remarkable thing – an arranged marriage which had turned out well. 'You are right; it is an unusual sight to see the heiress to a kingdom making a love match,' she told one friend who complimented her on her good luck. 'Perfect happiness is by no means common and I will be delighted if you will come and observe it at Claremont.'[144] In September 1816, Princess Mary decided to do just that. She drove down to Surrey, hoping to witness for herself such a remarkable example of royal matrimonial affection. Once there, she found herself a superfluous presence, her visit hardly acknowledged by 'two people engrossed with each other. I doubt the sort of life they are now leading can last,' she said, 'but I wish it may, with all my heart.'[145]

*

Mary's cool assessment of the long-term prospects for happy married love came surprisingly from a woman who had just become a wife herself. She was almost forty when she finally found a husband. But Mary's marriage, although it had its origins in pragmatic considerations very similar to those which had initially motivated Charlotte's alliance with Leopold, was never transformed into a partnership of genuine affection. It began as an act of practical convenience, and, on Mary's side at least, never amounted to much more than that.

It is surprising that Mary had not been more sought after as a bride. She was still handsome enough in early middle age for her niece to regard her as competition in the marriage market. When Charlotte had been captivated by the Duke of Devonshire, she feared that Mary had designs on him for herself; and in the early days of her courtship with the Prince of Coburg, Charlotte wondered whether, despite the difference in their ages, Leopold would pursue her aunt if disappointed in his attentions to herself. But since her youth, only one name had been consistently linked with Mary's: that of her cousin William, later Duke of Gloucester, whose father was the king's younger brother. His dogged, unrequited devotion was well known within the family, where it was regarded with amused condescension. Gloucester was not, it seemed, taken seriously by anyone as a credible marriage prospect. Perhaps that was why Princess Charlotte once named him to the regent as one of the few men she might consider as a husband. In doing so, she may have hoped simply to annoy Mary, for whom at that point she harboured jealous and angry feelings. Perhaps she intended to provoke her father, whom she knew was not fond of his cousin. If so, even she was astonished by the ferocity of his response. The regent treated his daughter to a tirade of abuse about the duke 'that became so excessively indecent that I hardly knew which way to look, and especially as he repeated it twice over'.[146]

Exactly what the regent told his daughter about the duke can only be imagined; but it was a surprising outburst, for Gloucester's failings were generally thought to be intellectual rather than moral. He was not considered very bright – one of his many family nicknames was 'Silly Billy' – but he was generally thought to make up for his lack of cleverness by the decent moderation of his conduct. Gloucester took his religious duties seriously. He was a regular church-goer, a Sabbatarian with strict views about activities which might properly be undertaken on Sundays. He was actively charitable – a generous benefactor to a wide range of good causes. In later life, in contrast to many of his relations, he was a committed supporter of the anti-slave trade movement. But if he lived a more sober life than his ducal cousins, he had none of their worldliness or wit, and was often the butt of their heavy-handed satire. The Duke of Cumberland once stopped his cousin as they walked through Piccadilly, demanding to know who his tailor was. When the hapless Gloucester told him, Cumberland roared with laughter. 'I only wanted to know because whoever he is, he ought to be avoided like the pestilence.'[147] In their letters to each other, the royal brothers referred to him as 'the Cheese', or 'Slice'.

Gloucester had none of the confidence and easy insouciance that were considered the marks of a man of rank. He was self-conscious about his status, and thought to stand too much on his dignity. This may have resulted from an uncomfortable awareness that his antecedents were far from unimpeachably aristocratic. His mother, Maria Waldegrave, was the illegitimate daughter of Sir Edward Walpole (son of the former first minister) and his mistress Dorothy Clement, who was said to have been the daughter of a rag-and-bone man. It cannot have been easy for a man as stiff and self-conscious as Gloucester to acknowledge that his grandmother had once ridden on a cart, shouting out her wares. As children, Gloucester and his sister Sophia were not always treated well by the king and queen, both of whom harboured a simmering resentment about their father's unauthorised marriage, and lost few opportunities to remind them of their ambiguous status. It was perhaps not surprising that, once he had become an adult, Gloucester relished displays of social deference. At a house party he attended in 1805, 'he never allowed a gentleman to be seated in his presence, and expected the ladies to hand him coffee on a salver, to stand while he drank it, and then to remove the cup'.[148]

Gloucester was said to have proposed to Mary thirty or forty times over the years. Finally, in 1815, she decided to accept him. A number of motives might have contributed to her change of heart. Her father, unreachable in his sickness, was no longer able to express his opinions on the match, which perhaps made it possible for Mary to persuade herself that he would not have opposed an alliance with a man who was already a member of the family. Her relations with her mother were the worst of all the sisterhood; she had been candid in her criticism of her since Amelia's death, and during the horrible year of 1812 had told the queen bluntly that living with her was affecting her health. The desire to escape from an uncongenial home seems to have weighed most strongly with Mary in making up her mind to accept her cousin after so many refusals. It was certainly more important than any feelings of love. Whilst she never spoke of Gloucester with anything less than respect, there is nothing in her letters to suggest she felt more than a companionable familiarity for a man she had known all her life, and who she knew admired her.

She became genuinely animated only when she considered the freedoms her marriage would allow her. As a wife, she hoped she would have more opportunities to decide for herself where she would go and whom she would see. Once removed from her mother's control, she was especially keen to spend time with her brothers in their own homes. She told the regent she could not wait to experience 'the unspeakable comfort' of visiting him when she liked. 'If I might feel empowered to do this, and you promise to come as often as you please to my house, it will be the joy of my life to see you there.'[149] She had made it very clear to her husband-to-be that she expected no obstacles to be put in the way of this new liberty. Indeed, as she explained to Lady Harcourt, she had refused to give her final consent to the marriage until she had secured from Gloucester full agreement to her terms. Fortunately, she had now received 'a very satisfactory answer … therefore I can say now we completely understand each other'. Mary had demanded assurances that her marriage would not remove her from her family, either physically or emotionally. She expected to live near them, to continue to involve herself in their affairs, and to play a continuing role in caring for her stricken father. 'My intended marriage will rather increase my affection, my attachment, my devotion to my family … as a married woman I can come forward and be of more use to all than I can now.' No longer a subordinate satellite to her mother, she hoped to be able to make a real difference to the conduct of family life. 'The Duke of Gloucester has so kindly entered into all my feelings, so faithfully promised I shall be as much with family as possible, and is so convinced how it is in my power to do my duty as his wife, as well as do my duty at Windsor (to a certain degree) that it makes me thank God.'[150]

It was the understanding that she would not be deprived of Mary's efficient, managing presence which smoothed away any potential opposition to the match from the queen. Mary's unsentimental pragmatism, which recalls the brisk, clear-eyed attitude towards matrimony of Mrs Collins in *Pride and Prejudice*, made possible for her what none of her sisters had achieved since Royal's wedding nearly twenty years before: a marriage sanctioned and publicly acknowledged by all the royal family. When the wedding day itself arrived, Mary greeted it with no great enthusiasm. 'I don't know what other people feel when going to be married,' she told Lady Harcourt, 'but as yet I have done nothing but cry.'[151] But whatever her private emotions, Mary carried off the event itself with characteristic style. She dressed for the ceremony, which took place at St James's Palace on 22 July 1816, with elegant understatement, her clothes, as ever, attracting much approving comment. 'Her dress a rich tissue of dead silver (no shine). No trimming upon it – lace round the neck only. Diamond necklace. The hair dressed rather high.'[152]

The newly married husband and wife went to live in the duke's house at Bagshot Park, near Windsor. They were close neighbours of Charlotte and Leopold, and often called on the younger couple. Charlotte did not look forward to their visits with much enthusiasm, but she acknowledged that 'though they are not the most agreeable people in the world, still, they are exceedingly good-humoured, good-natured, kind and easily to be pleased'. She thought the marriage had satisfied at least one of the partners. 'The duke seems to be very fond of Mary and to be very happy; he is certainly all attention to her, but I cannot say she looks the picture of happiness or as if she was much delighted with him.' This imbalance of affection between the Gloucesters always seemed painfully evident to Charlotte; but she could see that her aunt had nevertheless obtained something of what she hoped for from the match: 'being her own mistress, having her own house and being able to walk in the streets all delights her in various ways'.[153]

Mary's experience was not uncommon among her female contemporaries. She had married a man she did not love in order to secure to herself the freedoms she was denied as a middle-aged spinster. If she was unable to offer her husband the heartfelt devotion he must have hoped for, she never treated him with anything less than punctilious consideration. She always fulfilled what she saw as her obligations towards Gloucester with scrupulous dignity, managing his temper and indulging his whims. This became harder as the duke grew older and less malleable, complaining about the length of her stays at Brighton, and refusing to let her travel on Sundays; but she bore it all with resignation. 'Man is man and does not like to be put out of his way, and still less by a wife than anyone else.'[154] She never did or said anything to suggest that she thought she had made the wrong decision in marrying Gloucester; and she nursed him tirelessly during his final illness, in 1834. He asked that when the time came he should be buried with one of her rings on his fingers. It was Mary's sadness that, after so many years of loneliness, she linked herself to a man for whom she felt little more than mild affection, and it was Gloucester's tragedy that he cared for her with an intensity she never returned.

The Princess Royal, musing in far-off Württemberg on her sister's marriage, had no doubt that Mary had made the right decision. She was convinced that the unpredictable trials of matrimony were always to be preferred to the known horrors of the single state. 'The more I reflect on Mary's situation and mine,' she told Lady Harcourt, 'the more I regret my sisters not having been equally fortunate; as I am convinced they all would have been happier had they been properly established.'[155] Connubial happiness was much on her mind, as only three months after Mary's wedding, Royal's husband, now King of Württemberg, died. Royal was devastated. 'I believe there was never anybody more attached to another man than I was to the late king; this affection, which, during our union was the happiness of my life, makes me look forward with impatience to the end of my life, when I trust, through the mercy of Providence, I will be reunited with my husband in a better world.'[156]

Not everyone saw their relationship in such rosy terms. In February 1817, Royal felt compelled to write to the regent to contradict his suggestion that her and King Frederick's marriage had not always been happy. Her brother must surely understand 'how deeply you have wounded my feelings by attending to idle reports of those whose only object must be to do all mischief'.[157]

But in the wider world, the King of Württemberg's reputation was less benign than the shining image Royal chose to present. He had been an ambitious politician, one of Europe's great survivors, who played a canny hand throughout the wars that ruined so many other similarly placed rulers. An astute calculator, he had switched his allegiance from Britain to Napoleon when circumstances seemed to demand it, and saw his principality elevated by the emperor to the status of kingdom as a result. It was unsurprising that his erstwhile British allies regarded this as a betrayal, especially as he was George III's son-in-law. He was condemned by British diplomats as both slippery and disloyal. His own people were said to dislike him; he was an autocratic figure, resisting reforms and doing all he could to hold on to personal power at all costs. The politician Lord Castlereagh called him 'a tyrant, both in his public and private character'.

It was widely reported that he treated his wife with the same high-handed expectation of obedience with which he managed his subjects. The regent's friend Thomas Tyrwhitt had seen Württemberg's bullying nature exposed at first hand when he was sent to Germany in 1814 to invite Royal to attend the victory celebrations in London. Infuriated that the invitation had been made to his wife and not himself, the king forced his wife to pretend illness as a pretext for not attending. When Tyrwhitt threatened to confront him, Royal 'earnestly begged me to take as little notice of it as I consistently could, for, as she said, "I shall ultimately be the sufferer."'[158]

And yet, for all her tribulations, Royal never wavered in her conviction that her life had been far better as Württemberg's wife than if she had remained shut up at Windsor with her mother. Her husband was a difficult man, high-handed, arrogant and untrustworthy, who required a great deal of careful handling. Like her mother before her, Royal learnt quickly that her task was to bend to his will and offer no contradiction to any scheme he decided to pursue. Living with him had called on all her considerable reserves of patience and dedication; but for Royal, it had been worth it. She had spent her life in the active world, where she had well-defined and fulfilling roles to perform. She presided over her husband's court. She brought up his children, becoming a much-loved mother to her step-sons and -daughters. Even the most difficult times had at least been interesting. She had survived the turbulent changes of fortune that a lifetime of warfare had brought to the heart of her adopted home. She had entertained Napoleon, in whom she had observed a dangerous combination of charm and violence – and decided she rather admired him. She supported her husband's desire to advance and strengthen his possessions, and had certainly relished her elevation to queenship. As soon as her title was confirmed, she seized the opportunity to write to her mother, addressing her in the formal language of diplomacy as '*ma chère soeur*'. This implication of equals infuriated Charlotte, as her daughter must have known it would.

By the standards of most arranged marriages, Royal had not done too badly; but whilst Mary would have been content to stop there, coolly acknowledging the debits and credits of the matrimonial balance sheet, it had always been vital for her eldest sister to believe that her marriage had meant much more than that. She would not allow that the greatest relationship in her life had been anything less than a truly loving partnership, rooted in mutual affection. Whatever the daily reality of her marriage, that was the vision she had of it in her heart, and that was the version she was determined would be accepted and acknowledged as the last word on the partnership to which she had devoted her life.

*

Royal would surely have endorsed the devotion that linked her niece and namesake to her husband at their Claremont retreat. In February 1817 it looked as if Charlotte and Leopold's happiness was to be completed by the addition of a child to their 'earthly paradise'. Charlotte had miscarried twice since their marriage; but this time it seemed as though she would carry the baby to full term. She had appointed Sir Richard Croft, a fashionable *accoucheur*, to see her through her pregnancy. He encouraged her to stop wearing corsets, and put her on a diet consisting mainly of vegetables, perhaps in an attempt to reduce her weight. Like both her parents, Charlotte had a tendency to run to fat, and readily agreed to the regimen prescribed for her. It did not make her feel particularly well; she complained of tiredness and seemed overwhelmed by the physical changes in her body wrought by pregnancy. She certainly grew very large very quickly, which alarmed her grandmother. The queen, drawing on her own experience of childbearing, was concerned about Charlotte from the outset. 'God knows, from the moment I saw her advance in her pregnancy, I had a bad opinion of her, and named it to my daughters; for her figure was so immense (to me not natural) that I could not help being uneasy to a considerable degree.'[159]

As the birth approached, Charlotte was apprehensive, but tried to stay resilient. 'I am not in bad spirits about it, yet I think it is a very anxious and awful moment to expect, and one that I cannot feel quite unconcerned about.'[160] The baby was due in mid-October, but it was not until the early hours of 4 November that Charlotte finally went into labour. In the first stages, Croft declared that 'nothing could be going on better'; but by the morning of the 5th, he was more concerned. He and his colleague Dr Simms reported to the Cabinet that there had been little change overnight. They still hoped that 'the child may be safely born without artificial assistance, but still the progress of labour is so very slow that they cannot at present determine in what time it may be accomplished.'[161] Croft debated whether to make use of forceps, a relatively recent development in obstetrics, which were of proven efficacy in cases such as Charlotte's, although the risk of infection was considerable. He decided against, and Charlotte went on to endure another day of suffering. She had been in labour for fifty hours by the time the baby was delivered.

The outcome, after so much pain and effort, was a tragic one. Charlotte's child, 'a male and well formed', was stillborn. Every effort was made to revive the boy, who had not been dead for long, but nothing succeeded, and the doctors had no choice but to tell Charlotte that her protracted labour had all been in vain. She was surprisingly philosophical, telling Leopold that they would have other children. Soon, she was sitting up in bed taking tea and a little soup. Thinking the worst was over, Leopold left his wife for the first time in days and went to get some sleep. He was not with her when, a few hours later, Charlotte awoke in great pain. She complained of nausea and was very cold; the doctors gave her brandy in an attempt to warm her. 'They have made me tipsy,' she complained.[162] When she began to haemorrhage, there was nothing anyone could do; and at around half past two in the morning of the 6th, she died. She was twenty-one years old.

The queen was staying in Bath, where she had gone for her health, accompanied by Elizabeth, Augusta and Sir Brent Spencer. It was to Spencer that the letter announcing Charlotte's death was delivered, leaving him to break the news to her grandmother and aunts. 'He came to my door,' wrote Augusta to Lady Harcourt, 'and his step was so heavy and his knock so short, it really was like the knell of death. But when I saw his face, I called out, "Oh! That look kills me."' The shock was all the worse because early bulletins had suggested Charlotte was not in danger. Augusta was stupefied by her niece's death. 'God knows what my feelings were and are.'[163] Elizabeth was equally devastated. 'What an awful blow to the family and the whole nation,' she wrote. 'So young, so happy, so sure she was to be a mother and so thoroughly contented with her lot ... all at one solemn moment knocked on the head.'[164] For the queen, it was 'a thunderstroke upon us.'[165]

Dr Baillie, who hurried to Bath to console Charlotte's family, had little real comfort to offer. He confessed 'that the last few hours were like a hurricane; all was so frightful, even to him as a medical man.'[166] Augusta blamed Dr Croft and what she considered his eccentric management of Charlotte's pregnancy. He had 'made the poor child change her whole system by taking her off from wine and meat, and just at the time when she ought to have taken nourishment for two, she was deprived of the sort of food which would have supported her in the hour of labour ... It is true that there was nothing wrong as to the birth of her baby, but the infant could not have the strength to assist her, nor she the child, to bring it forth with a few strong pains.' She thought Croft had been 'sadly neglectful and dreadfully obstinate'.[167] Croft himself was acutely aware that his conduct was much criticised; he felt very deeply his failure to bring Charlotte through her ordeal alive, and in February 1818, whilst attending another patient in a difficult childbirth, he shot himself.

It was not customary for women to attend public funerals. None of the princesses were present at Charlotte's burial, but they heard the carriages bearing her coffin toil up the hill at Windsor, 'a dreary heavy sound, which is sad and melancholy to the ear and most painful to the heart'. Leopold went with her remains into the chapel vault which was her final resting place. 'He said he had never left Charlotte while she was alive; and had therefore followed her corpse to the grave; and thus he felt that she had never been neglected by him.'[168] Their son – who, had he lived, would one day have been king – was buried with her. No one could remember such an outpouring of national grief as that which greeted the loss of two heirs to the throne. Princess Lieven, the wife of the Russian ambassador, had never seen anything like it: 'It is impossible to find in the history of nations or families an event which had evoked such heartfelt mourning. One met in the streets people of every class in tears, the churches full at all hours, the shops shut for a fortnight (an eloquent testimony from a shop-owning community) and everyone, from the highest to the lowest, in a state of despair which it is impossible to describe.'[169]

When the grief subsided, it was clear some action would need to be taken to fill the vacancy Charlotte's death had created. It was impossible for the regent to have another legitimate child, separated as he was from a wife who showed no sign of dying. This placed the responsibility for ensuring the succession firmly on his brothers, not one of whom had a legitimate child. Thus began the process of 'hunting the heir' as the middle-aged dukes cast off long-standing and long-suffering mistresses – the Duke of Kent had lived with the unfortunate Mme de St Laurent since 1790 – and applied themselves stoically to the business of courting eligible princesses. Not surprisingly, given the potential prize on offer, they soon found willing candidates, and in the course of a few short weeks in 1818, the regent gave his consent to the marriage of three of his brothers. But, to everyone's surprise, in the same year he also agreed to another wedding – that of the family's most forceful advocate of the married state, who had long since despaired of ever achieving it herself.

*

Elizabeth's life had been one of uninterrupted domesticity since the onset of her father's final illness. She painted and cut out pictures of cupids with mothers and babies. She planned fêtes and other small parties, and entertained guests at her cottage. When she had no company, she had learnt to depend on her own resources to make herself happy. 'I have read a great deal and seen nobody,' she told Lady Harcourt, 'and I can assure you I have been extremely agreeable to myself.' She worked hard to keep her temper sweet and was never angry, 'but when I read the papers'.[170] However, for all her apparent cheerfulness, she admitted her spirits were 'sadly broken' by all she had endured, and the energy which had once been the defining quality of her character had largely evaporated. Her hopes for the future were muted now, her ambitions for herself much diminished. 'Though I do not expect to be happy, believe me,' she told the regent, 'I shall ever be content.'[171] But for all her best intentions, barely suppressed bitterness at her single state lurked just below her superficial serenity. In 1813, she urged her friend Augusta Compton not to refuse a proposal she had received, even though the man who had made it was elderly. Any husband was better than no husband in Elizabeth's eyes. She put the wedding cake of more fortunate friends beneath her pillow, but with no effect. By 1814, she had all but given up hope of finding a partner. When her old friend Lady Harcourt visited her, 'we build castles in the air which amuses us, or rather, she builds them for me, and when she has worked up my imagination to the summit of bliss, I still find myself in my own fireside, with my own comforts around me … I don't disown that, like an infant, my card house is fallen to the ground.'[172]

Then, in January 1818, without warning a letter arrived that seemed to promise an entirely unexpected release. It informed her that the Hereditary Prince Frederick of Hesse-Homburg was on his way to London 'and his purpose of coming here to ask me in marriage. You may easily conceive the kind of flurry it threw me into.' The prince, perhaps aware of the fate of previous suitors, had informed neither the queen nor the Foreign Secretary of his plans, but had addressed himself directly to Elizabeth, who knew next to nothing about him, except that he was a middle-aged man whose character was said to be 'excellent'. She went to Augusta and Mary, 'and we agreed I must instantly inform the queen of it in the morning which I did before my sisters'. The queen's first response was surprisingly measured. 'She answered, upon my reading the letter, "You always wished to settle, and have always said that you thought a woman might be happier and more comfortable in having a home." I added that I have ever thought so, and a time may come when I shall bless God for a home.' Elizabeth was astonished that such an opportunity had arisen at a stage in life when she least expected it. She was nearly forty-eight years old, and she knew a chance like this would not come again. 'I therefore candidly own I wish to accept this offer.' She begged the regent to help her achieve her aim, as she suspected that without his support, the queen would soon renege on her initial approval of the proposal. As she reminded him, she and her sisters had always sacrificed themselves to the needs of others. 'God knows, our lives have been lives of trial, and ever will be so. I have tried to the utmost of my power to do my duty as a daughter and a sister.' Was she not now entitled to seize this last chance of fulfilment? She assured him that if allowed to do so, she would not abandon those principles of obligation that had guided her life till now. The values that had served her well as a spinster would, she was sure, be even more important in her role as a wife. 'If I did not feel I should in every sense try to make my husband happy, you may depend upon it that I should think it very wrong were I to wish to change my situation.'[173]

As Elizabeth had feared, her mother's mild response to the idea of her marriage did not last long. She had let Mary go without a protest; but she had moved only as far away as Bagshot, and was still actively involved in family life. If Elizabeth married, she would go to live in Germany, a separation Charlotte could not contemplate without horror. She was closer to Elizabeth than to any of her other daughters. Elizabeth had been her secretary, her companion and her confidante, her partner in so many of her schemes and plans. In the shifting balance of family politics, she was always considered the queen's staunchest ally, 'her oracle', according to Princess Charlotte. As her health grew increasingly precarious, the queen relied more and more on Elizabeth's good humour and cheerfulness for comfort and support. Mary's marriage was not, in the end, a source of much regret to the queen; Elizabeth's was a different matter. She could not and would not give the match her blessing.

In response to Elizabeth's increasingly desperate requests, the regent came to Windsor to try to reconcile his mother to the marriage. He had limited success. 'No sunshine,' Elizabeth told him after his departure, 'and the clouds are as thick, if not thicker, than when you arrived on Sunday.'[174] The queen was soon so cross and miserable that Halford was summoned to examine her. He was shocked to find her in such a state of fury that both her pulse and her breathing were affected. This was extremely upsetting for a daughter as dutiful as Elizabeth to witness, but she refused to be either bullied or blackmailed into renouncing the proposal. It had been ten long years since she had been forced to give up the idea of marrying the Duke of Orléans; she would not make the same mistake again. Perhaps the battles of 1812, and her mother's lacerating accusation that her attempts to obtain some small freedoms for herself were an insult to the king, had hardened her heart.

Certainly the Elizabeth of 1818 reached very different conclusions about what she owed her mother than the Elizabeth of a decade earlier. She was strengthened in her resolve by the support of her sisters, who took a bleak view of the queen's motives and encouraged Elizabeth to do the same. Augusta urged her to 'look on the bright side of the measure and don't kill yourself with pining over my mother's manner'. It was hard to ignore such a flamboyant display of frustration and ill humour, but she must not be swayed by it. 'My mother is a spoilt child,' Augusta declared, 'for my father spoilt her from the hour she came, and we have continued to do the same from the hour of our birth, and she is vexed that she cannot manage this her own way.'[175] As advised, Elizabeth held her nerve; and the prince was invited to attend the next Drawing Room. On 14 February, Valentine's Day, Elizabeth wrote in her prayer book: 'Saw the Hereditary Prince of Hesse-Homburg for the first time at the Queen's House.'[176]

If she did not recall having seen him before, it is possible that the prince had seen her, for Hesse-Homburg had been one of the many sovereigns to crowd into London during the celebratory summer of 1814. His name had even been suggested as a potential husband for

Charlotte, who had dismissed him without further thought as 'not a man at all calculated to make me happy'.[177] When the prince arrived at the Drawing Room, he did not make a good impression. One observer commented cruelly that he would make an ideal husband for Elizabeth as he was 'as fat as herself'.[178] He wore a beard and whiskers when most Englishmen were clean-shaven, and smoked a pipe when the acceptable English vice was drink. 'It is impossible to describe the monster of a man,' wrote another outraged observer, 'a vulgar-looking German corporal, whose breath and hide is a compound between tobacco and garlic. What can have induced her nobody knows; he has about £300 pa.'[179] When the prince was introduced to the queen, the formal presentation quickly descended into farce. The queen dropped her fan, and the prince politely bent to pick it up 'with such alacrity that the exertion created so parlous a split and produced such a display that there was nothing left to the bride's imagination'. The royal brothers suggested that he retire, but the prince declined to do so, saying that 'as the Duke of York was so much more large, that he was sure his breeches would go on over all'.[180] All this was a gift to the caricaturists and gossip-mongers. News of the proposed marriage even reached Napoleon in remote exile on St Helena. The fallen emperor was scornful, commenting that 'the English royal family lowered themselves with little petty princes to whom I would not have given a brevet of sub-lieutenant'.[181]

None of this did anything to deter Elizabeth. The disdain of the fashionable world was far easier to deal with than her mother's wrath. She made no comment on the prince's appearance. She had been assured he was a man of honour, and that was enough for her. 'In our situation, there is nothing but character to look to … and the prince's is excellent.'[182] Finally, in the face of her daughter's intransigence, weakened by ill health and assailed on all sides by the urgings of her sons and daughters, the queen gave up her opposition and bowed to the inevitable. On 7 April 1818, Elizabeth achieved the ambition of a lifetime and became a bride at last. The couple spent their honeymoon at the regent's house in Brighton, where the hereditary prince commented that he was not as bored as he expected to be, and enjoyed many serene hours 'in his dressing gown and slippers, smoking in the conservatory'.[183]

Having spent so long brooding on matrimony, Elizabeth was determined that her experience of it would be as fulfilling as she had always imagined. She made up her mind to adore her husband, and did so from the moment they were married. Nothing deflected her. On the journey down to Brighton, the prince 'through not being used to a closed carriage' was so sick that he was obliged to ride outside, holding on grimly at the back as the coach thundered down the road. Elizabeth did not care; her new husband's unlucky ability to put himself in embarrassing situations, his lack of urbane sophistication, his indifference to the requirements of polite behaviour meant nothing to her. She knew she would make him an excellent wife and was certain their marriage would be a success. 'The Princess of Hesse-Homburg will redeem the character of good behaviour in the conjugal bonds, lost or mislaid by her family,' wrote her friend Mrs Trench. 'She is delighted with her hero, as she calls him.'[184] Elizabeth was pleased, but not surprised, to discover that in private the prince was everything she hoped he would be – respectful, considerate and affectionate. The more she knew him, the more she liked him. She wrote to the regent from Brighton that she was 'grateful to God and you for having given me so excellent a being, whose one thought is to make me happy.'[185]

Elizabeth's high opinion of Homburg was justified, as, beneath his unprepossessing exterior, there was much to appreciate. The prince – or 'Bluff', as Elizabeth was soon calling him, perhaps in tribute to the straightforward, unpretentious candour that was his defining quality – was indeed a far more worthy and likeable figure than many of those who had mocked him so unmercifully when he arrived in London. He was a career soldier who had fought bravely in many engagements and had been wounded severely in the leg at the Battle of Leipzig. Cornelia Knight, who met him when she visited Homburg in 1824, was most impressed with him. He was a highly intelligent man, who spoke French 'without any unpleasant accent. He was well versed in history and geography, and had a good library of books, of that description, all of which he was most willing to lend me.' After six years of marriage, his appearance had also improved somewhat, and Miss Knight noted approvingly that he was now 'remarkably neat in his person, and never came into company without changing his dress if he had been smoking.' She admired his 'noble frankness of character' too, but it was 'his generous and humane care of his subjects' which she thought 'rendered him truly worthy of being loved by all who knew him.' He was a diligently paternal ruler in the old style who administered his kingdom with a genuine and active concern. He found physicians for the sick and sometimes paid for their medicines. If they recovered, he called to congratulate them. If they died, he attended their funerals. He was indeed, Miss Knight concluded, 'the father of the people'.[186] The prince's paternalism was made easier by the diminutive size of his principality, which was only fifty square miles. It was as poor as it was tiny. Elizabeth's substantial dowry transformed the finances of both Hesse-Homburg and its ruler; indeed, it was probably the prospect of her money that had inspired him to ask for her hand in the first place. But from the moment of their marriage, Bluff treated Elizabeth with great affection, and seems to have grown very fond of her. 'My beloved husband is kind enough to say he can well understand what my mother felt at parting from me now, knowing me as he does,' she told the regent proudly. Whenever they were apart, which happened rarely, she wrote him pages of loving letters. She knew they would provoke his amused laughter – '*Voilà des phrases!*' – but she wrote them nonetheless.[187]

Elizabeth confessed that leaving Britain gave her 'quite a pang which as long as I exist I shall never forget'.[188] She departed immediately after her honeymoon, in June 1818, without returning to Windsor to say goodbye to her mother, judging that the experience would be too painful for them to bear. Arriving some weeks later at Homburg, she found her new home very different from the solid grandeur of Windsor or the gilded sophistication of Carlton House. 'You would be astonished at the extreme filth and dirt one meets with – it drives me near wild, but I have a regiment of females who I keep to sweep, to wipe, to clean.'[189] For all her exasperation with the ramshackle provinciality of her new kingdom, she never played the *grande dame*, and worked hard to make Bluff's family like her. 'She is so good, so excellent, and loves Homburg and all of us,' enthused one of her many sisters-in-law, 'and she fits into everything so wonderfully that one cannot believe it unless one sees it.'[190] The only thing she missed was someone to share her jokes. 'Privately, I do not think the Germans have much humour. They are a sedate, quiet people whereas you know what a cheerful being I am,' she observed. She also thought most of the men were ugly, 'looking as if they had been picked out to prevent the dear prince being jealous, for I do declare such a frightful set of men was never seen – Monsters!'[191]

In everything that really mattered, Elizabeth was, however, genuinely and effusively happy with her new existence. She had always said that all she really wanted was to live simply in the company of a man who appreciated her – and after three decades of denial and subjection, she finally achieved her long-desired dream. At the age of forty-eight, it was too late for her to translate the paper images of mothers and babies she was so expert in creating into the real thing – the obstructive attitude of her parents had ensured that the princess who most loved children never had any of her own. She satisfied her maternal urges by founding in Hanover a school 'for the infant children of mothers who go out to work all day'. There, watching the older ones play whilst the babies slept, she was satisfied. 'There is nothing I love more than children.'[192]

She refused to regret what might have been. On her honeymoon, she had reflected that 'my trial has been severe', but was determined that the sadness of the past should not overshadow her present joy. 'I thoroughly believe few in my situation of life are as happy as I am', she wrote in 1826. It had taken half a lifetime for that happiness to arrive; when it was finally offered, she had grasped it eagerly, determined to do everything possible to make it work. Elizabeth had no doubt to whom she owed the great transformation of her life. Until her death, she never failed to mark the anniversary of her first meeting with her adored Bluff. Each year on that day, armed with 'the blessing and pleasure of memory', she would 'look back at the sun beginning to shine on me as it did when he arrived, and I am sure it never set afterwards'.[193]

*

It weighed very heavily on Elizabeth that she had left her home just as the queen's health began to break up. She did not regret the decisions she had made, but could not help feeling a sense of guilt that she might not be present, alongside her sisters, to support their mother as she grew ever more frail.

For most of her life, Charlotte's health had been remarkably robust. She suffered from severe headaches, and from a recurring 'complaint of the bowels', but she had few serious illnesses and seemed extraordinarily resilient for a woman who had endured so many eighteenth-century pregnancies. Her only untoward symptom had been a strange fluctuation in her weight. She had always been slender to the point of thinness, but in 1805 'had grown very fat' quite suddenly, and two years later was 'so enormous … that she looked as if she carried all the fifteen princes and princesses before her'.[194] By 1810, she was again very thin; a few years later, she was being treated for 'pain in her chest'. Her symptoms suggest she was suffering from the early stages of what contemporaries referred to as dropsy, but which would now be diagnosed as heart failure.

For as long as she could, she attempted to carry on as usual, but in 1817, at the age of seventy-three, she knew she was not well. Her eldest son did his best to raise her flagging spirits, insisting that 'you are blessed with a better, sounder and stronger constitution than any other person living'. He urged her to think no more about illness, assuring her that she was 'very well and very young also'.[195] But he agreed that she might benefit from a trip to Bath, where she could take the waters. It was whilst staying in the city that she heard the terrible news of Princess Charlotte's death in November. Despite the shock, for a while she seemed to rally, but her improvement did not last. In January 1818, the regent received a gloomy assessment of her condition from Halford: 'The principal symptom is a distressing shortness of breath … on any exertion, and this recurs with so much severity as to justify an apprehension … that it may be more than her nature could sustain.'[196]

By June, she was so ill that, making her way back from the Queen's House in London to Windsor, she was forced to stop and rest at Kew. She had spent a lifetime travelling up and down the roads that linked her three homes, shaken and harried as the royal coaches traversed them at bone-shaking speed. She could not have known that this was the last of countless such journeys; but, as her condition steadily worsened, she began to suspect that she would never get to Windsor, as she had so fervently hoped. Unable to manage the trip, she spent the summer at Kew. By September, her legs were badly swollen, making even the smallest movement impossible. She also complained of 'the drag on her chest' which caused her pain when breathing. When Augusta asked her whether her doctors thought that 'the swelling in the legs is connected with the compliant on the chest', Charlotte replied that she did not want to trouble them 'with my foolish fancies and questions'. In fact, fluid was accumulating throughout her body as a direct consequence of her failing heart; but it was only in the weeks immediately before her death that Halford was finally allowed to examine her properly. He placed his hand on her heart and 'found it labour and act most unequally and irregularly, so as to feel this was the cause of all the ill'. She told Halford that sometimes 'she saw her way out of the wood – but when she had made the least effort of any kind, then – alas – alas – she thought it would not do'.[197]

Throughout the autumn it was plain to everyone around her that she was dying; but the queen herself would not acknowledge the danger of her situation. Finally she asked her doctors to prepare a candid written assessment of her state. When Augusta read it to her, she was devastated. 'When I came to the conclusion, she said, "I had not thought it would have come to this. But pray read it again and read it very slow." I did so, and then she cried and said, "I had hoped to get better, but nobody knows what I suffer."' She asked if the doctors 'named immediate danger'. Augusta did what she could to soften the message, but could not conceal from her mother the physicians' belief that she was unlikely to recover. 'She then laid her head on the pillow and cried, but with some difficulty, and after a few minutes of continued silence she said, "I had hoped to see you all happy, and now I fear I shall not arrive at that wish of my heart."' Augusta could only reply that 'we are all very sensible of your affection and most grateful for it'.[198]

Charlotte did not have an easy death; she could not lie down, and remained propped upright in a chair, gasping for breath. One of her legs ruptured, and she was in great pain. She wanted, more than anything, to see her husband one last time. 'I wish I was with the king. I ought to be at dear, dear Windsor.'[199] In the midst of her final sufferings, she still hoped this might be achieved, explaining pathetically to Halford: 'I own, sir, that it is very near my heart to be removed to Windsor before – before – …'[200] She must have known that this was impossible. She died on 17 November 1818, with her eldest son holding her hand. The Duke of York was there too, as were Augusta and Mary. 'We had the consolation of seeing her expire without a pang, and with a sweet smile on her face,' Mary recalled. Between them they had 'nearly received her last breath'.[201]

'What a loss!' Elizabeth had declared sadly, as she waited for news of her ailing mother's expected death to reach her in far-off Homburg. 'What a blow to us all and the nation! You have often heard me say, "No one will thoroughly know the value of my mother till they have lost her."'[202] In the days that followed her death, Charlotte's daughters struggled to come to terms with the loss of the parent who had so dominated their lives. They returned again and again to what was, for them, their mother's lasting legacy – the 'bright example' she left behind her. Her moral conduct had been without reproach, even when tested by the severest difficulties. 'Hers was a long life of trials,' wrote Mary. 'Religion and her trust in God supported her under her various misfortunes, and so virtuous a life in this world must be happy in a far better.'[203] All the sisters agreed that their mother's virtues had been the glue which held the family together. Her tireless sense of duty and her dogged perseverance in doing right as she saw it were, they thought, the qualities that had preserved a semblance of family unity over the years, even when it felt as though the whole structure was falling apart. She was, Mary wrote, 'the great link of the chain that brought us all together ... and which we must feel the want of, and the loss of, more and more every hour'.[204] Royal agreed. When her mother was still alive, she had mused that there was, in every large family, 'a person at the head of them to whom all look up to. Through their influence a kind of friendly unanimity is preserved; but should they fail, all draw their different ways and outward union is no more to be thought of.' She had no doubt that Charlotte had fulfilled that role. She too used the term 'great link in the chain' to describe the queen's unique and irreplaceable role in the family hierarchy.[205]

Charlotte's daughters were eloquent in describing those qualities that did the queen credit; but there is a coolness to the epitaphs they composed so carefully. They found it far easier to pay tribute to what they had admired in their mother than to celebrate any of her more engaging, humane characteristics. Perhaps this was because, in recent times at least, they had seen so little of them. As grown women, it was Charlotte's 'inborn deficiency' in these areas, her inability to demonstrate 'warmth tenderness affection etc.', which had shaped their lives, frustrated their ambitions and depressed their spirits. The way in which her daughters chose to remember her perhaps reflects what they had all known for many, many years – that it was far easier to respect their mother than it was to love her.

It is certainly true that many of Charlotte's most agreeable traits were those she kept best hidden. She had learnt early in her marriage that her feelings were always to come second to those of her husband, and trained herself to bury deep any emotions or desires that appeared to contradict his wishes – the words 'subdue' and 'suppress' recur throughout her correspondence with depressing regularity. She was capable of genuine affection – her friendship for Lady Harcourt lasted until the day she died, and her granddaughter Charlotte seems to have won a special place in her heart – but she allowed herself to express her feelings only in very cautiously defined and carefully considered circumstances. As a young woman, especially in the company of favoured friends, there had been a vivacious and playful side to her character, but this was always fragile, and collapsed, slowly but surely, under the pressure of the king's repeated illnesses. Even at her most robust, there had never been much room for emotional spontaneity in her vision of things. She expected from her children a reflection of the obedience she considered she herself owed to the king. Submission was passed down the family, with no opportunity for debate or contradiction. Charlotte became the most visible enforcer of her husband's authority, with the result that she was blamed by her children for policies which were not always of her own making, and of which she herself sometimes secretly disapproved. Her sad deathbed admission to her daughters that she had hoped 'to see you all happy' suggests that she knew they were not content in the situations that had been forced upon them, and that, in that respect, she had failed them. She paid a high price for that failure. Her unwillingness to champion the princesses' interests tainted her relationships with them, and ensured that all the bitterness they felt for their unsatisfactory lives was directed at her and not their father. With the exception of Amelia, not one of the sisters was prepared to acknowledge the huge role the king had played in creating and maintaining the circumstances of their unhappiness. To the end of his days, he was, for his daughters, 'the Dear Angel', the recipient of their warmest feelings, which they rarely directed towards the queen.

Within the confines of what she considered her duty, Charlotte had tried to do the best she could for her children. She always found it easiest to express her feelings for her children by the concern she showed for their moral and intellectual development. She fought hard to carve out a private space where they could enjoy being young, and did all she could to surround them with people such as Charlotte Finch and Mary Hamilton, who were clever, affectionate and likeable. She had been determined to bring up her sons and daughters according to the most modern and forward-looking educational principles, convinced this would make them happier, better people. She knew all of them, in their different ways, faced complicated futures, and thought providing them with the means to navigate their destinies was the best legacy she could give them. Through all the difficulties that beset her, she always found peace in religion and did the best she could – without much success, in the case of her sons – to encourage her family to share this consolation.

In many ways, hers was a lonely journey. In an age that did not appreciate female intellectual ability, she was a clever woman who took pride in her learning and in that of other women, and never sought to disparage intelligence of any kind. In the company of other lively, intellectually curious female companions, she was seen at her very best – generous, sprightly and amusing. Her reward was their loyalty. The friendships she forged with Mrs Delany, Lady Charlotte Finch and the Duchess of Portland ended only with their deaths, and her relationship with Lady Harcourt came to a close only with her own. Fanny Burney remained in thrall to her mind and her character until the day Charlotte died, although she found it easier to admire the queen when she was no longer obliged to live with her. Others were not so troubled by proximity. Charlotte had only two Mistresses of the Robes from her arrival in 1761, and lower-ranking members of her household were equally happy to remain in her service. Jane Moore, her 'necessary woman', who ensured her baths were hot and her sheets clean, worked for Charlotte for fifty-three years. Anne Boscowen, her 'mistress laundress', also served the queen for over half a century.[206] The longevity of their commitment is mute testimony to Charlotte's virtues as employer and mistress.

She was brave, too, in her own way. She was cowed and broken by the terrifying experience of her husband's inexplicable illness but not destroyed by it. There was a core of tough self-preservation in Charlotte that outfaced threat after threat, and enabled her to endure what she could not change. She survived the deaths of her children, the physical and mental disintegration of her husband, and the hostility and contempt of other members of her family. She defied threats of revolution, assassination attempts, and mercurial swings of politics that forced her into a public world she hated and feared. None of this, as her daughters could testify, made her an easy person to live with. The vicissitudes of her experiences soured her temper and buried her good qualities – her intelligence, her wit, her loyalty – under an often impenetrable shroud of depression from which they only rarely emerged. But even at the very end of her life there was a certain courage about Charlotte, a refusal to accept defeat that made her, with all her many faults, neither an insignificant nor an ignoble character. In 1816, in the midst of great social and political turmoil, she was challenged by a crowd as she made her way through the streets of London to her Drawing Room. In an atmosphere that threatened to turn violent, she was 'hissed and reviled', but remained undaunted. 'They stopped her chair, and she put down the glass and said, "I am seventy-two years of age – I have been Queen of England for fifty-five years, and I was never hissed by a mob before." So they let her pass on, without further molestation.'[207]

With their mother gone, the sisters tried to adjust themselves to life without her. 'Our going to prayers yesterday was awful,' Mary told the regent nearly a month after Charlotte's death. 'Passing the queen's empty chair was quite a trial.' Little by little they were 'fumbling into our old ways, and doing all we can to exert ourselves, to be of use and comfort to each other'.[208] They had one final ordeal to get through, however.

It had been extremely difficult to persuade Charlotte to make a will. The first minister, Lord Liverpool, thought her immovable resistance to any suggestion it was time to ensure all her affairs were in order was rooted in terror of her approaching end, a fear he did not understand. 'For a person whose conduct through life has been so free from reproach, she has a strange and unaccountable dread of everything that pertains to death.'[209] When her secretary, General Sir Herbert Taylor, urged her to discuss it, she refused to see him. It was not until several weeks later, only days before she died, that she could be persuaded to draw up the necessary document. Her main concern had been to provide for her unmarried daughters. She left her beloved Frogmore to Augusta, and the Lower Lodge, where the young princesses had grown up, to Sophia. None of her possessions were included in the will's provisions, however, and her executors, including General Taylor, decided that these were to be sold, and the proceeds passed to the princesses. It was a puzzling decision. The king was believed to have ordered a similar sale when his mother died, and that seems to have been enough to convince the executors that 'it was proper measure'.[210] The princesses were too bereft to oppose it, unable even to visit their mother's apartments without dissolving into grief, and finding the sight of her familiar things painful. Even in their distracted state, however, the resulting auctions were, as Mary commented, 'a sad pill to swallow'. The queen's horses and carriages went first, sold at Tattersalls; the rest of her belongings went under the hammer at Christie's. China, glass, furniture and even some of her famously vast and valuable collection of jewels were all quickly acquired by eager buyers. The queen's library, a testament to her tireless intellectual curiosity, took over a month to sell, the catalogue listing over 4,500 lots.[211] Her daughters were allowed to choose a few keepsakes from what remained of the wholesale dispersal of a lifetime's acquisition. Royal's choices took nearly four months to get to Germany, but when they arrived she was 'most terribly affected'. She had asked for 'a little reading desk I remember her having in 1769', and a small tortoiseshell box 'she always made use of in her lyings-in. My mind still being oppressed with her loss, the looking over her things gave me a melancholy pleasure.'[212]

In his secluded apartments in the quietest part of the castle, Charlotte's husband had no idea his wife was dead. It was a long time since the king had asked about any of his family, or indeed about anything that related to his former life. 'He considers himself no longer an inhabitant of the world,' noted Elizabeth, 'and often when he has played one of his favourite tunes, observes he was very fond of it when he was in the world.'[213] Music was his only pleasure now. Several harpsichords were placed around his room and in the corridors where he took his meagre exercise. 'The monarch frequently stopped at them, ran over a few notes of Handel's Oratorios, and proceeded on his walk.'[214] His calmer days were spent in a haunting parody of the role he had played for so many years. He dressed for dinner, and insisted upon wearing his Orders. In his silent rooms, he arranged appointments and promotions, often for men long since dead, debating their virtues and shortcomings, and entering into 'cheerful conversation with some of his ideal friends'. His physicians noticed that he was 'disposed to laugh and then to shed tears upon very slight suggestions of persons or things that presented themselves to his imagination'.[215] Sometimes he occupied himself with trivia – the rearranging of handkerchiefs and nightcaps – for hours at a time. Food was a special treat. After a lifetime of abstinence, he was at last free to eat what he liked. His meals were the highlights of the day, especially when mutton was served – which he preferred to eat standing up – followed by cherry tart.[216]

The physicians made occasional attempts to relieve his solitude, arguing that he might respond to a more stimulating environment; but the 'system of exclusion' propounded by the Willises remained immovably in place, and there was little talk of any expected improvement in the king's condition. In January 1819, Halford was granted permission by the all-powerful Willises to see the king alone. For a moment, it looked as if the shock of seeing someone new, someone he had once known and liked, might jolt the king into a brief return of rationality. 'Having stated his name, and his humble desire to ask His Majesty how he did, the king appeared forcibly impressed – collected himself – used the manner of a silent, solemn enthusiastic appeal by lifting up his eyes and his hands – but returned no answer – and precluded all further address by striking rapidly the keys of a harpsichord.'[217] The experiment was not repeated. George began to go deaf, which pushed him even further into the private world he now much preferred to the dark, shrouded reality of his daily existence. He refused to be shaved, and grew a white beard. In this remote, withdrawn condition, he was glimpsed by the engraver Samuel Reynolds, who made a poignant drawing of him in his reduced state. In the picture, the king sits isolated in a dark room, with his head resting on his hand, his hair long and flowing, his beard by now reaching his chest. He gazes intently into the distance.

It is an image of deep and brooding loneliness. When he recovered from his first bout of illness in 1789, George had compared himself to King Lear. In this portrait, made at the very end of his life, that is indeed whom he most resembles, a defeated, exhausted man, overcome by circumstances, baffled by what has happened to him. He stares fixedly into nothingness in an attempt perhaps to comprehend the extent of his misfortune. It is, by any measure, a profoundly sad image. It was also a painfully accurate one. When Reynolds showed it to the regent, 'he was much struck with the good likeness', asking only for his father's hair to be shown in rather less disorder.

After the queen's death, the Duke of York was placed in charge of the king's care, and became his most frequent non-medical visitor. When he called at Windsor towards the end of 1819, he found his father at the harpsichord, 'singing with as strong and firm a voice as I ever heard him, and seemed as happy and cheerful as possible'. His appetite was good, but Frederick noticed he had become 'greatly emaciated within the last twelve months'. The duke concluded that 'we can no longer look forward with any confidence to his being preserved to us for any length of time'.[218] A month later, he had lost his few remaining teeth, and was 'reduced almost to a skeleton'. At Christmas, after such a long period of relative placidity, the king fell once more into 'a paroxysm' of frantic activity. For over fifty hours, he was unable to sleep or rest. The Duke of York was summoned, as the doctors feared the king's constitution was at last failing under this final onslaught. He was with him when he died on 29 January 1820. There was no sign that he recognised him, but the eighty-one-year-old king would surely have been glad to know that his beloved Frederick was by his side at the end. The last words he was heard to utter were 'an application for some jelly'.[219]

*

George was buried at Windsor, the place he had come to think of as his family's home. It was said that over 30,000 people travelled down to the castle to see him interred in St George's Chapel. His long absence from the world had not meant that he was forgotten. 'Never, I believe,' wrote Nathaniel Wraxall, 'did any prince … leave behind him a memory more cherished by his subjects! Confined as he was to his apartments, unseen except by his medical attendants … yet his people have clung to his memory with a sort of superstitious reverence, as if, while he still continued an inhabitant of the earth, his existence suspended or averted national calamities.'[220] In London, the shops shut as a mark of respect. Even the poor were seen to wear small marks of mourning. Once George had been the focus of passionate hostility, his passage through London's streets accompanied by jeers and hissing, or even more intimidating silence; in death, the prevailing tone was one of sympathy, respect and a great sense of loss. He had reigned for fifty-nine years, longer than any other British king. Few of his subjects could remember any other monarch. Even those who disliked him were accustomed to him, and no one looked forward to his successor with much enthusiasm. 'How much better it is to weep over departed excellence,' wrote Lord Sidmouth, the Home Secretary, 'than to be harassed by living profligacy.'[221]

With George's death, the great political and moral experiment that had begun with his accession to the throne came finally to an end. He had hoped to find a new way for the royal family to live, both with each other, and within the 'peculiar situation' they occupied in the world. He had been determined to break what he rightly saw as the malign tradition of Hanoverian family dysfunction, which had passed a legacy of hatred and division down the generations, and replace it with a private world characterised by the more humane emotions – affection, harmony, comfort – all of which had taken on a greater prominence in the lives of his subjects, as the emotional climate had shifted. As so many of his contemporaries sought a greater, richer fulfilment from their relationships with each other as husbands and wives, parents and children, brothers and sisters, George, in his own way, did the same. On the foundation of this stable family life, he sought to remake the monarchy in the refracted glow of its virtues. The royal role, for George, was defined by service and duty, a sense of obligation to those he ruled. It was the task of the royal family to show they were worthy of the great task Providence had allotted them by embodying in themselves all the best qualities of their subjects. Their role did not exempt them from the rules by which others lived, as so many of his predecessors had believed; on the contrary, it required them to act as beacons of probity, examples for others to follow, a mirror in which the nation saw and recognised the best it could be.

This was the great mission to which George's life as both a public and private man was dedicated. In the immediate aftermath of his death, it was not clear that it would survive his passing. George IV operated by a very different moral compass from that of his parents. His court, especially in its latter years, more closely resembled that of George II than George III. There was no queen. His hated wife Caroline had died suddenly in 1821, her extraordinary career of international vagabondage and unsuitable lovers culminating in a trial for adultery engineered by her furious husband, determined she should never be crowned beside him. Instead, within the gloomily lavish interiors of Brighton, an increasingly sick and indolent king was dominated by a succession of strong-minded mistresses. If his daughter had succeeded him when he died in 1830, things might have been different. Perhaps the lost queen Charlotte, with Leopold by her side, might have carried into the next generation all the domestic virtues so celebrated by her grandparents, which she herself had so eagerly embraced after her happy marriage. But her early death meant the succession passed to her uncles and their lines. Frederick, Duke of York, died in 1827 without issue. He and his duchess had lived apart for years, she consoling herself for her lack of children with a huge menagerie of animals on which she lavished all her affection.

This meant that on the death of George IV, the crown passed to his younger brother William, Duke of Clarence. Bluff, cheerful, uncomplicated, William was in many ways the most faithful of the elder royal princes, producing ten illegitimate children on whom he doted, and living in happy contentment with the comic actress Dorothy Jordan for twenty years. But neither she nor her children were acceptable as the wife or heirs of a king, and despite his affection for her, William had few qualms about pensioning her off and in 1818 marrying the far more suitable Adelaide of Saxe-Meiningen. Plain but good-hearted, she was a loving, supportive wife, and William's kindness to her suggested that in different circumstances, he might have worked as hard as his father had before him to make a success of an arranged marriage. But for all the unexpected success of their relationship, William IV and his queen did not produce any heirs. After the sad loss of a baby daughter, there were no other children. This meant that, on William's death in 1837, it was Victoria, the daughter of George and Charlotte's fourth son Edward, Duke of Kent, who became queen.

George III's dilatoriness in finding suitable spouses for his children, combined with the capricious impact of fertility and mortality on those who did marry, meant that none of his immediate descendants was qualified either by character or situation to carry his monarchical project into the next generation. But in the reign of his granddaughter Victoria, his ideas were finally realised. She was the true inheritor of his thinking. Like George, she was naturally dutiful, with a strong moral sense. Her famous remark upon being told she had become queen – that she intended 'to be good' – would have met with George's wholehearted approval. Like him too, she was passionate but faithful, loyal but obstinate, inclined to pronounce judgement, and with a will of steel beneath an apparently calm demeanour that brooked little contradiction to her sense of what constituted right behaviour. She was neither as clever nor as cultivated as her grandfather, and she lacked entirely his occasional flashes of self-knowledge, his taste for wit and irony and occasional turn of a genuinely comic phrase; but like him she was lucky in her choice of a partner, finding in Albert, as George had done in Charlotte, a committed supporter in driving forward an image of the monarchy constructed to reflect the domestic virtues of the people over whom she reigned.

Victoria's is the name associated most closely with the values that have given the British monarchy much of its resilience over the last two hundred years. A sense of duty and obligation as its prevailing ideals, erected on a foundation of family stability, a willingness to identify itself wholeheartedly with the preoccupations and beliefs of the solid heartland of the population – these were the qualities that helped keep British sovereigns on their thrones when the revolutions of the mid-nineteenth century, the upheavals of the early 1900s, the conflagrations arising from the First World War and the global conflicts of the 1930s and 1940s toppled almost every other royal house in Europe. Many of these ideas were originally those of George III. He was the first British king to understand that these were the values which would best protect the institution of monarchy, and the first whose character and circumstances made it possible for him to establish them at the heart of his conception of his role. Others may have received more credit for this revolution in royal thinking; but George III was the trailblazer, the king who carved out the ideology that justified it, and, for over half a century, did all he could to live by its rules. In some ways, the continued existence of the monarchy itself is the best testimony to the success of what he himself knew was an enormous undertaking, the effective re-engineering of one of the central institutions of British life. In this respect at least, his great royal experiment left a legacy with which he himself would surely have been entirely satisfied.

The political outcome was, however, only one aspect of George's programme of royal reformation. He also hoped to change the experiences of those destined to live out their lives within its exacting framework, hoping to infuse into the often arid relationships that had been the lot of so many of his predecessors something of the warmth and affection that contemporary thinking believed was an essential quality of human existence. In this, his achievement was more ambivalent. There was little doubt that he was a far better family man than his father, his grandfather or his great-grandfather had been. Where they were practised serial adulterers, for whom a succession of mistresses was a necessary concomitant of their status as a man and a prince, he was rigidly – if sometimes painfully – faithful. He did not always find fidelity easy. As his outbursts during his illnesses suggest, he was a man of strong feelings, with deep attractions to other women, but he had seen for himself at first hand the results of this kind of liaison, the jealousy, bitterness and recrimination it produced. Above all, infidelity disrupted the established order of things, confusing existing hierarchies, allowing undue influence to flourish. Adultery was messy, chaotic, productive of deep unhappiness and, perhaps most powerfully for George, disrespectful to both God and himself. As a result, he was disinclined to follow in the footsteps of all his male relations. He was that rarest of things, a faithful royal husband who, when in good health, treated his wife with a respect and consideration many of her royal counterparts would have envied.

In his attitude to his family, he was again a great improvement on either George I or George II. He would never have treated his children with the eccentric perversity which both men exhibited towards their sons and daughters. George III could be selfish, narrow-minded and insensitive, but he was never deliberately cruel. He displayed qualities in his private life which his predecessors neither possessed nor valued; at his best, he was decent, loyal and kind. These virtues were most apparent when he was the father of a large young family. He was tirelessly solicitous for his children's wellbeing, taking time away from the pressures of his public role to visit them in their scattered quarters before breakfast and last thing at night. When they were small, sweet and malleable, he loved them with an open-hearted cheerfulness, abandoning his dignity to join them in their games. It is impossible to imagine George II surrendering his self-regard to play on the carpet with a lively toddler, or taking the trouble to send his daughter a delightfully eccentric present of a nutmeg-grater shaped as a shoe; when, on one of his rare absences from home, George III took care to arrange this gift for Amelia, it was accompanied by the loving note 'from your dear Papa'.

Yet, despite the pleasure he took in informality and affection, George III found it hard to abandon the authority over his family that had been such an important part of the old domestic dispensation. For all its humanity, his benevolence was in practice as absolute as the harsher regimes of his grandfather and great-grandfather. He expected total conformity to the vision of family life he had implemented and, as his brothers, sons and daughters discovered, he was implacable in his opposition to any action that deviated from it. He was not much troubled with feelings of doubt, convinced that it was the exercise of his will and the assiduous consideration of his interests which alone could ensure the success of the great family project in which he was so passionately engaged. His love for his wife and children never led him to acknowledge that their desires might occasionally and legitimately conflict with his own.

As a result, for all his good intentions, there was a whiff of familial despotism in George's behaviour. He justified his actions by reference to the importance of the outcome – the ends, in his eyes, legitimised the means – but the lives of all his children were, in the end, blighted by his insistence on total emotional obedience. His struggles to enforce it with his sons ruined his relationship with nearly all of them. Only the adored Frederick, and the mild and compliant Adolphus, Duke of Cambridge, who lived most of his adult life abroad, escaped the icy and sometimes terrifying blasts of his displeasure. The Prince of Wales bore the brunt of his father's anger and disappointment. Though the prince's behaviour was often provocative and irresponsible, the king was reluctant to tailor his management of his eldest son to accommodate his obvious weaknesses and his increasingly squandered talents. The king was always keener to enforce rules that did little to bring out the best in the intelligent but lazy prince than in finding ways to nurture his virtues. Although his relationship with the Prince of Wales was always the most troubled – George III conspicuously failed to break the Hanoverian tradition of discord with his heir – the king's younger sons too paid the price for their father's inflexibility and rigidity. It took the inoffensive and inexperienced Augustus nearly half a lifetime to recover from the treatment meted out to him after his clandestine marriage to Lady Augusta Murray. The remaining brothers, William, Edward and Ernest, found themselves constantly lectured for their failings and on the receiving end of their father's unpredictable and capricious temper. Plucked from the professions they loved, or forced into roles they disliked, excluded for many years from returning home and conscious that each had failed to live up to the standards he expected from them, not one of them followed willingly in George's footsteps by becoming a morally upright paterfamilias of the kind their father had been.

George's daughters might be said to have suffered as much from their father's kindness as their brothers did from his misdirected intensity. He loved his daughters in a way that he found hard to love his sons, especially after the princes were old enough to defy him. He admired the sisters' piety, their loyalty and their profound sense of duty. He basked in their boundless consideration for him, their unqualified adoration and love. From them he derived much of the comfort that sustained him through the crises and difficulties of his later life, not least the disabling horror of his repeated illnesses. But for all the warmth of his feelings, the king's daughters always sensed a conditionality about their father's love, a suspicion that his affection might alter if they were to try to change. The princesses' task was to remain fixed for ever in the roles he had assigned them. He loved his daughters all the more because, unlike his sons, they remained the same dutiful, devoted acolytes at the shrine of paternal affection that they had always been. This was how George liked things; he could see no reason for such a satisfying relationship to take on different or more complicated forms. He did not want to consider the idea that the princesses might seek objects for their love other than himself. They were such excellent and extraordinary daughters that he would not entertain the thought of their becoming other men's wives. As Royal once acknowledged, their father had always loved little girls best. Their unmarried status consigned them to a condition of perpetual infantilism; in refusing to consider the possibility of marriage, he ensured that even as grown women, they could still be treated rather like children, subject to his will and obliged to put his happiness before their own.

It is hard to deny that, whatever his ambitions, the king's attempt to establish a new kind of family life for himself and his children was at best a qualified success. No one reading the letters of his daughters, begging to be allowed the opportunity to find happiness beyond the limitations of the life he had prescribed for them, can fail to feel the waste and suffering of such thwarted lives. And yet, for all the unhappiness his children endured, there was something positive that they inherited from their father's endeavours to reshape the nature of family life – an affection and sympathy for each other. This did not mean that they spent their lives in perpetual harmony: on the contrary, as Princess Charlotte had observed, 'they all draw their own separate ways', and the relationships between the brothers and sisters were often marked by conflict, betrayal and indifference. But, despite the many divisions and arguments that pushed and pulled them apart, some of the unity and affection that had been instilled in them back in the remote days of their Kew childhood survived intact throughout their lives.

In 1827, when he had been properly king for seven years, George IV sent an invitation to the Princess Royal in Württemberg, asking her to visit him in England. Royal was far from well, suffering from the same heart problems that had killed her mother. She was, by her own admission, enormous, and could hardly walk, 'my breath being so short that I must be carried downstairs as well as upstairs.'[222] Despite her many incapacities, and with no husband alive to prevent her (Frederick had died over a decade earlier), she was as determined to make the difficult journey across Europe to see her brother. His health was bad as hers, and she must have known this was her last opportunity to see him.

When she arrived in June, it was the first time she had been in England for thirty years. She found everything altered. The England she had known was transformed, and her adored, glamorous brother was now an old man, worn out by drink, sickness and laudanum at the age of sixty-four, as big and ungainly as she was; but nothing could detract from Royal's pleasure in being with her closest family once again. She stayed at Frogmore, where she spent her time with Mary and Augusta, the sisters working together quietly, much as they had done when they were young. She went to see her eight-year-old niece, the Duke of Kent's daughter Princess Victoria. With her love for little girls undimmed, Royal hoped 'she will take a little bit of a fancy to me.'[223] Best of all, she was able to spend time with George, whom she had looked up to since childhood. 'She stayed nearly two hours with the king,' wrote Augusta, 'who is enchanted with her company.'[224] So pleased was he to see his sister again that he organised a special party, held on the banks of Virginia Water. Dinner was served in a grand tent, and brother and sisters were then rowed across the lake in the moonlight to enjoy their coffee on a small island. Augusta was suffused with pleasure, delighted to see them all together once more, 'my sister and the dear king, as happy as it is possible to be.'[225]

The ability to take pleasure in each other's company might not have seemed fair compensation for the difficulties George's children endured in seeking love and happiness elsewhere. Yet it was in its own way a lasting testimony to their father's genuine desire to leave his family in a better state than he had found it. The affection his children felt for each other was a reflection of what he had once felt for them. One of George's greatest achievements was to show his children what love and affection looked like; his great tragedy was that as grown men and women he allowed them so few chances to enjoy them.

Notes

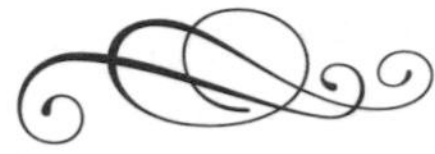

Prologue

1. Rev. L. V. Harcourt (ed.), *Diaries and Correspondence of the Rt Hon. George Rose* (4 vols, London, 1860), I, p. 188.
2. Romney Sedgwick (ed.), *Letters from George III to Lord Bute, 1756–1766* (London, 1939), p. 48.
3. Horace Walpole, *Memoirs of the Reign of King George III*, ed. Derek Jarrett (4 vols, London, 1999), I, p. 6.
4. Walpole to George Montagu, 22 July 1761, *The Yale Edition of Horace Walpole's Correspondence*, ed. W. S. Lewis (48 vols, New Haven, 1937–83), IX, p. 378.
5. César de Saussure, *A Foreign View of England in the Reigns of George I and George II*, ed. Mme van Muyden (London, 1902), p. 177.
6. Ibid., p. 179.
7. Ibid., p. 111.
8. Tim Blanning, *The Pursuit of Glory, Europe, 1648–1815* (London, 2007), p. 9.
9. Neil McKendrick, John Brewer and J. H. Plumb, *The Birth of a Consumer Society: The Commercialisation of Eighteenth-Century England* (London, 1982), p. 21.
10. Ibid.
11. Frederick A. Pottle (ed.), *Boswell's London Journal 1762–1763* (New Haven, 1950), p. 44.
12. Ibid., index, pp. 343–70.
13. Blanning, *Pursuit of Glory*, p. 95, quoting Paul Langford.
14. Ibid., p. 111.
15. McKendrick *et al.*, *Consumer Society*, p. 10.
16. Ibid., p. 80.
17. De Saussure, *A Foreign View*, p. 113.
18. McKendrick *et al.*, *Consumer Society*, p. 77.
19. Ibid., p. 26.
20. Blanning, *Pursuit of Glory*, p. 111.
21. Jeremy Black, *George III, America's Last King* (New Haven, 2006), p. 43.
22. Walpole to George Montagu, 13 November 1760, *Yale Edition of Walpole's Correspondence*, IX, p. 320.
23. James Greig (ed.), *The Diaries of a Duchess* (London, 1926), p. 35.

24. Walpole to Horace Mann, 28 October 1760, *Yale Edition of Walpole's Correspondence*, XXI, p. 442
25. The Countess of Ilchester and Lord Stavordale (eds), *The Life and Letters of Lady Sarah Lennox, 1745–1826* (London, 1904), p. 607.
26. Walpole, *Memoirs of the Reign of King George III*, I, p. 8.

Chapter 1 – The Strangest Family

1. Black, *George III*, p. 44.
2. Horace Walpole, *Lord Orford's Reminiscences* (London, 1818), pp. 6–8.
3. Alice Drayton Greenwood, *Lives of the Hanoverian Queens of England* (2 vols, London, 1909–11), I, p. 7.
4. Ibid.
5. Ragnhild Hatton, *George I* (New Haven, 2001), p. 27.
6. Hatton, *George I*, p. 27.
7. Greenwood, *Hanoverian Queens*, I, p. 20.
8. Hatton, *George I*, p. 34.
9. Ibid., p. 49.
10. Greenwood, *Hanoverian Queens*, I, p. 48.
11. Ibid., p. 64.
12. Walpole, *Reminiscences*, p. 20.
13. Hatton, *George I*, p. 59.
14. Walpole, *Reminiscences*, p. 21.
15. Hatton, *George I*, p. 64.
16. Greenwood, *Hanoverian Queens*, I, p. 110.
17. Dr Doran, *Lives of the Queens of England* (2 vols, London, 1855), I, pp. 194–95.
18. John, Lord Hervey, *Some Materials Towards Memoirs of the Reign of George II*, ed. Romney Sedgwick (3 vols, London, 1931), III, p. 918.
19. Walpole, *Reminiscences*, p. 35.
20. Hervey, *Memoirs*, III, p. 917.
21. Greenwood, *Hanoverian Queens*, I, p. 188.
22. Horace Walpole, *Memoirs of the Reign of George II*, ed. Lord Holland (3 vols, London, 1846), I, p. 175.
23. Andrew C. Thompson, *George II* (New Haven, 2011), p. 32.
24. Hervey, *Memoirs*, II, pp. 340–41.
25. Ibid., I, p. 261.
26. Walpole, *Reminiscences*, p. 29.
27. W. H. Wilkins, *Caroline the Illustrious* (2 vols, London, 1902), I, p. 30.
28. Ibid., p. 44.
29. Thompson, *George II*, p. 37.
30. Walpole, *Reminiscences*, p. 84.
31. Hervey, *Memoirs*, II, p. 641.
32. Ibid., I, p. 254.
33. Hervey, *Memoirs*, II, p. 445.
34. Ibid., I, p. 262.
35. Wilkins, *Caroline the Illustrious*, I, p. 34.
36. Walpole, *Memoirs of the Reign of George II*, ed. Holland, I, p. 176.
37. Hervey, *Memoirs*, I, p. 261.
38. Ibid., p. 488.
39. Wilkins, *Caroline the Illustrious*, I, p. 16.
40. Ibid., p. 201.
41. Ibid., p. 207.
42. Mary Clavering, Countess Cowper, *Diary of Mary Countess Cowper, 1714–1720* (London, 1864), p. 99.
43. Wilkins, *Caroline the Illustrious*, I, p. 162.
44. Ibid., p. 151
45. Ibid., p. 326.
46. Walpole, *Reminiscences*, p. 46.
47. Greenwood, *Hanoverian Queens*, I, p. 226.
48. Ibid., p. 237.
49. Ibid., p. 238.
50. Ibid., pp. 262–63.
51. Cowper, *Diary*, p. 132.
52. Ibid., p. 131.
53. Hervey, *Memoirs*, I, p. 68.

54. Greenwood, *Hanoverian Queens*, I, p. 236.

Chapter 2 – A Passionate Partnership

1. Walpole, *Reminiscences*, p. 22.
2. Thompson, *George II*, p. 73.
3. Ibid., p. 75.
4. Hervey, *Memoirs*, I, p. lv.
5. Ibid., p. xxiv.
6. Ibid., II, p. 349.
7. Ibid., I, p. 45.
8. Walpole, *Memoirs of the Reign of George II*, ed. Holland, I, p. 179.
9. Hervey, *Memoirs*, I, p. 69.
10. Thompson, *George II*, pp. 216–17.
11. Hervey, *Memoirs*, II, p. 487.
12. Ibid., p. 486.
13. Ibid., p. 487.
14. Greenwood, *Hanoverian Queens*, I, p. 342.
15. Walpole, *Reminiscences*, p. 74.
16. Hervey, *Memoirs*, I, p. 41.
17. Walpole, *Reminiscences*, p. 84.
18. Hervey, *Memoirs*, I, p. 43.
19. Ibid., II, p. 472.
20. Ibid., p. 278.
21. Ibid., p. 382.
22. Ibid., p. 458.
23. Ibid., p. 458–59.
24. Ibid., p. 496.
25. Ibid., p. 490.
26. Ibid., p. 599.
27. Ibid., p. 600.
28. Ibid., p. 603.
29. Ibid., p. 649.
30. Wilkins, *Caroline the Illustrious*, I, pp. 278–79.
31. Greenwood, *Hanoverian Queens*, I, p. 234.
32. Marples, Morris, *Poor Fred and the Butcher* (London, 1970), p. 13.
33. Hervey, *Memoirs*, I, p. 95.
34. Marples, *Poor Fred*, p. 20.
35. Hervey, *Memoirs*, I, p. 309.
36. Ibid., p. 306.
37. Marples, *Poor Fred*, p. 6.
38. Ibid., p.13.
39. Lucy Moore, *Amphibious Thing: The Life of a Georgian Rake* (London, 2000), p. 102.
40. Ibid., p. 104.
41. Robert Halsband, *Lord Hervey, Eighteenth-Century Courtier* (Oxford, 1973), p. 68.
42. Ibid., pp. 69, 71.
43. Moore, *Amphibious Thing*, p. 105.
44. Halsband, *Lord Hervey*, p. 127.
45. Marples, *Poor Fred*, p. 24.
46. Moore, *Amphibious Thing*, p. 96.
47. Ibid., p.144.
48. Hervey, *Memoirs*, I, p. 307.
49. Ibid., III, p. 820.
50. Walpole, *Memoirs of the Reign of George II*, ed. Holland, I, p. 72.
51. Hervey, *Memoirs*, I, p. 234.
52. Ibid.
53. Ibid., p. 305.
54. Ibid., II, p. 504.
55. Ibid., p. 371.
56. Ibid., III, p. 843.
57. Ibid., I, p. 310.
58. Ibid., II, pp. 550–51.
59. Ibid., p. 550.
60. Ibid., pp. 552–53.
61. Ibid., p. 614.
62. Ibid., p. 617.
63. Ibid., III, p. 757.
64. Ibid., pp. 758–59.
65. Ibid., p. 760.
66. Ibid., p. 762.
67. Ibid., p. 844.
68. Ibid., p. 677.
69. Ibid., p. 681.
70. Ibid., p. 806.
71. Ibid., p. 807.
72. Ibid., p. 820.
73. Ibid., p. 812.
74. Ibid., II, p. 372.
75. Ibid., III, p. 877.
76. Ibid., p. 881.
77. Ibid., p. 910.
78. Ibid., p. 883.
79. Ibid., pp. 891–92.
80. Ibid., p. 896.
81. Ibid., p. 884.

82. Ibid., p. 916.
83. Ibid., p. 909.

Chapter 3 – Son and Heir

1. Anon., *George III, His Court and Family* (London, 1821), p. 74.
2. Stella Tillyard, *A Royal Affair, George III and his Troublesome Siblings* (London, 2008), p. 20.
3. Black, *George III*, p. 6.
4. Anon., *Court and Family*, p. 74.
5. Marples, *Poor Fred*, p. 90.
6. Walpole, *Memoirs of the Reign of George II*, ed. Holland, I, p. 76.
7. Ibid., p. 145.
8. Ibid.
9. George Bubb Dodington, *The Political Journal of George Bubb Dodington*, ed. John Carswell and Leslie Dralle (Oxford, 1965), p. 75.
10. Marples, *Poor Fred*, p. 88.
11. Tillyard, *Royal Affair*, p. 22.
12. Anon., *Court and Family*, p. 97.
13. Tillyard, *Royal Affair*, p. 24.
14. Marples, *Poor Fred*, p. 79.
15. Dodington, *Political Journal*, p. 59.
16. Anon., *Court and Family*, p. 118.
17. Christopher Hibbert, *George III: A Personal History* (London, 1998), p. 13.
18. Tillyard, *Royal Affair*, p. 24.
19. Marples, *Poor Fred*, p. 79.
20. Tillyard, *Royal Affair*, p. 24.
21. J. A. Home (ed.), *The Letters and Journals of Lady Mary Coke* (4 vols, Edinburgh, 1889), I, p. lxxxiv.
22. Ibid.
23. Sedgwick (ed.), *Letters*, p. ix.
24. Home (ed.), *Coke*, I, p. lxxxv.
25. Dodington, *Political Journal*, p. 104.
26. John L. Bullion, '"George, Be a King!" The Relationship between Princess Augusta and George III', in Stephen Taylor, Richard Connors and Clyve Jones (eds), *Hanoverian Britain and Empire* (London, 1998), p. 182.
27. Dodington, *Political Journal*, p. 105.
28. Walpole, *Memoirs of the Reign of George II*, ed. Holland, I, p. 71.
29. Ibid., p. 77.
30. Hibbert, *George III*, p. 14.
31. Dodington, *Political Journal*, p. 112.
32. Walpole, *Memoirs of the Reign of George II*, ed. Holland, I, p. 83.
33. Marples, *Poor Fred*, p. 141.
34. Ibid., p. 154.
35. Ibid., p. 176.
36. Ibid., p. 153.
37. Sedgwick (ed.), *Letters*, p. xx.
38. Marples, *Poor Fred*, p. 197.
39. J. H. Jesse, *Memoirs of the Life and Reign of George III* (3 vols, London, 1867), I, p. 10.
40. Ibid., p. 11.
41. Bullion, 'George, Be a King!', p. 183.
42. Hervey, *Memoirs*, III, pp. 792–93.
43. Bullion, 'George, Be a King!', p. 188n.
44. Ibid., p. 183.
45. Walpole, *Memoirs of the Reign of George II*, ed. Holland, I, p. 78.
46. Ibid.
47. Dodington, *Political Journal*, p. 180.
48. Walpole, *Memoirs of the Reign of King George III*, ed. Jarrett, I, p. 15n.
49. Dodington, *Political Journal*, p. 190.
50. Ibid., p. 200.
51. Ibid., p. 208.
52. Walpole, *Memoirs of the Reign of King George III*, ed. Jarrett, I, p. 16.
53. Ibid., p. 105.
54. Doran, *Lives of the Queens of England*, I, p. 433.
55. Home (ed.), *Coke*, II, p. 264.

56. Walpole, *Memoirs of the Reign of King George III*, ed. Jarrett, II, p. 6.
57. Ibid., III, p. 176.
58. Dodington, *Political Journal*, pp. 240–41.
59. Ibid., p. 271.
60. Ibid., p. 300.
61. Hibbert, *George III*, p. 19.
62. Sedgwick (ed.), *Letters*, p. 21.
63. Walpole, *Memoirs of the Reign of King George III*, ed. Jarrett, I, p. 86.
64. Hibbert, *George III*, p. 16.
65. Tillyard, *Royal Affair*, p. 37.
66. Dodington, *Political Journal*, p. 318.
67. Ibid., p. 178.
68. Ibid., p. 207.
69. Ibid.
70. Ibid., p. 318.
71. Ibid., p. 178.
72. James, Earl Waldegrave, *Memoirs* (London, 1821), pp. 63–64.
73. Ibid., p. 63.
74. Dodington, *Political Journal*, p. 202.
75. Waldegrave, *Memoirs*, p. 10.
76. Ibid., p. 9.
77. Dodington, *Political Journal*, p. 178.
78. Nathaniel Wraxall, *The Historical and Posthumous Memoirs of Sir Nathaniel William Wraxall*, ed. Henry Wheatley (4 vols, London, 1884), I, p. 64.
79. Waldegrave, *Memoirs*, p. 38.
80. Sedgwick (ed.), *Letters*, p. xliv.
81. Wraxall, *Historical Memoirs*, I, p. 62.
82. Walpole, *Memoirs of the Reign of King George III*, ed. Jarrett, I, p. 196.
83. Ibid., p. 11n.
84. Ibid., p. xxxvi.
85. Ibid., p. 176.
86. Sedgwick (ed.), *Letters*, pp. 2–3.
87. Ibid., p. 4n.
88. Ibid., p. 4.
89. Ibid., p. 3.
90. Ibid., p. 21.
91. Ibid., p. 4.
92. Ibid., p. 45.
93. Ibid., p. liii.
94. Ibid.
95. Black, *George III*, p. 12.
96. Sedgwick (ed.), *Letters*, p. lii.
97. Ibid., p. liii.
98. Ibid., p. 31n.
99. Ibid., p. 4.
100. Ibid., p. 5.
101. Ibid., p. 45.
102. Tillyard, *Royal Affair*, p. 26.
103. Sedgwick (ed.), *Letters*, pp. 36, 13–14.
104. Ibid., p. 15.
105. Ibid., p. 20.
106. Ibid., p. 13.
107. Ibid., p. 46.
108. Ibid., p. 168.
109. Ibid., pp. 45–46.
110. Ibid., p. 6.
111. Ibid., pp. 26–27.
112. Ibid., p. 43.
113. Ibid., p. 37.
114. Walpole, *Memoirs of the Reign of King George III*, ed. Jarrett, I, p. 43.
115. Sedgwick (ed.), *Letters*, p. 37.
116. Ibid., p. 38.
117. Countess of Ilchester and Lord Stavordale (eds), *Lady Sarah Lennox* (London, 1904), p. 87.
118. Ibid., p. 88.
119. Ibid.
120. Stella Tillyard, *Aristocrats: Caroline, Emily and Sarah Lennox, 1740–1832* (London, 1994), p. 122.
121. Ibid.
122. Walpole to Montagu, 22 January 1761, *Yale Edition of Walpole's Correspondence*, IX, p. 335.
123. Tillyard, *Aristocrats*, p. 126.
124. Sedgwick (ed.), *Letters*, p. 38.
125. Ibid., pp. 39, 39n.
126. Ilchester and Stavordale (eds), *Lady Sarah Lennox*, p. 28.

127. Ibid.
128. Ibid., p. 102.
129. Ibid., p. 47.
130. Ibid., pp. 102–03.
131. Ibid., p. 107.
132. Ibid., pp. 104–05.
133. Ibid., p. 105.
134. Ibid., p. 94.

Chapter 4 – The Right Wife

1. Horace Walpole to Horace Mann, 28 October 1760, *Yale Edition of Walpole's Correspondence*, XXI, p. 442.
2. Horace Walpole to Montagu, 13 November 1760, ibid., IX, 9, p. 320.
3. Jeremy Black, *George II: Puppet of the Politicians?* (Exeter, 2007), p. 253.
4. Waldegrave, *Memoirs*, p. 7.
5. Black, *George II*, p. 254.
6. Sedgwick (ed.), *Letters*, p. 17n.
7. Ibid., p. 40.
8. Dodington, *Political Journal*, p. 319.
9. Romney Sedgwick, 'The Marriage of George III', *History Today*, 10, 6 (June 1960), p. 372.
10. Ibid.
11. Olwen Hedley, *Queen Charlotte* (London, 1975), p. 9.
12. Sedgwick, 'Marriage of George III', p. 373.
13. Ibid., p. 374.
14. Sedgwick (ed.), *Letters*, p. 53.
15. Ibid., p. 54.
16. Ibid., p. 55.
17. Lucille Iremonger, *Love and the Princesses* (London, 1958), p. 43.
18. Percy Fitzgerald, *The Good Queen Charlotte* (London, 1899), p. 14.
19. Ibid.
20. John Watkins, *Memoirs of Her Most Excellent Majesty Sophia Charlotte, Queen of Great Britain* (London, 1819), p. 30.
21. A term whose meaning of 'female intellectual' came into use around this time, in the middle of the eighteenth century. It originates in the fact that instead of formal black stockings, blue stockings were sometimes worn (by men) at literary assemblies in London hosted by society ladies; other women attending became known as 'bluestockings'.
22. Hedley, *Queen Charlotte*, p. 29.
23. Ibid., p. 28.
24. Ibid., p. 12.
25. Jesse, *Life and Reign of George III*, I, p. 88.
26. Walter Sichel (ed.), *The Glenbervie Journals* (London, 1910), pp. 119–20.
27. Sedgwick, 'Marriage of George III', p. 376.
28. Hedley, *Queen Charlotte*, p. 14.
29. Jesse, *Life and Reign of George III*, I, p. 94.
30. Hedley, *Queen Charlotte*, p. 32.
31. Ibid., p. 36.
32. Ibid., pp. 30–31.
33. Ibid., p. 28.
34. Horace Walpole to George Montagu, 10 July 1761, *Yale Edition of Walpole's Correspondence*, IX, p. 376.
35. Fitzgerald, *Good Queen Charlotte*, p. 22.
36. Sedgwick (ed.), *Letters*, p. 56.
37. Hedley, *Queen Charlotte*, p. 32.
38. Sedgwick (ed.), *Letters*, p. 58.
39. Horace Walpole to George Montagu, 22 July 1761, *Yale Edition of Walpole's Correspondence*, IX, p. 378.
40. Greig (ed.), *Diaries of a Duchess*, p. 28.
41. Hedley, *Queen Charlotte*, p. 19.
42. Ibid., p. 39.
43. Hedley, *Queen Charlotte*, p. 38. Horace Walpole to the Earl of Strafford, no date (summer

1761), *Yale Edition of Walpole's Correspondence*, XXXV, p. 309.
44. Hedley, *Queen Charlotte*, p. 40.
45. Horace Walpole to H. S. Conway, 9 September 1761, *Yale Edition of Walpole's Correspondence*, XXXVIII, p. 115.
46. Horace Walpole to the Earl of Strafford, no date, *Yale Edition of Walpole's Correspondence*, XXXV, p. 309.
47. Hedley, *Queen Charlotte*, p. 41.
48. Doran, *Lives of the Queens of England*, II, p. 14.
49. Horace Walpole to H. S. Conway, 9 September 1761, *Yale Edition of Walpole's Correspondence*, XXXVIII, p. 115.
50. Ibid.
51. Horace Walpole to Horace Mann, 9 September 1761, *Yale Edition of Walpole's Correspondence*, V, p. 359.
52. Horace Walpole to H. S. Conway, 9 September 1761, *Yale Edition of Walpole's Correspondence*, XXXVIII, p. 115.
53. Hedley, *Queen Charlotte*, p. 44.
54. Ibid.
55. Ibid., p. 46.
56. Horace Walpole to H. S. Conway, 9 September 1761, *Yale Edition of Walpole's Correspondence*, XXXVIII, p. 117.
57. Greig (ed.), *Diaries of a Duchess*, p. 32.
58. Horace Walpole to Horace Mann, 10 September 1761, *Yale Edition of Walpole's Correspondence*, XXI, p. 528.
59. Horace Walpole to H. S. Conway, 9 September 1761, *Yale Edition of Walpole's Correspondence*, XXXVIII, p. 115.
60. Greig (ed.), *Diaries of a Duchess*, p. 32.
61. Ibid., p. 34.
62. Ibid.
63. Horace Walpole to H. S. Conway, 9 September 1761, *Yale Edition of Walpole's Correspondence*, XXXVIII, p. 115.
64. Horace Walpole to George Montagu, 24 September 1761, *Yale Edition of Walpole's Correspondence*, IX, p. 386.
65. Hedley, *Queen Charlotte*, p. 51.
66. Horace Walpole to George Montagu, 24 September 1761, *Yale Edition of Walpole's Correspondence*, IX, p. 386.
67. Hedley, *Queen Charlotte*, p. 52.
68. Peter Quennell (ed.), *Memoirs of William Hickey* (London, 1975), p. 18.
69. Ibid., pp. 18–19.
70. Horace Walpole to H. S. Conway, 25 September 1761, *Yale Edition of Walpole's Correspondence*, XXXVIII, p. 119.
71. Greig (ed.), *Diaries of a Duchess*, p. 37.
72. Hedley, *Queen Charlotte*, p. 53.
73. Sedgwick (ed.), *Letters*, p. 62.

Chapter 5 – A Modern Marriage

1. Francis Bickley (ed.), *The Diaries of Sylvester Douglas, Lord Glenbervie* (2 vols, London, 1928,), II, p. 81.
2. Walpole, *Memoirs of the Reign of King George III*, ed. Jarrett, IV, p. 18.
3. Home (ed.), *Coke*, III, p. 52.
4. Walpole to H. S. Conway, 16 June 1768, quoted in *Dictionary of National Biography*.
5. Amanda Vickery, *Behind Closed Doors: At Home in Georgian England* (London, 2009), p. 82.
6. Lawrence Stone, *The Family, Sex and Marriage* (London, 1977), p. 218.
7. Amanda Vickery, *The Gentleman's Daughter* (London, 1998), p. 40.

8. Elizabeth Anson and Florence Anson (eds), *Mary Hamilton at Court and Home from Letters and Diaries* (London, 1925), p. 280.
9. Stone, *Family, Sex and Marriage*, p. 219.
10. Vickery, *Behind Closed Doors*, p. 147.
11. Sedgwick (ed.), *Letters*, p. 62.
12. Hedley, *Queen Charlotte*, p. 17.
13. Ibid., p. 43.
14. Stone, *Family, Sex and Marriage*, p. 220.
15. Horace Walpole to the Countess of Ailesbury, 27 September 1761, *Yale Edition of Walpole's Correspondence*, XXXVIII, p. 124.
16. Greig (ed.), *Diaries of a Duchess*, p. 41.
17. Ibid., p. 43.
18. Sedgwick (ed.), *Letters*, p. 132n.
19. Ibid., p. 125.
20. Greig (ed.), *Diaries of a Duchess*, p. 45.
21. Sedgwick (ed.), *Letters*, p. 126.
22. Home (ed.), *Coke*, III, p. 242.
23. Horace Walpole to George Montagu, 25 May 1762, *Yale Edition of Walpole's Correspondence*, X, p. 33.
24. Hedley, *Queen Charlotte*, p. 71.
25. Sedgwick (ed.), *Letters*, p. 93.
26. Ibid., p. 101.
27. Hedley, *Queen Charlotte*, pp. 83–84.
28. Emily Climenson (ed.), *Passages from the Diaries of Mrs Philip Lybbe Powys* (London, 1899), p. 116.
29. Greig (ed.), *Diaries of a Duchess*, pp. 78–79.
30. Hedley, *Queen Charlotte*, p. 71.
31. Sedgwick (ed.), *Letters*, p. 71.
32. Ibid., p. 68.
33. Ibid., p. 105.
34. Greig (ed.), *Diaries of a Duchess*, p. 79.
35. Jesse, *Life and Reign of George III*, I, p. 147.
36. Hibbert, *George III*, p. 89.
37. Sedgwick (ed.), *Letters*, p. lxi.
38. Ibid., p. 196.
39. Ibid., p. 166.
40. Jesse, *Life and Reign of George III*, I, p. 134.
41. Sedgwick (ed.), *Letters*, pp. 255–56.
42. Walpole, *Memoirs of the Reign of King George III*, ed. Jarrett, I, p. 196.
43. Sedgwick (ed.), *Letters*, p. 208.
44. Walpole, *Memoirs of the Reign of King George III*, ed. Jarrett, I, p. 15.
45. Greig (ed.), *Diaries of a Duchess*, p. 193.
46. Horace Walpole to the Earl of Hertford, 29 December 1763, *Yale Edition of Walpole's Correspondence*, XXXVIII, p. 272.
47. Francis A. Steuart (ed.), *The Last Journals of Horace Walpole* (2 vols, London, 1910), II, pp. 64–65.
48. Walpole, *Memoirs of the Reign of King George III*, ed. Jarrett, II, p. 5.
49. Earl of Malmesbury (ed.), *The Diaries and Correspondence of James Harris, First Earl of Malmesbury* (3 vols, London, 1844), III, pp. 154–55.
50. Home (ed.), *Coke*, III, p. 65.
51. Greig (ed.), *Diaries of a Duchess*, p. 43.
52. Queen Charlotte to Lady Harcourt, 22 April 1813, in William Harcourt (ed.), *The Harcourt Papers* (14 vols, privately printed, 1880–1905), VI.
53. Hedley, *Queen Charlotte*, p. 65.
54. Queen Charlotte to Lady Harcourt, 22 April 1813, *Harcourt Papers*, VI.
55. Mrs Papendiek, *Court and Private Life in the Time of Queen*

Charlotte, ed. Mrs V. Delves Broughton (2 vols, London, 1887), I, p. 14.
56. Ibid., p. 17.
57. Ibid.
58. Horace Walpole to the Earl of Hertford, 27 August 1764, *Yale Edition of Walpole's Correspondence*, XXXVIII, p. 428.
59. Walpole, *Memoirs of the Reign of King George III*, ed. Jarrett, I, p. 15.
60. Greig (ed.), *Diaries of a Duchess*, p. 79.
61. Mrs Harcourt, *Diary of the Court of King George III*, Miscellanies of the Philobiblon Society, XIII (London, 1871), p. 43.
62. Ibid., pp. 44–45.
63. Hedley, *Queen Charlotte*, p. 47.
64. Sedgwick (ed.), *Letters*, p. 99.
65. Harcourt, *Court of King George*, pp. 45–46.
66. Sedgwick (ed.), *Letters*, p. 62.

Chapter 6 – Fruitful

1. Paget Toynbee (ed.), *The Letters of Horace Walpole, Fourth Earl of Oxford* (16 vols, Oxford, 1903–05), V, p. 106.
2. Hedley, *Queen Charlotte*, p. 68.
3. Vickery, *Gentleman's Daughter*, p. 98.
4. Hedley, *Queen Charlotte*, p. 68.
5. Vickery, *Gentleman's Daughter*, p. 95.
6. Wendy Moore, *The Knife Man* (London, 2005). This is the fullest account of William Hunter's career.
7. William Hunter, 'Journal of Attendance on Her Majesty Queen Charlotte as Physician Extraordinary', p. 7, Hunterian Collection, University of Glasgow.
8. Ibid., pp. 11–12.
9. Greig (ed.), *Diaries of a Duchess*, p. 48.
10. Hunter, 'Journal', p. 12.
11. Greig (ed.), *Diaries of a Duchess*, p. 48.
12. Hunter, 'Journal', p. 14.
13. Ibid., pp. 23–25.
14. Sedgwick (ed.), *Letters*, p. 134.
15. Hunter, 'Journal', pp. 32–33.
16. Ibid., pp. 38–39.
17. Queen Charlotte to Prince Charles, 19 March 1776, Landeshauptarchiv Schwerin, Mecklenburg-Vorpommern, Germany.
18. Queen Charlotte to Prince Charles, 29 August 1779, Landeshauptarchiv Schwerin.
19. Home (ed.), *Coke*, I, p. 58.
20. Ibid., p. 54.
21. Ibid., p. 402.
22. Ibid., p. 414.
23. Queen Charlotte to Lady Harcourt, 31 August 1807, Harcourt Ms., Bodleian Library, University of Oxford.
24. Hedley, *Queen Charlotte*, p. 105.
25. Randolph Trumbach, *The Rise of the Egalitarian Family* (New York, 1978), p. 186.
26. Tillyard, *Aristocrats*, p. 244.
27. Jill Shefrin, *Such Constant Affectionate Care* (Los Angeles, 2003), p. 12.
28. Queen Charlotte to Prince Charles, no date (1776), Landeshauptarchiv Schwerin.
29. Thomas Gisborne, *An Enquiry into the Duties of the Female Sex* (London, 1797), p. 363.
30. Tillyard, *Aristocrats*, p. 233.
31. Greig (ed.), *Diaries of a Duchess*, p. 46.
32. Home (ed.), *Coke*, I, p. 243.
33. Christopher Lloyd, 'King, Queen and Family', in Jane Roberts (ed.), *George III and Queen Charlotte: Patronage, Collecting and Court Taste* (London, 2004), p. 28.

34. Walpole, *Memoirs of the Reign of King George III*, ed. Jarrett, I, p. 227.
35. Mme D'Arblay, *Diary and Letters of Mme D'Arblay*, ed. Charlotte Barrett (4 vols, London, 1854), II, p. 40.
36. Mrs Delany, *The Autobiography and Correspondence of Mary Granville, Mrs Delany*, ed. Lady Llanover (3 vols, London, 1861), II, p. 473.
37. Ibid., III, p. 308.
38. Schefrin, *Constant Affectionate Care*, p. 40.
39. Vickery, *Gentleman's Daughter*, p. 123.
40. Anon., *George III: His Court and Family* (2 vols, London, 1824), I, p. 422.
41. Papendiek, *Court and Private Life*, I, p. 119.
42. Dorothy Margaret Stuart, *The Daughters of George III* (London, 1939), p. 205.
43. Watkins, *Memoirs of Sophia Charlotte*, p. 189.
44. Shefrin, *Constant Affectionate Care*, p. 3.
45. Hedley, *Queen Charlotte*, p. 97.
46. Home (ed.), *Coke*, IV, p. 103.
47. Papendiek, *Court and Private Life*, I, p. 47.

Chapter 7 – Private Lives

1. Walpole to H. S. Conway, 5 July 1740, quoted in Shefrin, *Constant Affectionate Care*, p. 30.
2. Ibid.
3. Shefrin, *Constant Affectionate Care*, p. 13.
4. Diary of Lady Charlotte Finch, 22 July 1765, DG7, Leicester Record Office.
5. Shefrin, *Constant Affectionate Care*, p. 44.
6. Ibid.
7. Papendiek, *Court and Private Life*, I, p. 41.
8. Greig (ed.), *Diaries of a Duchess*, p. 63.
9. A. Aspinall (ed.), *The Correspondence of George, Prince of Wales, 1770–1812* (8 vols, Oxford, 1963–71), I, p. 4.
10. Home (ed.), *Coke*, IV, p. 378.
11. D'Arblay, *Diary and Letters*, II, p. 600.
12. Greig (ed.), *Diaries of a Duchess*, p. 48.
13. Diary of Lady Finch, 1 March 1765, DG7, Leicester Record Office.
14. Home (ed.), *Coke*, II, p. 205.
15. Ibid., p. 387.
16. Ibid., p. 435.
17. Greig (ed.), *Diaries of a Duchess*, p. 196.
18. Ibid., p. 195.
19. Ibid., p. 205.
20. Hedley, *Queen Charlotte*, p. 111.
21. Walpole, *Memoirs of the Reign of King George III*, ed. Jarrett, IV, p. 271.
22. Hedley, *Queen Charlotte*, p. 111.
23. Walpole, *Memoirs of the Reign of King George III*, ed. Jarrett, IV, p. 271.
24. Papendiek, *Court and Private Life*, I, p. 49.
25. Ibid., p. 52.
26. Ibid., p. 77.
27. D'Arblay, *Diary and Letters*, II, p. 95.
28. Hedley, *Queen Charlotte*, p. 114.
29. Papendiek, *Court and Private Life*, I, pp. 74, 49.
30. Ibid., pp. 93–94.
31. Queen Charlotte to Prince Charles, 18 May 1776, Landeshauptarchiv Schwerin.
32. Queen Charlotte to Prince Charles, 20 July 1777, Landeshauptarchiv Schwerin.
33. Queen Charlotte to Prince Charles, 9 July 1776, Landeshauptarchiv Schwerin.

34. Roberts (ed.), *George III and Queen Charlotte*, p. 133.
35. Queen Charlotte to Prince Charles, 6 July 1779, Landeshauptarchiv Schwerin.
36. Queen Charlotte to Prince Charles, 23 July 1779, Landeshauptarchiv Schwerin.
37. Queen Charlotte to Prince Charles, 6 July 1779, Landeshauptarchiv Schwerin.
38. Hedley, *Queen Charlotte*, p. 117.
39. Queen Charlotte to Prince Charles, 20 July 1776, Landeshauptarchiv Schwerin.
40. D'Arblay, *Diary and Letters*, II, p. 49.
41. Queen Charlotte to Lady Harcourt, 2 September 1798, Harcourt Ms.
42. Hedley, *Queen Charlotte*, p. 114.
43. Queen Charlotte to Prince Charles, 20 January 1776, Landeshauptarchiv Schwerin.
44. Queen Charlotte to Prince Charles, 29 December 1776 and 28 April and 13 June 1777, Landeshauptarchiv Schwerin.
45. Queen Charlotte to Prince Charles, 5 March 1776, Landeshauptarchiv Schwerin.
46. Ibid.
47. Queen Charlotte to Prince Charles, 18 May 1778, Landeshauptarchiv Schwerin.
48. Hedley, *Queen Charlotte*, p. 115.
49. Queen Charlotte to Prince Charles, 6 September 1780, Landeshauptarchiv Schwerin.
50. Ibid.
51. Ibid.
52. Queen Charlotte to Prince Charles, 14 January 1780, Landeshauptarchiv Schwerin.
53. Queen Charlotte to Mary Hamilton, 23 June 1780, Mary Hamilton Ms., John Rylands Library, University of Manchester.
54. Queen Charlotte to Prince Charles, 2 May 1777, Landeshauptarchiv Schwerin.
55. Queen Charlotte to Prince Charles, 17 October 1778, Landeshauptarchiv Schwerin.
56. Hedley, *Queen Charlotte*, p. 114.

Chapter 8 – A Sentimental Education

1. Shefrin, *Constant Affectionate Care*, pp. 11–12.
2. Watkins, *Memoirs of Sophia Charlotte*, p. 238.
3. Queen Charlotte to Prince Charles, 9 July 1782, Landeshauptarchiv Schwerin.
4. Flora Fraser, *Princesses: The Six Daughters of George III* (London, 2004), p. 36.
5. Shefrin, *Constant Affectionate Care*, p. 4.
6. Diary of Lady Finch, 10 November 1764, DG7, Leicester Record Office.
7. Shefrin, *Constant Affectionate Care*, p. 57.
8. Home (ed.), *Coke*, II, p. 363.
9. Ibid., III, p. 81.
10. Ibid., I, p. 30.
11. Ibid., IV, p. 430.
12. Shefrin, *Constant Affectionate Care*, pp. 11–12.
13. Steven Parissien, *George IV: The Grand Entertainment* (London, 2001), p. 20.
14. Augusta Murray, *Recollections* (London, 1868), p. 69.
15. Hibbert, *George III*, p. 101.
16. A. Aspinall (ed.), *The Later Correspondence of George III* (5 vols, Cambridge, 1966–70), I, p. xvi.
17. Ibid., p. 273.
18. Shefrin, *Constant Affectionate Care*, p. 62.
19. Aspinall (ed.), *Prince of Wales*, I, p. 5.

20. Bullion, 'George, Be a King!', p. 189n.
21. Aspinall (ed.), *Prince of Wales*, I, p. 5.
22. Bullion, 'George, Be a King!', p. 189n.
23. Ibid., p. 191n.
24. Aspinall (ed.), *Prince of Wales*, I, p. 5.
25. Bullion, 'George, Be A King!', p. 191n.
26. Home (ed.), *Coke*, IV, p. 178.
27. Watkins, *Memoirs of Sophia Charlotte*, p. 251.
28. Home (ed.), *Coke*, I, p. 30n.
29. Watkins, *Memoirs of Sophia Charlotte*, p. 250.
30. Home (ed.), *Coke*, IV, pp. 180–81.
31. Hibbert, *George III*, p. 101.
32. Greig (ed.), *Diaries of a Duchess*, p. 196.
33. Parissien, *George IV*, p. 21.
34. Aspinall (ed.), *Prince of Wales*, I, p. 33.
35. Malmesbury (ed.), *Diaries and Correspondence*, II, p. 124.
36. Aspinall (ed.), *Prince of Wales*, I, p. 33.
37. Home (ed.), *Coke*, II, p. 205.
38. Parissien, *George IV*, p. 24.
39. Papendiek, *Court and Private Life*, I, p. 132.
40. Anson and Anson (eds), *Mary Hamilton*, pp. 83–84.
41. Aspinall (ed.), *Prince of Wales*, I, p. 6.
42. Ibid., p. 18.
43. Ibid., p. 26.
44. Ibid., p. 28.
45. Queen Charlotte to Prince Charles, 1 June 1779, Landeshauptarchiv Schwerin.
46. Queen Charlotte to Prince Charles, 3 October 1780, Landeshauptarchiv Schwerin.
47. Aspinall (ed.), *Prince of Wales*, I, p. 41n.
48. Anson and Anson (eds), *Mary Hamilton*, p. 16.
49. Lady Louisa Stuart, *The Letters of Lady Louisa Stuart*, ed. R. Brimley Johnson (London, 1926), p. 212.
50. Clarissa Campbell Orr, 'Queen Charlotte, Scientific Queen', in Clarissa Campbell Orr (ed.), *Queenship in Britain 1660–1837* (Manchester, 2002), p. 250. This essay contains by far the fullest and most illuminating account of the Harcourt family and their milieu.
51. Delany, *Autobiography and Correspondence*, II, pp. 370–71.
52. Elizabeth, Countess Harcourt, 'Memoirs of the Years 1788 and 1789', *Harcourt Papers*, IV, p. 77.
53. D'Arblay, *Diary and Letters*, II, p. 50.
54. Harcourt, 'Memoirs of the Years 1788 and 1789', p. 77.
55. D'Arblay, *Diary and Letters*, II, p. 24.
56. Ibid., p. 209.
57. Queen Charlotte to Lady Harcourt, no date, *Harcourt Papers*, VI.
58. Campbell Orr, 'Scientific Queen', p. 236.
59. Queen Charlotte to Prince Charles, 6 July 1779, Landeshauptarchiv Schwerin.
60. Campbell Orr, 'Scientific Queen', pp. 253, 64n.
61. Queen Charlotte to Prince Charles, 9 July 1782, Landeshauptarchiv Schwerin.
62. Queen Charlotte to Lady Harcourt, no date, *Harcourt Papers*, VI.
63. Miss Goldsworthy to Mary Hamilton, 6 September 1779, Hamilton Ms.
64. Home (ed.), *Coke*, II, p. 247.
65. Shefrin, *Constant Affectionate Care*, p. 53.
66. Anson and Anson (eds), *Mary Hamilton*, p. 97.

67. Papendiek, *Court and Private Life*, I, p. 91.
68. Home (ed.), *Coke*, III, p. 258.
69. Shefrin, *Constant Affectionate Care*, p. 56.
70. Home (ed.), *Coke*, III, p. 291.
71. Shefrin, *Constant Affectionate Care*, p. 56.
72. Home (ed.), *Coke*, IV, p. 418.
73. Princess Augusta to Mrs Hamilton, 28 November 1777, Hamilton Ms.
74. Papendiek, *Court and Private Life*, I, p. 264.
75. Harcourt, *Court of King George*, p. 50.
76. Queen Charlotte to Prince Charles, 9 July 1782, Landeshauptarchiv Schwerin.
77. Watkins, *Memoirs of Sophia Charlotte*, p. 263.
78. Ibid., p. 319.
79. Delany, *Autobiography and Correspondence*, II, p. 55.
80. Ibid., p. 45.
81. D'Arblay, *Diary and Letters*, II, p. 110.
82. Anson and Anson (eds), *Mary Hamilton*, p. 50.
83. Ibid., p. 55.
84. Ibid., p. 60.
85. Ibid., p. 52.
86. Queen Charlotte to Mary Hamilton, 20 August 1780, Hamilton Ms.
87. Anson and Anson (eds), *Mary Hamilton*, p. 78.
88. Princesses Augusta and Elizabeth to Mary Hamilton, throughout 1777, Hamilton Ms.
89. Princess Augusta to Mary Hamilton, no date, Hamilton Ms.
90. Ibid.
91. Princess Augusta to Mary Hamilton, 14 August 1784, Hamilton Ms.
92. Princess Royal to Mary Hamilton, no date (1777), 13 January 1778, Hamilton Ms.
93. Princess Royal to Mary Hamilton, 3 January 1778, Hamilton Ms.
94. Princess Royal to Mary Hamilton 1 and 3 February 1778, Hamilton Ms.
95. Queen Charlotte to Prince Charles, 11 April 1777, Landeshauptarchiv Schwerin.
96. Fraser, *Princesses*, p. 50.
97. Queen Charlotte to Prince Charles, 20 July 1777, Landeshauptarchiv Schwerin.
98. Harcourt, 'Memoirs of the Years 1788 and 1789', p. 77.
99. Harcourt, *Court of King George*, p. 32.
100. Queen Charlotte to Mary Hamilton, no date (1780), Hamilton Ms.
101. Mrs Cheveley to Mary Hamilton, 24 November 1783, Hamilton Ms.
102. Shefrin, *Constant Affectionate Care*, p. 52.
103. Miss Goldsworthy to Mary Hamilton, 20 June 1780, Hamilton Ms.
104. Miss Goldsworthy to Mary Hamilton, 28 March 1780, Hamilton Ms.
105. Miss Goldsworthy to Mary Hamilton, no date, Hamilton Ms.
106. Anson and Anson (eds), *Mary Hamilton*, p. 77.
107. Queen Charlotte to Mary Hamilton, 25 June 1781, Hamilton Ms.
108. Anson and Anson (eds), *Mary Hamilton*, p. 193.
109. Queen Charlotte to Prince Charles, 13 June 1783, Landeshauptarchiv Schwerin.
110. Queen Charlotte to Mary Hamilton, no date (1780), Hamilton Ms.

Chapter 9 – Numberless Trials

1. Aspinall (ed.), *Prince of Wales*, I, p. 33.
2. Ibid.
3. Black, *George III*, p. 115.
4. Walpole, *Memoirs of the Reign of King George III*, ed. Jarrett, IV, p. 143.
5. Wraxall, *Historical Memoirs*, I, p. 37.
6. John Cannon, *Lord North: The Noble Lord in the Blue Ribbon* (London, 1970), pp. 7, 9.
7. John Fortescue, *The Correspondence of King George III* (6 vols, London, 1927), IV, p. 220.
8. Ibid., V, p. 62.
9. Hibbert, *George III*, p. 157.
10. Ibid., p. 145.
11. Ibid., p. 143.
12. Black, *George III*, p. 225.
13. Hibbert, *George III*, p. 158.
14. Cannon, *Lord North*, p. 25.
15. Queen Charlotte to Prince Charles, no date, Landeshauptarchiv Schwerin.
16. Queen Charlotte to Prince Charles, 1 June 1779, Landeshauptarchiv Schwerin.
17. Aspinall (ed.), *George III*, I, p. xvii.
18. Queen Charlotte to Prince Charles, 29 February 1780, Landeshauptarchiv Schwerin.
19. Aspinall (ed.), *George III*, I, p. xvii.
20. Hibbert, *George III*, p. 162.
21. Black, *George III*, p. 247.
22. Ibid., p. 101.
23. Hibbert, *George III*, p. 233.
24. Steuart (ed.), *Last Journals of Horace Walpole*, II, p. 496.
25. Hibbert, *George III*, p. 233.
26. Steuart (ed.), *Last Journals of Horace Walpole*, II, p. 496.
27. Hibbert, *George III*, p. 234.
28. Black, *George III*, p. 114.
29. Hibbert, *George III*, p. 164.
30. Aspinall (ed.), *Prince of Wales*, I, p. 104.
31. Lady Charlotte Finch to Mary Hamilton, 30 May 1782, Hamilton Ms.
32. Lady Charlotte Finch to Mary Hamilton, 3 July 1782, Hamilton Ms.
33. Lady Charlotte Finch to Mary Hamilton, 17 July 1782, Hamilton Ms.
34. Lady Charlotte Finch to Mary Hamilton, 22 August 1782, Hamilton Ms.
35. Lady Charlotte Finch to Mary Hamilton, 27 August 1782, Hamilton Ms.
36. Queen Charlotte to Prince Charles, 22 August 1782, Landeshauptarchiv Schwerin.
37. Miss Goldsworthy to Mary Hamilton, 24 August 1782, Hamilton Ms.
38. Papendiek, *Court and Private Life*, I, p. 271.
39. Mrs Cheveley to Mary Hamilton, 23 April 1783, Hamilton Ms.
40. Mrs Cheveley to Mary Hamilton, 26 April 1783, Hamilton Ms.
41. E. Sorell to Mary Hamilton, 4 May 1783, Hamilton Ms.
42. Lady Charlotte Finch to Mary Hamilton, 4 May 1783, Hamilton Ms.
43. Papendiek, *Court and Private Life*, I, p. 270.
44. Mrs Cheveley to Mary Hamilton, 5 May 1783, Hamilton Ms.
45. Miss Planta to Mary Hamilton, 5 May 1783, Hamilton Ms.
46. Aspinall (ed.), *Prince of Wales*, I, p. 108.
47. Mrs Cheveley to Mary Hamilton, 5 May 1783, Hamilton Ms.
48. Queen Charlotte to Lady Pembroke, 9 July 1785, Papers of

the Earls of Pembroke, 2057/F4/47, Wiltshire and Swindon Record Office.

49. Aspinall (ed.), *Prince of Wales*, I, p. 108n.
50. Hibbert, *George III*, p. 99.
51. Aspinall (ed.), *Prince of Wales*, I, p. 108n.
52. Ibid.
53. Ibid., pp. 66–68.
54. Ibid., p. 72.
55. Ibid., p. 60.
56. Ibid., p. 73.
57. Ibid., p. 76.
58. Ibid., p. 79.
59. Ibid., p. 134.
60. Ibid., p. 86.
61. Christopher Hibbert, *George IV: Prince of Wales* (London, 1973), p. 32.
62. Ibid., pp. 34–35.
63. Aspinall (ed.), *George III*, I, p. 77.
64. Aspinall (ed.), *Prince of Wales*, I, p. 138.
65. Hibbert, *George IV: Prince of Wales*, p. 39.
66. Ibid.
67. Ibid., p. 40.
68. Hibbert, *George III*, p. 249.
69. Ibid.
70. Aspinall (ed.), *Prince of Wales*, I, p. 73.
71. Ibid., p. 148.
72. Aspinall (ed.), *George III*, I, p. xxii.
73. Ibid., p. xviii.
74. Ibid., p. 107.
75. Ibid., p. xviii.
76. Aspinall (ed.), *Prince of Wales*, I, p. 153.
77. Aspinall (ed.), *George III*, I, p. 120.
78. Ibid., p. 175.
79. Aspinall (ed.), *Prince of Wales*, I, pp. 220–21.
80. Ibid., p. 330.
81. Steuart (ed.), *Last Journals of Horace Walpole*, II, p. 529.

Chapter 10 – Great Expectations

1. Campbell Orr, 'Scientific Queen', p. 255.
2. Bickley (ed.), *Diaries of Lord Glenbervie*, I, p. 213.
3. Lady Harcourt, *Harcourt Papers*, VI. Note made by Lady Harcourt attached to the voluminous collected correspondence from Princess Elizabeth.
4. Princess Elizabeth to Lord Harcourt, 4 December 1796, *Harcourt Papers*, VI.
5. George III to Lord Harcourt, 30 March and 1 April 1796, *Harcourt Papers*, VI.
6. Harcourt, 'Memoirs of the Years 1788 and 1789', p. 78.
7. Queen Charlotte to Lord Harcourt, 17 December 1786, *Harcourt Papers*, VI.
8. Queen Charlotte to Lady Harcourt, 27 September 1795, *Harcourt Papers*, VI.
9. Queen Charlotte to Lady Harcourt, 5 April 1789, *Harcourt Papers*, VI.
10. Queen Charlotte to Lord Harcourt, 9 June 1793, *Harcourt Papers*, VI.
11. Queen Charlotte to Lady Harcourt, 15 September 1784, *Harcourt Papers*, VI.
12. Princess Augusta to Lady Harcourt, September 1785, *Harcourt Papers*, VI.
13. Princess Augusta to Lady Harcourt, September 1785, *Harcourt Papers*, VI.
14. Queen Charlotte to Lady Harcourt, 19 September 1785, Harcourt Ms.
15. Mrs Cheveley to Mary Hamilton, 7 June 1781, Hamilton Ms.
16. Hester Davenport, *Faithful Handmaid; Fanny Burney at the Court of King George III* (London, 2000), p. 17.

17. D'Arblay, *Diary and Letters*, II, p. 10.
18. Delany, *Autobiography and Correspondence*, III, pp. 286–87.
19. Ibid., p. 308.
20. Aspinall (ed.), *Prince of Wales*, II, p. 446.
21. D'Arblay, *Diary and Letters*, II, p. 66.
22. Ibid., p. 28.
23. Ibid., p. 42.
24. Ibid., p. 297.
25. Ibid., p. 63.
26. Ibid.
27. Ibid., p. 76.
28. Ibid., p. 87.
29. Ibid., pp. 196–97.
30. Ibid., p. 366.
31. Ibid., p. 90.
32. Ibid., p. 91.
33. Ibid., p. 186.
34. Ibid., p. 372.
35. Ibid., p. 205.
36. Ibid., p. 42.
37. Ibid., p. 196.
38. Ibid., p. 258.
39. Ibid., p. 49.
40. Ibid., p. 48.
41. Ibid., p. 248
42. Ibid., p. 90.
43. Ibid., p. 164.
44. Ibid., p. 299.
45. Ibid., p. 231.
46. Ibid., p. 212.
47. Ibid., p. 65.
48. Ibid., p. 98.
49. Ibid., p. 99.
50. Ibid., p. 92.
51. Ibid., p. 235.
52. Ibid., p. 227
53. Ibid., pp. 193–94.
54. Ibid., p. 277.
55. Ibid., p. 94.
56. Ibid., p. 91.
57. Oliver Millar, *The Later Georgian Pictures in the Collection of Her Majesty the Queen* (2 vols, London, 1969), p. 36.
58. Princess Elizabeth to Lady Harcourt, 3 October 1792, *Harcourt Papers*, VI.
59. Delany, *Autobiography and Correspondence*, III, p. 317.
60. Aspinall (ed.), *Prince of Wales*, III, p. 106.
61. Princess Elizabeth to Lord Harcourt, 12 November 1797, *Harcourt Papers*, VI.
62. Philip Yorke (ed.), *Letters of Princess Elizabeth of England* (London, 1898), p. 143.
63. Princess Elizabeth to Lady Harcourt, 5 July 1794, *Harcourt Papers*, VI.
64. Harcourt, *Court of King George*, p. 49.
65. D'Arblay, *Diary and Letters*, III, p. 186.
66. Stuart, *Daughters of George III*, p. 73.
67. D'Arblay, *Diary and Letters*, II, p. 342.
68. Princess Augusta to Lord Harcourt, 5 November 1802, *Harcourt Papes*, VI.
69. Aspinall (ed.), *George III*, I, pp. xi, xin.
70. E. P. Thompson, *The Making of the English Working Class* (London, 1963), pp. 173–74.
71. D'Arblay, *Diary and Letters*, IV, pp. 60–61.
72. Aspinall (ed.), *George III*, I, p. xiv.
73. Stuart, *Daughters of George III*, p. 81.
74. Aspinall (ed.), *George III*, I, p. 274n.
75. D'Arblay, *Diary and Letters*, IV, p. 38.
76. Harcourt, *Court of King George*, p. 35.
77. Susan Buchan, *Lady Louisa Stuart* (London, 1932), p. 196.
78. Ibid.; Aspinall (ed.), *George III*, I, p. xiv.
79. Papendiek, *Court and Private Life*, I, p. 229.
80. Ibid., p. 229.

81. Stuart, *Daughters of George III*, p. 28.
82. Aspinall (ed.), *Prince of Wales*, I, p. 349n.
83. Delany, *Autobiography and Correspondence*, III, p. 386.
84. Fraser, *Princesses*, p. 99.
85. Ibid., pp. 96–97.
86. D'Arblay, *Diary and Letters*, II, p. 41.
87. Ibid., III, p. 242.
88. Davenport, *Faithful Handmaid*, p. 69.
89. Walpole, *Memoirs of the Reign of King George III*, ed. Jarrett, IV, pp. 272, 272n.
90. John Brooke, *King George III* (London, 1972), p. 434.
91. Ibid., p. 439.
92. Home (ed.), *Coke*, I, p. 94.
93. Walpole, *Memoirs of the Reign of King George III*, ed. Jarrett, IV, pp. 103–04.
94. Ibid., p. 176.
95. Steuart (ed.), *Last Journals of Horace Walpole*, II, p. 132.
96. Home (ed.), *Coke*, I, p. xcvii.
97. Brooke, *King George III*, pp. 446–47.
98. Aspinall (ed.), *Prince of Wales*, II, p. 339n.
99. Harcourt, *Court of King George*, p. 39.
100. Malmesbury (ed.), *Diaries and Correspondence*, III, p. 154.
101. Queen Charlotte to Prince Charles, 1 July 1783, Landeshauptarchiv Schwerin.
102. Fraser, *Princesses*, p. 79.
103. Malmesbury (ed.), *Diaries and Correspondence*, III, p. 160.
104. Harcourt, *Court of King George*, p. 40.
105. Ibid., p. 54.
106. Ibid., p. 40.
107. Ibid., p. 38.
108. Charlotte, Queen of Würtemberg to Lady Harcourt, 14 March 1823, Harcourt Ms.
109. William S. Childe-Pemberton, *The Romance of Princess Amelia* (New York, 1911), p. 23.
110. Greig (ed.), *Diaries of a Duchess*, p. 63.
111. Home (ed.), *Coke*, I, p. 33.
112. Tillyard, *Royal Affair*, p. 269.
113. Hibbert, *George III*, p. 175.
114. Brooke, *King George III*, p. 430.
115. Ibid., p. 426.
116. Queen Charlotte to Prince Charles, 20 July 1776, Landeshauptarchiv Schwerin.
117. Flora Fraser, *The Unruly Queen: The Life of Queen Caroline* (London, 1996), p. 15.
118. Delany, *Autobiography and Correspondence*, I, p. 188.
119. Harcourt, *Court of King George*, p. 55.
120. Queen Charlotte to Lady Harcourt, 2 September 1798, Harcourt Ms.
121. Harcourt, 'Memoirs of the Years 1788 and 1789', p. 20

Chapter 11 – An Intellectual Malady

1. D'Arblay, *Diary and Letters*, II, p. 593.
2. Ibid., III, p. 171.
3. Aspinall (ed.), *George III*, I, p. 378n.
4. Ibid.
5. Ida Macalpine and Richard Hunter, *George III and the Mad-Business* (London, 1969), p. 6.
6. D'Arblay, *Diary and Letters*, II, p. 557.
7. Ibid.
8. Ibid, p. 559.
9. Macalpine and Hunter, *George III*, p. 7.
10. Hibbert, *George III*, p. 256.
11. Macalpine and Hunter, *George III*, p. 11.
12. William Auckland, *Journal and Correspondence* (2 vols, London, 1861), II, p. 226.

13. Hibbert, *George III*, p. 255.
14. Harcourt, 'Memoirs of the Years 1788 and 1789', p. 9.
15. D'Arblay, *Diary and Letters*, III, pp. 25–26.
16. Aspinall (ed.), *George III*, I, p. 390.
17. Harcourt, 'Memoirs of the Years 1788 and 1789', p. 10.
18. Ibid., p. 11.
19. Sir Gilbert Elliot, *Life and Letters of Sir Gilbert Elliot, 1st Earl of Minto, 1751 to 1806* (3 vols, London, 1874), I, p. 228.
20. Macalpine and Hunter, *George III*, pp. 14–15.
21. D'Arblay, *Diary and Letters*, III, p. 49.
22. Aspinall (ed.), *George III*, I, p. 396.
23. Harcourt, 'Memoirs of the Years 1788 and 1789', p. 12.
24. Macalpine and Hunter, *George III*, pp. 16–17.
25. Aspinall (ed.), *George III*, I, p. 397.
26. Harcourt, 'Memoirs of the Years 1788 and 1789', p. 14.
27. Macalpine and Hunter, *George III*, p. 17.
28. F. McKno Bladon (ed.), *The Diaries of Robert Fulke Greville* (London, 1930), p. 79.
29. D'Arblay, *Diary and Letters*, III, p. 50.
30. Ibid.
31. Harcourt, 'Memoirs of the Years 1788 and 1789', p. 14.
32. Ibid., p. 15.
33. Ibid.
34. Ibid., p. 16.
35. Macalpine and Hunter, *George III*, p. 19.
36. Ibid., p. 20.
37. Harcourt, 'Memoirs of the Years 1788 and 1789', p. 17.
38. Macalpine and Hunter, *George III*, p. 21.
39. Harcourt, 'Memoirs of the Years 1788 and 1789', p. 18.
40. Hedley, *Queen Charlotte*, p. 142.
41. D'Arblay, *Diary and Letters*, III, pp. 52–53.
42. Harcourt, 'Memoirs of the Years 1788 and 1789', p. 20.
43. Ibid., p. 21
44. D'Arblay, *Diary and Letters*, III, p. 54.
45. Harcourt, 'Memoirs of the Years 1788 and 1789', p. 21.
46. D'Arblay, *Diary and Letters*, III, p. 56.
47. Ibid., pp. 57–58.
48. Harcourt, 'Memoirs of the Years 1788 and 1789', p. 22.
49. D'Arblay, *Diary and Letters*, III, p. 59.
50. Harcourt, 'Memoirs of the Years 1788 and 1789', pp. 23–24.
51. D'Arblay, *Diary and Letters*, III, pp. 60–61.
52. Harcourt, 'Memoirs of the Years 1788 and 1789', p. 25.
53. D'Arblay, *Diary and Letters*, III, p. 62.
54. Ibid.
55. Ibid., p. 63.
56. Ibid., p. 65.
57. Bland Burges letters, ff. 80, 87, quoted in Timothy J. Peters and Allan Beveridge, 'The Madness of King George III: A Psychiatric Reassessment', *History of Psychiatry* 21 (1)(2010), p. 24.
58. Harcourt, 'Memoirs of the Years 1788 and 1789', p. 25.
59. Ibid., p. 26.
60. D'Arblay, *Diary and Letters*, III, p. 66.
61. Ibid.
62. Harcourt, 'Memoirs of the Years 1788 and 1789', p. 28.
63. D'Arblay, *Diary and Letters*, III, p. 67.
64. Elliot, *Life and Letters*, I, p. 233.
65. Harcourt, 'Memoirs of the Years 1788 and 1789', p. 29.
66. Macalpine and Hunter, *George III*, p. 28.

67. Ibid., p. 30.
68. Ibid., p. 31.
69. Elliot, *Life and Letters*, I, p. 230.
70. D'Arblay, *Diary and Letters*, III, p. 79.
71. Elliot, *Life and Letters*, I, p. 233.
72. Macalpine and Hunter, *George III*, p. 30.
73. Ibid., p. 4.
74. Timothy J. Peters and D. Wilkinson, 'King George III and Porphyria: A Clinical Re-examination of the Historical Evidence', *History of Psychiatry* 21 (1)(2010), pp. 3–19.
75. Peters and Beveridge, 'The Madness of King George III', p. 20.
76. Ibid., p. 31.
77. D'Arblay, *Diary and Letters*, III, p. 77.
78. McKno Bladon (ed.), *Diaries of Robert Fulke Greville*, p. 81.
79. Ibid., p. 82.
80. Ibid., p. 83.
81. Ibid., p. 84.
82. D'Arblay, *Diary and Letters*, III, p. 87.
83. McKno Bladon (ed.), *Diaries of Robert Fulke Greville*, p. 86.
84. Ibid.
85. Harcourt, 'Memoirs of the Years 1788 and 1789', p. 54.
86. McKno Bladon (ed.), *Diaries of Robert Fulke Greville*, p. 89.
87. Ibid., p. 87.
88. Ibid., p. 88.
89. Ibid., p. 90.
90. Ibid., p. 96.
91. Ibid., p. 92.
92. Auckland, *Journal and Correspondence*, II, p. 244.
93. Ibid., p. 242.
94. McKno Bladon (ed.), *Diaries of Robert Fulke Greville*, p. 101.
95. Ibid., p. 94.
96. Macalpine and Hunter, *George III*, p. 42.
97. McKno Bladon (ed.), *Diaries of Robert Fulke Greville*, p. 102.
98. Ibid., p. 93.
99. Letter from Mrs Harcourt to Lady Harcourt in Harcourt, 'Memoirs of the Years 1788 and 1789', pp. 58–59.
100. Ibid., p. 60.
101. D'Arblay, *Diary and Letters*, III, p. 98.
102. Ibid., p. 96.
103. Letter from General Harcourt in Harcourt, *Court of King George*, p. 61.
104. McKno Bladon (ed.), *Diaries of Robert Fulke Greville*, p. 104.
105. Elliot, *Life and Letters*, I, p. 239.
106. Letter from Mrs Harcourt in Harcourt, 'Memoirs of the Years 1788 and 1789', pp. 62–63.
107. D'Arblay, *Diary and Letters*, III, p. 100.
108. Ibid., p. 102.
109. Letter from Mrs Harcourt in Harcourt, 'Memoirs of the Years 1788 and 1789', p. 61.
110. Ibid., p. 75.
111. D'Arblay, *Diary and Letters*, III, p. 105.
112. Ibid., p. 106.
113. McKno Bladon (ed.), *Diaries of Robert Fulke Greville*, p. 107.
114. Ibid., p. 109
115. Ibid., pp. 110–11.
116. Ibid., p. 112.
117. Ibid., p. 113.
118. Ibid., p. 114.
119. Ibid., p. 117.
120. D'Arblay, *Diary and Letters*, III, p. 111.
121. Ibid., p. 114.
122. Ibid., p. 112.
123. Auckland, *Journal and Correspondence*, II, p. 256.
124. D'Arblay, *Diary and Letters*, III, p. 118.
125. McKno Bladon (ed.), *Diaries of Robert Fulke Greville*, pp. 118–19.

126. Macalpine and Hunter, *George III*, p. 53.
127. Ibid.
128. Harcourt, 'Memoirs of the Years 1788 and 1789', p. 172.
129. McKno Bladon (ed.), *Diaries of Robert Fulke Greville*, pp. 120–21.
130. Macalpine and Hunter, *George III*, p. 57.
131. D'Arblay, *Diary and Letters*, III, p. 112.
132. Macalpine and Hunter, *George III*, p. 32.
133. Hedley, *Queen Charlotte*, p. 152.
134. Macalpine and Hunter, *George III*, pp. 54–55.
135. Ibid., p. 34.
136. Auckland, *Journal and Correspondence*, II, p. 245.
137. Elliot, *Life and Letters*, I, p. 252.
138. McKno Bladon (ed.), *Diaries of Robert Fulke Greville*, p. 149.
139. Harcourt, 'Memoirs of the Years 1788 and 1789', p. 123.
140. Ibid., p. 127.
141. Elliot, *Life and Letters*, I, p. 259.
142. Harcourt, 'Memoirs of the Years 1788 and 1789', p. 129.
143. Hedley, *Queen Charlotte*, p. 166.
144. Harcourt, 'Memoirs of the Years 1788 and 1789', p. 123.
145. Macalpine and Hunter, *George III*, p. 73.
146. McKno Bladon (ed.), *Diaries of Robert Fulke Greville*, p. 146.
147. Ibid., pp. 126, 146.
148. Ibid., p.127.
149. Macalpine and Hunter, *George III*, p. 65.
150. McKno Bladon (ed.), *Diaries of Robert Fulke Greville*, p. 129.
151. Ibid., p.133.
152. Ibid., p.138.
153. Ibid., p. 134
154. Harcourt, 'Memoirs of the Years 1788 and 1789', p. 74.
155. Hedley, *Queen Charlotte*, p. 162.
156. Elliot, *Life and Letters*, I, p. 246.
157. Harcourt, 'Memoirs of the Years 1788 and 1789', p. 74.
158. McKno Bladon (ed.), *Diaries of Robert Fulke Greville*, p. 139.
159. Ibid., p.142.
160. Ibid., p. 161.
161. Ibid., p. 165.
162. Ibid., p. 162.
163. Ibid., p. 169.
164. Ibid., pp. 170–71.
165. D'Arblay, *Diary and Letters*, III, p. 129.
166. Harcourt, 'Memoirs of the Years 1788 and 1789', p. 175.
167. D'Arblay, *Diary and Letters*, III, p. 137.
168. McKno Bladon (ed.), *Diaries of Robert Fulke Greville*, p. 175.
169. Ibid., pp. 187, 189, 191, 199.
170. Harcourt, 'Memoirs of the Years 1788 and 1789', p. 203.
171. Ibid., p. 196.
172. McKno Bladon (ed.), *Diaries of Robert Fulke Greville*, p. 201.
173. D'Arblay, *Diary and Letters*, III, pp. 152–55.
174. McKno Bladon (ed.), *Diaries of Robert Fulke Greville*, p. 205.
175. Ibid., p. 206.
176. Harcourt, 'Memoirs of the Years 1788 and 1789', p. 221.
177. McKno Bladon (ed.), *Diaries of Robert Fulke Greville*, p. 209.
178. Ibid., p. 213.
179. Ibid., p. 219.
180. Harcourt, 'Memoirs of the Years 1788 and 1789', p. 244.
181. Macalpine and Hunter, *George III*, pp. 83–84.
182. Harcourt, *Court of King George*, p. 7.
183. Macalpine and Hunter, *George III*, p. 86.
184. McKno Bladon (ed.), *Diaries of Robert Fulke Greville*, p. 237.
185. Harcourt (ed.), *Diaries and Correspondence of the Rt Hon. George Rose*, I, p. 97.

186. Harcourt, *Court of King George*, p. 4.
187. Elliot, *Life and Letters*, I, p. 274.
188. Harcourt, *Court of King George*, pp. 11–12.
189. Macalpine and Hunter, *George III*, p. 92.
190. McKno Bladon (ed.), *Diaries of Robert Fulke Greville*, p. 244.
191. Harcourt, *Court of King George*, pp. 12–13.
192. Macalpine and Hunter, *George III*, p. 85.
193. Hibbert, *George IV: Prince of Wales*, p. 78.
194. Hibbert, *George III*, p. 270.
195. Ibid., p. 271.
196. Jesse, *Life and Reign of George III*, III, p. 78.
197. Aspinall (ed.), *Prince of Wales*, I, p. 405.
198. Elliot, *Life and Letters*, I, p. 274.
199. Ibid., p. 287.
200. Ibid., p. 289.
201. Harcourt, *Court of King George*, p. 47.
202. Ibid., p. 10.
203. Papendiek, *Court and Private Life*, II, p. 133.
204. Ibid., p. 134.
205. Harcourt, *Court of King George*, p. 8.
206. Elliot, *Life and Letters*, I, p. 299.
207. Aspinall (ed.), *George III*, I, p. 405.
208. D'Arblay, *Diary and Letters*, III, p. 158.
209. Aspinall (ed.), *George III*, I, p. 403.
210. Elliot, *Life and Letters*, I, p. 286.
211. McKno Bladon (ed.), *Diaries of Robert Fulke Greville*, p. 254.

Chapter 12 – Three Weddings

1. D'Arblay, *Diary and Letters*, III, p. 187.
2. Ibid., p. 189.
3. Ibid., p. 191.
4. Ibid., p. 192.
5. Ibid., p. 194.
6. Ibid.
7. Harcourt, *Court of King George*, p. 32.
8. Black, *George III*, p. 138.
9. Stanley Ayling, *George III* (London, 1972), p. 207.
10. McKno Bladon (ed.), *Diaries of Robert Fulke Greville*, p. 298.
11. Eric Gillett (ed.), *Elizabeth Ham, by Herself, 1783–1820* (London, 1945), p. 35.
12. Ibid., p. 36.
13. McKno Bladon (ed.), *Diaries of Robert Fulke Greville*, p. 346.
14. D'Arblay, *Diary and Letters*, III, p. 196.
15. Ibid., p. 197.
16. Gillett (ed.), *Elizabeth Ham*, p. 45.
17. Aspinall (ed.), *Prince of Wales*, II, p. 202n.
18. McKno Bladon (ed.), *Diaries of Robert Fulke Greville*, p. 332.
19. Ibid., p. 291.
20. Aspinall (ed.), *Prince of Wales*, II, p. 202n.
21. McKno Bladon (ed.), *Diaries of Robert Fulke Greville*, p. 304–05.
22. Queen Charlotte to Lady Harcourt, 25 July 1800, Harcourt Ms.
23. Aspinall (ed.), *Prince of Wales*, III, p. 464.
24. Ibid., p. 456.
25. Hedley, *Queen Charlotte*, p. 181.
26. Ibid., p. 180.
27. Aspinall (ed.), *Prince of Wales*, II, p. 178n.
28. Ibid.
29. D'Arblay, *Diary and Letters*, III, p. 567.
30. Aspinall (ed.), *Prince of Wales*, II, p. 178n.
31. D'Arblay, *Diary and Letters*, III, p. 197.
32. Queen Charlotte to Prince Charles, 23 December 1789, Landeshauptarchiv Schwerin.

33. Harcourt, *Court of King George*, pp. 33–34.
34. Queen Charlotte to Prince Charles, 23 December 1789, Landeshauptarchiv Schwerin.
35. Brooke, *King George III*, p. 543.
36. D'Arblay, *Diary and Letters*, III, pp. 418–19.
37. Aspinall (ed.), *Prince of Wales*, II, p. 276.
38. Auckland, *Journal and Correspondence*, II, p. 211.
39. D'Arblay, *Diary and Letters*, II, pp. 101–02.
40. Black, *George III*, p. 186.
41. Ibid., p. 357.
42. Brooke, *King George III*, p. 499.
43. D'Arblay, *Diary and Letters*, II, pp. 102–03.
44. Queen Charlotte to Lady Harcourt, 8 July 1795, Harcourt Ms.
45. Aspinall (ed.), *Prince of Wales*, III, p. 79.
46. Queen Charlotte to Lady Harcourt, 8 July 1795, Harcourt Ms.
47. Black, *George III*, p. 360.
48. Kenneth Baker, *George III: A Life in Caricature* (London, 2007), p. 130.
49. Princess Elizabeth to Lady Harcourt, no date, Harcourt Ms.
50. Princess Elizabeth to Lady Harcourt, 2 November 1795, Harcourt Ms.
51. Ibid.
52. Princess Elizabeth to Lady Harcourt, 25 July 1794, Harcourt Ms.
53. Papendiek, *Court and Private Life*, II, p. 217.
54. Aspinall (ed.), *Prince of Wales*, II, p. 467.
55. Papers of James Bland Burges, Letter 132, 2 December 1794, Dep 10, Bodleian Library, University of Oxford.
56. Ibid.
57. Aspinall (ed.), *Prince of Wales*, II, p. 162.
58. Ibid., p. 163.
59. Ibid., p. 170.
60. Ibid., p. 168.
61. Ibid., p. xxxviii.
62. Ibid., p. 339n.
63. Roger Fulford, *Royal Dukes* (London, 1933), p. 256.
64. Aspinall (ed.), *Prince of Wales*, II, p. 410.
65. Aspinall (ed.), *George III*, II, p. 150.
66. Aspinall (ed.), *Prince of Wales*, II, p. 471n.
67. Aspinall (ed.), *George III*, II, p. 423.
68. Aspinall (ed.), *Prince of Wales*, II, p. 489.
69. Burges Papers, Letter 132, 2 December 1794.
70. Aspinall (ed.), *Prince of Wales*, II, p. 354.
71. Ibid., p. 174.
72. Parissien, *George IV*, p. 63.
73. Hibbert, *George IV: Prince of Wales*, p. 50.
74. Ibid., p. 51.
75. Ibid., p. 50.
76. Ibid., p. 56.
77. Egerton Castle (ed.), *The Jerningham Letters* (2 vols, London, 1896), I, p. 33.
78. Parissien, *George IV*, p. 66.
79. Hibbert, *George IV: Prince of Wales*, p. 52.
80. Ibid., p. 68.
81. Parissien, *George IV*, p. 70.
82. Fraser, *Unruly Queen*, p. 41.
83. Aspinall (ed.), *Prince of Wales*, II, pp. 443, 453.
84. Parissien, *George IV*, p. 74.
85. Aspinall (ed.), *Prince of Wales*, II, pp. 174–75.
86. Ibid., III, p. 9.
87. Ibid., II, p. 452.
88. Ibid., p. 465
89. Ibid., p. 469.

90. Malmesbury (ed.), *Diaries and Correspondence*, III, p. 153.
91. Ibid., p. 165.
92. Ibid., p. 166.
93. Ibid., p. 170.
94. Ibid., p. 179.
95. Ibid., p. 166.
96. Ibid., p. 167.
97. Ibid., p. 165.
98. Ibid., p. 166.
99. Ibid., p. 167.
100. Ibid., p. 177.
101. Ibid., p. 168.
102. Ibid., p. 167.
103. Ibid., p. 196.
104. Ibid., p. 216.
105. Ibid., p. 211.
106. Aspinall (ed.), *Prince of Wales*, II, p. 490.
107. Ibid., III, p. 53.
108. Malmesbury (ed.), *Diaries and Correspondence*, III, p. 218.
109. Ibid., p. 219.
110. Hibbert, *George IV: Prince of Wales*, p. 147.
111. Parissien, *George IV*, p. 76.
112. Ibid., p. 77.
113. Aspinall (ed.), *Prince of Wales*, III, p. 123.
114. Ibid., p. 72.
115. Queen Charlotte to Lady Harcourt, 29 August 1795, Harcourt Ms.
116. Aspinall (ed.), *George III*, II, p. 451.
117. Aspinall (ed.), *Prince of Wales*, III, p. 194.
118. Bickley (ed.), *Diaries of Lord Glenbervie*, I, p. 60.
119. Ibid., p. 71.
120. Lady Charlotte Bury, *The Diary of a Lady in Waiting*, ed. Francis Steuart (2 vols, London, 1908), I, p. 19.
121. Ibid., p. 23.
122. Aspinall (ed.), *Prince of Wales*, III, p. 198.
123. Castle (ed.), *Jerningham Letters*, I, p. 75.
124. Parissien, *George IV*, p. 73.
125. Fraser, *Unruly Queen*, p. 48.
126. Queen Charlotte to Lady Harcourt, 23 May 1796, *Harcourt Papers*, VI.
127. Aspinall (ed.), *Prince of Wales*, III, p. 243.
128. Aspinall (ed.), *George III*, II, p. 535.
129. Aspinall (ed.), *Prince of Wales*, III, p. 128.
130. Ibid., p. 149.
131. Ibid., p. 131.
132. Mrs Harcourt, 'Anecdotes Relating to the Years 1792–1795', *Harcourt Papers*, V, p. 620.
133. Aspinall (ed.), *Prince of Wales*, III, p. 119.
134. Aspinall (ed.), *George III*, II, p. xxxi.
135. Ibid., p. xxxii.
136. Ibid.
137. Sir John Hippesley to Lady Harcourt, no date, *Harcourt Papers*, VI.
138. Ibid.
139. D'Arblay, *Diary and Letters*, IV, p. 36.
140. Aspinall (ed.), *George III*, II, pp. xxxi, xxxin.
141. D'Arblay, *Diary and Letters*, III, p. 580.
142. Ibid., IV, p. 35.
143. Aspinall (ed.), *Prince of Wales*, III, p. 346.
144. Fraser, *Princesses*, p. 163.
145. Aspinall (ed.), *George III*, II, p. 591.
146. Ibid., p. 597.
147. Fraser, *Princesses*, p. 162.
148. Aspinall (ed.), *George III*, II, pp. 588–89.
149. Stuart, *Daughters of George III*, p. 33.
150. Princess Royal to Lady Harcourt, 14 March 1823, Harcourt Ms.
151. Aspinall (ed.), *George III*, II, p. 596.

152. Ibid., III, p. 30.
153. Aspinall (ed.), *Prince of Wales*, III, p. 421.
154. Stuart, *Daughters of George III*, p. 36.
155. Aspinall (ed.), *George III*, III, pp. 57–58.
156. Ibid., p. 58.
157. Aspinall (ed.), *Prince of Wales*, III, p. 435.
158. Stuart, *Daughters of George III*, p. 27.
159. Aspinall (ed.), *George III*, III, p. 66.
160. Aspinall (ed.), *Prince of Wales*, III, p. 266.

Chapter 13 – The Wrong Lovers

1. Papendiek, *Court and Private Life*, II, p. 216.
2. Ibid., p. 283.
3. Bickley (ed.), *Diaries of Lord Glenbervie*, II, p. 325.
4. Stuart, *Daughters of George III*, p. 213.
5. Aspinall (ed.), *Prince of Wales*, IV, p. 304.
6. Lloyd, 'King, Queen and Family', p. 66.
7. Aspinall (ed.), *Prince of Wales*, III, p. 479.
8. Ibid., p. 480.
9. Ibid., p. 478.
10. Ibid., IV, p. 41.
11. Childe-Pemberton, *Romance of Princess Amelia*, p. 157.
12. Stuart, *Daughters of George III*, p. 208.
13. A. Aspinall (ed.), *Letters of the Princess Charlotte* (London, 1949), p. 33.
14. Aspinall (ed.), *Prince of Wales*, VI, p. 390.
15. Lloyd, 'King, Queen and Family', p. 66.
16. D'Arblay, *Diary and Letters*, IV, pp. 56–57.
17. Ibid., p. 66.
18. Ibid., pp. 90–91.
19. Aspinall (ed.), *Prince of Wales*, III, p. 458.
20. Ibid., p. 460.
21. Ibid., p. 468.
22. Ibid., p. 476.
23. Ibid., IV, p. 36.
24. Ibid., pp. 92, 102.
25. Ibid., p. 548.
26. Ibid., p. 549.
27. Ibid., p. 227.
28. Ibid., p. 103.
29. Childe-Pemberton, *Romance of Princess Amelia*, p. 146.
30. John Wardroper, *Wicked Ernest* (London, 2002), p. 22.
31. Ibid.
32. Iremonger, *Love and the Princesses*, p. 184.
33. Aspinall (ed.), *Prince of Wales*, II, p. 388.
34. Wardroper, *Wicked Ernest*, p. 22; Princess Sophia to Lady Harcourt, 24 August 1794, *Harcourt Papers*, VI.
35. Wardroper, *Wicked Ernest*, p. 21.
36. Queen Charlotte to Lady Harcourt, 2 August 1800, Harcourt Ms.
37. Bickley (ed.), *Diaries of Lord Glenbervie*, I, p. 203.
38. Fraser, *Princesses*, p. 189.
39. Gillett (ed.), *Elizabeth Ham*, p. 47.
40. Ibid., pp. 47–48.
41. Bickley (ed.), *Diaries of Lord Glenbervie*, I, p. 363.
42. George Thomas Landmann, *Adventures and Recollections of Colonel Landmann* (2 vols, London, 1852), II, p. 321.
43. Gillett (ed.), *Elizabeth Ham*, p. 48.
44. Iremonger, *Love and the Princesses*, p. 202.
45. Aspinall (ed.), *Letters of the Princess Charlotte*, p. 151.
46. Glenbervie Diary, 11 October 1811, National Library of Scotland, Acc 10505.

47. Ibid.
48. Charles Greville, *The Greville Diaries*, quoted in Iremonger, *Love and the Princesses*, p. 204.
49. Charles Greville, quoted in Wardroper, *Wicked Ernest*, p. 19.
50. Aspinall (ed.), *Prince of Wales*, III, p. 464.
51. Fraser, *Princesses*, p. 192.
52. Iremonger, *Love and the Princesses*, p. 199.
53. Bickley (ed.), *Diaries of Lord Glenbervie*, II, pp. 94–95.
54. Glenbervie Diary, 11 October 1811.
55. Queen Charlotte to Lady Harcourt, no date (between July 1800 and October 1801), Harcourt Ms.
56. Bickley (ed.), *Diaries of Lord Glenbervie*, I, p. 364.
57. Iremonger, *Love and the Princesses*, p. 201.
58. Princess Sophia to Lady Harcourt, 30 December 1800, *Harcourt Papers*, VI.
59. Fraser, *Princesses*, p. 216.
60. Ibid.
61. Wardroper, *Wicked Ernest*, p. 85.
62. Ibid., p. 85.
63. Bickley (ed.), *Diaries of Lord Glenbervie*, II, pp. 75–76.
64. Ibid., p. 95.
65. Ibid., I, p. 363.
66. Glenbervie Diary, 11 October 1811.
67. Gillett (ed.), *Elizabeth Ham*, p. 48.
68. Aspinall (ed.), *Prince of Wales*, III, p. 154.
69. Harcourt, 'Anecdotes', *Harcourt Papers*, V, p. 414.
70. D'Arblay, *Diary and Letters*, IV, p. 46.
71. Princess Sophia to Lady Harcourt, 24 August 1794, *Harcourt Papers*, VI.
72. Aspinall (ed.), *Prince of Wales*, V, p. 484.
73. Aspinall (ed.), *Letters of Princess Charlotte*, p. 16.
74. Thompson, *English Working Class*, p. 155.
75. Black, *George III*, p. 366.
76. Malmesbury (ed.), *Diaries and Correspondence*, IV, p. 27.
77. Ibid., pp. 14, 10.
78. Bickley (ed.), *Diaries of Lord Glenbervie*, I, pp. 173, 185.
79. Malmesbury (ed.), *Diaries and Correspondence*, IV, p. 14.
80. Ibid., p. 14.
81. Bickley (ed.), *Diaries of Lord Glenbervie*, I, p. 217.
82. Malmesbury (ed.), *Diaries and Correspondence*, IV, p. 18.
83. Bickley (ed.), *Diaries of Lord Glenbervie*, I, p. 187.
84. Ibid., p. 352.
85. Malmesbury (ed.), *Diaries and Correspondence*, IV, p. 32.
86. Hedley, *Queen Charlotte*, p. 208.
87. Ibid., p. 209.
88. Ibid.
89. Bickley (ed.), *Diaries of Lord Glenbervie*, I, p. 211.
90. Hedley, *Queen Charlotte*, p. 210.
91. Macalpine and Hunter, *George III*, p. 126.
92. Ibid., p.127.
93. Hedley, *Queen Charlotte*, p. 210.
94. Bickley (ed.), *Diaries of Lord Glenbervie*, I, pp. 224–25.
95. Ibid., p. 225.
96. Wardroper, *Wicked Ernest*, p. 43.
97. Macalpine and Hunter, *George III*, p. 128.
98. Wardroper, *Wicked Ernest*, p. 43.
99. Bickley (ed.), *Diaries of Lord Glenbervie*, I, p. 236.
100. Ibid., p. 231.
101. Ibid., p. 322.
102. Malmesbury (ed.), *Diaries and Correspondence*, IV, p. 286.
103. Aspinall (ed.), *Prince of Wales*, IV, pp. 493–95.
104. Ibid., I, p. 496.

105. Princess Elizabeth to Lady Harcourt, 3 March 1804, Harcourt Ms.
106. Aspinall (ed.), *Prince of Wales*, V, p. 17.
107. Malmesbury (ed.), *Diaries and Correspondence*, IV, p. 319.
108. Aspinall (ed.), *Prince of Wales*, V, p. 70.
109. Ibid., p. 113.
110. Ibid., p. 117.
111. Ibid., p. 17.
112. Ibid., p. 6.
113. Ibid., p. 90.
114. Ibid., pp. 6–7.
115. Ibid., p. 90.
116. Ibid., p. 114.
117. Ibid., p. 126n.
118. Bickley (ed.), *Diaries of Lord Glenbervie*, II, p. 55.
119. Ibid.
120. Ibid., I, p. 378.
121. Hedley, *Queen Charlotte*, p. 216.
122. Aspinall (ed.), *Prince of Wales*, V, p. 29.
123. Fraser, *Princesses*, p. 206.
124. Aspinall (ed.), *Prince of Wales*, V, p. 90.
125. Ibid., p. 114.
126. Ibid.
127. Malmesbury (ed.), *Diaries and Correspondence*, IV, p. 337.
128. Fraser, *Princesses*, p. 210.
129. Ibid., p. 208.
130. Aspinall (ed.), *Prince of Wales*, V, pp. 160–61.
131. Bickley (ed.), *Diaries of Lord Glenbervie*, I, p. 401.
132. Auckland, *Journal and Correspondence*, IV, pp. 212, 213.
133. Queen Charlotte to Lady Harcourt, 6 November 1804, Harcourt Ms.
134. Queen Charlotte to Lady Harcourt, 8 March 1805, Harcourt Ms.
135. Fraser, *Princesses*, p. 209.
136. Hedley, *Queen Charlotte*, p. 223.
137. Ibid.
138. Queen Charlotte to Lady Harcourt, no date, *Harcourt Papers*, VI.
139. Queen Charlotte to Lady Harcourt, 6 December 1808, Harcourt Ms.
140. Queen Charlotte to Lord Harcourt, 5 December 1807, *Harcourt Papers*, VI.
141. Princess Elizabeth to Lady Harcourt, 23 July 1802, Harcourt Ms.
142. Aspinall (ed.), *Prince of Wales*, VI, p. 308 (11 September 1808).
143. Ibid., p. 309.
144. Princess Elizabeth to Lady Harcourt, 20 June 1808, Harcourt Ms.
145. Princess Elizabeth to Lady Harcourt, 18 June 1808, Harcourt Ms.
146. Princess Elizabeth to Lady Harcourt, 17 September 1807, Harcourt Ms.
147. Princess Elizabeth to Lady Harcourt, 20 June 1808, Harcourt Ms.
147. Aspinall (ed.), *Prince of Wales*, VI, p. 265.
149. Princess Elizabeth to Lady Harcourt, 23 July 1802, Harcourt Ms.
150. John Wardroper, *Wicked Ernest*, p. 97.
151. Aspinall (ed.), *Prince of Wales*, V, p. 243.
152. Ibid., VI, p. 323.
153. Ibid., p. 316 (25 September 1808).
154. Ibid.
155. Ibid., p. 323.
156. Ibid.
157. Ibid.
158. Ibid.
159. Bickley (ed.), *Diaries of Lord Glenbervie*, I, p. 397.
160. Ibid.
161. Ibid.

162. Princess Elizabeth to Lady Harcourt, 10 December 1808, Harcourt Ms.
163. Aspinall (ed.), *Prince of Wales*, VII, p. 45.
164. Childe-Pemberton, *Romance of Princess Amelia*, pp. 53–54.
165. Bickley (ed.), *Diaries of Lord Glenbervie*, II, pp. 23–24.
166. Childe-Pemberton, *Romance of Princess Amelia*, pp. 61–62.
167. Ibid., pp. 66–67.
168. Ibid., p. 173.
169. Ibid.
170. Ibid., p. 73.
171. Fraser, *Princesses*, p. 233.
172. Bickley (ed.), *Diaries of Lord Glenbervie*, II, p. 94.
173. Childe-Pemberton, *Romance of Princess Amelia*, p. 142.
174. Fraser, *Princesses*, p. 233.
175. Bickley (ed.), *Diaries of Lord Glenbervie*, II, p. 94.
176. Childe-Pemberton, *Romance of Princess Amelia*, p. 173.
177. Ibid., p. 181.
178. Ibid., pp. 124–25.
179. Ibid., pp. 136–37.
180. Ibid., p. 138.
181. Ibid., pp. 146–47.
182. Ibid., pp. 148–49.
183. Ibid., pp. 177–78.
184. Ibid., p. 174.
185. Ibid., p. 175.
186. Aspinall (ed.), *Prince of Wales*, VI, p. 517.
187. Childe-Pemberton, *Romance of Princess Amelia*, p. 200.
188. Ibid., p. 193.
189. Aspinall (ed.), *Prince of Wales*, VI, p. 412.
190. Aspinall (ed.), *George III*, V, p. 320.
191. Aspinall (ed.), *Prince of Wales*, VI, p. 422.
192. Aspinall (ed.), *George III*, V, p. 354.
193. Aspinall (ed.), *Prince of Wales*, VI, p. 441.
194. Ibid.
195. Ibid., p. 458.
196. Ibid., p. 452.
197. Aspinall (ed.), *George III*, V, p. 393.
198. Ibid., p. 414.
199. Bickley (ed.), *Diaries of Lord Glenbervie*, I, pp. 383–84.
200. Stuart, *Daughters of George III*, pp. 356–57.
201. Aspinall (ed.), *Prince of Wales*, VI, p. 502.
202. Ibid., p. 516.
203. Aspinall (ed.), *George III*, V, p. 592.
204. Aspinall (ed.), *Prince of Wales*, VII, p. 48.
205. Aspinall (ed.) *George III*, V, p. 607.
206. Halford Papers, DG 24/822/4, Leicester Record Office.
207. Ibid.
208. Ibid.
209. Childe-Pemberton, *Romance of Princess Amelia*, p. 222.
210. Aspinall (ed.), *Prince of Wales*, VII, p. 56.
211. Childe-Pemberton, *Romance of Princess Amelia*, p. 225.
212. Ibid., p. 233.
213. Ibid., pp. 228–29.
214. Hedley, *Queen Charlotte*, p. 242.
215. Childe-Pemberton, *Romance of Princess Amelia*, p. 227.
216. Ibid., p. 260n.
217. Ibid., p. 249.

Chapter 14 – Established

1. Hibbert, *George III*, p. 391.
2. Ibid., pp. 390–91.
3. Cornelia Knight, *Autobiography of Miss Cornelia Knight* (2 vols, London, 1861), I, pp. 174–75.
4. Aspinall (ed.), *Prince of Wales*, VII, p. 67n.
5. Princess Elizabeth to Lady Harcourt, 9 November 1810, *Harcourt Papers*, VI.

6. Macalpine and Hunter, *George III*, p. 144.
7. Aspinall (ed.), *Prince of Wales*, VII, p. 67n.
8. Macalpine and Hunter, *George III*, p. 146.
9. Princess Mary to Lady Harcourt, 2 December 1810, *Harcourt Papers*, VI.
10. Queen Charlotte to Lady Harcourt, December 1810, *Harcourt Papers*, VI.
11. Macalpine and Hunter, *George III*, p. 154.
12. Aspinall (ed.), *Prince of Wales*, VII, p. 219.
13. Ibid., VIII, p. 386.
14. Macalpine and Hunter, *George III*, p. 155.
15. Ibid., p. 157.
16. Ibid., pp. 157–58.
17. Ibid., p. 159.
18. Aspinall (ed.), *Prince of Wales*, VIII, p. 68.
19. Childe-Pemberton, *Romance of Princess Amelia*, p. 281.
20. Ibid., p. 282.
21. Macalpine and Hunter, *George III*, pp. 160–61.
22. Ibid., p. 162.
23. Aspinall (ed.), *Prince of Wales*, VIII, p. 68n.
24. Hedley, *Queen Charlotte*, p. 252.
25. Princess Elizabeth to Lady Harcourt, 16 November 1811, *Harcourt Papers*, VI.
26. Aspinall (ed.), *Prince of Wales*, VII, p. 223.
27. Queen Charlotte to Lady Harcourt, December 1810, *Harcourt Papers*, VI.
28. Queen Charlotte to Lady Harcourt, 10 July 1812, Harcourt Ms.
29. Hedley, *Queen Charlotte*, p. 251.
30. Stuart, *Daughters of George III*, p. 215.
31. Hedley, *Queen Charlotte*, p. 251.
32. Stuart, *Daughters of George III*, pp. 215–16.
33. Queen Charlotte to Lady Harcourt, 10 July 1812, Harcourt Ms.
34. Aspinall (ed.), *Prince of Wales*, VIII, p. 296.
35. Ibid., p. 299.
36. Stuart, *Daughters of George III*, p. 217.
37. Aspinall (ed.), *Prince of Wales*, VIII, p. 252.
38. Ibid., p. 349.
39. Princess Elizabeth to Lady Harcourt, 12 February 1812, Harcourt Ms.
40. Macalpine and Hunter, *George III*, p. 166.
41. Stuart, *Daughters of George III*, pp. 99–100.
42. Ibid., pp. 100–01.
43. Ibid., p. 223.
44. Ibid., p. 222.
45. A. Aspinall (ed.), *The Letters of King George IV: 1812 to 1830* (3 vols, Cambridge, 1938) I, p. 175.
46. Stuart, *Daughters of George III*, p. 175.
47. Ibid., p. 104.
48. Ibid., p. 105.
49. Ibid.
50. Ernest Taylor (ed.), *The Taylor Papers* (London, 1913), p. 78.
51. Ibid., p. 81.
52. Aspinall (ed.), *Letters of Princess Charlotte*, p. 37.
53. Princess Elizabeth to William, 3rd Lord Harcourt, 26 April 1812, Harcourt Ms.
54. Stuart, *Daughters of George III*, p. 110.
55. Ibid., p. 107.
56. Ibid., pp. 110–11.
57. Ibid., p. 109.
58. Ibid., p. 115.
59. Entry for Sir Brent Spencer, *Dictionary of National Biography*.

60. Princess Augusta to Lady Harcourt, 17 September 1807, Harcourt Ms.
61. Princess Augusta to Lady Harcourt, 28 September 1807, Harcourt Ms.
62. Stuart, *Daughters of George III*, p. 109.
63. Ibid., p. 111.
64. Ibid.
65. Aspinall (ed.), *Letters of Princess Charlotte*, p. 42.
66. Wardroper, *Wicked Ernest*, p. 88.
67. Aspinall (ed.), *Letters of Princess Charlotte*, p. 88.
68. Wardoper, *Wicked Ernest*, p. 88.
69. Ibid., p. 87.
70. Stuart, *Daughters of George III*, p. 289.
71. Aspinall (ed.), *Letters of Princess Charlotte*, p. 152.
72. Wardoper, *Wicked Ernest*, pp. 87–89.
73. Aspinall (ed.), *Letters of George IV*, I, p. 467.
74. Hibbert, *George IV: Prince of Wales*, p. 219.
75. George Thomas Keppel, Earl of Albemarle, *Fifty Years of My Life* (New York, 1876), p. 36.
76. Rose Weigall, *A Brief Memoir of the Princess Charlotte of Wales* (London, 1874), p. 34.
77. Ibid., p. 33.
78. Keppel, *Fifty Years*, p. 71.
79. Bury, *Lady in Waiting*, I, p. 38.
80. Keppel, *Fifty Years*, p. 53.
81. Ibid., p. 57.
82. Ibid., p. 47.
83. Bury, *Lady in Waiting*, I, p. 38.
84. Sichel (ed.), *Glenbervie Journals*, pp. 119–20 (21 October 1811).
85. Aspinall (ed.), *Letters of Princess Charlotte*, p. xi.
86. Bury, *Lady in Waiting*, I, p. 101.
87. Aspinall (ed.), *Letters of Princess Charlotte*, p. 102.
88. Bury, *Lady in Waiting*, I, p. 186.
89. Aspinall (ed.), *Letters of Princess Charlotte*, p. xv.
90. Aspinall (ed.), *Prince of Wales*, VIII, p. 30.
91. Knight, *Autobiography*, I, p. 212.
92. Ibid., p. 213.
93. Aspinall (ed.), *Letters of Princess Charlotte*, p. 21.
94. Ibid., pp. xvi, 85.
95. Ibid., p. 6.
96. Ibid., p. 7.
97. Princess Elizabeth to Lady Harcourt, 24 October 1811, Harcourt Ms.
98. Aspinall (ed.), *Letters of Princess Charlotte*, p. 23.
99. Ibid., p. 33.
100. Ibid., p. 28.
101. Knight, *Autobiography*, I, p. 240.
102. Bury, *Lady in Waiting*, I, p. 126.
103. Aspinall (ed.), *Letters of Princess Charlotte*, p. 108.
104. Ibid., p. 231.
105. Ibid., p. 26.
106. Ibid., pp. 74–75.
107. Ibid., p. 82.
108. Ibid., p. 69.
109. Aspinall (ed.), *Letters of George IV*, I, p. 289.
110. Aspinall (ed.), *Letters of Princess Charlotte*, p. 87.
111. Ibid., p. 89.
112. Ibid., p. 92.
113. Ibid., p. 94.
114. Ibid., p. 95.
115. Ibid., pp. 95, 96.
116. Ibid., p. 96.
117. Ibid., pp. 117–18.
118. Ibid., p. xviii; Fraser, *Unruly Queen*, p. 247.
119. Aspinall (ed.), *Letters of Princess Charlotte*, pp. 127–28.
120. Ibid., pp. 137–38.
121. Ibid., p. 140.
122. Ibid., p. 145.
123. Ibid., pp. 147, 148.
124. Ibid., p. 148.
125. Ibid., pp. 180–81.
126. Ibid., p. 155.

127. Ibid., p. 160.
128. Aspinall (ed.), *Letters of George IV*, I, p. 516.
129. Ibid., II, p. 30.
130. Ibid., p. 31.
131. Aspinall (ed.), *Letters of Princess Charlotte*, pp. 191–92.
132. Ibid., p. 165.
133. Ibid., p. 180.
134. Ibid., p. 190.
135. Ibid., p. 224.
136. Ibid., p. 225.
137. Ibid., p. 242.
138. Aspinall (ed.), *Letters of Princess Charlotte*, p. 243.
139. Alison Plowden, *Caroline and Charlotte* (London, 2005), p. 253.
140. Aspinall (ed.), *Letters of Princess Charlotte*, p. 231.
141. Ibid., pp. 224–25.
142. Bury, *Lady in Waiting*, I, p. 203.
143. Aspinall (ed.), *Letters of Princess Charlotte*, pp. 224–25.
144. Bury, *Lady in Waiting*, II, p. 81.
145. Fraser, *Princesses*, p. 294.
146. Aspinall (ed.), *Letters of Princess Charlotte*, p. 78.
147. Princess Elizabeth to Lord Harcourt, 20 June 1808, Harcourt Ms.
148. Stuart, *Daughters of George III*, p. 233.
149. Ibid., p. 229.
150. Princess Mary to Lady Harcourt, no date, *Harcourt Papers*, VI.
151. Ibid.
152. Childe-Pemberton, *Romance of Princess Amelia*, p. 296.
153. Aspinall (ed.), *Letters of Princess Charlotte*, pp. 245, 243.
154. Stuart, *Daughters of George III*, p. 249.
155. Princess Royal to Lady Harcourt, 1 April 1817, *Harcourt Papers*, VI.
156. Aspinall (ed.), *Letters of George IV*, II, p. 171.
157. Ibid., p. 187.
158. Ibid., I, p. 423.
159. Queen Charlotte to Lady Harcourt, 11 November 1817, *Harcourt Papers*, VI.
160. Plowden, *Caroline and Charlotte*, p. 257.
161. Aspinall (ed.), *Letters of George IV*, II, p. 211.
162. Plowden, *Caroline and Charlotte*, p. 263.
163. Princess Augusta to Lady Harcourt, 8 November 1817, *Harcourt Papers*, VI.
164. Princess Elizabeth to Lady Harcourt, 11 November 1817, *Harcourt Papers*, VI.
165. Queen Charlotte to Lady Harcourt, 11 November 1817, *Harcourt Papers*, VI.
166. Princess Augusta to Lady Harcourt, 8 November 1817, *Harcourt Papers*, VI.
167. Princess Augusta to Lady Harcourt, 13 November 1817, *Harcourt Papers*, VI.
168. Princess Augusta to Lady Harcourt, 19 November 1817, *Harcourt Papers*, VI.
169. Plowden, *Caroline and Charlotte*, p. 264.
170. Princess Elizabeth to Lady Harcourt, 22 January 1812, Harcourt Ms.
171. Stuart, *Daughters of George III*, p. 175.
172. Ibid., p. 176.
173. Ibid., pp. 178–79.
174. Ibid., p. 181.
175. Stuart, *Daughters of George III*, p. 180.
176. Ibid., p. 181.
177. Aspinall (ed.), *Letters of Princess Charlotte*, p. 212.
178. Iremonger, *Love and the Princesses*, p. 154.
179. Stuart, *Daughters of George III*, p. 182.
180. Iremonger, *Love and the Princesses*, p. 154.

181. Stuart, *Daughters of George III*, p. 182.
182. Ibid., pp. 178–79.
183. Yorke (ed.), *Letters of Princess Elizabeth*, p. 86.
184. Ibid.
185. Stuart, *Daughters of George III*, p. 185.
186. Knight, *Autobiography*, II, p. 139.
187. Stuart, *Daughters of George III*, p. 188.
188. Ibid., p. 185.
189. Ibid., p. 187.
190. Yorke (ed.), *Letters of Princess Elizabeth*, p. 94.
191. Stuart, *Daughters of George III*, pp. 196, 187.
192. Yorke (ed.), *Letters of Princess Elizabeth*, p. 319.
193. Stuart, *Daughters of George III*, pp. 191, 198.
194. Hedley, *Queen Charlotte*, p. 264.
195. Aspinall (ed.), *Letters of George IV*, II, p. 184.
196. Hedley, *Queen Charlotte*, p. 288.
197. Ibid., pp. 294–96.
198. Stuart, *Daughters of George III*, pp. 123–24.
199. Ibid., p. 125.
200. Hedley, *Queen Charlotte*, p. 296.
201. Ibid., p. 298.
202. Princess Elizabeth to Lady Harcourt, 9 September 1818, *Harcourt Papers*, VI. See also Yorke (ed.), *Letters of Princess Elizabeth*, p. 89.
203. Hedley, *Queen Charlotte*, p. 298.
204. Ibid.
205. Princess Royal to Lady Harcourt, 1 April 1817, Harcourt Ms.
206. Hedley, *Queen Charlotte*, p. 291.
207. Bury, *Lady in Waiting*, II, p. 92.
208. Stuart, *Daughters of George III*, p. 244.
209. Hedley, *Queen Charlotte*, p. 294.
210. Ibid., p. 303.
211. Ibid., p. 304.
212. Princess Royal to Lady Harcourt, 22 March 1819, *Harcourt Papers*, VI.
213. Yorke (ed.), *Letters of Princess Elizabeth*, p. 88.
214. Anon., *Court and Family*, p. 434.
215. Macalpine and Hunter, *George III*, p. 170.
216. Hibbert, *George III*, p. 407.
217. Macalpine and Hunter, *George III*, p. 170.
218. Aspinall (ed.), *Letters of George IV*, II, p. 298.
219. Anon., *Court and Family*, p. 445.
220. Hibbert, *George III*, p. 410.
221. Black, *George III*, p. 410.
222. Stuart, *Daughters of George III*, p. 64.
223. Ibid.
224. Ibid., p. 66.
225. Ibid.

Bibliography

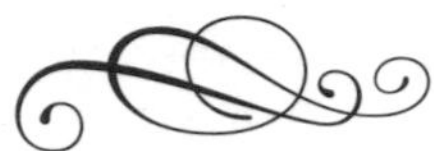

Archives

Bodleian Library, University of Oxford (Harcourt Ms.; Papers of James Bland Burges)

Hunterian Collection, University of Glasgow (William Hunter, 'Journal of Attendance'; Ms. Hunter)

Landeshauptarchiv Schwerin, Schwerin, Mecklenburg-Vorpommern, Germany (correspondence of Charlotte of Mecklenburg-Strelitz)

Leicester Record Office (Diary of Lady Charlotte Finch, DG7; Halford Papers, DG 24/822/4)

National Library of Scotland, Edinburgh (Glenbervie Papers)

John Rylands Library, University of Manchester (Mary Hamilton Papers)

Published Sources

Albemarle, George Thomas Keppel, *Fifty Years of My Life* (New York, 1876)

Ambrose, Tom, *Prinny and His Pals: George IV and His Remarkable Gift of Friendship* (London, 2009)

Anon., *George III: His Court and Family* (London, 1821)

Anson, Elizabeth, and Anson, Florence, eds, *Mary Hamilton at Court and Home from Letters and Diaries* (London, 1925)

Aspinall A., *Mrs Jordan and Her Family* (London, 1951)

Aspinall A., ed., *The Letters of King George IV: 1812 to 1830* (3 vols, Cambridge, 1938)

——ed., *Letters of the Princess Charlotte* (2 vols, London, 1949)

——ed., *The Correspondence of George, Prince of Wales* (8 vols, Oxford, 1963–71)

——ed., *The Later Correspondence of George III* (5 vols, Cambridge, 1962–70)

Auckland, William, Lord, *Journal and Correspondence*, ed. R. J. Eden (2 vols, London, 1861)

Ayling, Stanley, *George the Third* (London, 1972)

Baker, Kenneth, *George III: A Life in Caricature* (London, 2007)

Barrett, Charlotte, *Diary and Letters of Madame D'Arblay* (2 vols, London, 1879)

Bickley, Francis, ed., *The Diaries of Sylvester Douglas, Lord Glenbervie* (2 vols, London, 1928)

Bird, Anthony, *The Damnable Duke of Cumberland* (London, 1966)

Black, Jeremy, *George III: America's Last King* (New Haven and London, 2006)

——— *George II: Puppet of the Politicians?* (Exeter, 2007)

Bladon, F. McKno, ed., *The Diaries of Robert Fulke Greville* (London, 1930)

Blanning, Tim, *The Pursuit of Glory: Europe 1648–1815* (London, 2007)

Boswell, James, *London Journal, 1762–63*, ed. Frederick A. Pottle (New Haven, 1950)

Brewer, John, *The Pleasures of the Imagination: English Culture in the Eighteenth Century* (London, 1997)

Brooke, John, *King George III* (London, 1972)

Brooke, John, ed., *Horace Walpole: Memoirs of King George II* (3 vols, New Haven and London, 1985)

Brown, Irene Q., 'Domesticity, Feminism and Friendship: Female Aristocratic Marriage in England, 1660–1860', *Journal of Family History*, 7 (1982)

Buchan, Susan, *Lady Louisa Stuart* (London, 1932)

Buckingham, Duke of, *Memoirs of the Court of the Regency* (2 vols, London, 1856)

Bullion, John L., '"George Be a King!" The Relationship between Princess Augusta and George III', in Stephen Taylor, Richard Connors and Clyve Jones, eds, *Hanoverian Britain and Empire* (London, 1998)

Bury, Lady Charlotte, *The Diary of a Lady In Waiting*, ed. Francis Steuart (2 vols, London, 1908)

Campbell Orr, Clarissa, 'Queen Charlotte: Scientific Queen', in Clarissa Campbell Orr, ed., *Queenship in Britain 1660–1837* (Manchester, 2002)

Cannon, John, *Lord North: The Noble Lord in the Blue Ribbon* (London, 1970)

Chedzoy, Alan, *Seaside Sovereign: King George III at Weymouth* (Wimbourne, 2003)

Childe-Pemberton, William S., *The Romance of Princess Amelia* (New York, 1911)

Climenson, Emily, ed., *Passages from the Diaries of Mrs Philip Lybbe Powys* (London, 1899)

Cody, Lisa Forman, *Birthing the Nation: Sex, Science, and the Conception of Eighteenth-Century Britons* (Oxford, 2005)

Colley, Linda, *Britons: Forging the Nation 1707–1837* (New Haven and London, 1992)

Cowper, Mary Clavering, *Diary of Mary Countess Cowper, Lady of the Bedchamber to the Princess of Wales* (London, 1864)

D'Arblay, Mme, *Diary and Letters*, ed. Charlotte Barrett (4 vols, London, 1854)

Davenport, Hester, *Faithful Handmaid: Fanny Burney at the Court of King George III* (Stroud, 2000)

Delany, Mrs, *The Autobiography and Correspondence of Mary Granville, Mrs Delany*, ed. Lady Llanover (3 vols, London, 1861)

Dodington, George Bubb, *The Political Journal of George Bubb Dodington*, ed. John Carswell and Leslie Dralle (Oxford, 1965)

Doran, Dr, *Lives of the Queens of England* (2 vols, London, 1855)

Elliot, Sir Gilbert, *Life and Letters of Sir Gilbert Elliot, 1st Earl of Minto, 1751 to 1806*, ed. the Countess of Minto (3 vols, London, 1874)

Esher, Viscount, ed., *The Girlhood of Queen Victoria* (2 vols, London 1912)

Fitzgerald, Percy, *The Good Queen Charlotte* (London, 1899)

Fortescue, The Hon. Sir John, ed., *The Correspondence of King George the Third* (6 vols, London, 1927)

Fraser, Flora, *The Unruly Queen: The Life of Queen Caroline* (London, 1996)

——*Princesses: The Six Daughters of George III* (London, 2004)

Fulford, Roger, *Royal Dukes* (London, 1933)

Gillett, Eric, ed., *Elizabeth Ham by Herself 1783–1820* (London, 1945)

Gisbourne, Thomas, *An Enquiry into the Duties of the Female Sex* (London, 1797)

Green, Vivian, *The Madness of Kings: Personal Trauma and the Fate of Nations* (Stroud, 1993)

Greenwood, Alice Drayton, *Lives of the Hanoverian Queens of England* (2 vols, London, 1909–11)

Greig, James, ed., *The Diaries of a Duchess* (London, 1926)

Gronow, Captain Rees Howell, *Reminiscences of Captain Gronow* (London, 1862)

Halsband, Robert, *Lord Hervey: Eighteenth-Century Courtier* (Oxford, 1973)

Hamilton, Lady Anne, *Secret History of the Court of England* (London, 1903)

Hammersley, Violet, ed., *Letters from Madame de Sévigné* (London, 1955)

Harcourt, Mrs, *Diary of the Court of King George III*, Miscellanies of the Philobiblon Society, XIII (London, 1871)

Harcourt, Rev. L. V., ed., *Diaries and Correspondence of the Rt Hon. George Rose* (4 vols, London, 1860)

Harcourt, William, ed., *The Harcourt Papers* (14 vols, privately printed, 1880–1905)

Harris, James, First Earl of Malmesbury, *Diaries and Correspondence of James Harris, First Earl of Malmesbury*, III (London, 1844)

Hatton, Ragnhild, *George I* (New Haven, 2001)

Hedley, Olwen, *Queen Charlotte* (London, 1975)

Hervey, John Lord, *Some Materials Towards Memoirs of the Reign of George II*, ed. Romney Sedgwick (3 vols, London, 1931)

Hibbert, Christopher, *George IV: Prince of Wales* (London, 1972)

——*George IV: Regent and King* (London, 1973)

——*George III: A Personal History* (London, 1998)

Hickey, William, Memoirs, ed., *Peter Quennell* (London, 1975)

Home, J. A., ed., *The Letters and Journals of Lady Mary Coke* (4 vols, Edinburgh, 1889)

Ilchester, the Countess of, and Stavordale, Lord, eds, *The Life and Letters of Lady Sarah Lennox 1745–1826* (London, 1904)

Ilchester, the Earl of, *The Journal of Elizabeth Lady Holland 1791–1811* (2 vols, London 1908)

Iremonger, Lucille, *Love and the Princesses: The Strange Lives of Mad King George III and His Daughters* (London, 1958)

Jerningham, Lady Frances Dillon, *The Jerningham Letters 1780–1843*, ed. Egerton Castle (2 vols, London, 1896)

Jesse, J. Heneage, *Memoirs of Life &c. of George III* (3 vols, London, 1867)

Keppel, George Thomas, *Fifty Years of my Life* (New York, 1876)
Knight, Cordelia, *Autobiography of Miss Cordelia Knight* (2 vols, London 1861)
Laird, Mark, and Weisberg-Roberts, Alicia, eds, *Mrs Delaney and Her Circle* (New Haven and London, 2009)
Landmann, George Thomas, *Adventures and Recollections of Colonel Landmann* (2 vols, London, 1852)
Langford, P. A., *Polite and Commercial People: England 1727–1783* (Oxford, 1989)
Langford, Paul, *Englishness Identified: Manners and Character 1650–1850* (Oxford, 2000)
Levey, Michael, *A Royal Subject: Portraits of Queen Charlotte* (London, 1977)
Lloyd, C., 'King, Queen and Family', in Jane Roberts, ed., *George III and Queen Charlotte: Patronage, Collecting and Court Taste* (London, 2004)
Macalpine, Ida, and Hunter, Richard, *George III and the Mad-Business* (London, 1969)
McKendrick, Neil, Brewer, John, and Plumb, J. H., *The Birth of a Consumer Society: The Commercialization of Eighteenth-Century England* (London, 1982)
McKno Bladen, F., ed., *The Diaries of Robert Fulke Greville* (London, 1930)
Marples, Morris, *Six Royal Sisters: Daughters of George III* (London, 1969)
——*Poor Fred and the Butcher: Sons of George II* (London, 1970)
Millar, Oliver, *Pictures in the Royal Collection: Later Georgian Pictures* (London, 1969)
Moore, Lucy, *Amphibious Thing: The Life of a Georgian Rake* (London, 2000)
Moore, Wendy, *The Knife Man: The Extraordinary Life and Times of John Hunter, Father of Modern Surgery* (London, 2005)
Morrell, Philip, ed., *Leaves from the Greville Diary* (New York, 1929)
Murray, Augusta, *Recollections* (London, 1868)
Papendiek, Mrs, *Court and Private Life in the Time of Queen Charlotte*, ed. Mrs V. Delves Broughton (2 vols, London, 1887)
Parissien, Steven, *George IV: The Grand Entertainment* (London, 2001)
Peters, Timothy J., and Beveridge, Allan, 'The Madness of King George III: A Psychiatric Reassessment', in *History of Psychiatry* 21 (1) (2010)
Peters, T. J., and Wilkinson, D., 'King George III and Porphyria: A Clinical Re-examination of the Historical Evidence', in *History of Psychiatry* 21 (1) (2010)
Plowden, Alison, *Caroline and Charlotte: Regency Scandals* (London, 2005)
Pottle, Frederick A., ed., *Boswell's London Journal 1762–1763* (London, 1950)
Quennell, Peter, ed., *Private Letters of Princess Lieven* (London, 1937)
Roberts, Jane, ed., *George III and Queen Charlotte: Patronage, Collecting and Court Taste* (London, 2004)
Robins, Jane, *Rebel Queen: The Trial of Caroline* (London and New York, 2006)
Saussure, César de, *A Foreign View of England in the Reigns of George I and George II*, ed. Mme van Muyden (London, 1902)
Schama, Simon, *A History of Britain* (3 vols, London, 2000)
Sedgwick, Romney, 'The Marriage of George III', *History Today*, 10 (6) (June 1960)
Sedgwick, Romney, ed., *Letters from George III to Lord Bute 1756–1766* (London, 1939)

Shefrin, Jill, *Such Constant Affectionate Care: Lady Charlotte Finch – Royal Governess and the Children of George III* (Los Angeles, 2003)
Sichel, Walter, ed., *The Glenbervie Journals* (London, 1910)
Steuart, Francis A., ed., *The Last Journals of Horace Walpole* (2 vols, New York and London, 1910)
Stone, Lawrence, *The Family, Sex and Marriage in England 1500–1800* (London, 1977)
Stuart, Dorothy Margaret, *The Daughters of George III* (London, 1939)
Stuart, Lady Louisa, *The Letters of Lady Louisa Stuart*, ed. R. Brimley Johnson (London, 1926)
Taylor, Ernest, ed., *The Taylor Papers* (London, 1913)
Thompson, Andrew C., *George II* (New Haven and London, 2011)
Thompson, E. P., *The Making of the English Working Class* (London, 1963)
Tillyard, Stella, *Aristocrats: Caroline, Emily, Louisa and Sarah Lennox 1740–1832* (London, 1994)
——*A Royal Affair: George III and His Troublesome Siblings* (London, 2006)
Trumbach, Randolph, *The Rise of the Egalitarian Family* (New York, 1978)
Van Der Kiste, John, *George III's Children* (Stroud, 1992)
——*The Georgian Princesses* (London, 2000)
Vickery, A., 'Golden Age to Separate Spheres?', *Historical Journal*, 36 (2) (1993)
Vickery, Amanda, *The Gentleman's Daughter: Women's Lives in Georgian England* (New Haven and London, 1998)
——*Behind Closed Doors: At Home in Georgian England* (London, 2009)
Waldegrave, James, Earl, *Memoirs* (London, 1821)
Walpole, Horace, *Lord Orford's Reminiscences* (London, 1818)
——*Memoirs of the Reign of George II*, ed. Lord Holland (3 vols, London, 1846)
——*The Yale Edition of Horace Walpole's Correspondence*, ed. W. S. Lewis (48 vols, New Haven, 1937–83)
——*Memoirs of the Reign of King George III*, ed. Derek Jarrett (4 vols, New Haven and London, 2000)
Wardroper, John, *Wicked Ernest: The Truth about the Man who Was almost Britain's King* (London, 2002)
Watkins, John, *Memoirs of Her Most Excellent Majesty, Sophia Charlotte, Queen of Great Britain* (London, 1819)
Weigall, Rose Sophia M., *A Brief Memoir of the Princess Charlotte of Wales* (London, 1874)
Wilkins, W. H., *Caroline the Illustrious* (2 vols, London, 1901)
Wraxall, Sir Nathaniel William, *The Historical and Posthumous Memoirs of Sir Nathaniel William Wraxall* (London, 1884)
Yale Center for British Arts, *Johann Zoffany RA: Society Observed* (New Haven and London, 2011)
Yorke, Philip, ed., *Letters of Princess Elizabeth of England* (London, 1898)

Acknowledgements

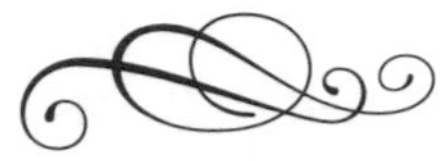

IT HAS TAKEN ME TEN years to write this book, during which time I have incurred many debts. I would like to thank the John Rylands Library, University of Manchester, and the Bodleian Library, Oxford, for allowing me to consult letters and journals in their collections. I am similarly grateful to the Landeshauptarchiv Schwerin, the Leicestershire Record Office and the Hunterian Collection, University of Glasgow, for making papers and documents available to me. I am also indebted to the London Library, whose extensive holdings of eighteenth- and nineteenth-century diaries and correspondence, together with their generous policy of allowing members to borrow them, made it possible for someone like me, with a full-time job, to access historical sources in my limited free time.

Many publishers might have given up on a book with such a lengthy gestation, but neither of mine did so. I will always be grateful to HarperCollins and Henry Holt for their faith in the project, and their remarkable patience and forbearance. I have benefited more than I can say from the wise advice and stewardship of all my editors, who have guided me through a decade of new learning and experience. I'd like to thank Richard Johnson of HarperCollins who commissioned *The Strangest Family* and who made a first-time writer feel confident enough to begin upon such an ambitious undertaking. His successor, Martin Redfern, has never wavered in his support for the book, and has been a beacon of encouragement and calming kindness throughout. Stephen Guise's painstaking care in managing the latter stages of the production process was a model of efficiency and engagement.

My American editor, Barbara Jones, has been equally generous; her trenchant comments and up-beat appreciation of my efforts kept me going when completion sometimes seemed a very long way off. I also owe a great deal to Stephen Rubin, whose personal enthusiasm for the book has been so important to me. Bold, forceful and very sure of what he likes, Steve's conviction that this was a book worth having inspired and energised me, and I shall always be grateful for his exuberant and powerfully expressed support.

The manuscript was read by two brilliant editors, David Milner and Kate Johnson, whose comments and suggestions were extremely helpful. I am likewise indebted to Professors Amanda Vickery and Jeremy Black, who read the finished manuscript, passing it through the prism of their unrivalled historical scholarship. I have benefitted hugely from their advice and friendly corrections, which are reflected in the final text. I am also grateful to Daniel Mitchell for his help in transcribing correspondence. Any remaining errors or infelicities are, of course, my own.

I should also like to pay tribute to some of those writers whose books so inspired me as a reader and fed my passion for the world I have sought to capture in my own writing. Of course, there are far too many to list here in their entirety, but I have always been stimulated by the work of Stella Tillyard, Amanda Foreman, Flora Fraser and Amanda Vickery. All these writers bring a new understanding to the inner lives of eighteenth-century families, especially the experiences of women and children. I have also learned a great deal from the pioneering work of Clarissa Campbell Orr and Irene Brown.

I am profoundly grateful to Peter Robinson, my agent for many years, without whose belief and fortitude this book would probably never have got off the starting block. Peter was stalwart, loyal and endlessly supportive, always ready with advice and encouragement, often delivered over a large glass of wine whilst he smoked a surreptitious cigarette. His contribution to the book is huge and will always be deeply appreciated. He is a wonderful man and a great friend. I should also like to thank Caroline Michel, who has shepherded the book through the final stages of its journey, and who has been unremitting in both her thoughtful kindness and steely sense of purpose. I have been very lucky to work with two such talented people.

While writing this book, I had a very demanding job as a channel controller at the BBC. I owe a great deal to my television colleagues, who, over the years, have listened politely as I have explained to them exactly what I was attempting to write. They were all very patient and understanding, at least when I was around! My thanks are due to everyone in broadcasting who has had to hear at length my views on the importance of the eighteenth century and all its works, but there are some people who have been more exposed to the full force of my passion than others. Special thanks go to Jana Bennet, Alan Yentob, George Entwistle, Danny Cohen, Michael Jackson, Denys Blakeway, Emma Swain, Ben Stephenson, Charlotte Moore, Claire Powell, Adam Barker, Mark Bell and Kate Mordaunt. None of my colleagues, however, has heard more about the book and its progress than Don Cameron. We worked together for the ten years of this book's gestation and he was party to all the many ups and downs along the way. He never looked bored while hearing about them, for which I owe him much. Great thanks too are due to Daisy Goodwin, not just for sharing her own experiences of the pleasures and challenges of writing, but also as a sympathetic listener, tough-minded adviser and much-valued friend.

Finally, I'd like to thank my family for all their support and encouragement. No one could have been more generous with his time and expertise than my brother John, who travelled across the country on more than one occasion to rescue me from disastrous computer malfunctions without a word of complaint. His wife, Jane, was just as understanding. My two sons, Alexander and Louis, were small children when I began writing. Now they are strapping teenagers. They have probably heard more about George III and his preoccupations than most boys of their age. Sometimes this has made them laugh – and who can blame them? – but they have borne without complaint the evenings, weekends and school holidays that have been devoted to writing and research. Perhaps one day they will read the book; if so, I hope they will feel it was all worthwhile.

There have been many people to thank here, but no one deserves my heartfelt gratitude more than my husband, Martin Davidson. It is inconceivable that this book would have been written without him. He ushered it into life. No one had a better understanding of what I hoped to achieve than he did, and no one did more to help me get there. An accomplished writer himself, he was tireless in doing all he could to improve my work, suggesting, correcting, editing, making me persevere in tough times and exulting when things went well. His opinion has always been the standard by which I judge everything I write. We have been partners in this enterprise, as in so much else. He is the love of my life and I am very proud to dedicate this book to him.

Illustration Credits

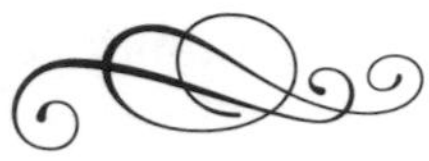

Frontispiece: Royal Collection Trust © Her Majesty Queen Elizabeth II, 2014/Bridgeman Images

Section One

Page 1: © National Portrait Gallery, London (top and bottom)
Page 2: © National Portrait Gallery, London (top and bottom)
Page 3: © National Portrait Gallery, London (top); Royal Collection Trust © Her Majesty Queen Elizabeth II, 2014/Bridgeman Images (bottom)
Page 4: © Yale Center for British Art, Paul Mellon Collection, USA/ Bridgeman Images (top); © National Portrait Gallery, London (bottom left); Royal Collection Trust © Her Majesty Queen Elizabeth II, 2014/Bridgeman Images (bottom right)
Page 5: Royal Collection Trust © Her Majesty Queen Elizabeth II, 2014/Bridgeman Images (top and bottom)
Page 6: © National Portrait Gallery, London (top and bottom)
Page 7: Royal Collection Trust © Her Majesty Queen Elizabeth II, 2014/Bridgeman Images (top and bottom)
Page 8: Royal Collection Trust © Her Majesty Queen Elizabeth II, 2014/Bridgeman Images (top and bottom)

Section Two

Page 1: Royal Collection Trust © Her Majesty Queen Elizabeth II, 2014/Bridgeman Images

Page 2: Royal Collection Trust © Her Majesty Queen Elizabeth II, 2014/Bridgeman Images
Page 3: © National Portrait Gallery, London (top and bottom)
Page 4: Royal Collection Trust © Her Majesty Queen Elizabeth II, 2014/Bridgeman Images (top left, top right and bottom)
Page 5: Royal Collection Trust © Her Majesty Queen Elizabeth II, 2014/Bridgeman Images (top and bottom)
Page 6: Royal Collection Trust © Her Majesty Queen Elizabeth II, 2014/Bridgeman Images (top left, top right, bottom left and bottom right)
Page 7: © National Portrait Gallery, London (top and bottom)
Page 8: © National Gallery, London/Bridgeman Images (top); Royal Collection Trust © Her Majesty Queen Elizabeth II, 2014/ Bridgeman Images (bottom)

Index

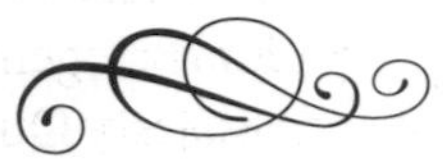